CHRISTIAN WORSHIP

A Lutheran Hymnal

Authorized by the
Wisconsin Evangelical Lutheran Synod

NORTHWESTERN PUBLISHING HOUSE
Milwaukee, Wisconsin

The logo for this hymnal is a version of the Chi-Rho, a symbol for Christ. In the Greek language these are the first letters of the name Christ. He is the center of our faith and worship, our prayers, our praise and thanksgiving. This hymnal reflects in its name, logo, liturgies, and hymns the story of God's love and salvation in Christ.

Fifth Printing, 1999

Northwestern Publishing House
1250 N. 113th St., Milwaukee, WI 53226-3284
© 1993 Northwestern Publishing House.
Published 1993
Printed in the United States of America

All rights reserved. No part of this book may be reproduced in any manner whatsoever without written permission from the publisher or from the other copyright holders. For further copyright information, see Acknowledgments on pages 925-936.

Manufactured in the United States of America.

ISBN 0-8100-0422-4

03N3000

CONTENTS

	Page
Introduction	8
Personal Prayers—For Worship	10
Holy Baptism	12
The Common Service	15
Service of Word and Sacrament	26
Service of the Word	38
Morning Praise	45
Evening Prayer	52
Index to the Psalms	62
Singing the Psalms	63
Psalms for Worship	64
Prayers of the Church	123
Athanasian Creed	132
Personal Prayers	134
Christian Marriage	140
Christian Funeral	144
Devotions	150
Private Confession	154
Personal Preparation for Holy Communion	156
The Christian Church Year	157
Calendar Dates for the Church Year	162
Lectionary	163
Indexes	924

HYMNS

	Hymn
Advent	1-32
Christmas	33-68
New Year	69-75
Name of Jesus/Presentation	76-78
Epiphany	79-94
Transfiguration	95-97
Lent	98-129
Palm Sunday	130-134
Maundy Thursday	135-136
Good Friday	137-140
Easter	141-168
Ascension	169-175
Pentecost	176-190
Holy Trinity	191-195
St. Michael and All Angels	196-198
Reformation	199-205
End Time	206-220
Opening of Service	221-232
Worship and Praise	233-261
Hymns of the Liturgy	262-278
Word of God	279-293
Baptism	294-301
Confession and Absolution	302-308
Holy Communion	309-318
Close of Service	319-334

Invitation	335-339
Redeemer	340-375
Justification	376-401
Faith	402-406
Prayer	407-413
Trust	414-451
Commitment	452-479
Stewardship	480-489
Christian Love	490-499
Christian Home	500-507
Christian Education	508-516
Social Concern	517-527
Church	528-541
Ministry	542-548
Saints and Martyrs	549-555
Evangelism	556-566
Missions	567-579
Morning	580-586
Evening	587-595
Confirmation	596-599
Marriage	600-604
Death and Burial	605-608
Thanksgiving	609-616
Nation	617-620
Church Anniversary	621-623

INTRODUCTION

The story of *Christian Worship: A Lutheran Hymnal* actually began in 1953 when the Lutheran Church—Missouri Synod (LCMS) initiated work on a revision of *The Lutheran Hymnal* (1941), the hymnal shared by the synods constituting the Synodical Conference. In 1959 the Wisconsin Evangelical Lutheran Synod (WELS) accepted the invitation to share in the revision work. In 1965, however, the LCMS abandoned this project in favor of a new pan-Lutheran hymnal, leading to the publication of *Lutheran Book of Worship* (1978) and *Lutheran Worship* (1982). After studying various options, the WELS in its 1983 convention resolved: "That the Synod now begin work on a new/revised hymnal of its own, one that under the blessings of God will be scripturally sound and edifying, welcomed and judged to be highly satisfactory by a majority of our members, in harmony with the character and heritage of our church body, and reflecting the larger perspective and mainstream of the worship of the Christian church."

In 1984 the Conference of Presidents called a full-time project director and appointed working committees. The Liturgy Committee, Hymn Committee, and Commission on Worship formed the Joint Hymnal Committee. Later in the project a full-time music editor was called. The hymnal group worked steadily for seven years to finish the hymnal manuscript, followed by a year and a half of layout, design, and promotion. In 1993, the completed hymnal was introduced along with *Christian Worship: Accompaniment for Liturgy and Psalms* and *Christian Worship: Manual.*

The phrase "new/revised" in the synodical resolutions was interpreted to mean a hymnal which **preserved** the Christian and Lutheran heritage of liturgy and hymns from *The Lutheran Hymnal* and at the same time **improved** and **expanded** it. Much of the familiar content of *The Lutheran Hymnal* has been preserved. The three historic liturgies, the Common Service, Matins, and Vespers are retained with some revision. Two new liturgies are included, the Service of Word and Sacrament and the Service of the Word, following the structure of historic Lutheran liturgy, but with new or revised texts and with newly composed music. These liturgies were added to provide some of the liturgical variety sought by many congregations and individuals. Also included in the book are rites for the Sacrament of Holy Baptism, Christian Marriage, and Christian Funeral. Three brief liturgies, Morning, Evening, and General Devotions, are designed for use in schools, conferences, and congregational organizations.

The regular use of Psalms is a new liturgical feature. In addition to its traditional use in Morning Praise and Evening Prayer (Matins and Vespers), the Psalm serves as response to the first lesson in The Common Service, Service of Word and Sacrament, and Service of the Word. The most important and most familiar of the Psalms were selected and arranged for liturgical use by careful shortening to six or seven verses. All the psalms or psalm sections are responsorial and have been furnished with easy and attractive congregational refrains. Sixteen melodies have been provided for singing the psalm verses.

The hymn section of the new hymnal has a familiar look. Over 400 hymns have been retained from *The Lutheran Hymnal*, though many have undergone a slight updating of language. The hymns are arranged according to the Christian year and topical headings.The hymn section also has a new look and sound. The last three decades have seen a strong resurgence of creativity and interest in the writing of hymns. Therefore, congregations will enjoy a greater variety of hymns than formerly. In addition to Lutheran chorales and traditional English hymnody, a wide selection of plainsong hymns, spirituals, folk hymns from Appalachia, Wales, Ireland, and elsewhere, gospel hymns, and contemporary hymns in different styles are included. In addition to new texts and new melodies, a somewhat freer and fresher type of harmonization has been furnished for some of the hymns; descants and guitar chords are supplied for a few others.

The hymnal is a unique tool for worship. It is a treasury of theology, poetry, music, history, liturgy, and praise. Because it is truly "the people's book," a good deal of care was taken to solicit opinion and reaction from the field. In addition to the *Sampler* of liturgy, hymnody, psalmody, and prayer distributed to all congregations early in the project, field testing among groups of congregations was carried on throughout the project. Thanks is due the many critical reviewers, proofreaders, and writers of several thousand letters of advice and reaction.

The overall intent of those who prepared *Christian Worship: A Lutheran Hymnal* was to produce a Lutheran hymnal that was at once forward-looking and also enriched by the faith and worship experience of the whole Christian church of the past. Specifically the goal was to deliver to the church a strongly Christ-centered book, bringing together liturgies and a large number of hymns celebrating the life and atoning work of Jesus. May the new book continue to proclaim the power of the Word of God and the foundation doctrine of forgiveness by God's grace through faith in Christ. May its use among us foster and strengthen appreciation of liturgical worship and enrich and enliven our relationship with God and each other.

IN THE NAME OF JESUS

PERSONAL PRAYERS
For Worship

In the Name of Jesus

FOR PEACE

O God of peace, I turn aside from an unquiet world, seeking rest for my spirit and light for my thoughts. I bring my work to be sanctified, my wounds to be healed, my sins to be forgiven, my hopes to be renewed. In you there is perfect harmony. Draw me to yourself, and silence the discords of my wasteful life. Your greatness is beyond my highest praise. Take me out of the loneliness of self, and fill me with the fullness of your peace.

REMEMBRANCE OF BAPTISM

Father, Son, and Holy Spirit: in the water of baptism you forgave my sin and delivered me from death and the devil. You raised me to a new life in Christ and clothed me with his merit. Help me rejoice in your washing of salvation and live before you in righteousness and purity forever.

A PERSONAL CONFESSION OF SIN

Father, I have sinned against you and am no longer worthy to be called your child. Especially am I sorry for _____. Yet in mercy you sacrificed your only Son to purge away my guilt. For his sake, O God, be merciful to me, a sinner, and in the joy of your Holy Spirit let me serve you all my days.

PRAISE AND THANKSGIVING

Praise to you, O God, maker of all things. You gave me life and breath. You sent your Son to cleanse me from sin and your Spirit to make me glad. Thank you for providing me with all that I need to live. Especially do I thank you for _____. To you be honor and glory now and forever.

BEFORE WORSHIP

Heavenly Father, I have come to worship you. Draw near to me in your gracious Word, and assure me of your loving kindness. Curb my wandering thoughts, that with undivided attention I may hear your voice and sing your praise.

O Lord—our Maker, Redeemer, and Comforter—we are assembled in your presence to hear your holy Word. We pray that you would open our hearts by your Holy Spirit, that through the preaching of your Word we may repent of our sins, believe in Jesus, and grow day by day in grace and holiness. Hear us for Jesus' sake.

BEFORE COMMUNION

Lord, I am not worthy to be a guest at your holy table. But you are the friend of sinners, and you will not cast me out. This bread is your body, which bore my sins upon the tree. This wine is your blood, which purifies me from all guilt. At your invitation, I come rejoicing. Receive me, my Savior.

AFTER COMMUNION

Thank you, Lord Jesus Christ, for nourishing me in this sacrament with your body and blood. You have given me forgiveness, life, and salvation. Let me always remain in you as a branch remains in the vine. Send me out in the power of your Spirit to live and work to your praise and glory.

O living Bread from heaven, how richly you have fed your guest!
   The gifts you now have given have filled my heart with joy and rest.
Lord, grant me that thus strengthened with heavenly food, while here
   my course on earth is lengthened, I serve with holy fear.
And when you call my spirit to leave this world below,
   I enter through your merit where joys unmingled flow.

AFTER WORSHIP

Good Shepherd, I was glad to be here, gathered with your flock to worship you. Cause the Word I have heard to take root in my heart and bear fruit in my life. Guide me in paths of righteousness, that my words and actions might lead others to glorify you.

Grant, O Lord, that the lips which here have sung your praise
     may continue to glorify you in the world;
 that the ears which have heard you speak
     may be open always to your Word and closed to hatred and discord;
 that the tongues which have confessed your name
     may always speak the truth without fear;
 that all of us who have worshiped together today
     may be united in true love for each other as you have loved us in Jesus.

BY THOSE SERVING AT WORSHIP

Father, Son, and Holy Spirit: I am happy for the privilege of ministering in your house. Help me to be reverent and humble in my service, setting a good example by my words and actions. Enable me to fulfill my duties in such a way that I may assist others to worship you joyfully.

Additional Personal Prayers are found on pages 134-139.
Suggested Psalms for private meditation are found on page 62.
Appropriate readings for ministry to the sick are found on pages 148-149.
A Personal Preparation for Holy Communion is found on page 156.

HOLY BAPTISM

This order incorporates Holy Baptism *into congregational worship by combining the sacrament of baptism with the confession of sins. Martin Luther said that confessing sins and receiving forgiveness is nothing else than a reliving of baptism. Thus this order provides opportunity not only to baptize but also to recall the lasting blessings of baptism.*

A baptism hymn may be sung.

REMAIN SEATED

M: The grace of our Lord ✠ Jesus Christ and the love of God and the fellowship of the Holy Spirit be with you.

C: **And also with you.**

CONFESSION OF SINS

M: Our Savior Jesus Christ commanded baptism when he said: "Go and make disciples of all nations, baptizing them in the name of the Father and of the Son and of the Holy Spirit." All of us are born into this world with a deep need for baptism. From our parents we inherit a sinful nature; we are without true fear of God and true faith in God and are condemned to eternal death. But Jesus took away our sin by giving his life on the cross. At our baptism he clothes us with the robe of his righteousness and gives us a new life. Our sinful nature need not control us any longer. We recall what baptism means for our daily lives as we speak these words:

C: **Baptism means that the sinful nature in us should be drowned by daily sorrow and repentance, and that all its evil deeds and desires be put to death. It also means that a new person should daily arise to live before God in righteousness and purity forever.**

M: As baptized children of God we confess our sins:

The congregation may kneel.

C: **Holy and merciful Father, I confess that I am by nature sinful, and that I have disobeyed you in my thoughts, words, and actions. I have done what is evil and failed to do what is good. For this I deserve your punishment both now and in eternity. But I am truly sorry for my sins, and trusting in my Savior Jesus Christ, I pray: Lord, have mercy on me, a sinner.**

M: God, our heavenly Father, has been merciful to us and has given his only Son to be the atoning sacrifice for our sins. Therefore, as a called servant of Christ and by his authority, I forgive you all your sins in the name of the Father and of the Son ✠ and of the Holy Spirit.

C: **Amen.**

The Rite of Baptism continues at the font.

SACRAMENT OF BAPTISM

For the baptism of children

M: In obedience to the command of our Lord and trusting in his promise, you have brought *this child* to be baptized. Jesus told us: "Let the little children come to me and do not hinder them, for the kingdom of God belongs to such as these." It is in baptism that God grants the new life of forgiveness, joy, and peace to little children. By the power of God's Word, this gracious water of life washes away sin, delivers from death and the devil, and gives eternal salvation to all who believe.

For the baptism of adults

M: ____, by the power of the Word, the Holy Spirit has led you to believe that this new life in Christ is yours. Now in Holy Baptism the Lord Jesus assures you of your salvation. That you may give public testimony of your faith, I therefore ask you:

Do you believe that you were born in sin and therefore eternally lost?

A: **Yes, I believe.**

M: Do you believe in the Triune God: Father, Son, and Holy Spirit?

A: **Yes, I believe.**

M: Do you believe that this Triune God planned and carried out your salvation?

A: **Yes, I believe.**

M: Do you believe that God grants you the forgiveness of sins in Holy Baptism?

A: **Yes, I believe.**

M: Do you desire to be baptized?

A: **Yes, I do.**

M: Receive the sign of the cross on the head and heart ✠ to mark you as a redeemed child of Christ.

The minister applies water to the person presented for baptism as he says:

____, I baptize you in the name of the Father and of the Son and of the Holy Spirit.

The Almighty God—Father, Son, and Holy Spirit—has forgiven all your sins. By your baptism, you are born again and made a dear child of your Father in heaven. May God strengthen you to live in your baptismal grace all the days of your life. Peace be with you.

STAND

EXHORTATION

M: Brothers and sisters in Christ:

Our Lord commands that we teach his precious truths to all who are baptized. Christian love therefore urges all of us, especially parents and sponsors, to assist in whatever manner possible so that ____ may remain a child of God until death. If you are willing to carry out this responsibility, then answer: Yes, as God gives me strength.

C: Yes, as God gives me strength.

M: Let us pray:

Merciful Father in heaven, we thank you for the blessing of baptism by which you offer and grant the forgiveness of sins, life, and salvation. Help us to regard our baptism as the robe of righteousness we are to wear all the days of our life. Look with special favor on ____ and grant *him* a rich measure of your Spirit that *he* may grow in faith and godly living. Make us willing to carry out our responsibilities to those who have been baptized, so that all of us may finally come to the blessed joys of heaven, through Jesus our Lord.

C: Amen.

The Common Service continues on page 16.
The Service of Word and Sacrament continues on page 28.
The Service of the Word continues on page 39.

Emergency Baptism

In urgent cases any Christian may administer Holy Baptism. Apply water to the person and say:

I baptize you in the name of the Father and of the Son and of the Holy Spirit. Amen.

If there is time, the baptism may be followed by the Lord's Prayer, or the prayer at the close of the service above, or another suitable prayer.

THE COMMON SERVICE

"The Common Service" is a version of the historic liturgy of the Christian church. It became the service commonly used by English-speaking Lutherans in America and appeared as "The Order of the Holy Communion" in The Lutheran Hymnal. *The present revision may be used either with or without the sacrament.*

HYMN

STAND

M: In the name of the Father and of the Son and of the Holy Spirit.

C: A - men.

CONFESSION OF SINS

M: Beloved in the Lord: let us draw near with a true heart and confess our sins to God our Father, asking him in the name of our Lord Jesus Christ to grant us forgiveness.

The congregation may kneel.

C: Holy and merciful Father, I confess that I am by nature sinful and that I have disobeyed you in my thoughts, words, and actions. I have done what is evil and failed to do what is good. For this I deserve your punishment both now and in eternity. But I am truly sorry for my sins, and trusting in my Savior Jesus Christ, I pray: Lord, have mercy on me, a sinner.

LORD, HAVE MERCY
  Kyrie

C: Lord, have mer - cy on us. Christ, have mer - cy on us. Lord, have mer - cy on us.

THE COMMON SERVICE

M: God, our heavenly Father, has been merciful to us and has given his only Son to be the atoning sacrifice for our sins. Therefore, as a called servant of Christ and by his authority, I forgive you all your sins in the name of the Father and of the Son ✠ and of the Holy Spirit.

C: A - men.

When there is a baptism, the Invocation and Confession of Sins are omitted and replaced by the rite for Holy Baptism on page 12.

Prayer and Praise

M: In the peace of forgiveness, let us praise the Lord.

GLORY BE TO GOD or another song of praise is sung.

GLORY BE TO GOD
Gloria in Excelsis

C: Glory be to God on high, and on earth peace, good will toward men.

We praise you, we bless you, we wor-ship you, we glorify you,

we give thanks to you, for your great glory, O Lord God, heav'n-ly King,

God the Fa-ther al - mighty. O Lord, the only begotten Son, Je-sus Christ;

O Lord God, Lamb of God, Son of the Father, you take away the

sin of the world; have mercy on us. You take away the

THE COMMON SERVICE

sin of the world; re-ceive our prayer. You sit at the right hand of God the Father; have mercy on us. For you on-ly are holy; you on-ly are the Lord. You only, O Christ, with the Ho-ly Spirit, are most high in the glory of God the Father. A-men.

PRAYER OF THE DAY

M: The Lord be with you.

C: And al-so with you.

M: Let us pray.

The minister says the Prayer of the Day.

C: A - men.

BE SEATED

THE WORD

FIRST LESSON

PSALM OF THE DAY

SECOND LESSON

THE COMMON SERVICE

VERSE OF THE DAY

The choir sings the proper VERSE OF THE DAY. If the minister speaks the Verse, the congregation sings the following Alleluia. During Lent the Alleluia may be omitted.

C: Al-le-lu - ia! Al-le-lu - ia! Al-le-lu - ia!

STAND

GOSPEL

After the announcement of the Gospel, the congregation sings:

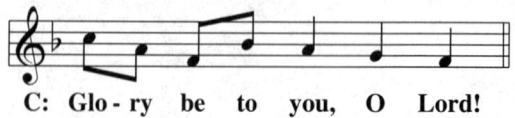

C: Glo-ry be to you, O Lord!

After the Gospel, the congregation sings:

C: Praise be to you, O Christ!

NICENE CREED

    We believe in one God, the Father, the Almighty,
        maker of heaven and earth,
        of all that is,
        seen and unseen.

    We believe in one Lord, Jesus Christ, the only Son of God,
        eternally begotten of the Father,
        God from God, Light from Light, true God from true God,
        begotten, not made,
        of one being with the Father.
    Through him all things were made.
    For us and for our salvation, he came down from heaven,
        was incarnate of the Holy Spirit and the virgin Mary,
        and became fully human.
    For our sake he was crucified under Pontius Pilate.
    He suffered death and was buried.

On the third day he rose again in accordance with the Scriptures.
He ascended into heaven
    and is seated at the right hand of the Father.
He will come again in glory to judge the living and the dead,
    and his kingdom will have no end.

We believe in the Holy Spirit,
    the Lord, the giver of life,
    who proceeds from the Father and the Son,
    who in unity with the Father and the Son is worshiped and glorified,
    who has spoken through the prophets.
We believe in one holy Christian and apostolic Church.
We acknowledge one baptism for the forgiveness of sins.
We look for the resurrection of the dead
    and the life of the world to come. Amen.

or

APOSTLES' CREED

I believe in God, the Father almighty,
    maker of heaven and earth.

I believe in Jesus Christ, his only Son, our Lord,
    who was conceived by the Holy Spirit,
    born of the virgin Mary,
    suffered under Pontius Pilate,
    was crucified, died, and was buried.
He descended into hell.
The third day he rose again from the dead.
He ascended into heaven
    and is seated at the right hand of God the Father almighty.
From there he will come to judge the living and the dead.

I believe in the Holy Spirit,
    the holy Christian Church,
        the communion of saints,
    the forgiveness of sins,
    the resurrection of the body,
    and the life everlasting. Amen.

BE SEATED

HYMN OF THE DAY

SERMON

STAND

THE COMMON SERVICE

After the sermon, the congregation sings:

C: Create in me a clean heart, O God, and renew a right spirit within me. Cast me not away from your presence, and take not your Holy Spirit from me. Restore unto me the joy of your salvation, and uphold me with your free Spirit. Amen.

BE SEATED

OFFERING

STAND

PRAYER OF THE CHURCH

LORD'S PRAYER

C: Our Father in heaven,
    hallowed be your name,
    your kingdom come,
    your will be done
        on earth as in heaven.
Give us today our daily bread.
Forgive us our sins,
    as we forgive those
    who sin against us.
Lead us not into temptation,
but deliver us from evil.
For the kingdom, the power,
    and the glory are yours
    now and forever. Amen.
	or	Our Father, who art in heaven,
		    hallowed be thy name,
		    thy kingdom come,
		    thy will be done
		        on earth as it is in heaven.
		Give us this day our daily bread;
		and forgive us our trespasses,
		    as we forgive those
		    who trespass against us;
		and lead us not into temptation,
		but deliver us from evil.
		For thine is the kingdom
		    and the power and the glory
		    forever and ever. Amen.

When there is no Communion, the service continues on page 25.

THE SACRAMENT

PREFACE

M: The Lord be with you.

C: And also with you.

M: Lift up your hearts.

C: We lift them up unto the Lord.

M: Let us give thanks to the Lord, our God.

C: It is good and right so to do.

M: It is truly good and right that we should at all times and in all places give you thanks, O Lord, holy Father, almighty and everlasting God, through Jesus Christ, our Lord,

PROPER PREFACES

> **Advent:** whose way John the Baptist prepared when he called people to repentance and pointed to Jesus as the Lamb of God who takes away the sin of the world. (Therefore . . .)
>
> **Christmas:** for in the wonder and mystery of his birth you have opened our eyes to the glory of your grace and renewed in our hearts the fervor of your love. (Therefore . . .)
>
> **Epiphany:** who lived among us as a human being and revealed his glory as your only Son, full of grace and truth. (Therefore . . .)
>
> **Lent:** who brought the gift of salvation to all people by his death on the tree of the cross, so that the devil, who overcame us by a tree would in turn by a tree be overcome. (Therefore . . .)
>
> **Easter/Ascension:** and we praise you especially for the glorious resurrection of your Son, the true Passover Lamb, who by his sacrifice took away the sins of the world and by his resurrection restored everlasting life. (Therefore . . .)

Pentecost: who on this day kept his promise and poured out the Holy Spirit to empower his Church to proclaim the gospel in all the world. (Therefore . . .)

The Holy Trinity: and now we confess that you, with your Son and the Holy Spirit, are one God and one Lord, and we acknowledge you as our Creator, Redeemer, and Sanctifier. (Therefore . . .)

Sundays after Pentecost: who promised that wherever two or three come together in his name, there he is with them to shepherd his flock till he comes again in glory. (Therefore . . .)

End Time: who preserves his Church to the end of time when he will come again as king to judge all people and take his own to glory. (Therefore . . .)

Minor Festivals: who in blessing his saints of the past has given us glorious assurance and hope that, following their example of faith, we may run with perseverance the race marked out for us, and receive the crown of glory that will never fade away. (Therefore . . .)

Therefore, with all the saints on earth and hosts of heaven, we praise your holy name and join their glorious song:

HOLY, HOLY, HOLY
Sanctus

C: Holy, holy, holy Lord God of heavenly hosts: heav'n and earth are full of your glory. Hosanna, hosanna, hosanna in the highest. Blessed is he, blessed is he, blessed is he who comes in the name of the Lord. Hosanna, hosanna, hosanna in the highest.

WORDS OF INSTITUTION

M: Our Lord Jesus Christ, on the night he was betrayed, took bread; and when he had given thanks, he broke it and gave it to his disciples, saying, "Take and eat; this is my body, which is given for you. Do this in remembrance of me."

Then he took the cup, gave thanks, and gave it to them, saying, "Drink from it, all of you; this is my blood of the new covenant, which is poured out for you for the forgiveness of sins. Do this, whenever you drink it, in remembrance of me."

M: The peace of the Lord be with you always.

C: A - men.

O CHRIST, LAMB OF GOD
Agnus Dei

C: O Christ, Lamb of God, you take a-way the sin of the world; have mer-cy on us. O Christ, Lamb of God, you take a-way the sin of the world; have mer-cy on us. O Christ, Lamb of God, you take a-way the sin of the world; grant us your peace. A - men.

BE SEATED

DISTRIBUTION
During the distribution the congregation may sing one or more hymns.

THE COMMON SERVICE

THANKSGIVING

STAND

The SONG OF SIMEON or a song of thanksgiving is sung.

SONG OF SIMEON
Nunc Dimittis

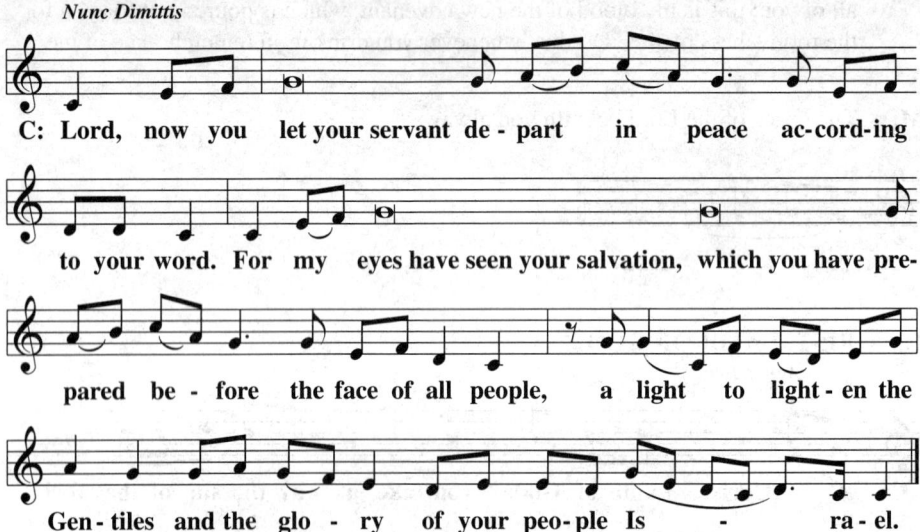

C: Lord, now you let your servant de-part in peace ac-cord-ing to your word. For my eyes have seen your salvation, which you have pre-pared be-fore the face of all people, a light to light-en the Gen-tiles and the glo-ry of your peo-ple Is - ra-el.

M: O give thanks to the Lord, for he is good.

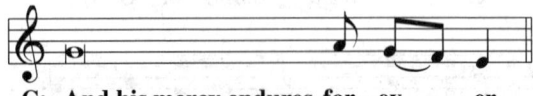

C: And his mercy endures for-ev - er.

M: We give thanks, almighty God, that you have refreshed us with this holy supper. We pray that through it you will strengthen our faith in you and increase our love for one another. We ask this in the name of Jesus Christ, our Lord, who lives and reigns with you and the Holy Spirit, one God, now and forever.

or

O God the Father, source of all goodness, in your loving kindness you sent your Son to share our humanity. We thank you that through him you have given us pardon and peace in this sacrament. We also pray that you will not forsake us but will rule our hearts and minds by your Holy Spirit so that we willingly serve you day after day, through Jesus Christ, our Lord, who lives and reigns with you and the Holy Spirit, one God, now and forever.

C: A - men.

M: The Lord bless you and keep you.
The Lord make his face shine on you and be gracious to you.
The Lord look on you with favor and ✢ give you peace.

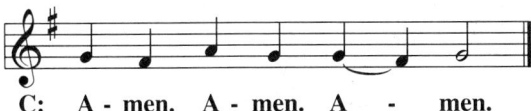

C: A-men. A-men. A-men.

When there is no Communion, the service concludes as follows:

BE SEATED

HYMN

STAND

M: Blessed Lord, you have given us your Holy Scriptures for our learning. May we so hear them, read, learn, and take them to heart, that being strengthened and comforted by your holy Word, we may cling to the blessed hope of everlasting life, through Jesus Christ, our Lord, who lives and reigns with you and the Holy Spirit, one God, now and forever.

or

Almighty God, grant to your Church the Holy Spirit and the wisdom that comes from above. Let nothing hinder your Word from being freely proclaimed to the joy and edifying of Christ's holy people, so that we may serve you in steadfast faith and confess your name as long as we live, through Jesus Christ, our Lord, who lives and reigns with you and the Holy Spirit, one God, now and forever.

C: A-men.

M: The Lord bless you and keep you.
The Lord make his face shine on you and be gracious to you.
The Lord look on you with favor and ✢ give you peace.

C: A-men. A-men. A-men.

SERVICE OF WORD AND SACRAMENT

The "Service of Word and Sacrament" is a version of the historic liturgy of the Christian church. This order may be used as an alternate to "The Common Service" when Holy Communion is celebrated.

HYMN

STAND

M: The grace of our Lord ✠ Jesus Christ and the love of God and the fellowship of the Holy Spirit be with you.

C: **And also with you.**

CONFESSION OF SINS

M: God invites us to come into his presence and worship him with humble and penitent hearts. Therefore, let us acknowledge our sinfulness and ask him to forgive us.

The congregation may kneel.

C: **Holy and merciful Father, I confess that I am by nature sinful, and that I have disobeyed you in my thoughts, words, and actions. I have done what is evil and failed to do what is good. For this I deserve your punishment both now and in eternity. But I am truly sorry for my sins, and trusting in my Savior Jesus Christ, I pray: Lord, have mercy on me, a sinner.**

M: God, our heavenly Father, has been merciful to us and has given his only Son to be the atoning sacrifice for our sins. Therefore, as a called servant of Christ and by his authority, I forgive you all your sins in the name of the Father and of the Son ✠ and of the Holy Spirit.

C: **Amen.**

PRAYER AND PRAISE

LORD, HAVE MERCY
Kyrie

M: For all that we need in life and for the wisdom to use all your gifts with gratitude and joy, hear our prayer, O Lord.

C: Lord, have mer - cy.

M: For the steadfast assurance that nothing can separate us from your love and for the courage to stand firm against the assaults of Satan and every evil, hear our prayer, O Christ.

C: Christ, have mer - cy.

M: For the well-being of your holy Church in all the world and for those who offer here their worship and praise, hear our prayer, O Lord.

C: Lord, have mer - cy.

M: Merciful God, maker and preserver of life, uphold us by your power and keep us in your tender care:

C: A - men.

When there is a baptism, the Greeting, the Confession of Sins, and the Kyrie are omitted and replaced by the rite for Holy Baptism on page 12.

M: The works of the Lord are great and glorious; his name is worthy of praise.

O LORD, OUR LORD or another song of praise is sung.

O LORD, OUR LORD

C: O Lord, our Lord, how glorious is your name in all the earth. Almighty God, merciful Father, you crown our life with your love. You take away our sin; you comfort our spirit; you make us pure and holy in your sight. You did not spare your only Son, but gave him up for us all. O Lord, our Lord, how glorious is your name in all the earth.

O Son of God, eternal Word of the Father, you came to live with us; you made your Father known;

SERVICE OF WORD AND SACRAMENT

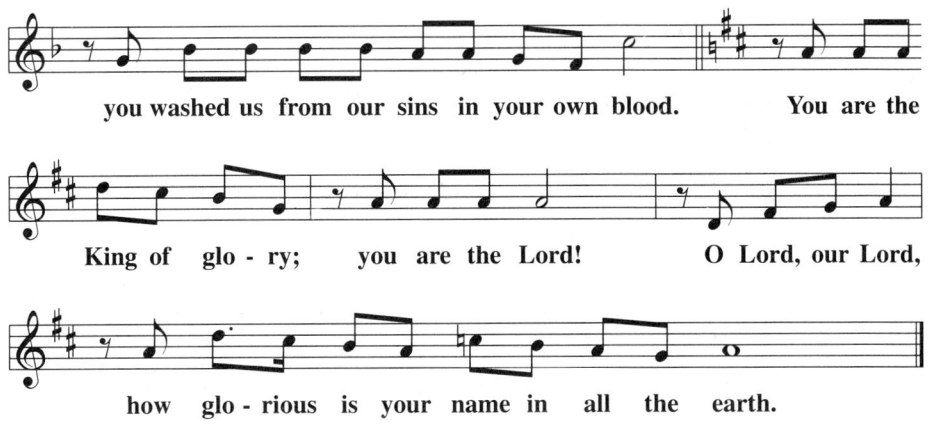

you washed us from our sins in your own blood. You are the King of glory; you are the Lord! O Lord, our Lord, how glorious is your name in all the earth.

PRAYER OF THE DAY

M: Let us pray.

The minister says the Prayer of the Day.

C: A - men.

BE SEATED

The Word

FIRST LESSON

PSALM OF THE DAY

SECOND LESSON

SERVICE OF WORD AND SACRAMENT

VERSE OF THE DAY

The choir sings the proper VERSE OF THE DAY or the congregation sings the following general verse. During Lent the general verse may be omitted.

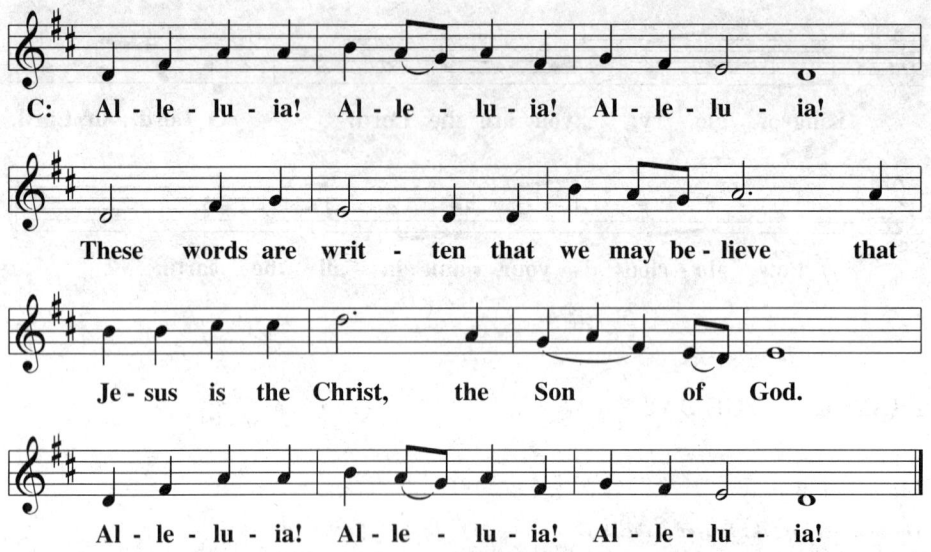

C: Alleluia! Alleluia! Alleluia! These words are written that we may believe that Jesus is the Christ, the Son of God. Alleluia! Alleluia! Alleluia!

STAND

GOSPEL

After the Gospel, the congregation sings:

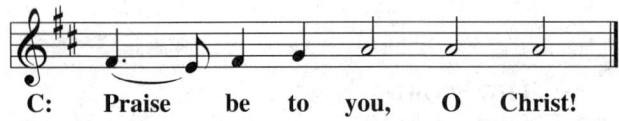

C: Praise be to you, O Christ!

BE SEATED

HYMN OF THE DAY

SERMON

STAND

NICENE CREED

We believe in one God, the Father, the Almighty,
>   maker of heaven and earth,
>   of all that is,
>   seen and unseen.

We believe in one Lord, Jesus Christ, the only Son of God,
>   eternally begotten of the Father,
>   God from God, Light from Light, true God from true God,
>   begotten, not made,
>   of one being with the Father.
> Through him all things were made.
> For us and for our salvation, he came down from heaven,
>   was incarnate of the Holy Spirit and the virgin Mary,
>   and became fully human.
> For our sake he was crucified under Pontius Pilate.
> He suffered death and was buried.
> On the third day he rose again in accordance with the Scriptures.
> He ascended into heaven
>   and is seated at the right hand of the Father.
> He will come again in glory to judge the living and the dead,
>   and his kingdom will have no end.

We believe in the Holy Spirit,
>   the Lord, the giver of life,
>   who proceeds from the Father and the Son,
>   who in unity with the Father and the Son is worshiped and glorified,
>   who has spoken through the prophets.
> We believe in one holy Christian and apostolic Church.
> We acknowledge one baptism for the forgiveness of sins.
> We look for the resurrection of the dead
>   and the life of the world to come. Amen.

BE SEATED

OFFERING

STAND

PRAYER OF THE CHURCH
Another prayer may be used.

M: Gracious God and Father, we praise you for the countless blessings, which we receive from your hand: the beauties of creation and the bounties of the earth, the joy of life and the pleasure of friendship, the good of work and the gift of rest, the privilege to share happiness and sorrow with one another. Above all we praise and thank you for your saving Word and for your Son's body and blood, which you give us to eat and to drink in the sacrament. Through these means of grace, you send the Holy Spirit into our hearts and unite us to Jesus and to the whole Christian Church on earth.

C: **Strengthen us through this heavenly food; increase our trust in Christ and our love for one another.**

M: Great God and Lord, without your continuing help we easily waver in our faith, lose courage, and grow careless in our watchfulness. The times and days are perilous. Give us strength to face the evils of each day with fresh confidence. Open our lips to speak of your grace, and move us to use the gifts that you give us to share your Word of salvation with all people. Protect and prosper the family, the school, the government, and all good institutions that you have established for the benefit of society. Remember in mercy those who are sick and suffering, and bring your healing to troubled homes and lives.

C: **Move us to pray for those in need and to help them with deeds of kindness.**

Special prayers and intercessions may follow.

M: Hear us, Lord, as we bring you our private petitions.

Silent prayer.

M: Now, eternal God and Father, keep us in the saving faith and so enable us to overcome all things through our Lord Jesus Christ.

LORD'S PRAYER

C: **Our Father in heaven,**   *or*   **Our Father, who art in heaven,**
    hallowed be your name,   **hallowed be thy name,**
    your kingdom come,   **thy kingdom come,**
    your will be done   **thy will be done**
        on earth as in heaven.   **on earth as it is in heaven.**
    Give us today our daily bread.   **Give us this day our daily bread;**
    Forgive us our sins,   **and forgive us our trespasses,**
        as we forgive those   **as we forgive those**
        who sin against us.   **who trespass against us;**
    Lead us not into temptation,   **and lead us not into temptation,**
    but deliver us from evil.   **but deliver us from evil.**
    For the kingdom, the power,   **For thine is the kingdom**
        and the glory are yours   **and the power and the glory**
        now and forever. Amen.   **forever and ever. Amen.**

SERVICE OF WORD AND SACRAMENT

THE SACRAMENT

Our Lord Jesus has given us a holy supper in which we receive his true body and blood for the forgiveness of sins and the strengthening of our faith. In this supper we celebrate the gift of his redemption, we bear witness to the fellowship we share as confessors of the truth, and we proclaim his death until he returns.

M: The Lord be with you.

C: And al - so with you.

M: Lift up your hearts.

C: We lift them up to the Lord.

M: Let us give thanks to the Lord our God.

C: It is right to give him thanks and praise.

M: Praise to the God and Father of our Lord Jesus Christ! In love he has blessed us with every spiritual blessing.

SEASONAL SENTENCES

Advent: Through his holy prophets, he promised a King to bring light to those living in darkness and in the shadow of death.

Christmas: When the time had fully come, he sent his Son, born of a woman, born under law, to redeem those under law, that we might receive the full rights of sons.

Epiphany: In the past he spoke to us through the prophets, but in these last days he has spoken to us by his Son, who is the radiance of his glory.

Lent: He made his Son to be the atoning sacrifice for our sins, and not only for ours but also for the sins of the whole world.

Easter/Ascension: He raised Christ from the dead and seated him at his right hand in the heavenly realms and placed all things under his feet for the benefit of the Church.

Pentecost: By the outpouring of the Holy Spirit, he empowered his Church to be witnesses of Christ to the ends of the earth.

The Holy Trinity: In perfect unity with his Son and the Holy Spirit, he is the source, guide, and goal of our lives now and always.

Sundays after Pentecost: He sends the Holy Spirit to testify that we are his children and to strengthen us when we are weak.

End Time: He protects and preserves his Church in every age and gives us confidence to lift up our heads and watch for Jesus with joy.

Minor Festivals: By his saints and witnesses of the past he encourages us to run with perseverance the race marked out for us and to live in righteousness and peace.

Now have come the salvation and the power and the kingdom of our God and the authority of his Christ. To him who sits on the throne and to the Lamb be praise and thanks and honor and glory for ever and ever.

HOLY, HOLY, HOLY
Sanctus

C: Holy, holy, holy is the Lord of hosts. The whole earth is full of your glory. You are my God, and I will exalt you. I will give you thanks, for you have become my salvation. Holy, holy, holy is the Lord of hosts. The whole earth is full of your glory.

WORDS OF INSTITUTION

M: Our Lord Jesus Christ, on the night he was betrayed, took bread; and when he had given thanks, he broke it and gave it to his disciples, saying, "Take and eat; this is my body, which is given for you. Do this in remembrance of me."

Then he took the cup, gave thanks, and gave it to them, saying, "Drink from it, all of you; this is my blood of the new covenant, which is poured out for you for the forgiveness of sins. Do this, whenever you drink it, in remembrance of me."

M: The peace of the Lord be with you always.

C: A - men.

O CHRIST, LAMB OF GOD
Agnus Dei

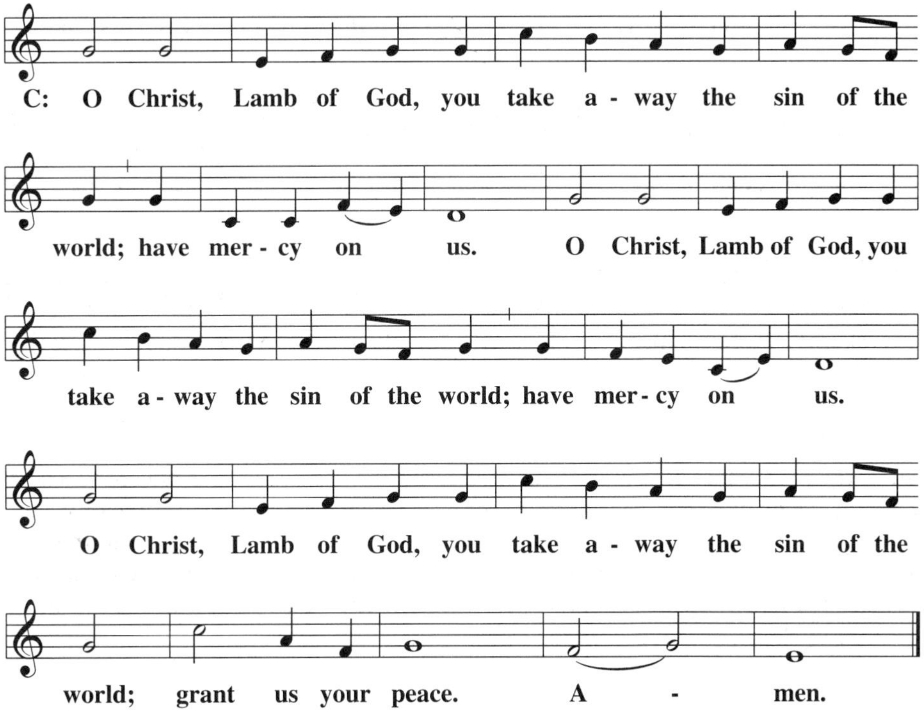

C: O Christ, Lamb of God, you take a-way the sin of the world; have mer-cy on us. O Christ, Lamb of God, you take a-way the sin of the world; have mer-cy on us. O Christ, Lamb of God, you take a-way the sin of the world; grant us your peace. A - men.

BE SEATED

SERVICE OF WORD AND SACRAMENT

DISTRIBUTION
During the distribution the congregation may sing one or more hymns.

THANKSGIVING

STAND

THANK THE LORD

During Lent the first stanza of "O Lord, We Praise You," Hymn 317, may be sung in place of THANK THE LORD.

C: Thank the Lord and sing his praise. Tell ev-'ry-one what he has done.

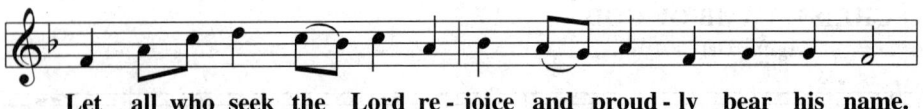
Let all who seek the Lord re-joice and proud-ly bear his name.

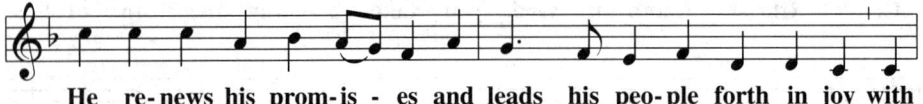
He re-news his prom-is-es and leads his peo-ple forth in joy with

shouts of thanks-giv-ing. Al-le-lu-ia! Al-le-lu - ia!

M: Hear the prayer of your people, O Lord, that the lips which have praised you here may glorify you in the world, that the eyes which have seen the coming of your Son may long for his coming again, and that all who have received in his true body and blood the pledge of your forgiveness may be restored to live a new and holy life, through Jesus Christ, our Lord, who lives and reigns with you and the Holy Spirit, one God, now and forever.

C: A - men.

SERVICE OF WORD AND SACRAMENT

M: Brothers and sisters, go in peace. Live in harmony with one another. Serve the Lord with gladness.

The Lord bless you and keep you.
The Lord make his face shine on you and be gracious to you.
The Lord look on you with favor and ✠ give you peace.

C: A - men.   A - men.   A - men.

SERVICE OF THE WORD

This service offers the congregation a form of worship that focuses on the proclamation of God's Word. Believers respond to this divine gift with prayer, praise, and thanksgiving.

HYMN

STAND

M: The grace of our Lord ✠ Jesus Christ and the love of God and the fellowship of the Holy Spirit be with you.

C: And also with you.

CONFESSION OF SINS

M: We have come into the presence of God, who created us to love and serve him as his dear children. But we have disobeyed him and deserve only his wrath and punishment. Therefore, let us confess our sins to him and plead for his mercy.

C: Merciful Father in heaven, I am altogether sinful from birth. In countless ways I have sinned against you and do not deserve to be called your child. But trusting in Jesus, my Savior, I pray: Have mercy on me according to your unfailing love. Cleanse me from my sin, and take away my guilt.

M: God, our heavenly Father, has forgiven all your sins. By the perfect life and innocent death of our Lord Jesus Christ, he has removed your guilt forever. You are his own dear child. May God give you strength to live according to his will.

C: Amen.

When there is a baptism, the Greeting and Confession of Sins are omitted and replaced by the rite for Holy Baptism on page 12.

SERVICE OF THE WORD

PRAYER AND PRAISE

M: In the peace of forgiveness, let us praise the Lord.

OH, TASTE AND SEE or another song of praise is sung.

OH, TASTE AND SEE

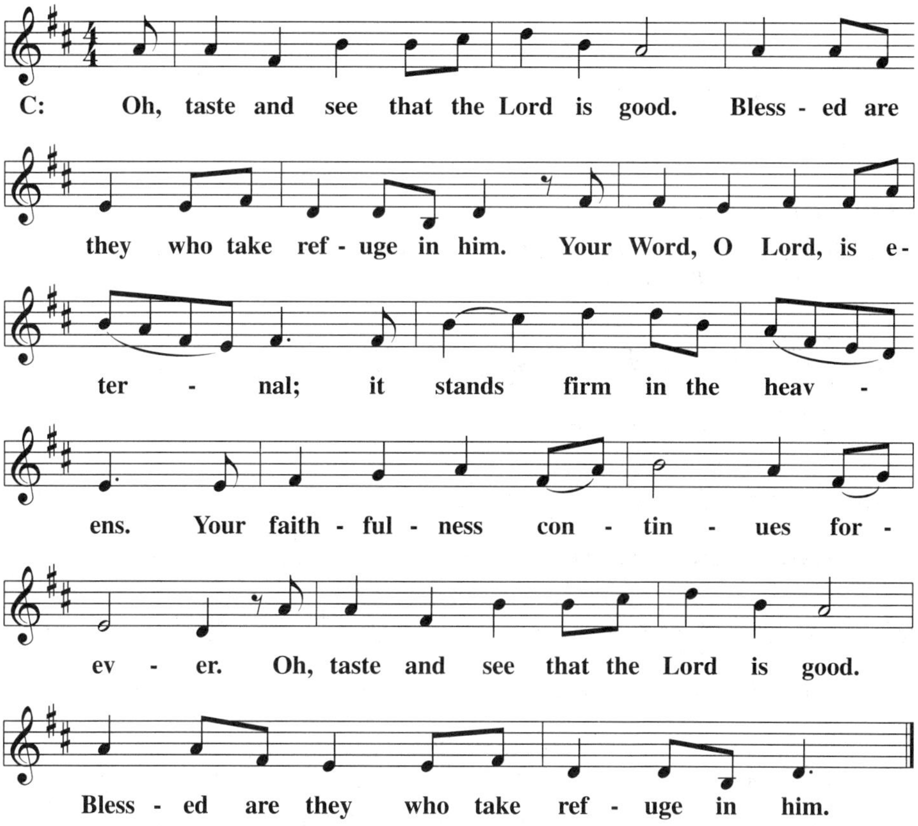

C: Oh, taste and see that the Lord is good. Blessed are they who take refuge in him. Your Word, O Lord, is eternal; it stands firm in the heavens. Your faithfulness continues forever. Oh, taste and see that the Lord is good. Blessed are they who take refuge in him.

PRAYER OF THE DAY

M: Let us pray.

The minister says the Prayer of the Day.

C: Amen.

BE SEATED

SERVICE OF THE WORD

THE WORD

FIRST LESSON

PSALM OF THE DAY

SECOND LESSON

VERSE OF THE DAY

The choir sings the proper VERSE OF THE DAY or the congregation sings the following general verse. During Lent the general verse may be omitted.

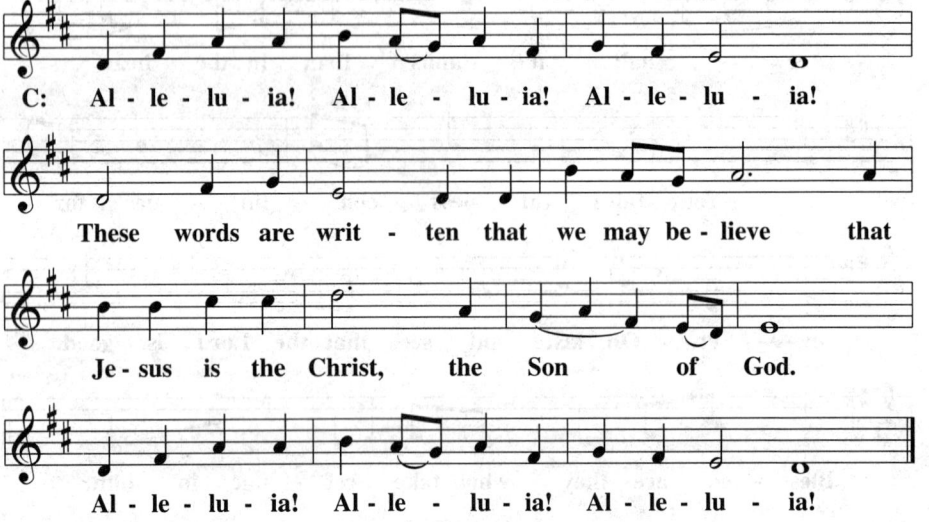

C: Alleluia! Alleluia! Alleluia! These words are written that we may believe that Jesus is the Christ, the Son of God. Alleluia! Alleluia! Alleluia!

STAND

GOSPEL

After the Gospel, the congregation sings:

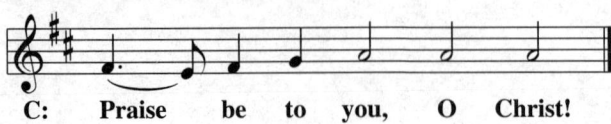

C: Praise be to you, O Christ!

BE SEATED

HYMN OF THE DAY

SERMON

STAND

APOSTLES' CREED

I believe in God, the Father almighty,
   maker of heaven and earth.

I believe in Jesus Christ, his only Son, our Lord,
   who was conceived by the Holy Spirit,
   born of the virgin Mary,
   suffered under Pontius Pilate,
   was crucified, died, and was buried.
He descended into hell.
The third day he rose again from the dead.
He ascended into heaven
   and is seated at the right hand of God the Father almighty.
From there he will come to judge the living and the dead.

I believe in the Holy Spirit,
   the holy Christian Church,
      the communion of saints,
   the forgiveness of sins,
   the resurrection of the body,
   and the life everlasting. Amen.

BE SEATED

Thanksgiving

OFFERING

STAND

PRAYER OF THE CHURCH

Another prayer may be used.

M: Lord God, our maker and preserver, we praise and thank you for all that you give us day after day.

C: We are not worthy of all the mercies you show us.

M: You have given us your precious Word to nourish our souls and to protect us from the temptations of the devil, the world, and our sinful nature.

C: We thank you for those who teach and preach your saving truth at this place and everywhere. Grant them a rich measure of patience, wisdom, and love.

M: Heavenly Father, we pray that you shield us from every kind of danger: sudden catastrophe, terrors of crime, and the pain of disease. Watch over those who travel by land, sea, and air. Keep our loved ones from whatever perils may threaten them.

C: Heal those who are sick, cheer those who are sad, calm those who are distressed, and comfort all who are old and infirm.

M: Bless our land, our people, and those who hold offices of high trust. Keep our government and schools upright and strong for the advancement of good citizenship and useful vocations, that we may enjoy your gifts of peace, security, and well-being.

C: Grant your blessing to every nation on earth. Where there are wars, may there be peace. Where there is hatred, let it be healed. Where there is poverty, danger, or disaster, come with your almighty power to help and restore.

Special prayers and intercessions may follow.

M: Hear us, Lord, as we bring you our private petitions.

Silent prayer.

M: We bring these requests before you in the name of Jesus our Lord, and ask you to hear us. Take all that we have, our bodies and minds, our time and skills, our ministries and offerings, and use them to your glory.

C: We give ourselves to you that we may serve you in whatever way is pleasing in your sight. Amen.

LORD'S PRAYER

C: Our Father in heaven,   *or*   Our Father, who art in heaven,
      hallowed be your name,   hallowed be thy name,
      your kingdom come,   thy kingdom come,
      your will be done   thy will be done
          on earth as in heaven.   on earth as it is in heaven.
      Give us today our daily bread.   Give us this day our daily bread;
      Forgive us our sins,   and forgive us our trespasses,
          as we forgive those   as we forgive those
          who sin against us.   who trespass against us;
      Lead us not into temptation,   and lead us not into temptation,
      but deliver us from evil.   but deliver us from evil.
      For the kingdom, the power,   For thine is the kingdom
          and the glory are yours   and the power and the glory
          now and forever. Amen.   forever and ever. Amen.

BE SEATED

HYMN

STAND

M: O Lord God, our heavenly Father, pour out the Holy Spirit on your faithful people. Keep us strong in your grace and truth, protect and comfort us in all temptation, and bestow on us your saving peace, through Jesus Christ, our Lord, who lives and reigns with you and the Holy Spirit, one God, now and forever.

or

Almighty God, we thank you for teaching us the things you want us to believe and do. Help us by your Holy Spirit to keep your Word in pure hearts that we may be strengthened in faith, guided in holiness, and comforted in life and in death, through Jesus Christ, our Lord, who lives and reigns with you and the Holy Spirit, one God, now and forever.

C: A - men.

M: Brothers and sisters, go in peace. Live in harmony with one another. Serve the Lord with gladness.

The Lord bless you and keep you.
The Lord make his face shine on you and be gracious to you.
The Lord look on you with favor and ✠ give you peace.

C: A - men. A - men. A - men.

MORNING PRAISE
MATINS

"Morning Praise" is based on the historic service called "Matins." Joined to Christ, our risen Lord, we glorify God as we rise to the activities of this new day.

STAND

MORNING HYMN
Another hymn may be sung.

1 Fa - ther, we praise you, now the night is o - ver, Ac - tive and
2 Mon - arch of all things, fit us for your man - sions; Ban - ish our
3 All - ho - ly Fa - ther, Son, and e - qual Spir - it, Trin - i - ty

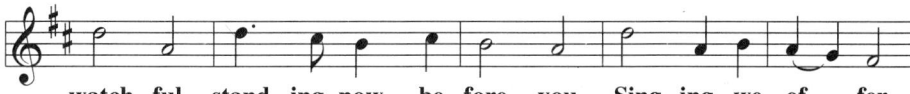

watch - ful, stand - ing now be - fore you. Sing - ing, we of - fer
weak - ness, health and whole - ness send - ing. Bring us to heav - en,
bless - ed, send us your sal - va - tion. Yours is the glo - ry,

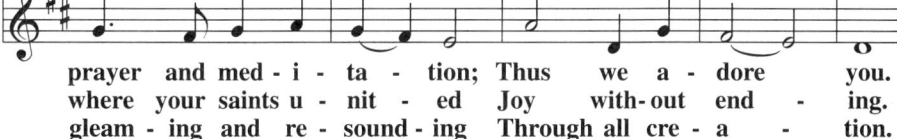

prayer and med - i - ta - tion; Thus we a - dore you.
where your saints u - nit - ed Joy with - out end - ing.
gleam - ing and re - sound - ing Through all cre - a - tion.

M: O Lord, o - pen my lips.

C: And my mouth shall de - clare your praise.

MORNING PRAISE

M: Has-ten to save me, O God.

C: O Lord, come quick-ly to help me.

M: (Advent) Behold the _____ King comes: let us wor-ship him.
   (Christmas) Unto us the _____ Christ is born: let us wor-ship him.
   (Epiphany) The glory of Christ _____ is re-vealed: let us wor-ship him.
   (Lent) Behold the _____ Lamb of God: let us wor-ship him.
   (Easter) The Lord is _____ ris - en: let us wor-ship him.
   (Pentecost) The Spirit of the Lord _____ fills the world: let us wor-ship him.
   (General) Praise be to God, the Father,
            the Son, and the Holy _____ Spir - it: let us wor-ship him.

OH, COME, LET US SING TO THE LORD
Venite

C: Oh, come, let us sing to the Lord, let us make a joyful noise to the rock of

our sal-va-tion. Let us come into his presence with thanks-giv-ing,

let us make a joyful noise to him with songs of praise. For the Lord is a

great God and a great king a-bove all gods. The deep places of the earth are

BE SEATED

PSALM

The PSALM is sung or said.

LESSON

Following the lesson, the SEASONAL RESPONSE may be sung or said.

Advent: The Lord will come again in glory. The Spirit and the Church cry out: Come, Lord Jesus, come.

Christmas/Epiphany: We have seen his glory, the glory of the one and only Son, who came from the Father, full of grace and truth.

Lent: All we like sheep have gone astray, and the Lord has laid on him the iniquity of us all. By his wounds we are healed.

Easter/Ascension: The Lord is risen! He is risen indeed! Alleluia! Death has been swallowed up in victory. Alleluia!

Pentecost: Come, Holy Spirit! Fill the hearts of your faithful people, and kindle in us the fire of your love. Alleluia!

General/Thanksgiving: Give thanks to the Lord; call on his name; make known among the nations what he has done.

HYMN

The SERMON may follow.

MORNING PRAISE

STAND

WE PRAISE YOU, O GOD or the SONG OF ZECHARIAH, Hymn 276, or another hymn is sung.

WE PRAISE YOU, O GOD
Te Deum

C: We praise you, O God, we acclaim you as Lord; all creation worships you, Father everlasting. To you all angels, all the pow'rs of heav'n, cherubim and seraphim, sing in endless praise: Holy, holy, holy Lord, God of heav'nly hosts, heaven and earth are full of your glory. The glorious company of apostles praise you. The noble fellowship of prophets praise you. The white–robed army of martyrs praise you. Throughout the world the holy Church acclaims you: Father of majesty unbounded, your glorious, true, and only Son,

and the Holy Spirit, ad - vo - cate and guide. You, Christ, are the King of glo - ry, the eternal Son of the Fa - ther. When you became man to set us free, you humbled yourself to be born of a vir-gin. You overcame the sting of death and opened the kingdom of heaven to all be-liev - ers. You sit at the right hand of God in the glory of the Fa - ther. We believe that you will come to be our judge. Come then, Lord, and help your peo - ple, bought with the price of your own blood, and bring us with your saints to glory ev - er - last - ing.

BE SEATED

The OFFERING may follow.

STAND

LORD, HAVE MERCY
Kyrie

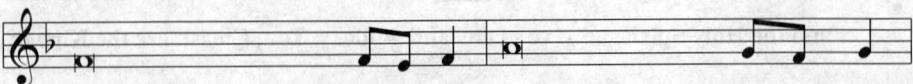

M: In the morning, O Lord, I call to you; be merciful to me and hear my prayer.

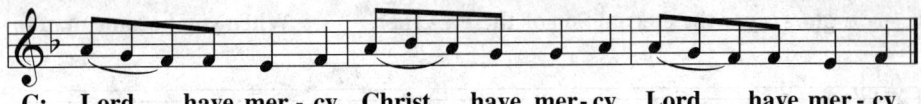

C: Lord, have mer-cy. Christ, have mer-cy. Lord, have mer-cy.

LORD'S PRAYER

C: Our Father in heaven,   *or*   Our Father, who art in heaven,

Our Father in heaven,	Our Father, who art in heaven,
hallowed be your name,	hallowed be thy name,
your kingdom come,	thy kingdom come,
your will be done	thy will be done
on earth as in heaven.	on earth as it is in heaven.
Give us today our daily bread.	Give us this day our daily bread;
Forgive us our sins,	and forgive us our trespasses,
as we forgive those	as we forgive those
who sin against us.	who trespass against us;
Lead us not into temptation,	and lead us not into temptation,
but deliver us from evil.	but deliver us from evil.
For the kingdom, the power,	For thine is the kingdom
and the glory are yours	and the power and the glory
now and forever. Amen.	forever and ever. Amen.

The PRAYER OF THE DAY or a prayer for the season or another prayer may follow, concluding with the PRAYER FOR GRACE.

PRAYER FOR GRACE

M: O Lord, our heavenly Father, almighty and everlasting God, you have brought us safely to this new day. Defend us with your mighty power, and grant that this day we neither fall into sin nor run into any kind of danger; and in all we do, direct us to what is right in your sight, through Jesus Christ, your Son, our Lord.

C: Amen.

MORNING PRAISE

M: Let us praise the Lord.

C: Thanks be to God.

BLESSING

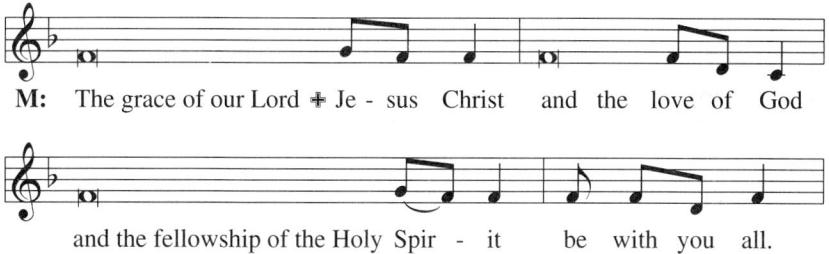
M: The grace of our Lord ✠ Jesus Christ and the love of God and the fellowship of the Holy Spirit be with you all.

C: A - men.

EVENING PRAYER
VESPERS

"Evening Prayer" is based on the historic service called "Vespers." Christians gather at the end of the day to raise their voices in thankful praise and prayer. Congregations may use the "Service of Light" (page 54) as an alternate beginning. The "Service of Light" portrays the comforting and ever-present light of Christ as daylight disappears.

OPENING HYMN

STAND

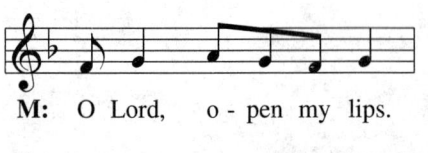

M: O Lord, o-pen my lips.

C: And my mouth shall de-clare your praise.

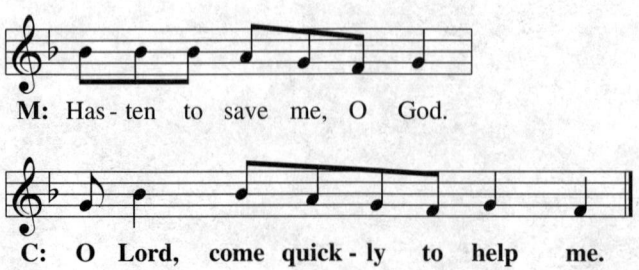

M: Has-ten to save me, O God.

C: O Lord, come quick-ly to help me.

EVENING PRAYER

M: The Lord be with you.

C: And al - so with you.

M: Lord God, you have brought us safely to this hour of evening prayer. We thank you for providing all that we need for body and life. Bless us who have gathered in your name. Forgive our sins. Speak to our hearts. Dispel our sorrows with the comfort of your Word, and receive our hymns of thanks and praise, through Jesus Christ, our living Savior, who reigns with you and the Holy Spirit, one God, now and forever.

C: **Amen.**

BE SEATED

> The service continues on page 55 with
> **LET MY PRAYER RISE BEFORE YOU**

EVENING PRAYER

SERVICE OF LIGHT
(Alternate Beginning)

STAND

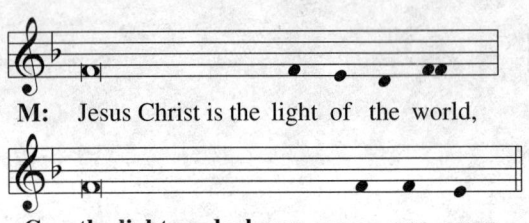

M: Jesus Christ is the light of the world,

C: the light no darkness can o-ver-come.

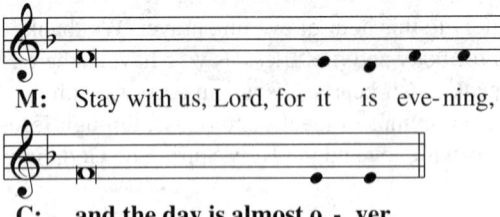

M: Stay with us, Lord, for it is eve-ning,

C: and the day is almost o - ver.

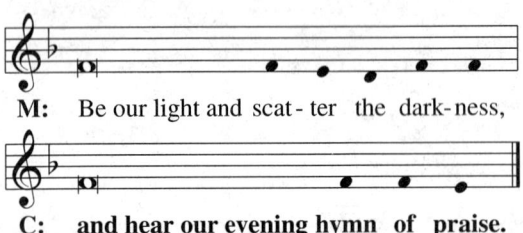

M: Be our light and scat-ter the dark-ness,

C: and hear our evening hymn of praise.

Candles may be lighted as this hymn is sung.

1 O gra-cious Light, Lord Je-sus Christ, In you the Fa-ther's glo-ry shone. Im-mor-tal, ho-ly, blest is he, And blest are you, his on-ly Son.

2 Now sun-set comes, but light shines forth; The lamps are lit to pierce the night. Praise Fa-ther, Son, and Spir-it: God Who dwells in the e-ter-nal light.

3 Wor-thy are you of end-less praise, O Son of God, life-giv-ing Lord; Where-fore you are through all the earth And in the high-est heav'n a-dored.

M: Blessed are you, O Lord our God, King of the universe, who led your people Israel with a pillar of cloud by day and a pillar of fire by night. Enlighten our darkness by the light of your Christ. May his Word be a lamp to our feet and a light to our path; for you are merciful, and you love your whole creation. We, your creatures, glorify you: Father, Son, and Holy Spirit.

or

Lord God, we thank you for this day of grace now drawing to a close. Stay with us and warm our hearts with your forgiving love in Christ. May your Word keep our faith burning brightly that we may walk in the light of your presence through the darkness of this world. Come and bless us as we worship you: Father, Son, and Holy Spirit.

C: Amen.

BE SEATED

LET MY PRAYER RISE BEFORE YOU
Psalm 141

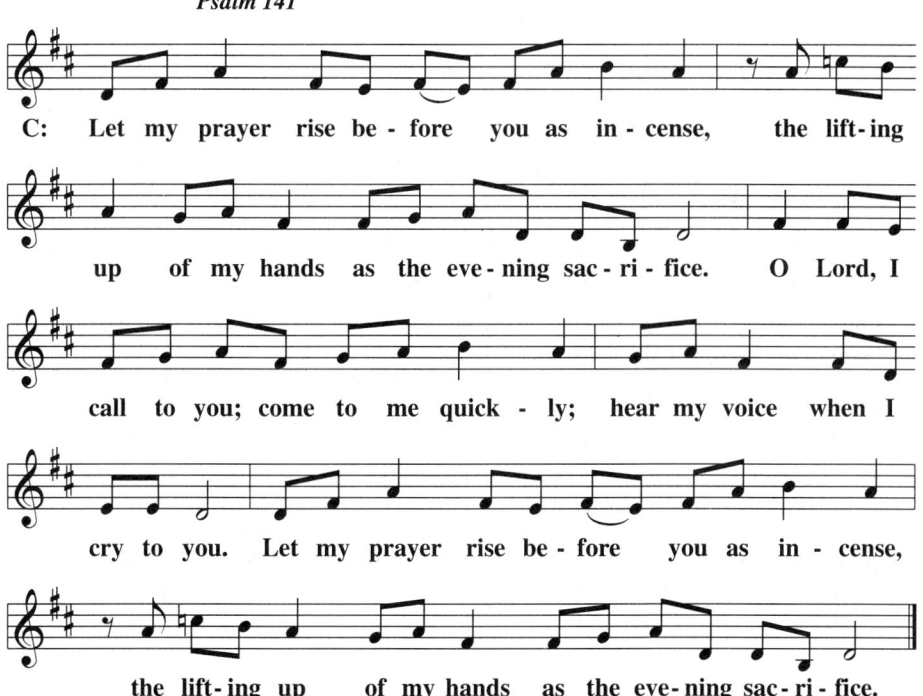

M: Let our prayers be acceptable in your sight. Come and help us in time of need that we may sing your praise in holy joy now and forever, through Jesus Christ, our Lord.

C: **Amen.**

PSALM

The PSALM is sung or said.

Silence for meditation.

The appointed psalm prayer or the following prayer is said.

M: Lord God, grant us your Holy Spirit that we may hear and believe your Word. Cleanse our minds and renew our hearts that we may live for you here and hereafter; through Jesus Christ, our Lord.

C: **Amen.**

LESSON

Following the lesson, the SEASONAL RESPONSE may be sung or said.

Advent: The Lord will come again in glory. The Spirit and the Church cry out: Come, Lord Jesus, come.

Christmas/Epiphany: We have seen his glory, the glory of the one and only Son, who came from the Father, full of grace and truth.

Lent: All we like sheep have gone astray, and the Lord has laid on him the iniquity of us all. By his wounds we are healed.

Easter/Ascension: The Lord is risen! He is risen indeed! Alleluia! Death has been swallowed up in victory. Alleluia!

Pentecost: Come, Holy Spirit! Fill the hearts of your faithful people, and kindle in us the fire of your love. Alleluia!

General/Thanksgiving: Give thanks to the Lord; call on his name; make known among the nations what he has done.

HYMN

EVENING PRAYER

The SERMON may follow.

STAND

The SONG OF MARY or a hymn is sung.

SONG OF MARY
Magnificat

C: My soul proclaims the greatness of the Lord; my spirit rejoices in God my Savior, for he has looked with favor on his lowly servant. From this day all generations will call me blessed. The Almighty has done great things for me, and holy is his name. He has mercy on those who fear him in ev-'ry generation.

He has shown the strength of his arm; he has scattered the

EVENING PRAYER

BE SEATED

The OFFERING may follow.

STAND

The following prayer or other prayers may be used concluding with the LORD'S PRAYER and the PRAYER FOR PEACE.

LORD, HAVE MERCY
Kyrie

M: In the closing hours of this day, hear us as we pray, O Lord:

C: Lord, have mer - cy.

M: For the well-being of people everywhere, for the growth of your church in all the world, and for the strengthening of all who serve and worship here, we pray, O Lord:

C: Christ, have mer - cy.

M: For one another, young and old, for your blessings that come with every stage of life, and for joy in doing your will, we pray, O Lord:

C: Lord, have mer - cy.

M: For our public servants who work day and night to bring protection, justice, learning, and health to this and every place, we pray to you, O Lord:

C: Lord, hear our prayer.

M: For favorable weather and bountiful harvests, for clothing and food, for health of body, mind, and spirit, and for deliverance from all sin and every form of evil, we pray to you, O Lord:

C: Lord, hear our prayer.

M: For the faithful who have gone before us, who have shared with us your good news, whose souls are now at rest in your heavenly kingdom, we give you thanks, O Lord:

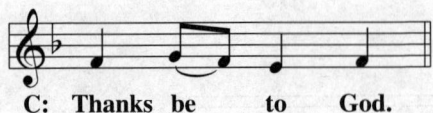

C: Thanks be to God.

M: In thanksgiving for your many and varied gifts to us, we now commend ourselves to your care. Be our shield and strength, O Lord.

C: A - men.

LORD'S PRAYER

C: Our Father in heaven,
   hallowed be your name,
   your kingdom come,
   your will be done
     on earth as in heaven.
Give us today our daily bread.
Forgive us our sins,
   as we forgive those
   who sin against us.
Lead us not into temptation,
but deliver us from evil.
For the kingdom, the power,
   and the glory are yours
   now and forever. Amen.

or

Our Father, who art in heaven,
   hallowed be thy name,
   thy kingdom come,
   thy will be done
     on earth as it is in heaven.
Give us this day our daily bread;
and forgive us our trespasses,
   as we forgive those
   who trespass against us;
and lead us not into temptation,
but deliver us from evil.
For thine is the kingdom
   and the power and the glory
   forever and ever. Amen.

PRAYER FOR PEACE

M: Lord God, all holy desires, all good counsels, and all just works come from you. Give to us, your servants, that peace which the world cannot give, that our hearts may be set to obey your commandments. Defend us also from the fear of our enemies that we may live in peace and quietness, through the merits of Jesus Christ our Savior, who lives and reigns with you and the Holy Spirit, one God, now and forever.

C: Amen.

EVENING PRAYER

SONG OF SIMEON
Nunc Dimittis

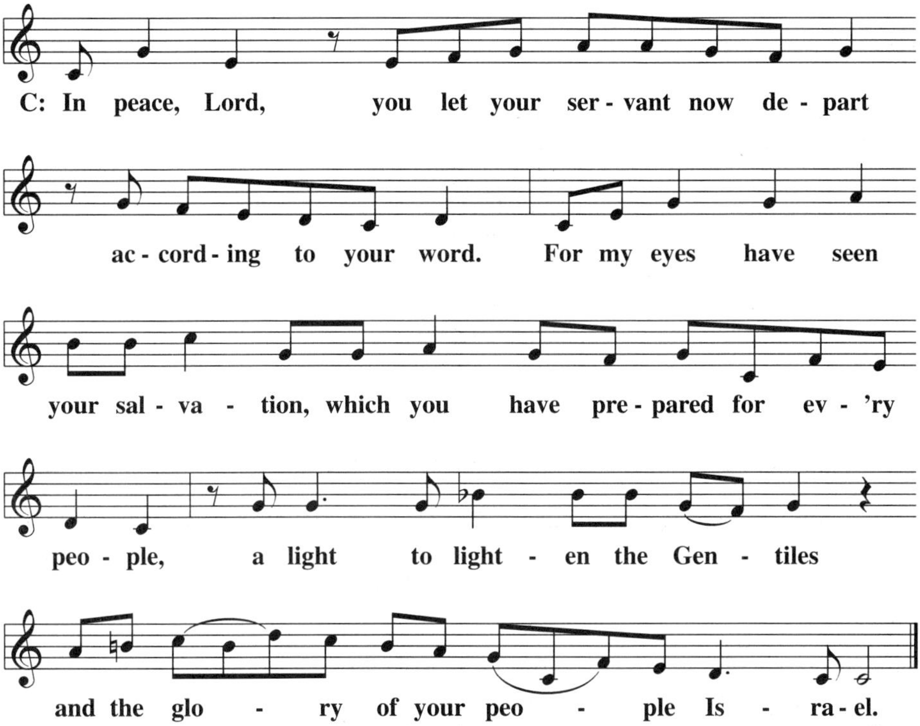

C: In peace, Lord, you let your servant now depart according to your word. For my eyes have seen your salvation, which you have prepared for ev-'ry people, a light to lighten the Gentiles and the glory of your people Israel.

BLESSING

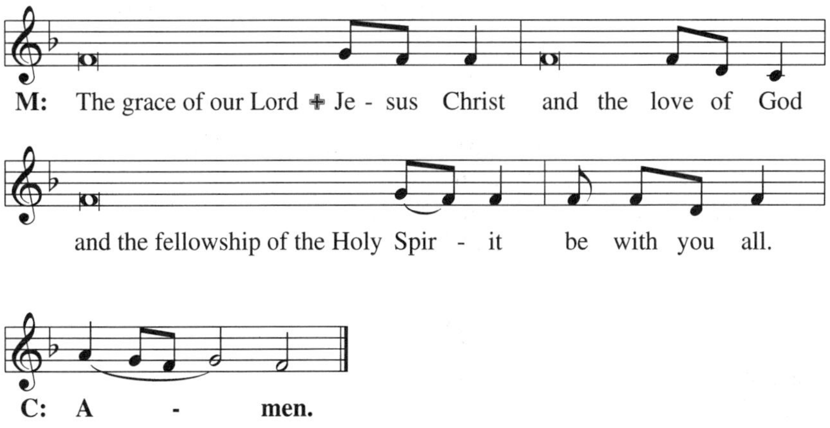

M: The grace of our Lord ✠ Jesus Christ and the love of God and the fellowship of the Holy Spirit be with you all.

C: Amen.

INDEX TO THE PSALMS

THE CHURCH YEAR

Advent 2, 8, 24, 85, 89, 96
Christmas 45, 72, 96, 98
Epiphany 2, 45, 47, 67, 72
Lent 2, 22, 51a, 118, 130
Easter 16, 96, 98, 118
Ascension 8, 24, 45, 47
Pentecost 51b, 67, 85, 96
End Time 1, 45, 46, 90

OCCASIONS IN LIFE

Sin, Confession, Forgiveness 6, 25, 30, 32, 38, 51a, 85, 90, 103, 130, 139a, 143

Trouble, Persecution, Danger 2, 18, 22, 23, 27, 31, 34, 38, 42-43, 46, 91, 121, 146
Deliverance 30, 34, 66, 116, 118, 126
Comfort 27, 42-43, 62
Angels 34, 91

Sickness 6, 23, 27, 103, 130, 143
Old Age 16, 71, 91
Death 16, 23, 31, 73, 90, 103, 118

Creation, Nature, Providence 8, 19, 23, 31, 33, 65, 96, 111, 139a, 145, 146, 148
Sanctity of Life 139b

Word 19, 119b, 119c
Worship 8, 33, 47, 51b, 65, 84, 89, 92, 96, 98, 100, 103, 118, 148, 150

Thanksgiving 65, 66, 103

Sanctification 1, 24, 51a, 51b, 62, 85, 119a, 119c
Stewardship 45, 62, 65
Evangelism 45, 51a, 51b, 66, 71, 89
Missions 45, 47, 67, 72, 98
Education 1, 78, 119b, 145

Anniversary 78, 90, 118

Close of Meeting 133-134
Christian Unity 133-134

Morning 8, 19, 51b, 84, 85, 100, 111, 145
Evening 23, 27, 31, 91, 121, 130

SINGING THE PSALMS

The following psalms have been printed for use in worship. Some of these psalms appear in their entirety; many others include only a selection of verses. The psalm verses were chosen and arranged to make them functional for corporate worship as well as suitable for private devotion. The psalms may be read or sung.

Each psalm includes a refrain and a psalm tone. The psalms may be sung with or without the refrain. If the refrain is sung, it should be sung at the beginning of the psalm and then repeated at the appointed places. The text of the psalm may be sung to the psalm tone. Each verse of the psalm is divided into two parts. The (*) marks the division. Each psalm tone also is divided into two parts marked by the (*). The first note of each half of the psalm tone is a reciting tone. One or more syllables of the text are sung on this tone. The point (´) indicates the syllable where the singer moves from the reciting tone to the last three notes of the psalm tone formula. Two or three syllables are sung on these three tones.

EXAMPLE:

    The LORD is my ´shepherd,*
      I shall not ´be in want.

The Lord is my shep - herd, I shall not be in want.

One way to sing the psalms is to have the congregation sing the refrain and have a choir or soloist sing the verses of the psalm. The refrain should be introduced by the organ or the choir with the congregation repeating the refrain at the beginning of the psalm. The choir or soloist then sings the verses of the psalm and the congregation joins in singing the refrain. The congregation may also join the choir in the singing of the "Glory be to the Father," which appears at the end of each psalm and is sung to the psalm tone formula.

These simple psalm settings provide materials that can lead to a great deal of variety as the psalms are used in worship. Choirs, soloists, and the congregation can become involved in singing the psalms in any number of interesting combinations. For a complete discussion of psalm performance, refer to *Christian Worship: Manual*.

Psalm 1

Refrain

Bless-ed are they who hope, who hope in the Lord.

Psalm tone

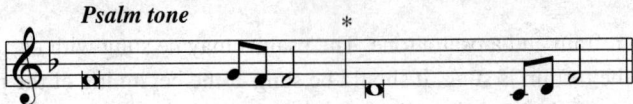

Blessed is the man
>   who does not walk in the counsel of the wícked*
>   or stand in the way of sínners.

But his delight is in the law óf the LORD,*
>   and on his law he meditates dáy and night.

He is like a tree planted by streams of wáter,
>   which yields its fruit in séason*
>   and whose leaf does not wither.
>   Whatever he does próspers.

Refrain

Therefore the wicked will not stand in the júdgment,*
>   nor sinners in the assembly of the ríghteous.

For the LORD watches over the way of the ríghteous,*
>   but the way of the wicked will pérish.

Glory be to the Father and tó the Son*
>   **and to the Holy Spírit,**
as it was in the begínning,*
>   **is now, and will be forever. Ámen.**

Refrain

Psalm 2

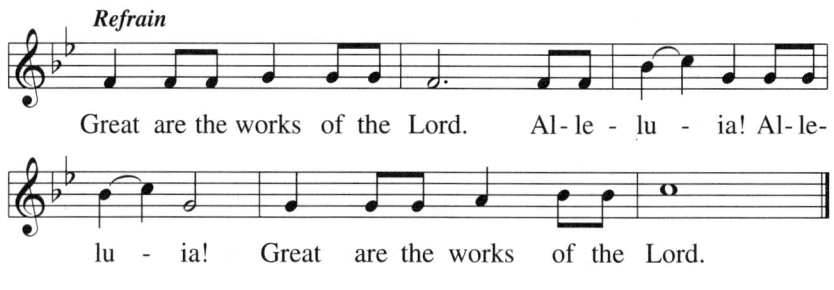

    Why do the nations conspire*
        and the peoples plot in vain?

    The kings of the earth take their stand and the rulers
        gather together against the LORD*
        and against his Anointed One.

Refrain

    The One enthroned in heaven laughs;*
        the Lord scoffs at them.

    Then he rebukes them in his anger
        and terrifies them in his wrath, saying,*
        "I have installed my King on Zion, my holy hill."

    I will proclaim the decree of the LORD:*
        He said to me, "You are my Son;
        today I have become your Father."

Glory be to the Father and to the Son*
    and to the Holy Spirit,
as it was in the beginning,*
    is now, and will be forever. Amen.

Refrain

Psalm 6

O Lord, do not rebuke me in your anger*
    or discipline me in your wrath.

Be merciful to me, Lord, for I am faint;*
    O Lord, heal me, for my soul is in anguish.

Turn, O Lord, and deliver me;*
    save me because of your unfailing love.

Refrain

I am worn out from groaning.*
    My eyes grow weak with sorrow.

Away from me, all you who do evil,*
    for the Lord has heard my weeping.

The Lord has heard my cry for mercy;*
    the Lord accepts my prayer.

Glory be to the Father and to the Son*
    and to the Holy Spirit,
as it was in the beginning,*
    is now, and will be forever. Amen.

Refrain

Psalm 8

I will praise your name for-ev-er, my King and my God.

O LORD, our Lord, how majestic is your name in all the earth!*
    You have set your glory above the heavens.

When I consider your heavens,*
    the work of your fingers,

what is man that you are mindful of him,*
    the Son of Man that you care for him?

Refrain

You made him a little lower than the heavenly beings*
    and crowned him with glory and honor.

You made him ruler over the works of your hands;*
    you put everything under his feet.

Glory be to the Father and to the Son*
    and to the Holy Spirit,
as it was in the beginning,*
    is now, and will be forever. Amen.

Refrain

Psalm 16

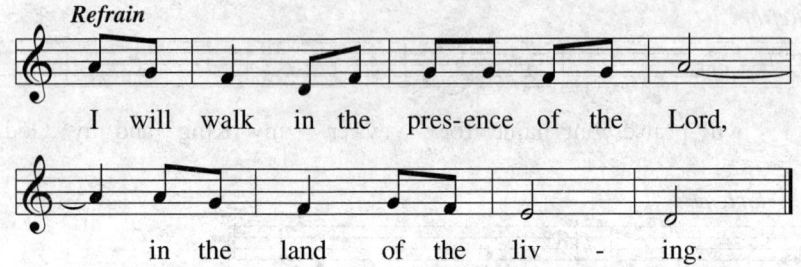

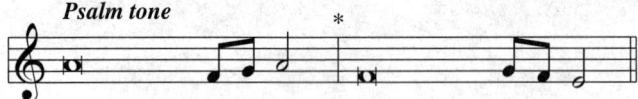

Keep me safe, O God,*
   for in you I take refuge.

I said to the LORD, "You are my Lord;*
   apart from you I have no good thing."

I have set the LORD always before me.*
   Because he is at my right hand, I will not be shaken.

Refrain

My heart is glad and my tongue rejoices;*
   my body also will rest secure,

because you will not abandon me to the grave,*
   nor will you let your Holy One see decay.

You have made known to me the path of life;*
   you will fill me with joy in your presence.

Glory be to the Father and to the Son*
   and to the Holy Spirit,
as it was in the beginning,*
   is now, and will be forever. Amen.

Refrain

Psalm 18

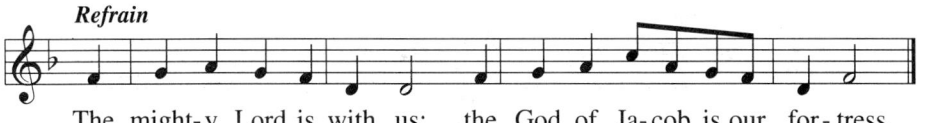

Refrain

The might-y Lord is with us; the God of Ja-cob is our for-tress.

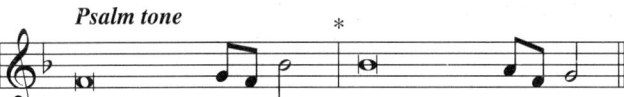

Psalm tone

The LORD is my rock, my fortress and my delíverer;*
 my God is my rock, in whom I take réfuge.

He reached down from on high and took hóld of me;*
 he rescued me from my powerful énemy.

He brought me out into a spácious place;*
 he rescued me because he delightéd in me.

Refrain

You, O LORD, keep my lamp búrning;*
 my God turns my darkness ínto light.

You save the húmble*
 but bring low those whose eyes are háughty.

You give me your shield of víctory,*
 and your right hand sustáins me.

Glory be to the Father and tó the Son*
 and to the Holy Spírit,
as it was in the begínning,*
 is now, and will be forever. Ámen.

Refrain

Psalm 19

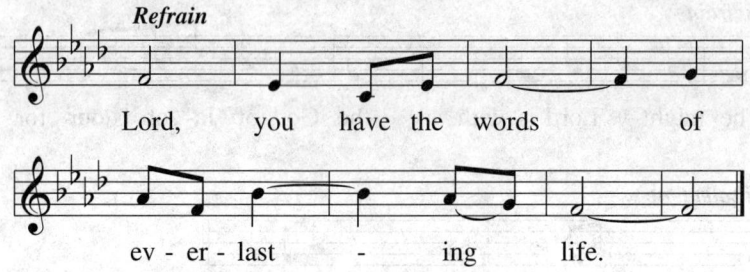

The heavens declare the glory of God;*
 the skies proclaim the work of his hands.

Their voice goes out into all the earth,*
 their words to the ends of the world.

Refrain

The law of the LORD is perfect,*
 giving joy to the heart.

The commands of the LORD are radiant,*
 giving light to the eyes.

They are more precious than gold;*
 they are sweeter than honey.

By them is your servant taught;*
 in keeping them there is great reward.

Refrain

May the words of my mouth and the meditation of my heart*
 be pleasing in your sight, O LORD, my Redeemer.

Glory be to the Father and to the Son*
 and to the Holy Spirit,
as it was in the beginning,*
 is now, and will be forever. Amen.

Refrain

Psalm 22

My God, my God, why have you forsaken me?*
 Why are you so far from saving me?

I am a worm and not a man,*
 scorned by men and despised by the people.

All who see me mock me;*
 they hurl insults, shaking their heads:

"He trusts in the LORD; let the LORD rescue him.*
 Let him deliver him, since he delights in him."

Refrain

My strength is dried up, and my tongue sticks to the roof of my mouth;*
 you lay me in the dust of death.

A band of evil men has encircled me,*
 they have pierced my hands and my feet.

They divide my garments among them*
 and cast lots for my clothing.

But you, O LORD, be not far off;*
 O my Strength, come quickly to help me.

Glory be to the Father and to the Son*
 and to the Holy Spirit,
as it was in the beginning,*
 is now, and will be forever. Amen.

Refrain

Psalm 23

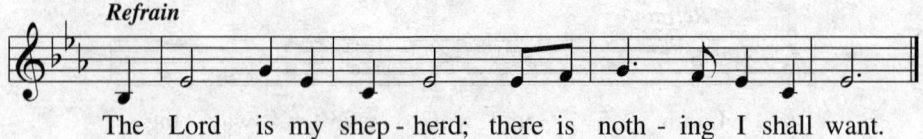

Refrain

The Lord is my shep-herd; there is noth-ing I shall want.

Psalm tone

                     The Lord is my shépherd,*
                         I shall not bé in want.

                     He makes me lie down in green pástures;*
                         he leads me beside quiet wáters.

                     He restóres my soul;*
                         he guides me in paths of righteousness
                         for his náme's sake.

                     Even though I walk through the valley
                         of the shadow of death, I will fear no évil,*
                         for you are with me;
                         your rod and your staff, they cómfort me.

                    Refrain

                     You prepare a table before me in the presence of my énemies.*
                         You anoint my head with oil;
                         my cup óverflows.

                     Surely goodness and love will follow me
                         all the days óf my life,*
                         and I will dwell in the house of the Lord foréver.

**   Glory be to the Father and tó the Son***
**   and to the Holy Spírit,**
**   as it was in the begínning,***
**   is now, and will be forever. Ámen.**

                  Refrain

Psalm 24

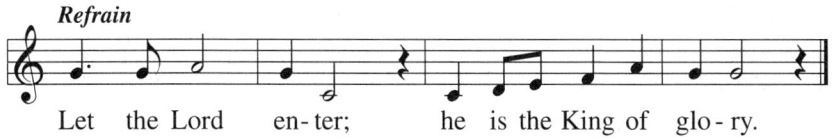

Refrain: Let the Lord enter; he is the King of glory.

Psalm tone

The earth is the LORD'S, and everything in it,*
 the world, and all who live in it;

for he founded it upon the seas*
 and established it upon the waters.

Who may ascend the hill of the LORD?*
 Who may stand in his holy place?

He who has clean hands and a pure heart,*
 he will receive blessing from God his Savior.

Refrain

Lift up your heads, O you gates;
be lifted up, you ancient doors,*
 that the King of glory may come in.

Who is this King of glory?*
 The LORD strong and mighty,
 the LORD mighty in battle.

Lift up your heads, O you gates;
lift them up, you ancient doors,*
 that the King of glory may come in.

Who is he, this King of glory?*
 The LORD Almighty—he is the King of glory.

Glory be to the Father and to the Son*
 and to the Holy Spirit,
as it was in the beginning,*
 is now, and will be forever. Amen.

Refrain

Psalm 25

Refrain: To you, O Lord, I lift my soul; in you I trust, my God.

Psalm tone

To you, O Lord, I lift úp my soul;*
 in you I trust, Ó my God.

Remember, O Lord, your great mércy and love,*
 for they are fróm of old.

Remember not the sins of my youth and my rebéllious ways;*
 according to your love remémber me,
 for you are góod, O Lord.

Refrain

Turn to me and be grácious to me,*
 for I am lonely and afflícted.

Look upon my affliction and my distress*
 and take away áll my sins.

Guard my life and réscue me,*
 for I take refúge in you.

Glory be to the Father and tó the Son*
 and to the Holy Spirit,
as it was in the begínning,*
 is now, and will be forever. Ámen.

Refrain

Psalm 27

Hear my voice when I call, O LORD;*
  be merciful to me and answer me.

Do not hide your face from me,*
  do not turn your servant away in anger; you have been my helper.

Do not reject me or forsake me,*
  O God my Savior.

Refrain

Though my father and mother forsake me,*
  the LORD will receive me.

I am still confident of this:*
  I will see the goodness of the LORD in the land of the living.

Wait for the LORD;*
  be strong and take heart and wait for the LORD.

Glory be to the Father and to the Son*
  and to the Holy Spirit,
as it was in the beginning,*
  is now, and will be forever. Amen.

Refrain

Psalm 30

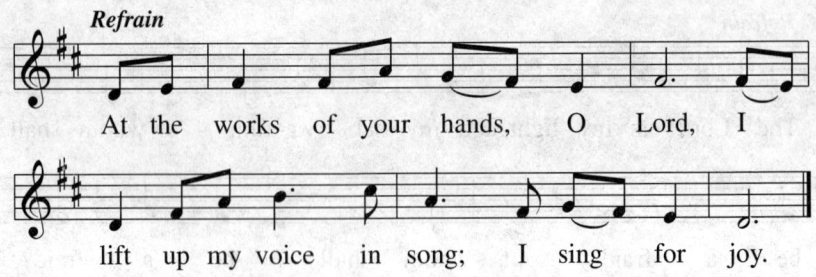

Sing to the Lord, you saints of his;*
 praise his holy name.

For his anger lasts only a moment,*
 but his favor lasts a lifetime;

weeping may remain for a night,*
 but rejoicing comes in the morning.

Refrain

To you, O Lord, I called;*
 to the Lord I cried for mercy.

Hear, O Lord, and be merciful to me;*
 O Lord, be my help.

You turned my wailing into dancing,*
 that my heart may sing to you and not be silent.

Glory be to the Father and to the Son*
 and to the Holy Spirit,
as it was in the beginning,*
 is now, and will be forever. Amen.

Refrain

Psalm 31

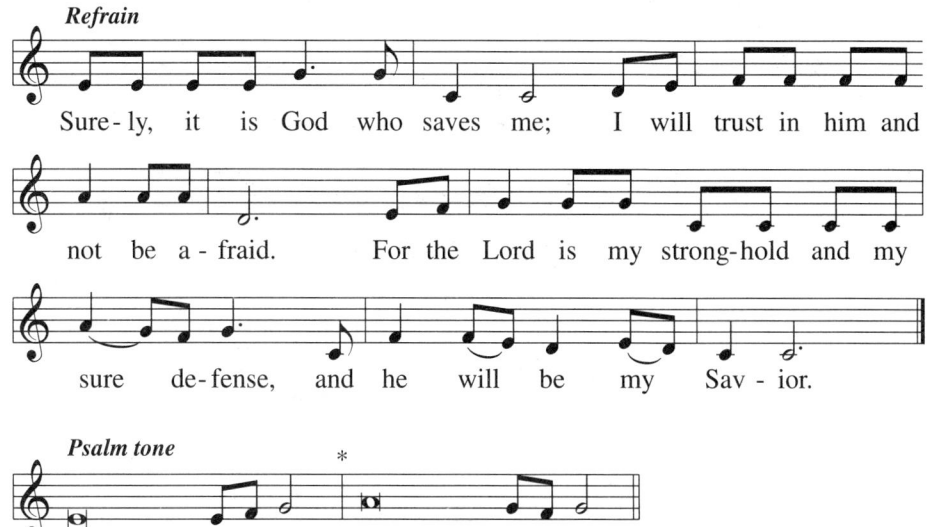

In you, O LORD, I have taken refuge;*
  deliver me in your righteousness.

Be my rock of refuge,*
  a strong fortress to save me.

Into your hands I commit my spirit;*
  redeem me, O LORD, the God of truth.

Refrain

My times are in your hands;*
  save me in your unfailing love.

How great is your goodness,*
  which you have stored up for those who fear you.

You heard my cry for mercy*
  when I called to you for help.

Glory be to the Father and to the Son*
  and to the Holy Spirit,
as it was in the beginning,*
  is now, and will be forever. Amen.

Refrain

Psalm 32

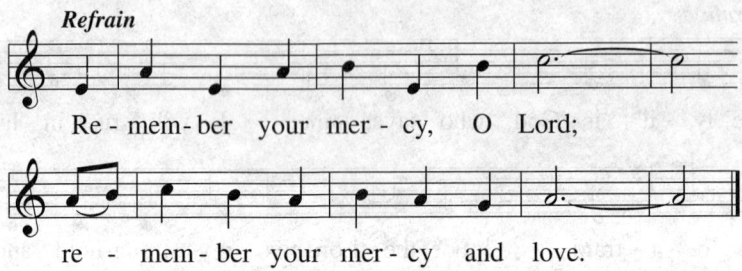

Refrain
Re-mem-ber your mer-cy, O Lord;
re-mem-ber your mer-cy and love.

Psalm tone

Blessed is he whose transgréssions are forgíven,*
    whose sins are cóvered.

When I kept silent, your hand was heavy upón me;*
    my strength was sapped as in the heat of súmmer.

Then I acknowledged my sín to you*
    and did not cover up my iníquity.

I said, "I will confess my transgressions tó the LORD,"*
    and you forgave the guilt óf my sin.

Refrain

You are my híding place;*
    you will protect me from tróuble.

Many are the woes of the wícked,*
    but the LORD's unfailing love surrounds
    those who trúst in him.

Glory be to the Father and tó the Son*
    and to the Holy Spírit,
as it was in the begínning,*
    is now, and will be forever. Ámen.

Refrain

Psalm 33

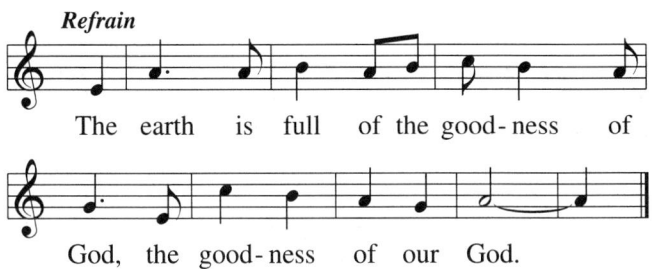

The earth is full of the good-ness of God, the good-ness of our God.

Psalm tone

Sing joyfully to the LORD, you righteous;*
 it is fitting for the upright to praise him.

For the Word of the LORD is right and true;*
 he is faithful in all he does.

By the word of the LORD were the heavens made,*
 their starry host by the breath of his mouth.

For he spoke, and it came to be;*
 he commanded, and it stood firm.

Refrain

The LORD foils the plans of the nations;*
 he thwarts the purposes of the peoples.

But the plans of the LORD stand firm forever,*
 the purposes of his heart through all generations.

The LORD loves righteousness and justice;*
 the earth is full of his unfailing love.

Glory be to the Father and to the Son*
 and to the Holy Spirit,
as it was in the beginning,*
 is now, and will be forever. Amen.

Refrain

Psalm 34

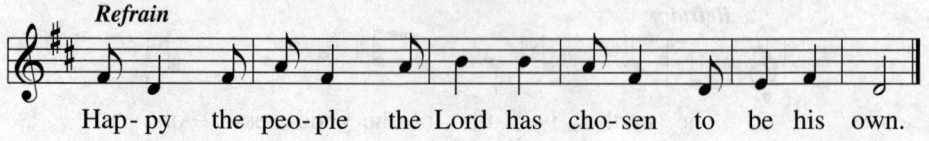

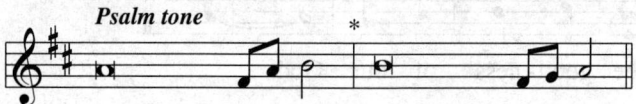

Taste and see that the LORD is good;*
   blessed are they who take refuge in him.

The eyes of the LORD are on the righteous*
   and his ears are attentive to their cry.

The angel of the LORD encamps around those who fear him,*
   and he delivers them.

Refrain

The righteous cry out, and the LORD hears them;*
   he delivers them from all their troubles.

The LORD is close to the brokenhearted*
   and saves those who are crushed in spirit.

The LORD redeems his servants;*
   no one who takes refuge in him will be condemned.

Glory be to the Father and to the Son*
   and to the Holy Spirit,
as it was in the beginning,*
   is now, and will be forever. Amen.

Refrain

Psalm 38

Refrain: Be mer-ci-ful, O Lord, for we have sinned.

Psalm tone

O LORD, do not rebuke me in your anger*
 or discipline me in your wrath.

For your arrows have pierced me,*
 and your hand has come down upon me.

My guilt has overwhelmed me*
 like a burden too heavy to bear.

Refrain

All my longings lie open before you, O LORD;*
 my sighing is not hidden from you.

I wait for you, O LORD;*
 you will answer, O Lord my God.

Come quickly to help me,*
 O Lord my Savior.

Glory be to the Father and to the Son*
 and to the Holy Spirit,
as it was in the beginning,*
 is now, and will be forever. Amen.

Refrain

Psalm 42-43

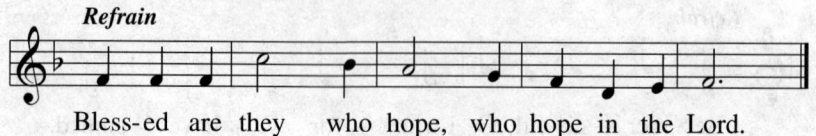

As the deer pants for streams of ́water,*
   so my soul pants for ́you, O God.

My soul thirsts for God, for the ĺiving God.*
   Where can I go and ́meet with God?

Why are you downcast, Ó my soul?*
   Why so disturbed withín me?

Put your ́hope in God,*
   for I will yet praise him, my Savior ́and my God.

Refrain

Send forth your light and your truth, let them ́guide me;*
   let them bring me to the place ́where you dwell.

Then will I go to the altar of God, my joy and ḿy delight.*
   I will praise you with the harp, O God, my God.

Glory be to the Father and t́o the Son*
   and to the Holy Śpirit,
as it was in the begínning,*
   is now, and will be forever. Ámen.

Refrain

Psalm 45

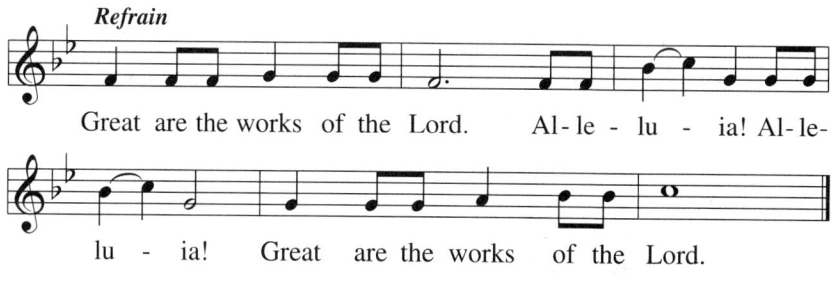

My heart is stirred by a noble theme*
    as I recite my verses for the King.

You are the most excellent of men,*
    and your lips have been anointed with grace.

Gird your sword upon your side, O Mighty One;*
    clothe yourself with splendor and majesty.

In your majesty ride forth victoriously;*
    let your right hand display awesome deeds.

Refrain

Your throne, O God, will last for ever and ever;*
    a scepter of justice will be the scepter of your kingdom.

You love righteousness and hate wickedness;*
    therefore God has anointed you with the oil of joy.

I will perpetuate your memory through all generations;*
    therefore the nations will praise you for ever and ever.

Glory be to the Father and to the Son*
    and to the Holy Spirit,
as it was in the beginning,*
    is now, and will be forever. Amen.

Refrain

Psalm 46

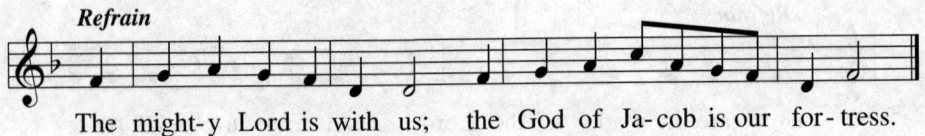

Refrain: The might-y Lord is with us; the God of Ja-cob is our for-tress.

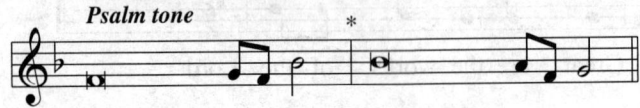

Psalm tone

God is our refúge and strength,*
    an ever-present help in tróuble.

Therefore we will not fear, though the éarth give way*
    and the mountains fall into the heart óf the sea,

though its waters róar and foam*
    and the mountains quake with their súrging.

Refrain

There is a river whose streams make glad the citý of God,*
    the holy place where the Most Hígh dwells.

God is within her, she will not fall;*
    God will help her at bréak of day.

"Be still, and know that Í am God;*
    I will be exalted amóng the nations,
    I will be exalted ín the earth."

Glory be to the Father and tó the Son*
    and to the Holy Spírit,
as it was in the begínning,*
    is now, and will be forever. Ámen.

Refrain

84

Psalm 47

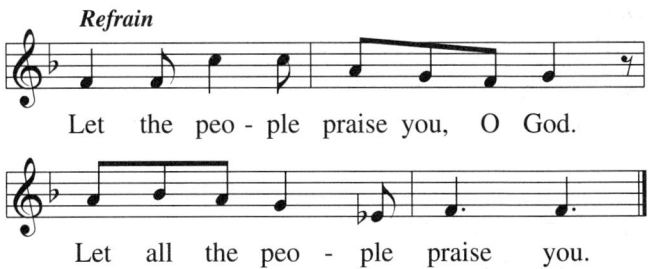

Clap your hands, all you nátions;*
　　shout to God with críes of joy.

How awesome is the LÓRD Most High,*
　　the great King over áll the earth!

God reigns over the nátions;*
　　God is seated on his hóly throne.

Refrain

God has ascended amid shóuts of joy,*
　　the LORD amid the sounding of trúmpets.

Sing praises to God, sing práises;*
　　sing praises to our King, sing práises.

For God is the King of áll the earth;*
　　sing to him a psálm of praise.

Glory be to the Father and tó the Son*
　　and to the Holy Spírit,
as it was in the begínning,*
　　is now, and will be forever. Ámen.

Refrain

Psalm 51a

Refrain

Be mer-ci-ful, O Lord, for we have sinned.

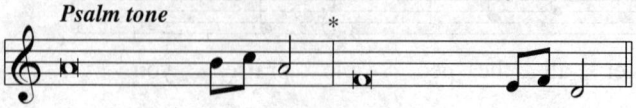

Psalm tone

Have mercy on me, O God,*
    according to your unfailing love.

Wash away all my iniquity,*
    and cleanse me from my sin.

For I know my transgressions,*
    and my sin is always before me.

Refrain

Against you, you only, have I sinned*
    and done what is evil in your sight.

Surely I was sinful at birth,*
    sinful from the time my mother conceived me.

Hide your face from my sins,*
    and blot out all my iniquity.

Restore to me the joy of your salvation,*
    and grant me a willing spirit, to sustain me.

Glory be to the Father and to the Son*
    and to the Holy Spirit,
as it was in the beginning,*
    is now, and will be forever. Amen.

Refrain

Psalm 51 b

O Lord, open my lips,*
   and my mouth will declare your praise.

You do not delight in sacrifice, or I would bring it;*
   you do not take pleasure in burnt offerings.

The sacrifices of God are a broken spirit;*
   a broken and contrite heart, O God, you will not despise.

Refrain

Create in me a pure heart, O God,*
   and renew a steadfast spirit within me.

Do not cast me from your presence*
   or take your Holy Spirit from me.

Restore to me the joy of your salvation,*
   and grant me a willing spirit, to sustain me.

Then I will teach transgressors your ways,*
   and sinners will turn back to you.

Glory be to the Father and to the Son*
   and to the Holy Spirit,
as it was in the beginning,*
   is now, and will be forever. Amen.

Refrain

Psalm 62

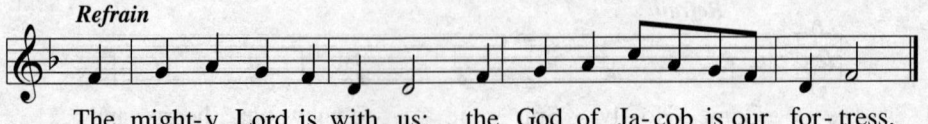
The might-y Lord is with us; the God of Ja-cob is our for-tress.

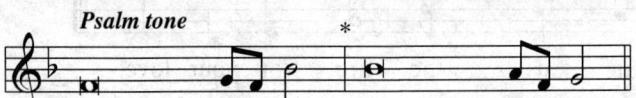

My soul finds rest in God alone;*
  my salvation comes from him.

He alone is my rock and my salvation;*
  he is my fortress, I will never be shaken.

Find rest, O my soul, in God alone;*
  my hope comes from him.

Refrain

Though your riches increase,*
  do not set your heart on them.

My salvation and my honor depend on God;*
  he is my mighty rock, my refuge.

Trust in him at all times, O people;*
  pour out your hearts to him, for God is our refuge.

Glory be to the Father and to the Son*
  and to the Holy Spirit,
as it was in the beginning,*
  is now, and will be forever. Amen.

Refrain

Psalm 65

Praise awaits you, O God,*
   you call forth songs of joy.

You care for the land and water it;*
   you soften it with showers and bless its crops.

The streams of God are filled with water*
   to provide the people with grain.

Refrain

You crown the year with your bounty,*
   and your carts overflow with abundance.

The grasslands of the desert overflow;*
   the hills are clothed with gladness.

The meadows are covered with flocks
   and the valleys are mantled with grain;*
   they shout for joy and sing.

Glory be to the Father and to the Son*
**   and to the Holy Spirit,**
as it was in the beginning,*
**   is now, and will be forever. Amen.**

Refrain

Psalm 66

Shout with joy to God, all the earth!*
  Sing the glory of his name; make his praise glorious!

Praise our God, O peoples,*
  let the sound of his praise be heard.

He has preserved our lives*
  and kept our feet from slipping.

Refrain

Come and listen, all you who fear God;*
  let me tell you what he has done for me.

If I had cherished sin in my heart,*
  the Lord would not have listened;

but God has surely listened*
  and heard my voice in prayer.

Glory be to the Father and to the Son*
  and to the Holy Spirit,
as it was in the beginning,*
  is now, and will be forever. Amen.

Refrain

Psalm 67

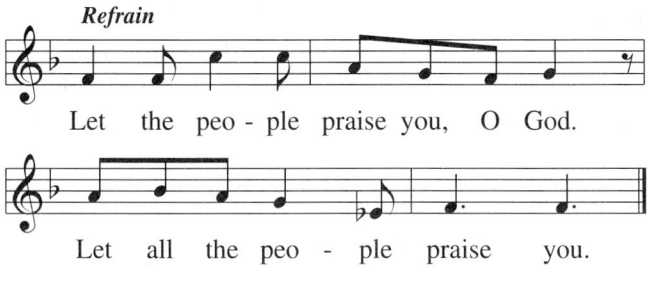

May God be gracious to us and bléss us*
   and make his face shine upón us;

may your ways be knówn on earth,*
   your salvation among all nátions.

May the nations be glad and síng for joy,*
   for you rule the peoples justly
   and guide the nations óf the earth.

Refrain

Then the land will yield its hárvest,*
   and God, our God, will bléss us.

God will bléss us,*
   and all the ends of the earth will féar him.

Glory be to the Father and tó the Son*
   and to the Holy Spírit,
as it was in the begínning,*
   is now, and will be forever. Ámen.

Refrain

Psalm 71

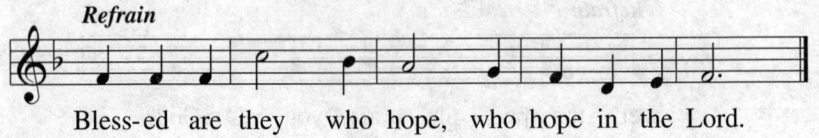

Bless-ed are they who hope, who hope in the Lord.

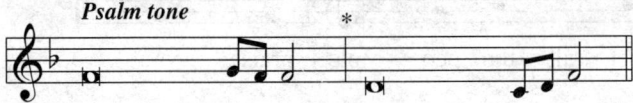

In you, O LORD, I have taken refuge;*
   let me never be put to shame.

Rescue me and deliver me in your righteousness;*
   turn your ear to me and save me.

Be my rock of refuge to which I can always go;*
   for you are my rock and my fortress.

Refrain

Since my youth, O God, you have taught me,*
   and to this day I declare your marvelous deeds.

Even when I am old and gray,*
   do not forsake me, O God,

till I declare your power to the next generation,*
   your might to all who are to come.

Glory be to the Father and to the Son*
   and to the Holy Spirit,
as it was in the beginning,*
   is now, and will be forever. Amen.

Refrain

Psalm 72

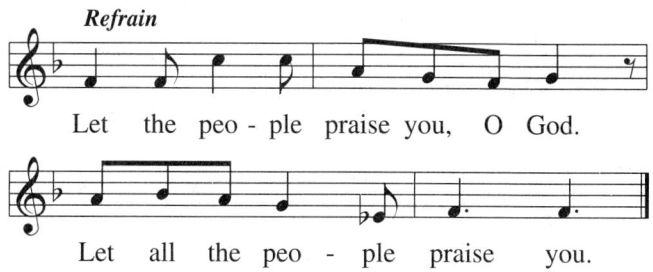

Endow the King with your justice, Ó God,*
 the royal Son with your ríghteousness.

He will defend the afflicted among the péople*
 and save the children of the néedy.

He will endure as long ás the sun,*
 as long as the moon, through all generátions.

He will be like rain falling on a mówn field,*
 like showers watering the earth.

Refrain

All kings will bow dówn to him,*
 and all nations will śerve him.

All nations will be bléssed through him,*
 and they will call him blessed.

Praise be to the LORD God, who alone does marvélous deeds.*
 May the whole earth be filled with his glóry.

Glory be to the Father and tó the Son*
 and to the Holy Śpirit,
as it was in the begínning,*
 is now, and will be forever. Ámen.

Refrain

Psalm 73

I am always with yóu, O Lord;*
   you hold me by my ríght hand.

You guide me with your cóunsel,*
   and afterward you will take me into glóry.

Whom have I in heavén but you?*
   And earth has nothing I desire besídes you.

My flesh and my héart may fail,*
   but God is the strength of my heart
   and my portion foréver.

Glory be to the Father and tó the Son*
   and to the Holy Spírit,
as it was in the begínning,*
   is now, and will be forever. Ámen.

Refrain

Psalm 78

Refrain: Your Word is a lamp to my feet and a light for my path.

Psalm tone

O my people, hear my teaching;*
 listen to the words of my mouth.

I will utter things from of old,*
 what we have heard and what our fathers have told us.

We will not hide them from our children;*
 we will tell the next generation
 the praiseworthy deeds of the LORD.

Refrain

The LORD decreed statutes for Jacob*
 and established the law in Israel,

so the next generation would know them,*
 and they in turn would tell their children.

Then they would put their trust in God*
 and would not forget his deeds but would keep his commands.

Glory be to the Father and to the Son*
 and to the Holy Spirit,
as it was in the beginning,*
 is now, and will be forever. Amen.

Refrain

Psalm 84

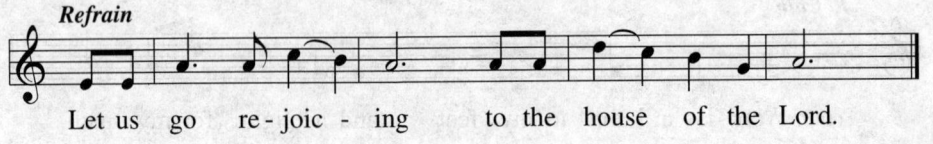

Refrain: Let us go rejoicing to the house of the Lord.

Psalm tone

How lovely is your dwélling place,*
   O Lord Almíghty!

My soul yearns, éven faints,*
   for the courts óf the Lord.

Blessed are those who dwell ín your house;*
   they are ever práising you.

Refrain

Better is one day ín your courts*
   than a thousand élsewhere;

I would rather be a doorkeeper in the house óf my God*
   than dwell in the tents of the wícked.

O Lord Almíghty,*
   blessed are they who trúst in you.

Glory be to the Father and tó the Son*
   and to the Holy Spírit,
as it was in the begínning,*
   is now, and will be forever. Ámen.

Refrain

Psalm 85

Refrain: I will hear what the Lord proclaims: peace to his people.

Psalm tone

You showed favor to your land, O LORD;*
 you restored the fortunes of Jacob.

You forgave the iniquity of your people*
 and covered all their sins.

Show us your unfailing love, O LORD,*
 and grant us your salvation.

Refrain

I will listen to what God the LORD will say;*
 he promises peace to his people, his saints.

Surely his salvation is near those who fear him,*
 that his glory may dwell in our land.

Love and faithfulness meet together;*
 righteousness and peace kiss each other.

Glory be to the Father and to the Son*
 and to the Holy Spirit,
as it was in the beginning,*
 is now, and will be forever. Amen.

Refrain

Psalm 89

I will sing of the LORD's great love foréver;*
 I will make your faithfulness known through all generátions.

I will declare that your love stands firm foréver,*
 that you established your faithfulness in heavén itself.

The heavens praise your wónders, O LORD,*
 your faithfulness too, in the assembly of the hóly ones.

Refrain

O LORD God Almighty, who ís like you?*
 You are mighty, O LORD, and your faithfulness surróunds you.

Blessed are those who have learned to acclaim you,*
 who walk in the light of your presénce, O LORD.

They rejoice in your name áll day long;*
 they exult in your ríghteousness.

Glory be to the Father and tó the Son*
 and to the Holy Spírit,
as it was in the begínning,*
 is now, and will be forever. Ámen.

Refrain

Psalm 90

Refrain

In ev-'ry age, O Lord, you have been our ref - uge.

Psalm tone

Lord, you have been our dwelling place*
   throughout all generations.

Before the mountains were born
   or you brought forth the earth and the world,*
   from everlasting to everlasting you are God.

For a thousand years in your sight are like a day
   that has just gone by,*
   or like a watch in the night.

Refrain

You have set our iniquities before you,*
   our secret sins in the light of your presence.

You turn mortals back to dust.*
   You sweep them away in the sleep of death.

The length of our days is seventy years—
   or eighty, if we have the strength;*
   yet their span is but trouble and sorrow.

Teach us to number our days aright,*
   that we may gain a heart of wisdom.

Refrain

Satisfy us in the morning with your unfailing love,*
   that we may sing for joy and be glad all our days.

Glory be to the Father and to the Son*
   and to the Holy Spirit,
as it was in the beginning,*
   is now, and will be forever. Amen.

Refrain

Psalm 91

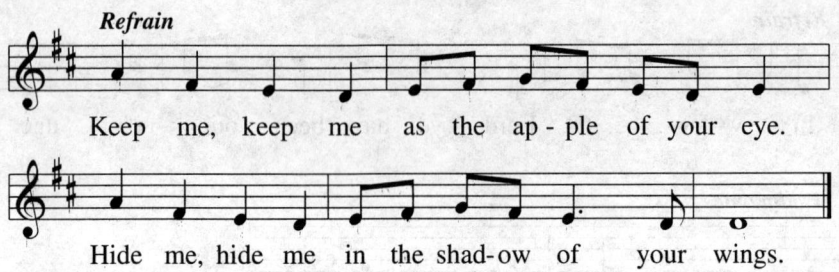

He who dwells in the shelter of the Most High*
   will rest in the shadow of the Almighty.

I will say of the LORD,*
   "He is my refuge and my fortress,
   my God, in whom I trust."

Refrain

You will not fear the terror of the night,*
   nor the arrow that flies by day.

If you make the Most High your dwelling,*
   then no harm will befall you,
   no disaster will come near your tent.

For he will command his angels concerning you*
   to guard you in all your ways;

they will lift you up in their hands,*
   so that you will not strike your foot against a stone.

Glory be to the Father and to the Son*
   and to the Holy Spirit,
as it was in the beginning,*
   is now, and will be forever. Amen.

Refrain

Psalm 92

Refrain

Psalm tone

How great are your works, O LORD,*
    how profound your thoughts!

The senseless man does not know,*
    fools do not understand,

that though the wicked spring up like grass*
    and all evildoers flourish,

they will be forever destroyed.*
    But you, O LORD, are exalted foréver.

Refrain

The righteous will flourish like a palm tree,*
    they will flourish in the courts of our God.

They will still bear fruit in old age,*
    they will stay fresh and green,

proclaiming, "The LORD is upright;*
    he is my rock, and there is no wickedness in him."

Glory be to the Father and to the Son*
    and to the Holy Spirit,
as it was in the beginning,*
    is now, and will be forever. Ámen.

Refrain

Psalm 96

Refrain
Sing to the Lord a new song; sing to the Lord a new song.

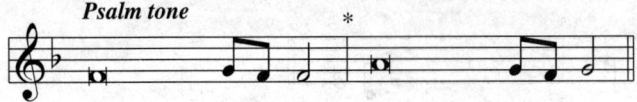
Psalm tone

Sing to the Lord, praise his name;*
 proclaim his salvation day after day.

Declare his glory among the nations,*
 his marvelous deeds among all peoples.

Worship the Lord in the splendor of his holiness;*
 tremble before him, all the earth.

Refrain

Let the heavens rejoice, let the earth be glad;*
 let the sea resound, and all that is in it;

let the fields be jubilant, and everything in them.*
 Then all the trees of the forest will sing for joy;

for he comes to judge the world in righteousness*
 and the peoples in his truth.

Glory be to the Father and to the Son*
 and to the Holy Spirit,
as it was in the beginning,*
 is now, and will be forever. Amen.

Refrain

Psalm 98

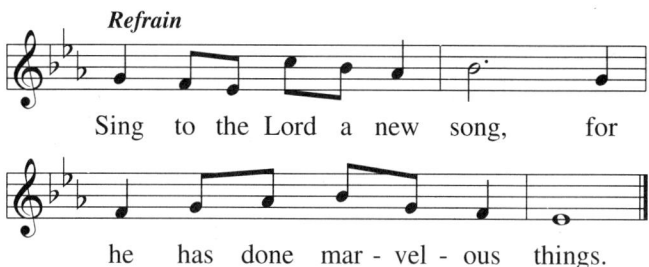

Sing to the LORD a new song,*
 for he has done marvelous things.

The LORD has made his salvation known*
 and revealed his righteousness to the nations.

He has remembered his love and his faithfulness
 to the house of Israel;*
 all the ends of the earth have seen
 the salvation of our God.

Refrain

Shout for joy to the LORD, all the earth,*
 burst into jubilant song with music;

make music to the LORD with the harp,*
 with the harp and the sound of singing.

Shout for joy before the LORD, the King.*
 He will judge the world in righteousness
 and the peoples with equity.

Glory be to the Father and to the Son*
 and to the Holy Spirit,
as it was in the beginning,*
 is now, and will be forever. Amen.

Refrain

Psalm 100

Refrain

Sing to the Lord a new song; sing to the Lord a new song.

Psalm tone

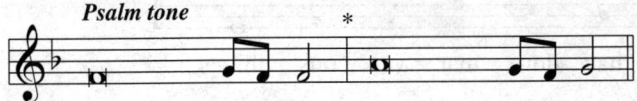

Shout for joy to the Lord, all the earth.*
    Worship the Lord with gladness;

come before him with joyful songs.*
    Know that the Lord is God.

It is he who made us, and we are his;*
    we are his people, the sheep of his pasture.

Refrain

Enter his gates with thanksgiving
    and his courts with praise;*
    give thanks to him and praise his name.

For the Lord is good and his love endures forever;*
    his faithfulness continues through all generations.

Glory be to the Father and to the Son*
    and to the Holy Spirit,
as it was in the beginning,*
    is now, and will be forever. Amen.

Refrain

Psalm 103

Refrain: I will hear what the Lord pro-claims: peace to his peo-ple.

Psalm tone

Praise the LORD, O my soul;*
 all my inmost being, praise his holy name.

He forgives all your sins*
 and heals all your diseases;

he redeems your life from the grave*
 and crowns you with love and compassion.

Refrain

The LORD is compassionate and gracious,*
 slow to anger, abounding in love.

He does not treat us as our sins deserve*
 or repay us according to our iniquities.

For as high as the heavens are above the earth,*
 so great is his love for those who fear him;

as far as the east is from the west,*
 so far has he removed our transgressions from us.

Refrain

As a father has compassion on his children,*
 so the LORD has compassion on those who fear him;

for he knows how we are formed,*
 he remembers that we are dust.

Our days are like grass, like a flower of the field;*
 the wind blows over it and it is gone.

But the LORD'S love is with those who fear him*
 from everlasting to everlasting.

Glory be to the Father and to the Son*
 and to the Holy Spirit,
as it was in the beginning,*
 is now, and will be forever. Amen.

Refrain

Psalm 111

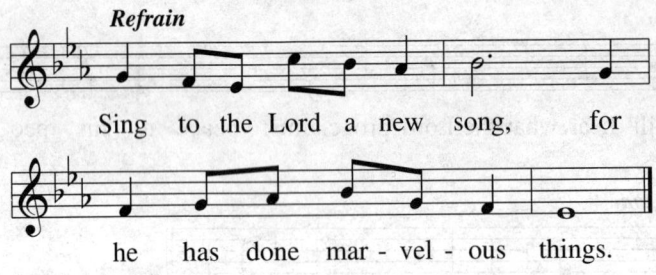

Great are the works of the LORD;*
    they are pondered by all who delight in them.

Glorious and majestic are his deeds,*
    and his righteousness endures forever.

He has caused his wonders to be remembered;*
    the LORD is gracious and compassionate.

Refrain

The works of his hands are faithful and just;*
    all his precepts are trustworthy.

He provided redemption for his people;*
    he ordained his covenant forever.

The fear of the LORD is the beginning of wisdom;*
    all who follow his precepts have good understanding.

Glory be to the Father and to the Son*
    and to the Holy Spirit,
as it was in the beginning,*
    is now, and will be forever. Amen.

Refrain

Psalm 116

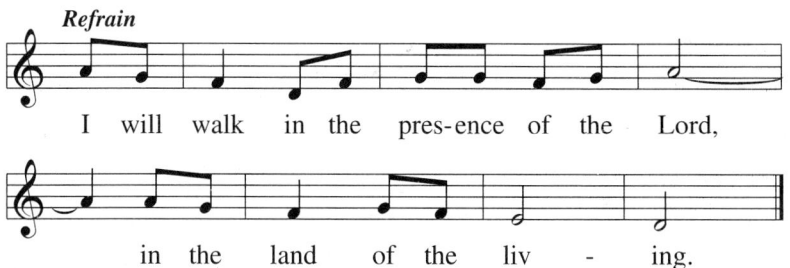

Refrain: I will walk in the presence of the Lord, in the land of the living.

Psalm tone

I love the LORD, for he heard my voice;*
 he heard my cry for mercy.

Because he turned his ear to me,*
 I will call on him as long as I live.

The LORD is gracious and righteous;*
 when I was in great need, he saved me.

Refrain

For you, O LORD, have delivered my soul from death,*
 my eyes from tears, my feet from stumbling.

How can I repay the LORD*
 for all his goodness to me?

I will lift up the cup of salvation*
 and call on the name of the LORD.

Glory be to the Father and to the Son*
 and to the Holy Spirit,
as it was in the beginning,*
 is now, and will be forever. Amen.

Refrain

Psalm 118

The LORD is my strength and my song;*
 he has become my salvation.

The LORD'S right hand is lifted high;*
 the LORD'S right hand has done mighty things!

I will not die but live,*
 and will proclaim what the LORD has done.

Refrain

I will give you thanks, for you answered me;*
 you have become my salvation.

The stone the builders rejected has become the capstone;*
 the LORD has done this, and it is marvelous in our eyes.

This is the day the LORD has made;*
 let us rejoice and be glad in it.

Glory be to the Father and to the Son*
 and to the Holy Spirit,
as it was in the beginning,*
 is now, and will be forever. Amen.

Refrain

Psalm 119 a

Your Word is a lamp to my feet and a light for my path.

Blessed are they whose ways are blámeless,*
 who walk according to the law óf the Lord.

Blessed are they who keep his státutes*
 and seek him with áll their heart.

You have laid down précepts*
 that are to be fullý obeyed.

Refrain

Oh, that my ways were stéadfast*
 in obeying ýour decrees!

Then I would not be pút to shame*
 when I consider all ýour commands.

I will praise you with an úpright heart*
 as I learn your ríghteous laws.

Glory be to the Father and tó the Son*
 and to the Holy Spírit,
as it was in the begínning,*
 is now, and will be forever. Ámen.

Refrain

Psalm 119b

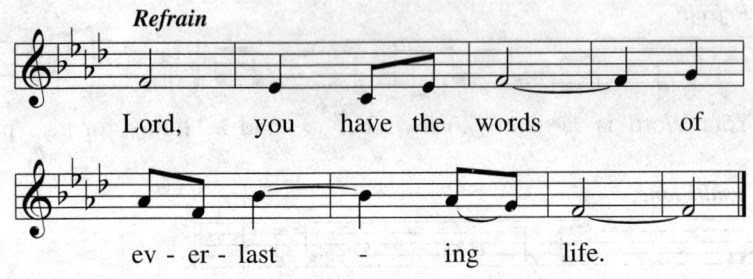

Teach me, O LORD, to follow your decrees;*
   then I will keep them to the end.

Give me understanding, and I will keep your law*
   and obey it with all my heart.

Direct me in the path of your commands,*
   for there I find delight.

Refrain

Turn my eyes away from worthless things;*
   preserve my life according to your Word.

Fulfill your promise to your servant,*
   so that you may be feared.

How I long for your precepts!*
   Preserve my life in your righteousness.

Glory be to the Father and to the Son*
   and to the Holy Spirit,
as it was in the beginning,*
   is now, and will be forever. Amen.

Refrain

Psalm 119 c

Your Word is a lamp to my feet and a light for my path.

Oh, how I love your law!*
 I meditate on it all day long.

I have more insight than all my teachers,*
 for I meditate on your statutes.

I have more understanding than the elders,*
 for I obey your precepts.

Refrain

I have kept my feet from every evil path*
 so that I might obey your Word.

I have not departed from your laws,*
 for you yourself have taught me.

How sweet are your words to my taste,*
 sweeter than honey to my mouth!

Glory be to the Father and to the Son*
 and to the Holy Spirit,
as it was in the beginning,*
 is now, and will be forever. Amen.

Refrain

Psalm 121

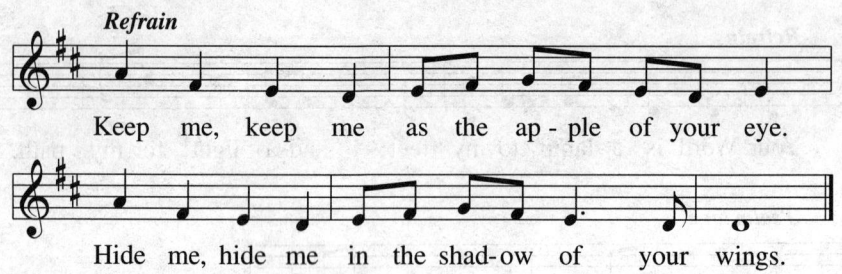

I lift up my eyes to the hills.*
  Where does my help come from?

My help comes from the Lord,*
  the maker of heaven and earth.

He will not let your foot slip,*
  he who watches over you will not slumber;

indeed, he who watches over Israel*
  will neither slumber nor sleep.

Refrain

The Lord watches over you,*
  the Lord is your shade at your right hand.

The Lord will keep you from all harm,*
  he will watch over your life;

the Lord will watch over your coming and going*
  both now and forevermore.

Glory be to the Father and to the Son*
  and to the Holy Spirit,
as it was in the beginning,*
  is now, and will be forever. Amen.

Refrain

Psalm 126

When the LORD brought back the captives to Zion,*
   we were like those who dreamed.

Our mouths were filled with laughter,*
   our tongues with songs of joy.

The LORD has done great things for us,*
   and we are filled with joy.

Refrain

Restore our fortunes, O LORD, like streams in the desert.*
   Those who sow in tears will reap with songs of joy.

He who goes out weeping, carrying seed to sow,*
   will return with songs of joy, carrying sheaves with him.

Glory be to the Father and to the Son*
   and to the Holy Spirit,
as it was in the beginning,*
   is now, and will be forever. Amen.

Refrain

Psalm 130

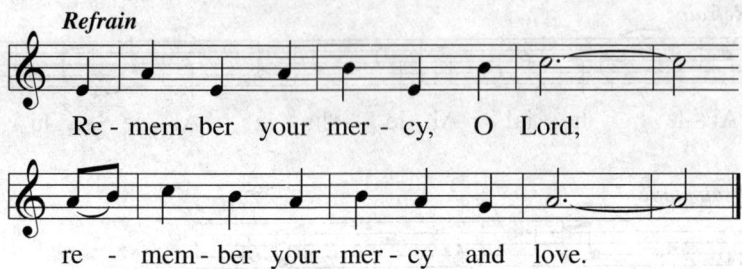

Out of the depths I cry toýou, O LORD;*
   O Lord, hear my voice.

Let your ears be atténtive*
   to my cry for mercy.

If you, O LORD, kept a recórd of sins,*
   O Lord, who could stand?

But with you there is forgíveness;*
   therefore ýou are feared.

Refrain

I wait for the LORD and in his Word I pút my hope.*
   My soul waits for the Lord more than
   watchmen wait for the morning.

O Israel, put your hope ín the LORD,*
   for with the LORD is unfailing love
   and with him is full redemption.

Glory be to the Father and tó the Son*
   and to the Holy Spirit,
as it was in the beginning,*
   is now, and will be forever. Ámen.

Refrain

Psalm 133-134

How good and pleásant it is*
 when brothers live together in únity!

For there the LORD bestows his blessing,*
 even life forévermore.

Refrain

Praise the LORD, all you servants óf the LORD*
 who minister in the house óf the LORD.

Lift up your hands in the sanctuáry*
 and práise the LORD.

May the LORD, the maker of heavén and earth,*
 bless you from Źion.

Glory be to the Father and tó the Son*
 and to the Holy Śpirit,
as it was in the beǵinning,*
 is now, and will be forever. Ámen.

Refrain

Psalm 139 a

O LORD, you have searched me and you knów me;*
 you perceive my thoughts fróm afar.

You discern my going out and my lýing down;*
 you are familiar with áll my ways.

Refrain

Where can I go from your Spírit?*
 Where can I flee from your présence?

If I go up to the heavens, ýou are there;*
 if I make my bed in the depths, ýou are there.

If I rise on the wings óf the dawn,*
 if I settle on the far side óf the sea,

even there your hand will gúide me,*
 your right hand will hóld me fast.

Glory be to the Father and tó the Son*
 and to the Holy Spírit,
as it was in the begínning,*
 is now, and will be forever. Ámen.

Refrain

Psalm 139 b

O LORD, you created my inmost being;*
 you knit me together in my mother's womb.

I praise you because I am fearfully and wonderfully made;*
 your works are wonderful, I know that full well.

My frame was not hidden from you;*
 your eyes saw my unformed body.

Refrain

All the days ordained for me*
 were written in your book before one of them came to be.

How precious to me are your thoughts, O God!*
 How vast is the sum of them!

Were I to count them,*
 they would outnumber the grains of sand.

Glory be to the Father and to the Son*
 and to the Holy Spirit,
as it was in the beginning,*
 is now, and will be forever. Amen.

Refrain

Psalm 143

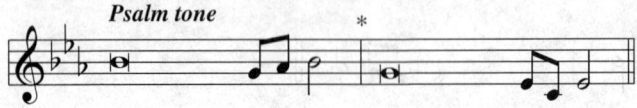

O LORD, hear my prayer, listen to my cry for mercy;*
    in your faithfulness and righteousness come to my relief.

Do not bring your servant into judgment,*
    for no one living is righteous before you.

My spirit grows faint within me;*
    my heart within me is dismayed.

Refrain

Answer me quickly, O LORD;*
    do not hide your face from me.

Let the morning bring me word of your unfailing love,*
    for I have put my trust in you.

Teach me to do your will, for you are my God;*
    may your good Spirit lead me on level ground.

Glory be to the Father and to the Son*
    and to the Holy Spirit,
as it was in the beginning,*
    is now, and will be forever. Amen.

Refrain

Psalm 145

Great is the LORD and most worthy of praise;*
 his greatness no one can fathom.

One generation will commend your works to another;*
 they will tell of your mighty acts.

The LORD upholds all those who fall*
 and lifts up all who are bowed down.

Refrain

The eyes of all look to you,
 and you give them their food at the proper time.*
 You open your hand
 and satisfy the desires of every living thing.

The LORD is near to all who call on him,*
 to all who call on him in truth.

He fulfills the desires of those who fear him;*
 he hears their cry and saves them.

Glory be to the Father and to the Son*
 and to the Holy Spirit,
as it was in the beginning,*
 is now, and will be forever. Amen.

Refrain

Psalm 146

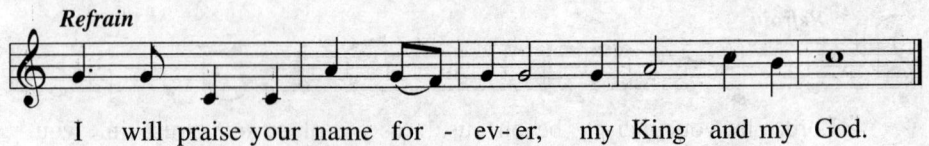

Refrain: I will praise your name for-ev-er, my King and my God.

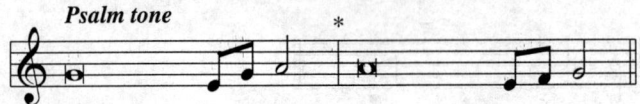

Psalm tone

Praise the Lord, Ó my soul.*
　I will sing praise to my God as long ás I live.

Do not put your trust in prínces,*
　in mortal men, who cánnot save.

Blessed is he whose hope is in the Lórd his God,*
　the maker of heavén and earth.

Refrain

The Lord gives food to the húngry,*
　the Lord sets prísoners free.

The Lord gives sight tó the blind,*
　the Lord lifts up those who are bówed down.

The Lord watches over the óutcast*
　and sustains the fatherless and the wídow.

The Lord remains faithful foréver.*
　He upholds the cause of thé oppressed.

Glory be to the Father and tó the Son*
　and to the Holy Spírit,
as it was in the begínning,*
　is now, and will be forever. Ámen.

Refrain

Psalm 148

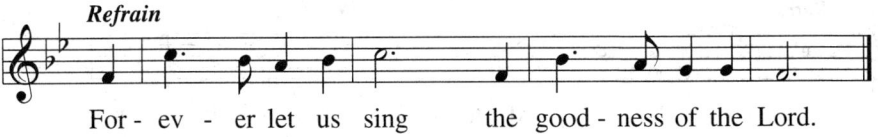

Refrain: For-ev-er let us sing the good-ness of the Lord.

Psalm tone

Praise the LORD from the heavens,*
 praise him in the heights above.

Praise him, all his angels,*
 praise him, all his heavenly hosts.

Praise him, sun and moon,*
 praise him, all you shining stars.

Refrain

Praise the LORD from the earth,*
 lightning and hail, stormy winds that do his bidding,

you mountains and all hills, fruit trees and all cedars,*
 wild animals and all cattle, small creatures and flying birds,

kings of the earth and all rulers on earth,*
 young men and maidens, old men and children.

Let them praise the name of the LORD,*
 for his splendor is above the earth and the heavens.

Glory be to the Father and to the Son*
 and to the Holy Spirit,
as it was in the beginning,*
 is now, and will be forever. Amen.

Refrain

Psalm 150

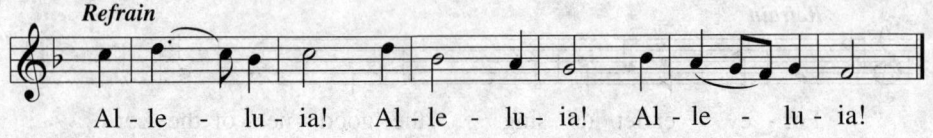

Praise God in his sanctuary;*
  praise him in his mighty heavens.

Praise him for his acts of power;*
  praise him for his surpassing greatness.

Refrain

Praise him with the sounding of the trumpet,*
  praise him with the harp and lyre,

praise him with tambourine and dancing,*
  praise him with strings and flute,

praise him with the clash of cymbals,*
  praise him with resounding cymbals.

Refrain

Let everything that has breath praise the Lord.*
  Praise the Lord.

Glory be to the Father and to the Son*
  and to the Holy Spirit,
as it was in the beginning,*
  is now, and will be forever. Amen.

Refrain

PRAYERS OF THE CHURCH

Advent

Eternal Father, throughout the centuries you repeated and affirmed your promise to send the offspring of the woman to crush the serpent's head. Through your prophets of old, you continually directed the eyes of your people to the advent of their Savior.

We praise you, O Lord, for keeping your promise and sending your Son to destroy the works of the devil.

As we prepare to celebrate the birth of our King, use your mighty Word to shatter our pride and to rouse us from spiritual slumber and apathy.

Move us to take to heart the words of John: "Repent, for the kingdom of heaven is near."

You sent your Son to redeem us from sin. Let this good news be our joy and strength. Use it to cheer the lonely, encourage the fearful, and give hope to the despairing. In these days before Christmas, spare us from the stress of deadlines and the frenzy of commercialism.

Fill our lives with the message of your peace and the music of your grace.

Direct our eyes not only to the manger but also to the skies, where we will see your Son coming again, not as a lowly child but as the Lord of lords.

Lift up our hearts in joyful anticipation of that day.

Special prayers and intercessions may follow.

Hear us, Lord, as we bring you our private petitions.

Silent prayer.

Come quickly, Lord Jesus, in your grace, in your power, and in your glory.

Come, Lord Jesus! Amen.

Epiphany

Lord Jesus Christ, Son of God and Mary's son, in the fullness of time you came into our world to save us from sin and death:

You ushered in the day of grace so long foretold.

Beloved Son of the Father, revered by the Magi, baptized by John, you came preaching and teaching, healing and comforting, forgiving and encouraging:

You brought the light of life to those walking in darkness, and the joy of salvation to those doomed to death.

Prince of Peace, shine like a beacon for us and the people of our world. Let the good news of salvation be heard in the remotest corners of the earth. Open our own lips to speak your name to those around us who still live without faith or hope:

Arouse us and our missionaries to flood the world with the light of your gospel.

Lord of the Church, let your peace rule our hearts that we may use our gifts to serve you and each other in willing gratitude and joy. Watch over our loved ones near and far, that they may remember your love and rejoice in your salvation. Strengthen the faith of the sick and the disheartened. Give hope to those in despair and comfort those who mourn:

Be gracious to all and lead us to reflect your love in everything we say and do.

Special prayers and intercessions may follow.

Hear us, Lord, as we bring you our private petitions.

Silent prayer.

Finally, bring us and all your believers to the heavenly home where we will stand in the full light of your glory and with all your saints and angels sing the everlasting song of triumph.

Amen.

Lent

Heavenly Father, you loved the world and gave your Son to liberate us from sin and death by his obedient death on the cross.

We confess that without your love we are lost.

Lord of the Church, we thank you for the treasure of the gospel. By your Spirit, keep our eyes fixed on Jesus, the author and perfecter of our faith.

Strengthen our determination to do what pleases you, no matter what the danger or the cost.

Let us pray for those who carry a cross in the name of Christ and face ridicule and persecution for the sake of the kingdom: missionaries and chaplains, young people who stand up for what is right in the face of pressure to do what is wrong, and all who pay a high price for their faith and their values as Christians.

By your Spirit, O Lord, grant them patience and endurance.

Let us pray for those who carry heavy burdens in life: the sick and the chronically ill, the depressed and the lonely, those torn by conflict in personal relationships, those victimized by war and injustice, and all who face the terrors of life with a heavy heart.

Grant them peace, O Lord, and in your mercy, be their guardian and friend, their comfort and hope.

Let us pray for those who care for others: pastors and counselors; physicians and nurses; social workers and caring friends; all who feed the hungry, comfort the hurting, and stand beside the dying.

Strengthen them in their work, O Lord, and do not let them become weary in doing good.

Special prayers and intercessions may follow.

Hear us, Lord, as we bring you our private petitions.

Silent prayer.

Help us run with perseverance the race marked out for us. Keep us faithful even to the point of death, that we may receive the crown of life, through Jesus Christ, our Lord.

Amen.

Easter

O Lord God, our strength, our song, and our salvation, you fulfilled your promises by the resurrection of your Son, Jesus Christ, from the dead.

Thanks be to God! You give us the victory through our Lord Jesus Christ.

In your compassion you sent Christ, the Good Shepherd, who laid down his life to rescue the lost.

Drive out all doubt and gloom that we may delight in your glorious triumph.

Lift our eyes heavenward to see him who lives to make intercession for the saints, and grant us confidence in the greatness of his power. Keep before us the vision of your redeemed people standing before your throne and singing the song of victory:

Worthy is the Lamb who was slain to receive wisdom and power and honor and glory and praise.

Make us instruments of your peace as we bring the good news of hope and new life to those around us. Guide us in the use of all that you have entrusted to us: our time, our talents, and our treasures.

Risen Lord, live in us that we may live for you.

Merciful Lord Jesus, grant healing to the sick, and strengthen the faith of the suffering and the dying. Assure them of your abiding presence, and comfort them with the hope of eternal life.

Special prayers and intercessions may follow.

Hear us, Lord, as we bring you our private petitions.

Silent prayer.

Gracious Father, you have restored to us the joy of your salvation. With happy hearts, we come before you and say:

Alleluia! Thanks be to God! Amen.

Sundays after Pentecost

O Lord, our God, you are wise and powerful, good and gracious. Your mercies are new every morning. Each day you open your hand and provide for the needs of your children on earth.

We praise you for every grace and blessing.

Strengthen your Church in all the world. Let your comforting message of salvation in Christ Jesus be proclaimed to troubled souls everywhere.

Use our ministries and offerings to extend your healing and your hope.

We bring you our requests for the various structures of our society. Bless our national, state (provincial), and local governments.

Grant us civil servants who are worthy of honor and respect.

Grant prosperity to our businesses and industries. Give employers a sense of fairness toward their workers, and employees a feeling of joy and pride in their workmanship.

Help us find satisfaction in all work well done.

Invigorate the schools of our land. Give success to every effort that helps students read, think, and communicate in ways that will promote an informed and responsible citizenry. Arouse curious minds to discover the wonders of your created order.

Give us teachers and students who pursue excellence.

Strengthen the families of our country. Give fathers and mothers a renewed commitment to be good parents. Give children and young people the wisdom to regard their parents as your representatives.

Lead us to love one another as you have loved us.

Special prayers and intercessions may follow.

Hear us, Lord, as we bring you our private petitions.

Silent prayer.

Gracious Father, we pray boldly as Jesus taught, with the confidence that you will hear and with the faith that you will respond for our welfare.

Amen.

PRAYERS OF THE CHURCH

GENERAL THANKSGIVING

Lord of heaven and earth, you made all things beautiful. You have provided green forests and refreshing streams. You have arranged the orderly procession of day and night for our work and rest.

Thank you for the mountains and the prairies, the roaring sea, and the gentle breeze.

Thank you for roofs that shelter us, for clothing that protects us, and for food and drink. Thank you for our work, for projects that are done well, and for the approval of supervisors and teachers. Thank you for all who serve at night to make our days more pleasant.

Thank you for associates at work, for their encouragement and praise, and for the joys of human friendships.

Thank you for our cities and our countrysides, for farms and factories, for streets and highways, and for all of life that flows so swiftly before us.

Thank you for children at play, their boundless energy, and their shouts of joy and laughter.

Thank you for the morning greetings we receive, and for all the smiles that come from faces loved by you.

Thank you for Christian parents, for their affection and their care.

Hear us, Lord, as we give thanks for personal blessings.

Silent prayer.

Thank you for your Son, Jesus Christ, for his coming to us in Word and sacraments, for his giving and forgiving, and for listening to our prayers. Receive our gifts and offerings as our sacrifice of praise.

Lead us in thankful living today and always. Amen.

Mission of the Church

Eternal God and Father, we give you thanks for the blessings we share as members of your holy Church, for your gracious Word and sacraments, for opportunities to worship and to grow in faith and knowledge, for occasions to serve and be served, for fellowship with believers in our congregation and in our synod.

Help us to rejoice in these blessings, dear Lord, and to use them faithfully.

Jesus Christ, Lord of the Church, you give grace to your people by calling us to be your witnesses in the world. Open our eyes to see the great and noble mission that lies before us. In the hurting eyes of the lonely, in the pained eyes of the sick, and in the searching eyes of the lost, help us to see your face, O Jesus, and to serve others as we would serve you.

Awaken us to the opportunities you give to proclaim your message of love.

Holy Spirit, giver of life, through Word and sacrament bestow on us the wisdom and power we need to witness clearly and to act boldly. Help us to speak the truth in love, to give the reason for the hope we have, and to conduct ourselves with gentleness and respect.

Set our hearts on fire as we work and witness for Christ.

Hear us, Lord, as we pray for a family member, an acquaintance, a neighbor, or a friend who does not believe in you, or whose faith is weak or troubled.

Silent prayer.

Bless the Church with men and women who are willing to proclaim your Word in places where we cannot go. Keep them and their loved ones in your care, and let nothing hinder their work. By the power of the gospel, restore their spirits each day, so that they do not lose heart as they serve us and others.

Move us to support them with our sincere prayers and generous offerings.

Special prayers and intercessions may follow.

Wherever your Word is proclaimed, O Lord, grant it success. Let your kingdom come to us and others, so that we and many more might join the assembly of saints and angels to sing your praise forever.

Savior of all, hear our prayer and help us in our mission. Amen.

The Nation

Almighty God, we acknowledge with thanks that all we have and enjoy is a gift from your gracious hand. We come before you today in heartfelt appreciation for our nation and its people.

We thank you for enabling us to worship you in freedom and to serve you without fear.

You have enriched us with the bounties of farm and factory, the beauty of forest and mountain, and the marvels of medicine and science.

For all these blessings, we praise and glorify you.

Look with favor upon our nation, and preserve our cherished liberties. Enable our leaders to govern with wisdom, honesty, courage, and justice. Protect those who serve in the armed forces and those who maintain peace and safety in our communities.

Give us willingness to obey our nation's laws and to work for the common good.

Keep our financial institutions secure and our economy strong. Bless our fields that they may produce abundant harvests. Guard us from calamities of nature and accident, and spare our land from the ravages of disease and epidemic.

Teach us not to worry but to cast all our cares on you.

Strengthen the homes of our nation. By your Spirit lead husbands and wives to love each other, parents to nurture their children, young adults to assume responsibility, and children to show respect.

Special prayers and intercessions may follow.

Hear us, Lord, as we bring you our private petitions.

Silent prayer.

To you, O Lord, we bring our thanks and our requests.

Hear our prayers for Jesus' sake. Amen.

Prayer of Intercession

Let us pray, brothers and sisters, for the holy Church of God throughout the world, that God the almighty Father gather and guide it so that we may worship him in peace and tranquility:

Almighty and eternal God, you have shown your glory to all nations in Jesus Christ. Guide the work of the Church. Help it to persevere in faith, proclaim your Word, and bring salvation to people everywhere. Lord, in your mercy,

Hear our prayer.

Let us pray for our pastors and teachers and all leaders of the Church, and for all the people of God:

Almighty and eternal God, your Spirit guides the Church and makes it holy. Strengthen and uphold all who serve you and your people. Keep them in health and safety for the good of the Church. Help each of us to do faithfully the work to which you have called us. Lord, in your mercy,

Hear our prayer.

Let us pray for those who do not believe in Christ, that the light of the Holy Spirit may show them the way to salvation:

Almighty and eternal God, enable those who do not acknowledge Christ to receive the truth of the gospel. Help us, your Church, to grow in love for you and for one another, so that we become more perfect witnesses of your love for all people. Lord, in your mercy,

Hear our prayer.

Let us pray for those who serve in public office, that God may guide their minds and hearts, so that all of us may live in true peace and freedom:

Almighty and eternal God, graciously direct those who have been set in positions of authority among us, so that people everywhere may enjoy justice, peace, freedom, and a share in the goodness of your creation. Lord, in your mercy,

Hear our prayer.

Let us pray that God, the almighty and merciful Father, may heal the sick, comfort the dying, give safety to travelers, and free those unjustly deprived of liberty:

Almighty and eternal God, you give strength to the weary and new courage to those who have lost heart. In your mercy hear the prayers of all who call on you in any trouble, that they may have the joy of receiving your help in their need. We ask this through Christ, our Lord.

Amen.

THE ATHANASIAN CREED

This creed is named after St. Athanasius, a staunch defender of the Christian faith in the fourth century. It was prepared to assist the Church in combating two errors that undermined Bible teaching. One error denied that God's Son and the Holy Spirit are of one being or Godhead with the Father. The other error denied that Jesus Christ is true God and true man in one person. The Athanasian Creed continues to serve the Christian Church as a standard of the truth. It declares that whoever rejects the doctrine of the Trinity and the doctrine of Christ is without the saving faith.

Whoever wishes to be saved must, above all else, hold to the true Christian faith.
> Whoever does not keep this faith pure in all points will certainly perish forever.

Now this is the true Christian faith:
> We worship one God in three persons and three persons in one God,
>> without mixing the persons or dividing the divine being.

For each person—the Father, the Son, and the Holy Spirit—is distinct,
> but the deity of Father, Son, and Holy Spirit is one,
>> equal in glory and coeternal in majesty.

What the Father is, so is the Son, and so is the Holy Spirit.
The Father is uncreated, the Son uncreated, the Holy Spirit uncreated;
the Father is infinite, the Son infinite, the Holy Spirit infinite;
the Father is eternal, the Son eternal, the Holy Spirit eternal;
> yet they are not three who are eternal, but there is one who is eternal,
>> just as they are not three who are uncreated, nor three who are infinite,
>>> but there is one who is uncreated and one who is infinite.

In the same way the Father is almighty, the Son is almighty, the Holy Spirit is almighty;
> yet they are not three who are almighty, but there is one who is almighty.

So the Father is God, the Son is God, the Holy Spirit is God;
> yet they are not three Gods, but one God.

So the Father is Lord, the Son is Lord, the Holy Spirit is Lord;
> yet they are not three Lords, but one Lord.

For just as Christian truth compels us to confess each person individually to be God and Lord,
> so the true Christian faith forbids us to speak of three Gods or three Lords.

The Father is neither made nor created nor begotten of anyone.
The Son is neither made nor created, but is begotten of the Father alone.
The Holy Spirit is neither made nor created nor begotten,
but proceeds from the Father and the Son.

So there is one Father, not three Fathers; one Son, not three Sons;
> one Holy Spirit, not three Holy Spirits.

And within this Trinity none comes before or after; none is greater or inferior,
> but all three persons are coequal and coeternal,

so that in every way, as stated before, all three persons are to be worshiped as one God and one God worshiped as three persons.
> Whoever wishes to be saved must have this conviction of the Trinity.

It is furthermore necessary for eternal salvation truly to believe
that our Lord Jesus Christ also took on human flesh.
Now this is the true Christian faith:
> We believe and confess that our Lord Jesus Christ, God's Son,
> is both God and man.

He is God, eternally begotten from the nature of the Father, and he is man, born in time from the nature of his mother, fully God, fully man, with rational soul and human flesh,
> equal to the Father as to his deity, less than the Father as to his humanity;

and though he is both God and man, Christ is not two persons but one,
> one, not by changing the deity into flesh, but by taking the humanity into God;

one, indeed, not by mixture of the natures, but by unity in one person;
> for just as the rational soul and flesh are one human being,
> so God and man are one Christ.

He suffered for our salvation, descended into hell, rose the third day from the dead.
> He ascended into heaven, is seated at the right hand of God the Father almighty,
> and from there will come to judge the living and the dead.

At his coming all people will rise with their own bodies
to answer for their personal deeds.
> Those who have done good will enter eternal life,
> but those who have done evil will go into eternal fire.

This is the true Christian faith.
> Whoever does not faithfully and firmly believe this cannot be saved.

PERSONAL PRAYERS

In the Name of Jesus

FOR GOD'S CREATION

Lord God, open my eyes to the beauty of your created world. You made all things to nourish my life and to fill me with wonder and joy. Open my mouth to praise and thank you for your gifts.

FOR GOD'S LOVE

God our Father, your Son welcomed all who came to him, even the outcasts and despised. Give me a faith that dares to come to you, trusting only in your love. Give me a love that accepts others, as I have been accepted by you.

FOR FAITH

O Holy Spirit, come to me with your comforting Word, which alone can drive away my doubts. Direct me to my Savior, Jesus, that I may trust in him with my whole heart.

FOR FORGIVENESS

Lord God, have mercy on me, a sinner. Forgive my open sins and my secret sins. Forgive the sins I know and the sins I do not know. Forgive the sins I did to please myself and the sins I did to please others. Forgive them all, gracious Lord, for Jesus' sake.

FOR PATIENCE

Lord Jesus, you promised to comfort those who mourn and to satisfy those who hunger. In time of trial remind me of your cross, where you endured the curse of my sin. When I am weak, teach me to depend on you for strength. At your own time, deliver me from suffering and distress.

FOR OBEDIENCE TO GOD'S WILL

Lord God, give me strength and willingness to say with your Son, "Not my will but your will be done." Make me cheerful and trusting to bear whatever you let happen to me. From your hand I am willing to take the good and the bad, the joy and the sorrow. Keep me from sin, gracious Father, and comfort me with your kind Word.

FOR THE FAMILY

Heavenly Father, thank you for my home and family, for love and gentleness, for laughter enjoyed and sorrows shared, for daily bread. Help me to be mindful of all your gifts and to rejoice in your goodness. May your peace be with us and your presence protect us.

FOR A MARRIED COUPLE

O God of tenderness and strength, bless our home and our love, our comings and our goings. Keep us from growing weary in doing good, and sustain us in the hour of trouble. Help us deal tenderly with each other, and knit our lives together in love for you and one another.

FOR THE SYNOD

Lord of the Church, you have joined me to a family of believers who walk together in faith, love, and service. Keep the congregations of our synod faithful to your Word, and make them eager to do your work. Guide our leaders, and help them fulfill their responsibilities with patience and understanding. Give me a vision which sees beyond the boundaries of my own congregation and a willingness to support the worldwide mission of your Church.

FOR WORKER TRAINING

Lord of the harvest, give to your Church men and women eager to prepare for service in your kingdom. Bless our schools with instructors who encourage and inspire their students to grow in grace and wisdom. Strengthen the resolve of students to complete their training for ministry, and send them out in the power of your Spirit.

FOR MISSIONARIES

Jesus, my risen Lord, you commanded your Church to preach the gospel to all nations. Prosper the work of missionaries sent out in your name. Protect them and their families from illness and danger. Give them joy in proclaiming the good news of salvation to people everywhere.

FOR PASTORS AND TEACHERS

O ascended Lord, thank you for the gift of pastors and teachers to feed your flock. Enable them, by the power of the Spirit, to stand firm in the midst of the trials and stresses of this world. Give them the courage to speak your Word faithfully and the grace to reflect your love in their actions.

FOR ZEAL TO DO GOD'S WORK

Too often I put my own concerns and priorities above your will and work, O Lord. Rid me of my selfishness, and fill me with the zeal to keep you first in my life.

FOR COURAGE TO SHARE THE GOSPEL

Give me a caring heart, O Lord, to love and seek the lost. Overcome my fear, and grant me courage to share my hope of salvation with those who have no hope. Make me faithful in my daily life so that all I say and do may glorify you.

FOR PROPER USE OF GOD'S GIFTS

Gracious God, all that I have comes from you: my body and mind, my strength and intelligence, my time and abilities, my energy and possessions. Guard me from the temptation to use these gifts only for my personal benefit. Make me willing to use them joyfully in service to you and to your people.

FOR THE GOVERNMENT

Lord of all nations, I praise you for the blessings you have showered on my country. Guide and guard your representatives in government as they care for the needs of all citizens. Give them wisdom to rule our society with honesty and justice, that we may have peace in our lives and opportunities to witness to your love.

FOR PEACE AMONG NATIONS

O God, my Father in heaven, bless every effort to establish peace among the nations of the world. Give wisdom and strength to those who lead, guide those who make decisions, and transform the hearts of people everywhere to exalt peace above war, justice above gain, and honor above glory.

FOR LOVE OF OTHERS

Lord Jesus, teach me to love others as you have loved me. Help me be more patient and alert to the needs of others, and always ready to serve them with the gifts you have given me.

Lord God, hear me as I speak to you about those near and dear:
  For all who travel: keep them safe.
  For all who are sick: heal them and make them strong.
  For all who are in pain: allow them to have relief.
  For all who are discouraged: let someone bring them cheer.
  For all who mourn losses: grant them understanding and recovery.
  For all who feel their hopes have been dashed through death: be the strong arm they need through Christ, who suffered death and rose again.
Dear Lord, let them know that nothing can separate them from your love in Christ Jesus.

FOR THE POOR AND HUNGRY

Compassionate Savior, too often I forget how many in our world are homeless, poor, and hungry. In your mercy relieve their suffering and pain. Remind me that when I help a person in need I am serving you.

IN TIME OF TROUBLE

O Lord, you promise that in all things you work for the good of those who love you. Help me see your loving hand in this time of trouble. Save me from doubt, relieve my anguish, and lead me through these dark days with the light of your presence.

FOR OTHERS IN TROUBLE

O Lord, be gracious and kind to all who are in trouble. Heal those who are sick, cheer those who are sad, and give your strength to those who are weary and weak. Do what is best for them according to your gracious will, and keep them faithful to our Lord Jesus Christ.

WHEN THERE IS STRIFE

O Lord, it grieves me that anger, strife, and bitterness have become a part of my life. Forgive my sins and renew my spirit so that I will pardon others, correct the mistakes I have made, and be more cheerful toward those around me. Remind me through your Word that your Son's peace provides the needed hope and reason for healing and change.

WHEN SICK

Great Physician of body and soul, I have been struggling with sickness and pain. If it is your will, let these days pass quickly. Guide the hands of those who care for me, and give me confidence in their skills. If I must continue to suffer, grant me the comfort of knowing that you will allow nothing to happen to me which is not for my eternal good.

FOR THE SICK

Almighty Father, giver of life and health, I pray for _____ and for all who are sick and suffering. Grant that in the midst of pain they may be comforted by your presence and sustained by your love. If it be your gracious will, restore them to health.

ON RECOVERING FROM INJURY OR ILLNESS

Lord of my life, in the day of trouble, I called to you and you delivered me. Receive my humble thanks. Bless those who prayed for me and those who served me in my time of illness. Enable me to use all my days in grateful praise and service.

FOR A LIFE OF SERVICE

Lord, make me an instrument of your peace:
   where there is hatred, let me sow love;
   where there is injury, pardon;
   where there is doubt, faith;
   where there is despair, hope;
   where there is darkness, light;
   and where there is sadness, joy.
O Divine Master, grant that I may not so much seek
   to be consoled, as to console;
   to be understood, as to understand;
   to be loved, as to love;
   for it is in giving that we receive,
   it is in pardoning that we are pardoned,
   and it is in dying that we are born to eternal life.

IN THE MORNING

I thank you, my heavenly Father, through Jesus Christ, your dear Son, that you have kept me this night from all harm and danger. Keep me this day also from sin and every evil, that all my doings and life may please you. Into your hands I commend my body and soul and all things. Let your holy angel be with me, that the wicked foe may have no power over me.

Almighty God, you divide the day from the night. Drive far from us all wrong desires, incline our hearts to keep your law, and guide our feet in the way of peace. And having done your will with cheerfulness while it is day, grant that when evening comes, we may rejoice in giving you thanks.

Grant us, O Lord, to live this day in gladness and peace, without stumbling and without stain, that reaching the evening victorious over all temptation, we may praise you, the eternal God, for you govern all things and are praised now and forever.

We give you thanks, O Lord, for the rest of the past night and for the gift of a new day with its opportunities for pleasing you. Grant that we may pass its hours in the freedom of your service and, when evening comes, give you thanks again.

IN THE EVENING

I thank you, my heavenly Father, through Jesus Christ, your dear Son, that you have graciously kept me this day. Forgive me all my sins, and graciously keep me this night. Into your hands I commend my body and soul and all things. Let your holy angel be with me, that the wicked foe may have no power over me.

Keep watch, dear Lord, with those who watch or work or weep this night, and give your angels charge over those who sleep. Tend the sick, give rest to the weary, pity the afflicted, soothe the suffering, bless the dying—and all for your love's sake.

O God our Father, by your mercy and might, the world turns safely into darkness and returns again to light. We place into your hands our unfinished tasks, our unsolved problems, and our unfulfilled hopes, knowing that only what you bless will prosper. To your great love and protection, we commit each other and all those we love, knowing that you alone are our sure defender.

O Lord, support us all the day long, till the shadows lengthen and the evening comes and the busy world is hushed and the fever of life is over and our work is done. Then in your mercy, grant us a safe lodging and a holy rest and peace at the last.

CHRISTIAN MARRIAGE

This order of worship celebrates God's gracious gift of marriage. The congregation shares the joy of the bride and groom as they publicly promise lifelong love and faithfulness to each other.

CALL TO WORSHIP

M: In the name of the Father and of the Son and of the Holy Spirit.

Our Lord Jesus Christ came as an invited guest to the wedding at Cana, and with his gracious presence, he brought joy and gladness to those who were there. Jesus is also with us who have gathered in his name to celebrate with the Word of God and prayer the marriage of _____ and _____. We are assured of God's gracious help and guidance in these words from the Psalms:

M: Give thanks to the Lord, for he is good.

C: His love endures forever.

M: The Lord is gracious and compassionate, slow to anger, and rich in love;

C: He is good to all.

M: God is our refuge and strength,

C: An ever-present help in trouble.

M: He is our God forever and ever;

C: He will be our guide even to the end.

M: May God be gracious to us and bless us

C: And make his face shine on us.

M: Loving Father, we are grateful for your goodness in permitting us to gather as the family and friends of _____ and _____ to share their joy on this special day. Look on them with favor, strengthen their confidence in your firm promises, and assure them of your abiding love. As your Son Jesus graced the wedding at Cana with his presence, so may he be with us who pray in his name.

C: Amen.

Congregational hymns or other music appropriate for worship may be sung here or at other places in the service.

Word of God

LESSONS

SERMON

Marriage Rite

M: Dear friends: When God in love created the world, he made man and woman in his own image and bonded them together in marriage. Through this blessed union of husband and wife, God established the family, provided for the physical and spiritual welfare of children, and fostered the peace and stability of society.

God intended marriage to bring loving companionship to the people of his world. But because of sin, the joy of marriage was soon overcast with sorrow, and the harmony of family life was shattered by strife. Out of love God sent his Son Jesus to die on the cross to take away the sins of all people. Everyone who believes in Jesus receives forgiveness and is enabled by the Holy Spirit to live in peace and joy.

God's love for you is boundless. He commands you, in response to his love, to love each other. Love is forgiving and enduring. Love shows itself in truth and faithfulness, in thoughtfulness and understanding, in patience and kindness. Marriage furnishes a unique opportunity to put this love into practice.

The pattern for Christian marriage is the intimate union of Christ and his Church, which the apostle Paul depicts in Ephesians 5. After urging believers to "submit to one another out of reverence for Christ," he makes this application for Christian spouses: "Wives, submit to your husbands as to the Lord. For the husband is the head of the wife as Christ is the head of the Church . . . Husbands, love your wives, just as Christ loved the Church and gave himself for her." It is reverence for Christ on the part of husband and wife that lays the foundation for Christian marriage.

You have come here to be united in marriage, which consists in your mutual consent, sincerely and freely given. You are now invited to declare this intent in the presence of God and these witnesses.

MARRIAGE PROMISES

M: *(to the groom):* _____, will you take _____ to be your wife? Will you be guided by the counsel and direction God has given in his Word and love your wife as Christ loved the Church? Will you be faithful to her, cherish her, support her, and help her in sickness and in health as long as you both shall live? If so, answer, "I will."

G: I will.

M: *(to the bride):* _____, will you take _____ to be your husband? Will you be guided by the counsel and direction God has given in his Word and submit to your husband as the Church submits to Christ? Will you be faithful to him, cherish him, support him, and help him in sickness and in health as long as you both shall live? If so, answer, "I will."

B: I will.

M: Join your right hands and make your promises to each other:

The groom and bride will say in turn:

I, _____, / in the presence of God and these witnesses, / take you, _____, to be my *wife/husband*. / I promise to be faithful to you / as long as we both shall live.

EXCHANGE OF RINGS

M: Exchange rings as a symbol of the lifelong commitment and abiding love which you as husband and wife have promised each other.

The groom and bride will say in turn:

_____, receive this ring / as a symbol of my love and faithfulness.

DECLARATION OF MARRIAGE

M: By their promises, _____ and _____ have bound themselves together in marriage before God and these witnesses. Therefore, I declare that they are husband and wife, in the name of the Father and of the Son ✠ and of the Holy Spirit. Those whom God has joined together, let no one separate.

MARRIAGE BLESSING

M: God the Father, God the Son, and God the Holy Spirit preserve you in faithfulness, strengthen you in love, and guide you to life's end.

HYMN

The following hymn or another hymn may be sung.

Now thank we all our God With hearts and hands and voices,
Who wondrous things has done, In whom his world rejoices,
Who from our mother's arms Has blessed us on our way
With countless gifts of love And still is ours today.

Oh, may this bounteous God Through all our life be near us,
With ever-joyful hearts And blessed peace to cheer us
And keep us in his grace And guide us when perplexed
And free us from all ills In this world and the next!

CHRISTIAN MARRIAGE

PRAYERS

Other prayers may be said

M: Let us pray:

Eternal God, source of love, help _____ and _____ to fulfill the promises they have made here today and to reflect your steadfast love in their love for each other. Give them kindness and patience, affection and understanding, happiness and contentment. Use their family and friends to support them in difficult days, that their love for each other may continue to grow as long as they live.

Gracious Father, in your goodness you bring people together into families and enrich their lives with abundant blessings. Renew the love of husbands and wives, parents and children, that they may strengthen and support each other on the way that leads to our heavenly home, through Jesus Christ, our Lord.

C: Amen.

LORD'S PRAYER

C: Our Father in heaven,
    hallowed be your name,
    your kingdom come,
    your will be done
        on earth as in heaven.
Give us today our daily bread.
Forgive us our sins,
    as we forgive those
    who sin against us.
Lead us not into temptation,
but deliver us from evil.
For the kingdom, the power,
    and the glory are yours
    now and forever. Amen.

or

Our Father, who art in heaven,
    hallowed be thy name,
    thy kingdom come,
    thy will be done
        on earth as it is in heaven.
Give us this day our daily bread;
and forgive us our trespasses,
    as we forgive those
    who trespass against us;
and lead us not into temptation,
but deliver us from evil.
For thine is the kingdom
    and the power and the glory
    forever and ever. Amen.

BLESSING

M: The Lord bless you and keep you.
The Lord make his face shine on you and be gracious to you.
The Lord look on you with favor and ✠ give you peace.

C: Amen.

CHRISTIAN FUNERAL

This order of worship is intended for the funeral or memorial service of one who has departed from this life in the Christian faith. With the Word of God, the Christian church comforts the bereaved family and friends and confesses its lasting hope in the resurrection of the dead in Christ.

GREETING AND PRAYER

M: In the name of the Father and of the Son and of the Holy Spirit. Amen.

We have come together to seek God's comfort in our sorrow and to rejoice in the promise of the resurrection. Grace and peace to you from God our Father and the Lord Jesus Christ, who said, "Come to me, all who are weary and burdened, and I will give you rest."

Let us pray.

Lord Jesus, you wept at the grave of your friend Lazarus, and you consoled Mary and Martha in their distress. Draw near to us who mourn for _____, and dry the tears of all who weep. Calm our troubled hearts, dispel our doubts and fears, and lead us to praise you for having brought *him* to faith. In your rising from the dead, you conquered death and opened the gates to eternal life. Strengthen us with your Word, and lead us through this earthly life until at last we are united with you and all the saints in glory everlasting. Amen.

PSALM 23

The L<small>ORD</small> is my shepherd, I shall not be in want.
He makes me lie down in green pastures,
   he leads me beside quiet waters, he restores my soul.
He guides me in paths of righteousness for his name's sake.
Even though I walk through the valley of the shadow of death,
I will fear no evil, for you are with me;
   your rod and your staff, they comfort me.
You prepare a table before me in the presence of my enemies.
You anoint my head with oil; my cup overflows.
Surely goodness and love will follow me all the days of my life,
   and I will dwell in the house of the L<small>ORD</small> forever.

Glory be to the Father and to the Son and to the Holy Spirit,
   as it was in the beginning, is now, and will be forever. Amen.

CHRISTIAN FUNERAL

A HYMN may be sung.

RESURRECTION COMFORT

M: Praise be to the God and Father of our Lord Jesus Christ, who comforts us in all our troubles, so that we can comfort those in any trouble with the comfort we ourselves have received from God. The apostle Paul writes to the Romans: "The wages of sin is death, but the gift of God is eternal life in Christ Jesus our Lord." Jesus gives us this comfort: "I am the resurrection and the life. He who believes in me will live, even though he dies; and whoever lives and believes in me will never die."

M: Death has been swallowed up in victory! Thanks be to God!

C: He gives us the victory through our Lord Jesus Christ.

M: When Christ, who is our life, appears,

C: Then we also will appear with him in glory.

M: We will be before the throne of God

C: And serve him day and night in his temple.

M: Never again will we hunger;

C: Never again will we thirst.

M: For the Lamb at the center of the throne will be our shepherd; he will lead us to springs of living water.

C: And God will wipe away every tear from our eyes.

M: Let us pray.

God of all grace, you sent your Son Jesus to destroy the power of death and to open the kingdom of heaven to all believers. Make us certain that because he lives, we too shall live. Comfort us with your promise that neither death nor life nor things present nor things to come shall be able to separate us from your love which is in Christ Jesus our Lord.

C: Amen.

LESSONS

HYMN

SERMON

APOSTLES' CREED

I believe in God, the Father almighty,
>   maker of heaven and earth.

I believe in Jesus Christ, his only Son, our Lord,
>   who was conceived by the Holy Spirit,
>   born of the virgin Mary,
>   suffered under Pontius Pilate,
>   was crucified, died, and was buried.
> He descended into hell.
> The third day he rose again from the dead.
> He ascended into heaven
>   and is seated at the right hand of God the Father almighty.
> From there he will come to judge the living and the dead.

I believe in the Holy Spirit,
>   the holy Christian Church,
>   the communion of saints,
>   the forgiveness of sins,
>   the resurrection of the body,
>   and the life everlasting. Amen.

HYMN

PRAYERS

The following responsive prayer or another prayer may be said.

M: Almighty God, we praise you for the great company of saints who have finished their lives in faith and now rest from their labors. We remember especially our loved one, _____, whom you have redeemed by the blood of your Son and received as your dear child through Holy Baptism. We thank you for giving *him* to us as a companion on our earthly pilgrimage. In your compassion, comfort all who are sad in this hour. Lord, in your mercy,

C: **Hear our prayer.**

M: We praise you for your love in Christ, which sustains us in life and death. In our earthly sorrows, help us find strength in the fellowship of the church, joy in the forgiveness of sins, and hope in the resurrection to eternal life. Lord, in your mercy,

C: Hear our prayer.

M: You do not leave us comfortless but strengthen and care for us through your Word and sacrament. You give us family, friends, and neighbors to help when there is loneliness now and in the days to come. Brighten our future with a firm trust in your promises and care. Lord, in your mercy,

C: Hear our prayer.

A special prayer or intercession may follow.

M: Remove our fears, and make us bold to pray with confidence as our Savior has taught us:

LORD'S PRAYER

C: Our Father in heaven,
    hallowed be your name,
your kingdom come,
your will be done
    on earth as in heaven.
Give us today our daily bread.
Forgive us our sins,
  as we forgive those
  who sin against us.
Lead us not into temptation,
but deliver us from evil.
For the kingdom, the power,
  and the glory are yours
  now and forever. Amen.

or

Our Father, who art in heaven,
    hallowed be thy name,
thy kingdom come,
thy will be done
    on earth as it is in heaven.
Give us this day our daily bread;
and forgive us our trespasses,
  as we forgive those
  who trespass against us;
and lead us not into temptation,
but deliver us from evil.
For thine is the kingdom
  and the power and the glory
  forever and ever. Amen.

BLESSING

M: The Lord bless you and keep you.
The Lord make his face shine on you and be gracious to you.
The Lord look on you with favor and ✠ give you peace.

C: Amen.

APPROPRIATE PSALMS AND LESSONS FOR CHRISTIAN FUNERALS AND FOR MINISTRY TO THE SICK, DYING, AND BEREAVED

Psalms

Psalm 16:5-11	The LORD has assigned me my portion
Psalm 23	The LORD is my shepherd
Psalm 27:1,4-9,13,14	The LORD is my light and my salvation
Psalm 31:1-3,9,10,14-17a,24	My times are in your hands
Psalm 32:1-7	Transgressions are forgiven
Psalm 34:1-9,17-19,22	A righteous man may have many troubles
Psalm 36:7-10	The fountain of life
Psalm 42:1-6a,9-11	Put your hope in God
Psalm 46:1-5,10,11	God is our refuge and strength
Psalm 50:15	Call on me in the day of trouble
Psalm 71:1-3,17-21	You will restore my life
Psalm 90:1-12	Teach us to number our days
Psalm 91	God is my refuge and my fortress
Psalm 103:1-17a	Praise the LORD, O my soul
Psalm 118:5-9	Take refuge in the LORD
Psalm 121	My help comes from the LORD
Psalm 130	Out of the depths I cry to you, O LORD
Psalm 139:1-18	O LORD, you know me
Psalm 145	The LORD is faithful to his promise
Psalm 146	I will praise the LORD all my life

Lessons

Job 19:23-27	I know that my Redeemer lives
Isaiah 25:6-9	God will swallow up death forever
Isaiah 26:1-4,19	Your dead will live
Isaiah 40:1-11	Comfort, comfort my people
Isaiah 40:28,29	God gives strength to the weary
Isaiah 43:1-3a,25	You are mine, says the LORD
Isaiah 44:6-8	I am the first and the last
Isaiah 55:1-3,6-13	Come, all you who are thirsty
Isaiah 57:1,2	The righteous find rest
Isaiah 61:1-3,10,11	Comfort for all who mourn
Isaiah 65:17-25	New heavens and a new earth
Lamentations 3:19-26,31-33,55-57	His compassions never fail
Daniel 12:1-3	Multitudes who sleep will awake
Hosea 6:1	Let us return to the LORD
Matthew 6:25-34	Do not worry
Matthew 11:28-30	Come to me, all you who are weary
Matthew 25:1-13	Wise and foolish virgins
Matthew 25:31-46	Take your inheritance
Mark 16:1-8	Jesus' resurrection
Luke 7:11-17	Young man, I say to you, get up
Luke 23:33,39-43	Today you will be with me in paradise

John 3:16-21	God so loved the world
John 5:24-29	The dead will hear his voice and come out
John 6:35-40	I shall raise them up at the last day
John 6:47-58	He who believes has everlasting life
John 10:11-16	I am the Good Shepherd
John 10:27-29	My sheep listen to my voice
John 11:3,4	The one you love is sick
John 11:17-27	I am the resurrection and the life
John 11:38-44	Lazarus, come out
John 14:1-6,25-27	Do not let your hearts be troubled
John 20:1-18	Jesus' resurrection
Romans 5:1-11	Rejoice in the hope of the glory of God
Romans 6:3-10	Baptized into Christ's death; raised to life
Romans 8:14-24a	Heirs of God
Romans 8:28-39	Chosen for salvation
Romans 14:7-9	Whether we live or die, we belong to the Lord
1 Corinthians 15:3-8,12-20	Christ died and rose again
1 Corinthians 15:20-24	In Christ shall all be made alive
1 Corinthians 15:35-44	Sown in dishonor, raised in glory
1 Corinthians 15:50-58	Death is swallowed up in victory
2 Corinthians 1:3-5	The God of all comfort
2 Corinthians 4:16—5:1	What is seen is temporary, unseen is eternal
2 Corinthians 5:1-10	Away from the body and at home with the Lord
Ephesians 1:3-8	Chosen in Christ
Ephesians 2:3b-10	Saved through faith
Philippians 3:7-14	Know Christ and the power of his resurrection
Philippians 3:20,21	Our citizenship is in heaven
Colossians 3:12-17	Let the peace of Christ rule in your hearts
1 Thessalonians 4:13-18	The dead in Christ will rise first
2 Timothy 2:8-13	If we died with him, we will also live with him
Hebrews 2:14-18	Christ also suffered
Hebrews 10:35-38	Do not throw away your confidence
Hebrews 11:1-3,13-16	Aliens and strangers on earth
Hebrews 12:1-3	Let us fix our eyes on Jesus
James 5:14-16	Confess your sins and pray for each other
1 Peter 1:3-9	A living hope through Christ's resurrection
1 Peter 5:6-11	Cast all your anxiety on him
1 John 3:1-3	Now we are children of God
Revelation 7:9-17	Standing before the throne in front of the Lamb
Revelation 14:6,7,12,13	Blessed are the dead who die in the Lord
Revelation 21:1-4,22-25	A new heaven and a new earth
Revelation 22:1-5	The Lord will give them light

At the death of a child:

Matthew 18:1-5,10	The greatest in the kingdom of heaven
Mark 5:35	Not dead, but asleep
Mark 10:13-16	Let the little children come to me

These devotions may be used in various settings: by organizations and committees as well as in schools, in classes, and in the home. Appropriate morning and evening psalm suggestions are found on page 62.

GENERAL DEVOTION

Leader: O Lord, teach us your ways,

Group: **That we may walk in your truth.**

           You comfort and help us day by day.

           We trust your loving care.

           You are the King of heaven and earth.

           We give you praise and thanks. Alleluia!

PRAYER

The following prayer or another prayer may be said.

Lord Jesus, you invite us to pray and promise that where two or three come together in your name, there you are with us. Answer our prayers, and fulfill our desires according to your wisdom and love. Strengthen us in the knowledge of your truth, and grant us life everlasting.

Amen.

HYMN OR PSALM

A hymn or psalm may be sung or said.

READING

A Scripture lesson or another devotional selection is read.

APOSTLES' CREED

I believe in God, the Father almighty,
    maker of heaven and earth.

I believe in Jesus Christ, his only Son, our Lord,
    who was conceived by the Holy Spirit,
    born of the virgin Mary,
    suffered under Pontius Pilate,
    was crucified, died, and was buried.
He descended into hell.
The third day he rose again from the dead.
He ascended into heaven
    and is seated at the right hand of God the Father almighty.
From there he will come to judge the living and the dead.

I believe in the Holy Spirit,
> the holy Christian Church,
>> the communion of saints,
> the forgiveness of sins,
> the resurrection of the body,
> and the life everlasting. Amen.

INTERCESSION

In peace, let us pray to the Lord.

Lord, hear our prayer.

For all people throughout the world, to strengthen believers and to enlighten unbelievers, we pray:

Lord, have mercy.

For peace and justice among nations, for honest leaders and good neighbors, for the gift of love, for steadfast faith and patient endurance, we pray:

Lord, have mercy.

For those who suffer pain or sorrow, for the lonely and depressed, for the poor and needy, for those who love us and those who hate us, we pray:

Lord, have mercy.

Be gracious to us, defend us by your power, and bring us to glory everlasting:

To you, O Lord, we entrust ourselves. Amen.

You have taught us to pray:

Our Father in heaven, hallowed be your name, your kingdom come, your will be done on earth as in heaven. Give us today our daily bread. Forgive us our sins, as we forgive those who sin against us. Lead us not into temptation, but deliver us from evil. For the kingdom, the power, and the glory are yours now and forever. Amen.

BLESSING

The almighty and merciful Lord, the Father, the Son, and the Holy Spirit, bless and preserve us.

Amen.

MORNING DEVOTION

Leader: God, our Father, each day is a gift of your grace.

Group: **Your mercies are new every morning.**

Guide our steps by the light of your Word.

Shield us from harm and keep us from evil.

Better than life is your love.

Put joy in our hearts and praise on our lips. Alleluia!

PRAYER FOR GRACE

O Lord, our heavenly Father, almighty and everlasting God, you have brought us safely to this new day. Defend us with your mighty power, and grant that this day we neither fall into sin nor run into any kind of danger; and in all we do, direct us to what is right in your sight, through Jesus Christ, your Son, our Lord.

Amen.

READING

A Scripture lesson, a portion of Luther's Small Catechism, or a devotional selection may be read.

HYMN OR PSALM

A hymn or psalm may be sung or said.

INTERCESSION

One or more prayers (see Personal Prayers on p. 134) may be used, concluding with all praying Luther's Morning Prayer.

LUTHER'S MORNING PRAYER

I thank you, my heavenly Father, through Jesus Christ, your dear Son, that you have kept me this night from all harm and danger. Keep me this day also from sin and every evil, that all my doings and life may please you. Into your hands I commend my body and soul and all things. Let your holy angel be with me, that the wicked foe may have no power over me. Amen.

BLESSING

May the love of the Lord Jesus draw us to himself. May the power of the Lord Jesus make us strong to do his will. May the peace of the Lord Jesus fill our lives.

Amen.

EVENING DEVOTION

Leader: Lord Jesus, you are the light of the world,

Group: The light no darkness can overcome.

Stay with us, for it is evening,

And the day is almost over.

Let your light scatter the darkness.

Let it shine in our hearts and lives. Amen.

PRAYER FOR PEACE

Lord God, all holy desires, all good counsels, and all just works come from you. Give to us, your servants, that peace which the world cannot give, that our hearts may be set to obey your commandments. Defend us also from the fear of our enemies, that we may live in peace and quietness, through the merits of Jesus Christ our Savior, who lives and reigns with you and the Holy Spirit, one God, now and forever.

Amen.

READING

A Scripture lesson, psalm, or devotional selection may be read.

HYMN OR PSALM

A hymn or psalm may be sung or said.

INTERCESSION

One or more prayers (see Personal Prayers on p. 134) may be used, concluding with all praying Luther's Evening Prayer.

LUTHER'S EVENING PRAYER

I thank you, my heavenly Father, through Jesus Christ, your dear Son, that you have graciously kept me this day. Forgive me all my sins, and graciously keep me this night. Into your hands I commend my body and soul and all things. Let your holy angel be with me, that the wicked foe may have no power over me. Amen.

BLESSING

May the blessing of the eternal God be upon us: his light to guide us, his presence to shelter us, his peace to unite us.

Amen.

PRIVATE CONFESSION

Luther writes in the Large Catechism: *"Christ himself entrusted absolution to his Church and commanded us to absolve one another from sins. So if there is a heart that feels its sin and desires consolation, it has here a sure refuge when it hears in God's Word that through a fellow human being, God absolves a person from sin."*

The following order may be used when someone seeks the ministry of a pastor or other fellow Christian to make personal confession.

Minister:

> In the name of our God, to whom all hearts are open and from whom no secrets are hidden. Amen.

Minister and Penitent:

> O Lord, hear my prayer, listen to my cry for mercy,
>   and in your faithfulness, come to my relief.
> Do not bring your servant into judgment,
>   for no one living is righteous before you.
> Answer me quickly, O Lord; my spirit fails.
> Do not hide your face from me, for I have put my trust in you.
> Show me the way I should go,
>   for to you I lift up my soul.
> Teach me to do your will, for you are my God.

Penitent:

> Almighty God, merciful Father, I, a troubled and repentant sinner, confess that I have sinned against you in my thoughts, my words, and my actions. I have not loved you with my whole heart; I have not loved others as I should. I am distressed by the sins that trouble me and am deeply sorry for them.

Here the penitent may confess specific sins.

Minister:

> Jesus says to his people: "If you forgive the sins of any, they are forgiven."
> His death paid for the guilt of your sins and the sins of the whole world.
> Do you believe this?

Penitent:

> Yes, I believe.

Minister:

Because of the promise of our Savior Jesus, I forgive you all your sins. Be assured that you are a dear child of God and an heir of eternal life.

Minister and Penitent:

O Lord, my God, I called to you for help, and you answered me. I thank you for the love you have shown me in Jesus Christ, my Savior. Through him you have rescued me from the guilt of my sin and given me the peace of forgiveness. Help me fight against temptation, correct whatever wrongs I can, and serve you and those around me with love and good works. In Jesus' name, I pray. Amen.

Minister:

Go in peace. The Lord be with you.

PERSONAL PREPARATION FOR HOLY COMMUNION

Q: What does God tell me about myself in his holy Word?

A: *He says that I am a sinner and deserve only his punishment.*

Q: What should I do if I am not aware of my sins or am not troubled by them?

A: *I should examine myself according to the Ten Commandments and ask how well I have carried out my responsibilities as a husband or wife or single person, as a parent or child, an employer or employee, a teacher or student. Have I loved God with all my heart, gladly heard his Word, and patiently endured affliction? Have I been disobedient, proud, or unforgiving? Have I been selfish, lazy, envious, or quarrelsome? Have I lied or deceived, taken something not mine, or given anyone a bad name? Have I abused my body or permitted indecent thoughts to linger in my mind? Have I failed to do what is right and good?*

Q: When I realize that I have sinned against God and deserve his punishment, what should I do?

A: *I will confess before God all my sins, those which I remember as well as those of which I am unaware. I will pray to God for his mercy and forgiveness.*

Q: How do I receive his gracious forgiveness?

A: *His Word assures me that Jesus led a pure and holy life for me and died on the cross for me to pay the full price for all my sins. Through faith in Jesus, I have been clothed in my Savior's perfect righteousness and holiness.*

Q: What further assurance do I have that Jesus is mine and I am his?

A: *In Holy Communion he gives me his body and blood together with the bread and wine as a truly life-giving food and drink to unite me with him and my fellow believers. By means of this sacrament, Jesus not only forgives my sins but sweeps away all my doubts about his love for me, gives me his own strength to live a God-pleasing life, and grants me a joyful foretaste of heaven.*

Q: How can I be sure that I receive all these blessings in the Lord's Supper?

A: *I have his own word spoken as his last will and testament on the night before he died. There he tells me: "Take and eat; this is my body. Drink from it, all of you; this is my blood which is poured out for you for the forgiveness of sins. Do this in remembrance of me."*

Q: How will I respond to this priceless gift from Jesus?

A: *I will daily thank and praise him for his love to me. With his help I will fight temptation, do my best to correct whatever wrongs I have done, and serve him and those around me with love and good works.*

Lord Jesus, with joy and gratitude I now come to your table to receive the precious food of your life-giving body and blood. May it strengthen me to remain in you as you remain in me, so that I bear much fruit in devoted service to you and in acts of kindness to others. Amen.

THE CHRISTIAN CHURCH YEAR

Sundays and Major Festivals

THE TIME OF CHRISTMAS

Advent Season

First Sunday in Advent	*Blue/Purple*
Second Sunday in Advent	*Blue/Purple*
Third Sunday in Advent	*Blue/Purple*
Fourth Sunday in Advent	*Blue/Purple*

Christmas Season

THE NATIVITY OF OUR LORD — *White*
   Christmas Eve
   Christmas Day

First Sunday after Christmas	*White*
Second Sunday after Christmas	*White*

Epiphany Season

THE EPIPHANY OF OUR LORD	*White*
First Sunday after the Epiphany *The Baptism of Our Lord*	*White*
Second Sunday after the Epiphany	*Green*
Third Sunday after the Epiphany	*Green*
Fourth Sunday after the Epiphany	*Green*
Fifth Sunday after the Epiphany	*Green*
Sixth Sunday after the Epiphany	*Green*
Seventh Sunday after the Epiphany	*Green*
Eighth Sunday after the Epiphany	*Green*
Last Sunday after the Epiphany *The Transfiguration of Our Lord*	*White*

THE TIME OF EASTER

Lenten Season

Ash Wednesday	*Black/Purple*
First Sunday in Lent	*Purple*
Second Sunday in Lent	*Purple*
Third Sunday in Lent	*Purple*
Fourth Sunday in Lent	*Purple*
Fifth Sunday in Lent	*Purple*

Holy Week

Sixth Sunday in Lent	*Purple*
Palm Sunday	
Maundy Thursday	*Purple/White*
Good Friday	*Black*

Easter Season

THE RESURRECTION OF OUR LORD	*White/Gold*
Easter Dawn	
Easter Day	
Second Sunday of Easter	*White*
Third Sunday of Easter	*White*
Fourth Sunday of Easter	*White*
Fifth Sunday of Easter	*White*
Sixth Sunday of Easter	*White*
THE ASCENSION OF OUR LORD	*White*
Seventh Sunday of Easter	*White*

THE TIME OF PENTECOST

Pentecost Season

THE COMING OF THE HOLY SPIRIT	*Red*
The Day of Pentecost	
First Sunday after Pentecost	*White*
The Holy Trinity	
Second Sunday after Pentecost	*Green*
Third Sunday after Pentecost	*Green*
Fourth Sunday after Pentecost	*Green*
Fifth Sunday after Pentecost	*Green*
Sixth Sunday after Pentecost	*Green*
Seventh Sunday after Pentecost	*Green*
Eighth Sunday after Pentecost	*Green*
Ninth Sunday after Pentecost	*Green*
Tenth Sunday after Pentecost	*Green*
Eleventh Sunday after Pentecost	*Green*
Twelfth Sunday after Pentecost	*Green*
Thirteenth Sunday after Pentecost	*Green*
Fourteenth Sunday after Pentecost	*Green*
Fifteenth Sunday after Pentecost	*Green*
Sixteenth Sunday after Pentecost	*Green*

Seventeenth Sunday after Pentecost	*Green*
Eighteenth Sunday after Pentecost	*Green*
Nineteenth Sunday after Pentecost	*Green*
Twentieth Sunday after Pentecost	*Green*
Twenty-first Sunday after Pentecost	*Green*
Twenty-second Sunday after Pentecost	*Green*
Twenty-third Sunday after Pentecost	*Green*
Twenty-fourth Sunday after Pentecost	*Green*

End Time Season

First Sunday of End Time *Reformation Sunday*	*Red*
Second Sunday of End Time *Last Judgment*	*Red*
Third Sunday of End Time *Saints Triumphant*	*White*
Last Sunday of End Time *Christ the King*	*White*

Minor Festivals

January

1	The Name of Jesus *New Year's Day*	*White*
18	The Confession of St. Peter	*White*
24	St. Timothy, Pastor and Confessor	*White*
25	The Conversion of St. Paul	*White*
26	St. Titus, Pastor and Confessor	*White*

February

2	The Presentation of Our Lord	*White*
24	St. Matthias, Apostle	*Red*

March

19	St. Joseph	*White*
25	The Annunciation of Our Lord	*White*

April

25	St. Mark, Evangelist	*Red*

May

1	St. Philip and St. James, Apostles	*Red*
31	The Visitation	*White*

June

11	St. Barnabas, Apostle	*Red*
24	The Nativity of St. John the Baptist	*White*
25	Presentation of the Augsburg Confession	*White*
29	St. Peter and St. Paul, Apostles	*Red*

July

22	St. Mary Magdalene	*White*
25	St. James the Elder, Apostle	*Red*

August

15	St. Mary, Mother of Our Lord	*White*
24	St. Bartholomew, Apostle	*Red*

September

21	St. Matthew, Apostle	*Red*
29	St. Michael and All Angels	*White*

October

18	St. Luke, Evangelist	*Red*
23	St. James of Jerusalem	*Red*
28	St. Simon and St. Jude, Apostles	*Red*
31	Reformation Day	*Red*

November

1	All Saints' Day	*White*
30	St. Andrew, Apostle	*Red*

December

21	St. Thomas, Apostle	*Red*
26	St. Stephen, Deacon and Martyr	*Red*
27	St. John, Apostle and Evangelist	*White*
28	The Holy Innocents, Martyrs	*Red*
31	New Year's Eve	*White*

Occasions

Christian Education	*Color of the Season*
Church Anniversary	*Red*
Church Dedication	*Red*
Environment	*Color of the Season*
Evangelism	*Color of the Season*
Family	*Color of the Season*
Home Missions	*Red*
Installation/Ordination	*Red*
Nation	*Color of the Season*
Organ Dedication	*Red*
School Dedication	*Red*
Social Concern	*Color of the Season*
Stewardship	*Color of the Season*
Synod	*Red*
Thanksgiving Day	*White*
Time of Crisis	*Color of the Season*
Worker Training	*Color of the Season*
World Missions	*Red*

The liturgical color for Christian Marriage or Christian Funeral is the color of the season.

CALENDAR DATES FOR THE CHRISTIAN CHURCH YEAR

	Ash Wednesday	Easter	Ascension	Pentecost	First Sunday in End Time	First Sunday in Advent
1993	Feb. 24	Apr. 11	May 20	May 30	Oct. 31	Nov. 28
1994	Feb. 16	Apr. 3	May 12	May 22	Oct. 30	Nov. 27
1995	Mar. 1	Apr. 16	May 25	June 4	Nov. 5	Dec. 3
1996	Feb. 21	Apr. 7	May 16	May 26	Nov. 3	Dec. 1
1997	Feb. 12	Mar. 30	May 8	May 18	Nov. 2	Nov. 30
1998	Feb. 25	Apr. 12	May 21	May 31	Nov. 1	Nov. 29
1999	Feb. 17	Apr. 4	May 13	May 23	Oct. 31	Nov. 28
2000	Mar. 8	Apr. 23	June 1	June 11	Nov. 5	Dec. 3
2001	Feb. 28	Apr. 15	May 24	June 3	Nov. 4	Dec. 2
2002	Feb. 13	Mar. 31	May 9	May 19	Nov. 3	Dec. 1
2003	Mar. 5	Apr. 20	May 29	June 8	Nov. 2	Nov. 30
2004	Feb. 25	Apr. 11	May 20	May 30	Oct. 31	Nov. 28
2005	Feb. 9	Mar. 27	May 5	May 15	Oct. 30	Nov. 27
2006	Mar. 1	Apr. 16	May 25	June 4	Nov. 5	Dec. 3
2007	Feb. 21	Apr. 8	May 17	May 27	Nov. 4	Dec. 2
2008	Feb. 6	Mar. 23	May 1	May 11	Nov. 2	Nov. 30
2009	Feb. 25	Apr. 12	May 21	May 31	Nov. 1	Nov. 29
2010	Feb. 17	Apr. 4	May 13	May 23	Oct. 31	Nov. 28
2011	Mar. 9	Apr. 24	June 2	June 12	Oct. 30	Nov. 27
2012	Feb. 22	Apr. 8	May 17	May 27	Nov. 4	Dec. 2
2013	Feb. 13	Mar. 31	May 9	May 19	Nov. 3	Dec. 1
2014	Mar. 5	Apr. 20	May 29	June 8	Nov. 2	Nov. 30
2015	Feb. 18	Apr. 5	May 14	May 24	Nov. 1	Nov. 29
2016	Feb. 10	Mar. 27	May 5	May 15	Oct. 30	Nov. 27
2017	Mar. 1	Apr. 16	May 25	June 4	Nov. 5	Dec. 3
2018	Feb. 14	Apr. 1	May 10	May 20	Nov. 4	Dec. 2
2019	Mar. 6	Apr. 21	May 30	June 9	Nov. 3	Dec. 1
2020	Feb. 26	Apr. 12	May 21	May 31	Nov. 1	Nov. 29
2021	Feb. 17	Apr. 4	May 13	May 23	Oct. 31	Nov. 28
2022	Mar. 2	Apr. 17	May 26	June 5	Oct. 30	Nov. 27
2023	Feb. 22	Apr. 9	May 18	May 28	Nov. 5	Dec. 3
2024	Feb. 14	Mar. 31	May 9	May 19	Nov. 3	Dec. 1
2025	Mar. 5	Apr. 20	May 29	June 8	Nov. 2	Nov. 30
2026	Feb. 18	Apr. 5	May 14	May 24	Nov. 1	Nov. 29
2027	Feb. 10	Mar. 28	May 6	May 16	Oct. 31	Nov. 28
2028	Mar. 1	Apr. 16	May 25	June 4	Nov. 5	Dec. 3
2029	Feb. 14	Apr. 1	May 10	May 20	Nov. 4	Dec. 2
2030	Mar. 6	Apr. 21	May 30	June 9	Nov. 3	Dec. 1
2031	Feb. 26	Apr. 13	May 22	June 1	Nov. 2	Nov. 30
2032	Feb. 11	Mar. 28	May 6	May 16	Oct. 31	Nov. 28
2033	Mar. 2	Apr. 17	May 26	June 5	Oct. 30	Nov. 27
2034	Feb. 22	Apr. 9	May 18	May 28	Nov. 5	Dec. 3
2035	Feb. 7	Mar. 25	May 3	May 13	Nov. 4	Dec. 2
2036	Feb. 27	Apr. 13	May 22	June 1	Nov. 2	Nov. 30
2037	Feb. 18	Apr. 5	May 14	May 24	Nov. 1	Nov. 29
2038	Mar. 10	Apr. 25	June 3	June 13	Oct. 31	Nov. 28
2039	Feb. 23	Apr. 10	May 19	May 29	Oct. 30	Nov. 27
2040	Feb. 15	Apr. 1	May 10	May 20	Nov. 4	Dec. 2

LECTIONARY
THREE YEAR SERIES
YEAR A

	First Lesson	Second Lesson	Gospel	Psalm
Advent 1	Is 2:1-5	Ro 13:11-14	Mt 24:37-44	18
Advent 2	Is 11:1-10	Ro 15: 4-13	Mt 3:1-12	130
Advent 3	Is 35:1-10	Jas 5:7-11	Mt 11:2-11	146
Advent 4	Is 7:10-14	Ro 1:1-7	Mt 1:18-25	24
Christmas Eve	Is 9:2-7	Tit 2:11-14	Lk 2:1-20	96
Christmas Day	Is 52:7-10	Heb 1:1-9	Jn 1:1-14	98
Christmas 1	Is 63:7-9	Ga 4:4-7	Mt 2:13-15, 19-23	2
Christmas 2	Is 61:10—62:3	Eph 1:3-6, 15-18	Jn 1:14-18	148
Epiphany	Is 60:1-6	Eph 3:2-12	Mt 2:1-12	72
Baptism of Our Lord	Is 42:1-7	Ac 10:34-38	Mt 3:13-17	45
Epiphany 2	Is 49:1-6	1 Co 1:1-9	Jn 1:29-41	89
Epiphany 3	Is 9:1-4	1 Co 1:10-17	Mt 4:12-23	27
Epiphany 4	Mic 6:1-8	1 Co 1:26-31	Mt 5:1-12	1
Epiphany 5	Is 58:5-9a	1 Co 2:1-5	Mt 5:13-20	111
Epiphany 6	Dt 30:15-20	1 Co 2:6-13	Mt 5:21-37	119a
Epiphany 7	Lev 19:1,2, 17,18	1 Co 3:10,11, 16-23	Mt 5:38-48	103
Epiphany 8	Is 49:13-18	1 Co 4:1-13	Mt 6:24-34	119b
Transfiguration	Ex 24:12, 15-18	2 Pe 1:16-21	Mt 17:1-9	148
Ash Wednesday	Is 59:12-20	2 Co 5:20b—6:2	Lk 18:9-14	51a
Lent 1	Ge 2:7-9, 15-17; 3:1-7	Ro 5:12-19	Mt 4:1-11	130
Lent 2	Ge 12:1-8	Ro 4:1-5, 13-17	Jn 4:5-26	121
Lent 3	Is 42:14-21	Eph 5:8-14	Jn 9:1-7, 13-17, 34-39	143
Lent 4	Hos 5:15—6:3	Ro 8:1-10	Mt 20:17-28	42-43
Lent 5	Eze 37:1-14	Ro 8:11-19	Jn 11:17-27, 38-45	116
Palm Sunday	Zec 9:9,10	Php 2:5-11	Mt 21:1-11	24
Maundy Thursday	Ex 12:1-14	1 Co 11:23-28	Jn 13:1-15, 34	116
Good Friday	Is 52:13—53:12	Heb 4:14-16; 5:7-9	Jn 19:17-30	22
Easter Dawn	Is 12:1-6	1 Co 15:51-57	Jn 20:1-18	30
Easter Day	Jnh 2:2-9	Col 3:1-4	Mt 28:1-10	118
Easter 2	Ac 2:14a, 22-32	1 Pe 1:3-9	Jn 20:19-31	16
Easter 3	Ac 2:14a, 36-47	1 Pe 1:17-21	Lk 24:13-35	67
Easter 4	Ac 6:1-9; 7:2a, 51-60	1 Pe 2:19-25	Jn 10:1-10	23
Easter 5	Ac 17:1-12	1 Pe 2:4-10	Jn 14:1-12	33
Easter 6	Ac 17:22-31	1 Pe 3:15-22	Jn 14:15-21	66
Ascension	Ac 1:1-11	Eph 1:16-23	Lk 24:44-53	47
Easter 7	Ac 1:1-14	1 Pe 4:12-17; 5:6-11	Jn 17:1-11a	8
Pentecost	Joel 2:28,29	Ac 2:1-21	Jn 16:5-11	51b
Holy Trinity	Ge 1:1—2:3	2 Co 13:11-14	Mt 28:16-20	150
Pentecost 2	Dt 11:18-21, 26-28	Ro 3:21-25a, 27,28	Mt 7:15-29	78
Pentecost 3	Hos 5:15—6:6	Ro 4:18-25	Mt 9:9-13	119c
Pentecost 4	Ex 19:2-8a	Ro 5:6-11	Mt 9:35—10:8	100
Pentecost 5	Jer 20:7-13	Ro 5:12-15	Mt 10:24-33	31
Pentecost 6	Jer 28:5-9	Ro 6:1b-11	Mt 10:34-42	89
Pentecost 7	Ex 33:12-23	Ro 7:15-25a	Mt 11:25-30	145
Pentecost 8	Is 55:10,11	Ro 8:18-25	Mt 13:1-9, 18-23	65
Pentecost 9	Joel 3:12-16	Ro 8:26,27	Mt 13:24-30, 36-43	18
Pentecost 10	1 Ki 3:5-12	Ro 8:28-30	Mt 13:44-52	119b
Pentecost 11	Is 55:1-5	Ro 8:35-39	Mt 14:13-21	42-43
Pentecost 12	1 Ki 19:9-18	Ro 9:1-5	Mt 14:22-33	73
Pentecost 13	Is 56:1, 6-8	Ro 11:13-15, 28-32	Mt 15:21-28	133-134
Pentecost 14	Ex 6:2-8	Ro 11:33-36	Mt 16:13-20	34
Pentecost 15	Jer 15:15-21	Ro 12:1-8	Mt 16:21-26	121
Pentecost 16	Eze 33:7-11	Ro 13:1-10	Mt 18:15-20	51a
Pentecost 17	Ge 50:15-21	Ro 14:5-9	Mt 18:21-35	103
Pentecost 18	Is 55:6-9	Php 1:18b-27	Mt 20:1-16	27
Pentecost 19	Eze 18:1-4, 25-32	Php 2:1-11	Mt 21:28-32	25
Pentecost 20	Is 5:1-7	Php 3:12-21	Mt 21:33-43	118
Pentecost 21	Is 25:6-9	Php 4:4-13	Mt 22:1-14	23
Pentecost 22	Is 45:1-7	1 Th 1:1-5a	Mt 22:15-21	96
Pentecost 23	Lev 19:1,2, 15-18	1 Th 1:5b-10	Mt 22:34-46	33
Pentecost 24	Mal 3:14-18	1 Th 3:7-13	Mt 25:14-30	92
Reformation	Da 6:10-12, 16-23	Ga 5:1-6	Mt 10:16-23	46
Last Judgment	Da 7:9,10	1 Th 5:1-11	Mt 25:31-46	90
Saints Triumphant	Is 52:1-6	1 Th 4:13-18	Mt 25:1-13	84
Christ the King	Eze 34:11-16, 23, 24	1 Co 15:20-28	Mt 27:27-31	47

LECTIONARY
THREE YEAR SERIES
YEAR B

	First Lesson	Second Lesson	Gospel	Psalm
Advent 1	Is 63:16b,17; 64:1-8	1 Co 1:3-9	Mk 13:32-37	24
Advent 2	Is 40:1-11	2 Pe 3:8-14	Mk 1:1-8	85
Advent 3	Is 61:1-3, 10,11	1 Th 5:16-24	Jn 1:6-8, 19-28	71
Advent 4	2 Sa 7:8-16	Ro 16:25-27	Lk 1:26-38	89
Christmas Eve	Is 9:2-7	Tit 2:11-14	Lk 2:1-20	96
Christmas Day	Is 52:7-10	Heb 1:1-9	Jn 1:1-14	98
Christmas 1	Is 45:20-25	Col 3:12-17	Lk 2:25-40	111
Christmas 2	Mic 5:2-5a	Heb 2:10-18	Jn 7:40-43	148
Epiphany	Is 60:1-6	Eph 3:2-12	Mt 2:1-12	72
Baptism of Our Lord	Is 49:1-6	Ac 16:25-34	Mk 1:4-11	2
Epiphany 2	1 Sa 3:1-10	1 Co 6:12-20	Jn 1:43-51	67
Epiphany 3	Jnh 3:1-5, 10	1 Co 7:29-31	Mk 1:14-20	62
Epiphany 4	Dt 18:15-20	1 Co 8:1-13	Mk 1:21-28	1
Epiphany 5	Job 7:1-7	1 Co 9:16-23	Mk 1:29-39	103
Epiphany 6	2 Ki 5:1-14	1 Co 9:24-27	Mk 1:40-45	32
Epiphany 7	Is 43:18-25	2 Co 1:18-22	Mk 2:1-12	130
Epiphany 8	Hos 2:14-16, 19,20	2 Co 3:1b-6	Mk 2:18-22	133-134
Transfiguration	2 Ki 2:1-12a	2 Co 3:12—4:2	Mk 9:2-9	148
Ash Wednesday	Is 59:12-20	2 Co 5:20b—6:2	Lk 18:9-14	51a
Lent 1	Ge 22:1-18	Ro 8:31-39	Mk 1:12-15	6
Lent 2	Ge 28:10-17	Ro 5:1-11	Mk 8:31-38	73
Lent 3	Ex 20:1-17	1 Co 1:22-25	Jn 2:13-22	19
Lent 4	Nu 21:4-9	Eph 2:4-10	Jn 3:14-21	38
Lent 5	Jer 31:31-34	Heb 5:7-9	Jn 12:20-33	143
Palm Sunday	Zec 9:9,10	Php 2:5-11	Mk 11:1-10	24
Maundy Thursday	Ex 12:1-14	1 Co 10:16,17	Mk 14:12-26	116
Good Friday	Is 52:13—53:12	Heb 4:14-16; 5:7-9	Jn 19:17-30	22
Easter Dawn	Is 12:1-6	1 Co 15:51-57	Jn 20:1-18	30
Easter Day	Is 25:6-9	1 Co 15:19-26	Mk 16:1-8	118
Easter 2	Ac 3:12-20	1 Jn 5:1-6	Jn 20:19-31	16
Easter 3	Ac 4:8-12	1 Jn 1:1—2:2	Lk 24:36-49	118
Easter 4	Ac 4:23-33	1 Jn 3:1,2	Jn 10:11-18	23
Easter 5	Ac 8:26-40	1 Jn 3:18-24	Jn 15:1-8	67
Easter 6	Ac 11:19-26	1 Jn 4:1-11	Jn 15:9-17	98
Ascension	Ac 1:1-11	Eph 1:16-23	Lk 24:44-53	47
Easter 7	Ac 1:15-26	1 Jn 4:13-21	Jn 17:11b-19	8
Pentecost	Eze 37:1-14	Ac 2:1-21	Jn 14:25-27	51b
Holy Trinity	Is 6:1-8	Ro 8:14-17	Jn 3:1-17	150
Pentecost 2	Dt 5:12-15	2 Co 4:5-12	Mk 2:23-28	126
Pentecost 3	Ge 3:8-15	2 Co 4:13-18	Mk 3:20-35	51a
Pentecost 4	Eze 17:22-24	2 Co 5:1-10	Mk 4:26-34	92
Pentecost 5	Job 38:1-11	2 Co 5:14-21	Mk 4:35-41	46
Pentecost 6	La 3:22-33	2 Co 8:1-9, 13,14	Mk 5:21-24a, 35-43	30
Pentecost 7	Eze 2:1-5	2 Co 12:7-10	Mk 6:1-6	143
Pentecost 8	Am 7:10-15	Eph 1:3-14	Mk 6:7-13	78
Pentecost 9	Jer 23:1-6	Eph 2:13-22	Mk 6:30-34	23
Pentecost 10	Ex 24:3-11	Eph 4:1-7, 11-16	Jn 6:1-15	84
Pentecost 11	Ex 16:2-15	Eph 4:17-24	Jn 6:24-35	145
Pentecost 12	1 Ki 19:3-8	Eph 4:30—5:2	Jn 6:41-51	34
Pentecost 13	Pr 9:1-6	Eph 5:15-20	Jn 6:51-58	1
Pentecost 14	Jos 24:1,2a, 14-18	Eph 5:21-31	Jn 6:60-69	71
Pentecost 15	Dt 4:1,2, 6-8	Eph 6:10-20	Mk 7:1-8, 14,15, 21-23	119c
Pentecost 16	Is 35:4-7a	Jas 1:17-27	Mk 7:31-37	146
Pentecost 17	Is 50:4-10	Jas 2:1-5, 8-10, 14-18	Mk 8:27-35	116
Pentecost 18	Jer 11:18-20	Jas 3:13-18	Mk 9:30-37	31
Pentecost 19	Nu 11:16, 24-29	Jas 4:7-12	Mk 9:38-50	51b
Pentecost 20	Ge 2:18-24	Heb 2:9-11	Mk 10:2-16	139b
Pentecost 21	Am 5:6,7, 10-15	Heb 3:1-6	Mk 10:17-27	90
Pentecost 22	Is 53:10-12	Heb 4:9-16	Mk 10:35-45	22
Pentecost 23	Jer 31:7-9	Heb 5:1-10	Mk 10:46-52	126
Pentecost 24	Dt 6:1-9	Heb 7:23-28	Mk 12:28-34	119a
Reformation	Jer 18:1-11	Rev 14:6,7	Mk 13:5-11	46
Last Judgment	Mal 4:1,2a	Heb 9:24-28	Jn 5:19-24	90
Saints Triumphant	Da 12:1-3	Heb 10:11-18	Jn 5:25-29	118
Christ the King	Da 7:13,14	Rev 1:4b-8	Jn 18:33-37	45

LECTIONARY
THREE YEAR SERIES
YEAR C

	First Lesson	Second Lesson	Gospel	Psalm
Advent 1	Jer 33:14-16	1 Th 3:9-13	Lk 21:25-36	25
Advent 2	Mal 3:1-4	Php 1:3-11	Lk 3:1-6	24
Advent 3	Zeph 3:14-17	Php 4:4-7	Lk 3:7-18	130
Advent 4	Mic 5:2-5a	Heb 10:5-10	Lk 1:39-55	85
Christmas Eve	Is 9:2-7	Tit 2:11-14	Lk 2:1-20	96
Christmas Day	Is 52:7-10	Heb 1:1-9	Jn 1:1-14	98
Christmas 1	1 Sa 2:18-20, 26	Heb 2:10-18	Lk 2:41-52	111
Christmas 2	Ge 17:1-7	Ga 4:4-7	Lk 1:68-75	148
Epiphany	Is 60:1-6	Eph 3:2-12	Mt 2:1-12	72
Baptism of Our Lord	1 Sa 16:1-13	Tit 3:4-7	Lk 3:15-17, 21,22	2
Epiphany 2	Is 62:1-5	1 Co 12:1-11	Jn 2:1-11	133-134
Epiphany 3	Is 61:1-6	1 Co 12:12-21, 26,27	Lk 4:14-21	19
Epiphany 4	Jer 1:4-10	1 Co 12:27—13:13	Lk 4:20-32	78
Epiphany 5	Is 6:1-8	1 Co 14:12b-20	Lk 5:1-11	85
Epiphany 6	Jer 17:5-8	1 Co 15:12, 16-20	Lk 6:17-26	1
Epiphany 7	Ge 45:3-8a, 15	1 Co 15:35-38a, 42-49	Lk 6:27-38	103
Epiphany 8	Jer 7:1-7	1 Co 16:5-9, 13,14	Lk 6:39-49	92
Transfiguration	Ex 34:29-35	2 Co 4:3-6	Lk 9:28-36	148
Ash Wednesday	Is 59:12-20	2 Co 5:20b—6:2	Lk 18:9-14	51a
Lent 1	Dt 26:5-10	Ro 10:8b-13	Lk 4:1-13	91
Lent 2	Jer 26:8-15	Php 3:17—4:1	Lk 13:31-35	42-43
Lent 3	Ex 3:1-8b, 10-15	1 Co 10:1-13	Lk 13:1-9	38
Lent 4	Is 12:1-6	1 Co 1:18-25	Lk 15:1-3,11b-32	32
Lent 5	Is 43:16-21	Php 3:8-14	Lk 20:9-19	73
Palm Sunday	Zec 9:9,10	Php 2:5-11	Lk 19:28-40	24
Maundy Thursday	Ex 12:1-14	Heb 10:15-25	Lk 22:7-20	116
Good Friday	Is 52:13—53:12	Heb 4:14-16; 5:7-9	Jn 19:17-30	22
Easter Dawn	Is 12:1-6	1 Co 15:51-57	Jn 20:1-18	30
Easter Day	Ex 15:1-11	1 Co 15:1-11	Lk 24:1-12	118
Easter 2	Ac 5:12, 17-32	Rev 1:4-18	Jn 20:19-31	16
Easter 3	Ac 9:1-19a	Rev 5:11-14	Jn 21:1-14	67
Easter 4	Ac 13:15,16a, 26-33	Rev 7:9-17	Jn 10:22-30	23
Easter 5	Ac 13:44-52	Rev 21:1-6	Jn 13:31-35	145
Easter 6	Ac 14:8-18	Rev 21:10-14, 22,23	Jn 14:23-29	65
Ascension	Ac 1:1-11	Eph 1:16-23	Lk 24:44-53	47
Easter 7	Ac 16:6-10	Rev 22:12-17, 20	Jn 17:20-26	8
Pentecost	Ge 11:1-9	Ac 2:1-21	Jn 15:26,27	51b
Holy Trinity	Nu 6:22-27	Ro 5:1-5	Jn 16:12-15	150
Pentecost 2	1 Ki 8:22,23, 41-43	Ga 1:1-10	Lk 7:1-10	100
Pentecost 3	1 Ki 17:17-24	Ga 1:11-24	Lk 7:11-17	30
Pentecost 4	2 Sa 11:26—12:10, 13-15	Ga 2:11-21	Lk 7:36-50	32
Pentecost 5	Zec 13:7-9	Ga 3:23-29	Lk 9:18-24	22
Pentecost 6	1 Ki 19:14-21	Ga 5:1, 13-25	Lk 9:51-62	62
Pentecost 7	Is 66:10-14	Ga 6:1-10, 14-16	Lk 10:1-12, 16-20	66
Pentecost 8	Dt 30:9-14	Col 1:1-14	Lk 10:25-37	25
Pentecost 9	Ge 18:1-14	Col 1:21-29	Lk 10:38-42	119a
Pentecost 10	Ge 18:20-32	Col 2:6-15	Lk 11:1-13	6
Pentecost 11	Ecc 1:2; 2:18-26	Col 3:1-11	Lk 12:13-21	34
Pentecost 12	Ge 15:1-6	Heb 11:1-3, 8-16	Lk 12:32-40	33
Pentecost 13	Jer 23:23-29	Heb 12:1-13	Lk 12:49-53	139a
Pentecost 14	Is 66:18-24	Heb 12:18-24	Lk 13:22-30	72
Pentecost 15	Pr 25:6,7	Heb 13:1-8	Lk 14:1, 7-14	119a
Pentecost 16	Pr 9:8-12	Phm 1:1,10-21	Lk 14:25-33	19
Pentecost 17	Ex 32:7-14	1 Ti 1:12-17	Lk 15:1-10	51a
Pentecost 18	Am 8:4-7	1 Ti 2:1-8	Lk 16:1-13	38
Pentecost 19	Am 6:1-7	1 Ti 6:6-16	Lk 16:19-31	146
Pentecost 20	Hab 1:1-3; 2:1-4	2 Ti 1:3-14	Lk 17:1-10	27
Pentecost 21	Ru 1:1-19a	2 Ti 2:8-13	Lk 17:11-19	111
Pentecost 22	Ge 32:22-30	2 Ti 3:14—4:5	Lk 18:1-8a	121
Pentecost 23	Dt 10:12-22	2 Ti 4:6-8, 16-18	Lk 18:18-27	119b
Pentecost 24	Ex 34:5-9	2 Th 1:1-5, 11,12	Lk 19:1-10	145
Reformation	Jer 31:31-34	Ro 3:19-28	Jn 8:31-36	46
Last Judgment	Jer 26:1-6	2 Th 1:5-10	Lk 19:11-27	90
Saints Triumphant	Is 65:17-25	2 Th 2:13—3:5	Lk 20:27-38	150
Christ the King	Jer 23:2-6	Col 1:13-20	Lk 23:35-43	98

LECTIONARY
ONE YEAR SERIES

	First Lesson	Second Lesson	Gospel	Psalm
Advent 1	Jer 33:14-18	Ro 13:11-14	Mt 21:1-9	24
Advent 2	Mal 4:1-6	Ro 15:4-13	Lk 21:25-36	85
Advent 3	Is 35:1-6	1 Co 1:26-31	Mt 11:2-10	111
Advent 4	Is 12:1-6	Php 4:4-7	Lk 1:46-55	92
Christmas Eve	Is 9:2-7	Tit 2:11-14	Lk 2:1-20	8
Christmas Day	Mic 5:2-5a	Heb 1:1-9	Jn 1:1-14	98
Christmas 1	Is 42:1-4	Ga 4:1-7	Lk 2:25-38	103
Christmas 2	Jer 31:15-20	1 Pe 4:12-19	Mt 2:13-23	18
Epiphany	Is 60:1-6	Eph 3:2-12	Mt 2:1-12	72
Baptism of Our Lord	Is 42:1-14	Ac 10:34-48	Mt 3:13-17	89
Epiphany 2	Is 61:1-3	Ro 12:1-5	Lk 2:41-52	84
Epiphany 3	Ex 15:22-27	Ro 12:6-16a	Jn 2:1-11	145
Epiphany 4	2 Ki 5:1-15a	Ro 12:16b-21	Mt 8:1-13	30
Epiphany 5	Ex 14:13-22	Ro 13:8-10	Mt 8:23-27	33
Epiphany 6	Ex 34:5-10	1 Co 9:24—10:5	Mt 20:1-16	46
Epiphany 7	Is 55:10-13	2 Co 11:19—12:9	Lk 8:4-15	1
Epipahny 8	Is 42:5-9	1 Co 13:1-13	Lk 18:31-43	71
Transfiguration	Dt 18:15-18	2 Pe 1:16-21	Mt 17:1-9	2
Ash Wednesday	Is 59:12-20	2 Co 5:17—6:2	Lk 7:36-50	130
Lent 1	Ge 3:1-15	2 Co 6:1-10	Mt 4:1-11	91
Lent 2	Is 49:5-9a	1 Th 4:1-7	Mt 15:21-28	25
Lent 3	2 Sa 22:1-7	Eph 5:1-9	Lk 11:14-28	73
Lent 4	Ex 16:11-17	Eph 3:14-20	Jn 6:1-15	145
Lent 5	Ex 3:1-15	Heb 9:11-15	Jn 8:46-59	45
Palm Sunday	Zec 9:9-12	Php 2:5-11	Mt 21:1-9	24
Maundy Thursday	Ex 12:1-14	1 Co 11:23-32	Jn 13:1-15	111
Good Friday	Is 52:13—53:12	Heb 7:26-28	Jn 18:1—19:42	22
Easter Dawn	Ps 16	1 Co 15:12-20	Jn 20:1-8	150
Easter Day	Job 19:23-27a	1 Co 5:6-8	Mk 16:1-8	118
Easter 2	Ge 15:1-6	1 Jn 5:4-10	Jn 20:19-31	116
Easter 3	La 3:18-26	1 Pe 2:11-20	Jn 16:16-23a	67
Easter 4	Eze 34:11-16	1 Pe 2:21-25	Jn 10:11-16	23
Easter 5	1 Ch 16:23-34	Jas 1:16-21	Jn 16:5-15	66
Easter 6	Jer 29:11-14	Jas 1:22-27	Jn 16:23b-30	85
Ascension	2 Ki 2:1-11	Ac 1:1-11	Lk 24:36-53	47
Easter 7	Eze 36:24-28	1 Pe 4:7-11	Jn 15:26—16:4	78
Pentecost	Joel 2:28-32	Ac 2:1-13	Jn 14:23-31	51b
Holy Trinity	Is 6:1-8	Ro 11:33-36	Jn 3:1-15	73
Pentecost 2	Dt 6:4-18	1 Jn 4:16-21	Lk 16:19-31	143
Pentecost 3	Is 25:6-9	1 Jn 3:13-18	Lk 14:16-24	100
Pentecost 4	Dt 32:3-12	1 Pe 5:6-11	Lk 15:1-10	103
Pentecost 5	Is 58:6-12	Ro 8:18-23	Lk 6:36-42	133-134
Pentecost 6	Jer 1:4-10	1 Pe 3:8-15	Lk 5:1-11	67
Pentecost 7	Ge 13:5-11	Ro 6:3-11	Mt 5:20-26	19
Pentecost 8	Ps 107:1-9	Ro 6:19-23	Mk 8:1-9	146
Pentecost 9	Jer 23:16-24	Ro 8:12-17	Mt 7:15-23	1
Pentecost 10	Ge 39:1-6a	1 Co 10:6-13	Lk 16:1-9	92
Pentecost 11	Da 9:15-18	1 Co 12:1-11	Lk 19:41-48	51a
Pentecost 12	2 Sa 12:1-13	1 Co 15:1-10	Lk 18:9-14	6
Pentecost 13	Mic 7:18-20	2 Co 3:4-11	Mk 7:31-37	34
Pentecost 14	Lev 19:9-18	Ga 3:15-22	Lk 10:23-37	133-134
Pentecost 15	Dt 8:10-18	Ga 5:16-24	Lk 17:11-19	116
Pentecost 16	1 Ki 17:8-16	Ga 5:25—6:10	Mt 6:24-34	62
Pentecost 17	1 Ki 17:17-24	Eph 3:13-21	Lk 7:11-17	126
Pentecost 18	Mic 6:6-8	Eph 4:1-6	Lk 14:1-11	143
Pentecost 19	Dt 10:12-21	1 Co 1:4-9	Mt 22:34-46	2
Pentecost 20	Ex 15:22-26	Eph 4:22-28	Mt 9:1-8	139a
Pentecost 21	Hos 1:2-11	Eph 5:15-21	Mt 22:1-14	27
Pentecost 22	Dt 1:26-36	Eph 6:10-17	Jn 4:46-54	139b
Pentecost 23	Ge 50:15-21	Php 1:3-11	Mt 18:23-35	38
Pentecost 24	Dt 10:12-20	Php 3:17-21	Mt 22:15-22	89
Reformation	Is 43:1-7	Ro 3:19-28	Jn 17:6-19	46
Last Judgment	Jer 8:4-7	1 Th 4:13-18	Mt 25:31-46	16
Saints Triumphant	Is 65:17-25	1 Th 5:1-11	Mt 25:1-13	121
Christ the King	Is 51:4-8	Rev 1:9-18	Jn 18:33-37	45

Let the word of Christ dwell in you richly as you teach and admonish one another with all wisdom, and as you sing psalms, hymns, and spiritual songs with gratitude in your hearts to God.

Colossians 3:16

ADVENT

1 The Advent of Our King

1 The advent of our King
  Our prayers must now employ,
  And we must hymns of welcome sing
  In strains of holy joy.

2 The everlasting Son
  Incarnate deigns to be,
  Himself a servant's form puts on
  To set his servants free.

3 O Zion's Daughter, rise
  To meet your lowly King,
  Nor let a faithless heart despise
  The peace he comes to bring.

4 As judge, on clouds of light,
  He soon will come again
  And his true members all unite
  With him in heav'n to reign.

5 Before the dawning Day
  Let sin's dark deeds be gone,
  The sinful self be put away,
  The new self now put on.

6 All glory to the Son,
  Who comes to set us free,
  With Father, Spirit, ever one
  Through all eternity.

Text: Charles Coffin, 1676-1749; tr. John Chandler, 1806-76, alt.
Tune: Aaron Williams, 1731-76
Setting © 1993 Elfred Bloedel

ST. THOMAS
SM
Alternate settings: 238, 533

ADVENT

Savior of the Nations, Come

2

1 Savior of the nations, come; Virgin's Son, make here your home. Marvel now, O heav'n and earth, That the Lord chose such a birth.

2 Not by human flesh and blood, By the Spirit of our God Was the Word of God made flesh, Woman's offspring, pure and fresh.

3 Wondrous birth! O wondrous Child Of the virgin undefiled, Though by all the world disowned, Yet to be in heav'n enthroned!

4 From the Father's throne he came And ascended to the same, Captive leading death and hell— High the song of triumph swell!

5 Praise to God the Father sing,
Praise to God the Son, our King,
Praise to God the Spirit be
Ever and eternally.

Text: Ambrose, 340-97, abr.; German version, Martin Luther, 1483-1546, abr.;
tr. William M. Reynolds, 1812-76, alt.
Tune: *Geystliche gesangk Buchleyn*, Wittenberg, 1524
Setting © 1993 Kermit G. Moldenhauer

NUN KOMM, DER HEIDEN HEILAND
77 77

Alternate setting: 28

ADVENT

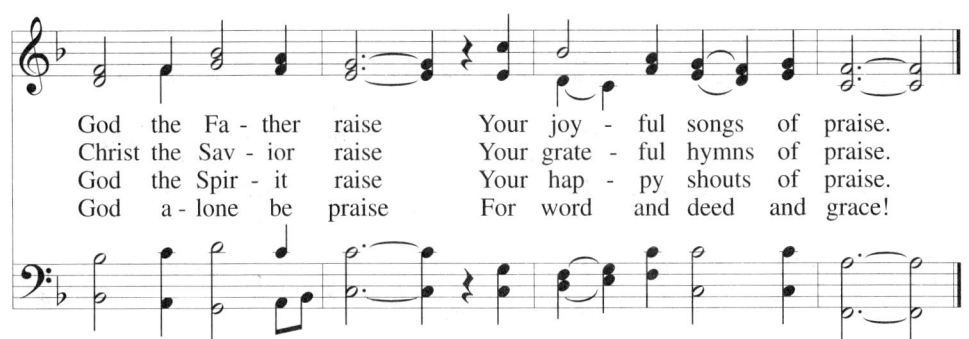

God the Fa - ther raise Your joy - ful songs of praise.
Christ the Sav - ior raise Your grate - ful hymns of praise.
God the Spir - it raise Your hap - py shouts of praise.
God a - lone be praise For word and deed and grace!

5 Redeemer, come! I open wide
   My heart to you; here, Lord, abide!
Oh, enter with your saving grace;
   Show me your kind and friendly face.
Your Holy Spirit guide us on
   Until our glorious goal is won.
Eternal praise and fame
   We offer to your name.

Text: Georg Weissel, 1590-1635; tr. Catherine Winkworth, 1827-78, alt.
Tune: Freylinghausen, *Geist-reiches Gesang-Buch*, Halle, 1704

MACHT HOCH DIE TÜR
88 88 88 66

ADVENT

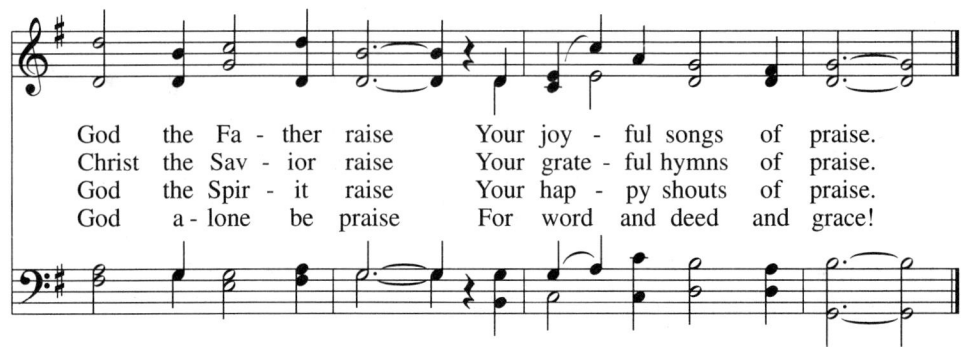

God the Father raise Your joyful songs of praise.
Christ the Savior raise Your grateful hymns of praise.
God the Spirit raise Your happy shouts of praise.
God alone be praise For word and deed and grace!

5 Redeemer, come! I open wide
My heart to you; here, Lord, abide!
Oh, enter with your saving grace;
Show me your kind and friendly face.
Your Holy Spirit guide us on
Until our glorious goal is won.
Eternal praise and fame
We offer to your name.

Text: Georg Weissel, 1590-1635; tr. Catherine Winkworth, 1827-78, alt.
Tune: August Lemke, 1820-1913

MILWAUKEE
88 88 88 66

ADVENT

5 As Angels Joyed with One Accord

1 As angels joyed with one accord Upon the advent of our Lord, So laud we all and bless the name Of him who from the Father came.

2 He came, not clothed in majesty Nor pow'r that suits his deity. In lowly state he walked till he In dying set us captives free.

3 This done, he soared to God's right hand, Yet orphaned not his chosen band, For he, not bound in grace and pow'r, Attends his own each day and hour.

4 In ev'ry age— let praise abound— He comes; we hear his voice resound. His glorious gospel does not cease To bring us comfort, joy, and peace.

5 He comes in water to the child
And cleanses it, from birth defiled.
This washing seals his pard'ning grace
And shows the Father's kindly face.

6 He comes to us in bread and wine
To give himself — and gifts divine.
Oh, praise him for this sacrament,
Redeeming love's great testament!

7 Lift up your heads! All grief and pain
Shall vanish when he comes again.
Where we shall see him face to face,
There joy alone shall have a place.

Text: Werner H. Franzmann, 1905-96, abr., alt.
Tune: Latin melody, 15th century, adapt.

PUER NOBIS NASCITUR
LM

Text © 1993 Werner H. Franzmann; Setting © A. R. Mowbray & Co., Ltd.

Alternate setting: 53

ADVENT

Come, O Long-Expected Jesus 6

1 Come, O long-ex-pect-ed Je-sus, Born to set your peo-ple free;
From our sins and fears re-lease us By your death on Cal-va-ry.
Is-rael's Strength and Con-so-la-tion, Hope to all the earth im-part,
Dear De-sire of ev-'ry na-tion, Joy of ev-'ry long-ing heart.

2 Born your peo-ple to de-liv-er, Born a child and yet a king,
Born to reign in us for-ev-er, Now your gra-cious king-dom bring.
By your own e-ter-nal Spir-it Rule in all our hearts a-lone;
By your all-suf-fi-cient mer-it Raise us to your glo-rious throne.

Text: Charles Wesley, 1707-88, alt.
Tune: Unknown

ST. HILARY
87 87 D

ADVENT

Come, O Precious Ransom, Come 8

1 Come, O precious Ransom, come, Only Hope for sinful mortals! Come, O Savior of the world! Open are to you all portals. Come, your beauty let us view; Anxiously we wait for you.

2 Enter now my waiting heart, Glorious King and Lord most holy. Dwell in me and ne'er depart, Though I am but poor and lowly. Ah, what riches will be mine When you are my guest divine!

3 My hosannas and my palms Graciously receive, I pray you. Evermore, as best I can, Savior, I will homage pay you, And in faith I will embrace, Lord, your merit through your grace.

4 Hail, hosanna, David's Son! Help, Lord; hear our supplication! Let your kingdom, scepter, crown Bring us blessing and salvation That forever we may sing Hail, hosanna! to our King.

Text: Johann G. Olearius, 1635-1711; tr. August Crull, 1845-1923, alt.
Tune: *Neu-verfertigtes Darmstädtisches Gesang-Buch*, Darmstadt, 1699, alt.

MEINEN JESUM LASS ICH NICHT
78 78 77

ADVENT

9 Jesus, Your Church with Longing Eyes

1 Jesus, your Church with longing eyes For your expected coming waits. When will the promised light arise And glory beam from heaven's gates?

2 E'en now, when tempests round us fall And wintry clouds o'ercast the sky, Your words with pleasure we recall And know that our redemption's nigh.

3 Come, gracious Lord, our hearts renew, Our sins forgive, our foes suppress, Our rooted enmity subdue, And crown your gospel with success.

4 Oh, come and reign o'er ev'ry land; Let Satan from his throne be hurled. Let nations bow to your command; Let grace revive a dying world.

5 Teach us in watchfulness and prayer
To wait for your appointed hour,
And fit us by your grace to share
The triumphs of your conqu'ring pow'r.

Text: William H. Bathurst, 1796-1877, abr., alt.
Tune: *Andächtige Haus-Kirche*, Nürnberg, 1676, alt.
Setting © 1993 Elfred Bloedel

O JESU CHRISTE, WAHRES LICHT
LM

Alternate settings: 383, 569

ADVENT

The Bridegroom Soon Will Call Us 10

1 The Bridegroom soon will call us; Shake off your drowsy sleep!
  Lest carelessness befall us, A watchful vigil keep!
  May all our lamps be burning With oil enough and more
  That we, with him returning, May find an open door!

2 There shall we see in glory Our dear Redeemer's face;
  The long-awaited story Of heav'nly joy takes place:
  The patriarchs shall meet us, The prophets' holy band;
  Apostles, martyrs greet us In that celestial land.

3 There God shall from all evil Forever make us free,
  From sin and from the devil, From all adversity,
  From sickness, pain, and sadness, From troubles, cares, and fears,
  And grant us heav'nly gladness And wipe away our tears.

4 In that fair home shall never Be silent music's voice;
  With hearts and lips forever We shall in God rejoice,
  While angel hosts are raising With saints from great to least
  A mighty hymn for praising The giver of the feast.

Text: Johann Walter, 1496-1570, abr.; tr. composite, 1989
Tune: *Musae Sioniae*, VII, Wolfenbüttel, 1609

ACH GOTT VOM HIMMELREICHE
76 76 D

Alternate setting: 314

Hark the Glad Sound! The Savior Comes 12

1 Hark the glad sound! The Sav-ior comes, The Sav-ior
2 He comes the cap-tives to re-lease, In Sa-tan's
3 He comes the bro-ken heart to bind, The bleed-ing
4 Our glad ho-san-nas, Prince of Peace, Your wel-come

prom - ised long; Let ev - 'ry heart pre -
pris - on held. The gates of brass be -
soul to cure, And with the trea - sures
shall pro - claim, And heav'n's e - ter - nal

pare a throne And ev - 'ry voice a song.
fore him burst; The i - ron fet - ters yield.
of his grace To en - rich the hum - ble poor.
arch - es ring With your be - lov - ed name.

Text: Philip Doddridge, 1702-51, abr., alt.
Tune: Thomas Haweis, 1734-1820, alt.

CHESTERFIELD
CM

ADVENT

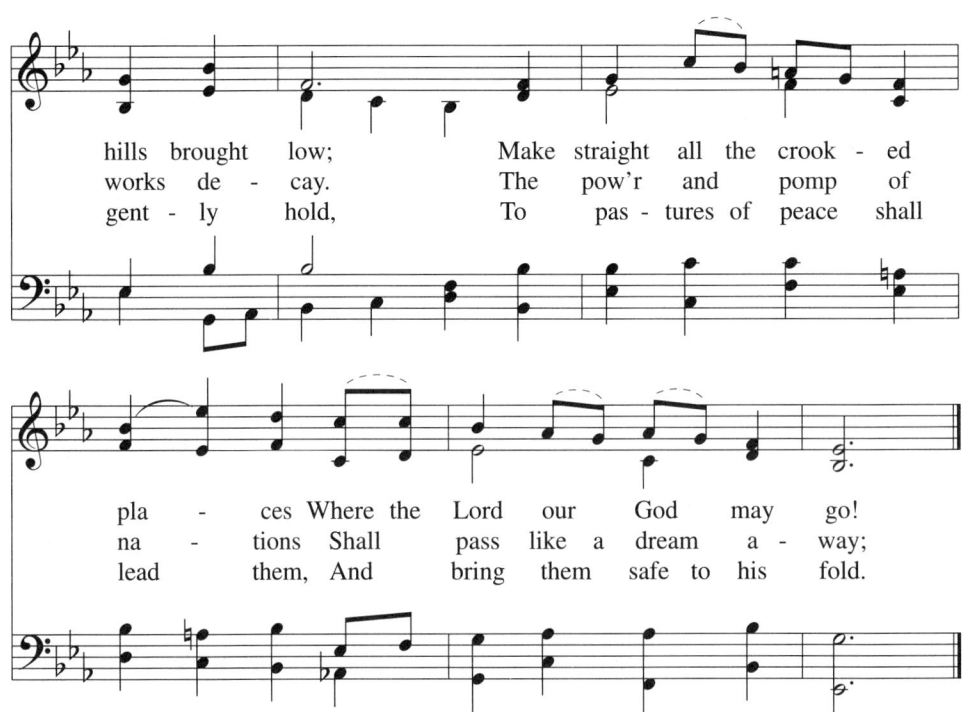

Text: James L. Milligan, 1876-1961, alt.
Tune: Henry H. Bancroft, b. 1904-1988
Setting © The Church Pension Fund

ASCENSION
Irregular

ADVENT

14 Arise, O Christian People

1. Arise, O Christian people! Prepare yourselves today; Prepare to greet the Savior, Who takes your sins away. To us by grace alone The truth and light were given; The promised Lord from heaven To all the world is shown.

2. Prepare the way before him; Prepare for him the best. Cast out what would offend him, This great, this heav'nly guest. Make straight, make plain the way: The lowly valleys raising, The heights of pride abasing, His path all even lay.

3. The humble heart and lowly God raises up on high; Beneath his feet in terror The haughty soul shall lie. The heart sincere and right, That heeds God's invitation And makes true preparation—It is the Lord's delight.

4. Prepare my heart, Lord Jesus; Turn not from me aside, And help me to receive you This blessed Adventtide. From stall and manger low Come now to dwell within me; I'll sing your praises gladly And forth your glory show.

Text: Valentin Thilo, 1607-62, alt.; tr. Arthur T. Russell, 1806-74, st. 1-3, alt.;
The Lutheran Hymnal, St. Louis, 1941, st. 4, alt.
Tune: *New Catechismus Gesangbüchlein*, Hamburg, 1598, alt.
Setting © 1993 Kermit G. Moldenhauer

AUS MEINES HERZENS GRUNDE
76 76 67 76

ADVENT

Hark! A Thrilling Voice Is Sounding 15

Text: Latin hymn, c. 6th century, abr., alt.; tr. Edward Caswall, 1814-78, alt.
Tune: William H. Monk, 1823-89; Desc. Alan Gray, 1855-1935

MERTON
87 87

ADVENT

16 On Jordan's Bank the Baptist's Cry

1. On Jordan's bank the Baptist's cry Announces that the Lord is nigh; Come, then, and listen, for he brings Good news about the King of kings.

2. Then cleansed be ev'ry life from sin And furnished for a guest within, And let us all our hearts prepare For Christ to come and enter there.

3. We hail you as our Savior, Lord, Our refuge and our great reward. Without your grace we waste away Like flow'rs that wither and decay.

4. Stretch forth your hand, our health restore, And lift us up to fall no more. Oh, make your face on us to shine, And fill the world with love divine.

5. All praise to you, eternal Son,
Whose advent has our freedom won,
Whom with the Father we adore
And Holy Spirit evermore.

Text: Charles Coffin, 1676-1749; tr. John Chandler, 1806-76, st. 1-3, alt.; composite, st. 4-5
Tune: Latin melody, 15th century, adapt.
Setting © A. R. Mowbray & Co., Ltd.

PUER NOBIS NASCITUR
LM
Alternate setting: 53

ADVENT

God's Own Son Most Holy   17

1 God's own Son most holy Came a servant lowly,
  Came to live among us, Came to suffer for us,
  Bore the cross to save us, Hope and freedom gave us.
2 Still he comes within us; Still his voice would win us
  From the sins that hurt us, Would to truth convert us
  From our foolish errors Ere he comes in terrors.
3 Thus, if we have known him And will not disown him
  Nor have loved him coldly But will trust him boldly,
  He will then receive us, Heal us, and forgive us.
4 Those who then are loyal Find a welcome royal.
  Come, then, O Lord Jesus, From our sins release us.
  Let us here confess you Till in heav'n we bless you.

Text: Johann Horn, c. 1490-1547, abr.; tr. Catherine Winkworth, 1827-78, alt.
Tune: attr. Michael Weisse, c. 1480-1534
Setting © 1984 Jack Warren Burnam.

GOTTES SOHN IST KOMMEN
66 66 66

ADVENT

Hosanna to the Coming Lord 21

1 Hosanna to the coming Lord! Hosanna to the incarnate Word! To Christ, Creator, Savior, King Let earth, let heav'n hosanna sing.
2 O Savior, with protecting care Abide in this your house of prayer, Where we your parting promise claim, Assembled in your sacred name.
3 O Advent King, our sins forgive; Come in our lives and hearts to live, And let our humble souls become A temple worthy of your name.
4 Then in the last and dreadful day, When earth and heav'n shall melt away, Your flock, redeemed from sinful stain, Shall swell the sound of praise again.

Text: Reginald Heber, 1783-1826, abr., alt.
Tune: Schumann, *Geistliche lieder auffs new gebessert*, Leipzig, 1539

VOM HIMMEL HOCH
LM

Alternate setting: 38

ADVENT

Oh, Come, Oh, Come, Emmanuel   23

1 Oh, come, oh, come, Emmanuel, And ransom captive
Israel That mourns in lonely exile here
Until the Son of God appear.

2 Oh, come, O Root of Jesse, free Your own from Satan's
tyranny; From depths of hell your people save,
And bring them vict'ry o'er the grave.

3 Oh, come, O Dayspring from on high, And cheer us by your
drawing nigh; Disperse the gloomy clouds of night,
And death's dark shadows put to flight.

4 Oh, come, O Key of David, come, And open wide our
heav'nly home. Make safe the way that leads on high,
And close the path to misery.

Refrain
Rejoice! Rejoice! Emmanuel Shall come to you, O Israel!

Text: Latin hymn, c. 12th century, abr.; tr. John M. Neale, 1818-66, alt.
Tune: Plainsong melody, 15th century, alt.

VENI, EMMANUEL
LM with Refrain

ADVENT

The King Shall Come 25

1. The King shall come when morning dawns And light triumphant breaks, When beauty gilds the eastern hills And life to joy awakes —
2. Not as of old a little child To bear and fight and die, But crowned with glory like the sun That lights the morning sky.
3. Oh, brighter than the rising morn When Christ, victorious, rose And left the lonesome place of death Despite the rage of foes.
4. Oh, brighter than that glorious morn Shall dawn upon our race The day when Christ in splendor comes And we shall see his face.

5 The King shall come when morning dawns
And light and beauty brings.
Hail, Christ the Lord! Your people pray:
Come quickly, King of kings!

Text: John Brownlie, 1857-1925, abr., alt.
Tune: *Repository of Sacred Music, Part Second,* Harrisburg, 1813
Setting © 1969 Concordia Publishing House

CONSOLATION
CM

ADVENT

26 Jesus Came, the Heavens Adoring

1 Jesus came, the heav'ns adoring, Came with peace from realms on high; Jesus came to win redemption, Lowly came on earth to die, Alleluia! Alleluia! Came in deep humility.

2 Jesus comes again in mercy When our hearts are worn with care; Jesus comes again in answer To an earnest, heartfelt prayer, Alleluia! Alleluia! Comes to save us from despair.

3 Jesus comes to hearts rejoicing, Bringing news of sins forgiv'n; Jesus comes with words of gladness, Leading souls redeemed to heav'n. Alleluia! Alleluia! Hope to all the world is giv'n.

4 Jesus comes on clouds triumphant When the heav'ns shall pass away. Jesus comes again in glory; Let us, then, our homage pay, Alleluia! ever singing Till the dawn of endless day.

Text: Godfrey Thring, 1823-1903, abr., alt.
Tune: *Geistreiches Gesang-Buch*, Darmstadt, 1698

SIEH, HIER BIN ICH, EHRENKÖNIG
87 87 87

ADVENT

O Jesus, Lamb of God, You Are 27

1. O Jesus, Lamb of God, you are My comfort and my guiding star; I come, a sinner, trustingly And bring my many sins with me.
2. O Lord, my sin indeed is great; I groan beneath the dreadful weight. Be merciful to me, I pray; Take guilt and punishment away.
3. Saint John the Baptist points to you And bids me cast my sin on you, For you have left your throne on high To suffer for the world and die.
4. Help me to change my ways, O Lord, And gladly to obey your Word. While here I live, abide with me, Then take me home eternally.

Text: Bartholomäus Helder, 1585-1635; tr. August Crull, 1845-1923, alt.
Tune: C. P. E. Bach, 1714-88

WEIMAR
LM

ADVENT

28 Let the Earth Now Praise the Lord

1 Let the earth now praise the Lord,
  Who has truly kept his word
  And at last to us did send
  Christ, the sinner's help and friend.

2 What the fathers most desired,
  What the prophets' heart inspired,
  What they longed for many a year
  Stands fulfilled in glory here.

3 Abram's promised great reward,
  Zion's helper, Jacob's Lord—
  Him of twofold race behold—
  Truly came, as long foretold.

4 Welcome, O my Savior, now!
  Joyful, Lord, to you I bow.
  Come into my heart, I pray;
  Oh, prepare yourself a way.

5 Crush for me the serpent's head
  That, set free from doubt and dread,
  I may cling to you in faith,
  Safely kept through life and death,

6 And, when you shall come again
  As a glorious king to reign,
  I with joy may see your face,
  Freely ransomed by your grace.

Text: Heinrich Held, 1620-59, abr.; tr. Catherine Winkworth, 1827-78, alt.
Tune: *Geystliche gesangk Buchleyn,* Wittenberg, 1524

NUN KOMM, DER HEIDEN HEILAND
77 77

Alternate setting: 2

ADVENT

O Lord of Light, Who Made the Stars   31

1 O Lord of light, who made the stars, O Dawn, by whom we see the way, O Christ, Redeemer of the world: Come now and listen as we pray.
2 In lowliness you came to earth To rescue us from Satan's snares, O wondrous Love that healed our wounds By taking on our mortal cares.
3 To pay the debt we owed for sin, Your painful cross was made the price; From blessed Mary's womb you came, A victim pure for sacrifice.
4 But now you reign, the King of kings, Adored in highest majesty; Your very name is held in awe From pole to pole and sea to sea. Amen.

5 Great Judge of all, on earth's last day
  Have pity on your children's plight.
  Rise up to shield us with your grace;
  Deliver us from Satan's might.

6 To God the Father and the Son
  And Holy Spirit, Three in One,
  Praise, honor, might, and glory be
  From age to age eternally. Amen.

Text: Latin hymn, c. 9th century; tr. Melvin Farrell, b. 1930, alt.
Tune: Sarum plainsong, c. 9th century

CONDITOR ALME SIDERUM
LM

Text © 1993 World Library Publications, Inc.; Setting © 1993 Kermit G. Moldenhauer

ADVENT

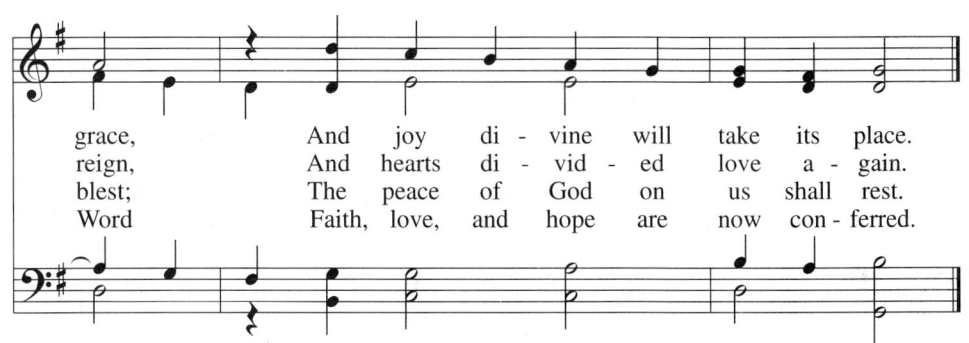

grace,   And joy di-vine will take its place.
reign,   And hearts di-vid-ed love a-gain.
blest;   The peace of God on us shall rest.
Word   Faith, love, and hope are now con-ferred.

5 Oh, may he soon to ev'ry nation
  Find entrance where he is unknown,
  With life and light and free salvation,
  That Satan's pow'r be overthrown,
  And healing to all hearts may come
  In heathen land and Christian home!

Text: Magnus B. Landstad, 1802-80, abr.; tr. Oluf H. Smeby, 1851-1929, alt.
Tune: Christian Möck, 1737-1818

WER WEISS, WIE NAHE
98 98 88

Setting © 1993 Elfred Bloedel

Alternate setting: 210

CHRISTMAS

33 All Praise to You, Eternal God

1 All praise to you, eternal God! Now clothed in human flesh and blood, You took a manger for your throne While worlds on worlds are yours alone. Alleluia!

2 Once did the skies before you bow; A virgin's arms contain you now While angels, who in you rejoice, Now listen for your infant voice. Alleluia!

3 O little Child, you were our guest That weary ones in you might rest; Forlorn and lowly was your birth That we might rise to heav'n from earth. Alleluia!

4 You came to us in darkest night To make us children of the light; Like angels in the realms divine Around your throne we, too, will shine. Alleluia!

5 All this your love for us has done;
By this our love for you is won;
For this our joyful songs we raise
And shout our thanks in ceaseless praise.
Alleluia!

Text: German hymn, c. 1370, abr., st. 1; Martin Luther, 1483-1546, st. 2-5;
tr. *The Sabbath Hymn Book*, New York, 1858, alt.
Tune: *Eyn Enchiridion oder Handbüchlein*, Erfurt, 1524

GELOBET SEIST DU, JESU CHRIST
LM with Alleluia

Now Sing We, Now Rejoice   34

CHRISTMAS

1 Now sing we, now rejoice, Now raise to heav'n our voice;
  He from whom joy streameth Poor in a manger lies;
  Not so brightly beameth The sun in yonder skies.
  Thou my Savior art! Thou my Savior art!

2 Come from on high to me; I cannot rise to thee.
  Cheer my wearied spirit, O pure and holy Child;
  Through thy grace and merit, Blest Jesus, Lord most mild,
  Draw me unto thee! Draw me unto thee!

3 Now through his Son doth shine The Father's grace divine.
  Death o'er us had reigned Through sin and vanity;
  He for us obtained Eternal joy on high.
  May we praise him there! May we praise him there!

4 Oh, where shall joy be found? Where but on heav'nly ground?
  Where the angels singing With all his saints unite,
  Sweetest praises bringing In heav'nly joy and light.
  Oh, that we were there! Oh, that we were there!

Text: Latin hymn, 14th century; tr. Arthur T. Russell, 1806-74, alt.
Tune: German melody, 14th century, alt.
Setting © 1993 Kermit G. Moldenhauer

IN DULCI JUBILO
66 66 66 55

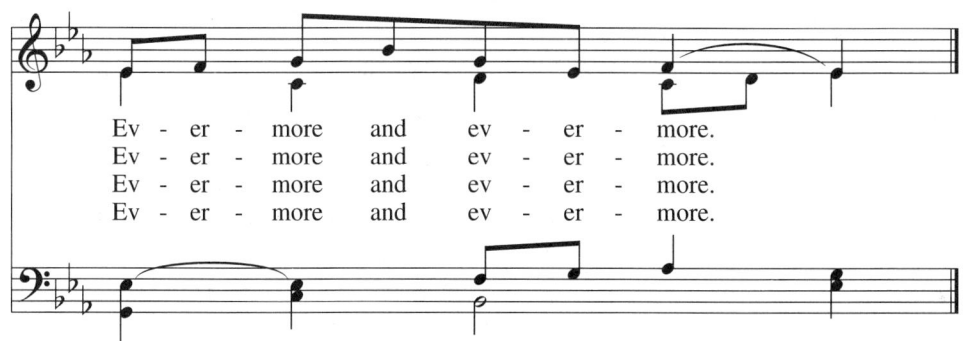

5 Christ, to you, with God the Father,
    And the Spirit ceaselessly
Hymn and chant and high thanksgiving
    And unending praises be,
Honor, glory, and dominion
    And eternal victory
Evermore and evermore.

Text: Aurelius Clemens Prudentius, 348-c.413, abr.;
    tr. John M. Neale, 1818-66, st. 1-4, alt.; Henry W. Baker, 1821-77, st. 5, alt.
Tune: Plainsong melody, 13th century
Setting © 1982 Concordia Publishing House

DIVINUM MYSTERIUM
87 87 877

CHRISTMAS

Once Again My Heart Rejoices 37

1 Once again my heart rejoices As I hear Far and near
  Sweetest angel voices. "Christ is born!" their choirs are
  singing Till the air Ev'rywhere Now with joy is ringing.

2 Hear! The conqueror has spoken: "Now the foe, Sin and woe,
  Death and hell are broken!" God is man, man to deliver,
  And the Son Now is one With our blood forever.

3 Should we still fear God's displeasure, Who, to save, Freely gave
  His most precious treasure? To redeem us he has given
  His own Son From the throne Of his might in heaven.

4 God becomes the victim, taking Mankind's place By his grace,
  Full atonement making. For our life his own he tenders,
  And his grace All our race Fit for glory renders.

5 Softly from his lowly manger
    Jesus calls
    One and all,
  "You are safe from danger.
  Children, from the sins that grieve you
    You are freed;
    All you need
  I will surely give you."

6 Come, then, banish all your sadness!
    One and all,
    Great and small,
  Come with songs of gladness;
  We shall live with him forever
    There on high
    In that joy
  Which will vanish never.

Text: Paul Gerhardt, 1607-76, abr., adapt.; tr. Catherine Winkworth, 1827-78, alt.   FRÖHLICH SOLL MEIN HERZE SPRINGEN
Tune: Johann Crüger, 1598-1662   8 33 6 D

CHRISTMAS

38 From Heaven Above to Earth I Come

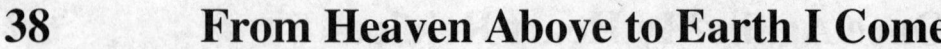

1 "From heav'n a-bove to earth I come To bear good
news to ev-'ry home; Glad ti-dings of great joy
I bring, Where-of I now will say and sing:

2 "To you this night is born a child Of Mar-y,
cho-sen vir-gin mild; This lit-tle child of lowly birth Shall be the joy of all the earth.

3 "This is the Christ, our God most high, Who hears your
sad and bit-ter cry; He will him-self your Savior be, From all your sins to set you free.

4 "He will on you the gifts be-stow Pre-pared by
God for all be-low, That in his king-dom, bright
and fair, You may with us his glo-ry share.

5 "These are the signs which you shall mark:
The swaddling clothes and manger dark.
There you will find the infant laid
By whom the heav'ns and earth were made."

6 How glad we'll be to find it so!
Then with the shepherds let us go
To see what God for us has done
In sending us his own dear Son.

7 Come here, my friends, lift up your eyes,
And see what in the manger lies.
Who is this child, so young and fair?
It is the Christchild lying there.

8 Welcome to earth, O noble Guest,
Through whom the sinful world is blest!
You came to share my misery
That you might share your joy with me.

CHRISTMAS

9 Ah, Lord, though you created all,
   How weak you are, so poor and small,
   That you should choose to lay your head
   Where lowly cattle lately fed!

10 Were earth a thousand times as fair
   And set with gold and jewels rare,
   It would be far too poor and small
   A cradle for the Lord of all.

11 Instead of soft and silken stuff
   You have but hay and straw so rough
   On which as King, so rich and great,
   To be enthroned in royal state.

12 And so it pleases you to see
   This simple truth revealed to me:
   That all the world's wealth, honor, might
   Are weak and worthless in your sight.

13 Ah, dearest Jesus, holy Child,
   Prepare a bed, soft, undefiled
   Within my heart, made clean and new,
   A quiet chamber kept for you.

14 My heart for very joy must leap;
   My lips no more can silence keep.
   I, too, must sing with joyful tongue
   That sweetest ancient cradle song:

15 Glory to God in highest heaven,
   Who unto us his Son has given!
   While angels sing with pious mirth
   A glad new year to all the earth.

Text: Martin Luther, 1483-1546; tr. Catherine Winkworth, 1827-78, alt.
Tune: Schumann, *Geistliche lieder auffs new gebessert*, Leipzig, 1539

VOM HIMMEL HOCH
LM

Alternate setting: 2

CHRISTMAS

39 Now Praise We Christ, the Holy One

1 Now praise we Christ, the Holy One, The blessed virgin Mary's Son. From east to west, from shore to shore Let earth its Lord and King adore.
2 He who himself all things did make A servant's form a-greed to take, That he as man mankind might win And save his creatures from their sin.
3 The grace and pow'r of God the Lord Upon the mother was outpoured; A virgin pure and undefiled In wondrous way conceived a child.
4 The noble mother bore a Son— For so did Gabriel's promise run— Whom John confessed and leaped with joy Before the mother knew her boy.

5 Upon a manger filled with hay
In poverty content he lay;
With milk was fed the Lord of all,
Who feeds the ravens when they call.

6 The heav'nly choirs rejoice and raise
Their voice to God in songs of praise.
To humble shepherds is proclaimed
The Shepherd who the world has framed.

7 All honor unto Christ the Lord,
Eternal and incarnate Word,
With Father and with Holy Ghost,
Till time in endless time be lost.

Text: Coelius Sedulius, 5th century, abr.;
   German version, Martin Luther, 1483-1546; tr. Richard Massie, 1800-87, alt.
Tune: *Eyn Enchiridion oder Handbüchlein*, Erfurt, 1524, alt.

CHRISTUM WIR SOLLEN LOBEN SCHON
LM

CHRISTMAS

O Jesus Christ, Your Manger Is 40

1. O Jesus Christ, Your manger is My paradise where my soul is reclining. For there, O Lord, We find the Word Made flesh for us — your grace is brightly shining.
2. He whom the sea And wind obey Comes down to serve the sinner in great meekness. Now God's own Son With us is one And joins us and our children in our weakness.
3. Dear Christian friend, On him depend; Be of good cheer and let no sorrow move you. For God's own child In mercy mild Joins you to him — how greatly God must love you!
4. Ponder again What glory then The Lord will give you for your earthly sadness. The angel host Can never boast Of greater glory, greater bliss or gladness.

5 The world may hold
    Her wealth and gold;
But you, my heart, keep Christ as your true treasure.
To him hold fast
    Until at last
A crown is yours and honor in full measure.

Text: Paul Gerhardt, 1607-76, abr.; tr. *The Lutheran Hymnal*, St. Louis, 1941, alt.
Tune: Johann Crüger, 1598-1662
Setting © 1993 Kermit G. Moldenhauer

O JESU CHRIST, DEIN KRIPPLEIN IST
44 11 D

CHRISTMAS

41 Let All Together Praise Our God

1 Let all together praise our God
Before his highest throne;
Today he opens heav'n again
And gives us his own Son,
And gives us his own Son.

2 He leaves his heav'nly Father's throne,
Is born an infant small,
And in a manger, poor and lone,
Lies in a humble stall,
Lies in a humble stall.

3 He veils in flesh his pow'r divine
A servant's form to take;
In want and lowliness must die
Who heav'n and earth did make,
Who heav'n and earth did make.

4 A wondrous change which he does make:
He takes our flesh and blood,
And he conceals for sinners' sake
His majesty as God,
His majesty as God.

5 He serves that I a lord may be —
A great exchange indeed!
Could Jesus' love do more for me
To help me in my need,
To help me in my need?

6 For us he opens wide the door
Of paradise today.
The angel guards the gate no more;
To God our thanks we pay,
To God our thanks we pay.

Text: Nikolaus Herman, c. 1480-1561, abr.; tr. August Crull, 1845-1923, alt.
Tune: Nikolaus Herman, c. 1480-1561

LOBT GOTT, IHR CHRISTEN
86 866

Alternate setting: 90

Come, Your Hearts and Voices Raising 42

1 Come, your hearts and voices raising, Christ the Lord with gladness praising; Loudly sing his love amazing, Worthy folk of Christendom.

2 See how God, for us providing, Gave his Son and life abiding; He our weary steps is guiding From earth's woe to heav'nly joy.

3 Christ, from heav'n to us descending And in love our race befriending, In our need his help extending, Saved us from the wily foe.

4 Jacob's Star in all its splendor Beams with comfort sweet and tender, Forcing Satan to surrender, Breaking all the pow'rs of hell.

5 Gracious Child, we pray you, hear us;
From your lowly manger cheer us.
Gently lead us and be near us
Till we join th' angelic choir.

Text: Paul Gerhardt, 1607-76, abr.; tr. *The Lutheran Hymnal*, St. Louis, 1941
Tune: *Ein Schlesich singebüchlein*, Breslau, 1555
Setting © 1993 Kermit G. Moldenhauer

QUEM PASTORES
88 87

CHRISTMAS

Break Forth, O Beauteous Heavenly Light 44

Text: Johann Rist, 1607-67, abr.; tr. John Troutbeck, 1832-99, alt.
Tune: Johann Schop, c. 1590-1667, alt.

ERMUNTRE DICH
87 87 88 77

Text © The Church Pension Fund

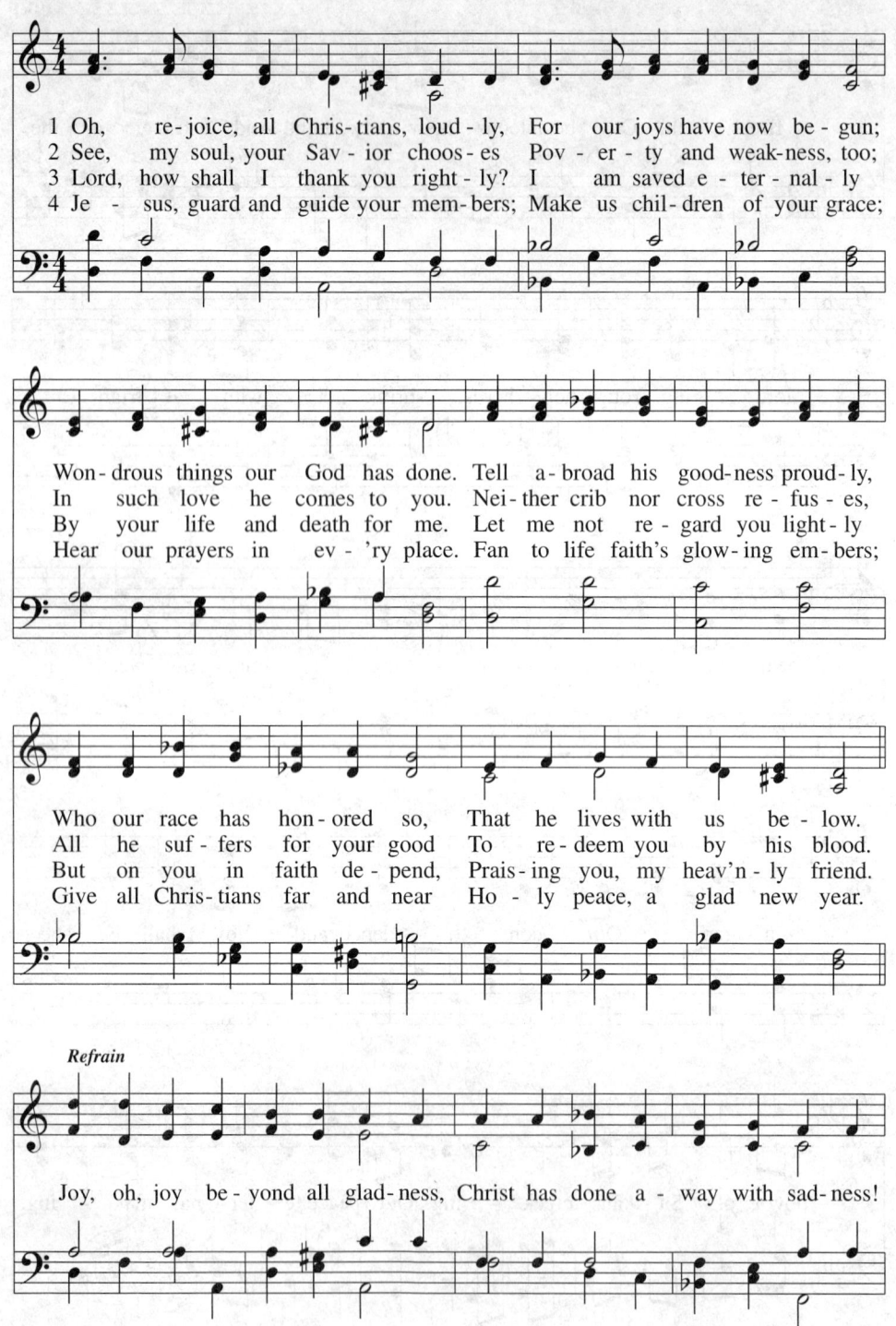

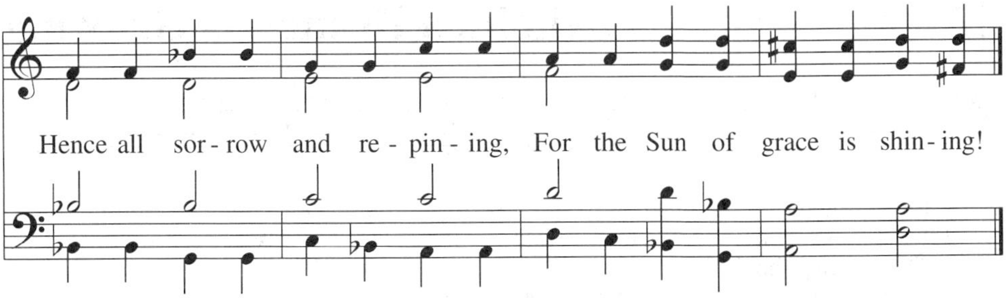

Hence all sor-row and re-pin-ing, For the Sun of grace is shin-ing!

Text: Christian Keimann, 1607-62; tr. Catherine Winkworth, 1827-78, alt.
Tune: Andreas Hammerschmidt, c. 1611-75, alt.
Setting © 1982 Concordia Publishing House

FREUET EUCH, IHR CHRISTEN ALLE
877 877 with Refrain

Your Little Ones, Dear Lord, Are We 46

1 Your lit-tle ones, dear Lord, are we And come your low-ly bed to see; En-light-en ev-'ry soul and mind That we the way to you may find.
2 With songs we has-ten you to greet And hum-bly fall be-fore your feet. Oh, bless-ed hour, oh, sweet-est night That gave you birth, our souls' de-light.
3 Oh, draw us whol-ly to you, Lord, And to us all your grace ac-cord; True faith and love to us im-part That we may hold you in our heart.
4 Un-til at last we, too, pro-claim, With all your saints, your glo-rious name; In par-a-dise our songs re-new And praise you as the an-gels do.

Text: Hans A. Brorson, 1694-1764; tr. Harriet R. K. Spaeth, 1845-1925, alt.
Tune: Johann A. P. Schulz, 1747-1800

HER KOMMER DINE ARME SMAA
LM

CHRISTMAS

5 O Savior, Child of Mary,
      Who felt our human woes,
   O Savior, King of glory,
      Who conquered all our foes,
   Bring us at last, we pray,
      To the bright courts of heaven
   And to the endless day.

Text: Alte Catholische Geistliche Kirchengeseng, Köln, 1599, abr.; tr. composite ES IST EIN ROS
Tune: Alte Catholische Geistliche Kirchengeseng, Köln, 1599 76 76 676

When Christmas Morn Is Dawning — 48

1 When Christ-mas morn is dawn-ing, I wish that I could be
2 How kind of you, my Sav-ior, To come to us on earth.
3 We need you, O Lord Je-sus, To be our dear-est friend.

There by the man-ger cra-dle God's Son, new-born, to see.
Oh, may we not by sin-ning De-spise your low-ly birth.
Your love will guard and guide us And keep us to life's end.

There by the man-ger cra-dle God's Son, new-born, to see.
Oh, may we not by sin-ning De-spise your low-ly birth.
Your love will guard and guide us And keep us to life's end.

Text: Abel Burckhardt, 19th century; tr. Joel W. Lundeen, 1918-90, alt. WIR HATTEN GEBAUET
Tune: German folk tune, c. 1800 76 76 76

Text © 1978 Lutheran Book of Worship

CHRISTMAS

49 Rejoice, Rejoice This Happy Morn

Rejoice, rejoice this happy morn! A Savior unto us is born, The Christ, the Lord of glory. His lowly birth in Bethlehem The angels from on high proclaim And sing redemption's story. My soul, Extol God's great favor; Bless him ever For salvation. Give him praise and adoration.

Text: Birgitte K. Boye, 1742-1824; tr. Carl Döving, 1867-1937
Tune: Philipp Nicolai, 1556-1608, alt.
Setting © 1981 Richard W. Gieseke

WIE SCHÖN LEUCHTET
887 887 22 44 48
Alternate setting: 79

5 And so I love each Christmas Eve,
   And I love Jesus, too;
   And that he loves me ev'ry day
   I know so well is true.

CHRISTMAS

On Christmas Night All Christians Sing   52

1 On Christ-mas night all Chris-tians sing To hear the news the
2 When sin de-parts be-fore your grace, Then life and health come
3 From out of dark-ness we have light Which made the an - gels

an - gels bring; On Christ-mas night all Chris-tians sing To
in its place. When sin de-parts be-fore your grace, Then
sing this night. From out of dark-ness we have light Which

hear the news the an - gels bring, News of great joy, news
life and health come in its place. An - gels and saints with
made the an - gels sing this night: "Glo - ry to God and

of great mirth, News of our mer - ci - ful King's birth.
joy may sing All for to see the new - born King.
peace to men Now and for - ev - er - more. A - men."

Text: English carol, abr., alt.   SUSSEX CAROL
Tune: English carol   88 88 88

Tune and Setting reproduced by permission of Stainer & Bell Ltd.

CHRISTMAS

53 To Shepherds as They Watched by Night

1. To shepherds as they watched by night Appeared a host of angels bright; "Behold the tender babe," they said, "In yonder lowly manger laid,
2. "At Bethlehem, in David's town, As Micah did of old make known. It is the Christ, your Lord and King, Who will to all salvation bring."
3. Oh, then rejoice that through his Son God is with sinners now at one; Made like yourselves of flesh and blood, Your brother is th' eternal God.
4. What harm can sin and death then do? The true God now abides with you. Let hell and Satan storm and rave, Christ is your brother — you are safe.

5. Not one he will or can forsake;
His cov'nant he will never break.
Let ev'ry scheme the tempter try,
You may his utmost pow'rs defy.

6. You shall and must at last prevail.
God's own you are; you cannot fail.
To God forever sing your praise
With joy and patience all your days.

Text: Martin Luther, 1483-1546; tr. Richard Massie, 1800-87, alt.
Tune: Latin melody, 15th century, adapt.

PUER NOBIS NASCITUR
LM

Alternate setting: 5

CHRISTMAS

Optional setting and descant for stanzas 3 and 4:

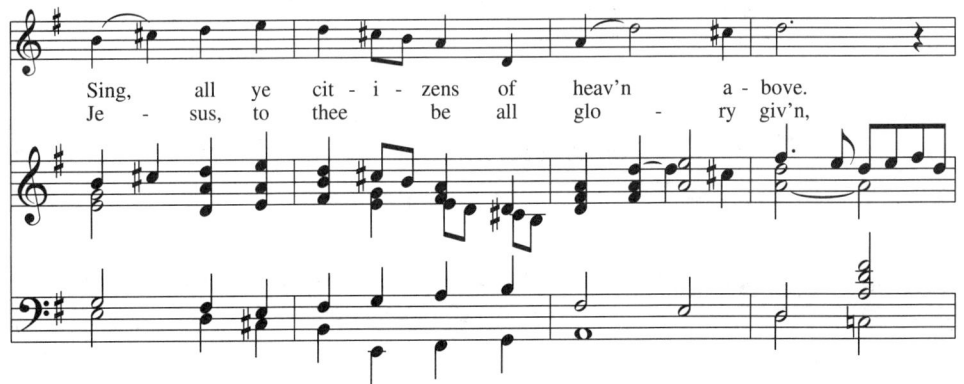

CHRISTMAS

Text: John F. Wade, c. 1711-86; tr. Frederick Oakeley, 1802-80, alt.
Tune: John F. Wade, c. 1711-86, alt.; Desc. with harm. by David V. Willcocks, b. 1919

ADESTE FIDELES
Irregular

Descant and harmony for st. 3,4 reprinted by permission of Oxford University Press

CHRISTMAS

57 Go, Tell It on the Mountain

Text: African-American spiritual, c. 19th century, refrain;
John W. Work, 1873-1925, stanzas, alt.
Tune: African-American spiritual, c. 19th century, alt.
Text reprinted with permission of Mrs. Edith M. Work

GO, TELL IT
78 76 76 76

See in Yonder Manger Low

CHRISTMAS

58

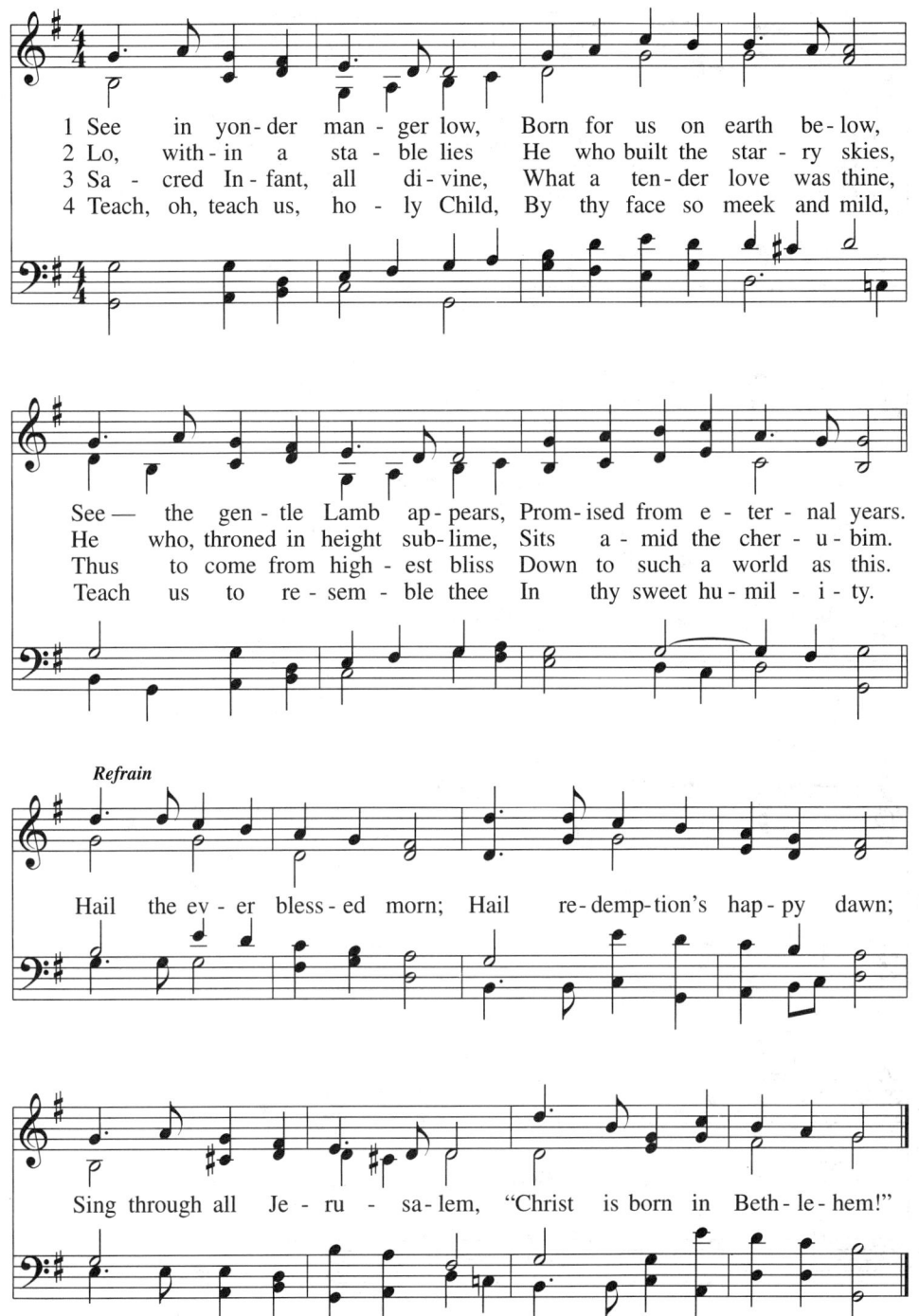

1. See in yonder manger low, Born for us on earth below,
   See the gentle Lamb appears, Promised from eternal years.
2. Lo, within a stable lies He who built the starry skies,
   He who, throned in height sublime, Sits amid the cherubim.
3. Sacred Infant, all divine, What a tender love was thine,
   Thus to come from highest bliss Down to such a world as this.
4. Teach, oh, teach us, holy Child, By thy face so meek and mild,
   Teach us to resemble thee In thy sweet humility.

Refrain
Hail the ever blessed morn; Hail redemption's happy dawn;
Sing through all Jerusalem, "Christ is born in Bethlehem!"

Text: Edward Caswall, 1814-78, alt.
Tune: John Goss, 1800-80

HUMILITY
77 77 with Refrain

CHRISTMAS

59 Christ the Lord to Us Is Born

1 Christ the Lord to us is born, Alleluia!
2 Prophesied in days of old, Alleluia!
3 Our poor human form he took, Alleluia!
4 God has saved us through his Son, Alleluia!

On this joyous Christmas morn, Alleluia!
God has sent him as foretold, Alleluia!
Realms of heaven he forsook, Alleluia!
Conquered lies the evil one, Alleluia!

Refrain

Of a virgin lowly, He, the King most holy, Born this day to save us.

Text: Bohemian carol, 15th century, abr.; tr. Vincent Pisek, 1859-1930, alt.
Tune: Bohemian carol, 15th century

NARODIL SE KRISTUS PAN
74 74 with Refrain

Text © 1941 Concordia Publishing House

CHRISTMAS

Silent Night! Holy Night

60

1 Silent night! Holy night! All is calm, all is bright, Round yon virgin mother and child. Holy Infant, so tender and mild, Sleep in heavenly peace, Sleep in heavenly peace.
2 Silent night! Holy night! Shepherds quake at the sight. Glories stream from heaven afar; Heav'nly hosts sing, Alleluia; Christ, the Savior, is born! Christ, the Savior, is born!
3 Silent night! Holy night! Son of God, love's pure light Radiant beams from thy holy face With the dawn of redeeming grace, Jesus, Lord, at thy birth, Jesus, Lord, at thy birth.

Text: Franz Joseph Mohr, 1792-1848, abr.; tr. John F. Young, 1820-85
Tune: Franz X. Gruber, 1787-1863, alt.

STILLE NACHT
Irregular

CHRISTMAS

Optional setting and descant for stanza 3:

CHRISTMAS

Text: Charles Wesley, 1707-88, abr., alt.
Tune: Felix Mendelssohn, 1809-47, alt.; Desc. with harm. by David V. Willcocks, b. 1919

MENDELSSOHN
77 77 D with Refrain

Descant and harmony for st. 3 reprinted by permission of Oxford University Press

CHRISTMAS

63 Angels We Have Heard on High

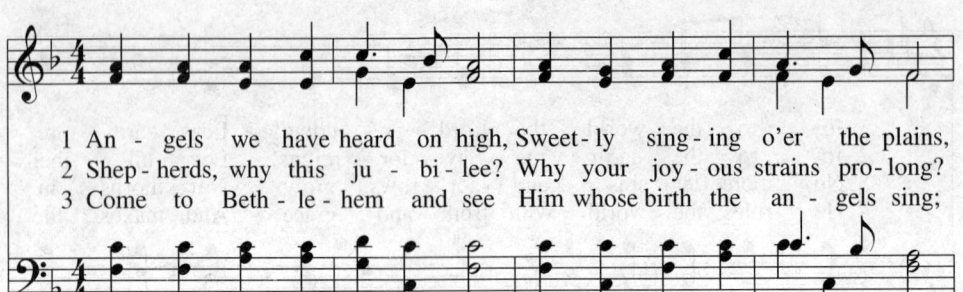

1 An-gels we have heard on high, Sweet-ly sing-ing o'er the plains,
2 Shep-herds, why this ju-bi-lee? Why your joy-ous strains pro-long?
3 Come to Beth-le-hem and see Him whose birth the an-gels sing;

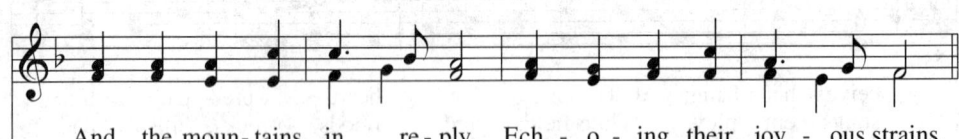

And the moun-tains in re-ply, Ech-o-ing their joy-ous strains.
What the glad-some ti-dings be Which in-spire your heav'n-ly song?
Come, a-dore on bend-ed knee Christ the Lord, the new-born King.

Refrain

Glo - ri - a

in ex-cel-sis De - o; Glo -

CHRISTMAS

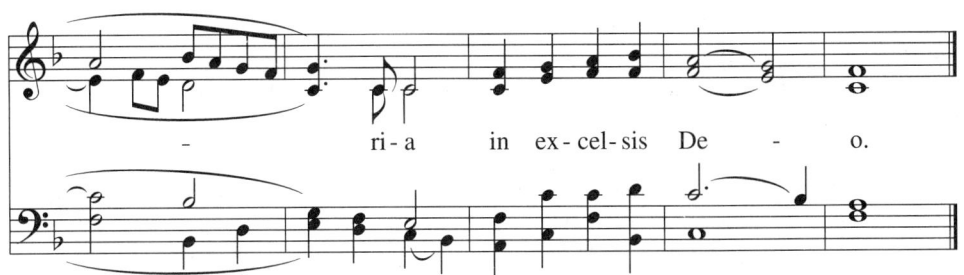

Text: *Nouveau recueil de cantiques*, 1855; tr. *The Crown of Jesus*, Part 2, London, 1862, alt.
Tune: *Nouveau recueil de cantiques*, 1855

GLORIA
77 77 with Refrain

Let Us All with Gladsome Voice 64

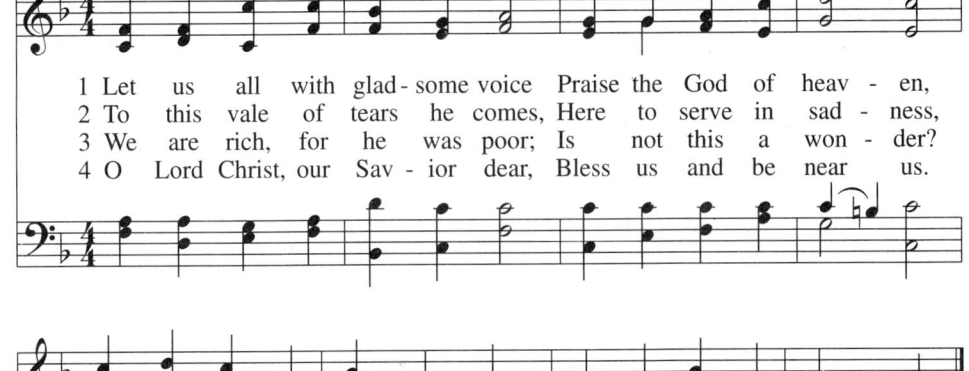

1 Let us all with glad-some voice Praise the God of heav-en,
  Who, to bid our hearts re-joice, His own Son has giv-en.
2 To this vale of tears he comes, Here to serve in sad-ness,
  That with him in heav'n's fair homes We may reign in glad-ness.
3 We are rich, for he was poor; Is not this a won-der?
  There-fore praise God ev-er-more Here on earth and yon-der.
4 O Lord Christ, our Sav-ior dear, Bless us and be near us.
  Grant us now a glad new year. A-men, Je-sus, hear us!

Text: *Ander Theil Des Dressdenischen GesangBuchs*, Dresden, 1632;
  tr. Catherine Winkworth, 1827-78, alt.
Tune: *Ander Theil Des Dressdenischen GesangBuchs*, Dresden, 1632, alt.

LASST UNS ALLE
76 76 Trochaic

CHRISTMAS

67 What Child Is This

1. What child is this who, laid to rest, On Mary's lap is sleeping? Whom angels greet With anthems sweet While shepherds watch are keeping? This, this is Christ the King, Whom shepherds guard and angels sing.

2. Why lies he in such mean estate Where oxen now are feeding? Good Christians, fear; For sinners here The silent Word is pleading. Nails, spear shall pierce him through; The cross he'll bear for me, for you.

3. So bring him incense, gold, and myrrh; Come, peasant, king, to own him. The King of kings Salvation brings; Let loving hearts enthrone him. Raise, raise the song on high; The virgin sings her lullaby.

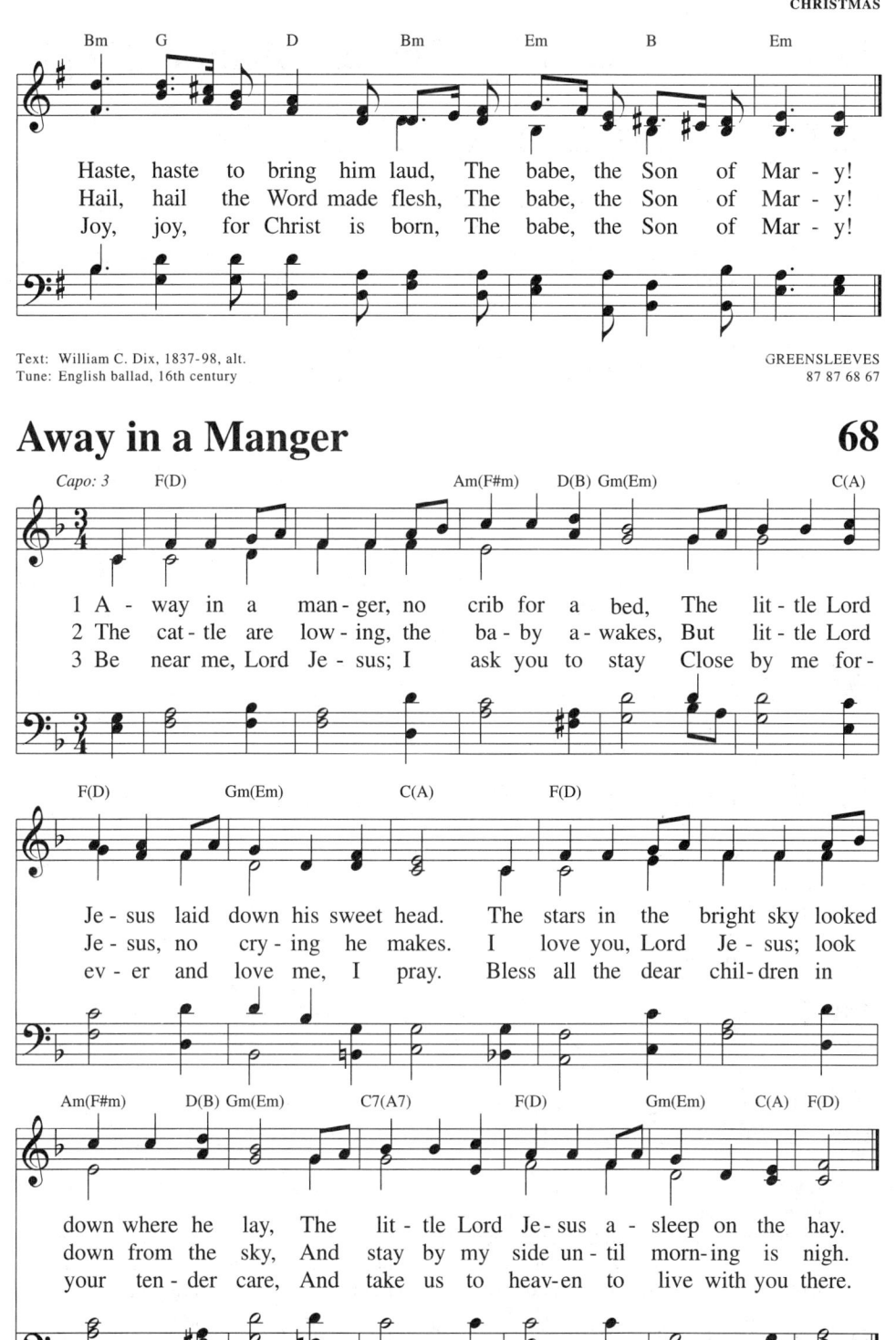

69 Across the Sky the Shades of Night

1. A-cross the sky the shades of night This New Year's Eve are fleet-ing. We deck your al-tar, Lord, with light, In sol-emn wor-ship meet-ing, And, as the year's last hours go by, We raise to you our ear-nest cry, Once more your love en-treat-ing.

2. We gath-er up in this brief hour The mem-'ry of your mer-cies. Your won-drous good-ness, love, and pow'r Our grate-ful song re-hears-es, For you have been our strength and stay In man-y a dark and drear-y day Of sor-row and re-vers-es.

3. Be-fore the cross, sub-dued, we bow, To you our prayers ad-dress-ing, Re-count-ing all your mer-cies now And all our sins con-fess-ing. We ask you, Lord, this com-ing year To keep us in your faith and fear And crown us with your bless-ing.

4. And while we pray, we lift our eyes To dear ones gone be-fore us, Safe home with you in Par-a-dise, Where Je-sus will reign o'er us, And ask of you, when life is past, To re-u-nite us all at last With those who've gone be-fore us.

5. Then, gra-cious God, in years to come, What-ev-er may be-tide us, Right on-ward through our jour-ney home, Oh, stay at hand to guide us, Nor leave us till, at close of life, Safe from all per-il, toil, and strife, Heav'n shall en-fold and hide us.

Text: James Hamilton, 1819-96, abr., alt.
Tune: attr. Nikolaus Decius, c. 1485-after 1546, alt.

ALLEIN GOTT IN DER HÖH SEI EHR
87 87 887

Alternate setting: 263

71 The Old Year Now Has Passed Away

1. The old year now has passed away; We thank you, O our God, today That you have kept us through the year When danger and distress were near.

2. We pray you, O eternal Son, Who with the Father reigns as one, To guard and rule your Christendom Through all the ages yet to come.

3. Take not your saving Word away, Which lights and cheers our souls each day. Abide with us and keep us free From error and hypocrisy.

4. Oh, help us to forsake all sin, A new and holier life begin! Forgive the old year's sins, and bless The new year with true happiness,

5. Wherein as Christians we may live
Or die in peace that you can give,
To rise again when you will come
And enter your eternal home.

6. There shall we thank you and adore
With all the angels evermore.
Lord Jesus Christ, increase our faith
To praise your name through life and death.

Text: attr. Johann Steurlein, 1546-1613; tr. Catherine Winkworth, 1827-78, alt.
Tune: *Cantionale Germanicum*, Gochsheim, 1628

HERR JESU CHRIST, DICH ZU UNS WEND
LM

Alternate settings: 230, 288

NEW YEAR

73   To God the Anthem Raising

1 To God the an-them rais - ing, Sing, Chris-tians, great and small;
  Sing out, his good-ness prais - ing; Oh, thank him, one and all!
  Be - hold how God this year, Which now is safe - ly end - ed,
  Has in his love be - friend - ed His chil - dren far and near.

2 Let us con-sid - er right - ly His mer - cies man - i - fold,
  And let us not think light - ly Of all his gifts un - told.
  Let thank-ful-ness re - call How God this year has led us,
  How he has clothed and fed us, The great ones and the small.

3 To church and state he grant - ed His peace in ev - 'ry place;
  His vine-yard he has plant - ed A - mong us by his grace.
  His ev - er - boun-teous hand Pros - per - i - ty has giv - en
  And want and fam - ine driv - en From this our na - tive land.

4 O Fa - ther, Lord of heav - en, For all your gifts of love
  Which you to us have giv - en We lift our thanks a - bove.
  In Je - sus' name we here, To you our prayers ad - dress - ing,
  Still ask you for your bless - ing: Grant us a joy - ful year.

Text: Paul Eber, 1511-69, abr.; tr. Carl Döving, 1867-1937, alt.
Tune: Wolfgang Figulus, 1520-91, alt.
Setting © 1993 Kermit G. Moldenhauer

HELFT MIR GOTTS GÜTE PREISEN
76 76 67 76

NEW YEAR

Now Let Us Come before Him 74

1. Now let us come before him, With song and prayer adore him, Who to our life has given All needed strength from heaven.
2. The stream of years is flowing, And we are onward going, From old to new surviving And by his mercy thriving.
3. Our God his own is shielding And help to them is yielding. Our work will prosper never Unless he bless it ever.
4. To all who bow before you And for your grace implore you, Grant, Lord, your benediction And patience in affliction.

5. Be with the sick and ailing,
Their Comforter unfailing;
Dispel their grief and sadness,
And give them joy and gladness!

6. Above all else, Lord, send us
Your Spirit to attend us,
Within our hearts abiding,
To heav'n our footsteps guiding.

Text: Paul Gerhardt, 1607-76, abr., adapt.; tr. John Kelly, 1833-90, alt.
Tune: Kermit G. Moldenhauer, b. 1949

Tune and Setting © 1993 Kermit G. Moldenhauer

NEW YEAR
77 77 Iambic

Jesus! Name of Wondrous Love 76

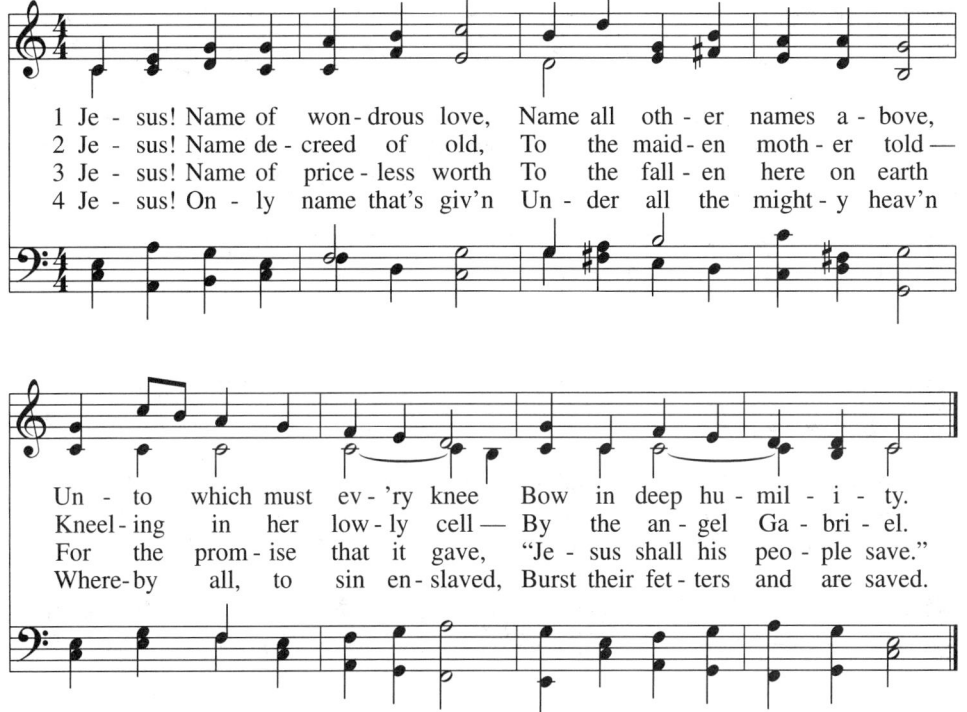

1 Jesus! Name of wondrous love, Name all other names above,
Unto which must ev'ry knee Bow in deep humility.

2 Jesus! Name decreed of old, To the maiden mother told—
Kneeling in her lowly cell— By the angel Gabriel.

3 Jesus! Name of priceless worth To the fallen here on earth
For the promise that it gave, "Jesus shall his people save."

4 Jesus! Only name that's giv'n Under all the mighty heav'n
Whereby all, to sin enslaved, Burst their fetters and are saved.

5 Jesus! Name of wondrous love,
Human name of God above;
Pleading only this, we, too,
Flee, O God, in faith to you.

EPIPHANY

79 How Lovely Shines the Morning Star

EPIPHANY

5 Grant us grace to see you, Lord,
   Mirrored in your holy Word.
 May our lives and all we do
   Imitate and honor you
 That we all like you may be
   At your great epiphany
 And may praise you, ever blest,
   God in man made manifest.

Text: Christopher Wordsworth, 1807-85, alt.
Tune: George J. Elvey, 1816-93

ST. GEORGE'S, WINDSOR
77 77 D

Alternate setting: 617

83 As with Gladness Men of Old

EPIPHANY

1. As with gladness men of old Did the guiding star behold, As with joy they hailed its light, Leading onward, beaming bright, So, most gracious Lord, may we Evermore your followers be.

2. As with joyful steps they sped, Savior, to your lowly bed, There to bend the knee before You whom heav'n and earth adore, So may we with willing feet Ever seek your mercy seat.

3. As they offered gifts most rare At your cradle, rude and bare, So may we with holy joy, Pure and free from sin's alloy, All our costliest treasures bring, Christ, to you, our heav'nly King.

4. Holy Jesus, ev'ry day Keep us in the narrow way; And, when earthly things are past, Bring our ransomed souls at last Where they need no star to guide, Where no clouds your glory hide.

5. In the heav'nly country bright
    Need they no created light;
  You its light, its joy, its crown,
    You its sun which goes not down.
  There forever may we sing
    Alleluias to our King!

Text: William C. Dix, 1837-98, alt.
Tune: Conrad Kocher, 1786-1872, alt.

DIX
77 77 77

EPIPHANY

Jesus Shall Reign Where'er the Sun   84

1 Jesus shall reign wher-e'er the sun Does its successive journeys run; His kingdom stretch from shore to shore Till moons shall wax and wane no more.

2 To him shall endless prayer be made And endless praises crown his head; His name like sweet perfume shall rise With ev-'ry morning sacrifice.

3 People and realms of ev-'ry tongue Praise his great love with sweetest song, And infant voices shall proclaim Their early blessings on his name.

4 Blessings abound wher-e'er he reigns: The pris-'ner leaps, unloosed his chains, The weary find eternal rest, And all who suffer want are blest.

5 Let ev'ry creature rise and bring
Worship and honor to our King;
Angels descend with songs again,
And earth repeat the loud amen.

Text: Isaac Watts, 1674-1748, abr., alt.
Tune: *Psalmodia Evangelica*, Part II, London, 1789

TRURO
LM

EPIPHANY

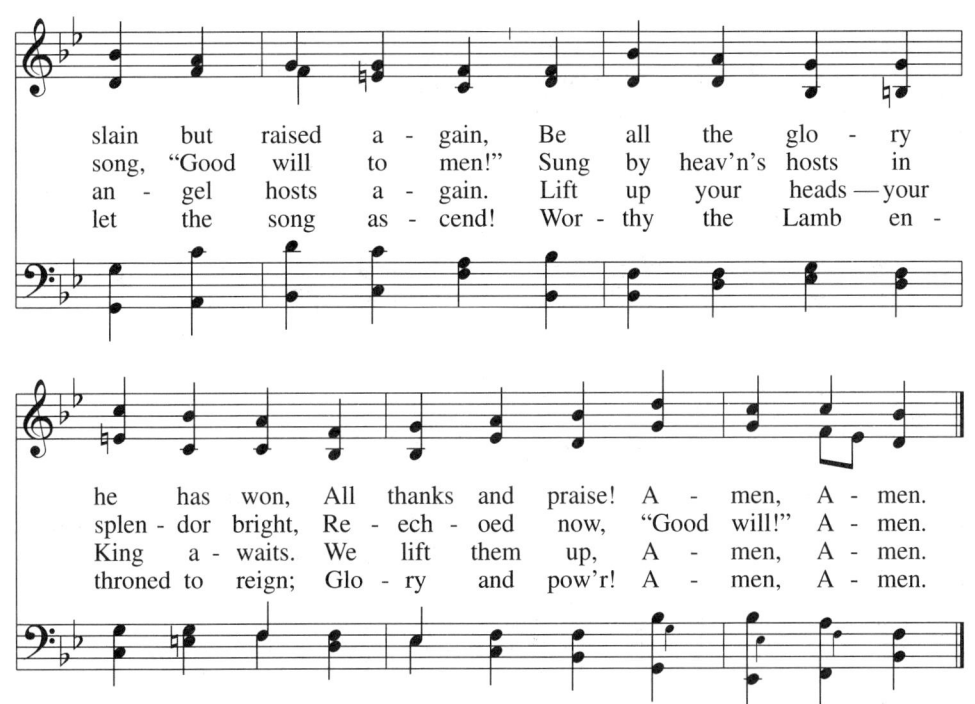

Text: John Julian, 1839-1913, abr., alt.
Tune: *Johann Störls . . . Schlag-Gesang-Und Noten-Buch,* Stuttgart, 1744

O GROSSER GOTT
LM D

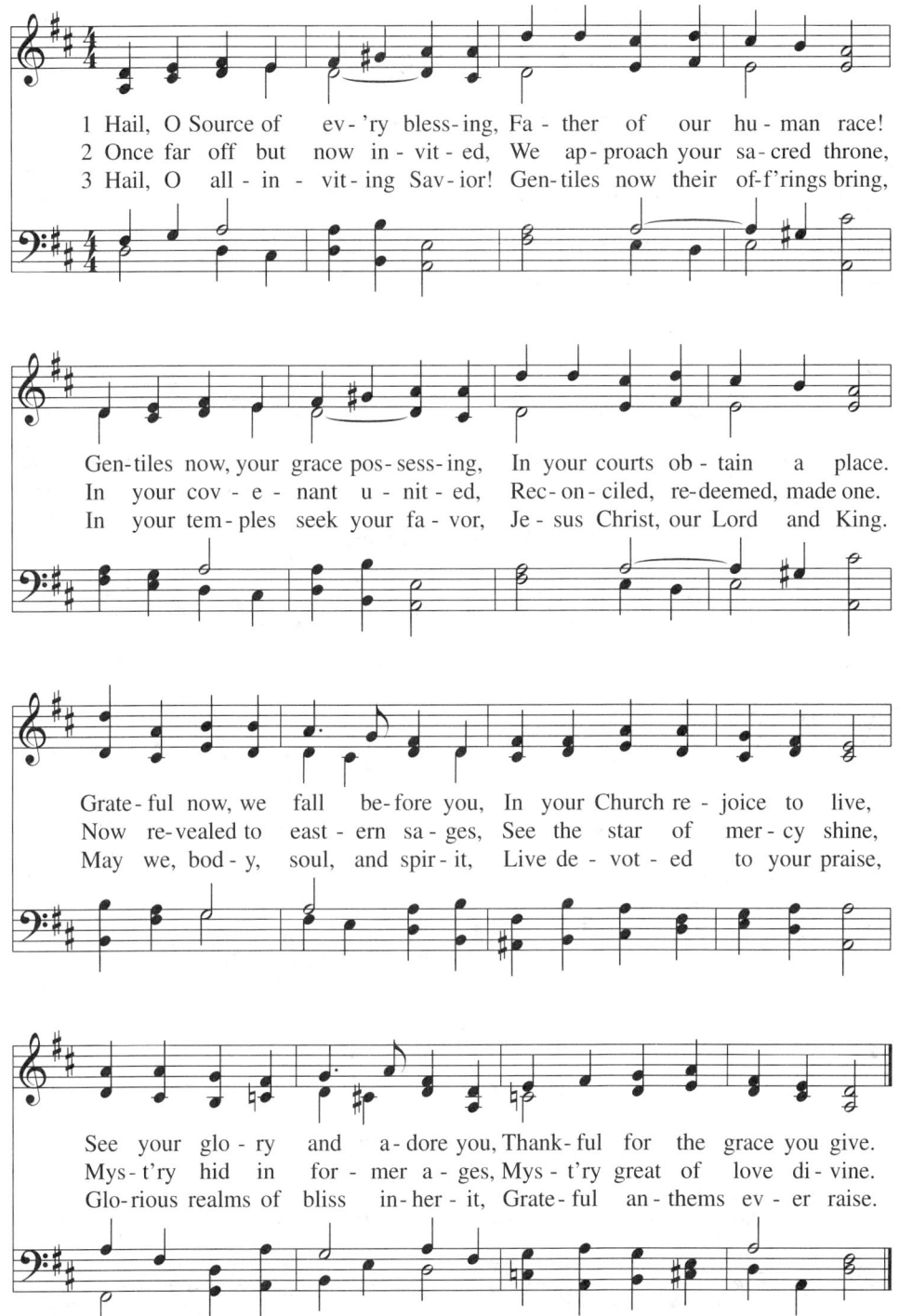

EPIPHANY

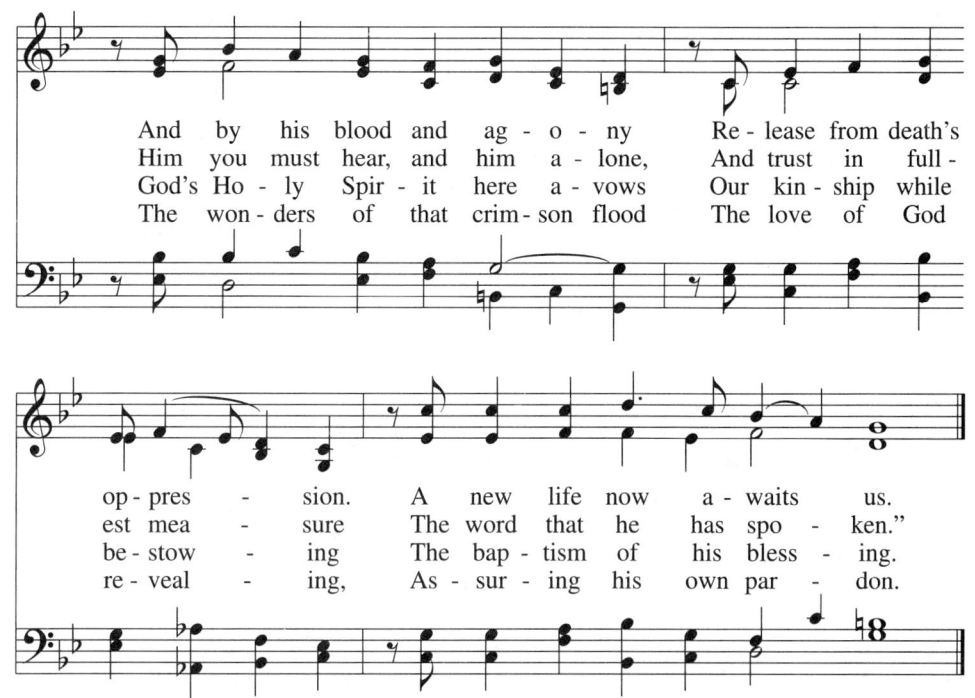

5 To his disciples spoke the Lord,
   "Go out to ev'ry nation
  And bring to them the living Word
   And this my invitation:
  Let ev'ryone abandon sin
   And come in true contrition
  To be baptized and thereby win
   Full pardon and remission
  And heav'nly bliss inherit."

Text: Martin Luther, 1483-1546, abr.; tr. Elizabeth Quitmeyer, 1911-88, alt.
Tune: *Geystliche gesangk Buchleyn*, Wittenberg, 1524

CHRIST UNSER HERR ZUM JORDAN KAM
87 87 87 87 7

Setting © 1978 *Lutheran Book of Worship*

EPIPHANY

89 To Jordan's River Came Our Lord

1 To Jordan's river came our Lord,
The Christ, whom heav'nly hosts adored,
The God from God, the Light from Light,
The Lord of glory, pow'r, and might.

2 The Savior came to be baptized—
The Son of God in flesh disguised—
To stand beneath the Father's will
And all his promises fulfill.

3 As Jesus in the Jordan stood
And John baptized the Lamb of God,
The Holy Spirit, heav'nly dove,
Descended on him from above.

4 Then from God's throne with thund'rous sound
Came God's own voice with words profound:
"This is my Son," was his decree,
"The one I love, who pleases me."

5 The Father's word, the Spirit's flight
Anointed Christ in glorious sight
As God's own choice, from Adam's fall
To save the world and free us all.

6 Now rise, faint hearts: be resolute!
This man is Christ, our substitute!
He was baptized in Jordan's stream,
Proclaimed Redeemer, Lord supreme.

Text: James P. Tiefel, b. 1949
Tune: *Musicalisch Hand-Buch der Geistlichen Melodien*, Hamburg, 1690, alt.

WINCHESTER NEW
LM

Text © 1993 James P. Tiefel; Setting © 1993 Elfred Bloedel

Alternate settings: 133, 607

EPIPHANY

The People that in Darkness Sat   90

1. The people that in darkness sat A glorious light have seen; The light has shone on them who long In shades of death have been, In shades of death have been.
2. To us a child of hope is born, To us a son is giv'n, And on his shoulders ever rests All pow'r in earth and heav'n, All pow'r in earth and heav'n.
3. His name shall be the Prince of Peace, The Everlasting Lord, The Wonderful, the Counselor, The God by all adored, The God by all adored.
4. His righteous government and pow'r Shall over all extend; On judgment and on justice based, His reign shall have no end, His reign shall have no end.

5. Lord Jesus, reign in us, we pray,
   And make us yours alone,
   For you are with the Father and
   The Spirit ever one,
   The Spirit ever one.

Text: John Morison, 1750-98, abr., alt.
Tune: Nikolaus Herman, c. 1480-1561

LOBT GOTT, IHR CHRISTEN
86 866

Alternate setting: 41

EPIPHANY

91   The Star Proclaims the King Is Here

1. The star proclaims the King is here;
But, Herod, why this senseless fear?
For he who came from heaven's throne
Does not desire an earthly crown.

2. The wiser Magi saw from far
And followed on his guiding star,
And, led by light, to Light they pressed
And by their gifts their God confessed.

3. Within the Jordan River stood
The pure and holy Lamb of God;
The Father's voice, the Spirit-dove,
Confirmed the Savior from above.

4. At Cana — miracle divine —
When water reddened into wine,
The faithful saw his glory shown
And put their trust in him alone.

5. All glory unto Jesus be
And praise for his epiphany,
Whom with the Father we adore
And Holy Spirit evermore.

Text: Coelius Sedulius, 5th century, abr.; tr. John M. Neale, 1818-66, alt.
Tune: *Rheinfelssisch Deutsches Catholisches Gesangbuch*, Augsburg, 1666

O HEILAND, REISS DIE HIMMEL AUF
LM

Alternate setting: 22

EPIPHANY

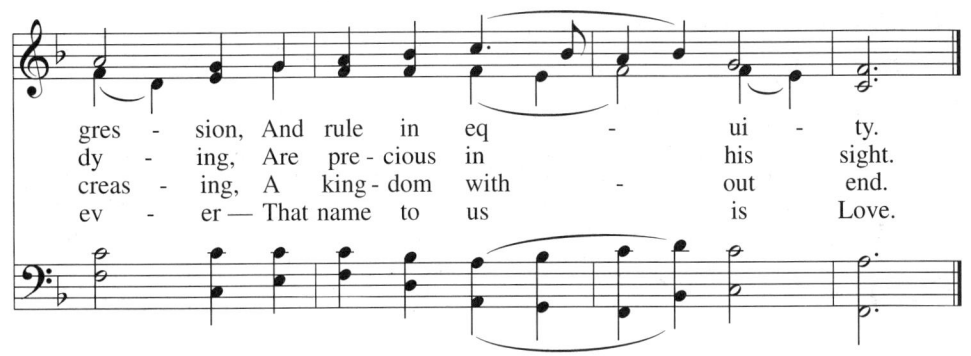

Text: James Montgomery, 1771-1854, abr., alt.
Tune: Leonhart Schröter, c. 1532-c. 1601

Setting © 1982 Concordia Publishing House

FREUT EUCH, IHR LIEBEN CHRISTEN
76 76 D

Alternate setting: 289

TRANSFIGURATION

How Good, Lord, to Be Here 95

1 How good, Lord, to be here! Your glory fills the night; Your
2 How good, Lord, to be here Your beauty to behold, Where
3 Fulfiller of the past, Promise of things to be, We
4 Before we taste of death, We see your kingdom come; We

face and garments, like the sun, Shine with unborrowed light.
Moses and Elijah stand, Your messengers of old.
hail your body glorified And our redemption see.
long to hold the vision bright And make this hill our home.

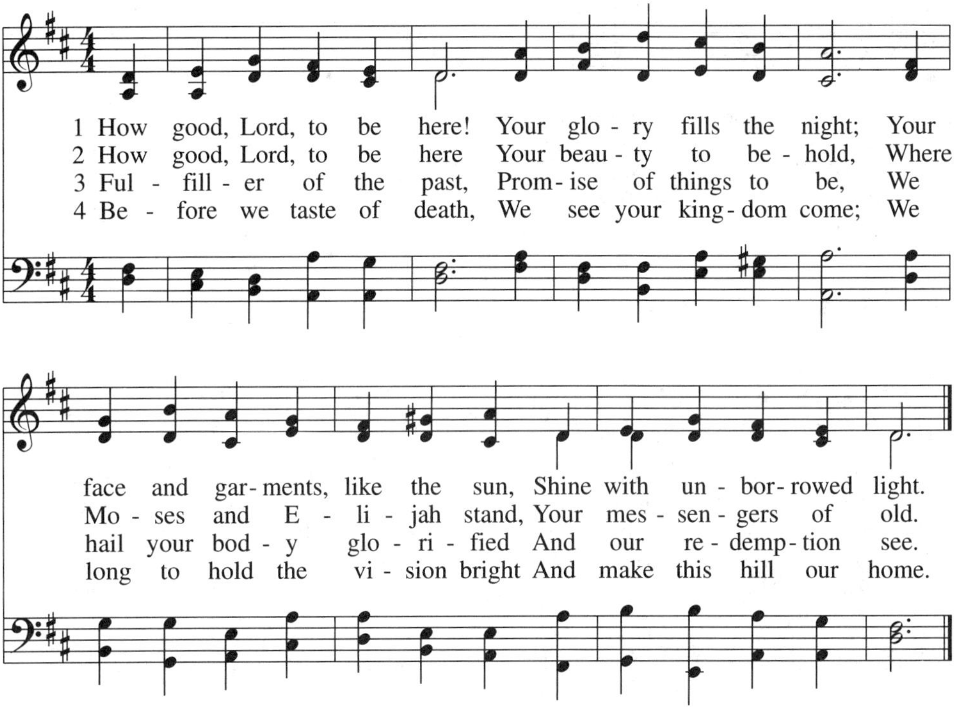

5 How good, Lord, to be here!
   Yet we may not remain;
   But since you bid us leave the mount,
   Come with us to the plain.

Text: Joseph A. Robinson, 1858-1933, alt.
Tune: J. S. Bach, 1685-1750, adapt.

POTSDAM
SM

TRANSFIGURATION

96 Oh, Wondrous Type! Oh, Vision Fair

1 Oh, wondrous type! Oh, vision fair
Of glory that the Church may share,
Which Christ upon the mountain shows,
Where brighter than the sun he glows!

2 With Moses and Elijah nigh
Th' incarnate Lord holds converse high,
And from the cloud the Holy One
Bears record to the only Son.

3 With shining face and bright array
Christ deigns to manifest today
What glory shall be theirs above
Who trust in his atoning love.

4 And faithful hearts are raised on high
By this great vision's mystery,
For which in joyful strains we raise
The voice of prayer, the hymn of praise.

5 O Father, with th' eternal Son
And Holy Spirit ever one,
We pray you, bring us by your grace
To see your glory face to face.

Text: Latin hymn, 15th century; tr. John M. Neale, 1818-66, alt.
Tune: English melody, 15th century
Setting © 1969 Concordia Publishing House

DEO GRACIAS
LM
Alternate setting: 371

LENT

5 Grant that I your passion view
　　With repentant grieving.
　Let me not bring shame to you
　　By unholy living.
　How could I refuse to shun
　　Ev'ry sinful pleasure
　Since for me God's only Son
　　Suffered without measure?

6 Graciously my faith renew;
　　Help me bear my crosses,
　Learning humbleness from you,
　　Peace mid pain and losses.
　May I give you love for love!
　　Hear me, O my Savior,
　That I may in heav'n above
　　Sing your praise forever.

Text: Sigmund von Birken, 1626-81; tr. August Crull, 1845-1923, alt.
Tune: Melchior Vulpius, c. 1570-1615, alt.

JESU KREUZ, LEIDEN UND PEIN
76 76 D Trochaic

Oh, Come, My Soul 99

1 Oh, come, my soul, your Sav-ior see Nailed to your cross on Cal-va-ry. Your pains he bears; Your thorns he wears That yours a crown of life might be.

2 'Tis yours, my soul, the sin, the shame, The cross, the nails, the thirst, the pain; In ag-o-ny His blood runs free To write in heav-en's book your name.

3 Oh, sing, my soul, sing end-less-ly The won-drous love that sets you free; His dy-ing breath Brings life from death, Makes heav'n your home e-ter-nal-ly.

Text: Kurt J. Eggert, 1923-93
Tune: Kurt J. Eggert, 1923-93

OH, COME, MY SOUL
88 44 8

Text, Tune, Setting © 1993 Kurt J. Eggert

LENT

100 A Lamb Goes Uncomplaining Forth

1. A Lamb goes uncomplaining forth, Our guilt and evil bearing And, laden with the sins of earth, None else the burden sharing. Goes patient on, grows weak and faint, To slaughter led without complaint,
2. This Lamb is Christ, the soul's great friend, The Lamb of God, our Savior; Him God the Father chose to send To gain for us his favor. "Go forth, my Son," the Father said, "And free my children from their dread
3. "Yes, Father, yes, most willingly I'll bear what you command me. My will conforms to your decree; I'll do what you have asked me." O wondrous Love, what have you done! The Father offers up his Son,
4. From morn till eve, in all I do, I'll praise you, Christ, my treasure. To sacrifice myself for you Shall be my aim and pleasure. My stream of life shall ever be A current flowing ceaselessly,

LENT

Text: Paul Gerhardt, 1607-76, abr.; tr. *The Lutheran Hymnal*, St. Louis, 1941, alt.
Tune: Wolfgang Dachstein, c. 1487-1553

AN WASSERFLÜSSEN BABYLON
87 87 887 887

LENT

Enslaved by Sin and Bound in Chains 102

1 En-slaved by sin and bound in chains, Beneath its
dread-ful ty-rant sway, And doomed to ev-er-
last-ing pains We wretch-ed, guilt-y cap-tives lay.

2 Nor gold nor gems could buy our peace, Nor all the
world's col-lect-ed store Suf-fice to pur-chase
our re-lease; A thou-sand worlds were all too poor.

3 Je-sus, the Lord, the might-y God, An all-suf-
fi-cient ran-som paid. O match-less price! His
pre-cious blood For vile, re-bel-lious trai-tors shed.

4 Je-sus the sac-ri-fice be-came To res-cue
guilt-y souls from hell; The spot-less, bleed-ing,
dy-ing Lamb Be-neath a-veng-ing jus-tice fell.

5 Amazing goodness! Love divine!
Oh, may our grateful hearts adore
The matchless grace nor yield to sin
Nor wear its cruel fetters more!

Text: Anne Steele, 1717-78
Tune: Louis Bourgeois, c. 1510-1561
Setting © 1982 Concordia Publishing House

WENN WIR IN HÖCHSTEN NÖTEN SEIN
LM
Alternate setting: 378

LENT

103 Glory Be to Jesus

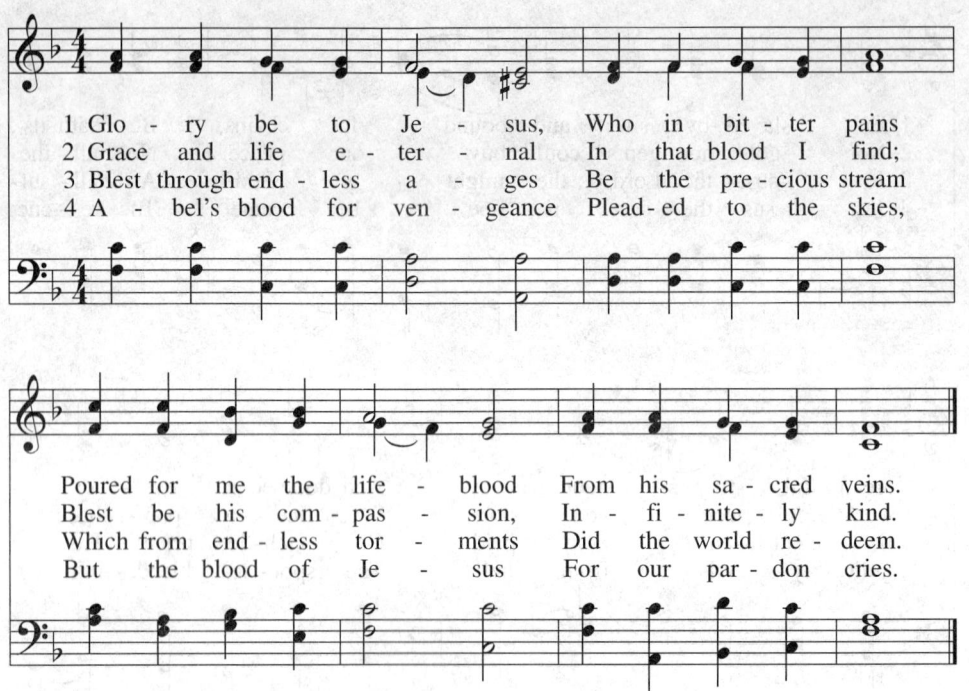

1 Glory be to Jesus, Who in bitter pains
  Poured for me the life-blood From his sacred veins.
2 Grace and life eternal In that blood I find;
  Blest be his compassion, Infinitely kind.
3 Blest through endless ages Be the precious stream
  Which from endless torments Did the world redeem.
4 Abel's blood for vengeance Pleaded to the skies,
  But the blood of Jesus For our pardon cries.

5 Oft as earth exulting
  Lifts its praise on high,
  Angel hosts rejoicing
  Make their glad reply.

6 Lift we, then, our voices,
  Swell the mighty flood;
  Louder still and louder
  Praise the precious blood!

Text: Italian hymn, 18th century, abr.; tr. Edward Caswall, 1814-78, alt.
Tune: Friedrich Filitz, 1804-76

WEM IN LEIDENSTAGEN
65 65

LENT

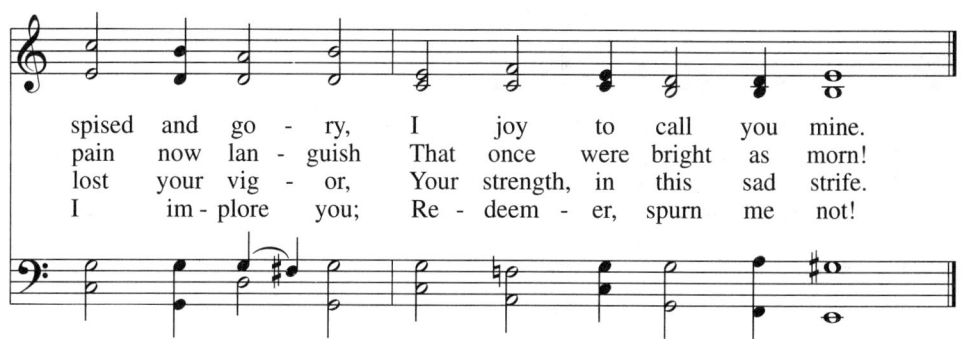

spised and go - ry, I joy to call you mine.
pain now lan - guish That once were bright as morn!
lost your vig - or, Your strength, in this sad strife.
I im - plore you; Re - deem - er, spurn me not!

5 What language shall I borrow
   To thank you, dearest Friend,
For this, your dying sorrow,
   Your pity without end?
Oh, make me yours forever,
   And keep me strong and true;
Lord, let me never, never
   Outlive my love for you.

6 My Savior, then be near me
   When death is at my door,
And let your presence cheer me;
   Forsake me nevermore!
When soul and body languish,
   Oh, leave me not alone,
But take away my anguish
   By virtue of your own!

7 Lord, be my consolation,
   My shield when I must die;
Remind me of your passion
   When my last hour draws nigh.
My eyes will then behold you,
   Upon your cross will dwell;
My heart will then enfold you —
   Who dies in faith dies well!

Text: attr. Bernard of Clairvaux, 1091-1153, abr.; German version,
   Paul Gerhardt, 1607-76; tr. *The Lutheran Hymnal,* St. Louis, 1941, alt.
Tune: Hans Leo Hassler, 1564-1612

HERZLICH TUT MICH VERLANGEN
76 76 D

LENT

5 They rise and needs will have
   My dear Lord made away.
A murderer they save;
   The Prince of life they slay.
Yet cheerful he
   To suff'ring goes
That he his foes
From death might free.

6 In life no house, no home
   My Lord on earth might have;
In death no friendly tomb
   But what a stranger gave.
What may I say?
   Heav'n was his home
But mine the tomb
Wherein he lay.

7 Here might I stay and sing;
   No story so divine,
Never was love, dear King,
   Never was grief like thine.
This is my friend,
   In whose sweet praise
I all my days
Could gladly spend!

Text: Samuel Crossman, c. 1624-83, alt.
Tune: John N. Ireland, 1879-1962

LOVE UNKNOWN
66 66 4444

Tune and Setting © John Ireland Trust

Sweet the Moments, Rich in Blessing 111

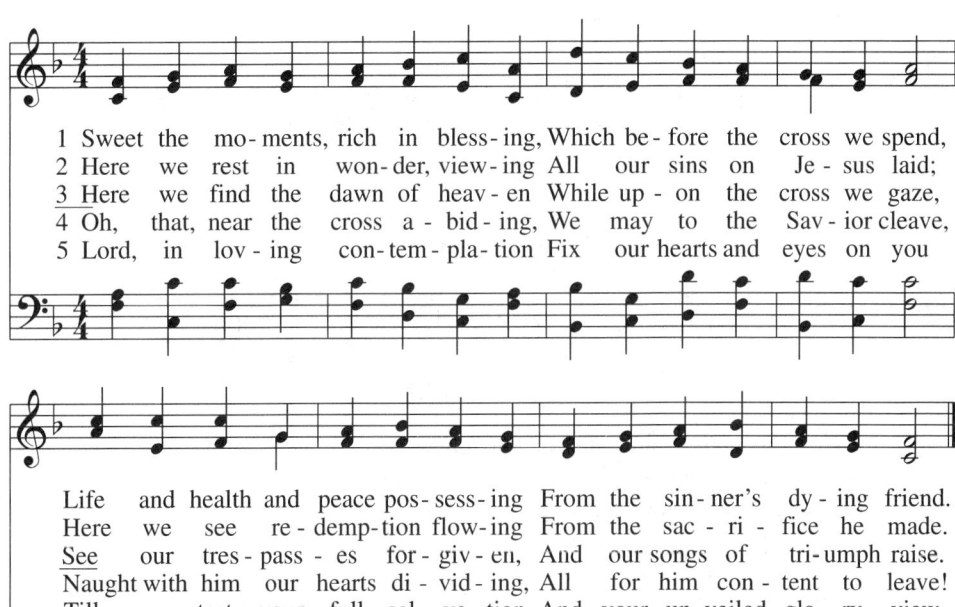

1 Sweet the moments, rich in bless-ing, Which be-fore the cross we spend,
2 Here we rest in won-der, view-ing All our sins on Je-sus laid;
3 Here we find the dawn of heav-en While up-on the cross we gaze,
4 Oh, that, near the cross a-bid-ing, We may to the Sav-ior cleave,
5 Lord, in lov-ing con-tem-pla-tion Fix our hearts and eyes on you

Life and health and peace pos-sess-ing From the sin-ner's dy-ing friend.
Here we see re-demp-tion flow-ing From the sac-ri-fice he made.
See our tres-pass-es for-giv-en, And our songs of tri-umph raise.
Naught with him our hearts di-vid-ing, All for him con-tent to leave!
Till we taste your full sal-va-tion And your un-veiled glo-ry view.

Text: Walter Shirley, 1725-86, alt.
Tune: *Erbaulicher Musicalischer Christen-Schatz,* Basel, 1745, alt.

RINGE RECHT
87 87

LENT

112 There Is a Fountain Filled with Blood

1 There is a fountain filled with blood— Immanuel was slain— And sinners who are washed therein Lose ev'ry guilty stain, Lose ev'ry guilty stain.
2 The dying thief rejoiced to see That fountain in his day; And there have I, as vile as he, Washed all my sins away, Washed all my sins away.
3 Dear dying Lamb, your precious blood Shall never lose its pow'r Till all the ransomed Church of God Be saved and sin no more, Be saved and sin no more.
4 E'er since by faith I saw the stream Your flowing wounds supply, Redeeming love has been my theme And shall be till I die, And shall be till I die.

5 When this poor lisping, stamm'ring tongue
  Lies silent in the grave,
  Then in a nobler, sweeter song
  I'll sing your pow'r to save,
  I'll sing your pow'r to save.

Text: William Cowper, 1731-1800, abr., alt.
Tune: Lowell Mason, 1792-1872

COWPER
CM

LENT

5 Thou hast suffered men to bruise thee
    That from pain I might be free;
Falsely did thy foes accuse thee —
    Thence I gain security.
Comfortless thy soul did languish
    Me to comfort in my anguish.
Thousand, thousand thanks shall be,
    Dearest Jesus, unto thee.

6 Thou hast suffered great affliction
    And hast borne it patiently,
Even death by crucifixion,
    Fully to atone for me.
Thou didst choose to be tormented
    That my doom should be prevented.
Thousand, thousand thanks shall be,
    Dearest Jesus, unto thee.

7 Then, for all that wrought my pardon,
    For thy sorrows deep and sore,
For thine anguish in the garden,
    I will thank thee evermore,
Thank thee for thy groaning, sighing,
    For thy bleeding and thy dying,
For that last triumphant cry,
    And shall praise thee, Lord, on high.

Text: Ernst C. Homburg, 1605-81, abr.; tr. Catherine Winkworth, 1827-78, st. 1-2, 5, 7, alt.;
    Evangelical Lutheran Hymn-Book, St. Louis, 1912, st. 3-4, 6
Tune: *Das grosse Cantional,* Darmstadt, 1687, alt.

JESU, MEINES LEBENS LEBEN
87 87 88 77

LENT

In the Hour of Trial 116

1 In the hour of trial, Jesus, plead for me
2 With forbidden pleasures Should this vain world charm
3 Should your mercy send me Sorrow, toil, and woe,
4 When my life is ending, Though in grief or pain,

Lest by base denial I unworthy be.
Or its tempting treasures Spread to work me harm,
Or should pain attend me On my path below,
When my body changes Back to dust again,

When you see me waver, With a look recall,
Bring to my remembrance Sad Gethsemane
Grant that I may never Fail your cross to view;
On your truth relying, Through that mortal strife,

Nor for fear or favor Ever let me fall.
Or, in darker semblance, Cross-crowned Calvary.
Grant that I may ever Cast my care on you.
Jesus, take me, dying, To eternal life.

Text: James Montgomery, 1771-1854, alt.
Tune: John B. Dykes, 1823-76

ST. MARY MAGDALENE
65 65 D

5 The sinless Son of God must die in sadness;
  The sinful child of man may live in gladness;
  We forfeited our lives, yet are acquitted —
  God is committed.

6 I'll think upon your mercy without ceasing,
  That earth's vain joys to me no more be pleasing;
  To do your will shall be my sole endeavor
  Henceforth forever.

7 And when, dear Lord, before your throne in heaven
  To me the crown of joy at last is given,
  Where sweetest hymns your saints forever raise you,
  I too shall praise you.

Text: Johann Heermann, 1585-1647, abr.; tr. Catherine Winkworth, 1827-78, st. 1-4, 6-7, alt.;
The Lutheran Hymnal, St. Louis, 1941, st. 5, alt.
Tune: Johann Crüger, 1598-1662

HERZLIEBSTER JESU
11 11 11 5

Setting © 1993 Kermit G. Moldenhauer

O Dearest Lord, Thy Sacred Head   118

1 O dearest Lord, thy sacred head With thorns was pierced for me;
2 O dearest Lord, thy sacred hands With nails were pierced for me;
3 O dearest Lord, thy sacred feet With nails were pierced for me;
4 O dearest Lord, thy sacred heart With spear was pierced for me;

Oh, pour thy blessing on my head That I may think for thee.
Oh, shed thy blessing on my hands That they may work for thee.
Oh, pour thy blessing on my feet That they may follow thee.
Oh, pour thy Spirit in my heart That I may live for thee.

Text: Henry E. Hardy, 1869-1946, alt.
Tune: *A Supplement to the Kentucky Harmony*, Harrisonburg, 1820

DETROIT
CM

Text reprinted by permission of A. R. Mowbray & Co. Ltd.; Setting © 1993 Bruce R. Backer

LENT

119 **Were You There**

Text: African-American spiritual, 19th century, abr.
Tune: African-American spiritual, 19th century, alt.

WERE YOU THERE
10 10 14 10

LENT

121 Jesus, Grant that Balm and Healing

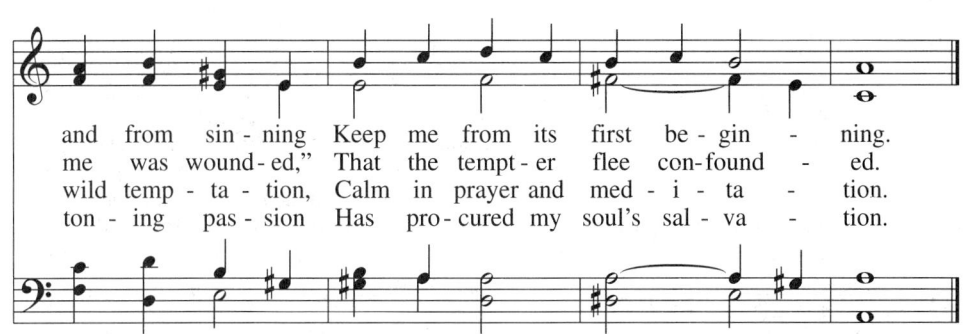

5 O my God, my Rock and Tower,
　　Grant that in your death I trust,
　Knowing death has lost his power
　　Since you crushed him in the dust.
Savior, let your agony
　Ever help and comfort me;
When I die be my protection,
　Light and life and resurrection.

Text: Johann Heermann, 1585-1647, abr.; tr. composite
Tune: Johann B. König, 1691-1758

DER AM KREUZ
87 87 77 88

Alternate setting: 319

LENT

Lord Jesus Christ, You Set Us Free 123

1 Lord Jesus Christ, you set us free — Accept our thanks eternally! Forgiven through your precious blood, We now are reconciled to God.
2 By virtue of the wounds you bore, True God and Man, our hope restore. Give courage when we yield our breath; Deliver us from hell and death.
3 Defend us, Lord, from sin and shame; Help us by your almighty name To bear our crosses patiently, Consoled by your great agony.
4 For thus the certainty we gain That you will always true remain And not forsake us in our strife But lead us out of death to life.

Text: Christoph Fischer, 1520-97; tr. August Crull, 1845-1923, alt.
Tune: Nikolaus Herman, c. 1480-1561

WIR DANKEN DIR, HERR JESU CHRIST
LM

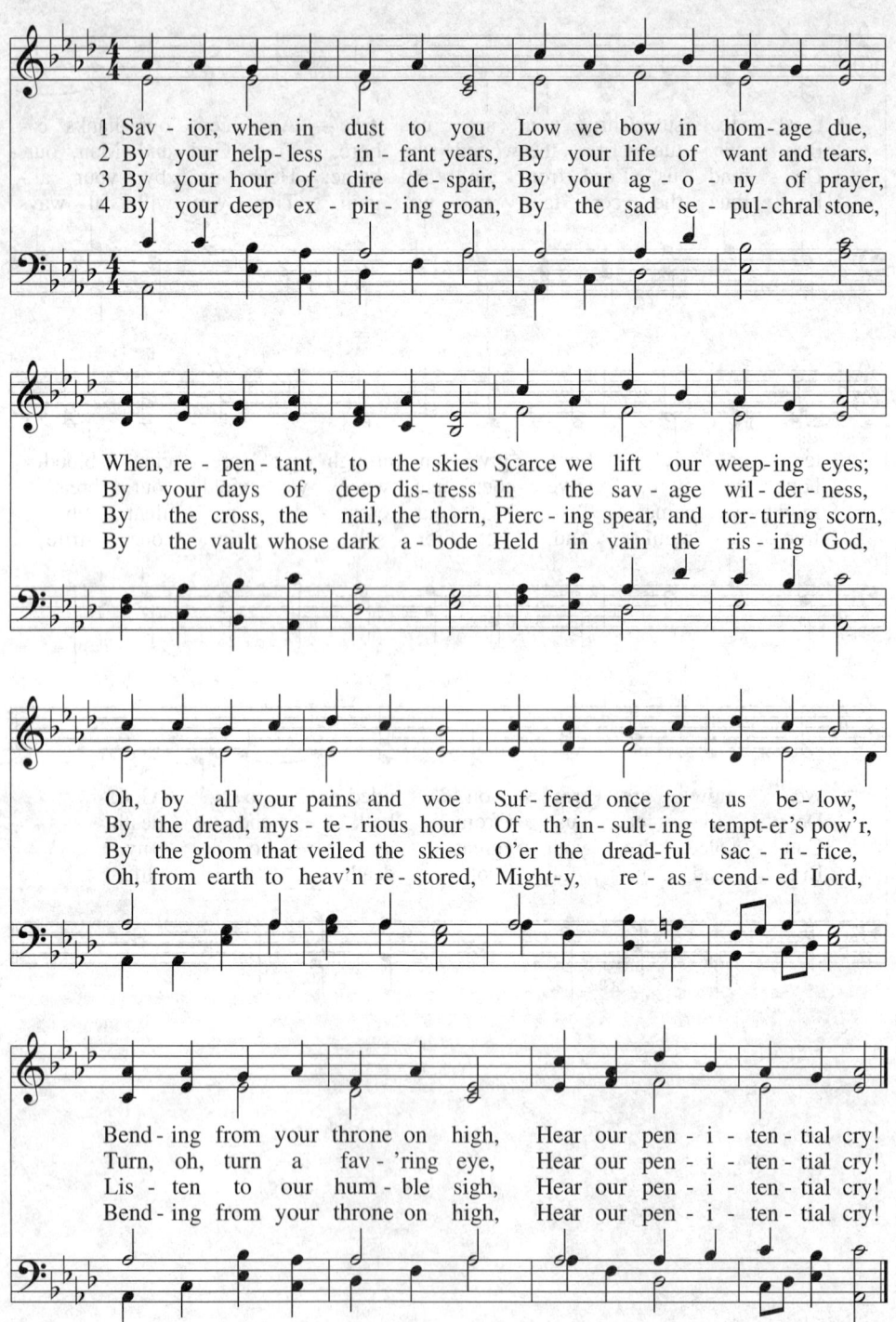

(The Soul:) 5 What can I for such love divine
To you, Lord Jesus, render?
No merit has this heart of mine;
Yet while I live I'll tender
Myself alone
And all I own
In love to serve before you.
Then when time's past,
Take me at last;
In heav'n I shall adore you.

Text: Kaspar F. Nachtenhöfer, 1624-85, st. 1-3, 5; Magnus D. Omeis, 1646-1708, st. 4;
tr. W. Gustave Polack, 1890-1950, alt.
Tune: *Geistreiches Gesang-Buch,* Darmstadt, 1698, alt.
Text © 1941 Concordia Publishing House

SO GEHST DU NUN
87 87 447 447 Iambic

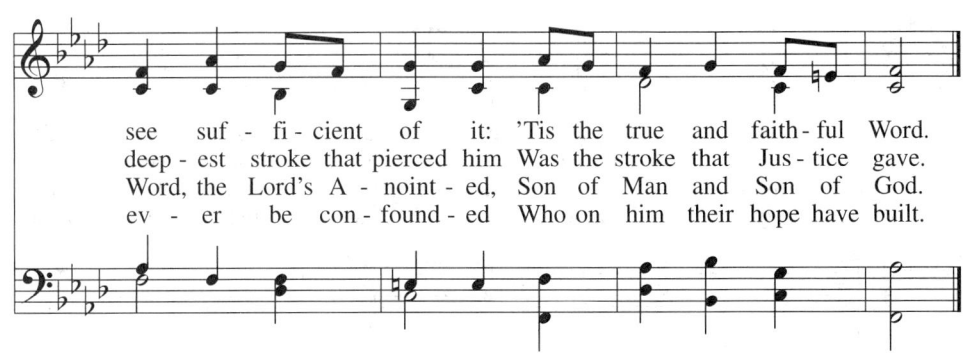

see suf-fi-cient of it: 'Tis the true and faith-ful Word.
deep-est stroke that pierced him Was the stroke that Jus-tice gave.
Word, the Lord's A-noint-ed, Son of Man and Son of God.
ev-er be con-found-ed Who on him their hope have built.

Text: Thomas Kelly, 1769-1855, alt.
Tune: *Geistliche Volkslieder*, Paderborn, 1850

Setting © 1982 Concordia Publishing House

O MEIN JESU, ICH MUSS STERBEN
87 87 D

Not All the Blood of Beasts 128

1 Not all the blood of beasts On Is-rael's al-tars slain
2 But Christ, the heav'n-ly Lamb, Takes all our sins a-way,
3 In faith I place my hand On that dear head di-vine,
4 My soul looks back to see The bur-den you did bear
5 Be-liev-ing, we re-joice To see the curse re-move;

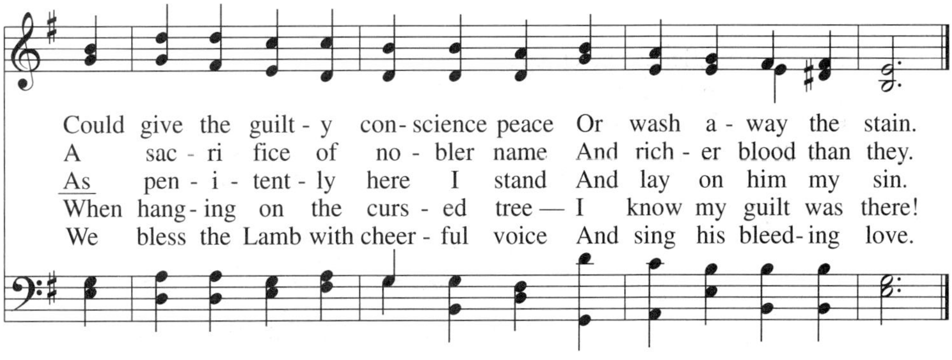

Could give the guilt-y con-science peace Or wash a-way the stain.
A sac-ri-fice of no-bler name And rich-er blood than they.
As pen-i-tent-ly here I stand And lay on him my sin.
When hang-ing on the curs-ed tree— I know my guilt was there!
We bless the Lamb with cheer-ful voice And sing his bleed-ing love.

Text: Isaac Watts, 1674-1748, alt.
Tune: William Daman, c. 1540-91

SOUTHWELL
SM

LENT

129 Alas! and Did My Savior Bleed

1 Alas! and did my Savior bleed, And did my Sov-'reign die? Would he de-vote that sa-cred head For sin-ners such as I?
2 Was it for crimes that I had done He groaned up-on the tree? A-maz-ing pit-y, grace un-known, And love be-yond de-gree!
3 Well might the sun in dark-ness hide And shut its glo-ries in When God, the might-y Mak-er, died For his own crea-tures' sin.
4 Thus might I hide my blush-ing face While his dear cross ap-pears, Dis-solve my heart in thank-ful-ness, And melt my eyes to tears.

5 But drops of grief can ne'er repay
The debt of love I owe;
Here, Lord, I give myself away —
'Tis all that I can do.

Text: Isaac Watts, 1674-1748, abr., alt.
Tune: Hugh Wilson, c. 1766-1824

MARTYRDOM
CM

PALM SUNDAY

Text: Theodulph of Orleans, c. 762-821; tr. John M. Neale, 1818-66, alt.
Tune: Melchior Teschner, 1584-1635, alt.; Desc. Kermit G. Moldenhauer, b. 1949
Setting © Bärenreiter-Verlag; Descant © 1993 Kermit G. Moldenhauer

VALET WILL ICH DIR GEBEN
76 76 D

Alternate settings: 94, 419

5 Ride on, ride on in majesty!
In lowly pomp ride on to die.
Bow your meek head to mortal pain,
Then take, O Christ, your power and reign.

Text: Henry H. Milman, 1791-1868, alt.
Tune: Graham George, b. 1912

THE KING'S MAJESTY
LM

Tune and Setting © 1941. Renewed 1969 H. W. Gray Co., Inc.

PALM SUNDAY

Ride On, Ride On in Majesty 133

1 Ride on, ride on in majesty! Hark! All the tribes hosanna cry. O Savior meek, pursue your road, With palms and scattered garments strowed.

2 Ride on, ride on in majesty! In lowly pomp ride on to die. O Christ, your triumphs now begin O'er captive death and conquered sin.

3 Ride on, ride on in majesty! The angel armies of the sky Look down with sad and wond'ring eyes To see th' approaching sacrifice.

4 Ride on, ride on in majesty! Your last and fiercest strife is nigh. The Father on his sapphire throne Awaits his own anointed Son.

5 Ride on, ride on in majesty!
In lowly pomp ride on to die.
Bow your meek head to mortal pain,
Then take, O Christ, your power and reign.

Text: Henry H. Milman, 1791-1868, alt.
Tune: *Musicalisch Hand-Buch der Geistlichen Melodien*, Hamburg, 1690, alt.

WINCHESTER NEW
LM

Alternate settings: 89, 607

PALM SUNDAY

134   O Bride of Christ, Rejoice

5. Then go your Lord to meet;
   Strew palm leaves at his feet;
   Your garments spread before him,
   And honor and adore him.
   Hosanna! Sing the story
   Of Christ, the King of glory!

Text: Danish hymn, c. 1600, abr., adapt.; tr. Victor O. Petersen, 1864-1929, alt.
Tune: *Der Bussfertige Sünder*, Nürnberg, 1679, alt.

WO SOLL ICH FLIEHEN HIN
66 77 77

MAUNDY THURSDAY

The Death of Jesus Christ, Our Lord 135

1. The death of Jesus Christ, our Lord, We celebrate with one accord; It is our comfort in distress, Our heart's sweet joy and happiness.

2. He blotted out with his own blood The judgment that against us stood; He full atonement for us made, And all our debt he fully paid.

3. That this forever true shall be He gives a solemn guarantee; In this his holy supper here We taste his love, so sweet, so near.

4. His Word proclaims and we believe That in this supper we receive His very body, as he said, His very blood for sinners shed.

5. A precious food is this indeed — It never fails us in our need — A heav'nly manna for our soul Until we safely reach our goal.

6. Oh, blest is each believing guest
Who in this promise finds his rest,
For Jesus will in love abide
With those who do in him confide.

7. The guest that comes with true intent
To turn to God and to repent,
To live for Christ, to die to sin,
Will thus a holy life begin.

8. They who his Word do not believe
This food unworthily receive,
Salvation here will never find —
May we this warning keep in mind!

9. Help us sincerely to believe
That we may worthily receive
Your supper and in you find rest.
Amen! They who believe are blest.

Text: Haquin Spegel, 1645-1714, abr.; tr. Olof Olsson, 1841-1900, alt.
Tune: Wagner, *Sammlung alter und neuer . . . Melodien,* 1742, alt.

GOTTLOB, ES GEHT NUNMEHR ZU ENDE
LM

Alternate setting: 500

MAUNDY THURSDAY

136   'Twas on that Dark, that Doleful Night

1. 'Twas on that dark, that doleful night When pow'rs of earth and hell arose Against the Son, our God's delight, And friends betrayed him to his foes.
2. Before the mournful scene began, He took the bread and blessed and broke. What love through all his actions ran! What wondrous words of grace he spoke!
3. "This is my body, slain for sin; Receive and eat the living food." Then took the cup and blessed the wine: "'Tis the new cov'nant in my blood."
4. "Do this," he said, "till time shall end, In mem'ry of your dying friend; Meet at my table and record The love of your departed Lord."

5. Jesus, your feast we celebrate;
We show your death; we sing your name
Till you return and we shall eat
The marriage supper of the Lamb.

Text: Isaac Watts, 1674-1748, abr., alt.
Tune: John B. Dykes, 1823-76

ST. CROSS
LM

GOOD FRIDAY

Oh, Darkest Woe 137

1. Oh, darkest woe! O tears, forth flow! Has earth so sad a wonder? God the Father's only Son Now is buried yonder.
2. Oh, sorrow dread! God's Son is dead! But by his expiation Of our guilt upon the cross Gained for us salvation.
3. Lo, stained with blood, The Lamb of God, The Bridegroom, lies before you, Pouring out his life that he May to life restore you.
4. How blest shall be Eternally Who oft in faith will ponder Why the glorious Prince of life Should be buried yonder.

5. O Jesus blest, My Help and Rest,
   With tears I now entreat you:
   Make me love you to the last
   Till in heav'n I greet you.

Text: Friedrich von Spee, 1591-1635, st. 1; Johann Rist, 1607-67, st. 2-5, abr.;
tr. Catherine Winkworth, 1827-78, st. 1, 3-5, alt.; composite, st. 2
Tune: *Himmlische Harmony*, Mainz, 1628, alt.
Setting © 1982 Concordia Publishing House

O TRAURIGKEIT, O HERZELEID
44 776

GOOD FRIDAY

138   Oh, Perfect Life of Love

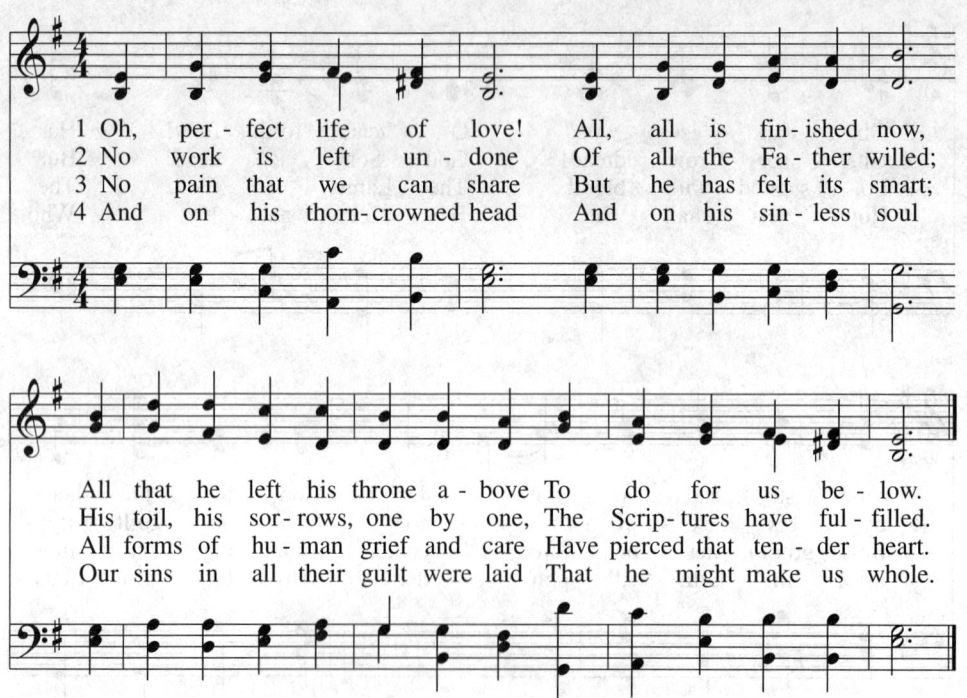

1. Oh, perfect life of love! All, all is finished now,
All that he left his throne above To do for us below.

2. No work is left undone Of all the Father willed;
His toil, his sorrows, one by one, The Scriptures have fulfilled.

3. No pain that we can share But he has felt its smart;
All forms of human grief and care Have pierced that tender heart.

4. And on his thorn-crowned head And on his sinless soul
Our sins in all their guilt were laid That he might make us whole.

5. In perfect love he dies;
For me he dies, for me!
O all-atoning Sacrifice,
You died to make me free!

6. In ev'ry time of need,
Before the judgment throne,
Your works, O Lamb of God, I'll plead,
Your merits, not my own.

Text: Henry W. Baker, 1821-77, abr., alt.
Tune: William Daman, c. 1540-91

SOUTHWELL
SM

GOOD FRIDAY

Jesus, in Your Dying Woes

139

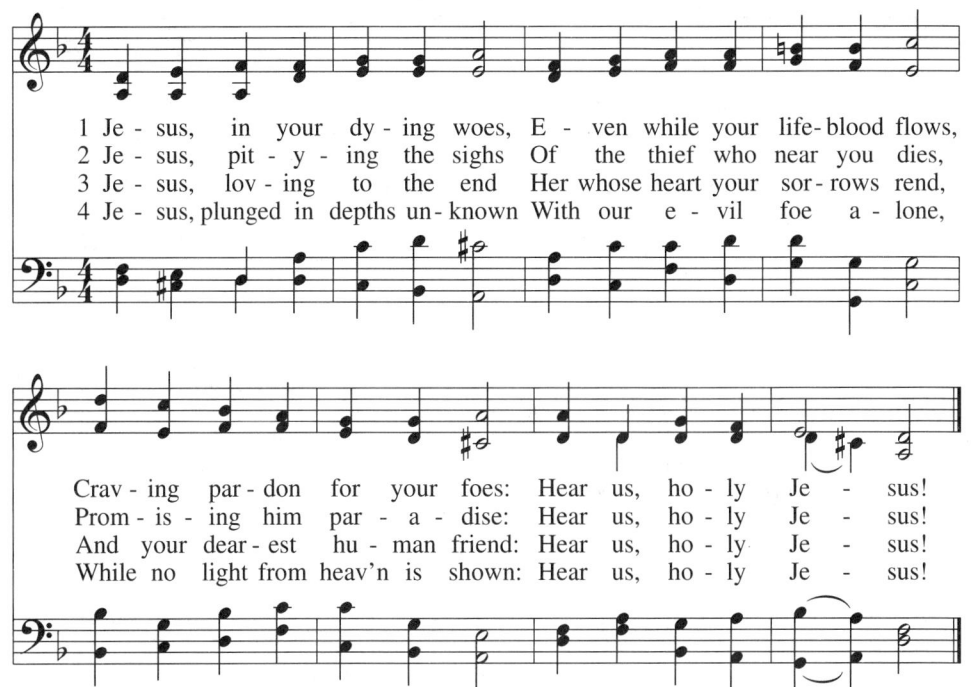

1 Jesus, in your dying woes, Even while your lifeblood flows, Craving pardon for your foes: Hear us, holy Jesus!
2 Jesus, pitying the sighs Of the thief who near you dies, Promising him paradise: Hear us, holy Jesus!
3 Jesus, loving to the end Her whose heart your sorrows rend, And your dearest human friend: Hear us, holy Jesus!
4 Jesus, plunged in depths unknown With our evil foe alone, While no light from heav'n is shown: Hear us, holy Jesus!

5 Jesus, in your thirst and pain,
  While your wounds the lifeblood drain,
  Thus fulfilling Scripture's plan:
  Hear us, holy Jesus!

6 Jesus, all our ransom paid,
  All your Father's will obeyed,
  By your suff'rings perfect made:
  Hear us, holy Jesus!

7 Jesus, all your labor vast,
  All your woe and conflict past,
  Yielding up your soul at last:
  Hear us, holy Jesus!

Text: Thomas B. Pollock, 1836-96, abr., alt.
Tune: Bernhard Schumacher, 1886-1978

SEPTEM VERBA
777 6

GOOD FRIDAY

140. God Was There on Calvary

1. God was there on Calvary, God the Father's only Son,
   Dying that the world might live, There on Calvary.

2. All the world on Calvary, Crucified the Prince of life,
   Pierced the hands of God's own Son, There on Calvary.

3. Sin was there on Calvary, All the sins of ev-'ry-one,
   Laid upon God's sinless Lamb There on Calvary.

4. Love was there on Calvary, Streaming from the heart of God,
   Reaching out for ev-'ry-one There on Calvary.

5. Life was there on Calvary,
   Flowing from his wounded side,
   Spent that death itself might die
   There on Calvary.

6. We were there on Calvary;
   We were pardoned, saved, set free,
   Saved to live eternally —
   Blessed Calvary!

Text: Kurt J. Eggert, 1923-93
Tune: Kurt J. Eggert, 1923-93

GOD WAS THERE ON CALVARY
77 75

Text and Tune © 1993 Kurt J. Eggert; Setting © 1993 Kermit G. Moldenhauer

EASTER

At the Lamb's High Feast We Sing 141

1 At the Lamb's high feast we sing Praise to our victorious King, Who has washed us in the tide Flowing from his pierced side. Alleluia!
2 Mighty Victim from the sky, Hell's fierce pow'rs beneath you lie. You have conquered in the fight; You have brought us life and light. Alleluia!
3 Now no more can death appall, Now no more the grave enthrall; You have opened paradise, And your saints in you shall rise. Alleluia!
4 Easter triumph, Easter joy! This alone can sin destroy; From sin's pow'r, Lord, set us free, New-born souls in you to be. Alleluia!

5 Father, who the crown shall give,
  Savior, by whose death we live,
  Spirit, guide through all our days,
  Three in One, your name we praise.
  Alleluia!

Text: Latin hymn, 17th century, abr.; tr. Robert Campbell, 1814-68, alt. SONNE DER GERECHTIGKEIT
Tune: *Kirchengeseng*, Ivančice, 1566 77 77 4
Setting © 1969 Concordia Publishing House

EASTER

Text: German hymn, c. 1100; tr. W. Gustave Polack, 1890-1950, alt.
Tune: Latin melody, c. 1100, alt.

CHRIST IST ERSTANDEN
PM

Text © 1941 Concordia Publishing House; Setting © 1993 Kermit G. Moldenhauer

EASTER

His Battle Ended There
146

1 His battle ended there, death was overcome.
  Jesus, alive again, wore the victor's crown.
  Clearly sin had failed; Goodness had prevailed.

2 Dread pow'rs of death and sin had him in their hold.
  When Jesus rose again all their plans were foiled.
  Jesus lived again, Triumphed over sin.

3 Dead in the grave he lay, mourned by ev'ry friend.
  Those dark and fearful days then did reach their end.
  God raised him to life, Victor in the strife.

4 He burst the chains of sin, opened death's dark jail.
  God filled him with new life, life that could not fail.
  Right before their eyes Jesus did arise.

Alleluia! Alleluia! Alleluia! Alleluia!

Text: African Chewa hymn, paraphrase Tom Colvin, b. 1925, abr.
Tune: African Angoni war song, adapt.
Text, Tune, Setting © 1976 Hope Publishing Co.

NCHEU
65 65 55 88

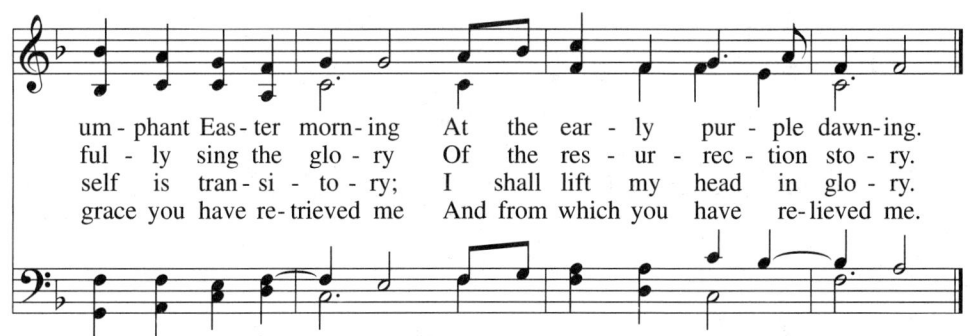

5 For the joy your advent gave me,
    For your gospel's great reward,
For your baptism which has saved me,
    For your supper and your Word,
For your death, the bitter scorn,
    For your resurrection morn:
Lord, I thank you and extol you,
    And in heav'n I shall behold you.

Text: Thomas H. Kingo, 1634-1703, abr.; tr. George A. T. Rygh, 1860-1942, alt.
Tune: Johann Schop, c. 1590-1667
Setting © 1982 Concordia Publishing House

WERDE MUNTER
87 87 77 88
Alternate settings: 283, 408

EASTER

Christ the Lord Is Risen Today 149

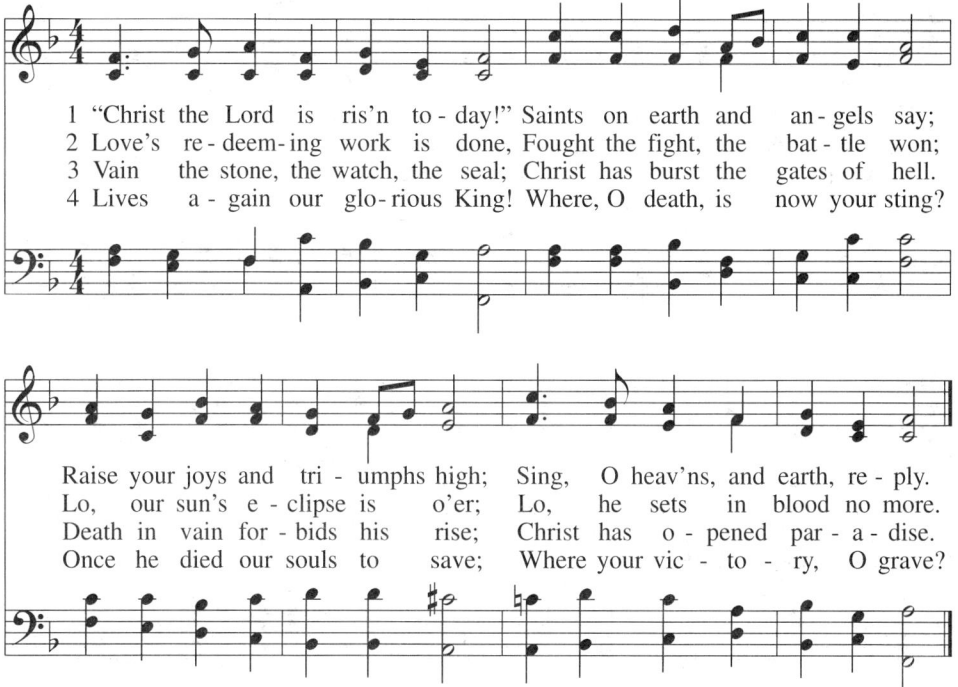

1 "Christ the Lord is ris'n to - day!" Saints on earth and an - gels say;
2 Love's re - deem - ing work is done, Fought the fight, the bat - tle won;
3 Vain the stone, the watch, the seal; Christ has burst the gates of hell.
4 Lives a - gain our glo - rious King! Where, O death, is now your sting?

Raise your joys and tri - umphs high; Sing, O heav'ns, and earth, re - ply.
Lo, our sun's e - clipse is o'er; Lo, he sets in blood no more.
Death in vain for - bids his rise; Christ has o - pened par - a - dise.
Once he died our souls to save; Where your vic - to - ry, O grave?

5 Soar we now where Christ has led,
Foll'wing our exalted head.
Made like him, like him we rise;
Ours the cross, the grave, the skies!

6 Hail the Lord of earth and heav'n!
Praise to you by both be giv'n!
God has now fulfilled his Word;
Praise the resurrected Lord!

Text: Charles Wesley, 1707-88, abr., alt.
Tune: Pierre de Corbeille, d. 1221, adapt.

ORIENTIS PARTIBUS
77 77

EASTER

Triumphant from the Grave 151

1 Tri-umphant from the grave Rose Jesus, strong to save.
2 Bur-ied like sinful man Who ends his mortal span,
3 Fierce though God's wrath had been On him because of sin,
4 Nailed fast to yonder tree See your iniquity!

He crushed — O Christian, mark it well — Sin, Satan, death, and hell.
Our Lord could not for long lie there, Our own decay to share.
The fi-'ry judgment burned no more; Its fury had passed o'er.
His cross has banished all your sin, Your pardon has brought in.

Refrain
Now sing your glad song And joyous praise to him prolong.

5 Sure bond and guarantee
God gave to you and me:
The Father has raised up his Son
To seal redemption won. *Refrain*

6 Now Satan is undone!
Now death's dread pow'r is gone!
From fear of hell you are set free
Through Jesus' victory! *Refrain*

Text: Werner H. Franzmann, 1905-96, alt.
Tune: Bruce R. Backer, b. 1929

TRIUMPH
SM with Refrain

Text, Tune, Setting © 1982 Concordia Publishing House

EASTER

152 I Know that My Redeemer Lives

EASTER

5 He lives to silence all my fears;
   He lives to wipe away my tears.
   He lives to calm my troubled heart;
   He lives all blessings to impart.

6 He lives, my kind, wise, heav'nly friend;
   He lives and loves me to the end.
   He lives, and while he lives I'll sing;
   He lives, my Prophet, Priest, and King.

7 He lives and grants me daily breath;
   He lives, and I shall conquer death.
   He lives my mansion to prepare;
   He lives to bring me safely there.

8 He lives, all glory to his name!
   He lives, my Jesus, still the same.
   Oh, the sweet joy this sentence gives:
   "I know that my Redeemer lives!"

Text: Samuel Medley, 1738-99, abr.
Tune: attr. John C. Hatton, d. 1793; Desc. Paul G. Bunjes, b. 1914

Descant © 1959 Concordia Publishing House

DUKE STREET
LM

Alleluia! Jesus Lives 153

1 Alleluia! Jesus lives! He is now the living one;
  From the gloomy house of death Forth the conqueror has gone,
  Bright forerunner to the skies Of his people, yet to rise.

2 Jesus lives! Let all rejoice; Praise him, ransomed ones of earth.
  Praise him in a nobler song, Cherubim of heav'nly birth.
  Praise the Victor-King, whose sway Sin and death and hell obey.

3 Jesus lives! Why do you weep? Why that sad and frequent sigh?
  He who died our brother here Lives our brother still on high,
  Lives forever to bestow Blessings on his Church below.

4 Jesus lives! And thus, my soul, Life is yours eternally;
  Joined to him, your living head, Where he is, you too shall be;
  You with him at his right hand Victor over death shall stand.

Text: Karl B. Garve, 1763-1841, abr.; tr. Jane L. Borthwick, 1813-97, alt.
Tune: Ludvig M. Lindeman, 1812-87

FRED TIL BOD
77 77 77

154 Alleluia, Alleluia, Give Thanks

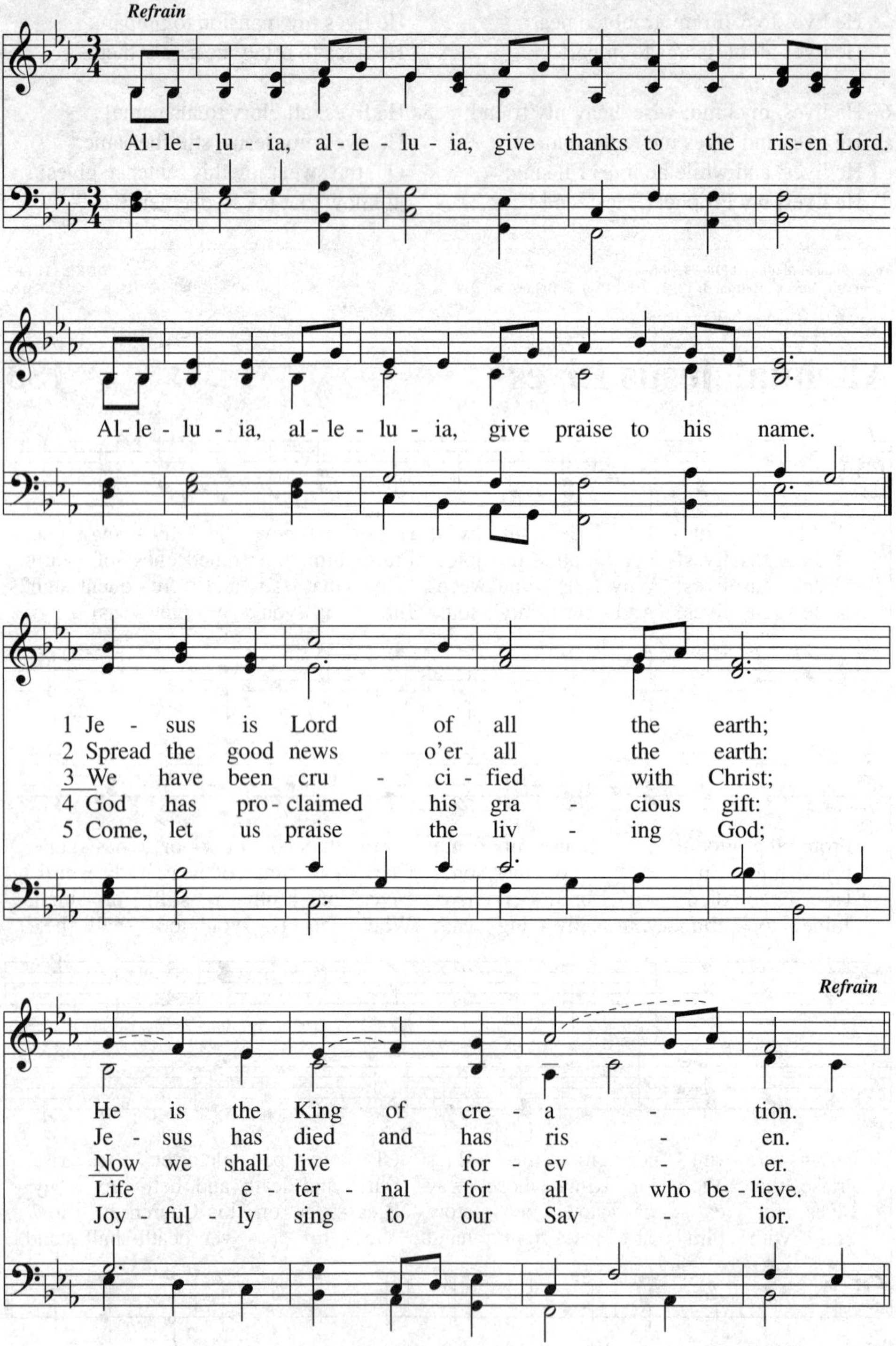

Text: Donald E. Fishel, b. 1950
Tune: Donald E. Fishel, b. 1950

ALLELUIA NO. 1
Irregular with Refrain

EASTER

Christ the Lord Is Risen Again 155

1 Christ the Lord is ris'n a-gain; Christ has broken death's strong chain. Hark, the angels shout for joy, Singing evermore on high: Hallelujah!
2 He who gave for us his life, Who for us endured the strife, Is our Paschal Lamb today. We, too, sing for joy and say: Hallelujah!
3 He who bore all pain and loss Comfortless upon the cross Lives in glory now on high, Pleads for us, and hears our cry: Hallelujah!
4 He whose path no records tell Has descended into hell; He the strong man armed has bound And in highest heav'n is crowned. Hallelujah!

5 He who slumbered in the grave
Is exalted now to save;
Now through Christendom it rings
That the Lamb is King of kings.
Hallelujah!

6 Now he bids us tell abroad
How the lost may be restored,
How the penitent forgiv'n,
How we, too, may enter heav'n.
Hallelujah!

Text: Michael Weisse, c. 1480-1534, abr.; tr. Catherine Winkworth, 1827-78, alt.
Tune: Latin melody, c. 1100, adapt.
Setting © The Church Pension Fund

CHRISTUS IST ERSTANDEN
77 77 4

EASTER

5 He brings me to the portal
  That leads to bliss untold,
 Whereon this rhyme immortal
  Is found in script of gold:
 "Who there my cross has shared
  Finds here a crown prepared;
 Who there with me has died
  Shall here be glorified."

Text: Paul Gerhardt, 1607-76, abr.; tr. John Kelly, 1833-90, alt.
Tune: Johann Crüger, 1598-1662

AUF, AUF, MEIN HERZ
76 76 66 66

EASTER

Text: Latin hymn, 14th century, st. 1-3; Charles Wesley, 1707-88, st. 4;
    tr. *Lyra Davidica,* London, 1708, st. 1-3, alt.
Tune: *Lyra Davidica,* London, 1708, alt.; Desc. *Hymns Ancient and Modern*, London, 1955
Descant © 1955. Renewal 1983 by Hope Publishing Co.

EASTER HYMN
77 77 with Alleluias

die for - ev - er. I am con - tent! I am con - tent!
res - ur - rec - tion. I am con - tent! I am con - tent!
ex - ul - ta - tion. I am con - tent! I am con - tent!
joice for - ev - er. I am con - tent! I am con - tent!

Text: Johann J. Möller, 1660-1733, abr.; August Crull, 1845-1923, alt.
Tune: Johann R. Ahle, 1625-73, alt.

ES IST GENUG
10 6 10 6 99 44

Morning Breaks upon the Tomb 159

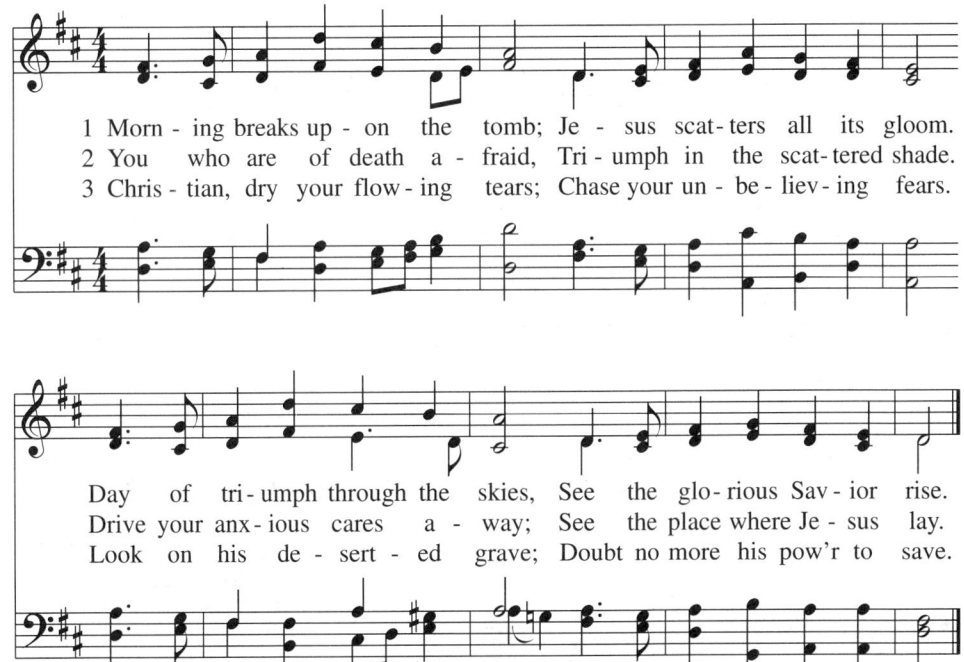

1 Morn - ing breaks up - on the tomb; Je - sus scat - ters all its gloom.
2 You who are of death a - fraid, Tri - umph in the scat - tered shade.
3 Chris - tian, dry your flow - ing tears; Chase your un - be - liev - ing fears.

Day of tri - umph through the skies, See the glo - rious Sav - ior rise.
Drive your anx - ious cares a - way; See the place where Je - sus lay.
Look on his de - sert - ed grave; Doubt no more his pow'r to save.

Text: William B. Collyer, 1782-1854, abr.
Tune: French melody, 13th century

INNOCENTS
77 77

EASTER

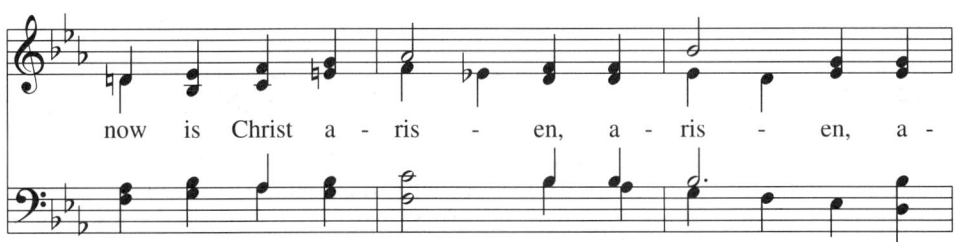

Text: George R. Woodward, 1848-1934
Tune: *Davids Psalmen*, Amsterdam, 1684

VRUECHTEN
67 67 with Refrain

Text reprinted by permission of A. R. Mowbray & Co., Ltd.; Setting © 1969 Concordia Publishing House

EASTER

He Is Arisen! Glorious Word 162

Text: Birgitte K. Boye, 1742-1824; tr. George A. T. Rygh, 1860-1942, alt.
Tune: Philipp Nicolai, 1556-1608, alt.
Setting © 1981 Richard W. Gieseke

WIE SCHÖN LEUCHTET
887 887 22 44 48
Alternate setting: 79

EASTER

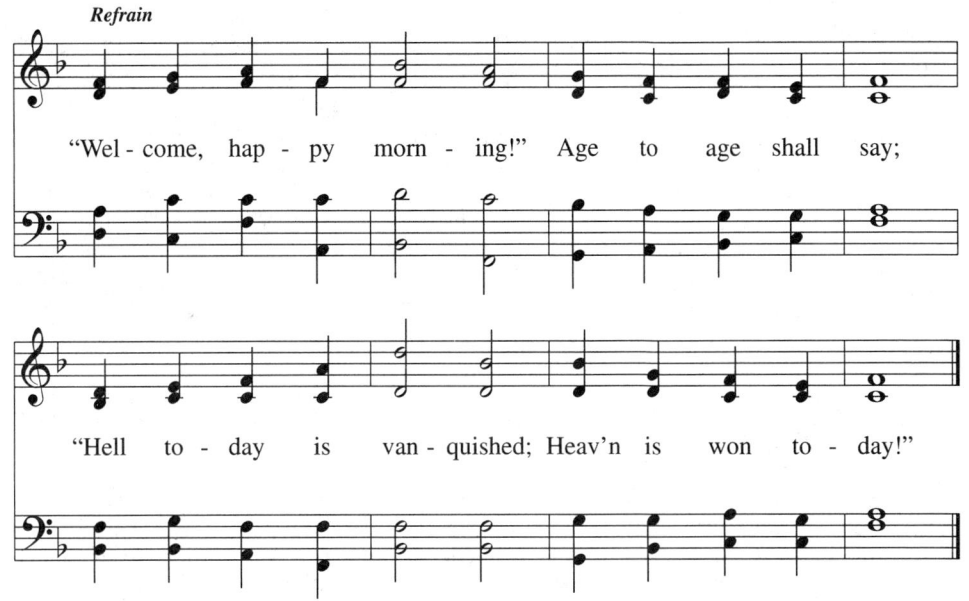

Text: Venantius Fortunatus, c. 530-609, abr.; tr. John Ellerton, 1826-93, alt.
Tune: *Enchiridion Geistlike Lede und Psalmen*, Lübeck, 1545

SEI DU MIR GEGRÜSSET
65 65 D with Refrain

EASTER

O Sons and Daughters of the King 165

1. O sons and daughters of the King, Whom heav'nly hosts in glory sing, Today the grave has lost its sting! Alleluia!

2. On that first morning of the week, Before the day began to break, The Marys went their Lord to seek. Alleluia!

3. An angel bade their sorrow flee, For thus he spoke unto the three, "Your Lord will go to Galilee." Alleluia!

4. That night th' apostles met in fear; Among them came their Lord most dear And said, "Peace be unto you here." Alleluia!

5. When Thomas afterwards had heard
That Jesus had fulfilled his word,
He doubted that it was the Lord.
Alleluia!

6. "Thomas, behold my side," said he,
"My hands, my feet, my body see;
And doubt not, but believe in me."
Alleluia!

7. No longer Thomas then denied;
He saw the feet, the hands, the side;
"You are my Lord and God," he cried.
Alleluia!

8. Blessèd are they that have not seen
And yet whose faith has constant been;
In life eternal they shall reign.
Alleluia!

9. On this most holy day of days
To God your hearts and voices raise
In laud and jubilee and praise.
Alleluia!

Text: attr. Jean Tisserand, d. 1494, abr.; tr. John M. Neale, 1818-66, alt.
Tune: Melchior Vulpius, c. 1570-1615, alt.

GELOBT SEI GOTT
888 with Alleluias

EASTER

Text: Georg Vetter, 1536-99; tr. Martin H. Franzmann, 1907-76, alt.
Tune: *Cinquante Pseaumes,* Geneva, 1543, alt.

Text and Setting © 1969 Concordia Publishing House

MIT FREUDEN ZART
448 448 44 44 8

ASCENSION

Draw Us to Thee 170

1 Draw us to thee, For then shall we Walk in thy steps forever And hasten on To be with thee, dear Savior.

2 Draw us to thee, Lord, lovingly; Let us depart with gladness That we may be Forever free From sorrow, grief, and sadness.

3 Draw us to thee; Oh, grant that we May walk the road to heaven! Direct our way Lest we should stray And from thy paths be driven.

4 Draw us to thee That also we Thy heav'nly bliss inherit And ever dwell Where sin and hell No more can vex our spirit.

5 Draw us to thee
  Unceasingly;
Into thy kingdom take us.
Let us fore'er
  Thy glory share;
Thy saints and joint heirs make us.

Text: Friedrich Funcke, 1642-99; tr. August Crull, 1845-1923, alt.
Tune: *As hymnodus sacer*, Leipzig, 1625, alt.

ACH GOTT UND HERR
447 447

ASCENSION

171 A Hymn of Glory Let Us Sing

ASCENSION

5 Be now our joy on earth, O Lord,
And be our future great reward.
  Alleluia! Alleluia!
Then, throned with you forever, we
Shall praise your name eternally.
  Alleluia! Alleluia! Alleluia!
    Alleluia! Alleluia!

6 O risen Christ, ascended Lord,
All praise to you let earth accord.
  Alleluia! Alleluia!
You are, while endless ages run,
With Father and with Spirit one.
  Alleluia! Alleluia! Alleluia!
    Alleluia! Alleluia!

Text: The Venerable Bede, 673-735, abr.; tr. composite
Tune: *Ausserlesene, Catholische, Geistliche Kirchengesäng*, Köln, 1623, alt.;
  Desc. composite
Setting reprinted by permission of Oxford University Press

LASST UNS ERFREUEN
888 888 with Alleluias

ASCENSION

172 Up through Endless Ranks of Angels

1. Up through endless ranks of angels, Cries of triumph in his ears, To his heav'nly throne ascending, Having vanquished all their fears, Christ looks down upon the faithful, Leaving them in happy tears.

2. Death destroying, life restoring, Proven equal to our need, Now for us before the Father As our brother intercede; Flesh that for the world was wounded, Living, for the wounded plead!

3. To our lives of wanton wand'ring Send your promised Spirit-guide; Through our lives of fear and failure With your pow'r and love abide; Welcome us, as you were welcomed, To an endless Eastertide.

4. Alleluia, alleluia! Oh, to breathe the Spirit's grace! Alleluia, alleluia! Oh, to see the Father's face! Alleluia, alleluia! Oh, to feel the Son's embrace!

Text: Jaroslav J. Vajda, b. 1919, abr., alt.
Tune: Henry V. Gerike, b. 1948
Text © Augsburg Publishing House; Tune and Setting © Henry V. Gerike

ASCENDED TRIUMPH
87 87 87

ASCENSION

174 See, the Conqueror Mounts in Triumph

ASCENSION

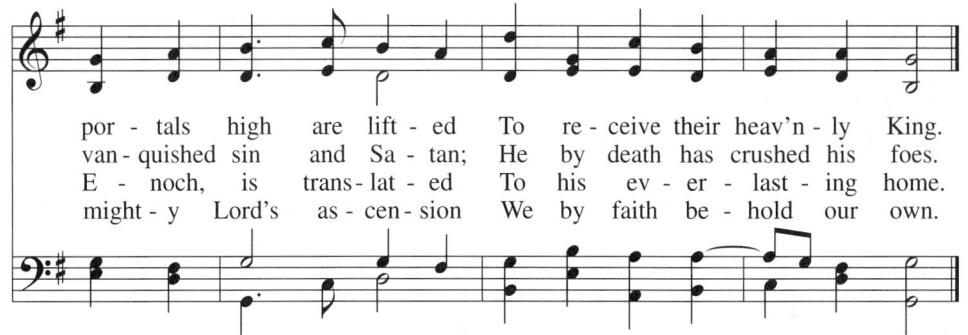

Text: Christopher Wordsworth, 1807-85, abr., alt.
Tune: Henry T. Smart, 1813-79

REX GLORIAE
87 87 D

Hail the Day that Sees Him Rise   175

1 Hail the day that sees him rise To his throne a-bove the skies!
2 There the glo-rious tri-umph waits: Lift your heads, e-ter-nal gates.
3 See, the heav'n its Lord re-ceives, Yet he loves the earth he leaves;
4 See, he lifts his hands a-bove; See, he shows the prints of love.

Christ, the Lamb for sin-ners giv'n, Re-as-cends his na-tive heav'n.
He has con-quered death and sin; Take the King of glo-ry in!
Though re-turn-ing to his throne, Still he calls man-kind his own.
Hark! His gra-cious lips be-stow Bless-ings on his Church be-low.

5 Still for us he intercedes;
   His prevailing death he pleads.
   He, the first of all our race,
   Near himself prepares a place.

6 There we shall with you remain
   Partners in your endless reign,
   There your face unclouded view,
   Find our heav'n of heav'ns in you.

Text: Charles Wesley, 1707-88, abr., alt.
Tune: Pierre de Corbeille, d. 1221, adapt.

ORIENTIS PARTIBUS
77 77

PENTECOST

176 Come, Holy Ghost, God and Lord

1 Come, Holy Ghost, God and Lord! May all your graces be out-poured On each believer's mind and heart; Your fervent love to them impart. Lord, by the brightness of your light In holy faith your church unite

2 Come, holy Light, Guide divine, And cause the Word of life to shine. Teach us to know our God aright And call him Father with delight. From ev'ry error keep us free; Let none but Christ our Master be

3 Come, holy Fire, Comfort true; Grant us the will your work to do And in your service to abide; Let trials turn us not aside. Lord, by your pow'r prepare each heart, And to our weakness strength impart

PENTECOST

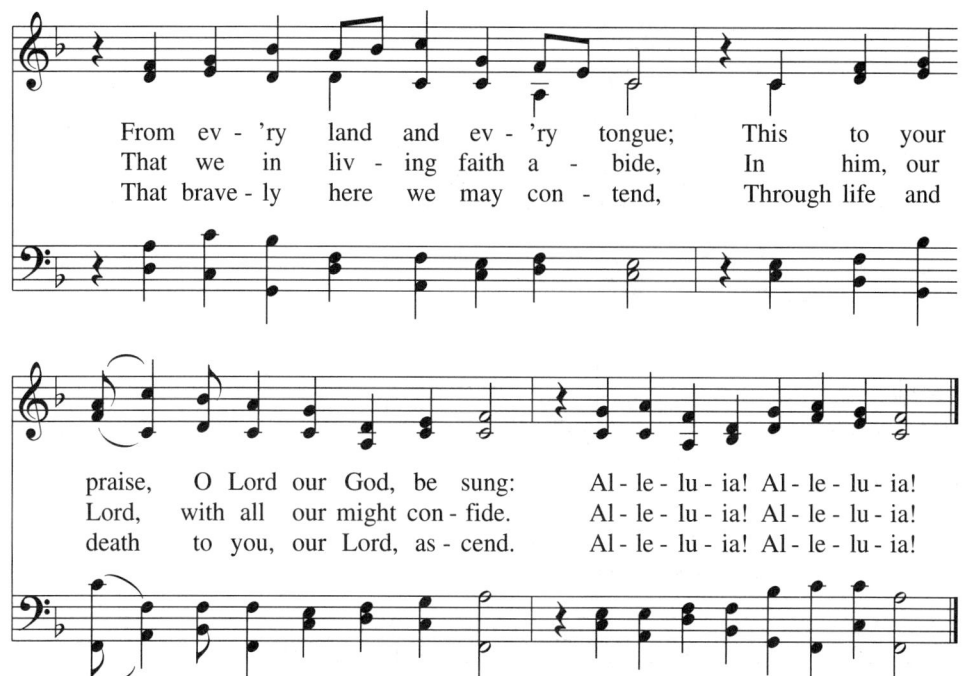

Text: German hymn, 15th century, st. 1; Martin Luther, 1483-1546, st. 2-3;
tr. *The Lutheran Hymnal,* St. Louis, 1941, alt.
Tune: *Eyn Enchiridion oder Handbüchlein,* Erfurt, 1524

KOMM, HEILIGER GEIST, HERRE GOTT
78 88 88 8 10 8

PENTECOST

177 Come, Holy Ghost, Creator Blest

1 Come, Holy Ghost, Creator blest, And make our hearts your place of rest; Come with your grace and heav'nly aid, And fill the hearts which you have made.

2 To you, the Counselor, we cry, To you, the gift of God most high; The fount of life, the fire of love, The soul's anointing from above.

3 Your light to ev'ry thought impart, And shed your love in ev'ry heart; The weakness of our mortal state With deathless might invigorate.

4 Drive far away our wily foe, And your abiding peace bestow; If you are our protecting guide, No evil can with us abide.

5 Teach us to know the Father, Son, And you, from both, as Three in One, That we your name may ever bless And in our lives the truth confess.

6 Praise we the Father and the Son And Holy Spirit, with them One, And may the Son on us bestow The gifts that from the Spirit flow!

Text: attr. Rhabanus Maurus, 776-856, abr.; tr. Edward Caswall, 1814-78, alt.
Tune: Klug, *Geistliche lieder auffs new gebessert*, Wittenberg, 1533

KOMM, GOTT SCHÖPFER
LM

PENTECOST

Come, Holy Ghost, Creator Blest   178

1 Come, Holy Ghost, Creator blest, And make our hearts your place of rest; Come with your grace and heav'nly aid, And fill the hearts which you have made.

2 To you, the Counselor, we cry, To you, the gift of God most high; The fount of life, the fire of love, The soul's anointing from above.

3 Your light to ev-'ry thought impart, And shed your love in ev-'ry heart; The weakness of our mortal state With deathless might invigorate.

4 Drive far away our wily foe, And your abiding peace bestow; If you are our protecting guide, No evil can with us abide. Amen.

5 Teach us to know the Father, Son,
And you, from both, as Three in One
That we your name may ever bless
And in our lives the truth confess.

6 Praise we the Father and the Son
And Holy Spirit, with them One,
And may the Son on us bestow
The gifts that from the Spirit flow!
Amen.

Text: attr. Rhabanus Maurus, 776-856, abr.; tr. Edward Caswall, 1814-78, alt.
Tune: Sarum plainsong, c. 9th century
Setting © 1993 Kermit G. Moldenhauer

VENI CREATOR SPIRITUS
LM

179 Hail Thee, Festival Day

PENTECOST

Text: Venantius Fortunatus, c. 530-609, abr., refrain, st. 1, 3;
  Mark A. Jeske, b. 1952, st. 2, 4; tr. composite, refrain, st. 1, 3
Tune: Ralph Vaughan Williams, 1872-1958
Text st.1,3, Tune and Setting reprinted by permission of Oxford University Press; Text st.2,4 © 1993 Mark A. Jeske

SALVE FESTA DIES
Irregular

PENTECOST

180 Holy Spirit, God of Love

Holy Spirit, God of love, Who our darkness brightens,
Poured on us from heav'n above, And our faith enlightens,
In your light we gather here; Show us that Christ's promise clear
Is Amen forever. Jesus, our ascended Lord,
Oh, fulfill your gracious Word; Bless us with your favor!

Text: Birgitte K. Boye, 1742-1824; tr. George A. T. Rygh, 1860-1942, alt.
Tune: *Ein New Gesengbuchlen,* Jungbunzlau, 1531, alt.

DER TAG, DER IST SO FREUDENREICH
76 76 776 776

PENTECOST

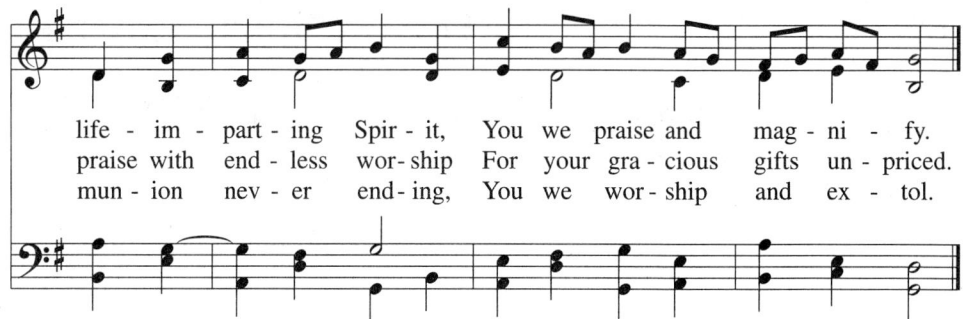

```
life - im - part - ing  Spir - it,    You we praise and      mag - ni - fy.
praise with  end - less  wor - ship   For your gra - cious   gifts un - priced.
mun - ion   nev - er    end - ing,    You we  wor - ship    and   ex - tol.
```

Text: Timothy Rees, 1874-1939, alt.
Tune: *Oude en Nieuwe Hollantse . . . Contradansen,* Amsterdam, c. 1710

IN BABILONE
87 87 D

Text reprinted by permission of A. R. Mowbray & Co., Ltd.; Setting © 1969 Concordia Publishing House

Alternate setting: 532

Holy Spirit, Light Divine 183

```
1 Ho - ly  Spir - it, Light di - vine,  Shine up - on    this   heart of mine;
2 Ho - ly  Spir - it, Love  di - vine,  Cleanse this guilt - y   heart of mine;
3 Ho - ly  Spir - it, Joy   di - vine,  Cheer this   sad - dened heart of mine;
4 Ho - ly  Spir - it, Pow'r di - vine,  Dwell with - in  this   heart of mine;
5 See, to you  I  give my heart;        Cleanse my life   in   ev - 'ry part;

Chase the gloom of   night a - way;  Turn the dark - ness in - to day.
In   your mer - cy   pit - y   me;   From sin's bond - age set me free.
Fill me  with your heav'n - ly peace; Let  it   grow  and  still in - crease.
Cast down ev - 'ry   i - dol throne;  Reign su - preme and reign a - lone.
Your own tem - ple   I  would be    Now and  for  e - ter - ni - ty.
```

Text: Andrew Reed, 1787-1862, abr., alt.
Tune: Orlando Gibbons, 1583-1625, alt.

SONG 13
77 77

PENTECOST

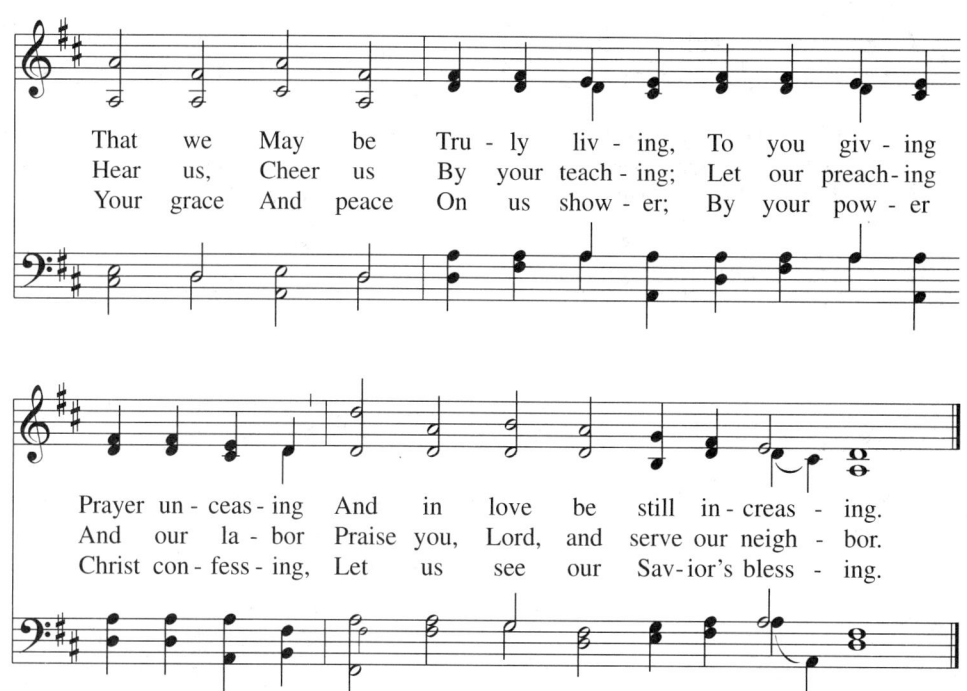

Text: Michael Schirmer, 1606-73, abr., adapt.; tr. Catherine Winkworth, 1827-78,
 st. 1,3, alt.; *The Lutheran Hymnal,* St. Louis, 1941, st. 2, alt.
Tune: Philipp Nicolai, 1556-1608, alt.

WIE SCHÖN LEUCHTET
887 887 22 44 48

Alternate setting: 49

PENTECOST

Creator Spirit, by Whose Aid   188

1. Creator Spirit, by whose aid The world's foundations first were laid, Come, visit ev'ry humble mind; Come, pour your joys on humankind. From sin and sorrow set us free; May we your living temples be.
2. O Source of light, our Counselor, The Father's help to us assure. Come down, as promised, with your fire, And hearts with heav'nly love inspire. Your sacred, healing message bring To sanctify us when we sing.
3. Giver of grace, descend from high In answer to our earnest cry. Help us eternal truths receive And practice all that we believe. Give us your wisdom that we see The glory of the Trinity.
4. Immortal honor, endless fame, Attend th' almighty Father's name; The Savior-Son be glorified, Who for all humankind has died; And equal adoration rise To you, O Spirit, in the skies.

Text: attr. Rhabanus Maurus, 776-856, abr.; tr. John Dryden, 1631-1700, alt.
Tune: *Gesangbuch . . . Psalmen, Geistliche Lieder*, Strassburg, 1541, alt.

ALL EHR UND LOB
88 88 88

Alternate settings: 262, 567

Text: Bartholomäus Crasselius, 1667-1724, abr.; tr. Catherine Winkworth, 1827-78, alt.
Tune: *Musicalisch Hand-Buch der Geistlichen Melodien,* Hamburg, 1690, alt.

DIR, DIR, JEHOVAH
9 10 9 10 10 10

HOLY TRINITY

Father Most Holy, Merciful, and Tender 191

1 Father most holy, merciful, and tender;
  Jesus, our Savior, with the Father reigning;
  Spirit of comfort, Advocate, Defender,
  Light never waning;

2 Trinity sacred, Unity unshaken;
  Deity perfect, giving and forgiving;
  Light of the angels, Life of the forsaken;
  Hope of the living;

3 Maker of all things, all your creatures praise you;
  All for your worship were and are created.
  Hear us, Almighty, hear us as we
  Our adoration;

4 To the all-ruling triune God be glory,
  Highest and greatest, over all exalted;
  We, too, would praise you, giving honor to you
  Now and forever.

Text: Latin hymn, 10th century; tr. Percy Dearmer, 1867-1936, alt.
Tune: K. Lee Scott, b. 1950

SHADES MOUNTAIN
11 11 11 5

Tune and Setting © 1987 MorningStar Music Publishers

192 Triune God, Oh, Be Our Stay

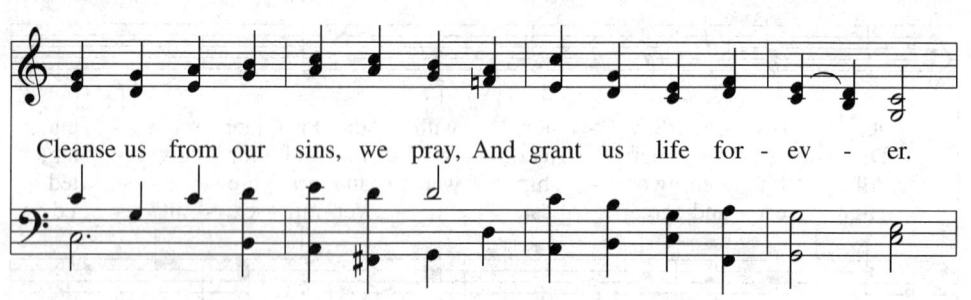

HOLY TRINITY

This hymn may also be sung as follows:

1 God the Father, be our stay …
2 Jesus Christ, oh, be our stay …
3 Holy Spirit, be our stay …

Text: German litany, 14th century, adapt.; tr. Richard Massie, 1800-87, alt.
Tune: *Geystliche gesangk Buchleyn,* Wittenberg, 1524, alt.
Setting © 1993 Kermit G. Moldenhauer

GOTT DER VATER WOHN UNS BEI
77 77 77 7 D

195 Holy, Holy, Holy! Lord God Almighty

HOLY TRINITY

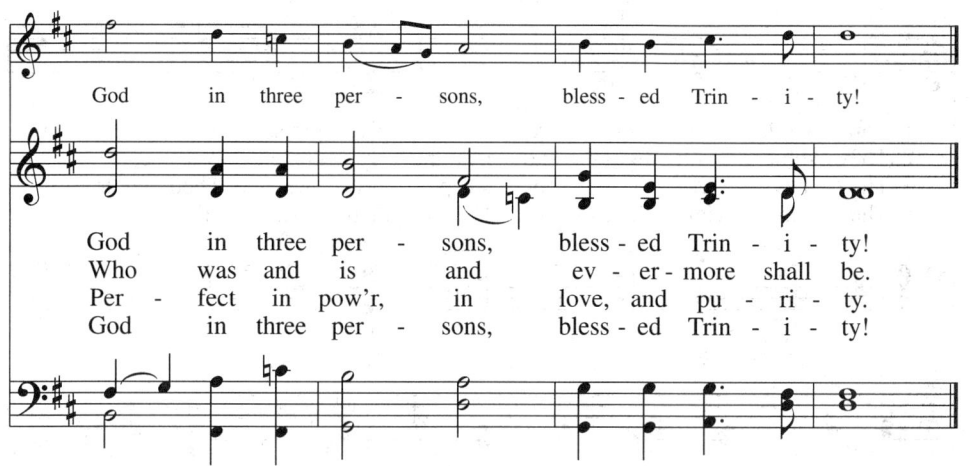

Text: Reginald Heber, 1783-1826, alt.
Tune: John B. Dykes, 1823-76; Desc. Kermit G. Moldenhauer, b. 1949

Descant © 1993 Kermit G. Moldenhauer

NICAEA
11 12 12 10

ST. MICHAEL AND ALL ANGELS

196 Lord God, to You We All Give Praise

1. Lord God, to you we all give praise;
To you our joyful hymns we raise
That angel hosts you did create
Around your glorious throne to wait.

2. They shine with light and heav'nly grace
And constantly behold your face.
They heed your voice; they know it well;
In godly wisdom they excel.

3. They never rest nor sleep as we;
Their whole delight is but to be
With you, Lord Jesus, and to keep
Your little flock, your lambs and sheep.

4. The ancient dragon is their foe;
His envy and his wrath they know.
So now he subtly lies in wait
To ruin school and church and state.

5. But watchful is the angel band
That follows Christ on ev'ry hand
To guard his people where they go
And break the counsel of the foe.

6. O Lord, awaken songs of praise
For angel hosts that guard our days;
Teach us to serve you and adore
As angels do forevermore.

Text: Philipp Melanchthon, 1497-1560, abr., adapt.; tr. Emanuel Cronenwett, 1841-1931, alt.
Tune: *Antiphoner*, Grenoble, 1753
Setting published by permission of the executors of the late Dr. Basil Harwood

DEUS TUORUM MILITUM
LM
Alternate setting: 502

REFORMATION

In Trembling Hands, Lord God, We Hold 199

1 In trembling hands, Lord God, we hold
Our heritage, your gift of grace,
Your gospel, bringing wealth untold:
All blessings here, in heav'n a place.

2 "In trembling hands"— for how could we
Retain your gift by our own pow'r?
The pearl of priceless worth would be
Soon lost — attend us ev'ry hour!

3 "In trembling hands"— with joyous awe,
Like Luther, we behold your Son:
For us he kept your holy law,
In dying full salvation won.

4 "In trembling hands"— and yet we cling
With grip of steel, which you must give,
To Christ, our all, our ev'rything,
To Christ, the life in whom we live.

5 "In trembling hands" — the treasure won
We only hold through Scripture, Lord.
Then keep us all, till life is done,
As people trembling at your Word.

6 "In trembling hands" — if it be so,
How can our hearts remain unstirred
While millions still in tatters go
Nor yet of wealth in Christ have heard?

7 In trembling hands, Lord God, we hold
Our heritage; now give us hands
That gladly share your heav'nly gold
With needy souls in many lands!

Text: Werner H. Franzmann, 1905-96, abr., alt.
Tune: Martin Albrecht, 1909-93

IN TREMBLING HANDS
LM

Text © 1993 Werner H. Franzmann; Tune and Setting © 1993 Martin Albrecht

REFORMATION

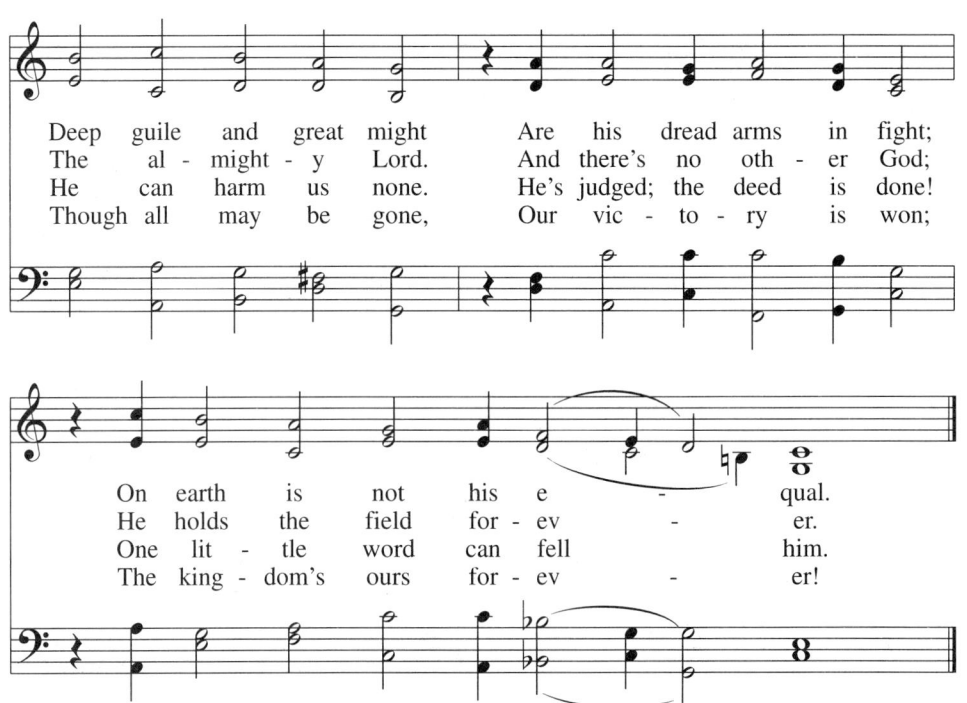

Text: Martin Luther, 1483-1546; tr. composite
Tune: Martin Luther, 1483-1546
Setting © 1970 by Bärenreiter-Verlag

EIN FESTE BURG
87 87 55 56 7

REFORMATION

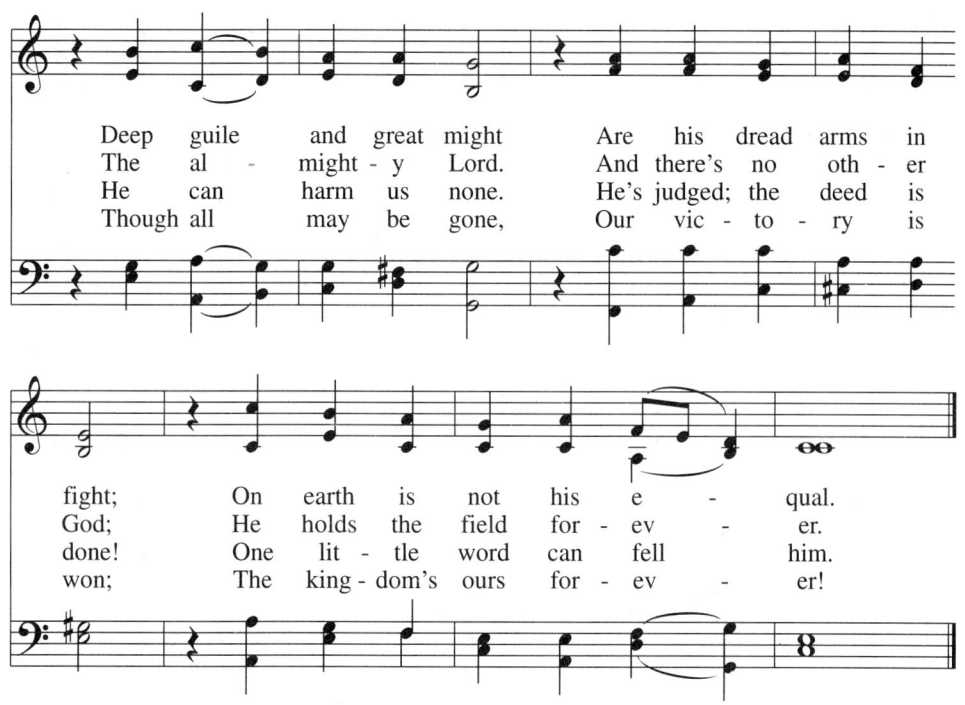

Text: Martin Luther, 1483-1546; tr. composite
Tune: Martin Luther, 1483-1546, alt.

EIN FESTE BURG
87 87 55 56 7

REFORMATION

```
near,  Who  rise   in      might  a  -  gainst   us.
soul   And  seeks  to      o  -  ver - whelm    us.
he     Who  made   the     earth  and  heav  -  ens.
```

Text: Martin Luther, 1483-1546; tr. *The Lutheran Hymnal,* St. Louis, 1941, alt.
Tune: Christian Egenolff, 1502-55, adapted by Ralph Vaughan Williams, 1872-1958

WÄCHTERLIED
87 87 887

Tune reprinted by permission of Oxford University Press

Lord, Keep Us Steadfast in Your Word   203

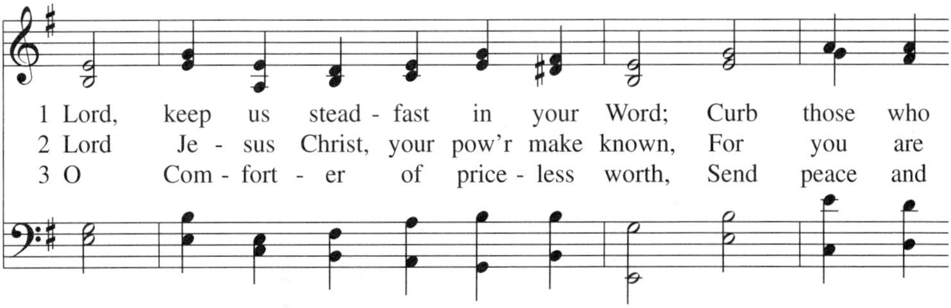

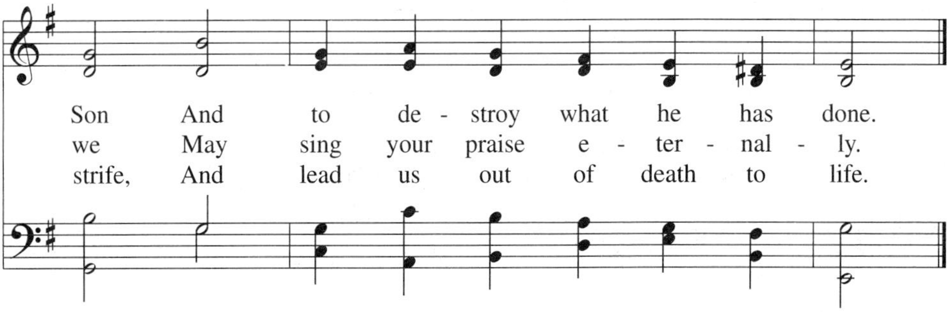

```
1 Lord,  keep   us     stead - fast   in     your  Word;   Curb   those   who
2 Lord           Je  - sus    Christ, your   pow'r make    known, For    you    are
3 O      Com - fort - er     of      price - less   worth, Send   peace  and

by    de  - ceit   or    sword   Would  seek   to    o  - ver - throw  your
Lord  of    lords  a   - lone;   De  - fend   your  Chris - ten - dom  that
u   - ni  - ty     on    earth.  Sup - port   us    in    our    fi   - nal

Son     And    to      de  - stroy   what  he     has    done.
we      May    sing    your  praise  e   - ter  - nal  - ly.
strife, And    lead    us    out     of    death  to    life.
```

Text: Martin Luther, 1483-1546; tr. composite
Tune: Klug, *Geistliche Lieder zu Wittemberg,* Wittenberg, 1543, alt.

ERHALT UNS, HERR
LM

Alternate settings: 282, 287

REFORMATION

204 — O God, Our Lord, Your Holy Word

1. O God, our Lord, Your holy Word Was long a hidden treasure Till to its place It was by grace Restored in fullest measure. For this today Our thanks we say And...

2. Salvation true By faith in you— That is your gospel's preaching, The heart and core Of Bible lore In all its sacred teaching. In Christ we must Put all our trust, Not...

3. Lord, you alone This work have done By your free grace and favor. All who believe Will grace receive Through Jesus Christ, our Savior. And though the foe Would overthrow Your...

4. Since you are mine, My Lord divine, Death holds no dreadful terrors; Your precious blood, My highest good, Has blotted out my errors. My thanks to you— Your Word is true! Ful-

REFORMATION

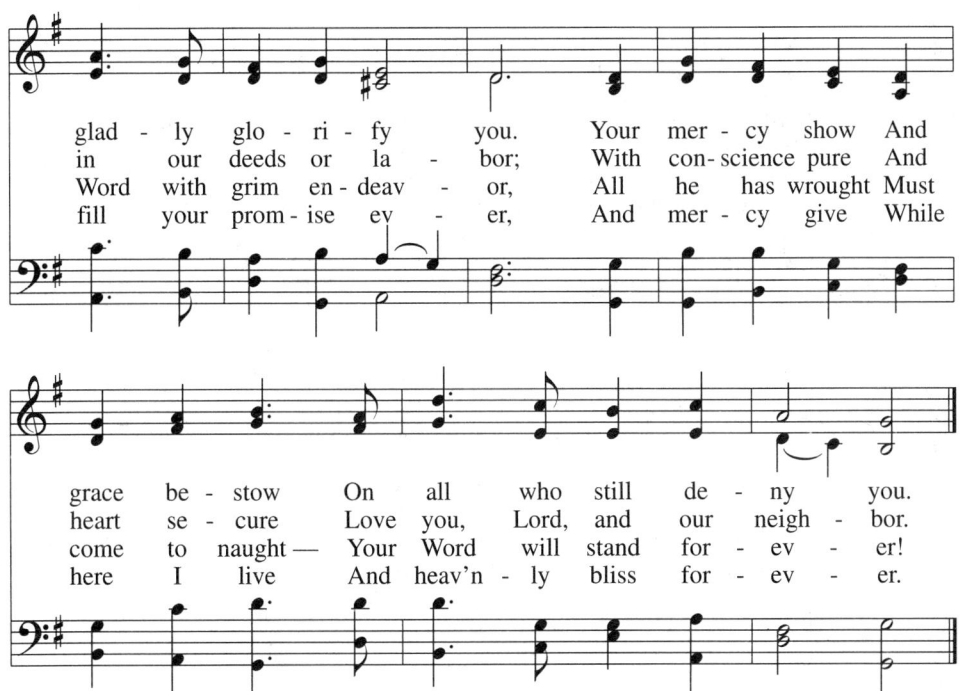

Text: *Enchiridion . . . zum Schwartzen Horn,* Erfurt, 1527, abr.;
tr. W. Gustave Polack, 1890-1950, alt.
Tune: *Enchiridion . . . zum Schwartzen Horn,* Erfurt, 1527
Text © 1941 Concordia Publishing House

O HERRE GOTT, DEIN GÖTTLICH WORT
447 447 D Iambic

REFORMATION

205   O Lord, Look Down from Heaven

1. O Lord, look down from heav'n, behold, And let your pity waken. How few are we within your fold, Your saints by all forsaken; True faith seems quenched on ev'ry hand; Your Word is not al-

2. O God, root out all heresy, And of false teachers rid us Who proudly say, "Now where is he Who shall our speech forbid us? By right or might we shall prevail; What we determine

3. Therefore said God, "I must arise— The poor my help are needing. To me ascend my people's cries, And I have heard their pleading. For them my saving Word shall fight And fearlessly and

4. Defend your truth, O God, and stay This evil generation, And from the error of its way Keep your own congregation. The wicked ev-'ry-where abound And would your little

REFORMATION

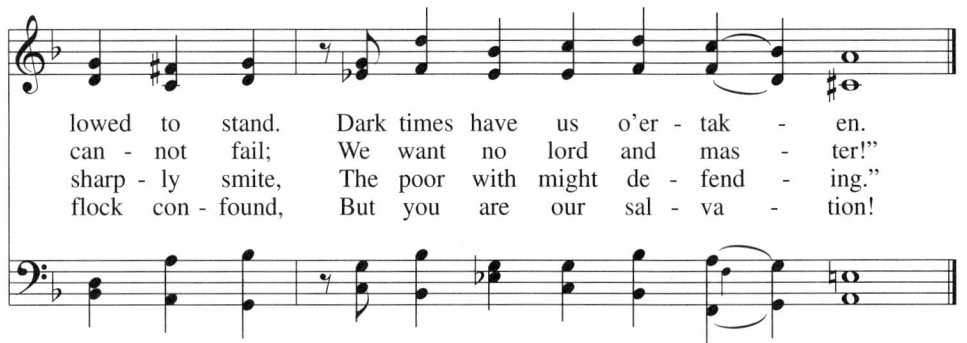

lowed to stand. Dark times have us o'er - tak - en.
can - not fail; We want no lord and mas - ter!"
sharp - ly smite, The poor with might de - fend - ing."
flock con - found, But you are our sal - va - tion!

Text: Martin Luther, 1483-1546, abr.;
    tr. *The Lutheran Hymnal,* St. Louis, 1941, alt.
Tune: *Eyn Enchiridion oder Handbüchlein,* Erfurt, 1524, alt.
Setting © 1993 Bruce R. Backer

ACH GOTT, VOM HIMMEL SIEH DAREIN
87 87 887

END TIME

Text: Philipp Nicolai, 1556-1608; tr. Catherine Winkworth, 1827-78, alt.
Tune: Philipp Nicolai, 1556-1608, alt.

Setting © 1993 Kermit G. Moldenhauer

WACHET AUF
898 898 664 448

Alternate setting: 455

END TIME

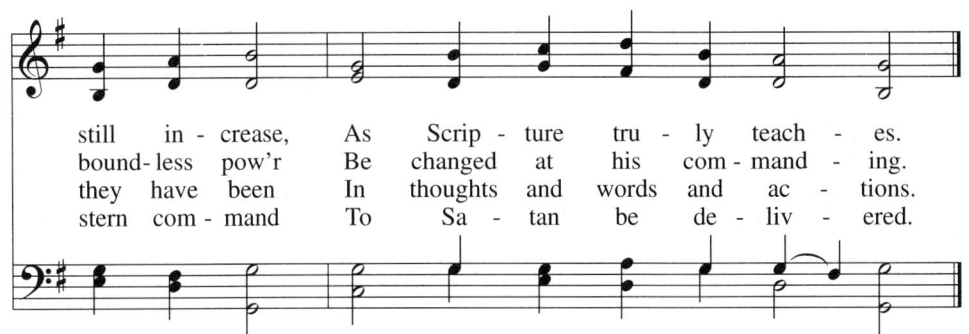

still in - crease, As Scrip - ture tru - ly teach - es.
bound-less pow'r Be changed at his com - mand - ing.
they have been In thoughts and words and ac - tions.
stern com - mand To Sa - tan be de - liv - ered.

5 My Savior paid the debt I owe
    And for my sin was smitten;
 Within the Book of Life I know
    My name has now been written.
 I will not doubt, for I am free,
    And Satan cannot threaten me;
 There is no condemnation!

6 O Jesus Christ, do not delay,
    But hasten our salvation;
 We often tremble on our way
    In fear and tribulation.
 Your saints are waiting patiently;
    Come soon, Redeemer; make us free
 From ev'ry evil. Amen.

Text: Bartholomäus Ringwaldt, 1532-99, abr.; tr. Philip A. Peter, 1832-1919, alt.
Tune: Klug, *Geistliche Lieder auffs new gebessert,* Wittenberg, 1535

ES IST GEWISSLICH
87 87 887

Alternate settings: 185, 208

END TIME

208   Great God, What Do I See and Hear

1. Great God, what do I see and hear? The end of things created; The judge of mankind shall appear On clouds of glory seated. The trumpet sounds; the graves restore The dead which they con-

2. The dead in Christ shall first arise At that last trumpet's sounding, Caught up to meet him in the skies, With joy their Lord surrounding. No gloomy fears their souls dismay; His presence sheds e-

3. But sinners filled with guilty fears Behold his wrath prevailing, For they shall rise and find their tears And sighs are unavailing; The day of grace is past and gone; They trembling stand be-

4. O Christ, you died, and yet you live; To me account your merit, My pardon seal, my sins forgive, And cleanse me by your Spirit. Beneath your cross I view the day When heav'n and earth shall

END TIME

tained be - fore:	Pre - pare, my soul, to meet him!
ter - nal day	On those pre - pared to meet him.
fore his throne,	All un - pre - pared to meet him.
pass a - way,	And thus pre - pare to meet you.

Text: *Psalms and Hymns,* Sheffield, 1802, st. 1, alt.;
William B. Collyer, 1782-1854, st. 2-4, alt.
Tune: Klug, *Geistliche Lieder auffs new gebessert,* Wittenberg, 1535
Setting © 1989 Ronald L. Shilling

ES IST GEWISSLICH
87 87 887

Alternate settings: 185, 207

Day of Wrath, Oh, Day of Mourning 209

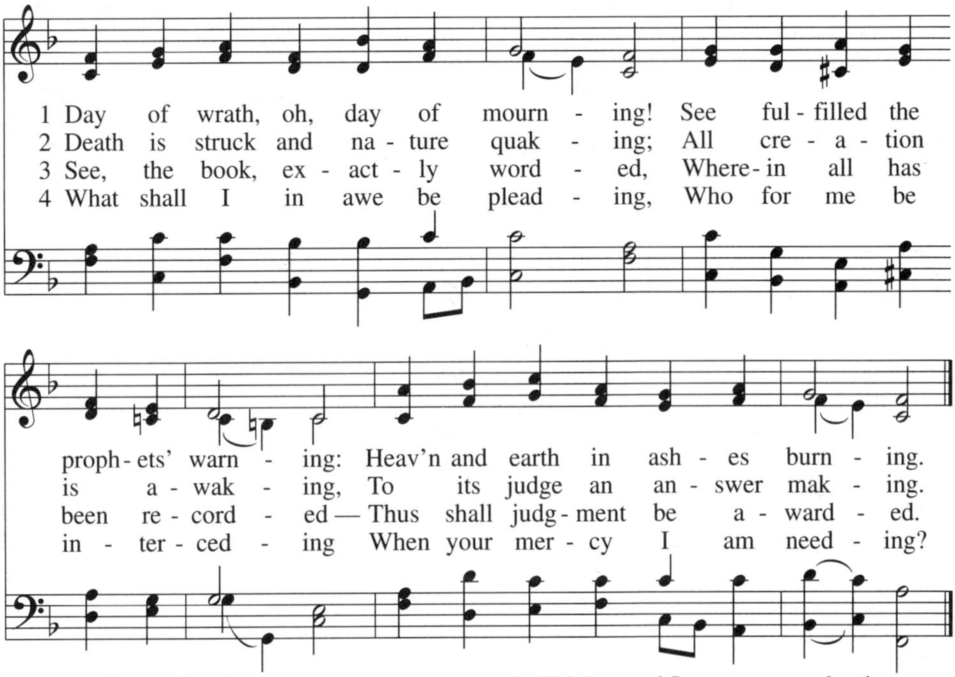

1 Day of wrath, oh, day of mourn - ing! See ful - filled the proph - ets' warn - ing: Heav'n and earth in ash - es burn - ing.
2 Death is struck and na - ture quak - ing; All cre - a - tion is a - wak - ing, To its judge an an - swer mak - ing.
3 See, the book, ex - act - ly word - ed, Where - in all has been re - cord - ed — Thus shall judg - ment be a - ward - ed.
4 What shall I in awe be plead - ing, Who for me be in - ter - ced - ing When your mer - cy I am need - ing?

5 King of majesty tremendous,
  Who does free salvation send us,
  Fount of pity, then befriend us.

6 Think, good Jesus — my salvation
  Caused your wondrous incarnation,
  Made you suffer my damnation!

7 On the cross your dying spared me;
  Just and righteous you declared me;
  I await the joy prepared me.

Text: attr. Thomas de Celano, c. 1190-c. 1260, abr., st. 1-6; Mark A. Jeske, b. 1952, st. 7;
tr. William J. Irons, 1812-83, st. 1-6, alt.
Tune: Latin melody, 13th century
Text st. 7 © 1993 Mark A. Jeske

DIES IRAE
888

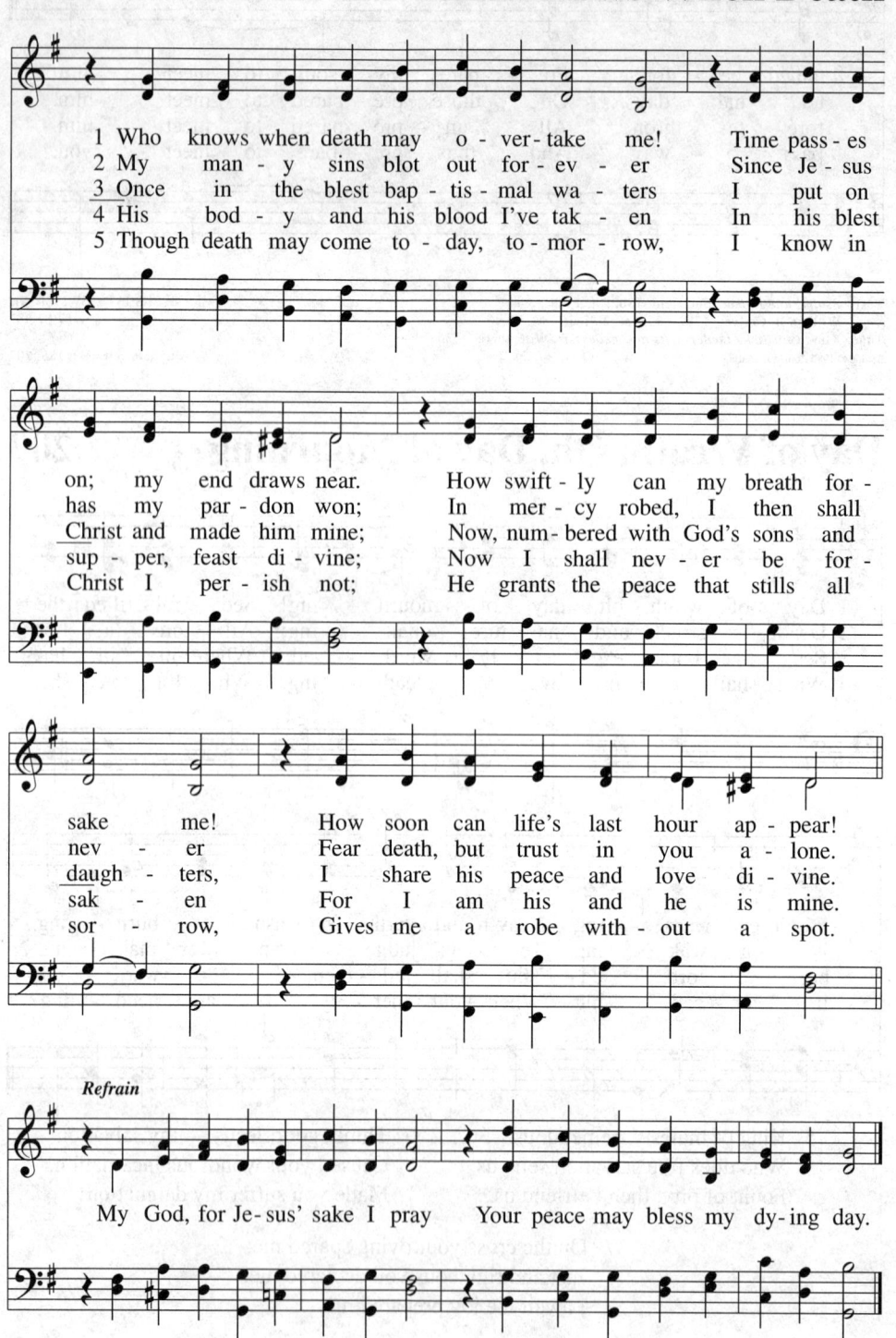

END TIME

212 — Jerusalem, Thou City Fair and High

1. Jerusalem, thou city fair and high,
   Would God I were in thee!
   My longing heart to thee would gladly fly;
   It will not stay with me.
   Far over vale and mountain,
   Far over field and plain,
   It hastes to thee again.

2. A moment's space, and gently, wondrously,
   Released from earthly ties,
   Elijah's chariot comes to carry me
   Through all these lower skies
   To yonder shining regions,
   While down to meet me come
   The blessed.

3. The patriarchs' and prophets' noble train,
   With all Christ's fol'wers true
   Who bore the cross and could the worst disdain
   That tyrants dared to do,
   I see them shine forever,
   All-glorious as the sun
   Mid light that.

4. Unnumbered choirs before the shining throne
   Their joyful anthems raise
   Till heaven's halls are echoing with the tone
   Of that great hymn of praise
   And all its host rejoices,
   And all its blessed throng
   Unite their.

END TIME

```
seek    its    foun -  tain    And  leave this   world  of    pain.
an -    gel    le -    gions   And  bid   me     wel -  come  home.
fa -    deth   nev -   er,     Their per - fect  free - dom   won.
myr -   iad    voic -  es      In   one   e -    ter -  nal   song.
```

Text: Johann M. Meyfart, 1590-1642, abr.; tr. Catherine Winkworth, 1827-78, alt.
Tune: *Christlich Neu-vermehrt . . . Gesangbuch*, Erfurt, 1663, alt.

JERUSALEM, DU HOCHGEBAUTE STADT
10 6 10 6 76 76

Forever with the Lord   213

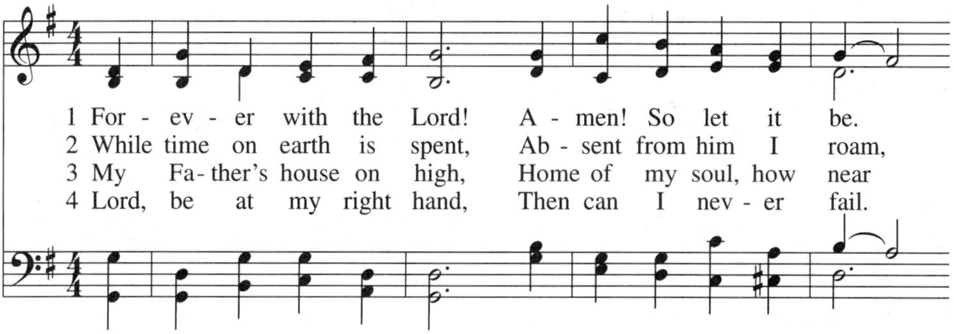

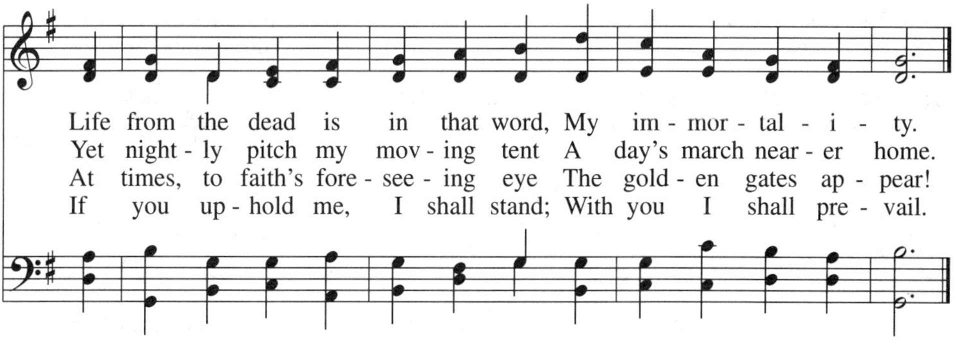

```
1 For - ev - er   with   the    Lord!  A - men! So   let  it   be.
2 While time on   earth  is     spent, Ab - sent from him I    roam,
3 My    Fa - ther's house on    high,  Home of   my   soul, how near
4 Lord, be   at   my     right  hand,  Then can  I    nev - er  fail.

Life  from  the   dead   is    in     that  word, My   im - mor - tal - i - ty.
Yet   night-ly    pitch  my    mov -  ing   tent  A    day's march near - er home.
At    times, to   faith's fore-see -  ing   eye   The  gold - en  gates ap - pear!
If    you   up -  hold   me,   I      shall stand; With you  I    shall pre - vail.
```

5 So when my dying breath
   Shall rend the veil in two,
   By death I shall escape from death
   To endless life with you.

6 I'll know as I am known;
   How shall I love that word
   And oft repeat before the throne,
   "Forever with the Lord!"

Text: James Montgomery, 1771-1854, abr., alt.
Tune: *Cantica Laudis,* Boston, 1850

SCHUMANN
SM

END TIME

Jerusalem, My Happy Home

215

5 O Christ, do thou my soul prepare
  For that bright home of love
  That I may see thee and adore
  With all thy saints above.

Text: F. B. P., 16th century, abr., alt.
Tune: American folk tune
Tune and Setting © 1938. Renewed 1966 J. Fischer & Bro.

LAND OF REST
CM

END TIME

The Head that Once Was Crowned 217

1. The head that once was crowned with thorns Is crowned with glory now; A royal diadem adorns The mighty victor's brow.
2. The highest place that heav'n affords Is his, is his by right, The King of kings and Lord of lords And heav'n's eternal light,
3. The joy of all who dwell above, The joy of all below To whom he manifests his love And grants his name to know.
4. To them the cross, with all its shame, With all its grace, is giv'n; Their name, an ever-lasting name; Their joy, the joy of heav'n.

5. They suffer with their Lord below;
They reign with him above,
Their profit and their joy, to know
The myst'ry of his love.

6. The cross he bore is life and health,
Though shame and death to him;
His people's hope, his people's wealth,
Their everlasting theme.

Text: Thomas Kelly, 1769-1855
Tune: Jeremiah Clarke, c. 1674-1707

ST. MAGNUS
CM

END TIME

218 Then the Glory

Then the glo-ry Then the rest Then the Sab-bath peace un-bro-ken

Then the gar-den Then the throne Then the crys-tal riv - er flow-ing

Then the splen-dor Then the life Then the new cre-a - tion sing-ing

Then the mar-riage Then the love Then the feast of joy un-end-ing

END TIME

Text: Jaroslav J. Vajda, b. 1919
Tune: Carl F. Schalk, b. 1929

NOW
78 78 78 78 78 87 63

Text © 1987 Hope Publishing Co.; Tune and Setting © 1969 Hope Publishing Co.

219. Lord, When Your Glory I Shall See

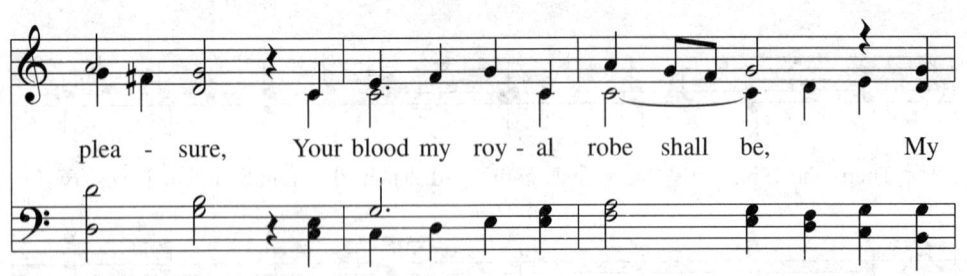

END TIME

Text: Paul Gerhardt, 1607-76, abr.; tr. *The Lutheran Hymnal,* St. Louis, 1941, alt.
Tune: Kurt J. Eggert, 1923-93

Tune and Setting © 1993 Kurt J. Eggert

WEDDING GLORY
87 87 887 887

OPENING OF SERVICE

222 Songs of Praise the Angels Sang

1. Songs of praise the angels sang,
Heav'n with alleluias rang,
When creation was begun,
When God spoke and it was done.

2. Songs of praise awoke the morn
When the Prince of Peace was born.
Songs of praise arose when he
Captive led captivity.

3. Heav'n and earth must pass away;
Songs of praise shall crown that day.
God will make new heav'ns and earth;
Songs of praise shall hail their birth.

4. And shall man alone be still?
Has he neither breath nor skill?
No, the Church delights to raise
Psalms and hymns and songs of praise.

5. Saints below, with heart and voice,
Still in songs of praise rejoice,
Learning here, by faith and love,
Songs of praise to sing above.

6. Whispered with their final breath,
Songs of praise shall conquer death.
Then, amidst eternal joy,
Songs of praise their pow'rs employ.

Text: James Montgomery, 1771-1854, alt.
Tune: French melody, 13th century

INNOCENTS
77 77

OPENING OF SERVICE

As We Begin Another Week 223

1 As we begin another week, In Jesus' name your grace we seek. God, grant that through these seven days No evil may befall our ways.
2 Your gentle blessings, Lord, outpour On all our labors evermore. Our hearts with your good Spirit fill That we may gladly do your will.
3 In ev-'ry season, ev-'ry place, May we recall your Word of grace Until, when life's brief day is past, We reach eternal joy at last
4 And keep with angels in your rest The endless Sabbath of the blest. Grant this to us through Christ, your Son, Who reigns with you upon your throne.

Text: Martin Wandersleben, 1608-68, abr.; tr. W. Gustave Polack, 1890-1950, alt.
Tune: *As hymnodus sacer,* Leipzig, 1625, alt.

Text © 1941 Concordia Publishing House

HERR JESU CHRIST, MEINS
LM
Alternate settings: 404, 547

OPENING OF SERVICE

224 God Himself Is Present

1 God himself is present— Let us now adore him
And with awe appear before him.
God is in his temple— All within keep silence,
Humbly kneel in deepest rev'rence.

2 God himself is present— Hear the harps resounding;
See the hosts the throne surrounding.
"Holy, holy, holy"— Hear the hymn ascending,
Songs of saints and angels blending.

3 Fount of ev'ry blessing, Purify my spirit,
Trusting only in your merit.
Like the holy angels, Worshiping before you,
May I ceaselessly adore you.

OPENING OF SERVICE

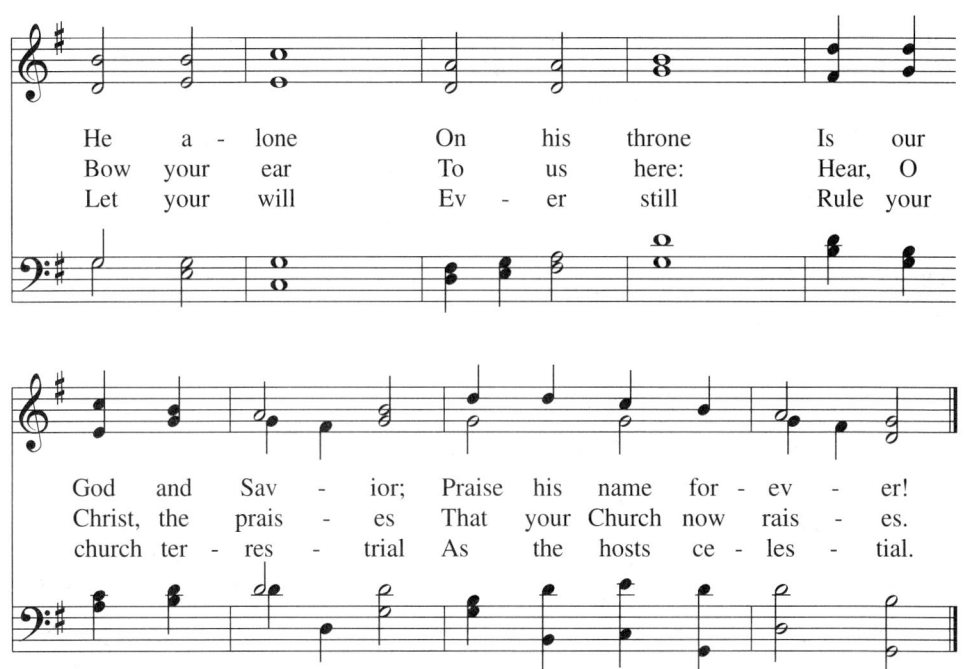

Text: Gerhard Tersteegen, 1697-1769, abr.;
tr. Frederick W. Foster, 1760-1835, and John Miller, 1756-90, alt.
Tune: Joachim Neander, 1650-80, alt.

WUNDERBARER KÖNIG
668 668 33 66

OPENING OF SERVICE

225 This Is the Day the Lord Has Made

1 This is the day the Lord has made; He
calls the hours his own. Let heav'n rejoice; let
earth be glad And praise surround the throne.

2 Today he rose and left the dead, And
Satan's empire fell; Today the saints his
triumphs spread And all his wonders tell.

3 Hosanna to the anointed King, To
David's holy Son! Help us, O Lord; descend and bring
Salvation from the throne.

4 Blessed is Jesus Christ, who came With
messages of grace, Who came in God the
Father's name To save our sinful race.

5 Hosanna in the highest strains
  The Church on earth shall raise;
  The highest heav'ns, in which he reigns,
  Shall give him nobler praise.

Text: Isaac Watts, 1674-1748, alt.
Tune: Johann Crüger, 1598-1662

NUN DANKET ALL
CM

Alternate settings: 227, 512

OPENING OF SERVICE

To Your Temple I Draw Near 226

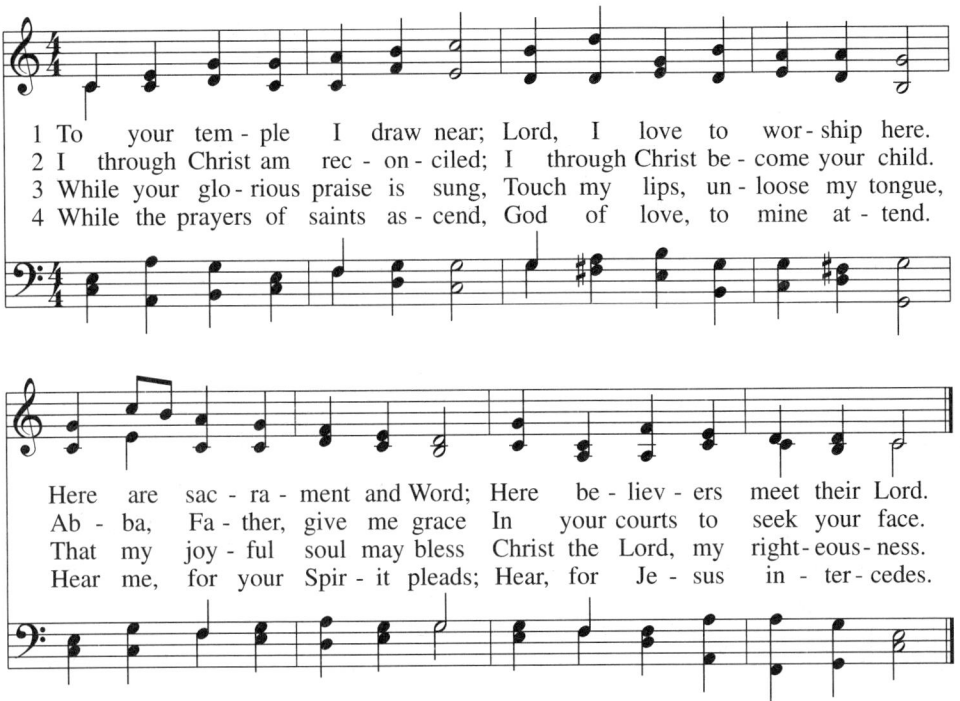

1 To your tem-ple I draw near; Lord, I love to wor-ship here.
2 I through Christ am rec-on-ciled; I through Christ be-come your child.
3 While your glo-rious praise is sung, Touch my lips, un-loose my tongue,
4 While the prayers of saints as-cend, God of love, to mine at-tend.

Here are sac-ra-ment and Word; Here be-liev-ers meet their Lord.
Ab-ba, Fa-ther, give me grace In your courts to seek your face.
That my joy-ful soul may bless Christ the Lord, my right-eous-ness.
Hear me, for your Spir-it pleads; Hear, for Je-sus in-ter-cedes.

5 While I listen to your law,
　Fill my soul with holy awe
　Till your gospel brings to me
　Life and immortality.

6 While your ministers proclaim
　Peace and pardon in your name,
　Through their voice, by faith, may I
　Hear you speaking from the sky.

7 From your house, when I return,
　May my heart within me burn,
　And at evening let me say,
　"I have walked with God today."

Text: James Montgomery, 1771-1854, alt.
Tune: Freylinghausen, *Geist-reiches Gesang-Buch,* Halle, 1704, alt.

GOTT SEI DANK DURCH ALLE WELT
77 77

Alternate setting: 76

OPENING OF SERVICE

227 Come, Let Us Join Our Cheerful Songs

1 Come, let us join our cheerful songs With angels round the throne. Ten thousand thousand are their tongues, But all their joys are one.
2 "Worthy the Lamb that died," they cry, "To be exalted thus." "Worthy the Lamb," our lips reply, "For he was slain for us."
3 Jesus is worthy to receive Honor and pow'r divine; And blessings more than we can give Be, Lord, forever thine.
4 Let all creation join in one To bless the sacred name Of him who sits upon the throne And to adore the Lamb.

Text: Isaac Watts, 1674-1748, abr., alt.
Tune: Johann Crüger, 1598-1662

NUN DANKET ALL
CM

Alternate settings: 225, 512

OPENING OF SERVICE

229 This Day at Your Creating Word

1 This day at your creating word First o'er the earth the light was poured: O Lord, this day upon us shine, And fill our souls with light divine.

2 This day the Lord for sinners slain In might victorious rose again: O Jesus, raise your people, too, From death of sin to life in you.

3 This day the Holy Spirit came With fiery tongues of cloven flame: O Spirit, fill our hearts this day With grace to hear and grace to pray.

4 This day of light and life and grace We gather in our worship-place: This holy hour, blest gift of love, Give we again to God above.

5 All praise to God the Father be,
To Christ, who set his people free,
Whom with the Spirit we adore
Forever and forevermore.

Text: William W. How, 1823-97, alt.
Tune: *Musicalisch Hand-Buch der Geistlichen Melodien*, Hamburg, 1690, alt.
Setting © 1993 Elfred Bloedel

WINCHESTER NEW
LM
Alternate settings: 133, 607

OPENING OF SERVICE

Lord Jesus Christ, Be Present Now 230

1 Lord Jesus Christ, be present now; Our hearts in
  true devotion bow. Your Spirit send with
  grace divine, And let your truth within us shine.

2 Unseal our lips to sing your praise; Our souls to
  you in worship raise. Make strong our faith; increase our light That we may know your name aright.

3 Until we join the hosts that cry, "Hosanna
  to the Lord most high." Then in the light of
  that blest place We shall behold you face to face.

4 Glory to God the Father, Son, And Holy
  Spirit, Three in One! To you, O blessed
  Trinity, Be praise throughout eternity!

Text: *Lutherische Hand-Büchlein,* 2nd ed., Altenburg, 1648;
    tr. Catherine Winkworth, 1827-78, alt.
Tune: *Cantionale Germanicum,* Gochsheim, 1628

HERR JESU CHRIST, DICH ZU UNS WEND
LM

Alternate settings: 71, 288

OPENING OF SERVICE

231 **Now the Silence**

OPENING OF SERVICE

Text: Jaroslav J. Vajda, b. 1919
Tune: Carl F. Schalk, b. 1929
Text, Tune, Setting © 1969 Hope Publishing Co.

NOW
78 78 78 78 78 87 63

WORSHIP AND PRAISE

All People that on Earth Do Dwell 233

1 All people that on earth do dwell, Sing to the Lord with cheerful voice. Him serve with fear; his praise forthtell; Come ye before him and rejoice.
2 Know that the Lord is God indeed; Without our aid he did us make. We are his folk; he doth us feed, And for his sheep he doth us take.
3 Oh, enter then his gates with praise; Approach with joy his courts unto. Praise, laud, and bless his name always, For it is seemly so to do.
4 For why? The Lord, our God, is good; His mercy is forever sure. His truth at all times firmly stood And shall from age to age endure.

5 To Father, Son, and Holy Ghost,
The God whom heav'n and earth adore,
From us and from the angel host
Be praise and glory evermore.

Text: William Kethe, d. c. 1593, alt.
Tune: *Trente quatre Pseaumes de David,* Geneva, 1551
Setting © 1982 Concordia Publishing House

OLD HUNDREDTH
LM
Alternate settings: 286, 323

234 Praise to the Lord, the Almighty

WORSHIP AND PRAISE

Text: Joachim Neander, 1650-80; tr. composite
Tune: *Ander Theil Des Erneuerten Gesang-Buchs*, Stralsund, 1665, alt.;
  Desc. Craig Sellar Lang, 1891-1971
Descant © 1953 Novello & Company Ltd.

LOBE DEN HERREN
14 14 478

WORSHIP AND PRAISE

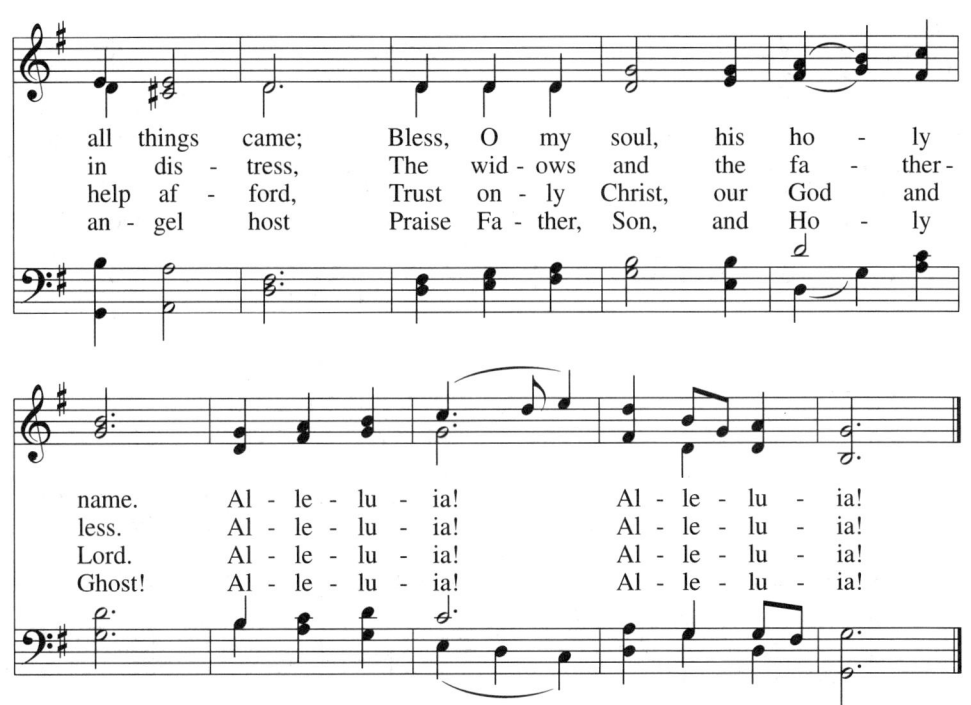

Text: Johann D. Herrnschmidt, 1675-1723, abr.; tr. Alfred E. R. Brauer, 1866-1949, alt.
Tune: *New-vermehrte Christliche Seelenharpf,* Ansbach, 1665, alt.

LOBE DEN HERREN, O MEINE SEELE
10 8 10 8 88 8

Text © 1941 Concordia Publishing House

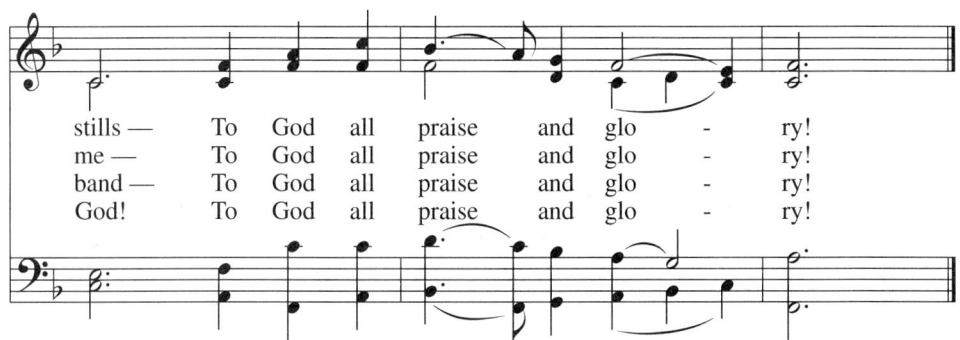

stills —	To God all praise and glory!
me —	To God all praise and glory!
band —	To God all praise and glory!
God!	To God all praise and glory!

5 Then come before his presence now
    And banish fear and sadness;
  To your Redeemer pay your vow
    And sing with joy and gladness.
  Though great distress my soul befell,
    The Lord my God did all things well —
  To God all praise and glory!

Text: Johann J. Schütz, 1640-90, abr.; tr. composite
Tune: Melchior Vulpius, c. 1570-1615

LOBT GOTT DEN HERREN, IHR HEIDEN ALL
87 87 887

WORSHIP AND PRAISE

see: Lord   of   might   and   maj - es - ty.
claim!   Lord   of   all,   we   praise your name!
days!   Lord   of   life,   we   sing   your praise.
true.   Lord   of   lords,   we   wor - ship you!

Text: Margaret Stinton, b. 1924
Tune: John Hughes, 1873-1932

CWM RHONDDA
87 87 877

Text © 1982 Margaret Stinton

Alternate setting: 523

Oh, Bless the Lord, My Soul

1 Oh, bless the Lord, my soul! Let all with-in me join
2 Oh, bless the Lord, my soul, Nor let his mer-cies lie
3 'Tis he for-gives my sins; 'Tis he re-lieves my pain;
4 He fills the poor with good; He gives the suf-f'rers rest;
5 His won-drous works and ways He made by Mo-ses known,

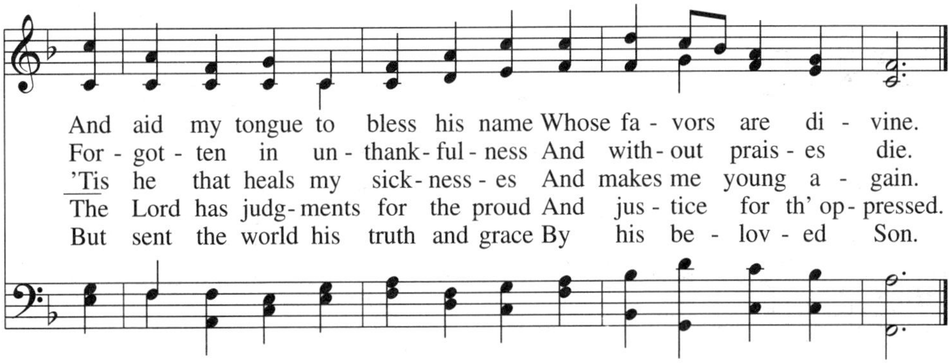

And aid my tongue to bless his name Whose fa-vors are di - vine.
For - got - ten in un - thank-ful-ness And with-out prais-es die.
'Tis he that heals my sick-ness-es And makes me young a-gain.
The Lord has judg-ments for the proud And jus-tice for th' op-pressed.
But sent the world his truth and grace By his be - lov - ed Son.

Text: Isaac Watts, 1674-1748, abr., alt.
Tune: Aaron Williams, 1731-76

ST. THOMAS
SM

Alternate settings: 1, 533

WORSHIP AND PRAISE

239 Glory Be to God the Father

1. Glory be to God the Father, Glory be to God the Son, Glory be to God the Spirit, Great Jehovah, Three in One! Glory, glory While eternal ages run!
2. Glory be to him who loved us, Washed us from each spot and stain; Glory be to him who bought us, Made us kings with him to reign! Glory, glory To the Lamb that once was slain!
3. Glory to the King of angels, Glory to the Church's King, Glory to the King of nations; Heav'n and earth, your praises bring! Glory, glory To the King of glory sing!
4. Glory, blessing, praise eternal! — Thus the choir of angels sings; Honor, riches, pow'r, dominion! — Thus its praise creation brings. Glory, glory, Glory to the King of kings!

Text: Horatius Bonar, 1808-89, alt.
Tune: Walter G. Whinfield, 1865-1919

WORCESTER
87 87 47

WORSHIP AND PRAISE

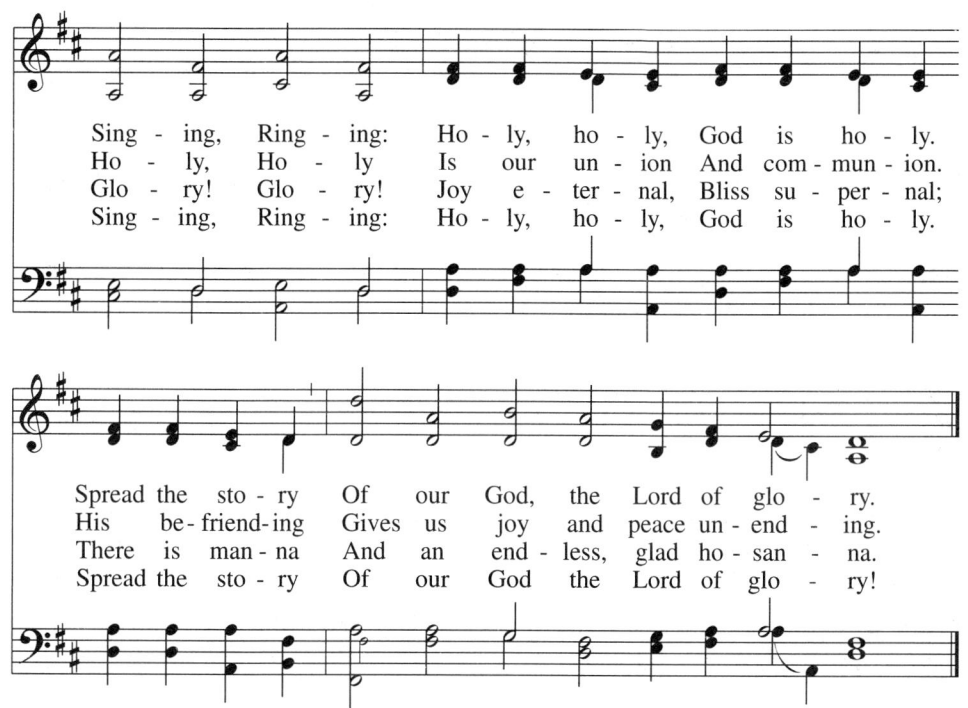

Sing - ing, Ring - ing: Ho - ly, ho - ly, God is ho - ly.
Ho - ly, Ho - ly Is our un - ion And com - mun - ion.
Glo - ry! Glo - ry! Joy e - ter - nal, Bliss su - per - nal;
Sing - ing, Ring - ing: Ho - ly, ho - ly, God is ho - ly.

Spread the sto - ry Of our God, the Lord of glo - ry.
His be - friend-ing Gives us joy and peace un - end - ing.
There is man - na And an end - less, glad ho - san - na.
Spread the sto - ry Of our God the Lord of glo - ry!

Text: *Geistreiches Gesangbuch,* Darmstadt, 1698; tr. composite
Tune: Philipp Nicolai, 1556-1608, alt.

WIE SCHÖN LEUCHTET
887 887 22 44 48

Alternate setting: 49

244 Arise, My Soul, Arise

1 A-rise, my soul, a-rise! Stretch forth to things e-ter-nal,
2 Now hear the harps of heav'n! Oh, hear the song vic-to-rious,

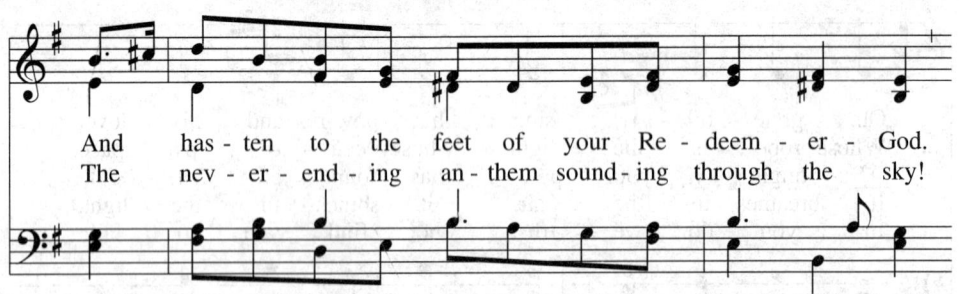

And has-ten to the feet of your Re-deem-er-God.
The nev-er-end-ing an-them sound-ing through the sky!

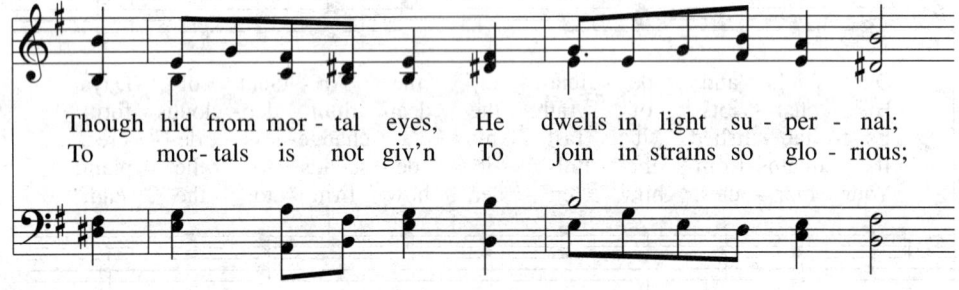

Though hid from mor-tal eyes, He dwells in light su-per-nal;
To mor-tals is not giv'n To join in strains so glo-rious;

Yet wor-ship him in hum-ble-ness and call him Lord.
Yet here on earth we, too, can sing our prais-es high!

WORSHIP AND PRAISE

Text: Johan Kahl, 1721-46; tr. Ernest E. Ryden, 1886-1981, alt.
Tune: Finnish folk tune, 19th century

NYT YLÖS, SIELUNI
PM

Text and Setting © 1958 *Service Book and Hymnal*

WORSHIP AND PRAISE

245 Sing a New Song to the Lord

1. Sing a new song to the Lord, He to whom wonders belong! Rejoice in his triumph and tell of his pow'r! Oh, sing to the Lord a new song!
2. Now to the ends of the earth, See, his salvation is shown, And still he remembers his mercy and truth, Unchanging in love to his own.
3. Sing a new song and rejoice! Publish his praises abroad! Let voices in chorus, with trumpet and horn, Resound for the joy of the Lord!
4. Join with the hills and the sea Thunders of praise to prolong! In judgment and justice he comes to the earth. Oh, sing to the Lord a new song!

Text: Timothy Dudley-Smith, b. 1926
Tune: David G. Wilson, b. 1940

CANTATE DOMINO
77 11 8

Text and Tune © 1973 Hope Publishing Co.; Setting © 1993 Hope Publishing Co.

WORSHIP AND PRAISE

The Stars Declare His Glory   246

1 The stars declare his glory; The vault of heaven springs— Mute witness of the Master's hand In all created things— And through the silences of space Their soundless music sings.

2 The dawn returns in splendor, The heavens burn and blaze, The rising sun renews the race That measures all our days And writes in fire across the skies God's majesty and praise.

3 So shine the Holy Scriptures To make the simple wise, More sweet than honey to the taste, More rich than any prize, His Word of love within our hearts, His light before our eyes.

4 So order, too, this life of mine; Direct it all my days. The meditations of my heart Be innocence and praise, My Rock and my redeeming Lord, In all my words and ways.

Text: Timothy Dudley-Smith, b. 1926, alt.
Tune: Richard T. Proulx, b. 1937

ALDINE
Irregular

Text © 1981 Hope Publishing Co.; Tune © 1986 GIA Publications, Inc.; Setting © 1993 Elfred Bloedel

WORSHIP AND PRAISE

5 Children of God,
    Dying and rising,
  Sing to the Lord a new song!
    Heaven and earth,
  Hosts everlasting,
    Sing to the Lord a new song! *Refrain*

Text: Herbert F. Brokering, b. 1926, abr.
Tune: David N. Johnson, 1922-87

EARTH AND ALL STARS
457 457 with Refrain

Text, Tune, Setting © 1968 Augsburg Publishing House

WORSHIP AND PRAISE

248 When in Our Music God Is Glorified

WORSHIP AND PRAISE

5 Let ev'ry instrument be tuned for praise;
  Let all rejoice who have a voice to raise,
  And may God give us faith to sing always:
  Alleluia!

Text: Fred Pratt Green, b. 1903, alt.
Tune: Charles V. Stanford, 1852-1924

ENGELBERG
10 10 10 with Alleluia

Text © 1972 Hope Publishing Co.

God of Mercy, God of Grace 249

1 God of mercy, God of grace, Show the brightness of your face.
  Shine upon us, Savior, shine; Fill your Church with light divine,
  And your saving health extend To the earth's remotest end.

2 Let the people praise you, Lord! Be by all that live adored.
  Let the nations shout and sing Glory to their Savior King,
  At your feet their tribute pay, And your holy will obey.

3 Let the people praise you, Lord, Then enjoy your rich reward!
  God to us his blessing give, We to God devoted live,
  All below and all above One in joy and light and love.

Text: Henry F. Lyte, 1793-1847, alt.
Tune: attr. Johann G. Werner, 1777-1822

RATISBON
77 77 77

WORSHIP AND PRAISE

Text: Isaac Watts, 1674-1748, alt.
Tune: *Ausserlesene, Catholische, Geistliche Kirchengesäng*, Köln, 1623, alt.

Setting reprinted by permission of Oxford University Press

LASST UNS ERFREUEN
888 888 with Alleluias

WORSHIP AND PRAISE

251 When Morning Gilds the Skies

1. When morning gilds the skies, My heart, awaking, cries, "May Jesus Christ be praised!" When evening shadows fall, Then sounds my vesper call: "May Jesus Christ be praised!"
2. When mirth for music longs, This is my song of songs: "May Jesus Christ be praised!" God's holy house of prayer Has none that can compare With "Jesus Christ be praised."
3. Let all of humankind In this their concord find: "May Jesus Christ be praised!" Let all the earth around Ring joyous with the sound: "May Jesus Christ be praised!"
4. Sing, sun and stars of space; Sing, all who see his face; Sing, "Jesus Christ be praised!" God's whole creation o'er, Today and evermore, Sing, "Jesus Christ be praised!"

Text: *Katholisches Gesangbuch*, Würzburg, 1828, abr.; tr. Robert S. Bridges, 1844-1930, alt.
Tune: Joseph Barnby, 1838-96

LAUDES DOMINI
666 666

Oh, Sing to the Lord

252

WORSHIP AND PRAISE

1 Oh, sing to the Lord; make a jubilant noise! Glory be to God! Oh, serve him with joy; in his presence now rejoice! Sing praise unto God out of Zion!
2 Not we, but the Lord is our Maker, our God; Glory be to God! His people we are, and the sheep led by his rod; Sing praise unto God out of Zion!
3 Oh, enter his gates with thanksgiving and praise; Glory be to God! To bless him and thank him our voices we will raise; Sing praise unto God out of Zion!
4 For good is the Lord, and his mercy is sure; Glory be to God! To all generations his truth shall still endure; Sing praise unto God out of Zion!

Text: Ulrik V. Koren, 1826-1910; tr. Harriet R. K. Spaeth, 1845-1925, alt.
Tune: Erik C. Hoff, 1832-94

GUDS MENIGHED, SYNG
11 5 12 9

WORSHIP AND PRAISE

Text: Paul Gerhardt, 1607-76, abr.; tr. composite
Tune: Johann Schop, c. 1590-1667, alt.
Setting © 1989 Ronald L. Shilling

SOLLT ICH MEINEM GOTT NICHT SINGEN
87 87 87 78 77

WORSHIP AND PRAISE

Text: Stuart W. K. Hine, 1899-1989
Tune: Swedish folk tune

Text, Tune, Setting © 1953. Renewed 1981 by Manna Music, Inc.

HOW GREAT THOU ART
11 10 11 10 with Refrain

WORSHIP AND PRAISE

Text: Johann Gramann, 1487-1541, abr.; tr. Catherine Winkworth, 1827-78, alt.
Tune: *Concentus novi*, Augsburg, 1540, alt.

NUN LOB, MEIN SEEL
78 78 76 76 76 76

Alternate setting: 403

WORSHIP AND PRAISE

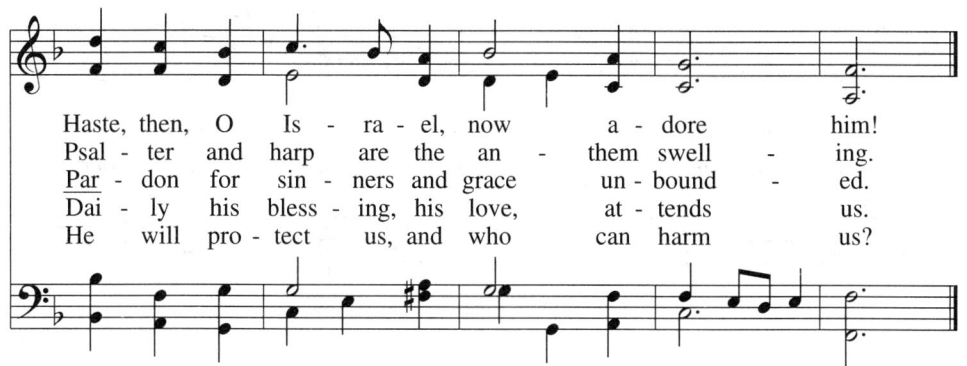

Haste, then, O Is - ra - el, now a - dore him!
Psal - ter and harp are the an - them swell - ing.
Par - don for sin - ners and grace un - bound - ed.
Dai - ly his bless - ing, his love, at - tends us.
He will pro - tect us, and who can harm us?

Text: Matthäus Apelles von Löwenstern, 1594-1648; tr. Catherine Winkworth, 1827-78, alt.
Tune: Matthäus Apelles von Löwenstern, 1594-1648, alt.

NUN PREISET ALLE
56 56 9 10 10

When All Your Mercies, O My God 259

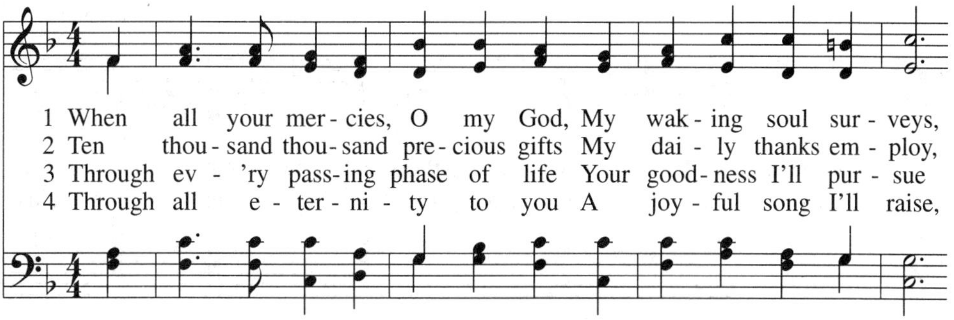

1 When all your mer - cies, O my God, My wak - ing soul sur - veys,
2 Ten thou - sand thou - sand pre - cious gifts My dai - ly thanks em - ploy,
3 Through ev - 'ry pass - ing phase of life Your good - ness I'll pur - sue
4 Through all e - ter - ni - ty to you A joy - ful song I'll raise,

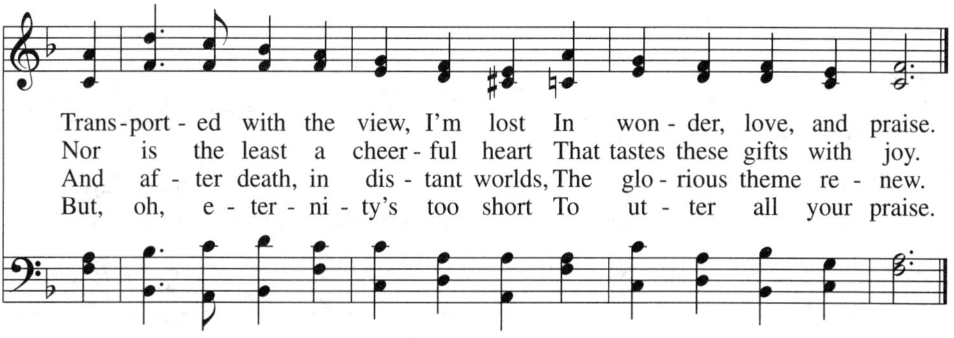

Trans - port - ed with the view, I'm lost In won - der, love, and praise.
Nor is the least a cheer - ful heart That tastes these gifts with joy.
And af - ter death, in dis - tant worlds, The glo - rious theme re - new.
But, oh, e - ter - ni - ty's too short To ut - ter all your praise.

Text: Joseph Addison, 1672-1719, abr., alt.
Tune: attr. George Kirbye, c. 1560-1634

WINCHESTER OLD
CM

WORSHIP AND PRAISE

260 Let All Things Now Living

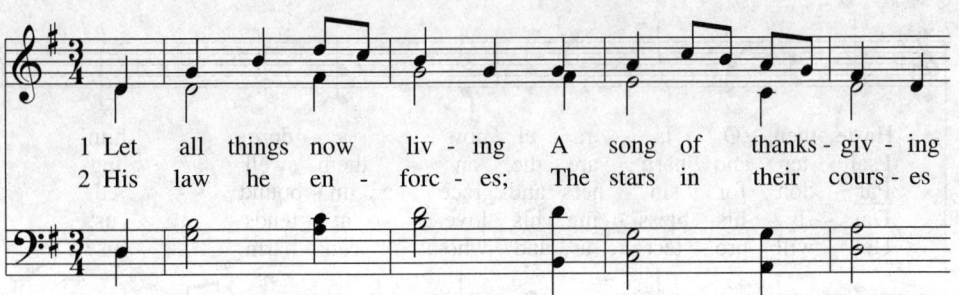

1 Let all things now living A song of thanks-giv-ing
2 His law he en - forc - es; The stars in their cours - es

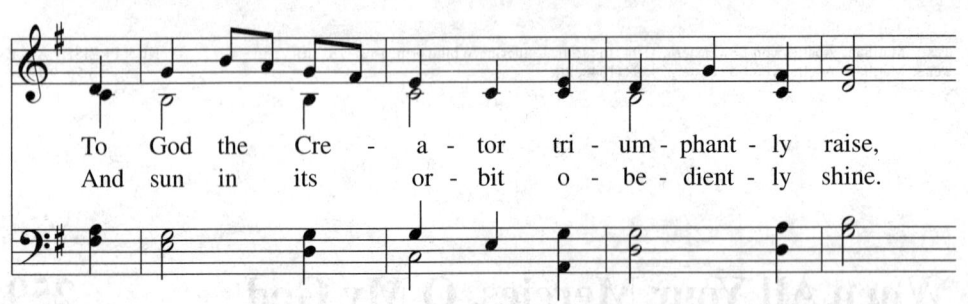

To God the Cre - a - tor tri - um - phant - ly raise,
And sun in its or - bit o - be - dient - ly shine.

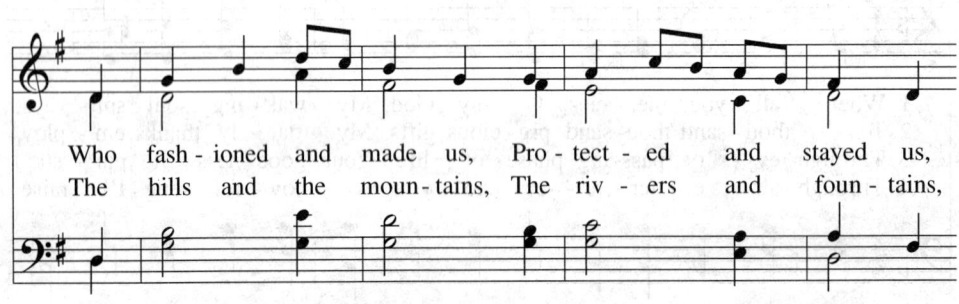

Who fash-ioned and made us, Pro - tect - ed and stayed us,
The hills and the moun-tains, The riv - ers and foun-tains,

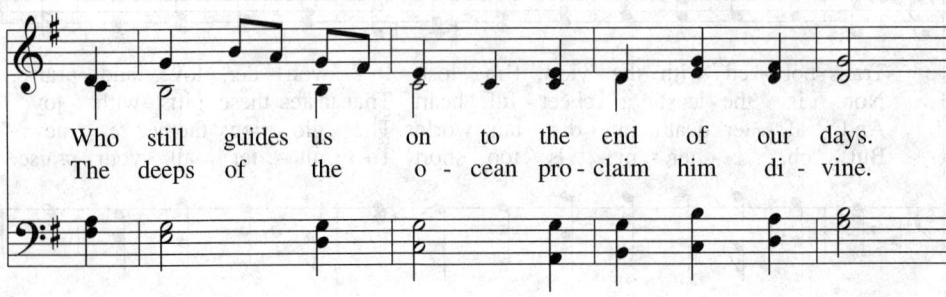

Who still guides us on to the end of our days.
The deeps of the o - cean pro - claim him di - vine.

WORSHIP AND PRAISE

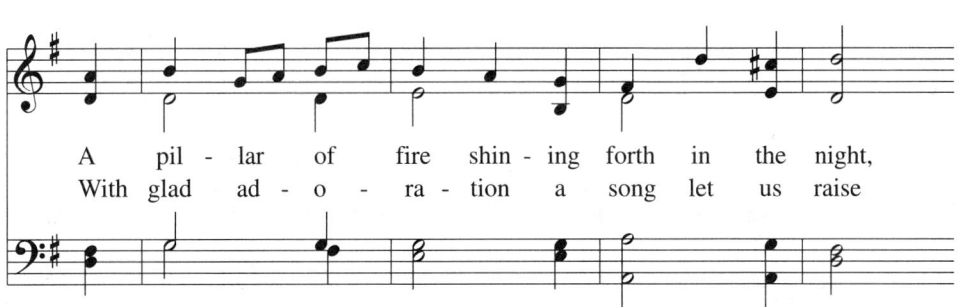

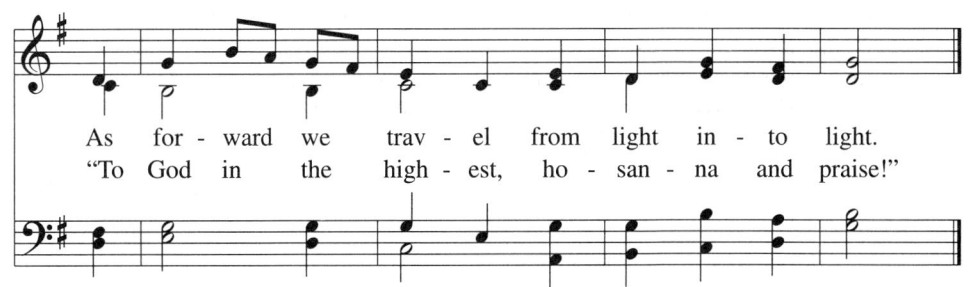

Text: Katherine K. Davis, 1892-1980, alt.
Tune: Welsh folk tune

THE ASH GROVE
66 11 66 11 D

Text © 1939. Renewed 1966 by E. C. Schirmer Music Co.; Setting © 1978 *Lutheran Book of Worship*

Alternate setting: 318

WORSHIP AND PRAISE

261 We Sing the Almighty Power of God

1. We sing th' almighty pow'r of God, Who made the mountains rise, Who spread the flowing seas abroad And built the lofty skies.
2. We sing the wisdom that ordained The sun to rule the day; The moon shines, too, at his command, And all the stars obey.
3. We sing the goodness of the Lord, Who fills the earth with food, Who formed the creatures by a word And then pronounced them good.
4. Lord, how your wonders are displayed Each time we turn our eyes To view the ground on which we tread Or gaze upon the skies.

5 There's not a plant or flow'r below
But makes your glories known,
And clouds arise and tempests blow
By order from your throne.

6 On you each moment we depend;
If you withdraw, we die.
Oh, may we never God offend,
Who is forever nigh!

Text: Isaac Watts, 1674-1748, alt.
Tune: *Harmonischer Lieder-Schatz,* Frankfurt, 1738, alt.

ICH SINGE DIR
CM

Alternate setting: 443

263 All Glory Be to God on High
Gloria in Excelsis

1. All glory be to God on high, Who has our race befriended! To us no harm shall now come nigh; The strife at last is ended. The Father's love, the Savior's birth, Bring peace, good will, to all the earth; Oh, thank him for his goodness!

2. We praise, we worship you, we trust; We give you thanks forever, O Father, that your rule is just And wise and changes never. In boundless pow'r, with mighty reign, Done is whatever you ordain; Your rule brings countless blessings!

3. O Jesus Christ, the only Son Of God, your heav'nly Father, You did for all our sins atone, And your lost sheep you gather. O Lamb of God, to you on high From depths of woe we sinners cry, Have mercy on us, Jesus!

4. O Holy Spirit, precious Gift, Our Comforter from heaven, Our weary hearts and souls uplift; For this our praise is given. Deliver us from doubt and fear; When Satan troubles us, be near; We trust your love and power.

Text: Nikolaus Decius, c. 1485-after 1546, abr., st. 1-3; Mark A. Jeske, b. 1952, st. 4;
tr. Catherine Winkworth, 1827-78, st. 1-3, alt.
Tune: attr. Nikolaus Decius, c. 1485-after 1546, alt.
Text st.4 © 1993 Mark A. Jeske; Setting © 1978 *Lutheran Book of Worship*
Alternate *Song of Praise*, pp. 16, 28, 39

ALLEIN GOTT IN DER HÖH SEI EHR
87 87 887

Alternate setting: 69

Glory Be to God in Heaven
Gloria in Excelsis

264

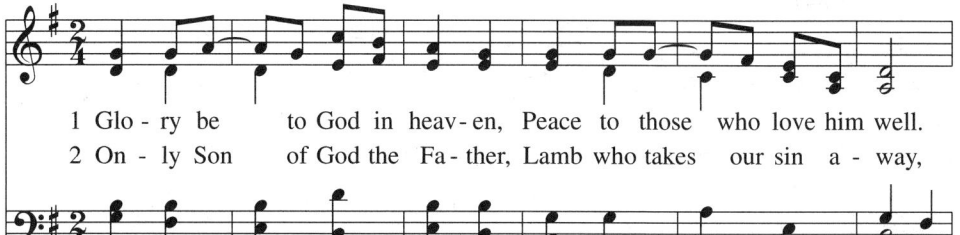

1 Glo-ry be to God in heav-en, Peace to those who love him well.
2 On-ly Son of God the Fa-ther, Lamb who takes our sin a-way,

On the earth let all his peo-ple Speak his grace, his won-ders tell:
Now with him in tri-umph seat-ed—For your mer-cy, Lord, we pray:

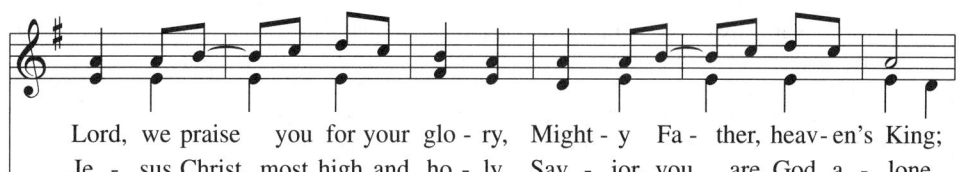

Lord, we praise you for your glo-ry, Might-y Fa-ther, heav-en's King;
Je-sus Christ, most high and ho-ly, Sav-ior, you are God a-lone

Hear our joy-ful ad-o-ra-tion, And ac-cept the thanks we bring.
In the glo-ry of the Fa-ther With the Spir-it, Three in One!

Text: Michael A. Perry, b. 1942
Tune: Ronald Arnatt, b. 1930
Text © 1982 Hope Publishing Co.; Tune © 1971 Walton Music Corporation; Setting © 1993 Elfred Bloedel

LADUE CHAPEL
87 87 D

Alternate *Song of Praise*, pp. 16, 28, 39

265 This Is the Feast of Victory
Dignus est Agnus

Refrain

This is the feast of vic-to-ry for our God,

Al-le-lu - ia, al-le-lu - ia, al-le-lu - ia!

1 Wor-thy is Christ, the Lamb who was slain, Whose
2 Pow - er, rich - es, wis - dom, and strength, And
3 Sing with all the peo - ple of God, And
4 Bless - ing, hon - or, glo - ry, and might Be to
5 For the Lamb who was slain Has be-

Refrain

blood set us free to be peo - ple of God.
hon - or, bless - ing, and glo - ry are his.
join in the hymn of all cre - a - tion.
God and the Lamb for - ev - er. A - men.
gun his reign. Al - le - lu - ia!

Text: John W. Arthur, 1922-80
Tune: Richard W. Hillert, b. 1923
Text © 1978 *Lutheran Book of Worship;* Tune and Setting © 1975, 1988 Richard Hillert

Alternate *Song of Praise,* pp. 16, 28, 39

FESTIVAL CANTICLE
Irregular with Refrain

266 Kyrie, God Father in Heaven Above
Kyrie

HYMNS OF THE LITURGY

Text: Latin trope, 9th century; German version, Wittenberg, 1541;
tr. W. Gustave Polack, 1890-1950, alt.
Tune: Plainsong melody, c. 800, adapt.
Text © 1941 Concordia Publishing House; Setting © 1993 Kermit G. Moldenhauer
May be sung in place of *Lord, Have Mercy,* pp. 15, 27

KYRIE, GOTT VATER
PM

HYMNS OF THE LITURGY

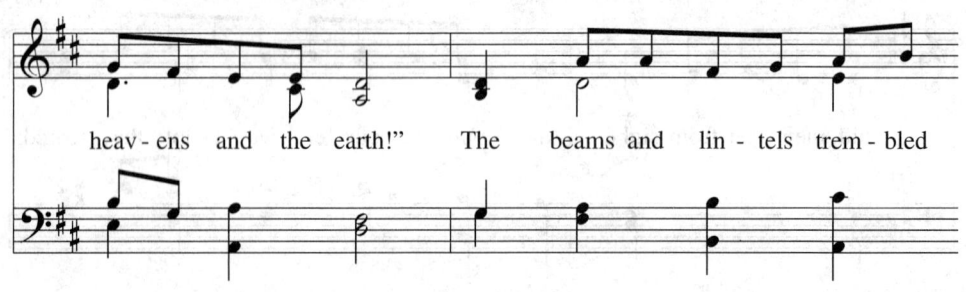

Text: Martin Luther, 1483-1546; tr. *The Lutheran Hymnal,* St. Louis, 1941, alt.
Tune: Martin Luther, 1483-1546, alt.
Setting © 1982 Concordia Publishing House

JESAIA, DEM PROPHETEN
PM

May be sung in place of *Holy, Holy, Holy,* pp. 22, 34

HYMNS OF THE LITURGY

Lamb of God, Pure and Holy 268
Agnus Dei

Stanzas 1, 2, 3

Lamb of God, pure and ho - ly, Who on the cross did suf - fer,

Ev - er pa - tient and low - ly, Your-self to scorn did of - fer.

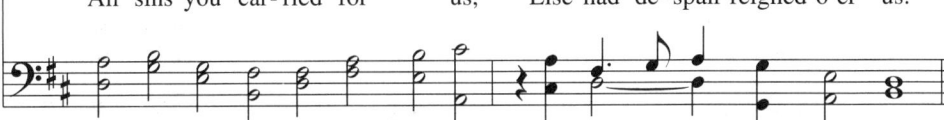

All sins you car-ried for us, Else had de-spair reigned o'er us:

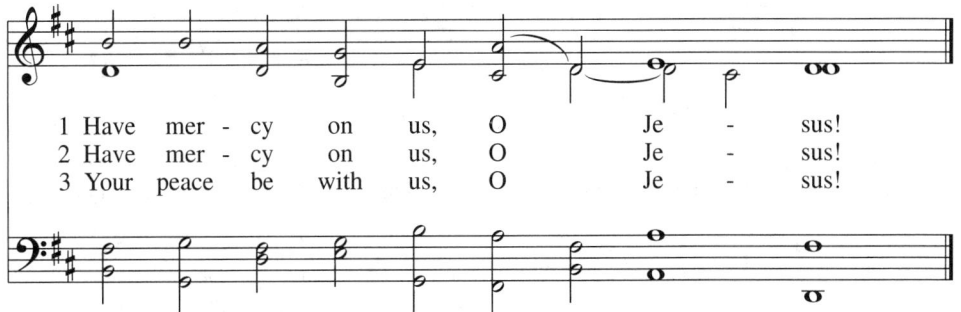

1 Have mer - cy on us, O Je - sus!
2 Have mer - cy on us, O Je - sus!
3 Your peace be with us, O Je - sus!

Text: Nikolaus Decius, c. 1485-after 1546; tr. composite
Tune: Nikolaus Decius, c. 1486-after 1546

O LAMM GOTTES, UNSCHULDIG
77 77 778

May be sung in place of *O Christ, Lamb of God*, pp. 23, 35

271. We All Believe in One True God
Credo

1. We all believe in one true God, Who created earth and heaven, The Father, who to us in love Has the right of children given. He in soul and body feeds us; All we need his hand provides us.

2. We all believe in Jesus Christ, His own Son, our Lord, possessing An equal Godhead, throne and might, Source of ev'ry grace and blessing, Born of Mary, virgin mother, By the power of the Spirit,

3. We all confess the Holy Ghost, Who, sweet hope and comfort giving, Now with the Father and the Son In eternal light is living, Who the Church, his own creation, Keeps in unity of spirit;

HYMNS OF THE LITURGY

He through snares and perils leads us, Watching that no harm betides us. He cares for us by day and night; All things are governed by his might.

Made true man, our elder brother, That the lost might life inherit, Was crucified by sinful men And raised by God to life again.

Here forgiveness and salvation Daily come through Jesus' merit. All flesh shall rise, and we shall be In bliss with God eternally.

Text: Martin Luther, 1483-1546; tr. composite
Tune: Latin credo melody, 14th century, adapt.
Setting © 1982 Concordia Publishing House

The Creed in song, pp. 18, 31, 41

WIR GLAUBEN ALL AN EINEN GOTT
88 88 88 88 88

HYMNS OF THE LITURGY

272 Create in Me a Clean Heart, O God

Create in me a clean heart, O God, and renew a right spirit within me. Cast me not away from your presence, and take not your Holy Spirit from me. Restore unto me the joy of your salvation, and uphold me with your free Spirit. Amen.

Text: Psalm 51:10-12
Tune: Johann G. Winer, 1583-1651, adapt.
Text, Tune, Setting reprinted by permission of Concordia Publishing House

SCHAFFE IN MIR, GOTT
PM

Alternate tune for *Create in Me*, p. 20

HYMNS OF THE LITURGY

Glory Be to the Father 273
Gloria Patri

Text: Latin chant, second century; tr. unknown
Tune: *Pfälzische Kirchenordnung*, 1550
Text, Tune, Setting reprinted by permission of Concordia Publishing House

GLORY BE TO THE FATHER
PM

HYMNS OF THE LITURGY

274 My Soul Now Magnifies the Lord
Magnificat — Song of Mary

1 My soul now magnifies the Lord;
My spirit shall in God rejoice.
My humble state he did regard,
Exalting me by gracious choice.

2 Henceforth shall people call me blest,
For great things he has done for me.
The mighty God is now my guest;
The Holy One has set me free.

3 His mercy is on all who fear,
Who trust in him from age to age.
His arm of strength to all is near;
The proud he scatters, though they rage.

4 He brings down rulers from their seat
And raises those of low degree.
He fills the hungry souls with meat;
The rich depart in poverty.

5 He helped his servant Israel,
Remem b'ring his eternal grace,
As from of old he did foretell
To Abraham and all his race.

6 So praise with me the Holy One,
Who comes in all humility.
To our Redeemer, God's own Son,
Be glory in eternity!

Text: Hermann Bonnus, c. 1504-48; tr. John T. Mueller, 1885-1967, alt.
Tune: Georg Joseph, 17th century, adapt.
Text © 1941 Concordia Publishing House

ANGELUS
LM

Alternate *Song of Mary*, p. 57

276 Praise Be to the Lord
Benedictus — Song of Zechariah

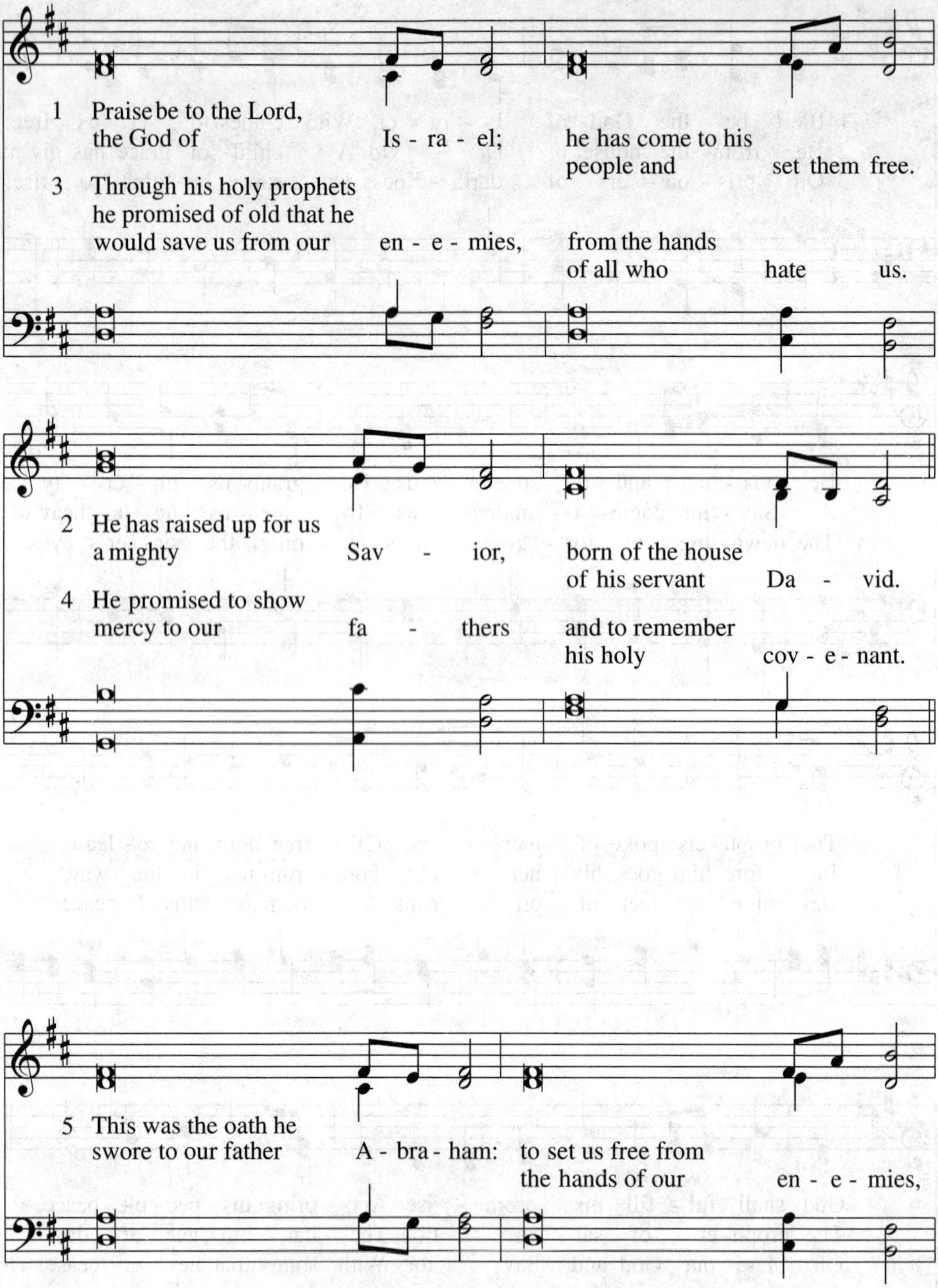

1. Praise be to the Lord, the God of Is-ra-el; he has come to his people and set them free.

2. He has raised up for us a mighty Sav-ior, born of the house of his servant Da-vid.

3. Through his holy prophets he promised of old that he would save us from our en-e-mies, from the hands of all who hate us.

4. He promised to show mercy to our fa-thers and to remember his holy cov-e-nant.

5. This was the oath he swore to our father A-bra-ham: to set us free from the hands of our en-e-mies,

HYMNS OF THE LITURGY

6 free to worship him without fear, holy and righteous in
his sight all the days of our life.

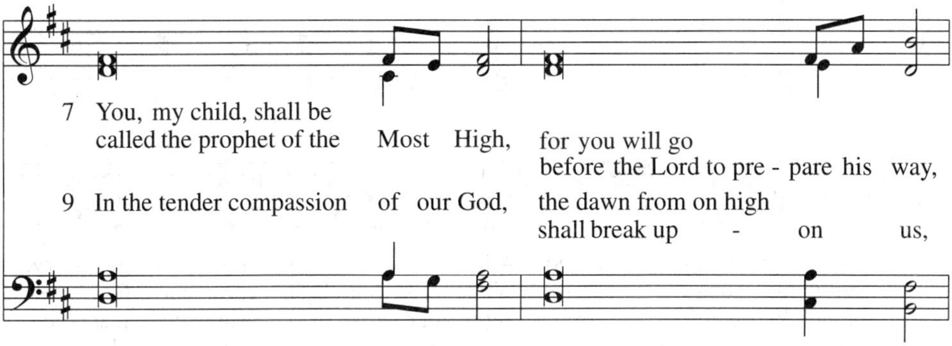

7 You, my child, shall be called the prophet of the Most High, for you will go before the Lord to prepare his way,

8 to give his people knowledge of salvation by the forgiveness of their sins.

9 In the tender compassion of our God, the dawn from on high shall break upon us,

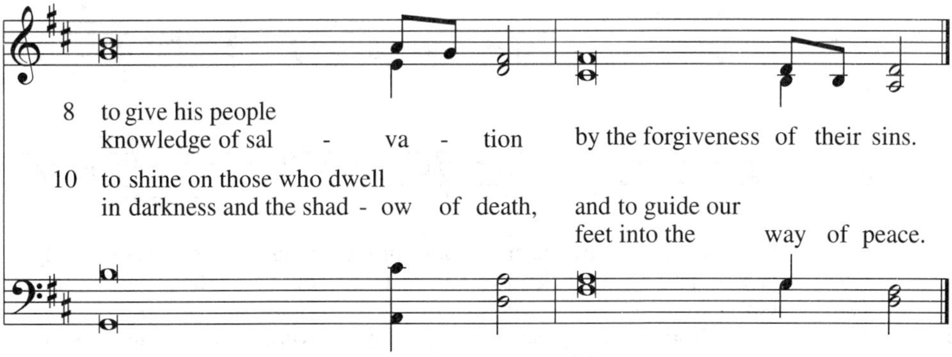

10 to shine on those who dwell in darkness and the shadow of death, and to guide our feet into the way of peace.

Text: International Consultation on English Texts, alt.
Tune: Kermit G. Moldenhauer, b. 1949
Tune and Setting © 1993 Kermit G. Moldenhauer

May be sung in place of *We Praise You, O God*, p. 48

277 God, We Praise You
Te Deum

1. God, we praise you! God, we bless you! God, we name you sov-'reign Lord! Mighty King whom angels worship, Father, by your Church adored: All creation shows your glory; Heav'n and earth draw near your throne, Singing, "Holy, holy, holy Lord!"

2. True apostles, faithful prophets, Saints who set their world ablaze, Martyrs, once unknown, unheeded, Join one growing song of praise, While your Church on earth confesses One majestic Trinity: Father, Son, and Holy Spirit, God who ever shall be.

3. Jesus Christ, the King of glory, Everlasting Son of God, Humble was your virgin mother, Hard the lonely path you trod: By your cross is sin defeated, Hell confronted face to face, Heaven opened to believers, Sinners justified by grace.

4. Christ, at God's right hand victorious, You will judge the world you made; Lord, in mercy help your servants For whose freedom you have paid: Raise us up from dust to glory; Guard us from all sin today. King enthroned above all praises, Save your people, God, we pray.

HYMNS OF THE LITURGY

ho - ly, ho - ly, Lord of hosts and God a - lone!"
Ho - ly Spir - it, God, our hope e - ter - nal - ly.
to be - liev - ers, Sin - ners jus - ti - fied by grace.
bove all prais - es, Save your peo - ple, God, we pray.

Text: Christopher M. Idle, b. 1938
Tune: Franz Joseph Haydn, 1732-1809
Text © 1982 Hope Publishing Co.

AUSTRIA
87 87 D

May be sung in place of *We Praise You, O God*, p. 48

HYMNS OF THE LITURGY

278 Holy God, We Praise Your Name
Te Deum

1 Holy God, we praise your name; Lord of all, we bow before you. All on earth your scepter claim; All in heav'n above adore you. Infinite your vast domain, Everlasting is your reign.

2 Hark! The glad celestial song Angel choirs above are raising; Prophets, martyrs join the throng, In unceasing chorus praising With the Church in one accord: Holy, holy, holy Lord!

3 Blest Redeemer, virgin's Son, Over death his vict'ry claiming, Now ascended to his throne, Judge and king, his grace proclaiming, Opens heav'n to all his own. Praise and thanks to God alone!

4 Holy Father, holy Son, Holy Spirit, three we name you; Though in essence only one, Undivided God we claim you, Then, adoring, bend the knee And confess the myst'ry.

Text: *Katholisches Gesangbuch,* Vienna, 1774, abr., adapt., st. 1-2, 4;
Ruth M. Glaeske, b. 1941, st. 3; tr. Clarence A. Walworth, 1820-1900, st. 1-2, 4, alt.
Tune: *Katholisches Gesangbuch,* Vienna, 1774, alt.
Text st. 3 © 1993 Ruth Backer Glaeske
May be sung in place of *We Praise You, O God,* p. 48

GROSSER GOTT, WIR LOBEN DICH
78 78 77

WORD OF GOD

280   Thy Strong Word

1. Thy strong word did cleave the darkness; At thy speaking it was done. For created light we thank thee While thine ordered seasons run. Alleluia! Alleluia! Praise to

2. Lo, on those who dwelt in darkness, Dark as night and deep as death, Broke the light of thy salvation, Breathed thine own life-giving breath. Alleluia! Alleluia! Praise to

3. Thy strong Word bespeaks us righteous; Bright with thine own holiness, Glorious now, we press toward glory, And our lives our hopes confess. Alleluia! Alleluia! Praise to

4. From the cross thy wisdom shining Breaketh forth in con-qu'ring might; From the cross forever beameth All thy bright redeeming light. Alleluia! Alleluia! Praise to

WORD OF GOD

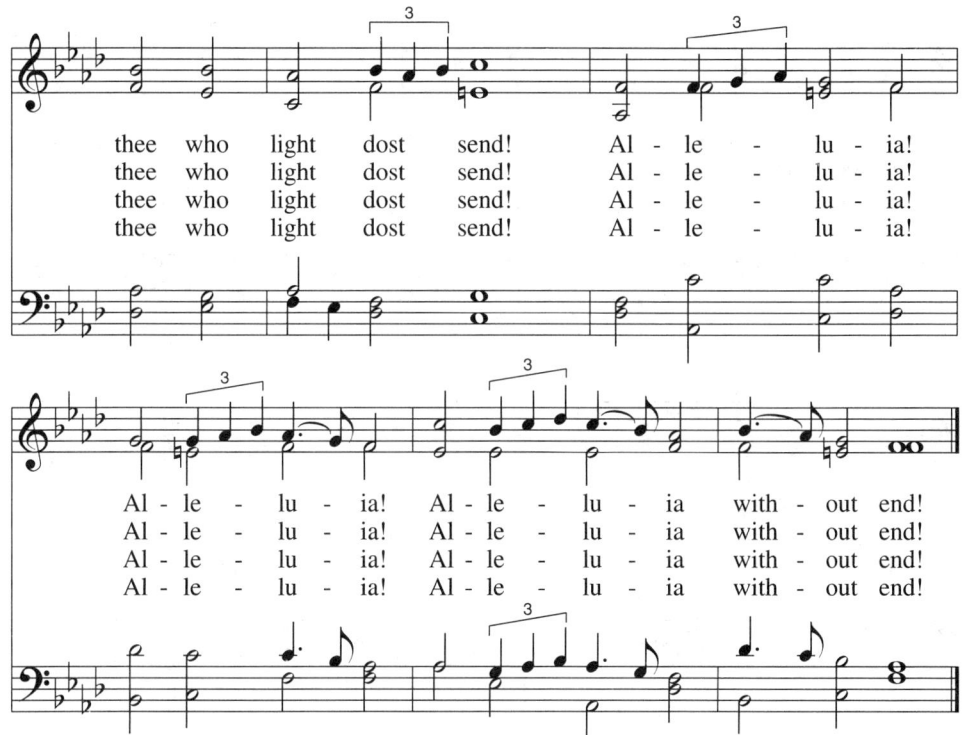

5 Give us lips to sing thy glory,
   Tongues thy mercy to proclaim,
  Throats to shout the hope that fills us,
   Mouths to speak thy holy name.
  Alleluia! Alleluia!
   May the light which thou dost send
  Fill our songs with alleluias,
  Alleluias without end!

6 God the Father, light-creator,
   To thee laud and honor be.
  To thee, Light from Light begotten,
   Praise be sung eternally.
  Holy Spirit, light-revealer,
   Glory, glory be to thee.
  Mortals, angels, now and ever
  Praise the holy Trinity!

Text: Martin H. Franzmann, 1907-76, alt.
Tune: Thomas J. Williams, 1869-1944
Text © 1969 Concordia Publishing House

EBENEZER
87 87 D

WORD OF GOD

Word e'er be my plea-sure And my heart's most pre - cious trea-sure.
all who feel sin's bur - den You give peace and words of par - don.
are my sword pre - vail-ing And my cup of joy un - fail - ing.
high - est praise is giv - en In the end - less joy of heav - en.

Text: Anna Sophia of Hesse-Darmstadt, 1638-83, abr.; tr. composite   WERDE MUNTER
Tune: Johann Schop, c. 1590-1667   87 87 77 88

Setting © 1993 Elfred Bloedel   Alternate settings: 147, 408

How Precious Is the Book Divine 284

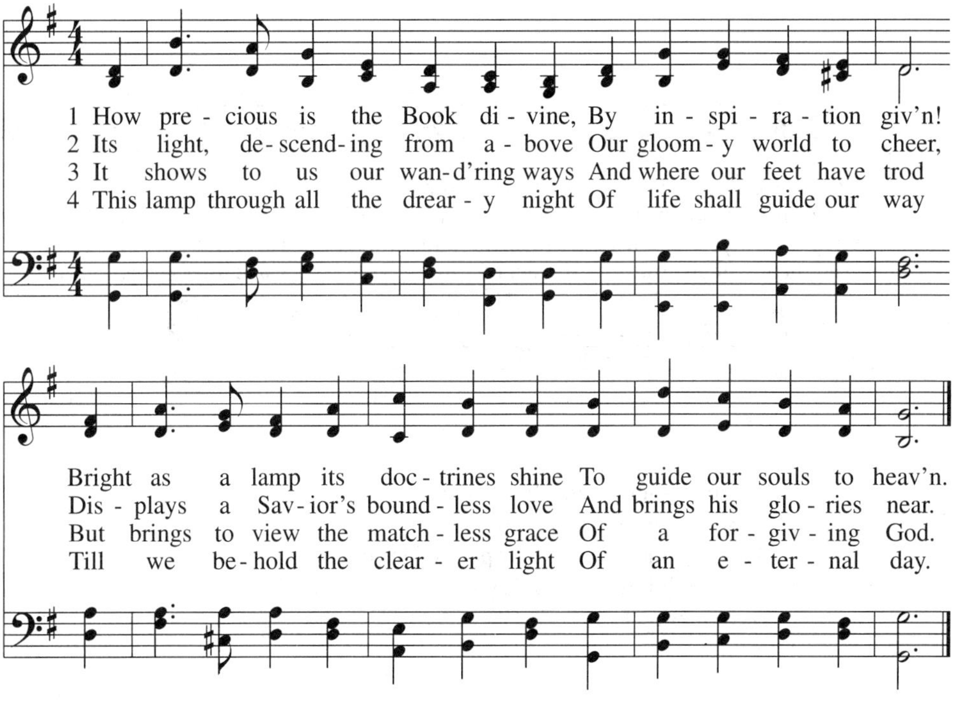

1 How pre - cious is the Book di - vine, By in - spi - ra - tion giv'n!
2 Its light, de - scend - ing from a - bove Our gloom - y world to cheer,
3 It shows to us our wan - d'ring ways And where our feet have trod
4 This lamp through all the drear - y night Of life shall guide our way

Bright as a lamp its doc - trines shine To guide our souls to heav'n.
Dis - plays a Sav - ior's bound - less love And brings his glo - ries near.
But brings to view the match - less grace Of a for - giv - ing God.
Till we be - hold the clear - er light Of an e - ter - nal day.

Text: John Fawcett, 1740-1817, abr., alt.   WALDER
Tune: Johann J. Walder, 1750-1817   CM

WORD OF GOD

285 The Ten Commandments Are the Law

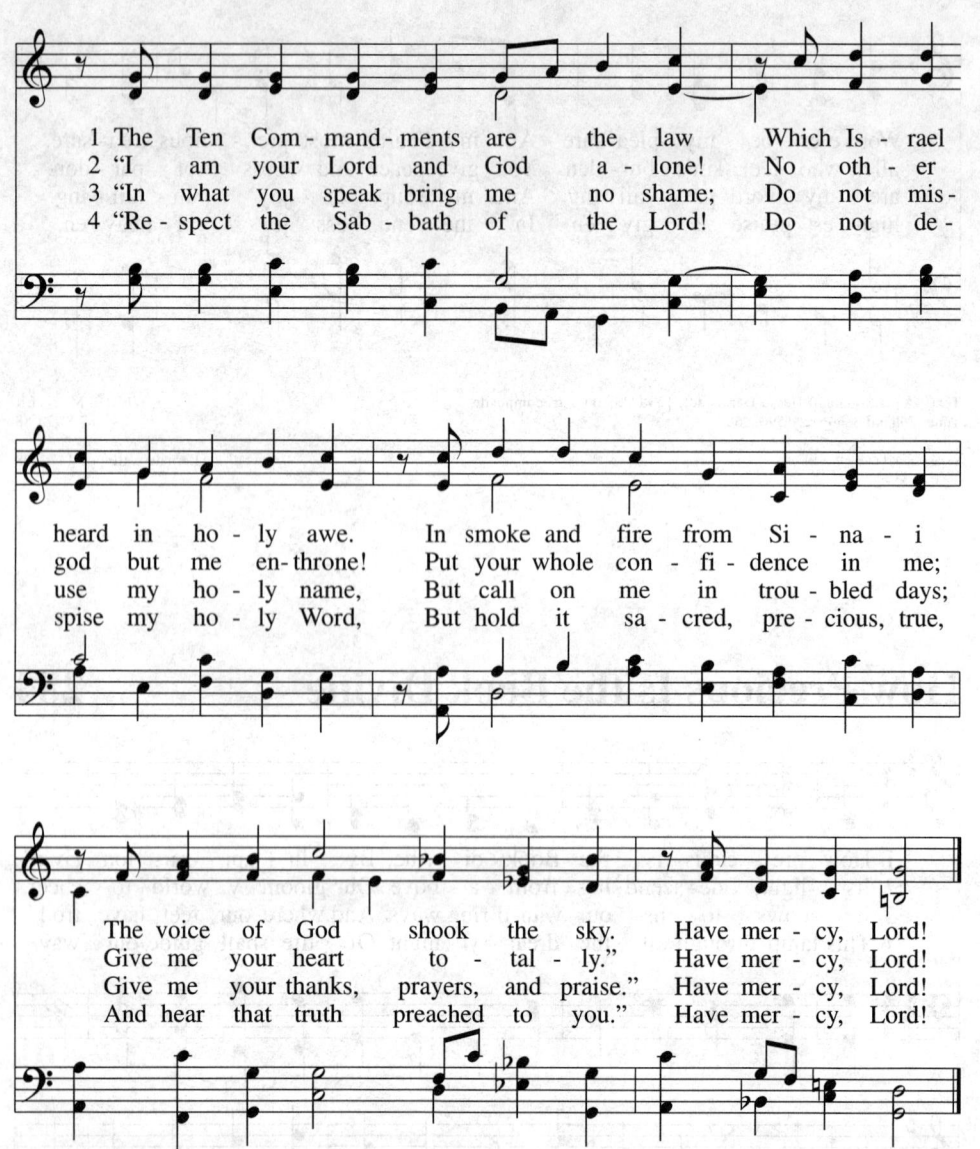

1 The Ten Commandments are the law Which Israel heard in holy awe. In smoke and fire from Sinai The voice of God shook the sky. Have mercy, Lord!

2 "I am your Lord and God alone! No other god but me enthrone! Put your whole confidence in me; Give me your heart totally." Have mercy, Lord!

3 "In what you speak bring me no shame; Do not misuse my holy name, But call on me in troubled days; Give me your thanks, prayers, and praise." Have mercy, Lord!

4 "Respect the Sabbath of the Lord! Do not despise my holy Word, But hold it sacred, precious, true, And hear that truth preached to you." Have mercy, Lord!

5 "Give to your parents honor due,
   Be dutiful and loving, too,
   And help them when their pow'rs are few;
   So shall it go well with you."
   Have mercy, Lord!

6 "You shall not murder, hurt, nor hate;
　　Your anger dare not dominate.
　Be kind and patient; help, defend,
　　And treat your foe as your friend."
　Have mercy, Lord!

7 "Be faithful to your marriage vow;
　　No lust or impure thoughts allow,
　But keep your body free from sin
　　With self-control, discipline."
　Have mercy, Lord!

8 "You shall not steal or take away
　　What others worked for night and day,
　But open wide a gen'rous hand
　　And help the poor in the land."
　Have mercy, Lord!

9 "Bear no false witness nor defame
　　Your neighbor and destroy his name,
　But view him in the kindest way;
　　Speak truth in all that you say."
　Have mercy, Lord!

10 "You shall not crave your neighbor's house
　　Nor covet money, goods, or spouse.
　Pray God he would your neighbor bless
　　As you yourself wish success."
　Have mercy, Lord!

11 God gave these laws to show therein,
　　O child of man, your life of sin,
　And help you rightly to perceive
　　How unto God you should live.
　Have mercy, Lord!

12 Our works cannot salvation gain;
　　They merit only endless pain.
　Forgive us, Lord! To Christ we fly,
　　Our mediator on high.
　Have mercy, Lord!

Text: Martin Luther, 1483-1546; tr. composite paraphrase
Tune: German melody, 13th century, alt.

IN GOTTES NAMEN FAHREN WIR
88 87 4

Setting © 1993 Kermit G. Moldenhauer

WORD OF GOD

286 The Law Commands and Makes Us Know

1 The law commands and makes us know What duties to our God we owe, But 'tis the gospel must reveal Where lies our strength to do his will.
2 The law uncovers guilt and sin And shows how vile our hearts have been; The gospel only can express Forgiving love and cleansing grace.
3 What curses does the law pronounce Against the one who fails but once! But in the gospel Christ appears, Pard'ning the guilt of num'rous years.
4 My soul, no more attempt to draw Your life and comfort from the law. Flee to the hope the gospel gives; The one who trusts the promise lives.

Text: Isaac Watts, 1674-1748, alt.
Tune: *Trente quatre Pseaumes de David,* Geneva, 1551

OLD HUNDREDTH
LM

Alternate settings: 233, 323

The Law of God Is Good and Wise   287

WORD OF GOD

1 The law of God is good and wise; It sets his will before our eyes, Shows us the way of righteousness, But dooms to death when we transgress.
2 The law is good, but since the fall Its holiness condemns us all; It dooms us for our sins to die And has no pow'r to justify.
3 Its light of holiness imparts The knowledge of our sinful hearts That we may see our lost estate And seek relief before too late.
4 To Jesus we for refuge flee, Who from the curse has set us free, And humbly worship at his throne, Saved by his grace through faith alone.

Text: Matthias Loy, 1828-1915, abr., alt.
Tune: Klug, *Geistliche Lieder zu Wittemberg,* Wittenberg, 1543, alt.

ERHALT UNS, HERR
LM

Alternate settings: 203, 282

WORD OF GOD

288 The Gospel Shows the Father's Grace

1. The gospel shows the Father's grace, Who sent his Son to save our race, Proclaims how Jesus lived and died That we might thus be justified.

2. It sets the Lamb before our eyes, Who made the atoning sacrifice And calls the souls with guilt oppressed To come and find eternal rest.

3. It brings the Savior's righteousness To robe our souls in royal dress; From all our guilt it brings release And gives the troubled conscience peace.

4. It is the pow'r of God to save From sin and Satan and the grave; It works the faith which firmly clings To all the treasures which it brings.

5. It bears to all the tidings glad
And bids their hearts no more be sad;
The weary, burdened souls it cheers
And banishes their guilty fears.

6. May we in faith its message learn
Nor thanklessly its blessings spurn;
May we in faith its truth confess
And praise the Lord, our righteousness.

Text: Matthias Loy, 1828-1915, alt.
Tune: *Cantionale Germanicum,* Gochsheim, 1628
Setting © 1993 Elfred Bloedel

HERR JESU CHRIST, DICH ZU UNS WEND
LM
Alternate settings: 71, 230

WORD OF GOD

Text: Johann H. Schröder, 1667-99, abr., adapt.; tr. Frances E. Cox, 1812-97, alt.
Tune: Friedrich L. C. Layriz, 1808-59

EINS IST NOT
87 87 12 12 11 11

WORD OF GOD

291 We Have a Sure Prophetic Word

1 We have a sure prophetic Word By inspiration of the Lord, And, though assailed on ev'ry hand, Jehovah's Word shall ever stand.
2 By pow'rs of empire banned and burned, By pagan pride rejected, spurned, The Word still stands, the Christian's trust, While haughty empires lie in dust.
3 What-e'er the Word in times of old Of future days and deeds foretold Is all fulfilled while ages roll, As traced on the prophetic scroll.
4 Abiding, steadfast, firm, and sure, The teachings of the Word endure. Blest all who trust this steadfast Word; Their anchor holds in Christ, the Lord.

Text: Emanuel Cronenwett, 1841-1931, alt.
Tune: Klug, *Geistliche Lieder auffs new gebessert*, Wittenberg, 1535

WO GOTT ZUM HAUS
LM
Alternate setting: 506

WORD OF GOD

The Lord Is God; There Is No Other 292

1 The Lord is God; there is no oth-er. The Lord our God a-lone be blessed. His name a-mong us shall be ho-ly. His Word will give us Sab-bath rest.

2 Fa-ther and moth-er we will hon-or. All hu-man life will we be-friend. All wives and hus-bands shall be faith-ful. Our neigh-bor's goods will we de-fend.

3 Truth-ful in speech our rep-u-ta-tion, By self-less-ness shall we be known. Un-end-ing love we pledge all peo-ple, Our high-est love for God a-lone.

Text: Daniel J. Meeter, b. 1953, alt.
Tune: Roy A. Hopp, b. 1951
Text © 1980 Daniel Meeter; Tune and Setting © 1987 CRC Publications

DENVER
98 98

Baptized into Your Name Most Holy 294

1 Baptized into your name most holy, O Father, Son, and Holy Ghost, I claim a place, though weak and lowly, Among your saints, your chosen host, Buried with Christ and dead to sin. Your Spirit now shall live within.

2 My loving Father, there you took me To be henceforth your child and heir. My faithful Savior, there you let me The fruit of all your sorrows share. O Holy Spirit, comfort me When threat'ning clouds around I see.

3 My faithful God, you fail me never; Your promise surely will endure. Oh, cast me not away forever If words and deeds become impure. Have mercy when I come defiled; Forgive, lift up, restore your child.

4 All that I am and love most dearly— Receive it all, O Lord, from me. Let me confess my faith sincerely And help me your own child to be! Let nothing that I am or own Serve any will but yours alone.

Text: Johann J. Rambach, 1693-1735, abr.;
tr. Catherine Winkworth, 1827-78, alt.
Tune: Johann B. König, 1691-1758
Setting © 1981 Richard W. Gieseke

O DASS ICH TAUSEND ZUNGEN HÄTTE (KÖNIG)
98 98 88

Alternate settings: 242, 386

5 Now into your heart we pour
   Prayers that from our hearts proceeded.
Our petitions heav'nward soar;
   May our warm desires be heeded!
Write the name we now have given;
   Write it in the book of heaven!

Text: Benjamin Schmolck, 1672-1737, abr.; tr. Catherine Winkworth, 1827-78, alt.
Tune: Johann R. Ahle, 1625-73, alt.

LIEBSTER JESU, WIR SIND HIER
78 78 88

Alternate settings: 330, 461

Our Children Jesus Calls 296

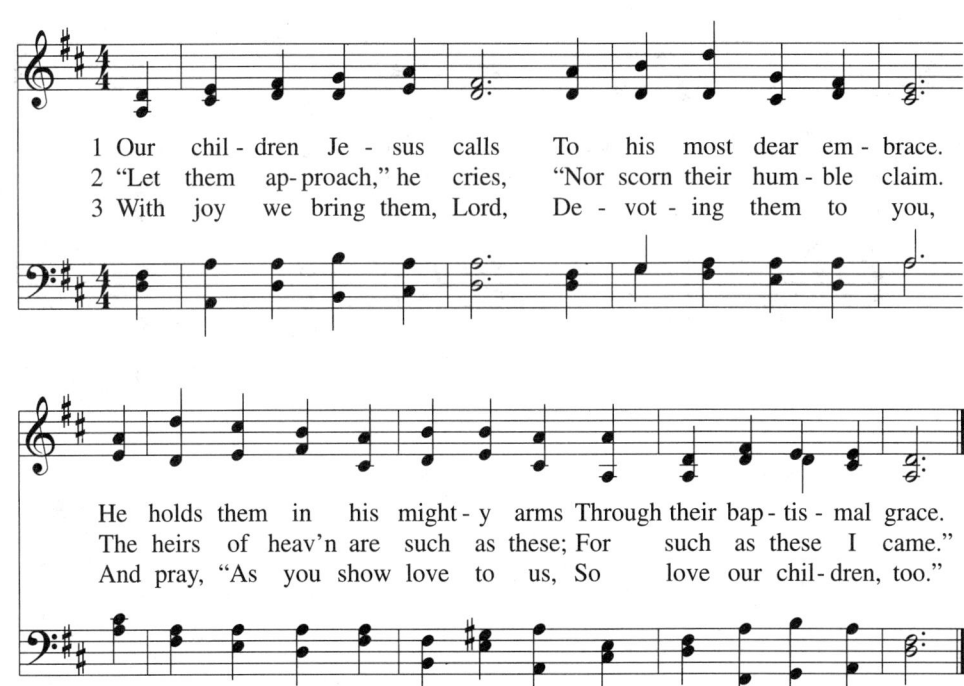

1 Our children Jesus calls To his most dear embrace.
  He holds them in his mighty arms Through their baptismal grace.
2 "Let them approach," he cries, "Nor scorn their humble claim.
  The heirs of heav'n are such as these; For such as these I came."
3 With joy we bring them, Lord, Devoting them to you,
  And pray, "As you show love to us, So love our children, too."

Text: Philip Doddridge, 1702-51, adapt., abr.
Tune: Johann B. König, 1691-1758, adapt.

FRANCONIA
SM

BAPTISM

Dear Father, You Have Made Us All 298

1 Dear Father, you have made us all; To you your people humbly pray: Look on this child, who at your call Now enters on life's narrow way.
2 Dear Savior, for your love untold, To you this little child we bring. Receive *him,* Shepherd, to your fold That *he* to you in faith may cling.
3 Dear Spirit, pour upon this child Your gifts of grace, your promise true, And make *him* pure and undefiled, A holy temple, kept for you.
4 O triune God, we humbly pray That all your blessings be conferred Upon this child, here cleansed today, By means of water and the Word.

Text: Albert Knapp, 1798-1864; tr. William M. Czamanske, 1873-1964, alt.
Tune: *Cantionale Germanicum,* Gochsheim, 1628, alt.
Text © 1941 Concordia Publishing House

HERR JESU CHRIST, DICH ZU UNS WEND
LM
Alternate settings: 71, 288

BAPTISM

See This Wonder in the Making 300

1 See this wonder in the making: God himself this child is taking As a lamb safe in his keeping, His to be, awake or sleeping.
2 Miracle each time it happens As the door to heaven opens And the Father beams, "Beloved, Heir of gifts a king would covet!"
3 Far more tender than a mother, Far more caring than a father, God, into your arms we place *him,* With your love and peace embrace *him.*
4 Here we bring a child of nature; Home we take a new-born creature, Now God's precious son or daughter, Born again by Word and water.

Text: Jaroslav J. Vajda, b. 1919
Tune: Swedish folk tune, 19th century

TRYGGARE KAN INGEN VARA
LM Trochaic

Text © 1984 Jaroslav J. Vajda

CONFESSION AND ABSOLUTION

303   With Broken Heart and Contrite Sigh

1. With broken heart and contrite sigh, A trembling sinner, Lord, I cry. Your par-d'ning grace is rich and free— O God, be merciful to me!

2. I smite upon my troubled breast, With deep and conscious guilt oppressed, Christ and his cross my only plea— O God, be merciful to me!

3. Far off I stand with tearful eyes Nor dare uplift them to the skies, But you can all my anguish see— O God, be merciful to me!

4. No gifts, no deeds that I have done Can for a single sin atone. To Calvary alone I flee— O God, be merciful to me!

5. And when, redeemed from sin and hell,
   With all the ransomed souls I dwell,
   My joyous song shall ever be:
   God has been merciful to me!

Text: Cornelius Elven, 1791-1873, alt.
Tune: Jeremiah Clarke, c. 1674-1707

ST. LUKE
LM

CONFESSION AND ABSOLUTION

Jesus Sinners Does Receive   304

1 Jesus sinners does receive; Oh, may all this saying ponder
2 We deserve but grief and shame, Yet his words, rich grace revealing,
3 Sheep that from the fold did stray Are not by the Lord forsaken;
4 Come, O sinners, one and all, Come, accept his invitation.

Who in sin's delusions live And from God and heaven wander.
Pardon, peace, and life proclaim; Here their ills have perfect healing
Weary souls who lost their way Are by Christ, the shepherd, taken
Come, obey his gracious call; Come and take his free salvation!

Here is hope for all who grieve — Jesus sinners does receive.
Who with humble hearts believe — Jesus sinners does receive.
In his arms that they may live — Jesus sinners does receive.
Firmly in these words believe — Jesus sinners does receive.

5 I, a sinner, come to you
   With a penitent confession.
Savior, show me mercy, too;
   Grant for all my sins remission.
Let these words my soul relieve —
Jesus sinners does receive.

6 Oh, how blest it is to know,
   Were as scarlet my transgression,
It shall be as white as snow
   By your blood and bitter passion,
For these words I do believe —
Jesus sinners does receive.

7 Jesus sinners does receive.
   Even I have been forgiven.
And when I this earth must leave,
   I shall find an open heaven.
Dying, still to him I cleave —
Jesus sinners does receive.

Text: Erdmann Neumeister, 1671-1756, abr.; tr. composite
Tune: *Neu-verfertigtes Darmstädtisches Gesang-Buch,* Darmstadt, 1699, alt.

MEINEN JESUM LASS ICH NICHT
78 78 77

CONFESSION AND ABSOLUTION

305   From Depths of Woe I Cry to You

1 From depths of woe I cry to you; Lord, hear me,
I implore you. Bend down your gracious ear to me;
My prayer let come before you. If you kept
record of my sin And held against me

2 Your love and grace alone avail To blot out
my transgression. The best and holiest deeds must fail
To break sin's dread oppression. Before you
none can boasting stand, But all must fear your

3 Therefore my hope is in the Lord And not in
my own merit; It rests upon his faithful Word
To them of contrite spirit. That he is
merciful and just— This is my comfort

4 My soul is waiting for the Lord As one who
longs for morning; No watcher waits with greater hope
Than I for his returning. I hope as
Israel in the Lord; He sends redemption

CONFESSION AND ABSOLUTION

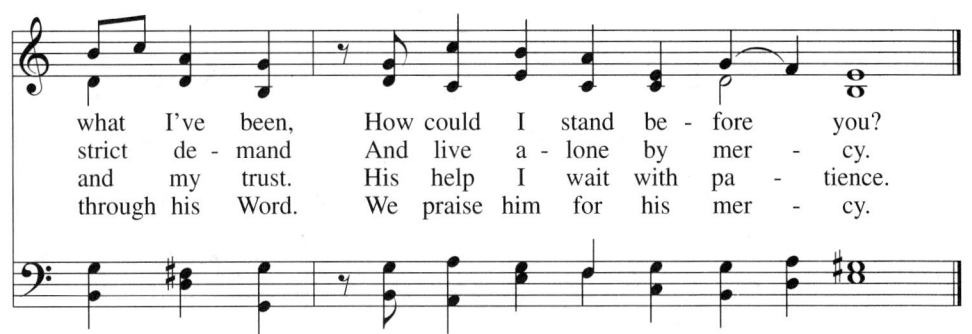

what I've been, How could I stand be - fore you?
strict de - mand And live a - lone by mer - cy.
and my trust. His help I wait with pa - tience.
through his Word. We praise him for his mer - cy.

Text: Martin Luther, 1483-1546, abr.; tr. Catherine Winkworth, 1827-78, st. 1-3, alt.;
 Gracia Grindal, b. 1943, st. 4
Tune: Martin Luther, 1483-1546, alt.
Text st. 4 © 1978 *Lutheran Book of Worship*

AUS TIEFER NOT
87 87 887

CONFESSION AND ABSOLUTION

306   Before You, God, the Judge of All

1. Before you, God, the Judge of all, With grief and shame I humbly fall. I see my sins against you, Lord, My sins of thought and deed and word. They press me sore; to you I flee: O God, be merciful to me!

2. O Lord, my God, to you I pray: Oh, cast me not in wrath away! Let your good Spirit ne'er depart, But let him draw to you my heart That truly penitent I be: O God, be merciful to me!

3. O Jesus, let your precious blood Be to my soul a cleansing flood. Turn not, O Lord, your guest away, But grant that justified I may Go to my house at peace to be: O God, be merciful to me!

Text: Magnus B. Landstad, 1802-80; tr. Carl Döving, 1867-1937, alt.
Tune: attr. Martin Luther, 1483-1546
Setting © 1981 Richard W. Gieseke

VATER UNSER IM HIMMELREICH, DER DU
88 88 88
Alternate settings: 407, 410, 479

CONFESSION AND ABSOLUTION

308 As Surely As I Live, God Said

1 "As surely as I live," God said, "I would not have the sinner dead, But that he turn from error's ways, Repent, and live through endless days."

2 To us, therefore, Christ gave command: "Go forth and preach in ev'ry land; Bestow on all my pard'ning grace Who will repent of sinful ways.

3 "All those whose sins you thus remit I truly pardon and acquit, And those whose sins you do retain Condemned and guilty shall remain.

4 "What you will bind, that bound shall be; What you will loose, that shall be free; Unto my Church the keys are giv'n To op'n and close the gates of heav'n."

5 The words which absolution give
Are his who died that we might live;
The minister whom Christ has sent
Is but his humble instrument.

6 When ministers lay on their hands,
Absolved by Christ the sinner stands;
He who by grace the Word believes
Forgiveness, sure and sweet, receives.

7 Praise God the Father and the Son
And Holy Spirit, Three in One,
As was, is now, and so shall be
Forever and eternally!

Text: Nikolaus Herman, c. 1480-1561, abr.; tr. Matthias Loy, 1828-1915, alt.
Tune: Jeremiah Clarke, c. 1674-1707

ST. LUKE
LM

5 Your heart is filled with fervent yearning
  That sinners may salvation see
  Who, Lord, to you in faith are turning;
  So let me, too, come trustingly.
  Refrain

6 Weary am I and heavy laden;
  With sin my soul is sore oppressed.
  Receive me graciously and gladden
  My heart, for I am now your guest.
  Refrain

7 You here will find a heart most lowly
  That feels unworthy in your sight,
  That duly weeps o'er sin, yet solely
  Your merit pleads, as it is right.
  Refrain

8 By faith I call your holy table
  The testament of your deep love,
  For by your gift I now am able
  To know the heart of God above.
  Refrain

9 What higher gift can we inherit?
  It is faith's bond and solid base;
  It is the strength of heart and spirit,
  The covenant of hope and grace.
  Refrain

10 This feast is manna, wealth abounding
   Unto the poor, to weak ones pow'r,
   To angels joy, to hell confounding,
   And life for me in death's dark hour.
   Refrain

11 Your body, giv'n for me, O Savior,
   Your blood, which you for me have shed —
   These are my life and strength forever;
   By them my hungry soul is fed.
   Refrain

12 With you, Lord, I am now united;
   I live in you and you in me.
   No sorrow fills my soul; delighted,
   It finds its peace on Calvary.
   Refrain

13 Who can condemn me now? For surely
   The Lord is near, who justifies.
   No hell I fear, and thus securely
   With Jesus I to heaven rise.
   Refrain

14 Though death may threaten with disaster,
   It cannot rob me of my cheer,
   For he who is of death the master
   With help and strength is always near.
   Refrain

15 My heart has now become your dwelling,
   O blessed, holy Trinity.
   With angels I, your praises telling,
   Shall live in joy eternally.
   Refrain

Text: Friedrich C. Heyder, 1677-1754, abr.; tr. *The Lutheran Hymnal,* St. Louis, 1941, alt.
Tune: *Emskirchner Choralbuch,* Leipzig, 1756, alt.

ICH STERBE TÄGLICH
98 98 88

Alternate setting: 70

HOLY COMMUNION

311 Soul, Adorn Yourself with Gladness

1 Soul, adorn yourself with gladness; Leave behind all gloom and sadness. Come into the daylight's splendor; There with joy your praises render Unto him whose grace unbounded Has this wondrous

2 Hasten as a bride to meet him, And with loving rev-'rence greet him, For with words of life immortal He is knocking at your portal. O-pen wide the gates before him, Saying, as you

3 He who craves a precious treasure Neither cost nor pain will measure, But the priceless gifts of heaven God to us has freely given. Though the wealth of earth were proffered, Naught would buy the

4 Now I kneel before you lowly, Filled with joy most deep and holy, As with trembling awe and wonder On your mighty work I ponder, How by mystery surrounded, Depths that no one

HOLY COMMUNION

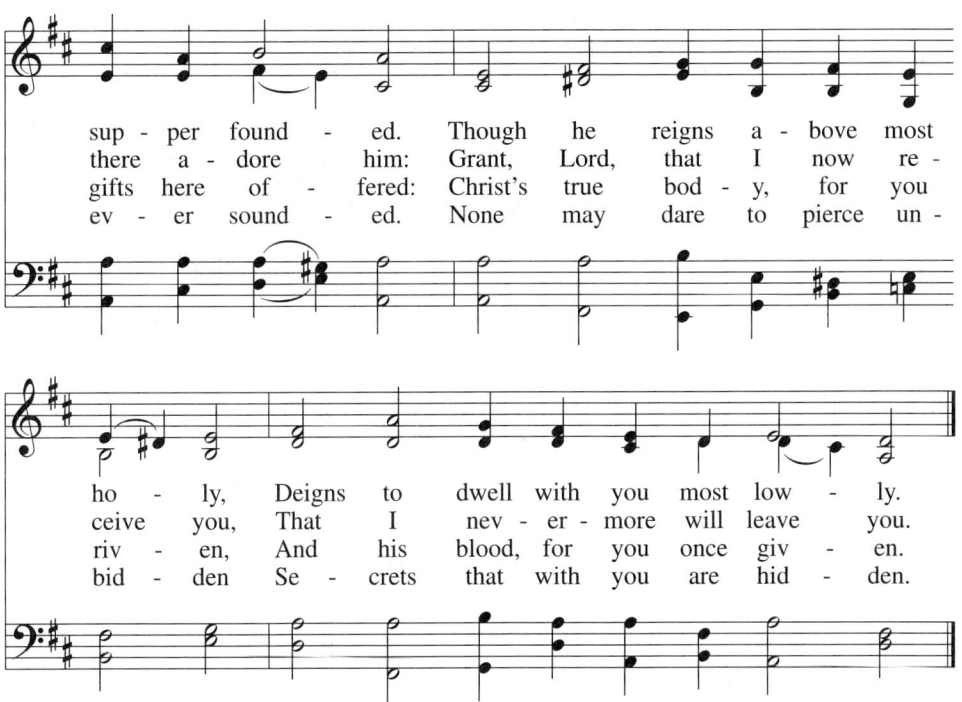

sup - per found - ed. Though he reigns a - bove most ho - ly, Deigns to dwell with you most low - ly.
there a - dore him: Grant, Lord, that I now re - ceive you, That I nev - er - more will leave you.
gifts here of - fered: Christ's true bod - y, for you riv - en, And his blood, for you once giv - en.
ev - er sound - ed. None may dare to pierce un - bid - den Se - crets that with you are hid - den.

5 Human reason, though it ponders,
  Cannot fathom these great wonders,
That Christ's body must be boundless
  Since the souls it feeds are countless,
And that he his blood is giving
  With the wine we are receiving.
These great mysteries unsounded
  Are by God alone expounded.

6 Lord, by love and mercy driven,
  You have left your throne in heaven
On the cross for me to languish
  And to die in bitter anguish,
To forgo all joy and gladness
  And to shed your blood in sadness.
By this blood redeemed and living,
  Lord, I praise you with thanksgiving.

7 Jesus, Sun of life, my Splendor,
  Jesus, Friend of friends most tender,
Jesus, Joy of my desiring,
  Fount of life, my soul inspiring —
At your feet I cry, my Maker:
  Let me be a fit partaker
Of this blessed food from heaven
  For our good, your glory, given.

8 Jesus, Lord of life, I pray you,
  Let me gladly here obey you.
By your love I am invited;
  Be your love with love requited.
By this supper let me measure,
  Lord, how vast and deep love's treasure.
Through the gift of grace you give me
  As your guest in heav'n receive me.

Text: Johann Franck, 1618-77, abr.; tr. Catherine Winkworth, 1827-78,
  st. 1-2, 4, alt.; *The Lutheran Hymnal*, St. Louis, 1941, st. 3, 5-6, alt.
Tune: Johann Crüger, 1598-1662, alt.

SCHMÜCKE DICH
LM D Trochaic

Alternate setting: 616

HOLY COMMUNION

    you for need-ed rest, For com-fort, and for par - don.
    and your maj-es-ty Till dawns the judg-ment morn - ing,
    an - y dar-ing hand Or sub-tle craft and cun - ning.
    naught you can-not do, For you, Lord, are al-might - y.

5 Though reason cannot understand,
    Yet faith this truth embraces:
 Your body, Lord, is ev'rywhere
    At once in many places.
 I leave to you how this can be;
    Your Word alone suffices me;
 I trust its truth unfailing.

6 Lord, I believe what you have said;
    Help me when doubts assail me.
 Remember that I am but dust,
    And let my faith not fail me.
 Your supper in this vale of tears
    Refreshes me and stills my fears
 And is my priceless treasure.

7 Grant that we worthily receive
    Your supper, Lord, our Savior,
 And, truly grieving for our sins,
    May prove by our behavior
 That we are thankful for your grace
    And day by day may run our race,
 In holiness increasing.

8 For your consoling supper, Lord,
    Be praised throughout all ages!
 Preserve it, for in ev'ry place
    The world against it rages.
 Grant that this sacrament may be
    A blessed comfort unto me
 When living and when dying.

Text: Samuel Kinner, 1603-68; tr. Emanuel Cronenwett, 1841-1931, alt.
Tune: Peter Sohren, c. 1630-c. 1692, alt.

DU LEBENSBROT, HERR JESU CHRIST
87 87 887

HOLY COMMUNION

313   Jesus Christ, Our Blessed Savior

1. Jesus Christ, our blessed Savior, Turned away God's wrath forever; By his bitter grief and woe He saved us from the evil foe.

2. As his pledge of love undying, He, this precious food supplying, Gives his body with the bread And with the wine the blood he shed.

3. Jesus here himself is sharing; Take heed how you are preparing, For if you do not believe, Judgment instead you shall receive.

4. Useless would be Jesus' passion If salvation you could fashion. Do not come if you suppose You need not him who died and rose.

5. Christ says, "Come, all you that labor,
And receive my grace and favor;
Those who feel no pain or ill
Need no physician's help or skill."

6. Then hold fast with faith unshaken
That this food is to be taken
By the souls who are distressed,
By hearts that long for peace and rest.

7. Praise the Father, who from heaven
Unto us such food has given
And, to mend what we have done,
Gave into death his only Son.

8. If your heart this truth professes
And your mouth your sin confesses,
Surely you will be his guest
And at his banquet ever blest.

Text: John Hus, c. 1369-1415; German version,
Martin Luther, 1483-1546, abr.; tr. composite
Tune: Klug, *Geistliche Lieder auffs new gebessert*, Wittenberg, 1535, alt.

JESUS CHRISTUS, UNSER HEILAND, DER VON UNS
88 78

HOLY COMMUNION

315 Here, O My Lord, I See You Face to Face

1 Here, O my Lord, I see you face to face;
Here would I touch and handle things unseen,
Here grasp with firmer hand eternal grace,
And all my weariness upon you lean.

2 This is the hour of banquet and of song;
Here is the heav'nly table spread anew.
Here let me feast and, feasting, still prolong
The brief bright hour of fellowship with you.

3 I have no help but yours nor do I need Another
arm but yours to lean upon.
It is enough, O Lord, enough indeed;
My strength is in your might, your might alone.

4 Mine is the sin but yours the righteousness;
Mine is the guilt but yours the cleansing blood.
Here is my robe, my refuge, and my peace:
Your blood, your righteousness, O Lord, my God.

5 Too soon we rise; the vessels disappear.
The feast, though not the love, is past and gone.
The bread and wine remove, but you are here,
Nearer than ever, still my shield and sun.

6 Feast after feast thus comes and passes by,
Yet, passing, points to that glad feast above,
Giving sweet foretaste of the festal joy,
The Lamb's great marriage feast of bliss and love.

Text: Horatius Bonar, 1808-89, abr., alt.
Tune: Henry Lawes, 1595-1662
Setting © 1969 Concordia Publishing House

FARLEY CASTLE
10 10 10 10

HOLY COMMUNION

O Jesus, Blessed Lord, to Thee 316

1 O Jesus, blessed Lord, to thee My heartfelt thanks forever be, Who hast so lovingly bestowed On me thy body and thy blood.

2 Break forth, my soul, for joy and say: What wealth is come to me this day! My Savior dwells within my heart — How blest am I! How good thou art!

Text: Thomas H. Kingo, 1634-1703; tr. Arthur J. Mason, 1851-1928
Tune: *Trente quatre Pseaumes de David,* Geneva, 1551
Setting © 1982 Concordia Publishing House

OLD HUNDREDTH
LM
Alternate settings: 286, 323

HOLY COMMUNION

317 O Lord, We Praise You

1. O Lord, we praise you, bless you, and a-dore you, In thanks-giving bow be-fore you. Here with your bod-y and your blood you nour-ish Our weak souls that they may flour-ish. O Lord, have mer - cy! May your bod-y,

2. Your ho-ly bod-y in-to death was giv-en, Life to win for us in heav-en. No great-er love than this to you could bind us; May this feast of that re-mind us! O Lord, have mer - cy! Lord, your love and

3. May God be-stow on us his grace and fa-vor To please him with our be-hav-ior And live to-geth-er here in love and u-nion, Cher-ish-ing our blest com-mu-nion. O Lord, have mer - cy! Let not your good

HOLY COMMUNION

Text: German folk hymn, 15th century, st. 1; Martin Luther, 1483-1546, st. 2-3;
tr. *The Lutheran Hymnal,* St. Louis, 1941, alt.
Tune: *Geystliche gesangk Buchleyn,* Wittenberg, 1524, alt.
Setting © 1993 Kermit G. Moldenhauer

GOTT SEI GELOBET UND GEBENEDEIET
PM

HOLY COMMUNION

318 Sent Forth by God's Blessing

1 Sent forth by God's bless-ing, Our true faith con-fess-ing, The
2 With praise and thanks-giv-ing, To God ev-er-liv-ing, The

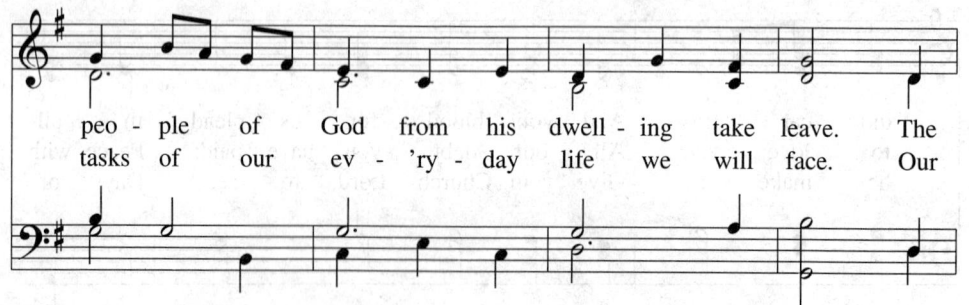

peo-ple of God from his dwell-ing take leave. The
tasks of our ev-'ry-day life we will face. Our

sup-per is end-ed; Oh, be now ex-tend-ed The
faith ev-er shar-ing, In love ev-er car-ing, Em-

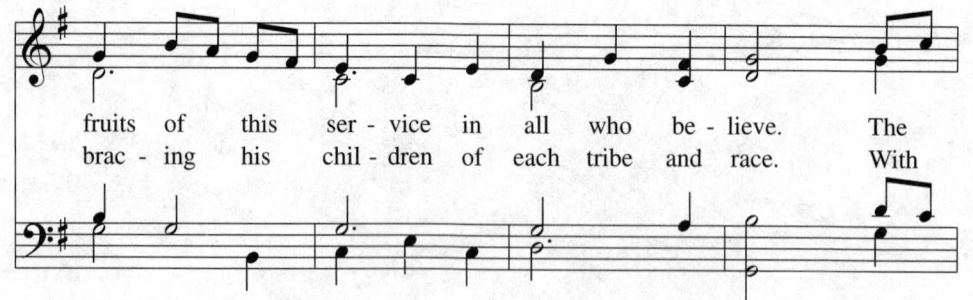

fruits of this ser-vice in all who be-lieve. The
brac-ing his chil-dren of each tribe and race. With

HOLY COMMUNION

Text: Omer Westendorf, b. 1916, alt.
Tune: Welsh folk tune

THE ASH GROVE
66 11 66 11 D

Text © 1964 World Library Publications, Inc.; Setting © 1978 *Lutheran Book of Worship*

Alternate setting: 260

CLOSE OF SERVICE

On My Heart Imprint Your Image 320

On my heart imprint your image, Blessed Jesus, King of grace, That life's riches, cares, and pleasures Have no pow'r to hide your face. This the superscription be: Jesus, crucified for me, Is my life, my hope's foundation, And my glory and salvation.

Text: Thomas H. Kingo, 1634-1703, abr.; tr. Peer O. Strömme, 1856-1921, alt.
Tune: *Trente quatre Pseaumes de David,* Geneva, 1551, alt.

FREU DICH SEHR
87 87 77 88

CLOSE OF SERVICE

323 Almighty Father, Bless the Word

1 Almighty Father, bless the Word Which through your grace we now have heard. Oh, may the precious seed take root, Spring up, and bear abundant fruit.

2 We praise you for the means of grace As homeward now our steps we trace. Grant, Lord, that we who worshiped here May all at last in heav'n appear.

Text: Scandinavian hymn; tr. *The Lutheran Hymnary,* Decorah, 1913, alt.
Tune: *Trente quatre Pseaumes de David,* Geneva, 1551

OLD HUNDREDTH
LM

Alternate settings: 233, 286

CLOSE OF SERVICE

Almighty God, Your Word Is Cast　　324

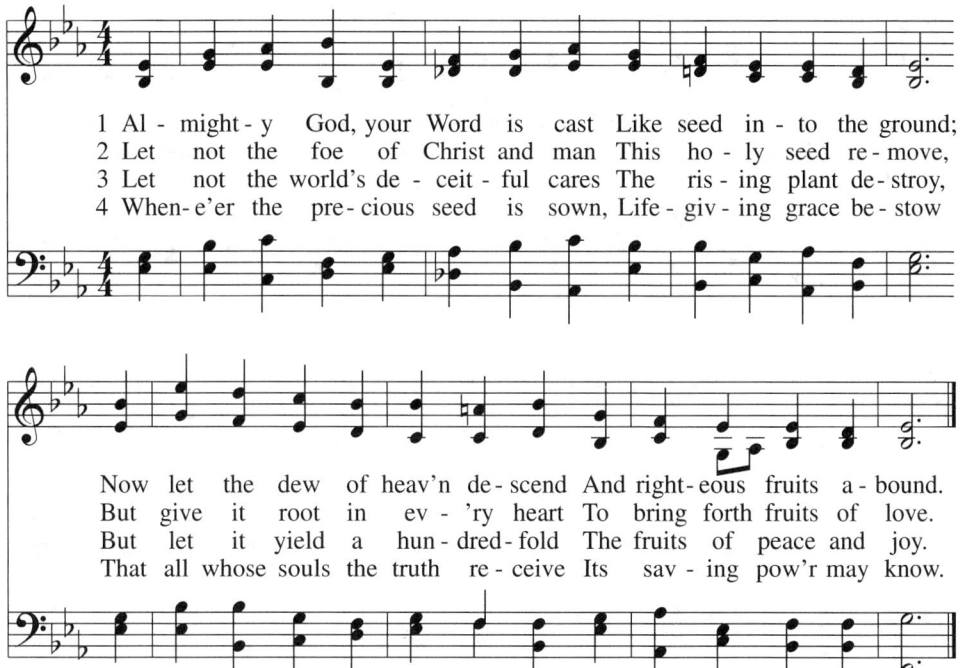

1 Almighty God, your Word is cast Like seed into the ground;
  Now let the dew of heav'n descend And righteous fruits abound.
2 Let not the foe of Christ and man This holy seed remove,
  But give it root in ev'ry heart To bring forth fruits of love.
3 Let not the world's deceitful cares The rising plant destroy,
  But let it yield a hundredfold The fruits of peace and joy.
4 When-e'er the precious seed is sown, Life-giving grace bestow
  That all whose souls the truth receive Its saving pow'r may know.

Text: John Cawood, 1775-1852, abr., alt.
Tune: *The CL Psalms of David,* Edinburgh, 1615

DUNDEE
CM

Alternate setting: 420

CLOSE OF SERVICE

May the Grace of Christ Our Savior 326

1 May the grace of Christ our Savior And the Father's boundless love With the Holy Spirit's favor Rest upon us from above.
2 So may we abide in union With each other and the Lord, Gathered here in blest communion By the power of his Word.
3 Now with all the saints in heaven Thanks and praise to you we sing, Father, Son, and Holy Spirit, Three in One, our triune King.

Text: John Newton, 1725-1807, st. 1-2, alt.; Carroll T. Andrews, b. 1918, st. 3, alt.
Tune: Christian F. Witt, 1660-1716, alt.
Text st.3 © 1971 by GIA Publications, Inc.

STUTTGART
87 87
Alternate setting: 463

CLOSE OF SERVICE

327 God Be with You till We Meet Again

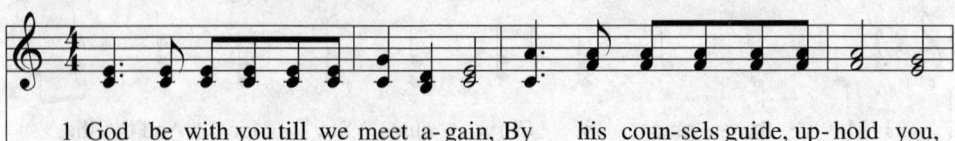

1 God be with you till we meet a-gain, By his coun-sels guide, up-hold you,
2 God be with you till we meet a-gain, 'Neath his wings pro-tect-ing hide you,

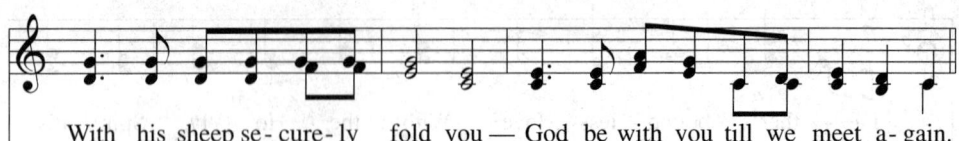

With his sheep se-cure-ly fold you— God be with you till we meet a-gain.
Dai-ly man-na still pro-vide you— God be with you till we meet a-gain.

Refrain

Till we meet, Till we meet, Till we meet at Je-sus' feet.

Till we meet, Till we meet— God be with you till we meet a-gain.

Text: Jeremiah E. Rankin, 1828-1904, abr., alt.
Tune: William G. Tomer, 1833-96

GOD BE WITH YOU
98 89 with Refrain

CLOSE OF SERVICE

God Be with You till We Meet Again   328

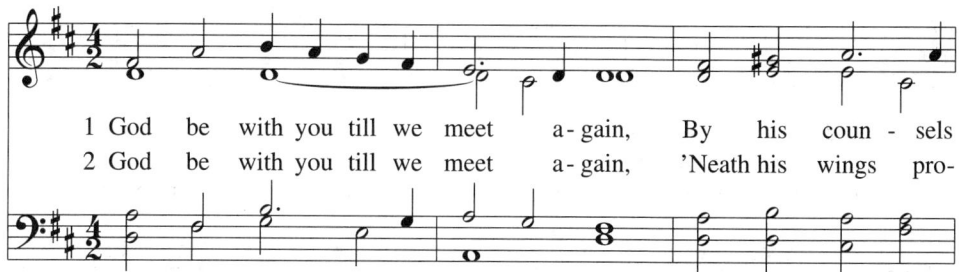

1 God be with you till we meet a-gain, By his coun-sels
2 God be with you till we meet a-gain, 'Neath his wings pro-

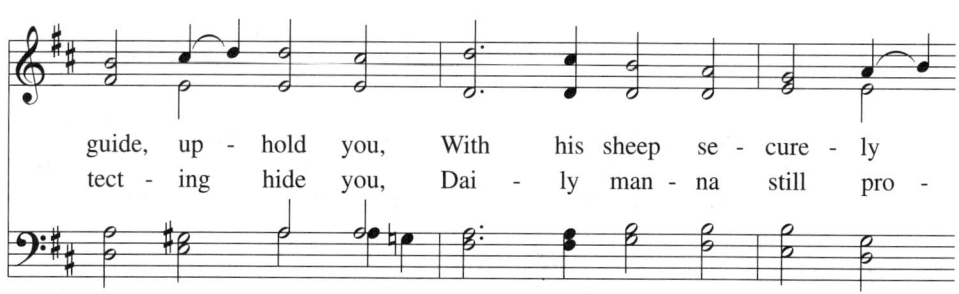

guide, up-hold you, With his sheep se-cure-ly
tect-ing hide you, Dai-ly man-na still pro-

fold you — God be with you till we meet a-gain.
vide you — God be with you till we meet a-gain.

Text: Jeremiah E. Rankin, 1828-1904, abr., alt.
Tune: Ralph Vaughan Williams, 1872-1958

RANDOLPH
98 89

Tune and Setting reprinted by permission of Oxford University Press

CLOSE OF SERVICE

329   Lord, Dismiss Us with Your Blessing

1. Lord, dismiss us with your blessing; Fill our hearts with joy and peace. Let us each, your love possessing, Triumph in redeeming grace. Oh, refresh us, oh, refresh us, Trav-'ling through this wilderness.

2. Thanks we give and adoration For the gospel's joyful sound; May the fruits of your salvation In our hearts and lives abound! Ever faithful, ever faithful To your truth may we be found.

3. So whene'er the signal's given Us from earth to call away, Borne on angels' wings to heaven, Glad the summons to obey, May we ever, may we ever Reign with Christ in endless day.

Text: John Fawcett, 1740-1817, alt.
Tune: Friedrich O. Reuter, 1863-1924

NEW ULM
87 87 87

CLOSE OF SERVICE

331 Guide Me, O Thou Great Jehovah

1 Guide me, O thou great Jehovah, Pilgrim through this barren land. I am weak, but thou art mighty; Hold me with thy pow'r-ful hand. Bread of heaven, Feed me till I want no more.

2 Open now the crystal fountain Whence the healing stream doth flow; Let the fiery, cloudy pillar Lead me all my journey through. Strong Deliv'rer, Be thou still my strength and shield.

3 When I tread the verge of Jordan, Bid my anxious fears subside; Death of death and hell's Destruction, Land me safe on Canaan's side. Songs of praises I will ever give to thee.

Text: William Williams, 1717-91, abr.; tr. Peter Williams, 1722-96, st. 1; William Williams, st. 2-3
Tune: George W. Warren, 1828-1902

GUIDE ME
87 87 47

CLOSE OF SERVICE

333   Abide, O Dearest Jesus

1 Abide, O dearest Jesus, Among us with your grace
   That Satan may not harm us Nor we to sin give place.
2 Abide, O dear Redeemer, Among us with your Word
   And thus now and hereafter True peace and joy afford.
3 Abide with heav'nly brightness Among us, precious Light;
   Your truth direct and keep us From error's gloomy night.
4 Abide with richest blessings Among us, bounteous Lord;
   Let us in grace and wisdom Grow daily through your Word.

5 Abide with your protection
   Among us, Lord, our Strength,
   Lest world and Satan fell us
   And overcome at length.

6 Abide, O faithful Savior,
   Among us with your love;
   Grant steadfastness and help us
   To reach our home above.

Text: Josua Stegmann, 1588-1632; tr. August Crull, 1845-1923, alt.
Tune: Melchior Vulpius, c. 1570-1615, alt.

CHRISTUS, DER IST MEIN LEBEN
76 76

Alternate setting: 606

CLOSE OF SERVICE

Praise God, from Whom All Blessings Flow 334

Text: Thomas Ken, 1637-1711, abr.
Tune: *Trente quatre Pseaumes de David,* Geneva, 1551

OLD HUNDREDTH
LM

Alternate settings: 233, 286

INVITATION

335   O Kingly Love, that Faithfully

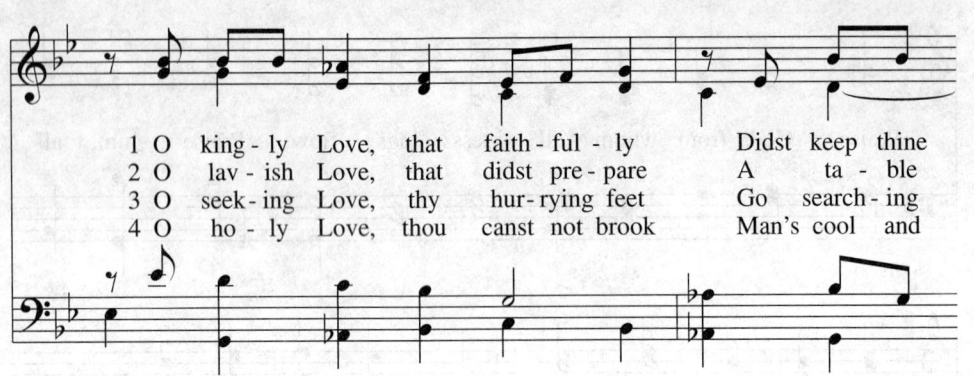

1 O kingly Love, that faithfully Didst keep thine ancient promises, Didst bid the bidden come to thee,
2 O lavish Love, that didst prepare A table bounteous as thy heart That men might leave their puny care
3 O seeking Love, thy hurrying feet Go searching still to urge and call The bad and good on ev-'ry street
4 O holy Love, thou canst not brook Man's cool and careless enmity; O ruthless Love, thou wilt not look

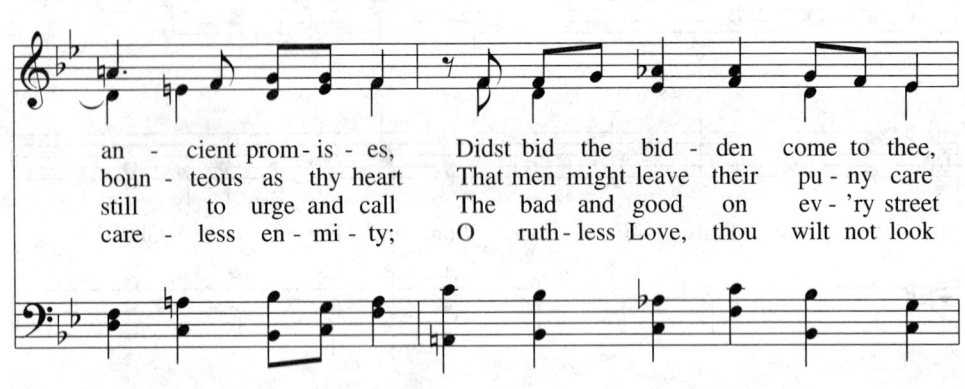

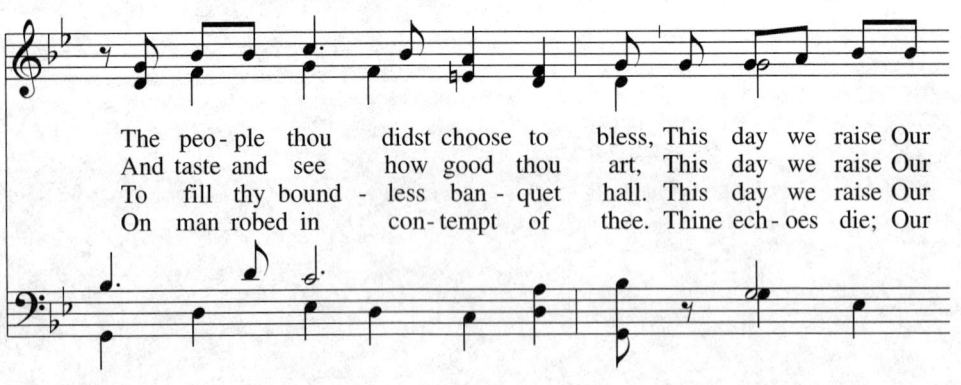

The people thou didst choose to bless, This day we raise Our
And taste and see how good thou art, This day we raise Our
To fill thy boundless banquet hall. This day we raise Our
On man robed in contempt of thee. Thine echoes die; Our

INVITATION

Text: Matthew Bridges, 1800-94, st. 1-2, 4, abr., alt.; Godfrey Thring, 1823-1903, st. 3
Tune: George J. Elvey, 1816-93; Desc. Walter L. Pelz, b. 1926

DIADEMATA
SM D

Descant © 1963 Augsburg Publishing House

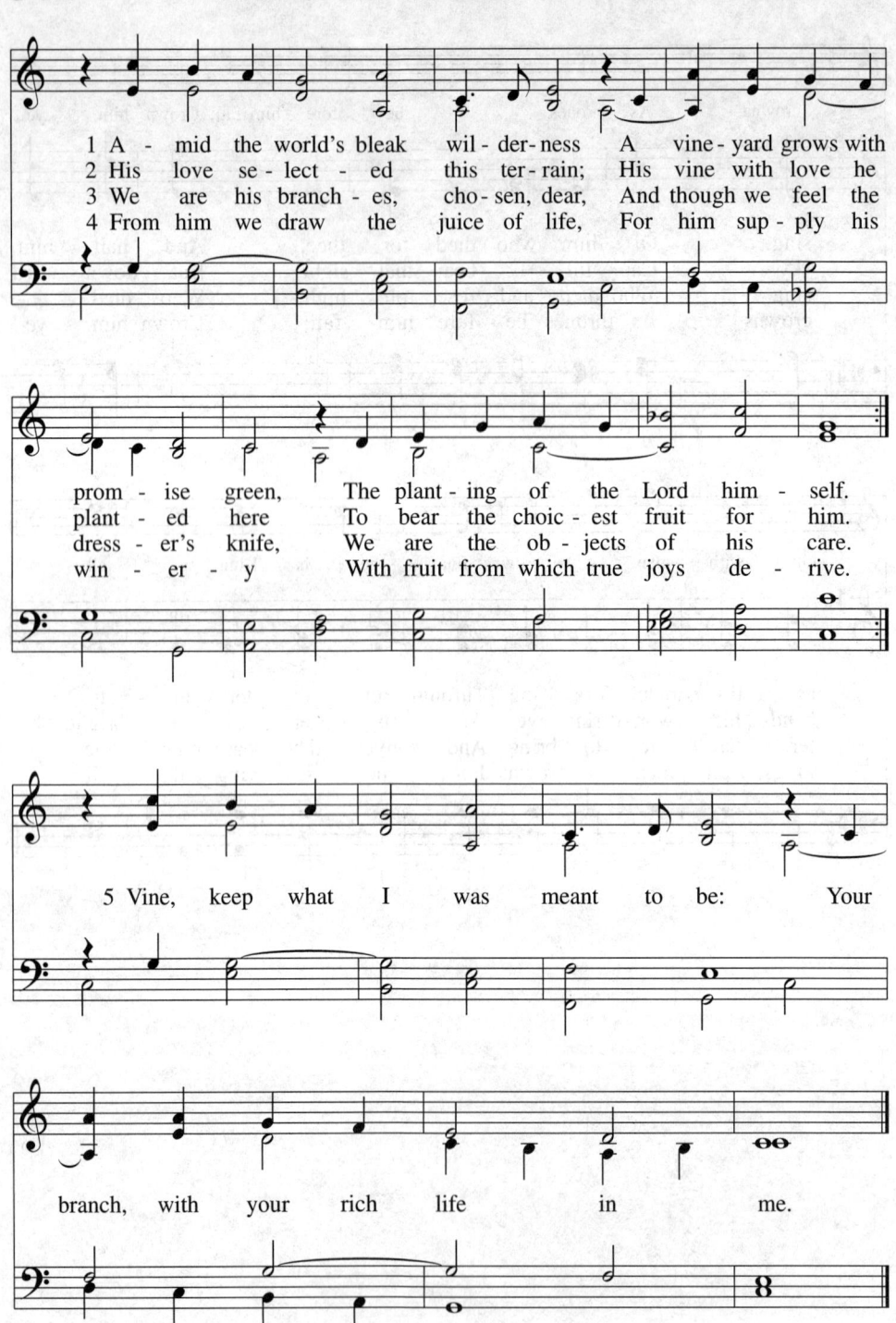

REDEEMER

Christ Is the World's Light 343

1 Christ is the world's light, Christ and none oth-er; Born in our darkness, he became our brother. If we have seen him, we have seen the Father: Glory to God on high!
2 Christ is the world's peace, Christ and none oth-er; No one can serve him and despise another. Who else unites us, one with God the Father? Glory to God on high!
3 Christ is the world's life, Christ and none oth-er; Sold once for silver, murdered here, our brother. He who redeemed us reigns with God the Father: Glory to God on high!
4 Give God the glory, God and none oth-er; Give God the glory, Spirit, Son, and Father; Give God the glory, God with us, my brother: Glory to God on high!

Text: Fred Pratt Green, b. 1903, alt.
Tune: *Antiphoner*, Paris, 1681

CHRISTE SANCTORUM
10 11 11 6

Text © 1969 Hope Publishing Co.; Setting © 1969 Concordia Publishing House

Alternate setting: 558

REDEEMER

5 In your hearts enthrone him;
  There let him subdue
All that is not holy,
  All that is not true.
Crown him as your captain
  In temptation's hour;
Let his will enfold you
  In its light and pow'r.

6 Christians, this Lord Jesus
  Shall return again
In his Father's glory,
  With his angel train;
For all wreaths of empire
  Meet upon his brow,
And our hearts confess him
  King of glory now.

Text: Caroline M. Noel, 1817-77, abr., alt.
Tune: Ralph Vaughan Williams, 1872-1958

KING'S WESTON
65 65 D

Tune and Setting reprinted by permission of Oxford University Press

In the Cross of Christ I Glory　　345

Text: John Bowring, 1792-1872
Tune: Ithamar Conkey, 1815-67

RATHBUN
87 87

346 In You Is Gladness

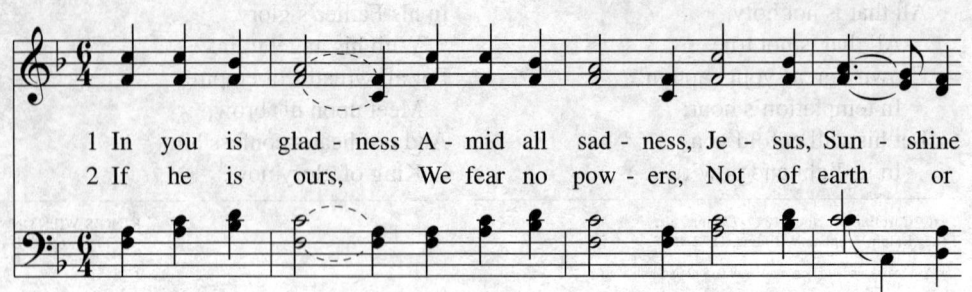

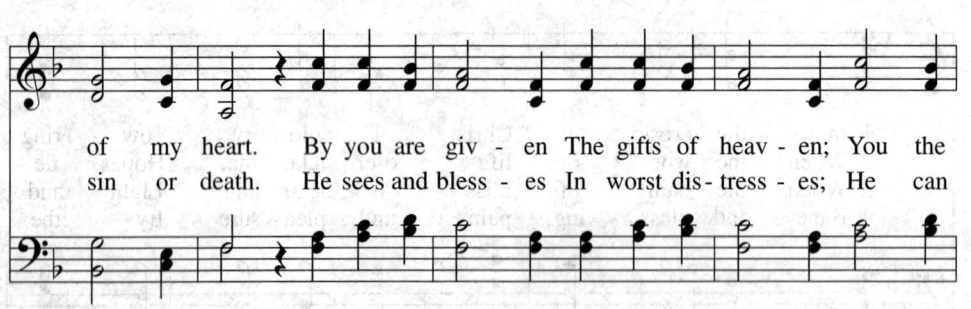

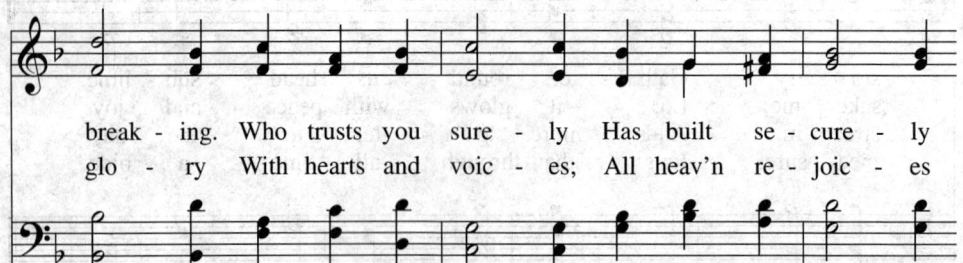

1. In you is gladness Amid all sadness, Jesus, Sunshine of my heart. By you are given The gifts of heaven; You the true Redeemer are. Our souls are waking; Our bonds are breaking. Who trusts you surely Has built securely

2. If he is ours, We fear no powers, Not of earth or sin or death. He sees and blesses In worst distresses; He can change them with a breath. Wherefore the story Tell of his glory With hearts and voices; All heav'n rejoices

REDEEMER

Text: Johann Lindemann, 1549-1631; tr. Catherine Winkworth, 1827-78, alt.
Tune: Giovanni G. Gastoldi, c. 1556-c. 1622
Setting © Oliver Ditson

IN DIR IST FREUDE
PM

REDEEMER

347 Jesus! and Shall It Ever Be

1. Jesus! and shall it ever be A mortal man ashamed of thee? Ashamed of thee, whom angels praise, Whose glories shine through endless days?
2. Ashamed of Jesus? Just as soon Let midnight be ashamed of noon. 'Tis midnight with my soul till he, Bright Morning Star, bids darkness flee.
3. Ashamed of Jesus, that dear friend On whom my hopes of heav'n depend? No; when I blush, be this my shame, That I no more revere his name.
4. Ashamed of Jesus? Yes, I may When I've no guilt to wash away, No tear to wipe, no good to crave, No fear to quell, no soul to save.
5. Till then — nor is my boasting vain —
   Till then I boast a Savior slain;
   And oh, may this my glory be:
   That Christ is not ashamed of me.

Text: Joseph Grigg, c. 1722-68, abr.; altered by Benjamin Francis, 1734-99
Tune: Henry K. Oliver, 1800-85

FEDERAL STREET
LM

REDEEMER

Jesus, Jesus, Only Jesus 348

1 Jesus, Jesus, only Jesus Can my heart-felt longing still.
  Lo, I pledge myself to Jesus, What he wills alone to will,
  For my heart, which he hath filled, Ever cries, "Lord, as thou wilt."

2 One there is for whom I'm living, Whom I love most tenderly;
  Unto Jesus I am giving What in love he gave to me.
  Jesus' blood hides all my guilt — Lord, oh, lead me as thou wilt.

3 What to me may seem a treasure But displeasing is to thee —
  Oh, remove such harmful pleasure; Give instead what profits me.
  Let my heart by thee be stilled; Make me thine, Lord, as thou wilt.

4 Let me earnestly endeavor Thy good pleasure to fulfill;
  In me, through me, with me ever, Lord, accomplish thou thy will.
  In thy holy image built, Let me die, Lord, as thou wilt.

5 Jesus, constant be my praises,
     For thou unto me didst bring
  Thine own self and all thy graces
     That I joyfully may sing:
  Be it unto me, my Shield,
     As thou wilt, Lord, as thou wilt.

Text: Ludämilia Elisabeth, 1640-72; tr. August Crull, 1845-1923, alt.
Tune: Das . . . vollkommenes Musikalisches Choral-Buch, Hamburg, 1715, alt.

JESUS, JESUS, NICHTS ALS JESUS
87 87 77

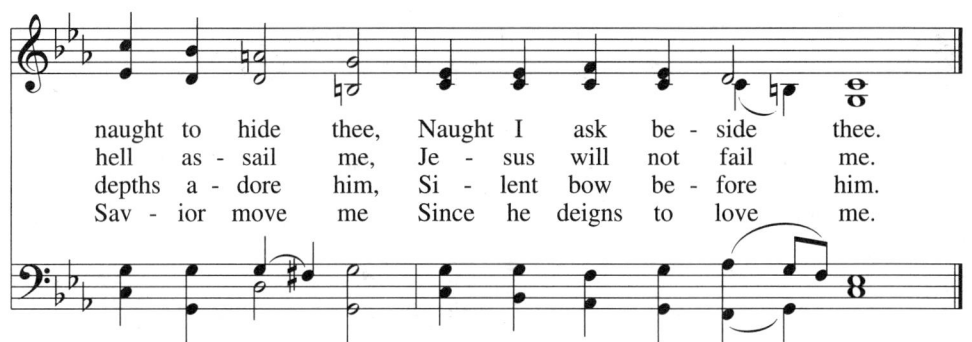

naught to hide thee, Naught I ask be - side thee.
hell as - sail me, Je - sus will not fail me.
depths a - dore him, Si - lent bow be - fore him.
Sav - ior move me Since he deigns to love me.

5 Hence, all fear and sadness!
For the Lord of gladness,
    Jesus, enters in.
Those who love the Father,
Though the storms may gather,
    Still have peace within.
Yea, whate'er I here must bear,
Thou art still my purest pleasure,
    Jesus, priceless treasure!

Text: Johann Franck, 1618-77, abr.; tr. Catherine Winkworth, 1827-78,
    st. 1-2, 4-5, alt.; *The Lutheran Hymnal*, St. Louis, 1941, st. 3
Tune: Johann Crüger, 1598-1662
Setting © 1982 Concordia Publishing House

JESU, MEINE FREUDE
665 665 34 86

350 All Praise Be Yours

1. All praise be yours, for you, O King divine, Your rightful glory freely did resign That in our darkened hearts your grace might shine. Alleluia!
2. You came to us in lowliness of thought; By you the outcast and the poor were sought, And by your death was God's salvation wrought. Alleluia!
3. O Jesus, let your mind within us be, For you were servant that we might be free And humbly stooped to death on Calvary. Alleluia!
4. Therefore you are, by God's eternal vow, Most high exalted o'er all creatures now And giv'n the name to which all knees shall bow. Alleluia!

5. Let ev'ry tongue confess with one accord
   In heav'n and earth that Jesus Christ is Lord,
   And God the Father be by all adored.
   Alleluia!

Text: F. Bland Tucker, 1895-1984, alt.
Tune: Lawrence P. Schreiber, b. 1933
Text © The Church Pension Fund; Tune and Setting © 1967 The Bethany Press

NATIONAL CITY
10 10 10 with Alleluia

REDEEMER

Hail, O Once-Despised Jesus 351

1 Hail, O once-despised Jesus! Hail, O Galilean King!
You have suffered to release us, Hope to give and peace to bring.
Hail, O universal Savior, Bearer of our sin and shame;
By your merits we find favor; Life is given through your name.

2 Paschal Lamb, by God appointed, All our sins on you were laid;
By almighty love anointed, You have full atonement made.
Ev'ry sin has been forgiven Through the power of your blood;
Open is the gate of heaven; We are reconciled to God.

3 Jesus, heav'nly hosts adore you, Seated at your Father's side.
Crucified this world once saw you; Now in glory you abide.
There for sinners you are pleading, And our place you now prepare,
Ever for us interceding Till in glory we appear.

4 Worship, honor, pow'r, and blessing You are worthy to receive;
Loudest praises, without ceasing, Right it is for us to give.
Help, O bright angelic spirits, All your noblest anthems raise;
Help to sing our Savior's merits; Help to chant Immanuel's praise.

Text: *A Collection of Hymns,* London, c. 1757, alt.
Tune: Freylinghausen, *Geist-reiches Gesang-Buch,* Halle, 1704, alt.

O DURCHBRECHER ALLER BANDE
87 87 D

Alternate setting: 87

REDEEMER

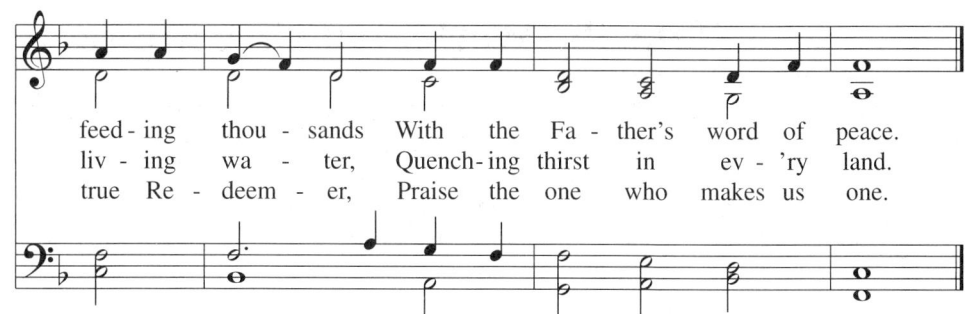

feed - ing thou - sands With the Fa - ther's word of peace.
liv - ing wa - ter, Quench-ing thirst in ev - 'ry land.
true Re - deem - er, Praise the one who makes us one.

Text: Rusty Edwards, b. 1955, alt.
Tune: attr. Benjamin F. White, 1800-79

BEACH SPRING
87 87 D

Text © 1987 Hope Publishing Co.; Setting © 1978 *Lutheran Book of Worship*

Lamb of God, We Fall before You   354

1 Lamb of God, we fall be - fore you, Hum - bly trust - ing in your cross.
2 Je - sus is the per - fect Sav - ior, On - ly source of all that's good;
3 Je - sus gives us true re - pent - ance By his Spir - it sent from heav'n,
4 Faith he grants us to be - lieve it, Grate - ful hearts his love to prize;

Our great joy is to a - dore you; All things else are on - ly dross.
Ev - 'ry grace and ev - 'ry fa - vor Come to us through Je - sus' blood.
Whis - pers this as - sur - ing sen - tence, "All your sins are now for - giv'n."
Want we wis - dom? He must give it, Hear - ing ears and see - ing eyes.

    5 Jesus gives us pure affections,
       Wills to do what he requires,
       Makes us follow his directions,
       And what he commands, inspires.

    6 All our prayers and all our praises,
       Rightly offered in his name —
       He that asks for them is Jesus;
       He that answers is the same.

Text: Joseph Hart, 1712-68, alt.
Tune: *Erbaulicher Musicalischer Christen-Schatz*, Basel, 1745, alt.

RINGE RECHT
87 87

REDEEMER

Text: Fanny J. Crosby, 1820-1915, abr., alt.
Tune: J. Paul Williams, b. 1937, and Donna L. Williams, b. 1940

GIVE ME JESUS
87 87 with Refrain

Tune © 1980 Hope Publishing Co.; Setting © 1993 Hope Publishing Co.

You Are the Way; through You Alone 356

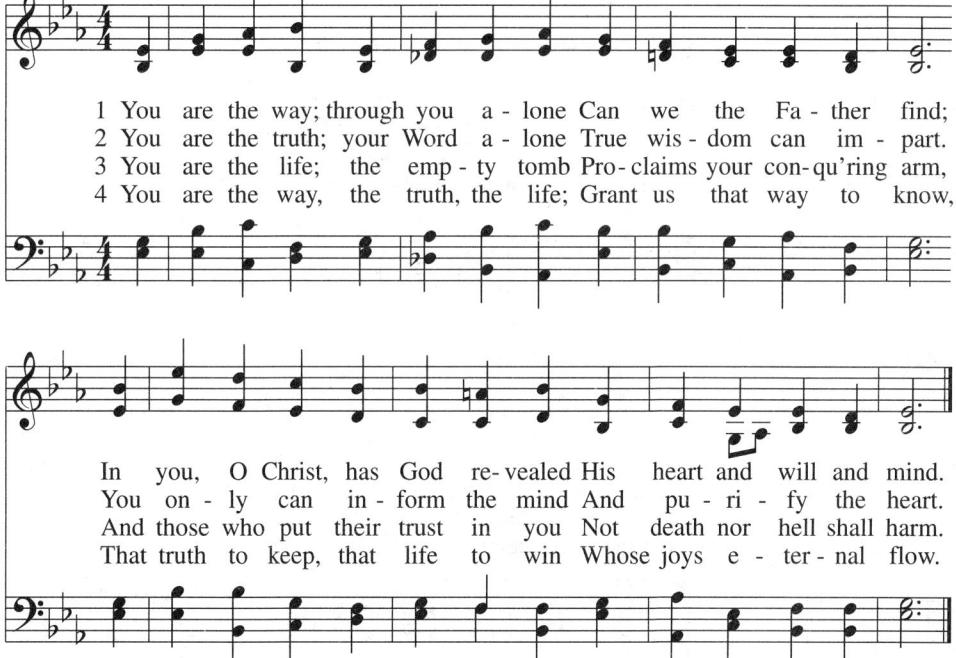

1 You are the way; through you alone Can we the Father find;
In you, O Christ, has God revealed His heart and will and mind.
2 You are the truth; your Word alone True wisdom can impart.
You only can inform the mind And purify the heart.
3 You are the life; the empty tomb Proclaims your conqu'ring arm,
And those who put their trust in you Not death nor hell shall harm.
4 You are the way, the truth, the life; Grant us that way to know,
That truth to keep, that life to win Whose joys eternal flow.

Text: George W. Doane, 1799-1859, alt.
Tune: *The CL Psalms of David,* Edinburgh, 1615

DUNDEE
CM

Alternate setting: 420

REDEEMER

How Sweet the Name of Jesus Sounds 358

1 How sweet the name of Jesus sounds In a believer's ear! It soothes our sorrows, heals our wounds, And drives away all fear.
2 It makes the wounded spirit whole And calms the heart's unrest; 'Tis manna to the hungry soul And to the weary, rest.
3 Dear name! The rock on which I build, My shield and hiding place, My never-failing treasury filled With boundless stores of grace.
4 By you my prayers acceptance gain Although with sin defiled; Satan accuses me in vain For God calls me his child.

5 O Jesus, Shepherd, Guardian, Friend,
  My Prophet, Priest, and King,
  My Lord, my Life, my Way, my End,
  Accept the praise I bring.

6 I praise in weakness from afar —
  How cold my warmest thought!
  But when I see you as you are,
  I'll praise you as I ought.

7 Till then I would your love proclaim
  With ev'ry fleeting breath;
  And may the music of your name
  Refresh my soul in death.

Text: John Newton, 1725-1807, alt.
Tune: Alexander R. Reinagle, 1799-1877
Setting © 1982 Concordia Publishing House

ST. PETER
CM
Alternate settings: 405, 509

REDEEMER

The Lord's My Shepherd; I'll Not Want 360

1. The Lord's my shepherd; I'll not want. He makes me down to lie In pastures green; he leadeth me The quiet waters by.
2. My soul he doth restore again And me to walk doth make With-in the paths of righteousness, E'en for his own name's sake.
3. Yea, though I walk in death's dark vale, Yet will I fear no ill; For thou art with me, and thy rod And staff me comfort still.
4. My table thou hast furnished In presence of my foes; My head thou dost with oil anoint, And my cup overflows.

5. Goodness and mercy, all my life,
Shall surely follow me,
And in God's house forevermore
My dwelling-place shall be.

Text: *The Psalms of David in Meeter,* Edinburgh, 1650
Tune: William Gardiner, 1770-1853, adapt.

BELMONT
CM

Lord Jesus Christ, My Savior Blest 362

1 Lord Jesus Christ, My Savior blest, My Hope and my Salvation! Lord, hear my plea: Deliver me From misery! Your Word brings consolation.
2 Lord, as you will, So lead me still; Your mercy fails me never. My God, I pray: Teach me your way To my last day; From evil keep me ever.
3 I have your Word, Christ Jesus, Lord: You never will forsake me! This will I plead In time of need. Oh, help with speed When troubles overtake me!
4 Now henceforth must I put my trust In you, O dearest Savior. Your gracious choice, Your Word and voice, Make me rejoice Though sinful my behavior.

5 Grant, Lord, I pray,
   Your grace each day,
   That I, your name revering,
      Your glory see
      And happy be
      Eternally,
   Before your throne appearing.

Text: Hans C. Sthen, b. c. 1540, abr.; tr. Harriet R. K. Spaeth, 1845-1925, alt.
Tune: Ludvig M. Lindeman, 1812-87

HERRE JESU KRIST
447 444 7

363 The King of Glory Comes

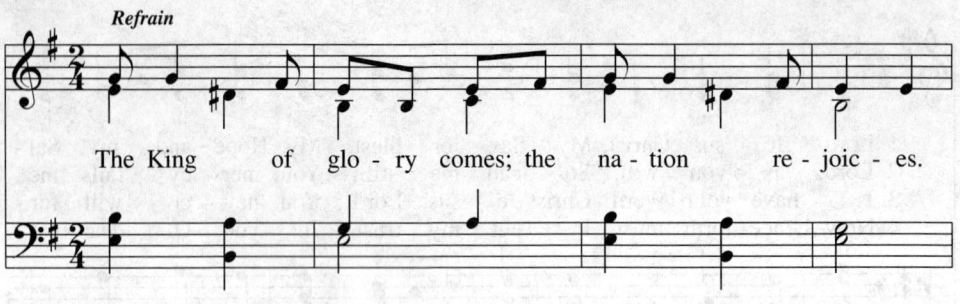

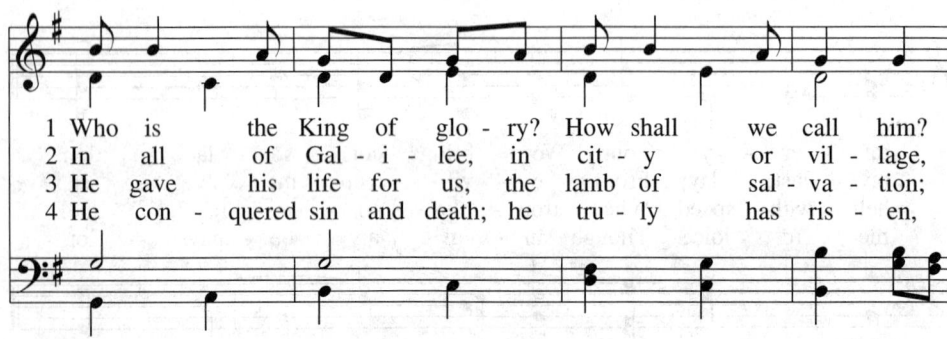

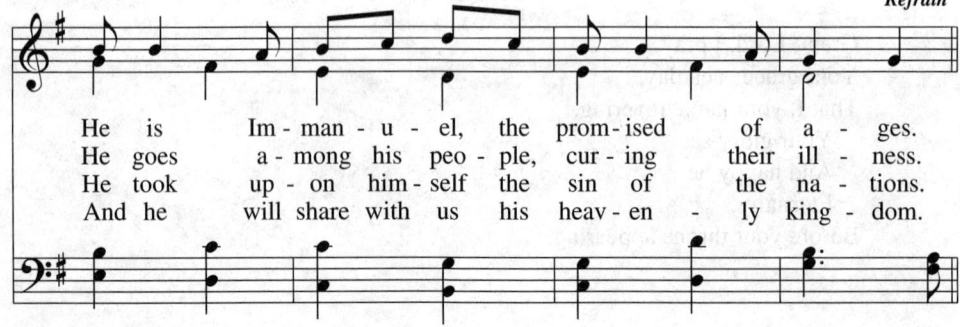

Text: Willard F. Jabusch, b. 1930, alt.
Tune: Israeli melody, 20th century

PROMISED ONE
12 12 with Refrain

Text © 1966, 1985 Willard F. Jabusch; Setting reprinted by permission of United Church Press

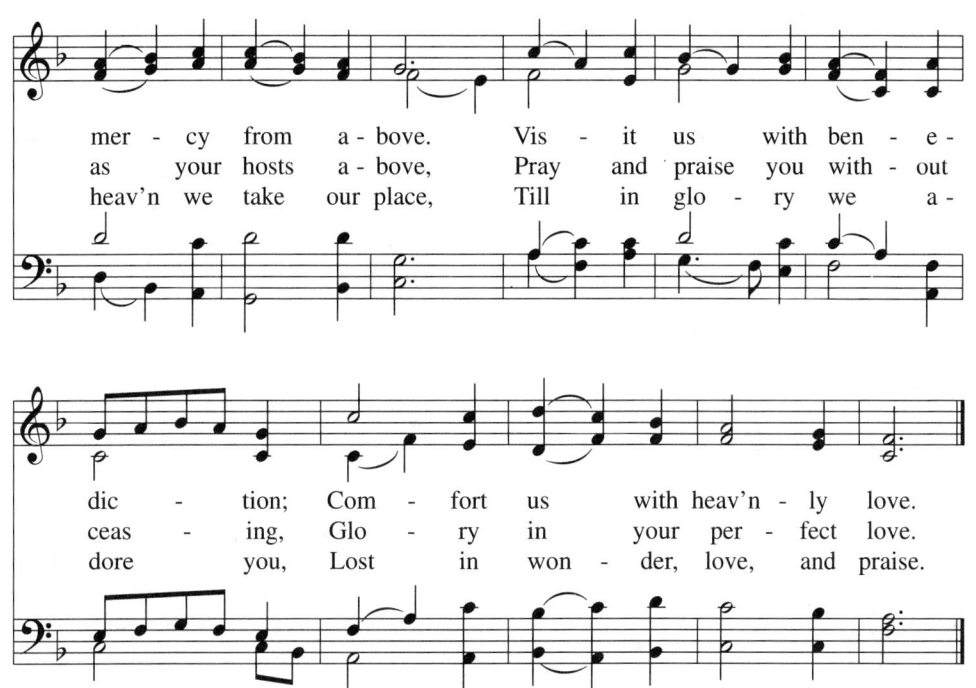

REDEEMER

Text: Charles Wesley, 1707-88, adapt., alt.
Tune: Rowland H. Prichard, 1811-87

HYFRYDOL
87 87 D

Alternate settings: 486, 603

370 All Hail the Power of Jesus' Name

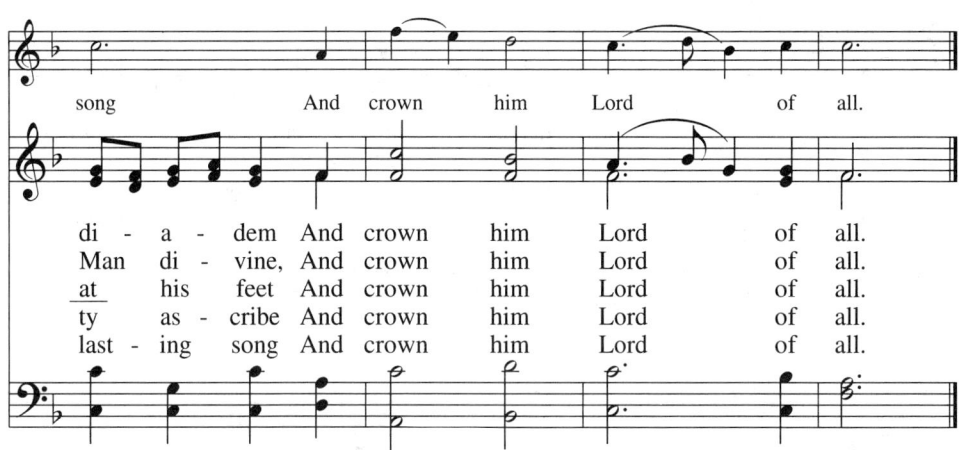

Text: Edward Perronet, 1726-92, st. 1-3, abr., alt.; *A Selection of Hymns,* London, 1787, st. 4-5, alt.
Tune: Oliver Holden, 1765-1844; Desc. Michael E. Young, b. 1939, alt.

CORONATION
86 86 86

Descant © 1979 by GIA Publications, Inc.

5 For us, by wickedness betrayed,
   For us, in crown of thorns arrayed,
   He bore the shameful cross and death;
   For us he gave his dying breath.

6 For us he rose from death again;
   For us he went on high to reign;
   For us he sent his Spirit here
   To guide, to strengthen, and to cheer.

7 All glory to our Lord and God
   For love so deep, so high, so broad,
   The Trinity whom we adore
   Forever and forevermore.

Text: attr. Thomas à Kempis, 1380-1471, abr.; tr. Benjamin Webb, 1819-85, alt.
Tune: English melody, 15th century; Setting: *Hymns Ancient & Modern, Revised,* 1950.

Setting © 1985 Hope Publishing Co.

DEO GRACIAS
LM

Alternate setting: 96

REDEEMER

O Jesus, King Most Wonderful 373

1 O Jesus, King most wonderful, / O Majesty renowned, / O Conqueror invincible, / In whom all joys are found,
2 When once you visit darkened hearts, / Then truth begins to shine, / Then earthly vanity departs, / Then kindles love divine.
3 O Jesus, Light of all below, / O Fount of life and fire, / Surpassing all the joys we know, / All that we can desire.
4 May ev'ry heart confess your name, / Forever you adore, / Enkindled with the Spirit's flame / To love you more and more.

5 Oh, may our tongues forever bless
And honor you alone,
And may we in our lives express
The image of your own!

Text: attr. Bernard of Clairvaux, 1091-1153, abr.; tr. Edward Caswall, 1814-78, alt.
Tune: John B. Dykes, 1823-76

ST. AGNES
CM

REDEEMER

374 My Shepherd Will Supply My Need

1. My shepherd will supply my need — Jehovah is his name.
   In pastures fresh he makes me feed Beside the living stream.
   He brings my wand'ring spirit back When I forsake his ways
   And ...

2. When I walk through the shades of death, His presence is my stay;
   One word of his supporting breath Drives all my fears away.
   His hand, in sight of all my foes, Will still my table spread;
   My ...

3. The sure provisions of my God Attend me all my days;
   Oh, may his house be my abode And all my work be praise.
   There would I find a settled rest While others go and come,
   No ...

REDEEMER

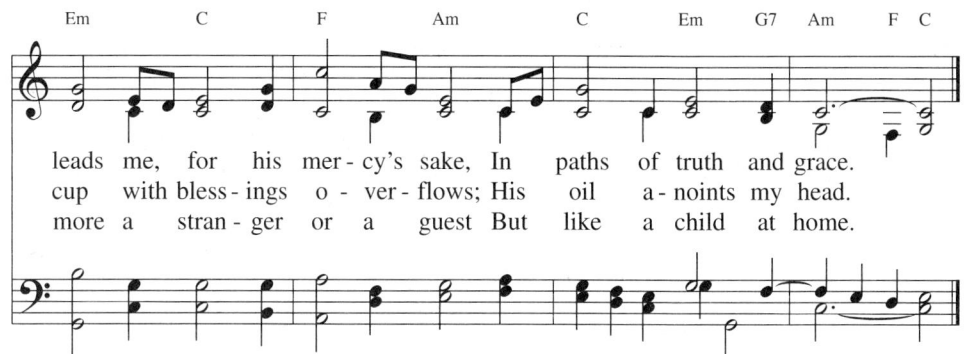

Text: Isaac Watts, 1674-1748, alt.
Tune: *A Compilation of Genuine Church Music,* Winchester, VA, 1832
Setting © 1993 Kermit G. Moldenhauer

RESIGNATION
CM D

REDEEMER

375 The King of Love My Shepherd Is

1 The King of love my shepherd is, Whose goodness fails me never; I nothing lack if I am his, And he is mine forever.

2 Where streams of living water flow, My Savior gently leads me; And where the verdant pastures grow, With food celestial feeds me.

3 Confused and foolish oft I strayed, But yet in love he sought me And on his shoulder gently laid And home, rejoicing, brought me.

4 In death's dark vale I fear no ill With you, dear Lord, beside me; Your rod and staff my comfort still, Your cross before to guide me.

5 You spread a table in my sight,
A banquet here bestowing;
Your oil of welcome, my delight;
My cup is overflowing!

6 And so through all the length of days
Your goodness fails me never.
Good Shepherd, may I sing your praise
Within your house forever!

Text: Henry W. Baker, 1821-77, alt.
Tune: Irish melody, c. 18th century, alt.

ST. COLUMBA
87 87 Iambic

JUSTIFICATION

Jesus, Your Blood and Righteousness 376

1 Jesus, your blood and righteousness
My beauty are, my glorious dress;
Mid flaming worlds, in these arrayed,
With joy shall I lift up my head.

2 Bold shall I stand in that great day —
Who can a word against me say?
Fully through you absolved I am
From sin and fear, from guilt and shame.

3 Lord, I believe your precious blood,
Which at the very throne of God
Forever will for sinners plead,
For me — e'en for my soul — was shed.

4 Lord, I believe were sinners more
Than sands upon the ocean shore,
You have for all a ransom paid,
For all a full atonement made.

5 When from the dust of death I rise
To claim my mansion in the skies,
E'en then this shall be all my plea:
Jesus has lived and died for me.

6 Jesus, be worshiped endlessly!
Your boundless mercy has for me,
For me and all your hands have made,
An everlasting ransom paid.

Text: Nicolaus L. von Zinzendorf, 1700-60, abr.; tr. John B. Wesley, 1703-91, alt.
Tune: George J. Elvey, 1816-93

ST. CRISPIN
LM

Alternate setting: 391

5 He spoke to his beloved Son:
 "'Tis time to have compassion.
 Then go, bright Jewel of my crown,
 And bring mankind salvation.
 From sin and sorrow set them free;
 Slay bitter death for them that they
 May live with you forever."

6 The Son obeyed his Father's will,
 Was born of virgin mother,
 And, God's good pleasure to fulfill,
 He came to be my brother.
 No garb of pomp or pow'r he wore;
 A servant's form like mine he bore
 To lead the devil captive.

7 To me he spoke, "Hold fast to me —
 I am your rock and castle.
 Your ransom I myself will be;
 For you I strive and wrestle.
 For I am yours, your friend divine,
 And evermore you shall be mine;
 The foe shall not divide us.

8 "The foe shall shed my precious blood,
 Me of my life bereaving.
 All this I suffer for your good;
 Be steadfast and believing.
 Life shall from death the vict'ry win;
 My innocence shall bear your sin,
 And you are blest forever.

9 "Now to my Father I depart,
 The Holy Spirit sending
 And, heav'nly wisdom to impart,
 My help to you extending.
 He will a source of comfort be,
 Teach you to know and follow me,
 And in all truth will guide you.

10 "What I on earth have lived and taught
 Be all your life and teaching;
 So shall my kingdom's work be wrought
 And honored in your preaching.
 Take care that no one's man-made laws
 Should e'er destroy the gospel's cause.
 This final word I leave you."

Text: Martin Luther, 1483-1546; tr. Richard Massie, 1800-87, alt.
Tune: *Etlich Cristlich lider,* Wittenberg, 1524

NUN FREUT EUCH, LIEBEN CHRISTEN
87 87 887

Alternate setting: 72

JUSTIFICATION

378 All Mankind Fell in Adam's Fall

1 All mankind fell in Adam's fall; One common sin infects us all. From one to all the curse descends, And o-ver all God's wrath impends.

2 Through all our pow'rs corruption creeps And us in dreadful bondage keeps; In guilt we draw our infant breath And reap its fruits of woe and death.

3 From hearts depraved, to evil prone, Flow thoughts and deeds of sin alone; God's image lost, the darkened soul Nor seeks nor finds its heav'nly goal.

4 But Christ, the second Adam, came To bear our sin and woe and shame, To be our life, our light, our way, Our only hope, our only stay.

5 As by one man all mankind fell
And, born in sin, was doomed to hell,
So by one Man, who took our place,
We all were justified by grace.

6 We thank you, Christ; new life is ours,
New light, new hope, new strength, new pow'rs;
This grace our ev'ry way attend
Until we reach our journey's end.

Text: Lazarus Spengler, 1479-1534, abr.; tr. Matthias Loy, 1828-1915, st. 1-4, 6, alt.; *The Lutheran Hymnal*, St. Louis, 1941, st. 5, alt.
Tune: Louis Bourgeois, c. 1510-c. 1561

WENN WIR IN HÖCHSTEN NÖTEN SEIN
LM

Alternate setting: 102

JUSTIFICATION

Amazing Grace—How Sweet the Sound 379

Text: John Newton, 1725-1807, st. 1-3, abr.; John P. Rees, 19th century, st. 4
Tune: *Columbian Harmony,* Cincinnati, 1829, alt.
Setting © 1964 Abingdon Press

NEW BRITAIN
CM

pur-	pose	you	or-dained	me,	That	I	live	for	you	a-	lone.
well	that,	if	I	love	you,	You,	O	Fa-	ther,	loved me	first.
vid-	ed	ad-	o-ra-	tion	To	the	great	Je-	ho-	vah	give.

Text: Josiah Conder, 1789-1855, alt.
Tune: *Erbaulicher Musicalischer Christen-Schatz,* Basel, 1745, alt.

Setting © 1993 Elfred Bloedel

O DU LIEBE MEINER LIEBE
87 87 D

Alternate setting: 108

Grace Has a Thrilling Sound   381

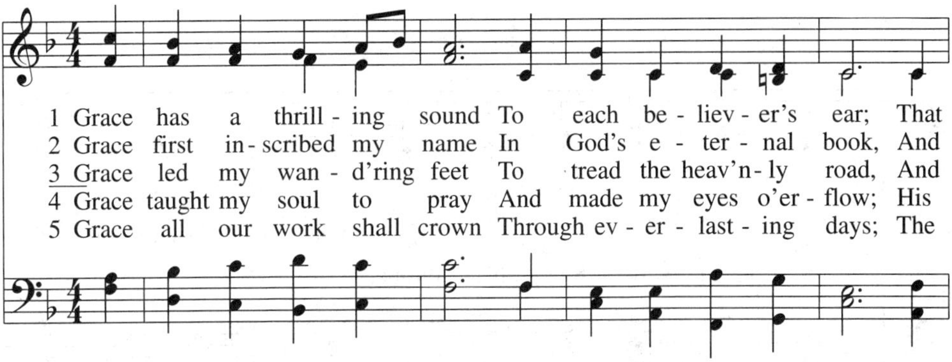

1 Grace has a thrill-ing sound To each be-liev-er's ear; That
2 Grace first in-scribed my name In God's e-ter-nal book, And
3 Grace led my wan-d'ring feet To tread the heav'n-ly road, And
4 Grace taught my soul to pray And made my eyes o'er-flow; His
5 Grace all our work shall crown Through ev-er-last-ing days; The

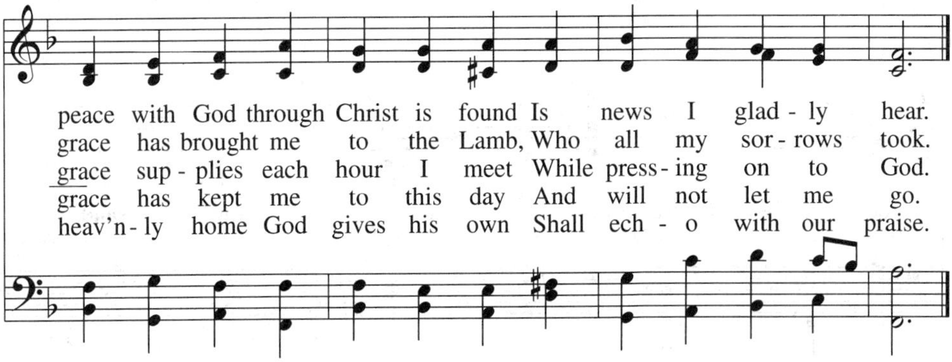

peace with God through Christ is found Is news I glad-ly hear.
grace has brought me to the Lamb, Who all my sor-rows took.
grace sup-plies each hour I meet While press-ing on to God.
grace has kept me to this day And will not let me go.
heav'n-ly home God gives his own Shall ech-o with our praise.

Text: Philip Doddridge, 1702-51, st. 1, 3, 5, alt.; Augustus M. Toplady, 1740-78, st. 2, 4, alt.
Tune: William H. Monk, 1823-89

ENERGY
SM

Alternate setting: 555

JUSTIFICATION

5 Let mercy cause me to be willing
    To bear my lot and not to fret.
   While he my restless heart is stilling,
    May I his mercy not forget!
   Whatever comes my heart to test,
    His mercy is my only rest.

6 Lord, I will stand on this foundation
    As long as I on earth remain;
   This will engage my meditation
    While I the breath of life retain.
   And then, when face to face with you,
   I'll sing your mercy great and true.

Text: Johann A. Rothe, 1688-1758, abr.; tr. composite
Tune: Johann B. König, 1691-1758

O DASS ICH TAUSEND ZUNGEN HÄTTE (KÖNIG)
98 98 88

Alternate settings: 242, 294

Drawn to the Cross 387

1 Drawn to the cross, which you have blessed With healing gifts for souls distressed, To find in you my life, my rest, Christ crucified, I come.
2 How well you know my griefs and fears, Your grace abused, my misspent years; So now to you with contrite tears, Christ crucified, I come.
3 Wash me and take away each stain; Let nothing of my sin remain. For cleansing through your cross and pain, Christ crucified, I come.
4 To pledge my labor willingly, Which shall so sweet a service be That angels well might envy me, Christ crucified, I come.

Text: Genevieve M. Irons, 1855-1928, alt.
Tune: Joseph Barnby, 1838-96
Setting © 1978 Lutheran Book of Worship

JUST AS I AM
888 6

JUSTIFICATION

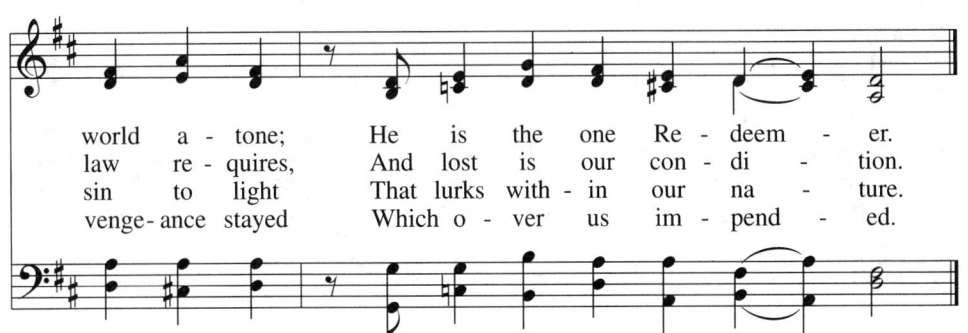

```
world a-tone;        He is the one Re-deem-er.
law re-quires,       And lost is our con-di-tion.
sin to light         That lurks with-in our na-ture.
venge-ance stayed    Which o-ver us im-pend-ed.
```

5 Since Christ has full atonement made
   And brought to us salvation,
Each Christian therefore may be glad
   And build on this foundation.
Your grace alone, dear Lord, I plead;
Your death is now my life indeed,
For you have paid my ransom.

6 All blessing, honor, thanks, and praise
   To Father, Son, and Spirit,
The God who saved us by his grace —
   All glory to his merit!
O Triune God in heav'n above,
You have revealed your saving love;
Your blessed name be hallowed!

Text: Paul Speratus, 1484-1551, abr.; tr. composite
Tune: *Etlich Cristlich lider*, Wittenberg, 1524, alt.

ES IST DAS HEIL
87 87 887

Alternate setting: 299

JUSTIFICATION

391 God Loved the World So that He Gave

1 God loved the world so that he gave His only
Son the lost to save That all who would in
him believe Should everlasting life receive.

2 Christ is the solid rock of faith, Who was made
flesh and suffered death. All who confide in
him alone Are built on this chief cornerstone.

3 God would not have the sinner die— His Son with
saving grace is nigh. His Spirit in the
Word does teach How we the blessed goal may reach.

4 Be of good cheer, for God's own Son Forgives the
sins that you have done. You're justified by
Jesus' blood; Baptized, you are a child of God.

5 When you are sick, when death draws near,
This truth your troubled heart can cheer:
Christ Jesus saves my soul from death —
This is the anchor of my faith!

6 Glory to God the Father, Son,
And Holy Spirit, Three in One!
To you, O blessed Trinity,
Be praise now and eternally!

Text: *Heiliges Lippen . . . Gesangbuch*, Stettin, c. 1778; tr. August Crull, 1845-1923, alt.
Tune: George J. Elvey, 1816-93

ST. CRISPIN
LM

Alternate setting: 376

JUSTIFICATION

5 My guilt, O Father, you have laid
    On Christ, your Son, my Savior.
  Lord Jesus, you my debt have paid
    And gained for me God's favor.
  O Holy Spirit, Fount of grace,
    The good in me to you I trace;
  In faith and hope preserve me.

Text: Johann Heermann, 1585-1647, st. 1-4, abr.;
Neu-vermehrtes vollständiges Gesangbuch, Braunschweig, 1661, st. 5; tr. composite
Tune: *Etlich Cristlich lider,* Wittenberg, 1524

NUN FREUT EUCH, LIEBEN CHRISTEN
87 87 887

Setting © 1993 Kermit G. Moldenhauer

Alternate setting: 173

Blessed Are the Saints of God 394

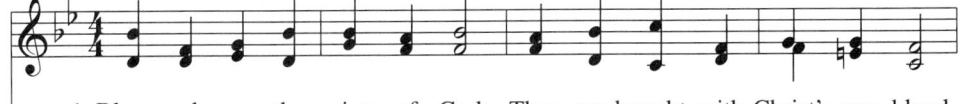
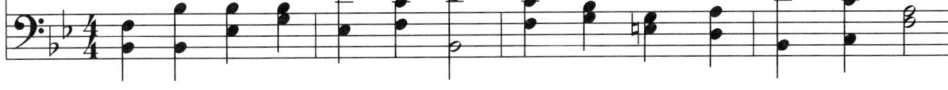

1 Bless-ed are the saints of God; They are bought with Christ's own blood.
2 They are jus-ti-fied by grace; They en-joy the Sav-ior's peace.
3 They are lights up-on the earth, Chil-dren of a heav'n-ly birth.

They are ran-somed from the grave; Life e-ter-nal they shall have.
All their sins are washed a-way; They shall stand in God's great day.
One with God, with Je-sus one, Glo-ry is in them be-gun.

With them num-bered may we be Here and in e-ter-ni-ty.
With them num-bered may we be Here and in e-ter-ni-ty.
With them num-bered may we be Here and in e-ter-ni-ty.

Text: Joseph Humphreys, b. 1720, alt.
Tune: Johann G. Ebeling, 1637-76

VOLLER WUNDER
77 77 77

Alternate setting: 580

JUSTIFICATION

395   Seek Where You May to Find a Way

1. Seek where you may To find a way That leads to your salvation. My heart is stilled; On Christ I build — He is the one foundation. His Word is sure; His works endure. He will o'erthrow My

2. Seek whom you may To be your stay; None can redeem his brother. All helpers failed; This man prevailed, The God-Man, and none other. The Servant-Lord Our life restored. We're justified, For

3. Seek him alone, Who did atone, Who did your souls deliver; Oh, seek him first, All you who thirst For grace that fails you never. In ev'ry need Seek him indeed; To ev'ry heart He

4. My heart's delight, My crown most bright, Jesus, you are forever. Not wealth or pride Or aught beside Our bond of love shall sever. You are my Lord; Your precious Word Shall be my guide What-

JUSTIFICATION

ev - 'ry foe; Through him I more than con - quer.
he has died, The guilt - less for the guilt - y.
will im - part His bless - ings with - out mea - sure.
e'er be - tide. Oh, teach me, Lord, to trust you!

Text: Georg Weissel, 1590-1635, abr.; tr. Arthur P. Voss, 1899-1955, alt.
Tune: Johann Stobäus, 1580-1646, alt.

SUCH, WER DA WILL
447 447 44 447

In Adam We Have All Been One 396

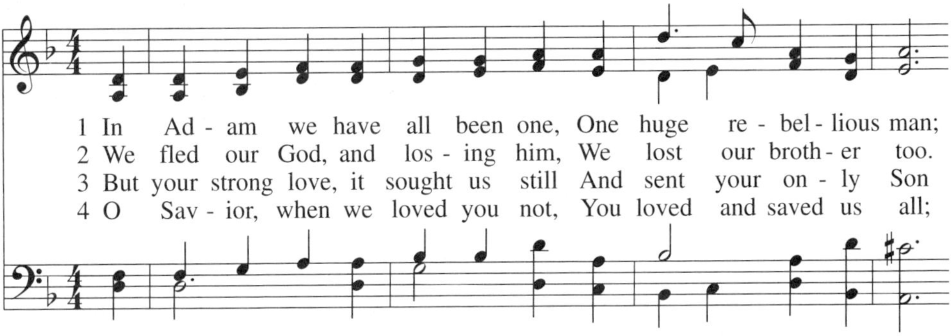

1 In Ad - am we have all been one, One huge re - bel - lious man;
2 We fled our God, and los - ing him, We lost our broth - er too.
3 But your strong love, it sought us still And sent your on - ly Son
4 O Sav - ior, when we loved you not, You loved and saved us all;

We all have fled that eve - ning voice That sought us as we ran.
Each sin - gly sought and claimed his own; Each man his broth - er slew.
That we might hear his shep - herd - voice And, hear - ing him, be one.
O great good Shep - herd of man - kind, Oh, hear us when we call.

5 Send us your Spirit; teach us truth
   To purge our vanity.
   From fancied wisdom, self-sought ways,
   O Savior, set us free.

6 Then shall our song united rise
   To your eternal throne,
   Where with the Father evermore
   And Spirit you are one.

Text: Martin H. Franzmann, 1907-76, alt.
Tune: Kurt J. Eggert, 1923-93

ADAM
CM

Text © 1969 Concordia Publishing House; Tune and Setting © 1993 Kurt J. Eggert

JUSTIFICATION

397 Just As I Am, without One Plea

1. Just as I am, without one plea
But that thy blood was shed for me
And that thou bidd'st me come to thee,
O Lamb of God, I come, I come.

2. Just as I am, and waiting not
To rid my soul of one dark blot,
To thee, whose blood can cleanse each spot,
O Lamb of God, I come, I come.

3. Just as I am, though tossed about
With many a conflict, many a doubt,
Fightings and fears within, without,
O Lamb of God, I come, I come.

4. Just as I am, poor, wretched, blind;
Sight, riches, healing of the mind,
Yea, all I need, in thee to find,
O Lamb of God, I come, I come.

5. Just as I am, thou wilt receive,
Wilt welcome, pardon, cleanse, relieve;
Because thy promise I believe,
O Lamb of God, I come, I come.

6. Just as I am; thy love unknown
Has broken ev'ry barrier down.
Now to be thine, yea, thine alone,
O Lamb of God, I come, I come.

Text: Charlotte Elliott, 1789-1871
Tune: William B. Bradbury, 1816-68

WOODWORTH
LM

JUSTIFICATION

Lord, We Confess Our Numerous Faults 398

1. Lord, we confess our num'rous faults, How great our guilt has been, How vain and foolish all our thoughts, How deeply stained with sin.
2. But oh, my soul, forever praise, Forever love, his name Who turns your feet from dan-g'rous ways Of folly, sin, and shame.
3. 'Tis not by works of righteousness Which our own hands have done, But we are saved by God's free grace Abounding through his Son.
4. 'Tis from the mercy of our God That all our hopes begin; 'Tis by the water and the blood Our souls are washed from sin.

5. 'Tis through the purchase of his death
Who hung upon the tree
The Spirit is sent down to breathe
On such dry bones as we.

6. Raised from the dead, we live anew;
And, justified by grace,
We shall appear in glory, too,
And see our Father's face.

Text: Isaac Watts, 1674-1748, alt.
Tune: *The Whole Booke of Psalmes,* London, 1562, alt.

ST. FLAVIAN
CM

Alternate setting: 412

JUSTIFICATION

400 O God, O Lord of Heaven and Earth

JUSTIFICATION

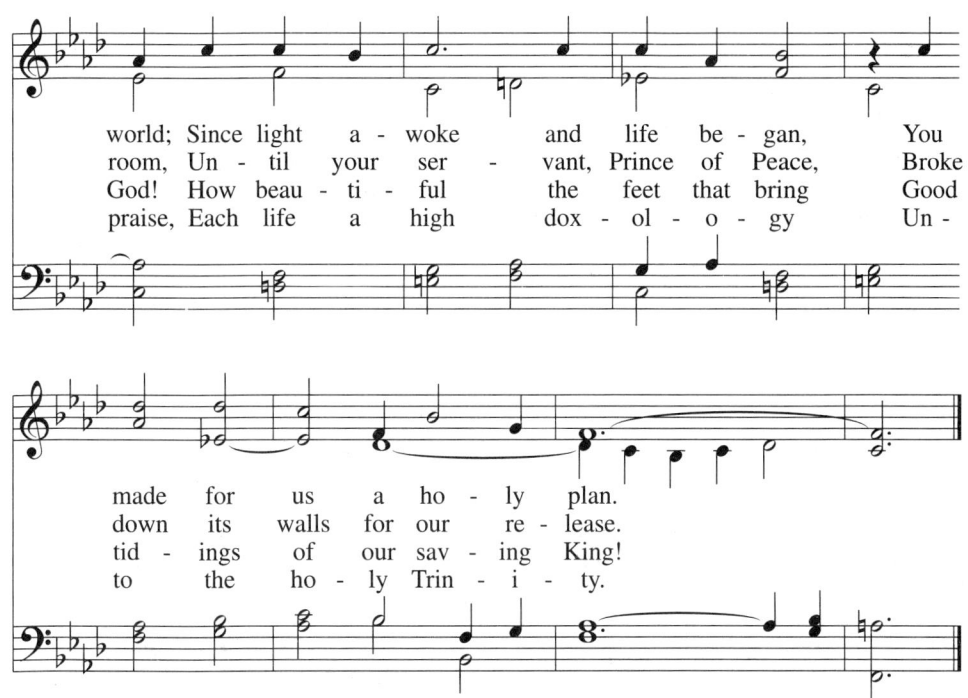

Text: Martin H. Franzmann, 1907-76, alt.
Tune: Jan O. Bender, 1909-94

WITTENBERG NEW
LM D

Text and Tune © 1978 *Lutheran Book of Worship;* Setting © 1969 Concordia Publishing House

JUSTIFICATION

401 Your Works, Not Mine, O Christ

1 Your works, not mine, O Christ, Speak gladness to this heart.
  They tell me all is done;
  They bid my fear depart.

2 Your blood, not mine, O Christ, Can heal my sinful soul;
  Your wounds, not mine, contain
  The balm that makes me whole.

3 Your cross, not mine, O Christ, Has borne the dreadful load
  Of sins that none could bear
  But the incarnate God.

4 Your death, not mine, O Christ, Has paid the ransom due;
  Ten thousand deaths like mine
  Would have been all too few.

Refrain
To whom but you, who can alone
For sin atone, Lord, shall I flee?

5 Your righteousness, O Christ,
  Alone can cover me;
  No other righteousness
  Can set a sinner free.
     Refrain

Text: Horatius Bonar, 1808-89, alt.
Tune: *The Parish Choir*, London, 1850

ST. JOHN
66 66 88

My Faith Looks Up to Thee 402

FAITH

1 My faith looks up to thee, Thou Lamb of Cal-va-ry, Sav-ior di-vine. Now hear me while I pray; Take all my guilt a-way; Oh, let me from this day Be whol-ly thine!
2 May thy rich grace im-part Strength to my faint-ing heart; My zeal in-spire! As thou hast died for me, Oh, may my love to thee Pure, warm, and change-less be, A liv-ing fire!
3 While life's dark maze I tread And griefs a-round me spread, Be thou my guide. Bid dark-ness turn to day, Wipe sor-row's tears a-way, Nor let me ev-er stray From thee a-side.
4 When ends life's tran-sient dream, When death's cold, sul-len stream Shall o'er me roll, Blest Sav-ior, then, in love, Fear and dis-trust re-move; Oh, bear me safe a-bove, A ran-somed soul!

Text: Ray Palmer, 1808-87
Tune: Lowell Mason, 1792-1872, alt.

OLIVET
664 6664

Text: Erdmann Neumeister, 1671-1756; tr. composite
Tune: *Concentus novi,* Augsburg, 1540, alt.

NUN LOB, MEIN SEEL
78 78 76 76 76 76

Alternate setting: 257

404 Faith Is a Living Power from Heaven

1. Faith is a living pow'r from heav'n
That grasps the promise God has giv'n,
A trust that cannot be o'erthrown,
Fixed heartily on Christ alone.

2. Faith finds in Christ whate'er we need
To save or strengthen us indeed,
Receiving grace from heaven's throne
And humbly sharing cross and crown.

3. Faith in the Savior brings us peace
And bids the mourner's weeping cease;
By faith the children's place we claim
And give all honor to one name.

4. We thank you, then, O God of heav'n,
That you to us this faith have giv'n
Through mighty Word and sacrament
To trust the one whom you have sent.

5. As you have promised, grant each soul
Its holy faith's true end and goal:
The blessedness no foes destroy,
Eternal love and light and joy.

Text: Petrus Herbert, d. 1571, abr.; tr. Catherine Winkworth, 1827-78, alt.
Tune: *As hymnodus sacer,* Leipzig, 1625, alt.

HERR JESU CHRIST, MEINS
LM

Alternate settings: 223, 547

Oh, for a Faith that Will Not Shrink 405

FAITH

1. Oh, for a faith that will not shrink Though pressed by many a foe, That will not tremble on the brink Of poverty or woe,
2. That will not murmur nor complain Beneath the chast'ning rod, But in the hour of grief or pain Can lean upon its God,
3. A faith that shines more bright and clear When tempests rage without, That, when in danger, knows no fear, In darkness feels no doubt,
4. That bears unmoved the world's dread frown Nor heeds its scornful smile, That sin's wild ocean cannot drown Nor Satan's arts beguile,

5. A faith that keeps the narrow way
Till life's last spark is fled
And with a pure and heav'nly ray
Lights up the dying bed.

6. Lord, give us such a faith as this,
And then, whate'er may come,
We'll taste e'en now the hallowed bliss
Of an eternal home.

Text: William H. Bathurst, 1796-1877
Tune: Alexander R. Reinagle, 1799-1877

ST. PETER
CM

Alternate settings: 358, 509

FAITH

406 This Is the Threefold Truth

1. This is the three-fold truth on which our faith depends;
And with this joyful cry worship begins and ends:
2. Made sacred by long use, new-minted for our time,
Our liturgies sum up the hope we have in him:
3. On this we fix our minds as, kneeling side by side,
We take the bread and wine, take him, the Crucified:
4. By this we are upheld when doubt or grief assails
Our Christian faith and love, and only grace avails:
5. This is the threefold truth which, if we hold it fast,
Changes the world and us and brings us home at last:

Refrain
Christ has died! Christ is risen! Christ will come again!

Text: Fred Pratt Green, b. 1903, alt.
Tune: Jack Schrader, b. 1942

ACCLAMATIONS
12 12 12

Text, Tune, Setting © 1980 Hope Publishing Co.

PRAYER

408 Christians, While on Earth Abiding

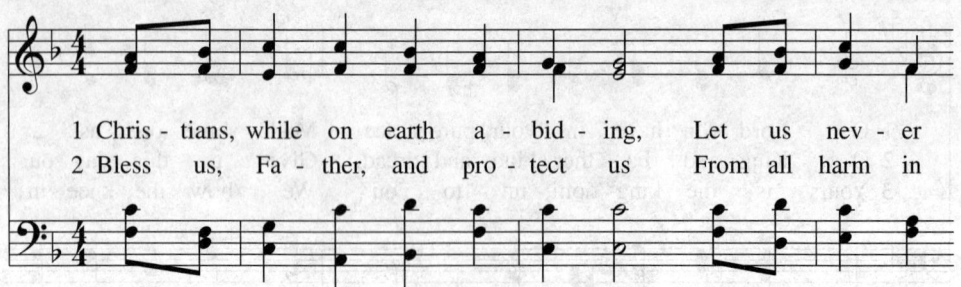

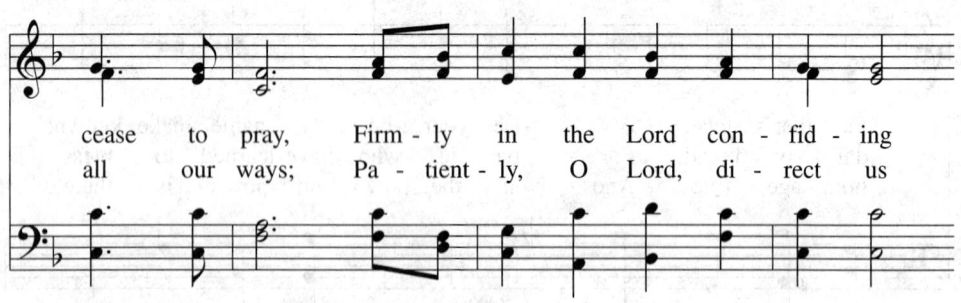

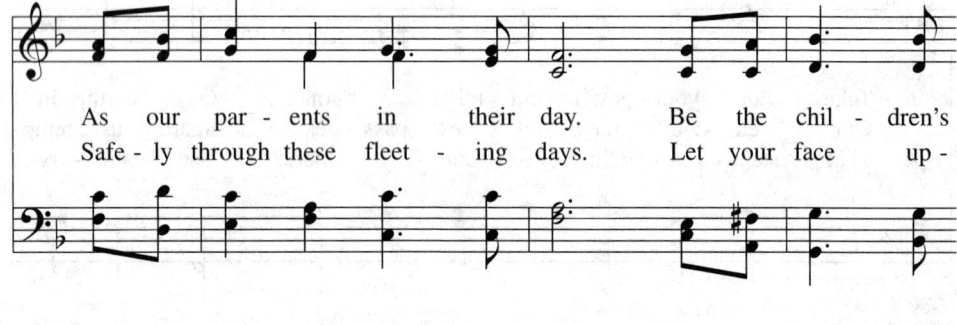

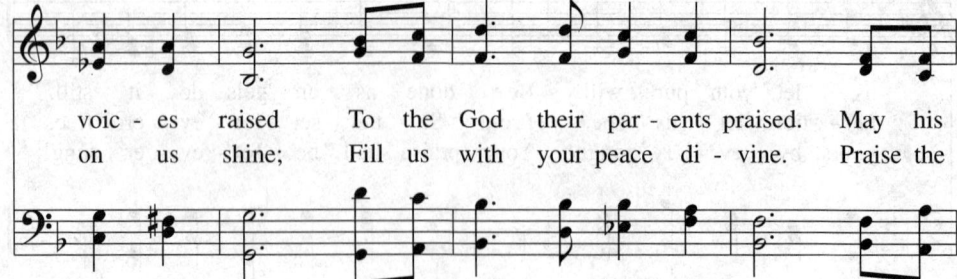

1 Christians, while on earth abiding, Let us never cease to pray, Firmly in the Lord confiding As our parents in their day. Be the children's voices raised To the God their parents praised. May his

2 Bless us, Father, and protect us From all harm in all our ways; Patiently, O Lord, direct us Safely through these fleeting days. Let your face upon us shine; Fill us with your peace divine. Praise the

PRAYER

| bless - ing, fail - ing nev - er, | Rest up - on his peo - ple ev - er.
| Fa - ther, Son, and Spir - it! | Praise him, all who life in - her - it!

Text: Johann Olof Wallin, 1779-1839, st. 1, abr.; Jesper Svedberg, 1653-1735, st. 2;
tr. *Hymnal and Order of Service,* Rock Island, 1901, alt.
Tune: Johann Schop, c. 1590-1667

WERDE MUNTER
87 87 77 88

Alternate settings: 147, 283

Come, My Soul, with Every Care 409

1 Come, my soul, with ev - 'ry care; Je - sus loves to an - swer prayer.
2 You are com - ing to a king — Large pe - ti - tions with you bring,
3 With my bur - den I be - gin: Lord, re - move this load of sin;
4 Lord, your rest to me im - part; Take pos - ses - sion of my heart.

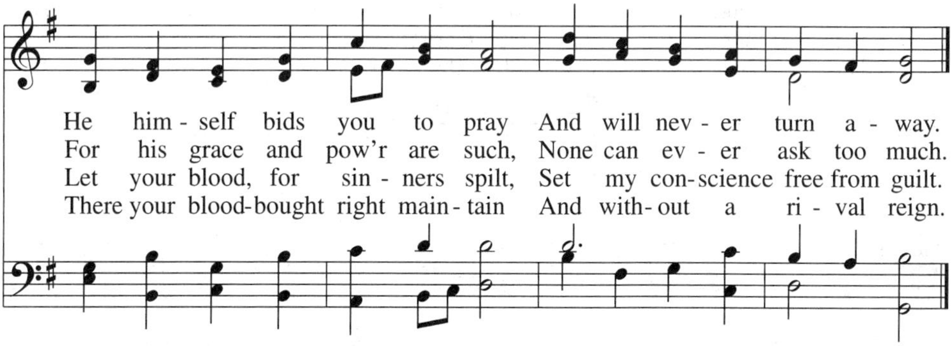

He him - self bids you to pray And will nev - er turn a - way.
For his grace and pow'r are such, None can ev - er ask too much.
Let your blood, for sin - ners spilt, Set my con - science free from guilt.
There your blood-bought right main - tain And with - out a ri - val reign.

5 While I am a pilgrim here,
  Let your love my spirit cheer.
  As my guide, my guard, my friend,
  Lead me to my journey's end.

6 Show me what I am to do;
  Ev'ry hour my strength renew.
  Let me live a life of faith;
  Let me die your people's death.

Text: John Newton, 1725-1807, abr., alt.
Tune: Justin H. Knecht, 1752-1817

VIENNA
77 77

Alternate setting: 426

5 Give us today our daily bread,
　　And let us all be clothed and fed.
　From hardship, war, and earthly strife,
　　From sickness, famine, spare our life.
　Let selfishness and worry cease
　　That we may live in godly peace.

6 Forgive our sins, Lord, we implore,
　　That they may trouble us no more;
　We, too, will gladly those forgive
　　Who hurt us by the way they live.
　Help us in our community
　　To serve each other willingly.

7 Into temptation lead us not.
　　When evil foes against us plot
　And vex our souls on ev'ry hand,
　　Oh, give us strength that we may stand
　Firm in the faith, a mighty host,
　　Through comfort of the Holy Ghost.

8 From evil, Lord, deliver us;
　　The times and days are perilous.
　Redeem us from eternal death,
　　And, when we yield our dying breath,
　Console us, grant us calm release,
　　And take our souls to you in peace.

9 Amen, that is, it shall be so.
　　Make strong our faith that we may know
　That we may doubt not but believe
　　What here we ask we shall receive.
　Thus in your name and at your Word
　　We say, "Amen. Oh, hear us, Lord!"

Text: Martin Luther, 1483-1546; tr. composite
Tune: attr. Martin Luther, 1483-1546

VATER UNSER IM HIMMELREICH, DER DU
88 88 88

Alternate settings: 306, 407, 479

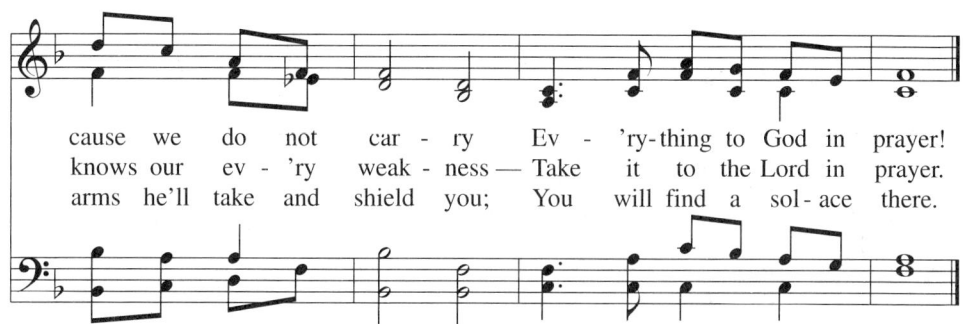

cause we do not car-ry Ev-'ry-thing to God in prayer!
knows our ev-'ry weak-ness— Take it to the Lord in prayer.
arms he'll take and shield you; You will find a sol-ace there.

Text: Joseph M. Scriven, 1820-86, alt.
Tune: Charles C. Converse, 1832-1918

CONVERSE
87 87 D

Lord, Teach Us How to Pray Aright 412

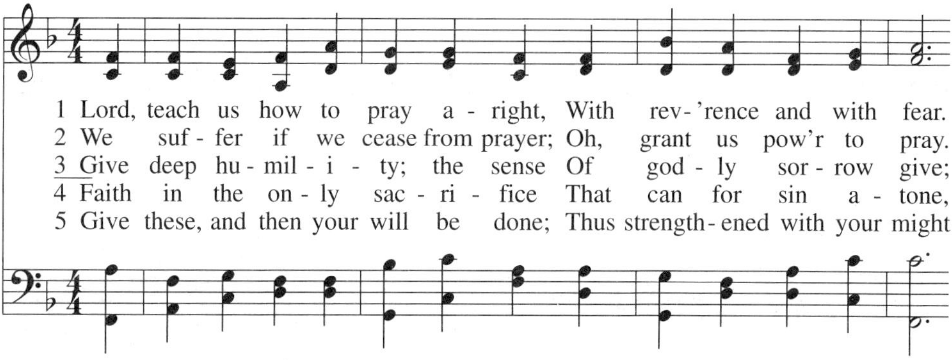

1 Lord, teach us how to pray a-right, With rev-'rence and with fear.
2 We suf-fer if we cease from prayer; Oh, grant us pow'r to pray.
3 Give deep hu-mil-i-ty; the sense Of god-ly sor-row give;
4 Faith in the on-ly sac-ri-fice That can for sin a-tone,
5 Give these, and then your will be done; Thus strength-ened with your might

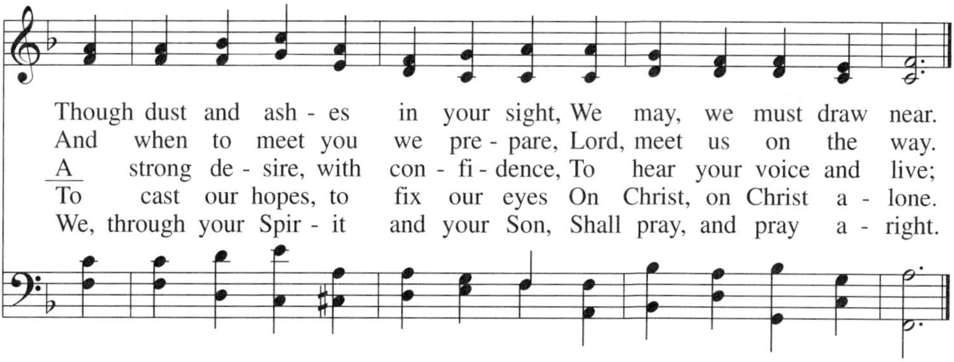

Though dust and ash-es in your sight, We may, we must draw near.
And when to meet you we pre-pare, Lord, meet us on the way.
A strong de-sire, with con-fi-dence, To hear your voice and live;
To cast our hopes, to fix our eyes On Christ, on Christ a-lone.
We, through your Spir-it and your Son, Shall pray, and pray a-right.

Text: James Montgomery, 1771-1854, abr., alt.
Tune: *The Whole Booke of Psalmes,* London, 1562, alt.
Setting © 1993 Kermit G. Moldenhauer

ST. FLAVIAN
CM
Alternate setting: 398

PRAYER

413 When in the Hour of Utmost Need

1 When in the hour of utmost need
  We know not where to look for aid,
  When days and nights of anxious thought
  Nor help nor counsel yet have brought,

2 Then is our comfort this alone
  That we may meet before your throne;
  To you, O faithful God, we cry
  For rescue in our misery.

3 For you have promised, Lord, to heed
  Your children's cries in time of need
  Through him whose name alone is great,
  Our Savior and our advocate.

4 And so we come, O God, today
  And all our woes before you lay.
  Be with us in our anguish still;
  Free us at last from ev'ry ill,

5 So that with all our hearts we may
  To you our glad thanksgiving pay,
  Then walk obedient to your Word
  And now and ever praise you, Lord.

Text: Paul Eber, 1511-69, abr., adapt.; tr. Catherine Winkworth, 1827-78, alt.
Tune: Louis Bourgeois, c. 1510-c. 1561
Setting © 1982 Concordia Publishing House

WENN WIR IN HÖCHSTEN NÖTEN SEIN
LM
Alternate setting: 378

TRUST

FINLANDIA
10 10 10 10 10 10

Text: Catharina A. von Schlegel, 1697-1752, abr.; tr. Jane L. Borthwick, 1813-97, alt.
Tune: Jean J. C. Sibelius, 1865-1957, adapt.
Tune © Breitkopf & Härtel; Setting © 1933 Presbyterian Board of Christian Education. Renewed 1961.

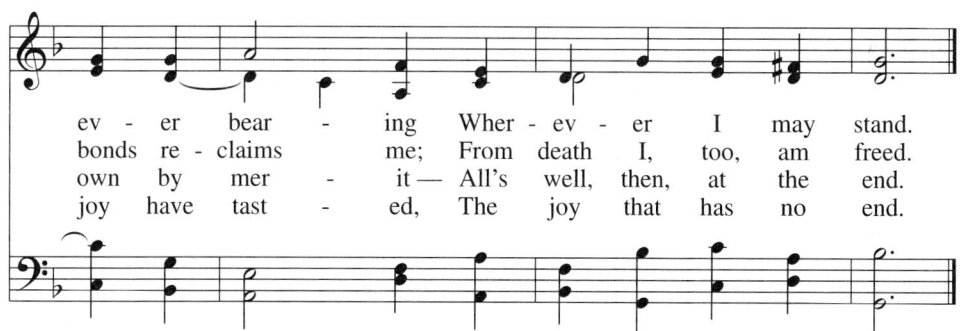

5 And when the world will perish
   With all its pride and pow'r,
All that the world may cherish
   Will vanish in that hour.
But though in death they make
   The deepest grave our cover,
When there our sleep is over,
   Our God will us awake.

Text: Ludwig Helmbold, 1532-98, abr.; tr. Catherine Winkworth, 1827-78,
   st. 1, 4-5, alt.; *The Lutheran Hymnal,* St. Louis, 1941, st. 2-3, alt.
Tune: *Recueil de plusieurs chansons,* Lyons, 1557, alt.

VON GOTT WILL ICH NICHT LASSEN
76 76 67 76

5 No sin can now condemn me
    Or set my hope aside.
  Now hell no more can claim me;
    Its fury I deride.
  No sentence now reproves me;
    No guilt destroys my peace,
  For Christ, my Savior, loves me
    And shields me with his grace.

6 No danger, thirst, or hunger,
    No pain or poverty,
  No earthly tyrant's anger
    Shall ever vanquish me.
  Though earth should break asunder,
    You are my Savior true;
  No fire or sword or thunder
    Shall sever me from you.

7 My heart for joy is springing
    And can no more be sad,
  'Tis full of joy and singing,
    Sees only sunshine glad.
  The sun that cheers my spirit
    Is Jesus Christ, my King;
  The heav'n I shall inherit
    Makes me rejoice and sing.

Text: Paul Gerhardt, 1607-76, abr.; tr. Richard Massie, 1800-87,
  st. 1-3, 6-7, alt.; unknown, st. 4-5, alt.
Tune: Melchior Teschner, 1584-1635, alt.
Setting © 1993 Kermit G. Moldenhauer

VALET WILL ICH DIR GEBEN
76 76 D

Alternate settings: 19, 94

God Moves in a Mysterious Way — 420

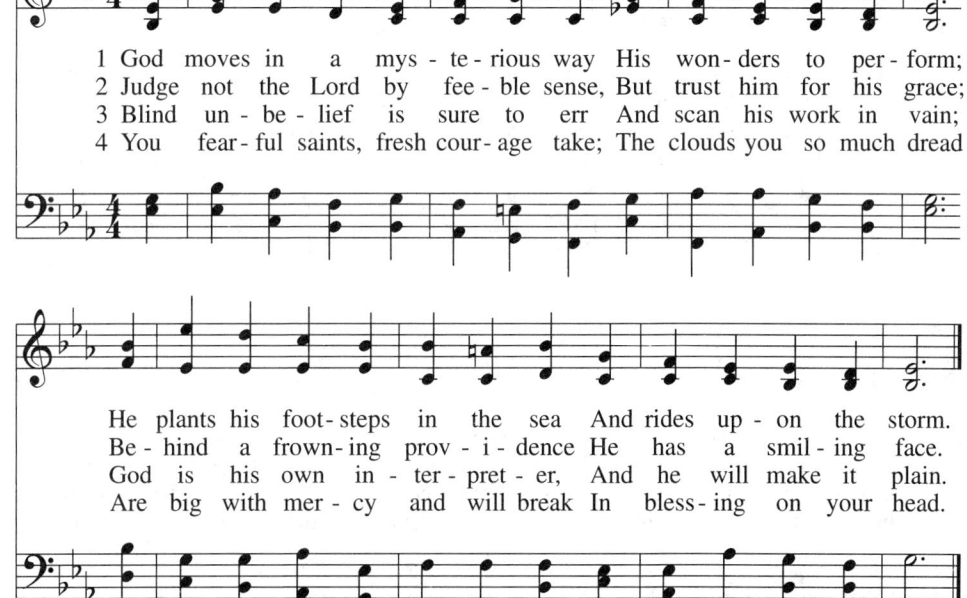

1 God moves in a mysterious way His wonders to perform;
  He plants his footsteps in the sea And rides upon the storm.
2 Judge not the Lord by feeble sense, But trust him for his grace;
  Behind a frowning providence He has a smiling face.
3 Blind unbelief is sure to err And scan his work in vain;
  God is his own interpreter, And he will make it plain.
4 You fearful saints, fresh courage take; The clouds you so much dread
  Are big with mercy and will break In blessing on your head.

Text: William Cowper, 1731-1800, abr., alt.
Tune: *The CL Psalms of David*, Edinburgh, 1615
Setting © 1993 Elfred Bloedel

DUNDEE
CM

Alternate setting: 324

421 All Depends on Our Possessing

1 All depends on our possessing God's abundant grace and blessing, Though all earthly wealth depart. They who trust with faith unshaken In their God are not forsaken And e'er keep a dauntless heart.

2 He who to this day has fed me And to many joys has led me Is and ever shall be mine. He who ever gently schools me, He who daily guides and rules me, Will remain my help divine.

3 Many spend their lives in fretting Over trifles and in getting Things that have no solid ground. I shall strive to win a treasure That will bring me lasting pleasure And that now is seldom found.

4 Well he knows what best to grant me; All the longing hopes that haunt me, Joy and sorrow, have their day. I shall doubt his wisdom never— As God wills, so be it ever— I to him commit my way.

5 If on earth my days he lengthen,
    He my weary soul will strengthen;
  All my trust in him I place.
    Earthly wealth is not abiding,
  Like a stream away is gliding;
    Safe I anchor in his grace.

Text: Andächtige Haus-Kirche, Nürnberg, 1676, abr.; tr. Catherine Winkworth, 1827-78, alt.
Tune: Johann Löhner, 1645-1705, alt.

ALLES IST AN GOTTES SEGEN
887 887

Jesus, Lead Us On 422

1 Jesus, lead us on Till our rest is won; And although the way be cheerless, We will follow, calm and fearless. Guide us by your hand To our fatherland.

2 If the way be drear, If the foe be near, Let not faithless fears o'ertake us; Let not faith and hope forsake us, For through many a woe To our home we go.

3 When we seek relief From a long-felt grief, When temptations come alluring, Make us patient and enduring; Show us that bright shore Where we weep no more.

4 Jesus, still lead on Till our rest is won. Heav'nly Leader, still direct us; Still support, console, protect us Till we safely stand In our fatherland.

Text: Nicolaus L. von Zinzendorf, 1700-60, adapt.; tr. Jane L. Borthwick, 1813-97, alt.
Tune: Adam Drese, 1620-1701

SEELENBRÄUTIGAM
55 88 55

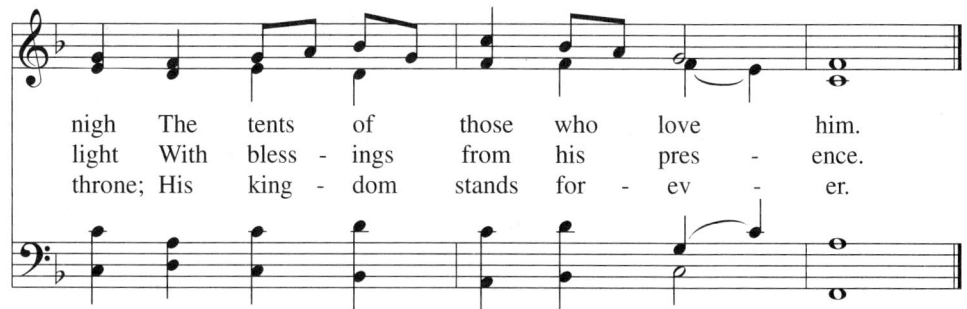

nigh The tents of those who love him.
light With bless - ings from his pres - ence.
throne; His king - dom stands for - ev - er.

Text: Julius L. Krohn, 1835-88; tr. Ernest E. Ryden, 1886-1981 and Toivo K. I. Harjunpaa, b. 1910, alt.
Tune: Christian Egenolff, 1502-55, adapted by Ralph Vaughan Williams, 1872-1958

WÄCHTERLIED
87 87 887

Text reprinted by permission of The Lutheran World Federation; Tune reprinted by permission of Oxford University Press

Yours Forever, God of Love   426

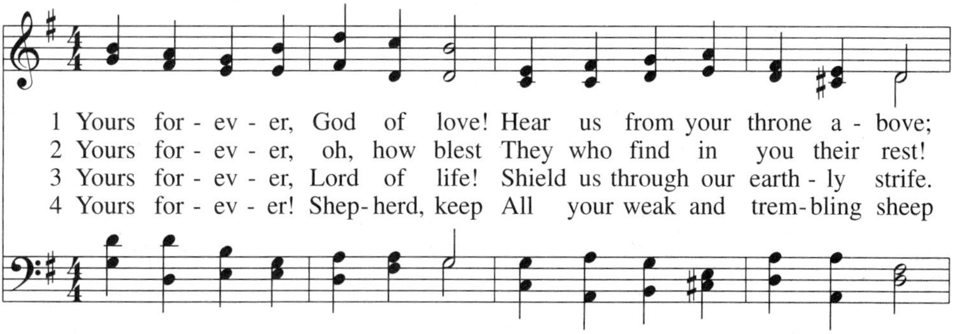

1 Yours for - ev - er, God of love! Hear us from your throne a - bove;
2 Yours for - ev - er, oh, how blest They who find in you their rest!
3 Yours for - ev - er, Lord of life! Shield us through our earth - ly strife.
4 Yours for - ev - er! Shep - herd, keep All your weak and trem - bling sheep

Yours for - ev - er may we be Here and in e - ter - ni - ty!
Sav - ior, Guard - ian, heav'n - ly Friend, Oh, de - fend us to the end.
You, the life, the truth, the way, Guide us to the realms of day.
Safe - ly in your ten - der care; Let us all your good - ness share.

    5 Yours forever! You our guide,
       All our needs by you supplied,
       All our sins by you forgiv'n,
       Lead us, Lord, from earth to heav'n.

Text: Mary F. Maude, 1819-1913, abr., alt.
Tune: Justin H. Knecht, 1752-1817

VIENNA
77 77

Alternate setting: 409

TRUST

429 What God Ordains Is Always Good

1 What God ordains is always good; His will is just and holy. As he directs my life for me, I follow meek and lowly. My God indeed In ev'ry need Knows well how he will shield me;

2 What God ordains is always good; He never will deceive me. He leads me in his righteous way And never will he leave me. I take content What he has sent; His hand that sends me sadness

3 What God ordains is always good; He is my friend and Father. He will not let me suffer harm Though many storms may gather. Now I may know Both joy and woe; Some day I shall see clearly

4 What God ordains is always good. Though I the cup am drinking Which savors now of bitterness, I take it without shrinking. For after grief God grants relief, My heart with comfort filling

5 What God ordains is always good;
   This truth remains unshaken.
Though sorrow, need, or death be mine,
   I shall not be forsaken.
   I fear no harm,
   For with his arm
He will embrace and shield me;
   So to my God I yield me.

Text: Samuel Rodigast, 1649-1708, abr.; tr. *The Lutheran Hymnal,* St. Louis, 1941, alt.
Tune: Severus Gastorius, 1646-82, alt.

WAS GOTT TUT
87 87 44 77

Text: Paul Gerhardt, 1607-76, abr.; tr. Richard Massie, 1800-87, alt.
Tune: Johann G. Ebeling, 1637-76

DIE GÜLDNE SONNE
PM

5 I walk with Jesus all the way;
   His guidance never fails me.
He takes my ev'ry fear away
   When Satan's pow'r assails me,
And, by his footsteps led,
  My path I safely tread.
In spite of ills that threaten may,
   I walk with Jesus all the way.

6 My walk is heav'nward all the way;
   Await, my soul, the morrow,
When you farewell can gladly say
   To all your sin and sorrow.
All worldly pomp, begone!
  To heav'n I now press on.
For all the world I would not stay;
   My walk is heav'nward all the way.

Text: Hans A. Brorson, 1694-1764; tr. Ditlef G. Ristad, 1863-1938, alt.
Tune: Freylinghausen, *Geist-reiches Gesang-Buch,* 4th ed., Halle, 1708

DER LIEBEN SONNE LICHT UND PRACHT
87 87 66 88

Text: Martin M. Schalling, 1532-1608; tr. Catherine Winkworth, 1827-78, alt.
Tune: *Zwey Bücher . . . Tabulatur,* Strassburg, 1577, alt.

HERZLICH LIEB HAB ICH DICH, O HERR
887 887 88 88 488

TRUST

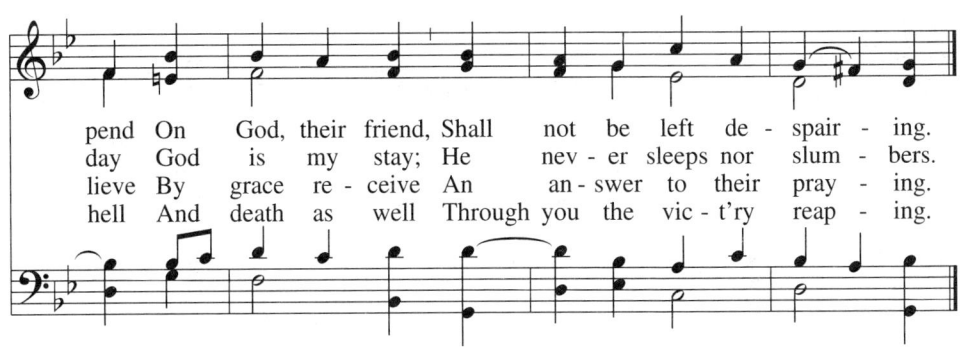

pend On God, their friend, Shall not be left de - spair - ing.
day God is my stay; He nev - er sleeps nor slum - bers.
lieve By grace re - ceive An an - swer to their pray - ing.
hell And death as well Through you the vic - t'ry reap - ing.

Text: Albrecht von Preussen, 1490-1568; tr. composite
Tune: Claude de Sermisy, c. 1490-1562, alt.

Setting © 1982 Concordia Publishing House

WAS MEIN GOTT WILL
87 87 447 447 Iambic

Alternate setting: 447

Jesus, Shepherd of the Sheep 436

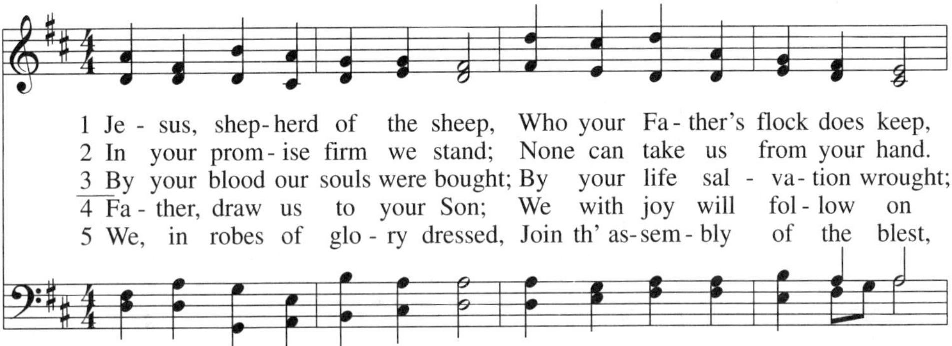

1 Je - sus, shep - herd of the sheep, Who your Fa - ther's flock does keep,
2 In your prom - ise firm we stand; None can take us from your hand.
3 By your blood our souls were bought; By your life sal - va - tion wrought;
4 Fa - ther, draw us to your Son; We with joy will fol - low on
5 We, in robes of glo - ry dressed, Join th' as - sem - bly of the blest,

Safe we wake and safe we sleep, Guard - ed still by you.
Speak — we hear — at your com - mand, We will fol - low you.
By your light our feet are taught, Lord, to fol - low you.
Till the work of grace is done, There to live with you.
Gath - ered to e - ter - nal rest In the fold with you.

Text: Henry Cook, 1788-1868, alt.
Tune: Friedrich Filitz, 1804-76, alt.

CAPETOWN
777 5

TRUST

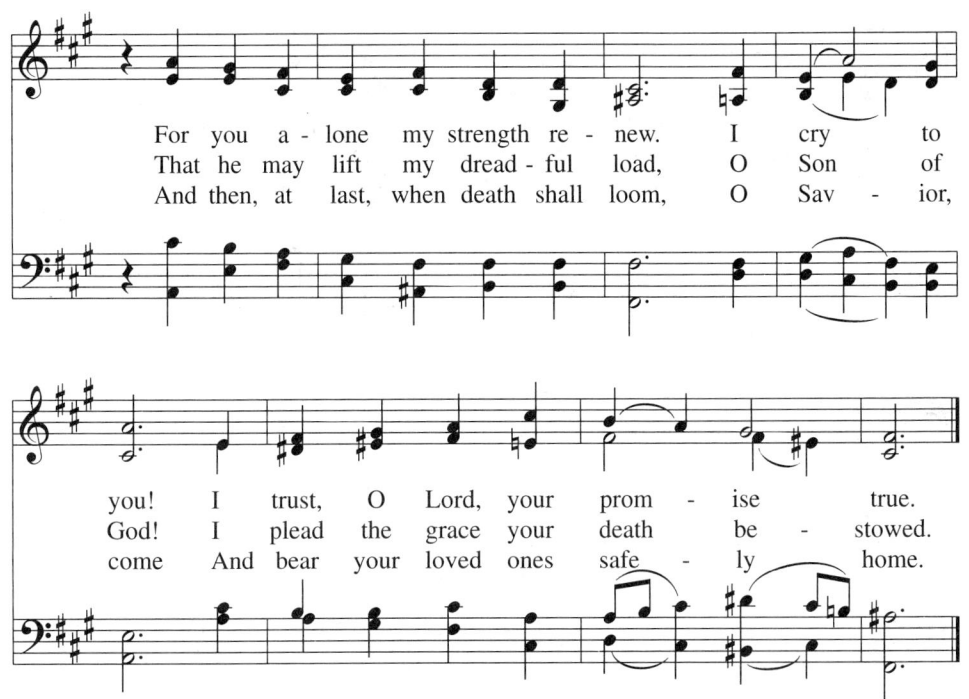

Text: Konrad Hubert, 1507-77, abr.; tr. Gilbert E. Doan, b. 1930
Tune: *Eyn schönn Lied,* Wittenberg, 1541, alt.

Text © 1967 Lutheran Council in the U.S.A.

ALLEIN ZU DIR
87 87 88 848

TRUST

Text: Michael Joncas, b. 1951, abr., alt.
Tune: Michael Joncas, b. 1951, alt.
Text and Tune © 1979, 1991, New Dawn Music, 5536 NE Hassalo, Portland, OR 97213. All rights reserved. Used by permission.
Setting © 1993 Elfred Bloedel

ON EAGLES' WINGS
Irregular

TRUST

5 Time, like an ever-rolling stream,
   Soon bears us all away;
   We fly, forgotten, as a dream
   Dies at the op'ning day.

6 O God, our help in ages past,
   Our hope for years to come,
   Still be our guard while troubles last
   And our eternal home!

Text: Isaac Watts, 1674-1748, abr., alt.
Tune: William Croft, 1678-1727, alt.; Desc. Michael E. Young, b. 1939

ST. ANNE
CM

Descant © 1979 by GIA Publications, Inc.

Have No Fear, Little Flock   442

1 Have no fear, little flock; Have no fear, little flock, For the Father has chosen To give you the kingdom; Have no fear, little flock!
2 Have good cheer, little flock; Have good cheer, little flock, For the Father will keep you In his love forever; Have good cheer, little flock!
3 Praise the Lord high above; Praise the Lord high above, For he stoops down to heal you, Up-lift and restore you; Praise the Lord high above!
4 Thankful hearts raise to God; Thankful hearts raise to God, For he stays close beside you, In all things works with you; Thankful hearts raise to God!

Text: Marjorie A. Jillson, b. 1931
Tune: Heinz W. Zimmermann, b. 1930

LITTLE FLOCK
66 76 6

Text and Tune © 1973 Concordia Publishing House

TRUST

443. Rejoice, My Heart, Be Glad and Sing

1. Rejoice, my heart, be glad and sing;
A cheerful trust maintain,
For God, the source of ev'rything,
Your treasure shall remain.

2. Why spend the day in blank despair,
In restless thought the night?
On your Creator cast your care;
He makes your burdens light.

3. Did not his love and truth and pow'r
Guard ev'ry childhood day?
And did he not in threat'ning hour
Turn dreaded ills away?

4. He always will with patience chide;
His rod falls gently down,
And all your sins he casts aside
In ocean depths to drown.

5. His wisdom never plans in vain
Nor falters nor mistakes;
All that his counsels did ordain
A happy ending makes.

6. Upon your lips, then, lay your hand,
And trust his guiding love;
Then like a rock your peace shall stand
Here and in heav'n above.

Text: Paul Gerhardt, 1607-76, abr.; tr. John Kelly, 1833-90, alt.
Tune: *Harmonischer Lieder-Schatz*, Frankfurt, 1738, alt.
Setting © 1981 Richard W. Gieseke

ICH SINGE DIR
CM

Alternate setting: 261

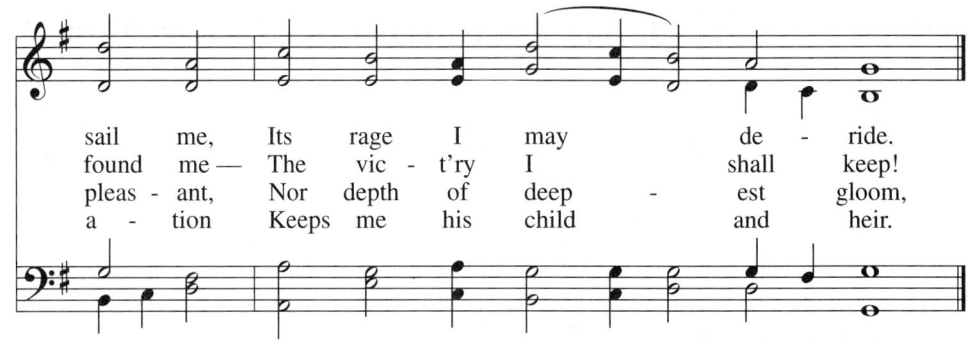

sail	me,	Its	rage	I	may	de -	ride.
found	me —	The	vic - t'ry	I		shall	keep!
pleas - ant,	Nor	depth	of	deep -	est		gloom,
a -	tion	Keeps	me	his	child	and	heir.

Text: Simon Dach, 1605-59, abr.; tr. composite
Tune: *Musika Teutsch*, Nürnberg, 1532, alt.

ICH DANK DIR, LIEBER HERRE
76 76 D

Setting © 1993 Elfred Bloedel

Alternate setting: 596

I Am Trusting You, Lord Jesus   446

1 I am trusting you, Lord Jesus, Trust-ing on-ly you,
2 I am trusting you for par-don; At your feet I bow,
3 I am trusting you for cleans-ing In the crim-son flood,
4 I am trusting you to guide me; You a-lone shall lead,

Trust-ing you for full sal - va-tion, Free and true.
For your grace and ten - der mer-cy Trust-ing now.
Trust-ing you who made me ho - ly By your blood.
Ev-'ry day and hour sup - ply-ing All my need.

5 I am trusting you for power;
   You can never fail.
   Words which you yourself shall give me
   Must prevail.

6 I am trusting you, Lord Jesus;
   Never let me fall.
   I am trusting you forever
   And for all.

Text: Frances R. Havergal, 1836-79, alt.
Tune: Henry W. Baker, 1821-77

STEPHANOS
85 83

Alternate setting: 504

447. Who Trusts in God, a Strong Abode

1. Who trusts in God, a strong abode In heav'n and earth possesses; Who looks in love To Christ above — No fear his heart oppresses. In you alone, Dear Lord, we own Sweet hope and consolation, Our shield from

2. Though Satan's wrath Beset our path And worldly scorn assail us, While you are near, We will not fear; Your strength will never fail us. Your rod and staff Will keep us safe And guide our steps forever; Nor shades of

3. In all the strife Of mortal life Our feet will stand securely. Temptation's hour Will lose its pow'r, For you will guard us surely. O God, renew With heav'nly dew Our body, soul, and spirit Until we

TRUST

5 All honor, praise, and majesty
   To Father, Son, and Spirit be,
 Our God forever glorious,
   In whose rich grace
   We run our race
 Till we depart victorious.

Text: Adam Reusner, 1496-c. 1575, abr.; tr. Catherine Winkworth, 1827-78, st. 1-4, alt.;
    The Lutheran Hymnal, St. Louis, 1941, st. 5, alt.
Tune: *Davids Himlische Harpffen*, Nürnberg, 1581, alt.

Setting © 1993 Bruce R. Backer

IN DICH HAB ICH GEHOFFET
887 447

Children of the Heavenly Father 449

1 Children of the heav'nly Father Safely in his bosom gather; Nestling bird or star in heaven Such a refuge ne'er was given.
2 God his own doth tend and nourish; In his holy courts they flourish. From all evil things he spares them; In his mighty arms he bears them.
3 Neither life nor death shall ever From the Lord his children sever; Unto them his grace he showeth, And their sorrows all he knoweth.
4 Though he giveth or he taketh, God his children ne'er forsaketh; His the loving purpose solely To preserve them pure and holy.

Text: Caroline V. Berg, 1832-1903; tr. Ernst W. Olson, 1870-1958
Tune: Swedish folk tune, 19th century

TRYGGARE KAN INGEN VARA
LM Trochaic

Text © Board of Publication, Lutheran Church in America

TRUST

450 God, My Lord, My Strength

1 God, my Lord, my strength, my place of hiding And confiding In all needs by night and day; Though foes surround me And Satan mark his prey, God shall have his way.
2 Christ in me, and I am freed for living And forgiving, Heart of flesh for lifeless stone, Now bold to serve him, Now cheered his love to own, Nevermore alone.
3 Up, weak knees and spirit bowed in sorrow! No tomorrow Shall arise to beat you down; God goes before you And angels all around; On your head a crown!

Text: *Pisne duchovni . . . Cithara Sanctorum*, Levoca, 1636; tr. Jaroslav J. Vajda, b. 1919, alt.
Tune: *Gradual*, Prague, 1567
Text © 1969 Concordia Publishing House

PÁN BŮH
10 47 56 5

COMMITMENT

Text: Sigmund von Birken, 1626-81; tr. J. Adam Rimbach, 1871-1941, alt.
Tune: Georg G. Boltze, 18th century, alt.

LASSET UNS MIT JESU ZIEHEN
87 87 877 877

COMMITMENT

I Gave My Life for Thee

454

1. I gave my life for thee; My precious blood I shed
That thou might'st ransomed be And quickened from the dead.
I gave my life for thee; Come, give thyself to me!

2. My Father's home of light, My rainbow-circled throne,
I left for earthly night, For wand'rings sad and lone.
I left it all for thee; Come now and follow me!

3. I spent long years for thee In weariness and woe
That an eternity Of joy thou mightest know.
I spent long years for thee; Come, spend thy years for me.

4. I suffered much for thee, More than my tongue may tell,
Of bit'rest agony, To rescue thee from hell.
I suffered much for thee; Come, bear thy cross with me.

5. And I have brought to thee
   Down from my home above
   Salvation full and free,
   My pardon and my love.
   Great gifts I brought for thee;
   Come, bring thy gifts to me.

6. Oh, let thy life be spent,
   Thy years for me be giv'n,
   As I for thee was sent
   To bear thee home to heav'n.
   I gave my life for thee;
   Come, give thy life to me.

Text: Frances R. Havergal, 1836-79, alt.
Tune: *The Whole Booke of Psalmes*, London, 1592

OLD 120TH
66 66 66

COMMITMENT

455 Rise! To Arms! With Prayer Employ You

1 Rise! To arms! With prayer employ you, O Christians, lest the foe destroy you, For Satan has designed your fall. Wield God's Word, a weapon glorious; Against each foe you'll be vic-

2 Jesus, all your children cherish, And keep them that they never perish Whom you have purchased with your blood. Let new life to us be given That we may look to you in

COMMITMENT

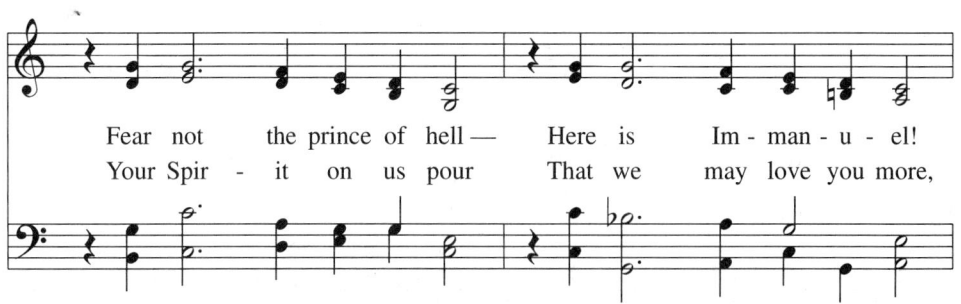
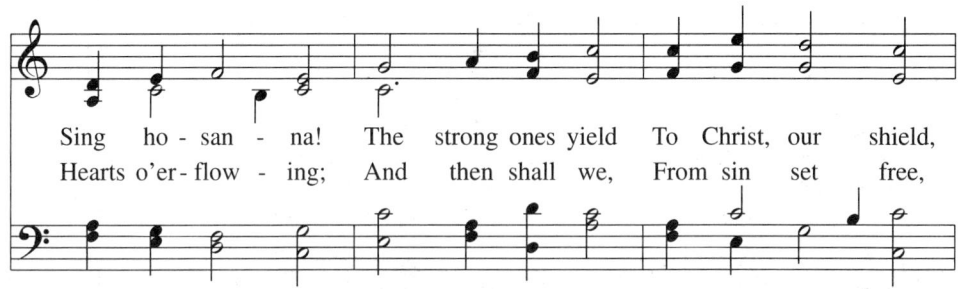

Text: Wilhelm E. Arends, 1677-1721, abr.; tr. John M. Sloan, 1835- after 1890, alt.
Tune: Philipp Nicolai, 1556-1608, alt.
Setting © 1970 Bärenreiter-Verlag

WACHET AUF
898 898 664 448
Alternate setting: 206

COMMITMENT

456 Forth in Your Name, O Lord, I Go

1 Forth in your name, O Lord, I go, My daily labor to pursue, Determined only you to know In all I think or speak or do.
2 Oh, let me cheerfully fulfill The task your wisdom has assigned And do your good and perfect will— In all my works your presence find!
3 May I find you at my right hand; Your eyes see truly what I do. I labor on at your command And offer all my works to you.
4 Give me to bear your easy yoke And ev'ry moment watch and pray And still to things eternal look And hasten to your glorious day.

5 For you I joyously employ
Whatever you in grace have giv'n;
I run my daily course with joy
And closely walk with you to heav'n.

Text: Charles Wesley, 1707-88, abr., alt.
Tune: Barry L. Bobb, b. 1951
Tune © 1981 Barry L. Bobb; Setting © 1982 Concordia Publishing House

LAKEWOOD
LM

COMMITMENT

458 May We Your Precepts, Lord, Fulfill

1 May we your pre-cepts, Lord, ful-fill   And do on
2 So may we join your name to bless,   Your grace a-
3 Spir-it of life, of love, and peace,   U-nite our

earth our Fa-ther's will   As an-gels do a-bove,
dore, your pow'r con-fess, To flee from sin and strife.
hearts, our joy in-crease, Your gra-cious help sup-ply.

Still walk in Christ, the liv-ing way,   With all your
One is our call-ing, one our name,   The end of
To each of us the bless-ing give   In Chris-tian

chil-dren, and o-bey   The law of Chris-tian love.
all our hopes the same: A glo-rious crown of life.
fel-low-ship to live,   In joy-ful hope to die.

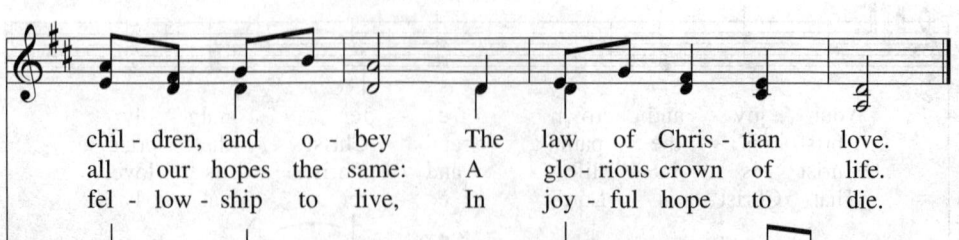

Text: Edward Osler, 1798-1863, alt.
Tune: Lowell Mason, 1792-1872

MERIBAH
886 886

COMMITMENT

O God, My Faithful God 459

1 O God, my faithful God, O Fountain ever flowing,
  Who good and perfect gifts In mercy are bestowing,
  Give me a healthy frame, And may I have within
  A conscience free from blame, A soul unhurt by sin.

2 Grant me the strength to do With ready heart and willing
  Whatever you command, My calling here fulfilling,
  That I do what I should While trusting you to bless
  The outcome for my good, For you must give success.

3 Keep me from saying things That later need recalling;
  Grant that no idle words May from my lips be falling,
  But then, when in my place I must and ought to speak,
  My words grant pow'r and grace Lest I offend the weak.

4 Lord, let me win my foes With kindly words and actions,
  And let me find good friends For counsel and correction.
  Help me, as you have taught, To love both great and small
  And by your Spirit's might To live in peace with all.

Text: Johann Heermann, 1585-1647, abr., adapt.; tr. Catherine Winkworth, 1827-78, alt.
Tune: *Neu-vermehrtes . . . Gesangbuch,* 3rd ed., Meiningen, 1693, alt.

O GOTT, DU FROMMER GOTT (II)
67 67 66 66

Alternate setting: 460

COMMITMENT

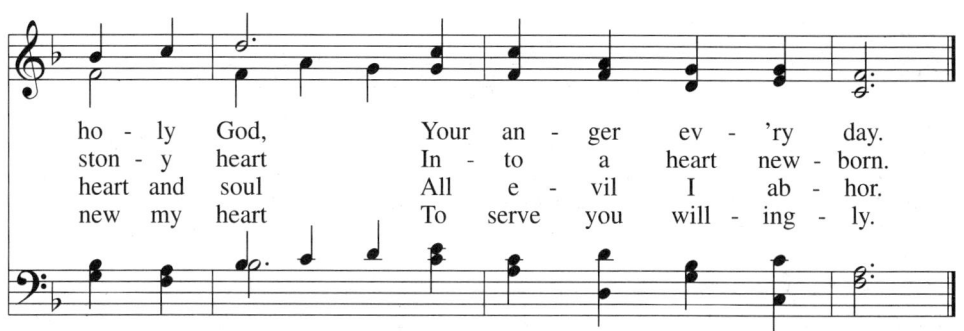

5 O Father, God of love,
   Now hear my supplication;
  O Savior, Son of God,
   Accept my adoration;
  O Holy Spirit, be
   My ever faithful guide
  That I may serve you here
   And there with you abide.

COMMITMENT

461 From Eternity, O God

1 From eternity, O God, In your Son you did elect me. Therefore, Father, on life's road Graciously to heav'n direct me; Send to me your Holy Spirit That his gifts I may inherit.

2 Born alive but dead in sin, Lost to all good things by nature, I was found and changed within And became a newborn creature. Sinful flesh works ruination, But the Spirit works salvation.

3 Drive away the gloomy night Of my darkened mind's reflection. Quench all thoughts that are not right; Hold my reason in subjection. For your truth may I be yearning, Heav'nly wisdom ever learning.

4 As a branch upon a vine, In my blessed head divine Lord implant me; Ever of my To remain a member grant me. Oh, let him, my Lord and Savior, Be my life and love forever!

COMMITMENT

5 Faith and hope and charity
   Graciously, O Father, give me;
 Be my guardian constantly
   That the devil may not grieve me.
 Grant me humbleness and gladness,
   Peace and patience in my sadness.

6 Help me speak what's right and good
   And keep silence on occasion.
 Help me pray, Lord, as I should;
   Help me bear my tribulation.
 Help me die and let my spirit
   Everlasting life inherit.

Text: Caspar Neumann, 1648-1715, abr.; tr. August Crull, 1845-1923, alt.
Tune: Johann R. Ahle, 1625-73, alt.

Setting © 1982 Concordia Publishing House

LIEBSTER JESU, WIR SIND HIER
78 78 88

Alternate settings: 221, 330

Oh, that the Lord Would Guide My Ways   462

1 Oh, that the Lord would guide my ways To keep his statutes still! Oh, that my God would grant me grace To know and do his will!
2 Order my footsteps by your Word, And make my heart sincere; Let sin have no dominion, Lord, But keep my conscience clear.
3 Assist my soul, too apt to stray, A stricter watch to keep; And should I e'er forget your way, Restore your wand'ring sheep.
4 Make me to walk in your commands— 'Tis a delightful road— Nor let my head or heart or hands Offend against my God.

Text: Isaac Watts, 1674-1748, abr., alt.
Tune: William H. Havergal, 1793-1870, adapt.

EVAN
CM

COMMITMENT

463 Jesus Calls Us O'er the Tumult

1 Jesus calls us o'er the tumult Of our life's wild, restless sea; Day by day his voice invites us, Saying, "Christian, follow me!"

2 As the first disciples heard it By the Galilean lake, Turned from home and toil and kindred, Leaving all for his dear sake.

3 Jesus calls us from the worship Of the vain world's golden store, From each idol that would keep us, Saying, "Christian, love me more."

4 In our joys and in our sorrows, Days of toil and hours of ease, Still he calls, in cares and pleasures, "Christian, love me more than these."

5 Jesus calls us! In your mercy,
Savior, help us hear your call;
Give our hearts to your obedience,
Serve and love you best of all!

Text: Cecil F. Alexander, 1818-95, alt.
Tune: Christian F. Witt, 1660-1716, alt.

STUTTGART
87 87

Alternate setting: 326

COMMITMENT

Jesus Christ, My Pride and Glory 464

1 Jesus Christ, my pride and glory, He, the true and living light, Strengthens me with glorious might. Christ, revealed in sacred story, Whom I now as Lord confess, Teaches me true holiness.

2 Let me live to praise you ever, Jesus, now my heart's delight; You are leading me aright. Let me cling to you forever, All the fleshly lusts deny, And the devil's hosts defy.

3 Grant me, Lord, your Holy Spirit That in all I follow him Lest the light of faith grow dim. Let me ever trust your merit; Let your blessing me attend; From all evil me defend.

4 From all pain and imperfection, Gracious Lord, deliver me; Heaven's glory let me see. Keep me under your direction That the grace you gave to me I may praise eternally.

Text: Johann G. Olearius, 1635-1711, abr.; tr. Paul E. Kretzmann, 1883-1965, alt.   ACH, WAS SOLL ICH SÜNDER MACHEN
Tune: *Schäffer-Belustigung . . . Hirthen-Lieder,* Altdorf, 1653, alt.   877 877

Text © 1941 Concordia Publishing House; Setting © 1993 Bruce R. Backer

COMMITMENT

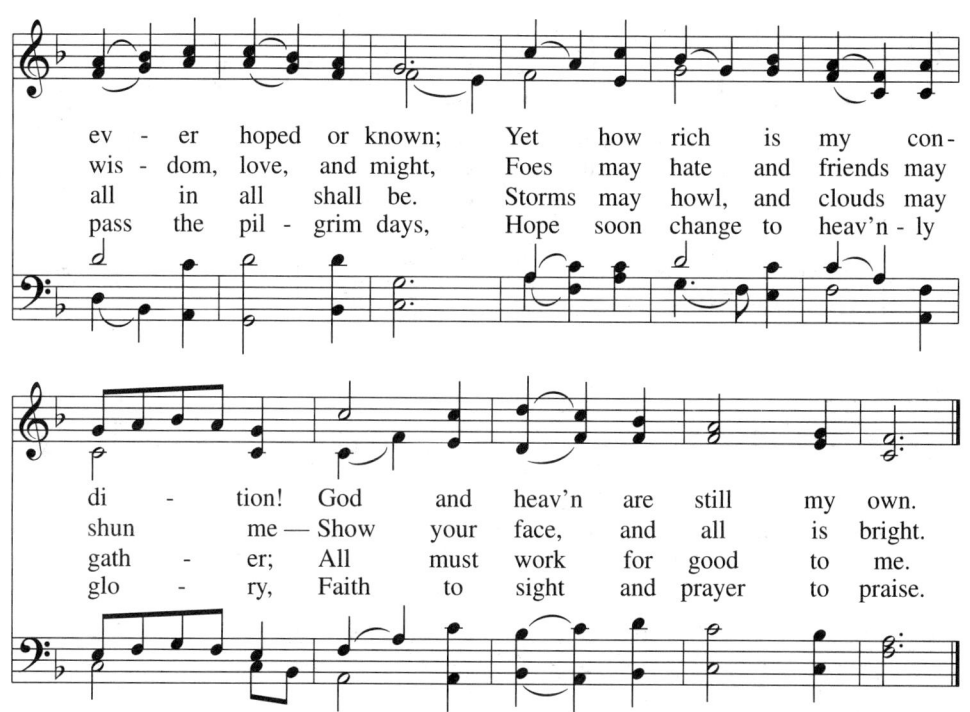

Text: Henry F. Lyte, 1793-1847, abr., alt.
Tune: Rowland H. Prichard, 1811-87

HYFRYDOL
87 87 D

Alternate settings: 486, 603

COMMITMENT

466 Though Thoughtless Thousands Choose

5. Soon will the saints in glory meet,
   Soon walk through ev'ry golden street
   And sing on ev'ry blissful plain,
   "To live is Christ; to die is gain."

Text: Joseph Hoskins, 1745-88, alt.
Tune: William Knapp, 1698-1768, alt.

WAREHAM
LM

Alternate settings: 198, 601

COMMITMENT

May the Mind of Christ My Savior 467

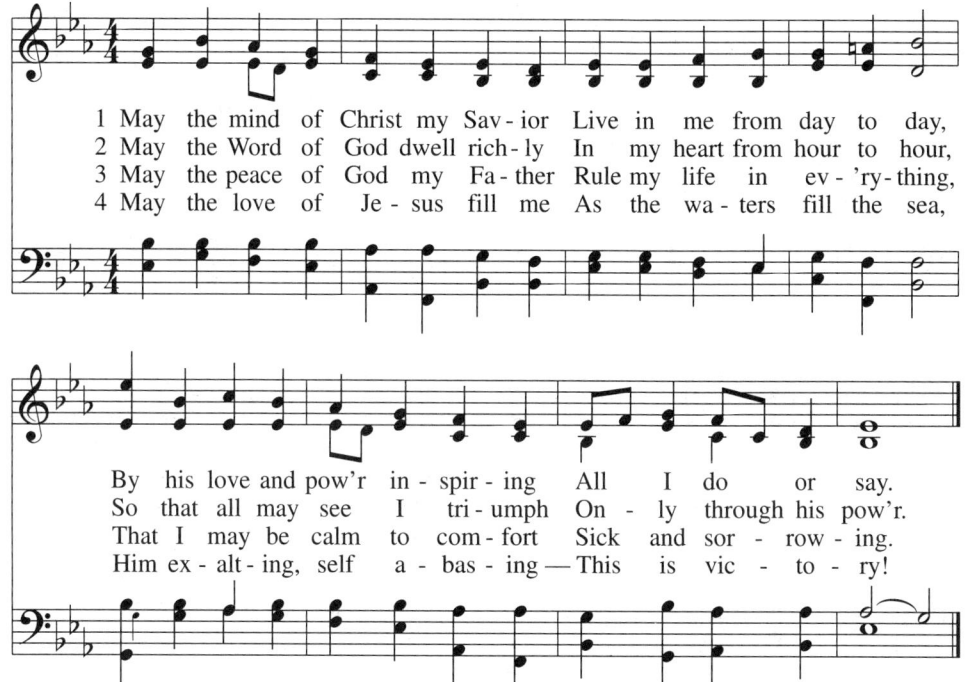

1 May the mind of Christ my Savior Live in me from day to day,
By his love and pow'r inspiring All I do or say.

2 May the Word of God dwell richly In my heart from hour to hour,
So that all may see I triumph Only through his pow'r.

3 May the peace of God my Father Rule my life in ev'rything,
That I may be calm to comfort Sick and sorrowing.

4 May the love of Jesus fill me As the waters fill the sea,
Him exalting, self abasing—This is victory!

5 May I run the race before me,
Strong and brave to face the foe,
Looking only unto Jesus
As I onward go.

6 May his spirit live within me
As I seek the lost to win,
And may they forget the channel,
Seeing only him.

Text: Kate B. Wilkinson, 1859-1928, alt.
Tune: A. Cyril Barham-Gould, 1891-1953

ST. LEONARD'S
87 85

COMMITMENT

468   My God, My Father, Make Me Strong

1. My God, my Father, make me strong, When tasks of life seem hard and long, To greet them with this triumph song: Your will be done.

2. Draw from my timid eyes the veil To show, where earthly forces fail, Your pow'r and love must still prevail— Your will be done.

3. With confident and humble mind In service freedom I will find, Praying through ev'ry toil assigned: Your will be done.

4. What seems impossible I dare; Yours is the call and yours the care. Your wisdom shall the way prepare— Your will be done.

5. Heav'n's music chimes the glad days in;
   Hope soars beyond death, pain, and sin;
   Faith shouts in triumph, Love must win —
   Your will be done!

Text: Frederick Mann, 1846-1928, abr., alt.
Tune: Johann D. Mayer, 1636-96, alt.

Text © 1941 Concordia Publishing House; Setting © 1993 Elfred Bloedel

ES IST KEIN TAG
888 4
Alternate setting: 487

COMMITMENT

Take My Life and Let It Be

469

1 Take my life and let it be Con-se-crated, Lord, to thee. Take my moments and my days; Let them flow in cease-less praise.
2 Take my hands and let them move At the im-pulse of thy love. Take my feet and let them be Swift and beau-ti-ful for thee.
3 Take my voice and let me sing Al-ways, on-ly for my King. Take my lips and let them be Filled with mes-sag-es from thee.
4 Take my sil-ver and my gold; Not a mite would I with-hold. Take my in-tel-lect and use Ev-'ry pow'r as thou shalt choose.

5 Take my will and make it thine;
   It shall be no longer mine.
   Take my heart — it is thine own;
   It shall be thy royal throne.

6 Take my love, my Lord, I pour
   At thy feet its treasure store.
   Take myself, and I will be
   Ever, only, all for thee.

Text: Frances R. Havergal, 1836-79
Tune: William H. Havergal, 1793-1870

PATMOS
77 77

COMMITMENT

470 Praise to You and Adoration

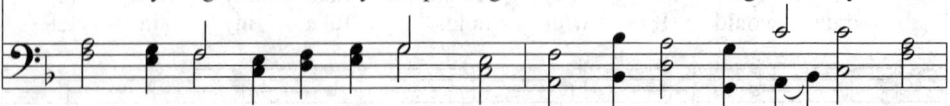

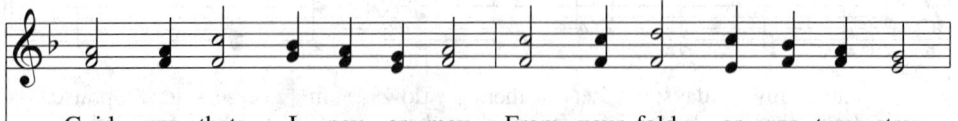

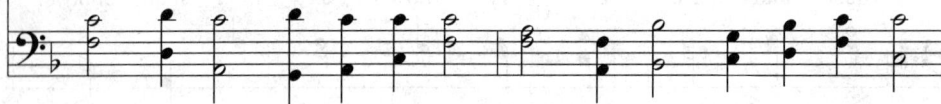

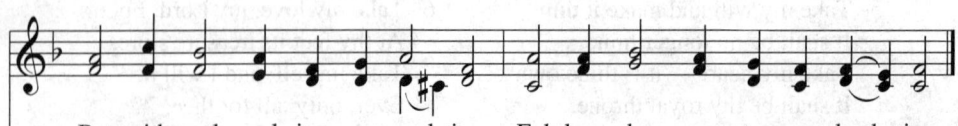

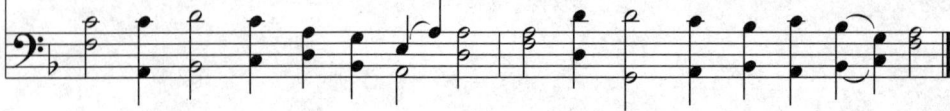

Text: Thomas H. Kingo, 1634-1703; tr. composite
Tune: *Trente quatre Pseaumes de David*, Geneva, 1551

FREU DICH SEHR
87 87 77 88

COMMITMENT

Renew Me, O Eternal Light 471

1 Renew me, O eternal Light, And let my heart and soul be bright, Illumined with the light of grace That issues from your holy face.
2 Destroy in me the lust of sin; From all impureness make me clean. Oh, grant me pow'r and strength, my God, To strive against my flesh and blood.
3 Create in me a new heart, Lord, That gladly I obey your Word. Oh, let your will be my desire And with new life my soul inspire.
4 Grant that I only you may love And seek those things which are above Till I behold you face to face, O Light eternal, through your grace.

Text: Johann F. Ruopp, 1672-1708, abr.; tr. August Crull, 1845-1923, alt.
Tune: *As hymnodus sacer,* Leipzig, 1625, alt.

HERR JESU CHRIST, MEINS
LM

Alternate settings: 404, 547

COMMITMENT

The Man Is Ever Blest
475

1. The man is ever blest / Who shuns the sinners' ways, / Nor takes the scorners' place, / Among their counsels never stands,
2. But makes the law of God / His study and delight / Amid the labors of the day / And watches of the night.
3. He like a tree shall thrive / With waters near the root. / Fresh as the leaf his name shall live; / His works are heav'nly fruit.
4. Not so the wicked man! / He no such blessing finds. / His hopes shall flee like empty chaff / Before the driving winds.

5. How will he bear to stand
   Before that judgment seat
   Where all the saints at Christ's right hand
   In full assembly meet?

6. God knows and he approves
   The way the righteous go,
   But sinners and their works shall meet
   A dreadful overthrow.

Text: Isaac Watts, 1674-1748, alt.
Tune: *Trente quatre Pseaumes de David*, Geneva, 1551, alt.

ST. MICHAEL
SM

COMMITMENT

Jesus, Your Boundless Love to Me 479

1 Jesus, your boundless love to me No thought can reach, no tongue declare. Dwell in my heart eternally, And reign without a rival there. To you alone, dear Lord, I live; Myself to you, dear Lord, I give.
2 Oh, grant that nothing in my soul May dwell but your pure love alone; Oh, may your love possess me whole, My joy, my treasure, and my crown! All coldness from my heart remove; My ev'ry act, word, thought be love.
3 This love unwearied I pursue And dauntlessly to you aspire. Oh, may your love my hope renew, Burn in my soul like heav'nly fire! And day and night be all my care To guard this sacred treasure there.
4 In suff'ring be your love my peace; In weakness be your love my pow'r; And when the storms of life shall cease, O Jesus, in that final hour Be then my rod and staff and guide And draw me safely to your side.

Text: Paul Gerhardt, 1607-76, abr.; tr. John B. Wesley, 1703-91, alt.
Tune: attr. Martin Luther, 1483-1546
Setting © 1990 Ronald L. Shilling

VATER UNSER IM HIMMELREICH, DER DU
88 88 88
Alternate settings: 306, 407, 410

STEWARDSHIP

480 Almighty Father, Heaven and Earth

1 Almighty Father, heav'n and earth With lavish wealth before you bow; Those treasures owe to you their birth, So richly furnished for us now.
2 The wealth of earth, of sky, of sea, The gold, the silver, sparkling gem, The waving corn, the bending tree Are yours; you are but lending them.
3 To you, as early morning's dew, Our praises, gifts, and prayers shall rise As rose, when joyous earth was new, Faith's patriarchal sacrifice.
4 We, Lord, would lay, at your request, The costliest off'rings on your shrine, And when we give and give our best, We but return your gifts divine.

5 O Father, whence all blessings come,
O Son, Dispenser of God's store,
O Spirit, bear our off'rings home —
Lord, make them yours forevermore!

Text: Edward A. Dayman, 1807-90, alt.
Tune: Nikolaus Herman, c. 1480-1561, alt.
Setting © 1982 Concordia Publishing House

O HEILIGE DREIFALTIGKEIT
LM
Alternate settings: 584, 591

STEWARDSHIP

Lord of All Good

483

1 Lord of all good, our gifts we bring you now; Use them your
holy purpose to ful-fill. To-kens of love and pledg-es
they shall be That our whole life is of-fered to your will.

2 We give our minds to un-der-stand your ways; Hands, eyes, and
voice to serve your great de-sign; Hearts with the flame of your own
love a-blaze — Thus for your glo-ry all our pow'rs com-bine.

3 Fa-ther, whose boun-ty all cre-a-tion shows; Christ, by whose
will-ing sac-ri-fice we live; Spir-it, from whom all life in
full-ness flows: To you with grate-ful hearts our-selves we give.

Text: Albert F. Bayly, 1901-84, alt.
Tune: Henry Lawes, 1595-1662

FARLEY CASTLE
10 10 10 10

Text © Albert F. Bayly; Setting © 1969 Concordia Publishing House

STEWARDSHIP

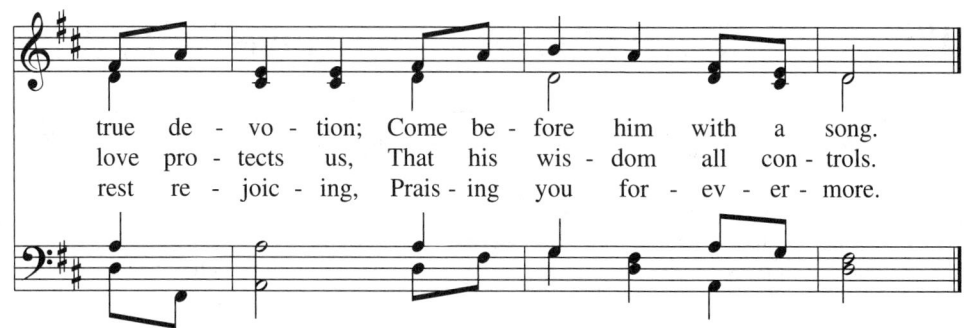

true de - vo - tion; Come be - fore him with a song.
love pro - tects us, That his wis - dom all con - trols.
rest re - joic - ing, Prais - ing you for - ev - er - more.

Text: Henry Bateman, 1802-72, alt.
Tune: *Repository of Sacred Music, Part Second*, Harrisburg, 1813, alt.

NETTLETON
87 87 D

We Give Thee but Thine Own 485

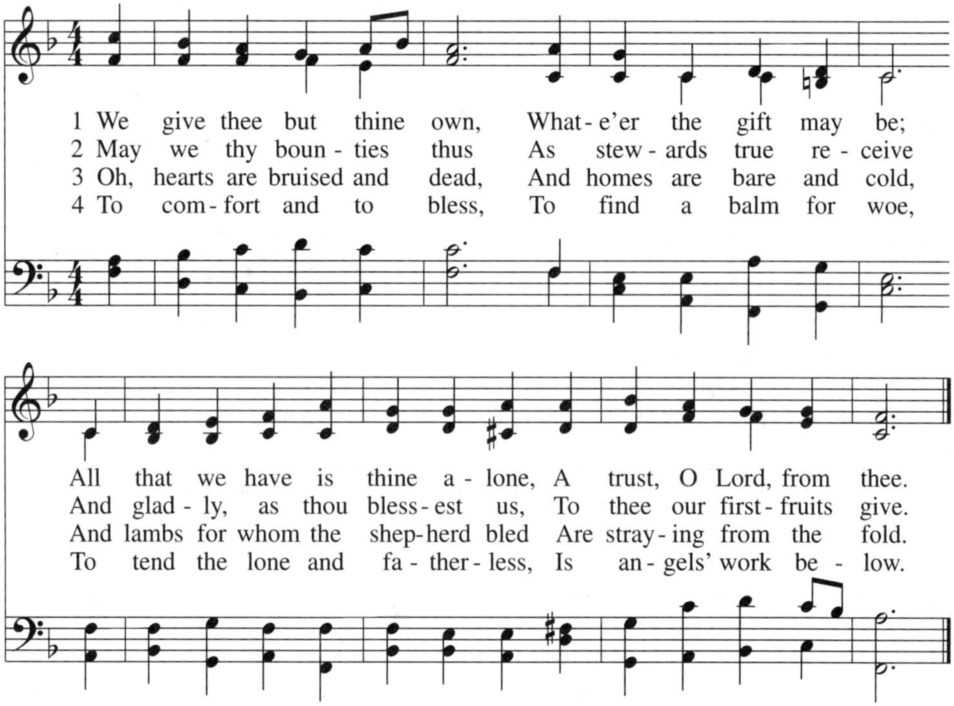

1 We give thee but thine own, What - e'er the gift may be;
2 May we thy boun - ties thus As stew - ards true re - ceive
3 Oh, hearts are bruised and dead, And homes are bare and cold,
4 To com - fort and to bless, To find a balm for woe,

All that we have is thine a - lone, A trust, O Lord, from thee.
And glad - ly, as thou bless - est us, To thee our first - fruits give.
And lambs for whom the shep - herd bled Are stray - ing from the fold.
To tend the lone and fa - ther - less, Is an - gels' work be - low.

5 The captives to release,
    To God the lost to bring,
  To teach the way of life and peace —
    It is a Christ-like thing.

6 And we believe thy Word
    Though dim our faith may be:
  Whate'er for thine we do, O Lord,
    We do it unto thee.

Text: William W. How, 1823-97
Tune: William H. Monk, 1823-89

ENERGY
SM

Alternate setting: 555

STEWARDSHIP

5 Lord of glory, you have bought us
   With your lifeblood as the price,
Never grudging for the lost ones
   That tremendous sacrifice.
Give us faith to trust you boldly,
   Hope, to stay our souls on you;
But, oh, best of all your graces,
   With your love our love renew.

Text: Eliza S. Alderson, 1818-89, alt.
Tune: Rowland H. Prichard, 1811-87

Setting © 1986 Bruce R. Backer

HYFRYDOL
87 87 D

Alternate settings: 365, 603

STEWARDSHIP

487 O Lord of Heaven and Earth and Sea

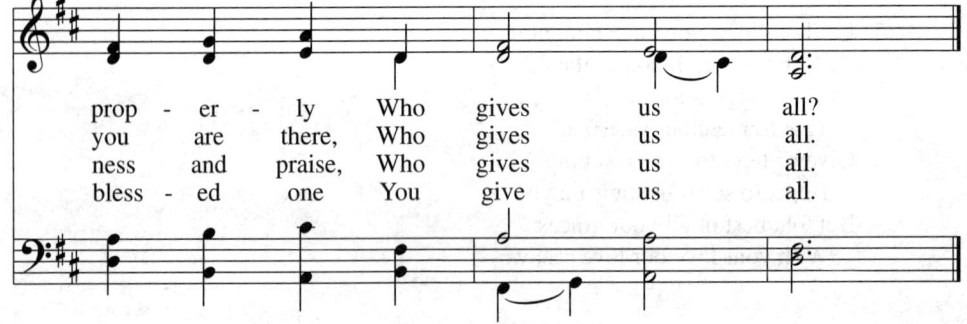

1. O Lord of heav'n and earth and sea, To you all praise and glory be! How can we thank you properly Who gives us all?
2. The golden sunshine, springtime air, Sweet flow'rs and fruit your love declare; When harvests ripen, you are there, Who gives us all.
3. For peaceful homes and healthful days, For all the blessings earth displays We owe you thankfulness and praise, Who gives us all.
4. You did not spare your only Son, But gave him for a world undone, And freely with that blessed one You give us all.

5. We have your Spirit ev'ry hour,
The Lord of life and love and pow'r,
He will his sev'nfold graces show'r
Upon us all.

6. For means of grace, for sins forgiv'n,
For souls redeemed and hopes of heav'n,
What can to you, O Lord, be giv'n,
Who gives us all?

7. We lose what on ourselves we spend;
We have as treasures without end
Whatever, Lord, to you we lend,
Who gives us all.

8. Dear Lord, from you we all derive
Our life, our gifts, our pow'r to give.
Oh, may we ever with you live,
Who gives us all!

Text: Christopher Wordsworth, 1807-85, alt.
Tune: Johann D. Mayer, 1636-96, alt.

ES IST KEIN TAG
888 4

Alternate setting: 468

Text: Robert Murray, 1832-1909, abr., alt.
Tune: *The Christian Lyre*, New York, 1831
Setting © 1986 by GIA Publications, Inc.

PLEADING SAVIOR
87 87 D

CHRISTIAN LOVE

O Master of the Loving Heart   491

1. O Master of the loving heart, The friend of all in need, We pray that we may be like you In thought and word and deed.
2. Your days were full of kindly acts; Your speech was true and plain; Of those who ever sought you, Lord, None came to you in vain.
3. Your face was warm with sympathy; Your hand God's strength revealed; Who saw your face or felt your touch Were comforted and healed.
4. Oh, grant us hearts like yours, dear Lord, So joyous, free, and true, That all your children, ev'rywhere, Be drawn by us to you.

Text: Calvin W. Laufer, 1874-1938, alt.
Tune: Carl G. Gläser, 1784-1829, alt.
Setting © 1993 Elfred Bloedel

AZMON
CM

CHRISTIAN LOVE

love   and   pit - y;   Heal our   wrongs and   help our   need.
thirst   for   plea - sure; Stem our   self - ish   greed for   gain.
crushed and   bro - ken?   Teach us,   Lord, to   soothe their care.
of   your boun - ty   Held in   sol - emn   trust will be.

Text: Somerset T. C. Lowry, 1855-1932, abr., alt.
Tune: *The Revivalist,* Troy, NY, 1868

LORD, REVIVE US
87 87 D

Setting © 1986 James E. Engel.

Forgive Our Sins as We Forgive   493

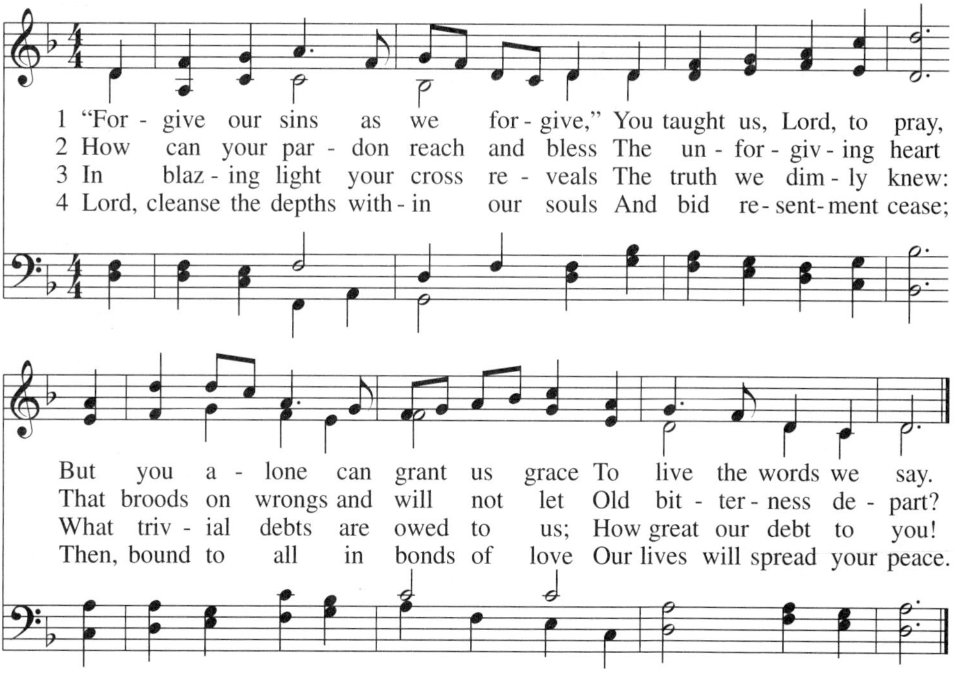

1 "For - give our   sins as   we   for - give," You taught us, Lord, to   pray,
2 How   can   your par - don   reach and   bless The un - for - giv - ing   heart
3 In   blaz - ing light your cross re - veals The truth we   dim - ly   knew:
4 Lord, cleanse the depths with - in   our   souls And bid   re - sent - ment cease;

But   you   a - lone can   grant us   grace To   live the   words we   say.
That   broods on   wrongs and   will not   let   Old   bit - ter - ness de - part.
What   triv - ial debts are   owed to   us;   How   great our   debt to   you!
Then, bound to   all   in   bonds of   love Our   lives will spread your peace.

Text: Rosamond E. Herklots, 1905-87, alt.
Tune: *A Supplement to the Kentucky Harmony,* Harrisonburg, 1820

DETROIT
CM

Text reprinted by permission of Oxford University Press; Setting © 1993 Bruce R. Backer

CHRISTIAN LOVE

494 Blest Be the Tie that Binds

1 Blest be the tie that binds / Our hearts in Christian love; / The fellowship of kindred minds / Is like to that above.

2 Before our Father's throne / We pour our ardent prayers; / Our fears, our hopes, our aims are one, / Our comforts and our cares.

3 We share our mutual woes, / Our mutual burdens bear, / And often for each other flows / The sympathizing tear.

4 When here our pathways part, / We suffer bitter pain; / Yet, one in Christ and one in heart, / We hope to meet again.

5 From sorrow, toil, and pain
And sin we shall be free
And perfect love and friendship reign
Through all eternity.

Text: John Fawcett, 1740-1817, abr., alt.
Tune: Lowell Mason, 1792-1872

BOYLSTON
SM

CHRISTIAN LOVE

Not for Tongues of Heaven's Angels

495

1. Not for tongues of heav-en's an-gels, Not for wis-dom to dis-cern, Not for faith that mas-ters moun-tains, For this bet-ter gift we yearn— May love be ours, O Lord!
2. Love is hum-ble; love is gen-tle; Love is ten-der, true, and kind. Love is gra-cious, ev-er pa-tient, Gen-er-ous of heart and mind— May love be ours, O Lord!
3. Nev-er jeal-ous, nev-er self-ish, Love will not re-joice in wrong; Nev-er boast-ful nor re-sent-ful, Love be-lieves and suf-fers long— May love be ours, O Lord!
4. Soon will fade the word of wis-dom, Faith and hope be one day past; When we see our Sav-ior clear-ly, Love it is a-lone will last— May love be ours, O Lord!

Text: Timothy Dudley-Smith, b. 1926, alt.
Tune: Peter W. Cutts, b. 1937
Text © 1985 Hope Publishing Co.; Tune and Setting © 1969 Hope Publishing Co.

BRIDEGROOM
87 87 6

CHRISTIAN LOVE

Text: Jeff Cothran, 1948-92
Tune: Jewish folk melody
Text and Setting © 1972 GIA Publications, Inc.

SHIBBOLET BASADEH
768 D with Refrain

CHRISTIAN LOVE

497

This Is My Will

1. "This is my will, my one command, That love should dwell among you all. This is my will, that you should love As I have shown that I love you.
2. "No greater love can any have Than that one die to save his friends. You are my friends if you obey What I command that you should do.
3. "I call you now no longer slaves; No slave knows all the master does. I call you friends, for all I hear My Father say, you hear from me.
4. "You chose not me, but I chose you, That you should go and bear much fruit. I chose you out that you in me Should bear much fruit that will abide.

5. "All that you ask my Father dear
For my name's sake you shall receive.
This is my will, my one command,
That love should dwell in each, in all."

Text: James Quinn, b. 1919, alt.
Tune: Gaelic melody, c. 19th century
Text © 1969 James Quinn, SJ; Setting © Estate of T. H. Weaving

SUANTRAI
LM

CHRISTIAN LOVE

499 O God of Mercy, God of Might

1 O God of mercy, God of might, In love and mercy infinite, Teach us, as ever in your sight, To live our lives to you.
2 You sent your Son for all to die That fallen man might live thereby. Oh, hear us, for to you we cry In hope, O Lord, to you.
3 Teach us the lesson Jesus taught: To feel for those his blood has bought, That ev'ry deed and word and thought May work a work for you.
4 All are redeemed, both far and wide, Since Jesus Christ for all has died; Grant us the will, and grace provide, To love them all in you.

5 In sickness, sorrow, want, or care
May we each other's burdens share;
May we, where help is needed, there
Give help as though to you.

6 And may your Holy Spirit move
All those who live to live in love
Till you receive in heav'n above
All those who lived for you.

Text: Godfrey Thring, 1823-1903, alt.
Tune: Samuel Howard, 1710-82

ISLEWORTH
888 6

Alternate setting: 572

CHRISTIAN HOME

For Christian Homes, O Lord, We Pray 500

1 For Christian homes, O Lord, we pray, That you might dwell with us each day. Make ours a place where you are Lord, Where all is governed by your Word.

2 We are the children of your grace; Our homes are now your dwelling-place. In you we trust and daily live; Teach us to serve and to forgive.

3 United in a bond of love, We lift our eyes to you above. From you we gain the strength to live, The wish to share, the joy to give.

4 Protect us and our loved ones dear From pain and sorrow, want and fear; Yet when we must our burdens bear, "Your will be done" shall be our prayer.

5 And when you call us all to rest,
  Then will we have a home more blest,
  See all our care and sorrow cease,
  And find with Christ eternal peace.

Text: Richard S. Armstrong, b. 1924, st. 1, 3-5, abr., alt.
Mark A. Jeske, b. 1952, st. 2, alt.
Tune: Wagner, *Sammlung alter und neuer . . . Melodien,* 1742, alt.
Text st. 2 © 1993 Mark A. Jeske; Setting © 1982 Concordia Publishing House

GOTTLOB, ES GEHT NUNMEHR ZU ENDE
LM

Alternate setting: 135

CHRISTIAN HOME

Lord of the Home 502

1. Lord of the home, the Son you love Received a mother's tender care, A father's strength like yours above, A home with warmth and kindness there.

2. Help us, O Lord, our homes to make Your Holy Spirit's dwelling-place; Our hands and hearts' devotion To be the servants of your grace.

3. We pray that all who with us dwell Your love and joy and peace may know. And while our lips your praises tell, May faithful lives your glory show.

4. Teach us to keep our homes so fair That, were our Lord a child once more, He might be glad our hearth to share And find a welcome at our door.

5. Lord, may your Spirit sanctify
   Each household duty we fulfill.
   May we our Savior glorify
   With glad obedience to your will.

Text: Albert F. Bayly, 1901-84, alt.
Tune: *Antiphoner*, Grenoble, 1753

Text © Albert F. Bayly; Setting © 1993 Kermit G. Moldenhauer

DEUS TUORUM MILITUM
LM

Alternate setting: 196

CHRISTIAN HOME

Text: Magnus B. Landstad, 1802-80, abr.; tr. Ole T. Arneson, 1853-1917, alt.
Tune: Kermit G. Moldenhauer, b. 1949

OH, BLESSED HOME
887 887 7

Tune and Setting © 1993 Kermit G. Moldenhauer

Bless Our Loved Ones, Holy Father 504

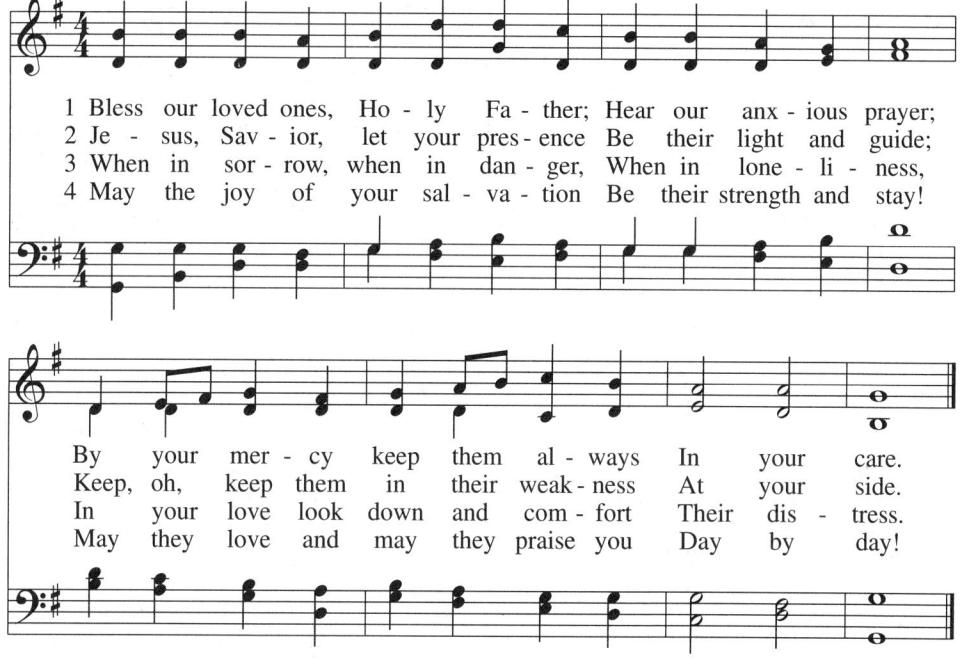

5 Holy Spirit, let your teaching
   Sanctify their life;
   Send your grace that they may conquer
   In the strife.

6 Father, Son, and Holy Spirit,
   God forever true,
   Bless them, guide them, save them, keep them
   Close to you.

Text: Isabella S. Stephenson, 1843-90, alt.
Tune: Henry W. Baker, 1821-77

STEPHANOS
85 83

Alternate setting: 446

CHRISTIAN HOME

505 Love Is the Gracious Gift

1. Love is the gracious gift of your goodness; Love is the patient fruit of your care; Love is the gentle work of your Spirit, Who is the source of love ev'ry-where.
2. You loved me first, Lord, sending me Jesus. Then I responded, trusting your Son. Now you invite me to love my neighbor, Showing your true love to ev'ry-one.
3. Love means forgiveness, patience, and kindness; Love is not jealous, boastful, or rude. Love endures all things, bearing, believing; Love hopes forever, rejoices in truth.
4. Love in a marriage, love freely given, Love of a husband, love of a wife— Made to continue, blossom, and flourish, Grow ever deeper throughout this life.
5. Love among Christians, love in the fam'ly, Love for the Savior, whose blood was shed, Love and submission one to another As unto Christ, who reigns as our head.

Text: Donald E. Smith, b. 1952, alt.
Tune: Gaelic melody, 19th century
Text © 1985 Donald E. Smith; Setting © 1993 Kermit G. Moldenhauer

BUNESSAN
Irregular

CHRISTIAN HOME

Oh, Blest the House, Whate'er Befall 506

5. Then here will I and mine today
   A solemn promise make and say:
   Though all the world forsake his Word,
   I and my house will serve the Lord!

Text: Christoph C. L. von Pfeil, 1712-84, abr.; tr. Catherine Winkworth, 1827-78, st. 1-2, 4-5, alt.; *Evangelical Lutheran Hymnal,* Columbus, OH, 1880, st. 3, alt.
Tune: Klug, *Geistliche Lieder auffs new gebessert,* Wittenberg, 1535

WO GOTT ZUM HAUS
LM

Alternate setting: 291

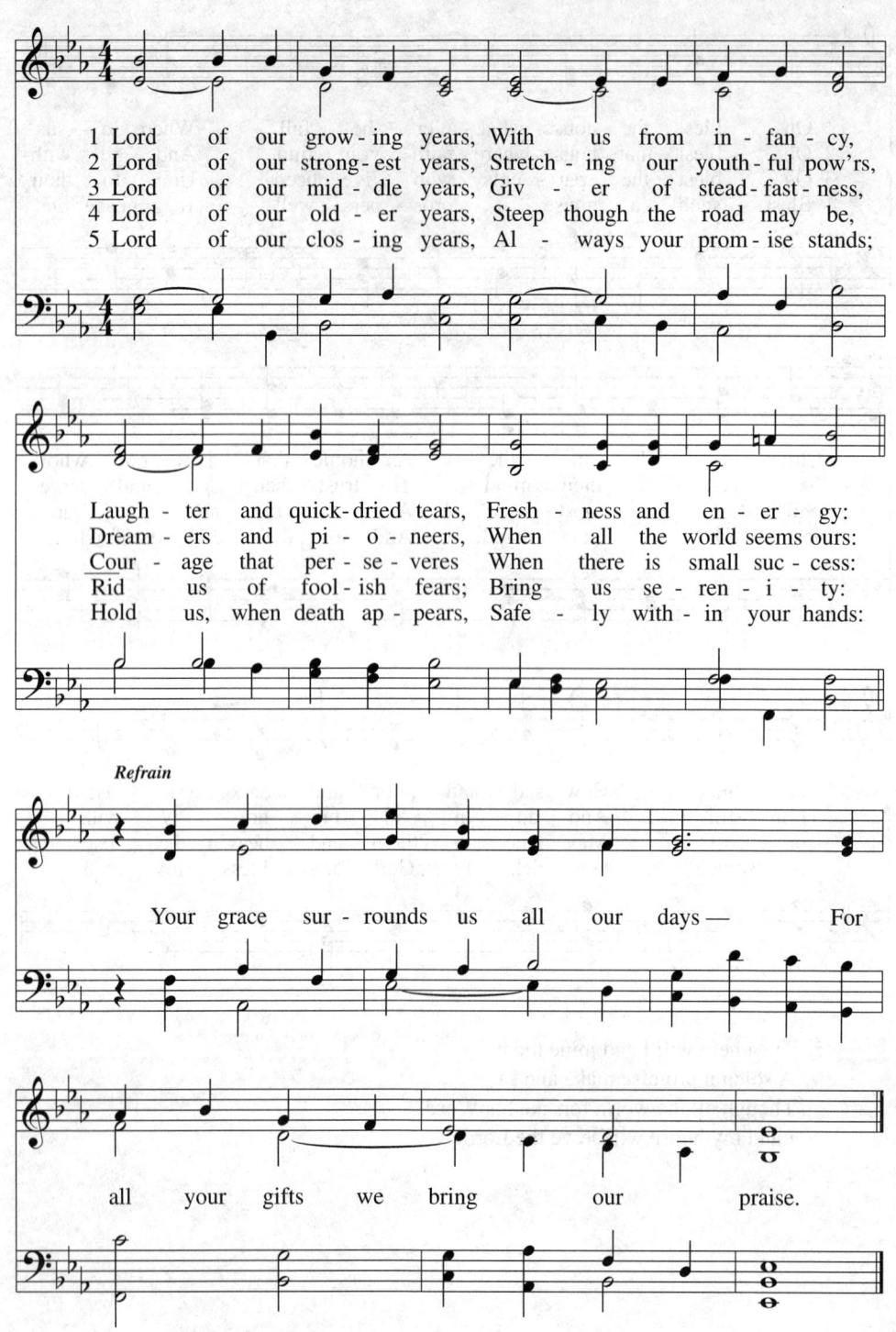

CHRISTIAN EDUCATION

509 How Shall the Young Secure Their Hearts

1. How shall the young secure their hearts And guard their lives from sin? Your Word, O Lord, the truth imparts To keep the conscience clean.
2. Your Word is like a heav'nly light That guides us all the day, And through the dangers of the night A lamp to lead our way.
3. The starry heav'ns your rule obey; The earth maintains its place; And these your servants night and day Your skill and pow'r express.
4. But still your law and gospel, Lord, Have lessons more divine; Not earth stands firmer than your Word Nor stars so nobly shine.

5. Your Word is everlasting truth;
   How pure is ev'ry page!
   That holy Book will guide our youth
   And well support our age.

Text: Isaac Watts, 1674-1748, abr., alt.
Tune: Alexander R. Reinagle, 1799-1877

ST. PETER
CM

Alternate settings: 358, 405

CHRISTIAN EDUCATION

I Pray You, Dear Lord Jesus 510

I pray you, dear Lord Jesus, My heart to keep and train
That I your holy temple From youth to age remain.
Oh, turn my thoughts forever From worldly wisdom's lore;
If I but learn to know you, I shall not want for more.

Text: Thomas H. Kingo, 1634-1703, abr.; tr. Norman A. Madson, 1886-1962, alt.
Tune: *Koral-Melodier,* 1801

JEG VIL MIG HERREN LOVE
76 76 D

CHRISTIAN EDUCATION

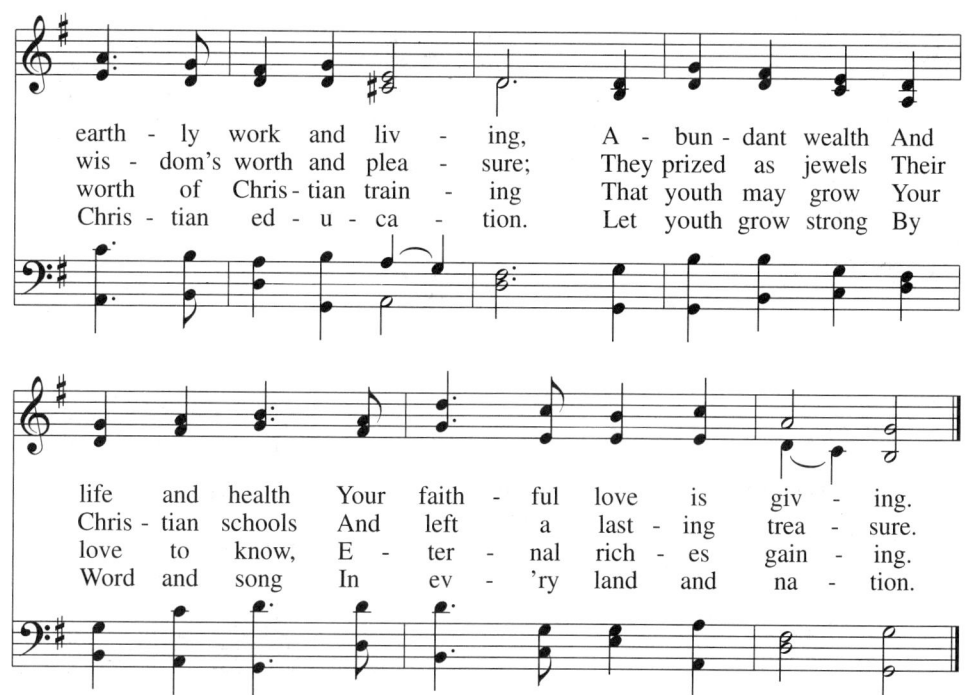

Text: Oliver C. Rupprecht, b. 1903, abr., alt.
Tune: *Enchiridion . . . zum Schwartzen Horn*, Erfurt, 1527

O HERRE GOTT, DEIN GÖTTLICH WORT
87 87 447 447 Iambic

Text © 1993 Dr. Oliver C. Rupprecht

CHRISTIAN EDUCATION

512 Let Children Hear the Mighty Deeds

1 Let children hear the mighty deeds Which God performed of old, Which in our younger years we saw, And which our fathers told.
2 Make unto them his glories known, His works of pow'r and grace, And we'll convey his wonders down Through ev'ry rising race.
3 Our lips shall tell them to our sons And they again to theirs That generations yet unborn May teach them to their heirs.
4 Oh, teach them with all diligence The truths of God's own Word, To place in him their confidence, To fear and trust their Lord,

5 To learn that in our God alone
Their hope securely stands,
That they may ne'er forget his works,
But walk in his commands.

Text: Isaac Watts, 1674-1748, st. 1-3, 5, alt.; Bernhard Schumacher, 1886-1978, st. 4
Tune: Johann Crüger, 1598-1662
Text © 1941 Concordia Publishing House

NUN DANKET ALL
CM

Alternate settings: 225, 227

CHRISTIAN EDUCATION

Lord Jesus Christ, the Children's Friend   513

1 Lord Jesus Christ, the children's friend, To each of them your presence send; Call them by name and keep them true In loving faith, dear Lord, to you.
2 In Christian homes, Lord, let them be Your blessing to their family; Let Christian schools your work extend In living truth as you intend,
3 That caring parents, gracious Lord, And faithful teachers find reward In leading these, whom you call, To find in Christ their all in all.
4 That all of us, your children dear, By Christ redeemed, may Christ revere. Lead us in joy that all we do Will witness to our love for you.

Text: Henry L. Lettermann, b. 1932, abr.
Tune: Barry L. Bobb, b. 1951

LAKEWOOD
LM

Text and Setting © 1982 Concordia Publishing House; Tune © 1981 Barry L. Bobb

CHRISTIAN EDUCATION

514   Lord, Help Us Ever to Retain

1. Lord, help us ever to retain The Catechism's doctrine plain As Luther taught the Word of truth In simple style to tender youth.
2. Help us your holy law to learn, To mourn our sin and from it turn In faith to you and to your Son And Holy Spirit, Three in One.
3. Hear us, dear Father, when we pray For needed help from day to day That as your children we may live, Whom you in baptism did receive.
4. Lord, when we fall or go astray, Absolve and lift us up, we pray; And through the sacrament increase Our faith till we depart in peace.

Text: Ludwig Helmbold, 1532-98; tr. Matthias Loy, 1828-1915, alt.
Tune: *As hymnodus sacer,* Leipzig, 1625, alt.

HERR JESU CHRIST, MEINS
LM

Alternate settings: 223, 547

CHRISTIAN EDUCATION

Shepherd of Tender Youth 515

1 Shepherd of tender youth, Guiding in love and truth
Through devious ways, Christ, our triumphant King, We come your
name to sing And here our children bring To join your praise.

2 You are our holy Lord, Christ, the incarnate Word,
Healer of strife. You did yourself abase That from sin's
deep disgrace You might thus save our race And give us life.

3 You are our great High Priest; You have prepared the feast
Of holy love; And in our mortal pain None calls on
you in vain; Our plea do not disdain: Help from above!

4 Oh, ever be our guide, Our shepherd and our pride,
Our staff and song. Jesus, O Christ of God, By your enduring Word
Lead us where you have trod; Make our faith strong.

5 So now and till we die
 Sound we your praises high
And joyful sing;
 Infants and all the throng
 Who to your Church belong
Unite to swell the song
 To Christ, our King.

Text: attr. Clement of Alexandria, c. 170 - c. 220; tr. Henry M. Dexter, 1821-90, alt.
Tune: Lowell Mason, 1792-1872, alt.

OLIVET
664 6664

SOCIAL CONCERN

Almighty Father, Strong to Save 517

1 Almighty Father, strong to save, Whose arm has bound the restless wave, Who bids the mighty ocean deep Its own appointed limits keep: Oh, hear our earnest, humble plea For those in peril on the sea.

2 O Christ, the Lord of hill and plain O'er which our traffic runs amain By mountain pass or valley low; Wherever, Lord, your people go, Protect them by your guarding hand From ev'ry peril on the land.

3 O Spirit, whom the Father sent To spread abroad the firmament; O Wind of heaven, by your might Save all who dare the eagle's flight, And keep them by your watchful care From ev'ry peril in the air.

4 O Trinity of love and pow'r, Your people shield in danger's hour; From rock and tempest, fire and foe, Protect them all where'er they go; Thus evermore to you shall be Glad praise from air and land and sea.

Text: William Whiting, 1825-78, st. 1, 4, alt.; Robert N. Spencer, 1877-1961, st. 2-3, alt.
Tune: John B. Dykes, 1823-76

MELITA
88 88 88

Text © The Church Pension Fund

SOCIAL CONCERN

518 Forth in the Peace of Christ We Go

5 We are the Church; Christ bids us show
  That in his Church all nations find
  Their hearth and home where Christ restores
  True peace, true love to humankind.

Text: James Quinn, b. 1919, st. 1-2, 4-5, abr., alt.; Mark A. Jeske, b. 1952, st. 3
Tune: *Llyfr Tonau Cynulleidfaol,* Wales, 1859

LLEDROD
LM

Text st.1,2,4,5 © 1969 James Quinn, SJ; Text st.3 © 1993 Mark A. Jeske

SOCIAL CONCERN

O God of Love, O King of Peace 519

Text: Henry W. Baker, 1821-77, alt.
Tune: Jeremiah Clarke, c. 1674-1707

ST. LUKE
LM

Text: Edward H. Plumptre, 1821-91, alt.
Tune: English folk tune, 19th century, adapt.

KINGSFOLD
CM D

Setting reprinted by permission of Oxford University Press

SOCIAL CONCERN

521   Lord of All Nations, Grant Me Grace

1. Lord of all nations, grant me grace
To love all people, ev'ry race,
And in each person help me view
My kindred, loved, redeemed by you.

2. Break down the wall that would divide
Your children, Lord, on ev'ry side.
My neighbors' good let me pursue;
Bind them to me and all to you.

3. Forgive me, Lord, where I have erred
By loveless act and thoughtless word.
Make me to see the wrong I do
Will hurt my neighbor, Lord, and you.

4. Give me your courage, Lord, to speak
Whenever strong oppress the weak.
And should I be a victim, too,
Help me forgive, remem'bring you.

5. With your own love may I be filled
And by your Holy Spirit willed,
That all I touch, whate'er I do,
May be divinely touched by you.

Text: Olive Wise Spannaus, b. 1916, alt.
Tune: attr. Matthias Kunwaldsky, 1442-1500

Text and Setting © 1969 Concordia Publishing House

BEATUS VIR
LM

SOCIAL CONCERN

Grant Peace, We Pray, in Mercy, Lord 522

Text: Latin antiphon, c. 6th century; German version, Martin Luther, 1483-1546; tr. *Laudamus,* Hannover, 1952
Tune: *Kirchen gesenge,* Nürnberg, 1531
Text reprinted by permission of The Lutheran World Federation

VERLEIH UNS FRIEDEN GNÄDIGLICH
87 87 8

SOCIAL CONCERN

hour, For the fac - ing of this hour.
days, For the liv - ing of these days.
goal, Lest we miss your king - dom's goal.
dore, Serv - ing you whom we a - dore.

Text: Harry E. Fosdick, 1878-1969, abr., alt.
Tune: John Hughes, 1873-1932

Setting © 1982 Concordia Publishing House

CWM RHONDDA
87 87 877

Alternate setting: 237

O Fount of Good, for All Your Love 524

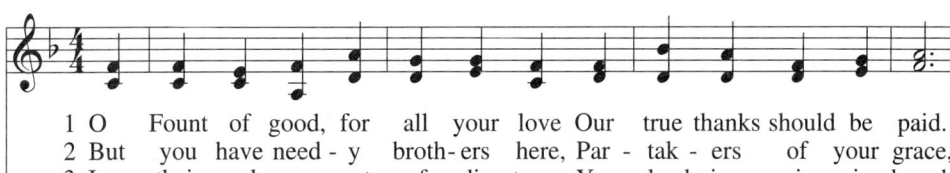

1 O Fount of good, for all your love Our true thanks should be paid.
2 But you have need-y broth-ers here, Par-tak-ers of your grace,
3 In their sad ac-cents of dis-tress Your plead-ing voice is heard;
4 Then help us, Lord, your yoke to wear And glad-ly do your will,

What can we ren-der, Lord, to you, When you own all that's made?
Whose names you will your-self con-fess Be - fore the Fa-ther's face.
You may in them be clothed and fed And vis - it - ed and cheered.
Each oth - er's dai - ly bur-dens share, The law of love ful - fill.

5 Your face with rev'rence and with love
  We in the poor will view,
  And, while we minister to them,
  We do it as to you.

Text: Philip Doddridge, 1702-51; altered by Edward Osler, 1798-1863, alt.
Tune: *The Whole Booke of Psalmes,* London, 1562, alt.

Setting © 1993 Kermit G. Moldenhauer

ST. FLAVIAN
CM

Alternate setting: 398

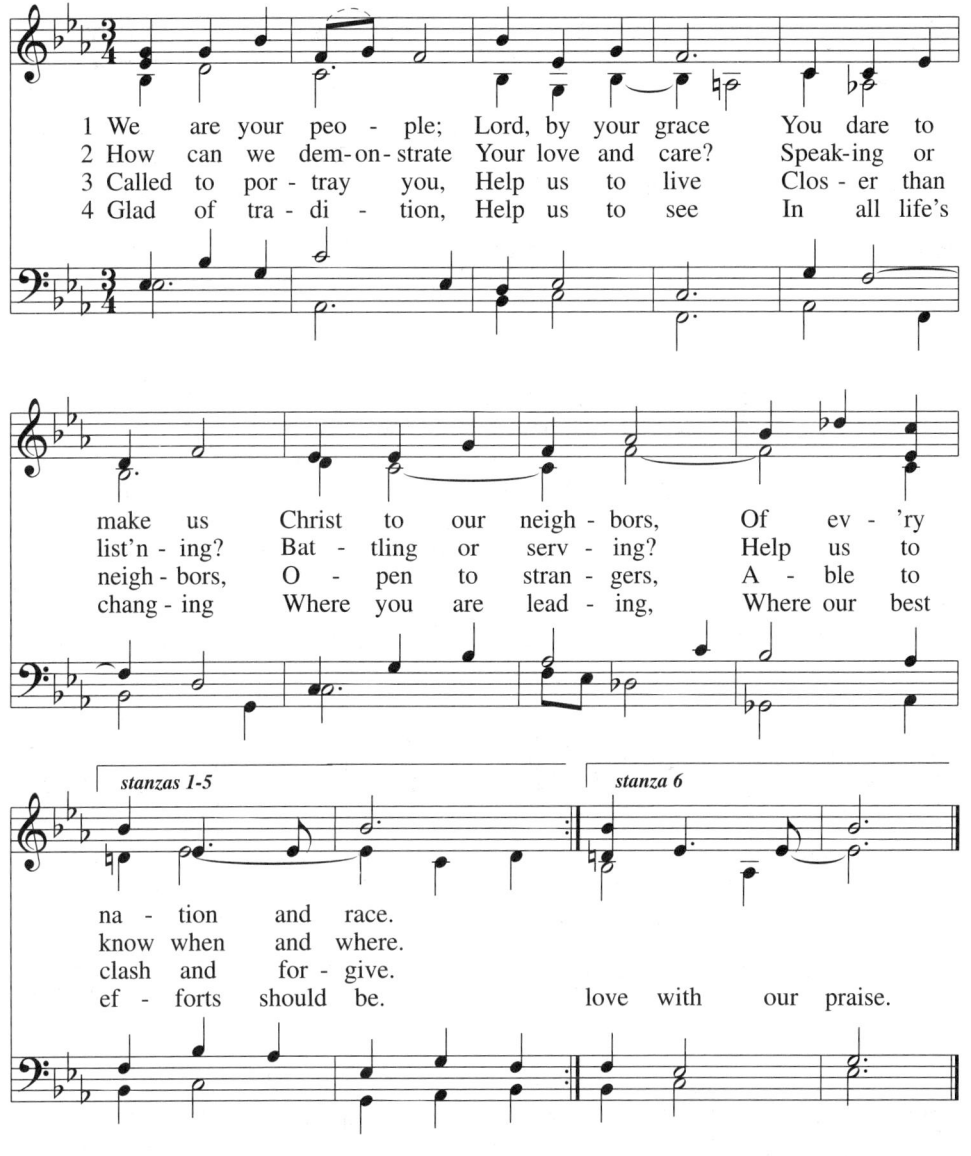

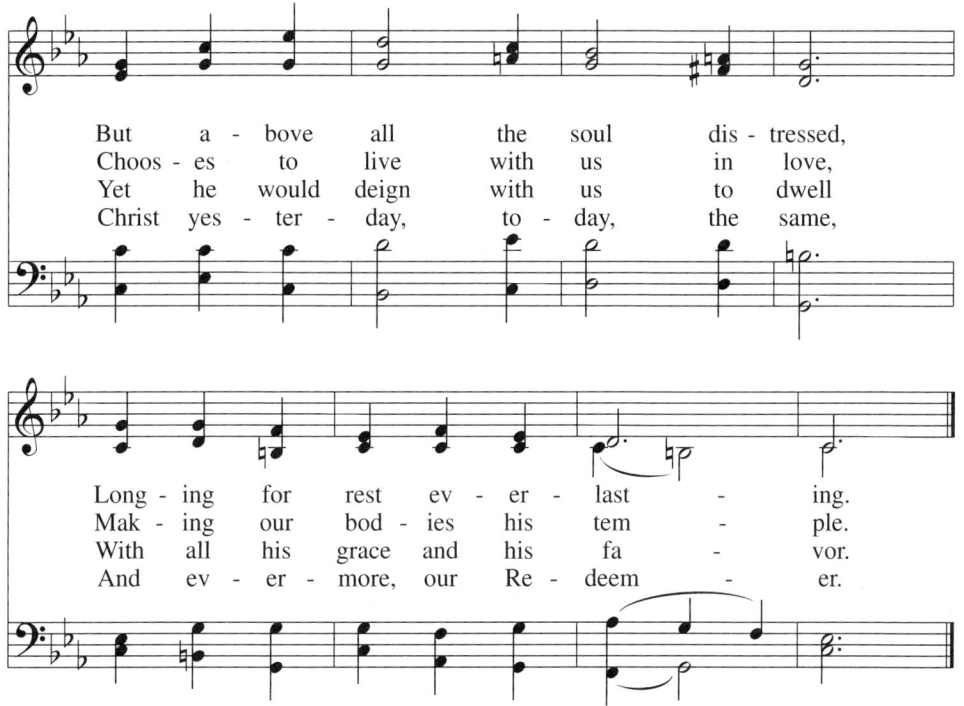

But a - bove all the soul dis - tressed,
Longing for rest ev - er - last - ing.

Choos - es to live with us in love,
Mak - ing our bod - ies his tem - ple.

Yet he would deign with us to dwell
With all his grace and his fa - vor.

Christ yes - ter - day, to - day, the same,
And ev - er - more, our Re - deem - er.

5 Grant then, O God, your will be done,
    That, when the church bells are ringing,
Many in saving faith may come
    Where Christ his message is bringing:
"I know my own; my own know me.
    You, not the world, my face shall see.
My peace I leave with you always."

Text: Nikolai F. S. Grundtvig, 1783-1872, abr.; tr. Carl Döving, 1867-1937, alt.
Tune: Ludvig M. Lindeman, 1812-87

KIRKEN DEN ER ET GAMMELT HUS
88 88 88 8

CHURCH

530 Hark! The Church Proclaims Her Honor

1 Hark! The Church proclaims her honor, And her strength is only this: God has laid his choice upon her, And the work she does is his.

2 He his Church has firmly founded; He will guard what he began. We, by sin and foes surrounded, Build her walls as best we can.

3 Frail and fleeting are our powers, Short our days, our foresight dim. We confess a choice not ours: We were chosen first by him.

4 Though we here must strive in weakness, Though in tears we often bend, What his might began in meekness Shall achieve a glorious end.

5 Onward, then, without despairing!
  Calm we follow at his Word,
  Thus through joy and sorrow bearing
  Faithful witness to our Lord.

Text: Samuel Preiswerk, 1799-1871; tr. Catherine Winkworth, 1827-78, alt.
Tune: Christian F. Witt, 1660-1716, alt.

STUTTGART
87 87

Alternate setting: 463

CHURCH

coming of his Spirit Into open minds and hearts.
newness and renewal, God the Spirit comes to each.
means in daily living To believe and to adore.
cannot live without you, We adore you! We believe!

Text: Fred Pratt Green, b. 1903
Tune: *Oude en Nieuwe Hollantse . . . Contradansen*, Amsterdam, c. 1710

Text © 1979 Hope Publishing Co.; Setting © F. E. Röntgen

IN BABILONE
87 87 D

Alternate setting: 182

I Love Your Kingdom, Lord

1 I love your kingdom, Lord, The place of your abode,
2 Beyond my highest joy I prize its heav'nly ways,
3 I love your Church, O God, Your saints in ev'ry land,
4 For them my tears shall fall; For them my prayers ascend;

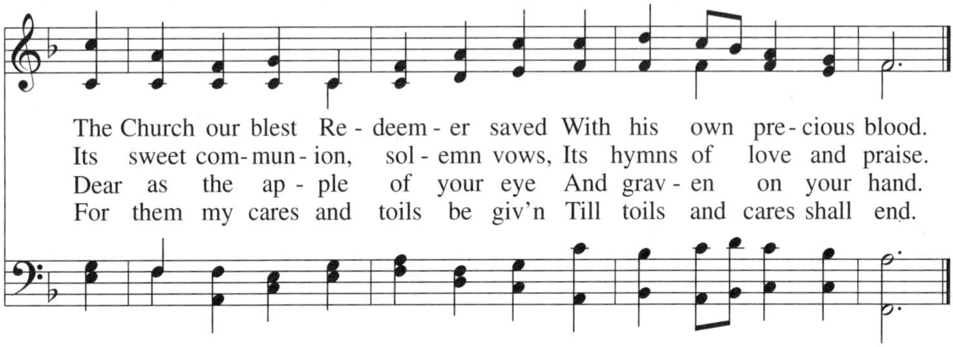

The Church our blest Redeemer saved With his own precious blood.
Its sweet communion, solemn vows, Its hymns of love and praise.
Dear as the apple of your eye And graven on your hand.
For them my cares and toils be giv'n Till toils and cares shall end.

5 Sure as your truth shall last,
   To Zion shall be giv'n
   The brightest glories earth can yield
   And brighter bliss of heav'n.

Text: Timothy Dwight, 1752-1817, abr., alt.
Tune: Aaron Williams, 1731-76

ST. THOMAS
SM

Alternate settings: 1, 238

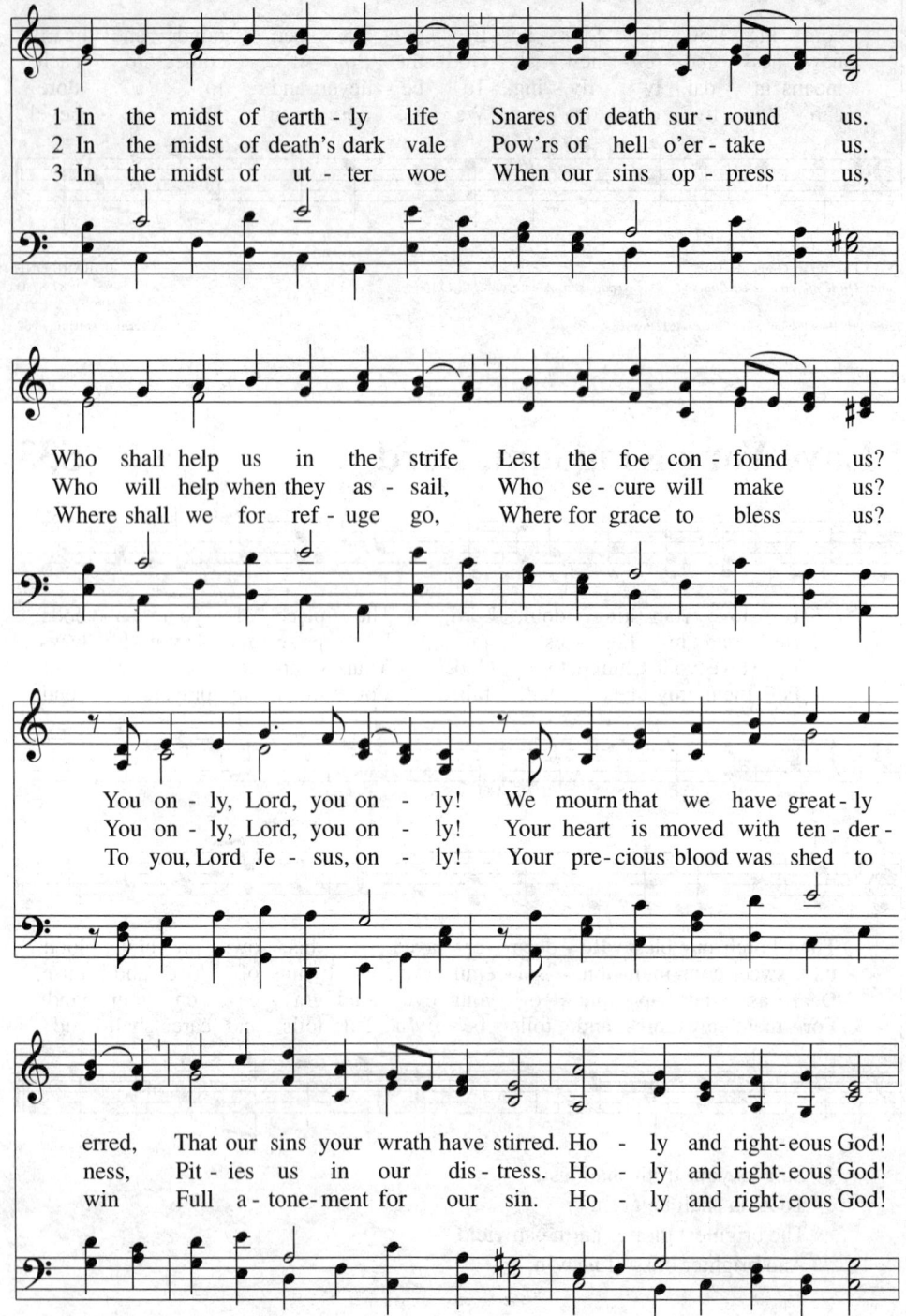

CHURCH

Text: Martin Luther, 1483-1546; tr. *The Lutheran Hymnal*, St. Louis, 1941, alt.
Tune: Latin melody, 13th century, adapt.

MITTEN WIR IM LEBEN SIND
PM

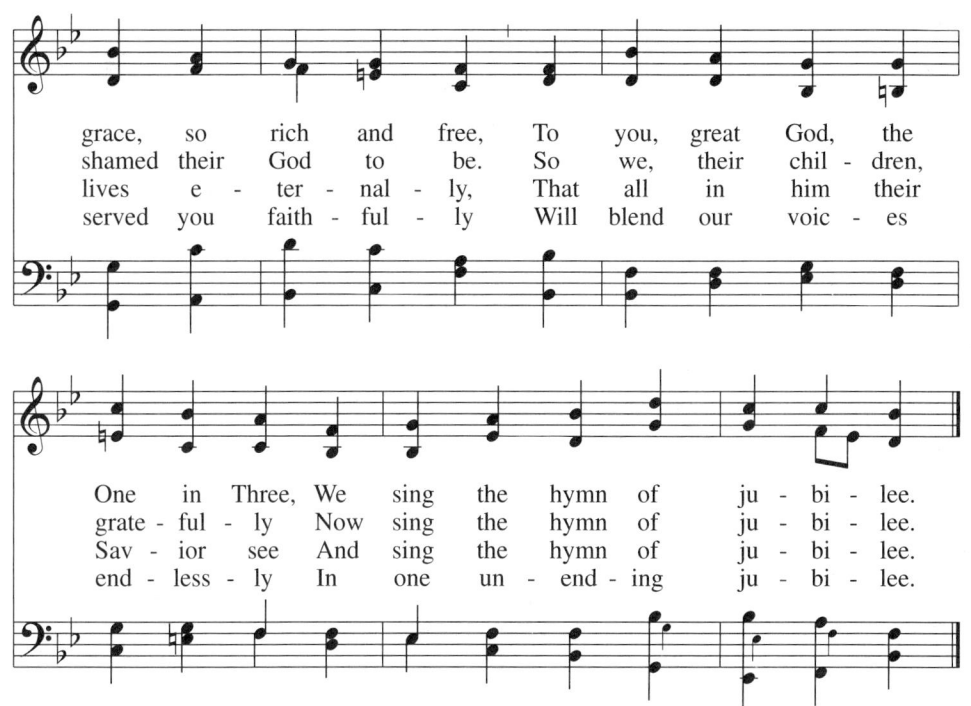

Text: W. Harry Krieger, 1914-74, abr., alt.
Tune: *Johann Störls . . . Schlag-Gesang-Und Noten-Buch,* Stuttgart, 1744
Text © 1972 Concordia Publishing House

O GROSSER GOTT
LM D

Text: Johann Mentzer, 1658-1734, abr.; tr. William J. Schaefer, 1891-1976, alt.
Tune: Friedrich O. Reuter, 1863-1924

REUTER
87 87 65 66 7

Alternate setting: 293

Text: Sabine Baring-Gould, 1834-1924, abr., alt.
Tune: Arthur S. Sullivan, 1842-1900

ST. GERTRUDE
65 65 D with Refrain

CHURCH

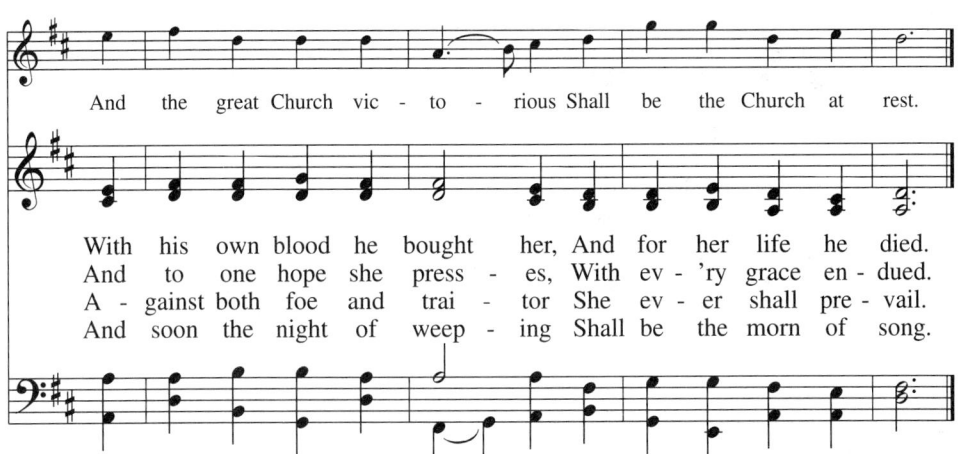

5 Mid toil and tribulation
　　And tumult of her war
She waits the consummation
　　Of peace forevermore
Till with the vision glorious
　　Her longing eyes are blest
And the great Church victorious
　　Shall be the Church at rest.

Text: Samuel J. Stone, 1839-1900, abr., alt.
Tune: Samuel S. Wesley, 1810-76; Desc. Kermit G. Moldenhauer, b. 1949

AURELIA
76 76 D

Descant © 1993 Kermit G. Moldenhauer

Alternate setting: 372

CHURCH

539   In Christ There Is No East or West

5 In Christ now meet both east and west;
In him meet south and north.
All Christly souls are one in him
Throughout the whole wide earth.

Text: John Oxenham, 1852-1941, st. 1, 4-5; Mark A. Jeske, b. 1952, st. 2; Michael Perry, b. 1942, st. 3
Tune: African-American spiritual, adapt.

MCKEE
CM

Text st. 2 © 1993 Mark A. Jeske; Text st. 3 © 1982 Hope Publishing Co.; Tune and Setting © Harry T. Burleigh

Rejoice, O Pilgrim Throng 540

5 At last the march shall end;
  The wearied ones shall rest;
  The pilgrims find their homes at last,
  Jerusalem the blest.
  Refrain

Text: Edward H. Plumptre, 1821-91, abr., alt.
Tune: Arthur H. Messiter, 1834-1916

MARION
SM with Refrain

541 Lord Jesus Christ, with Us Abide

1. Lord Jesus Christ, with us abide,
For round us falls the eventide,
Nor let your Word, that heav'nly light,
For us be ever veiled in night.

2. O God, how sin's dread works abound!
Throughout the earth no rest is found,
And falsehood's spirit wide has spread,
And error boldly rears its head.

3. In these last days of sore distress
Grant us, dear Lord, true steadfastness
That pure we keep, till life is spent,
Your holy Word and sacrament.

4. Lord Jesus, help, your Church uphold,
For we are sluggish, thoughtless, cold.
Oh, prosper well your Word of grace,
And spread its truth in ev'ry place.

5. Oh, keep us in your Word, we pray;
The guile and rage of Satan stay!
Oh, may your mercy never cease!
Give concord, patience, courage, peace.

6. The cause is yours, the glory, too,
So hear us, Lord, and keep us true.
Your Word alone is our defense,
The Church's glorious confidence.

7. Oh, grant that in your holy Word
We here may live and die, dear Lord,
And when our journey's ending here,
Receive us into glory there.

Text: *Geistliche Psalmen*, Nürnberg, 1611, st. 1, 3;
Nikolaus Selnecker, 1532-92, st. 2, 4-7, abr., adapt.; tr. composite
Tune: *Geistliche Lieder*, Leipzig, 1589, alt.

ACH BLEIB BEI UNS
LM

MINISTRY

Dear Lord, to Your True Servants Give 542

1 Dear Lord, to your true servants give The grace to you alone to live. Set free from sin to serve you, Lord, They go to share your living Word, The gospel message to proclaim That all may know your saving name.
2 They gladly go at your command To spread your Word o'er sea and land. Be with them, Lord, and make them strong To heal sin's ills, to right the wrong. Your rule is over wind and wave, And mighty is your arm to save.
3 When all their labor seems in vain, Revive their sinking hopes again; And when success crowns what they do, Oh, keep them humble, Lord, and true Until before your judgment seat They lay their trophies at your feet.

Text: W. Gustave Polack, 1890-1950, alt.
Tune: John B. Dykes, 1823-76
Text © 1941 Concordia Publishing House

MELITA
88 88 88

MINISTRY

Preach You the Word 544

1 Preach you the Word and plant it home To those who like or like it not, The Word that shall en-dure and stand When flow'rs and mor-tals are for-got.
2 We know how hard, O Lord, the task Your ser-vant bids us un-der-take: To preach your Word and nev-er ask What pride-ful prof-it it may make.
3 The sow-er sows; his reck-less love Scat-ters a-broad the good-ly seed, In-tent a-lone that there may be The whole-some loaves that peo-ple need.
4 Though some be snatched and some be scorched And some be choked and mat-ted flat, The sow-er sows; his heart cries out, "Oh, what of that, and what of that?"

5 Preach you the Word and plant it home
  And never faint; the Harvest-Lord
  Who gave the sower seed to sow
  Will watch and tend his planted Word.

Text: Martin H. Franzmann, 1907-76, alt.
Tune: *Rheinfelssisch Deutsches Catholisches Gesangbuch,* Augsburg, 1666
Text © 1971 Mrs. Martin H. Franzmann; Setting © 1969 Concordia Publishing House

O HEILAND, REISS DIE HIMMEL AUF
LM
Alternate setting: 91

MINISTRY

545 Send, O Lord, Your Holy Spirit

1 Send, O Lord, your Holy Spirit On your servants now, we pray;
   Let them all be faithful shepherds That no lamb is led astray.
   Your pure teaching to proclaim, To adore your holy name,
   And to

2 You, O Lord, yourself have called them For your precious lambs to care;
   But to prosper in their calling, They the Spirit's gifts must share.
   Grant them wisdom from above; Fill their hearts with holy love.
   In their

3 Help, Lord Jesus, help them nourish Our dear children with your Word,
   That in constant love they serve you Till in heav'n their song is heard.
   Boundless blessings, Lord, bestow On your servants' work below.
   Till by

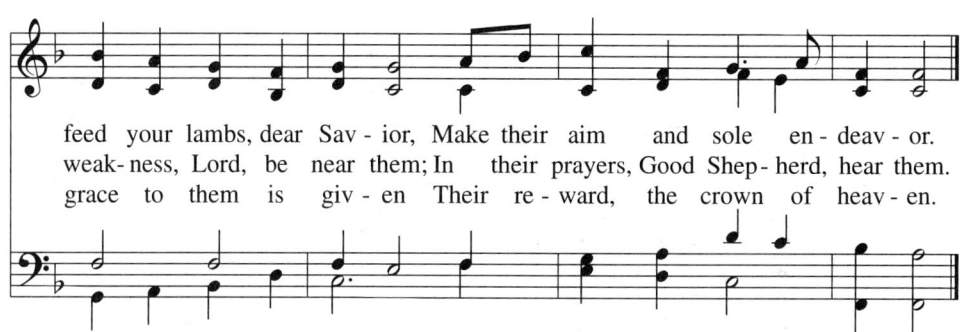

MINISTRY

We Bid You Welcome in the Name 547

1. We bid you welcome in the name Of Jesus, our exalted head. Come as a servant — so he came — We shall receive you in his stead.
2. Come as a shepherd; guard and keep This fold from hell and world and sin. Nourish the lambs and feed the sheep; The wounded heal; the lost bring in.
3. Come as a teacher sent from God With his whole counsel to declare. Our souls encourage with the Word, While we uphold your hands with prayer.
4. Come as a messenger of peace, Filled with the Spirit, fired with love. God bless your work, your strength increase, And guide us all to heav'n above.

Text: James Montgomery, 1771-1854, abr., alt.
Tune: *As hymnodus sacer,* Leipzig, 1625, alt.

HERR JESU CHRIST, MEINS
LM

Alternate settings: 223, 404

SAINTS AND MARTYRS

Around the Throne, a Glorious Band 549

1. A-round the throne, a glorious band, The saints in countless numbers stand, Of ev'ry tongue, redeemed to God, Arrayed in garments washed in blood.

2. Through tribulation great they came; They bore the cross, despised the shame. From all their labors now they rest In God's eternal glory blest.

3. They see their Savior face to face And sing the triumphs of his grace. Each day and night they sing his praise, To him the loud thanksgiving raise:

4. "Worthy the Lamb, for sinners slain, Through endless years to live and reign; You have redeemed us by your blood And made us kings and priests to God."

5. Oh, may we tread the sacred road
That saints and holy martyrs trod,
Wage to the end the glorious strife,
And win, like them, a crown of life.

Text: Rowland Hill, 1744-1833, abr., alt.
Tune: *Second Supplement to Psalmody in Miniature*, London, 1778, adapt.

ROCKINGHAM OLD
LM

SAINTS AND MARTYRS

Text: Hans A. Brorson, 1694-1764; tr. composite
Tune: Norwegian folk tune, 17th century

GREAT WHITE HOST
PM

Text st. 3 © 1978 *Lutheran Book of Worship*

SAINTS AND MARTYRS

552 By All Your Saints Still Striving

1 By all your saints still striving, For all your saints at rest,
Your holy name, O Jesus, Forevermore be blessed.
You rose, our King victorious, That they might wear the crown
And ever shine in splendor Reflected from your throne.

2 *(Insert the stanza appropriate for the day.)*

3 Then let us praise the Father And worship God the Son
And sing to God the Spirit, Eternal Three in One,
Till all the ransomed number Who stand before the throne
Ascribe all pow'r and glory And praise to God alone.

Text: Horatio B. Nelson, 1823-1913, st. 1-4, 6-27, alt.; Harlyn J. Kuschel, b. 1945, st. 5
Tune: Finnish folk tune, c. 19th century

KUORTANE
76 76 D

Text st. 1-4, 6-27 © The Church Pension Fund; Text st. 5 © 1993 Harlyn J. Kuschel; Setting reprinted by permission of Oxford University Press

Confession of St. Peter

4. We praise you, Lord, for Peter,
　　So eager and so bold,
　Thrice failing, yet repentant,
　　Thrice charged to feed your fold.
　Lord, make your pastors faithful
　　To guard your flock from harm,
　And hold them when they waver
　　With your almighty arm.

St. Timothy and St. Titus

5. All praise for faithful pastors,
　　Who preached and taught your Word,
　For Timothy and Titus,
　　True servants of their Lord.
　Lord, help your pastors nourish
　　The souls within their care,
　So that your Church may flourish
　　And all your blessings share.

Conversion of St. Paul

6. Praise for the light from heaven
　　And for the voice of awe;
　Praise for the glorious vision
　　The persecutor saw.
　O Lord, for Paul's conversion
　　We bless your name today.
　Come, shine within our darkness,
　　And guide us in the way.

St. Matthias

7. For one in place of Judas
　　Th' apostles sought God's choice;
　The lot fell to Matthias,
　　For whom we now rejoice.
　May we like true apostles
　　Your holy Church defend
　And not betray our calling
　　But serve you to the end.

St. Joseph

8. All praise, O God, for Joseph,
　　The guardian of your Son,
　Who saved him from King Herod
　　When safety there was none.
　He taught the trade of builder
　　When they to Naz'reth came;
　And Joseph's love as father
　　Blessed God the Father's name.

St. Mark

9. For Mark, O Lord, we praise you,
　　The weak by grace made strong;
　His witness in his Gospel
　　Becomes victorious song.
　May we in all our weakness
　　Receive your pow'r divine
　And all, as faithful branches,
　　Grow strong in you, the vine.

St. Philip and St. James

10. We praise you, Lord, for Philip,
　　Blest guide to Greek and Jew,
　And for young James the faithful,
　　Who heard and followed you.
　Oh, grant us grace to know you,
　　The victor in the strife,
　That we with all your servants
　　May wear the crown of life.

St. Barnabas

11. For Barnabas we praise you,
　　Who kept your law of love
　And, leaving earthly treasures,
　　Sought riches from above.
　O Christ, our Lord and Savior,
　　Let gifts of grace descend
　That your true consolation
　　May through the world extend.

St. John the Baptist

12 All praise for John the Baptist,
        Forerunner of the Word,
    Our true Elijah, making
        A highway for the Lord.
    The last and greatest prophet,
        He saw the dawning ray
    Of light that grows in splendor
        Until the perfect day.

St. Peter and St. Paul

13 We praise you for St. Peter;
        We praise you for St. Paul.
    They taught both Jew and Gentile
        That Christ is all in all.
    To cross and sword they yielded
        And saw the kingdom come;
    O God, your two apostles
        Reached life through martyrdom.

St. Mary Magdalene

14 All praise for Mary Magdalene,
        Whose wholeness was restored
    By you, her faithful master,
        Her Savior and her Lord.
    On Easter morning early
        A word from you sufficed;
    Her faith was first to see you,
        Her Lord, the risen Christ.

St. James the Elder

15 O Lord, for James we praise you,
        Who fell to Herod's sword.
    He drank the cup of suff'ring
        And thus fulfilled your Word.
    Lord, curb our vain impatience
        For glory and for fame;
    Equip us for such suff'rings
        As glorify your name.

St. Mary, Mother of Our Lord

16 We sing with joy of Mary,
        Whose heart with awe was stirred
    When, youthful and unready,
        She heard the angel's word.
    Yet she her voice upraises,
        God's glory to proclaim,
    As once for our salvation
        Your mother she became.

St. Bartholomew

17 Praise for your blest apostle
        Surnamed Bartholomew;
    We know not his achievements
        But know that he was true,
    For he at the ascension
        Was an apostle still.
    May we discern your presence
        And seek, like him, your will.

St. Matthew

18 Praise, Lord, for him whose Gospel
        Your human life declared,
    Who, worldly gain forsaking,
        Your path of suff'ring shared.
    From all unrighteous mammon,
        Oh, raise our eyes anew
    That we, like faithful Matthew,
        May rise and follow you.

St. Luke

19 For Luke, beloved physician,
        All praise, whose Gospel shows
    The healer of the nations,
        The one who shares our woes.
    Your wine and oil, O Savior,
        Upon our spirits pour,
    And with true balm of Gilead
        Anoint us evermore.

SAINTS AND MARTYRS

St. James of Jerusalem

20 Praise for the Lord's own brother,
    James of Jerusalem,
He saw the risen Savior
    And placed his faith in him.
Presiding at the council
    That set the Gentiles free,
He welcomed them as kindred
    On equal terms to be.

St. Simon and St. Jude

21 Praise, Lord, for your apostles,
    St. Simon and St. Jude.
One love, and hope, impelled them
    To tread the way, renewed.
May we with zeal as earnest
    The faith of Christ maintain,
Be bound in love together,
    And life eternal gain.

All Saints' Day

22 Apostles, prophets, martyrs,
    And all the noble throng
Who wear the spotless raiment
    And raise the ceaseless song —
For these, passed on before us,
    We offer praises due
And, walking in their footsteps,
    Would live our lives for you.

St. Andrew

23 All praise, O Lord, for Andrew,
    The first to welcome you,
Whose witness to his brother
    Named you Messiah true.
May we with hearts kept open
    To you throughout the year,
Confess to friend and neighbor
    Your advent ever near.

St. Thomas

24 All praise, O Lord, for Thomas,
    Whose short-lived doubtings prove
Your perfect twofold nature,
    The depth of your true love.
To all who live with questions
    A steadfast faith afford
And grant us grace to know you,
    Made flesh, yet God and Lord.

St. Stephen

25 All praise, O Lord, for Stephen,
    Who, martyred, saw you stand
To help in time of torment,
    To plead at God's right hand.
Like you, our suff'ring Savior,
    His enemies he blessed;
With "Lord, receive my spirit,"
    His faith, in death, confessed.

St. John the Evangelist

26 For John, your loved disciple,
    Exiled to Patmos' shore,
And for his faithful record
    We praise you evermore.
Praise for the mystic vision
    His words to us unfold.
Instill in us his longing
    Your glory to behold.

Holy Innocents

27 Praise for your infant martyrs,
    Whom your mysterious love
Called early from life's conflicts
    To share your peace above.
O Rachel, cease your weeping;
    They're free from pain and cares.
Lord, grant us crowns as brilliant
    And faith as sure as theirs.

SAINTS AND MARTYRS

553 Give Thanks to God on High

1. Give thanks to God on high For saints of other days, Whose hope it was to live and die In love's consuming blaze For Christ and his kingdom, His glory and his praise.

2. Their vision long-fulfilled, Our prayer is still the same: Upon their work of faith to build, Their word of truth proclaim For Christ and his kingdom And for his holy name.

3. New tasks today are ours Who serve a world in pain, New calls to challenge all our pow'rs Of heart and hand and brain, For Christ and his kingdom While life and breath remain.

4. Give thanks to God on high For all the future sends, In praise of Christ to live and die Who calls his servants friends, For Christ and his kingdom, Whose glory never ends.

Text: Timothy Dudley-Smith, b. 1926
Tune: Bruce R. Backer, b. 1929

FRANKLIN
66 86 66

Text © 1985 Hope Publishing Co.; Tune and Setting © 1993 Bruce R. Backer

SAINTS AND MARTYRS

Oh, How Blest Are They 554

1 Oh, how blest are they whose toils are ended,
  Who through death have unto God ascended!
  They have arisen
  From the cares which keep us still in prison.

2 We are still as in a dungeon living,
  Still oppressed with sorrow and misgiving;
  Our undertakings
  Are but toils and troubles and heartbreakings.

3 They meanwhile are in their chambers sleeping,
  Quiet and set free from all their weeping;
  No cross or sadness
  There can hinder their untroubled gladness.

4 Christ has wiped away their tears forever;
  They have that for which we still endeavor.
  To them are chanted
  Songs that ne'er to mortal ears were granted.

5 Come, O Christ, and loose the chains that bind us;
  Lead us forth and cast this world behind us.
  With you, th' Anointed,
  Finds the soul its joy and rest appointed.

Text: Simon Dach, 1605-59, abr.; tr. Henry W. Longfellow, 1807-92, alt.
Tune: Johann Störls . . . Schlag-Gesang-Und Noten-Buch, Stuttgart, 1744

O WIE SELIG
10 10 5 10

SAINTS AND MARTYRS

555   For All Your Saints, O Lord

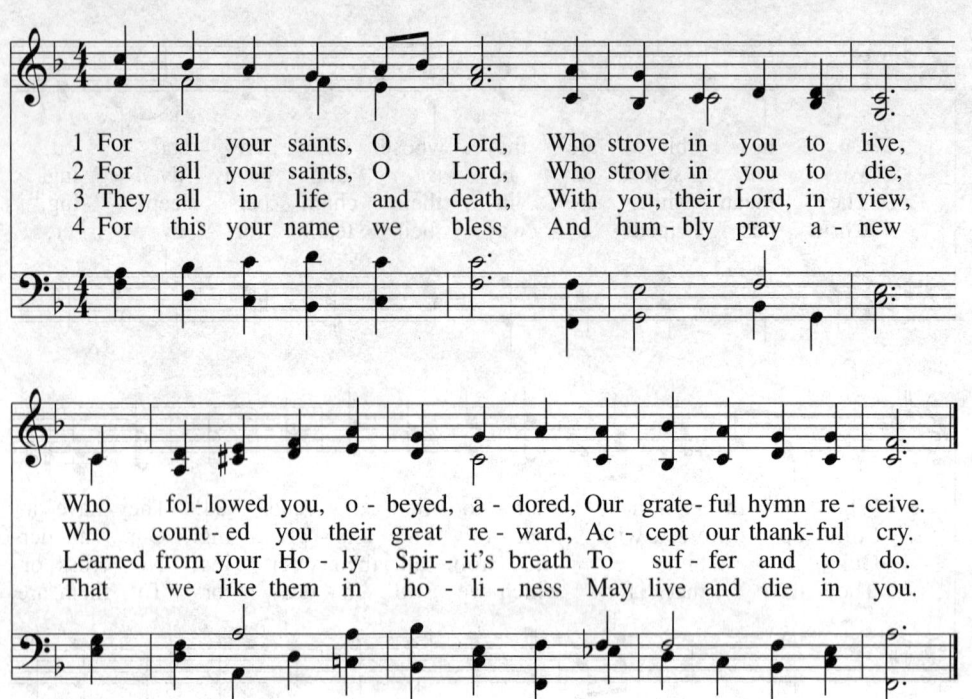

1 For all your saints, O Lord, Who strove in you to live,
Who fol-lowed you, o-beyed, a-dored, Our grate-ful hymn re-ceive.
2 For all your saints, O Lord, Who strove in you to die,
Who count-ed you their great re-ward, Ac-cept our thank-ful cry.
3 They all in life and death, With you, their Lord, in view,
Learned from your Ho-ly Spir-it's breath To suf-fer and to do.
4 For this your name we bless And hum-bly pray a-new
That we like them in ho-li-ness May live and die in you.

Text: Richard Mant, 1776-1848, abr., alt.
Tune: William H. Monk, 1823-89
Setting © 1982 Concordia Publishing House

ENERGY
SM
Alternate setting: 381

EVANGELISM

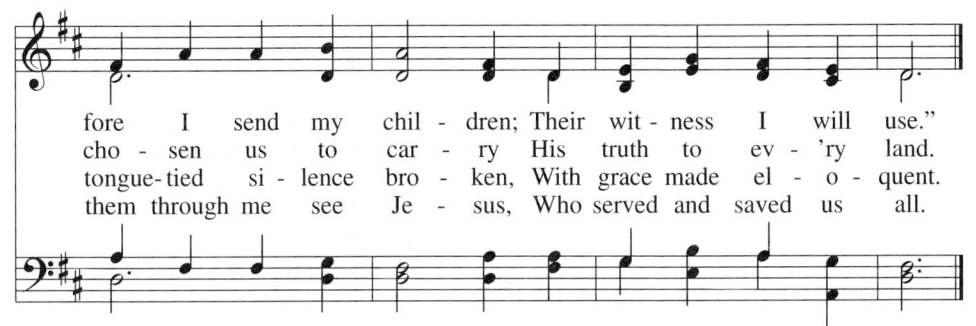

5 Lord, gather all your children,
    Wherever they may be,
And lead them on to heaven
    To live eternally
With you, our loving Father,
    And Christ, our brother dear,
Whose Spirit guards and gives us
    The joy to persevere.

Text: Henry L. Lettermann, b. 1932, abr.
Tune: Lowell Mason, 1792-1872
Text © 1982 Concordia Publishing House

MISSIONARY HYMN
76 76 D
Alternate setting: 571

EVANGELISM

558 Christ High-Ascended

1 Christ high-ascended, now in glory seated, Throned and exalted, victory completed, Death's dread dominion finally defeated— We are his witnesses.
2 Christ, from the Father ev-'ry pow'r possessing, Who on his chosen lifted hands in blessing, Sends forth his servants, still in faith confessing— We are his witnesses.
3 Christ, who in dying won for us salvation, Lives now the firstborn of the new creation; To win disciples out of ev-'ry nation, We are his witnesses.
4 Christ in his splendor, all dominion gaining, Christ with his people evermore remaining, Christ to all ages, gloriously reigning— We are his witnesses.

5 As at his parting, joy shall banish grieving,
Faith in his presence strengthen our believing;
Filled with his Spirit, love and pow'r receiving,
We are his witnesses.

Text: Timothy Dudley-Smith, b. 1926
Tune: *Antiphoner*, Paris, 1681
Text © 1984 Hope Publishing Co.

CHRISTE SANCTORUM
11 11 11 6
Alternate setting: 343

EVANGELISM

5 I hear the Savior calling! His call has urgency!
  Each moment souls are dying; Soon comes eternity.
  And so, my precious Savior, This is my humble plea:
  Prepare me for my mission For you are calling me!

Text: John C. Lawrenz, b. 1943
Tune: Friedrich K. Anthes, 1812 - after 1857

ANTHES
76 76 D

Text © 1993 John C. Lawrenz

Alternate setting: 336

Lord, Speak to Us that We May Speak   561

1 Lord, speak to us that we may speak In living ech-oes of your tone. As you have sought, so let us seek Your stray-ing chil-dren, lost and lone.
2 Oh, lead us, Lord, that we may lead The wan-d'ring and the wa-v'ring feet. Oh, feed us, Lord, that we may feed Your hun-g'ring ones with man-na sweet.
3 Oh, teach us, Lord, that we may teach The pre-cious truths which you im-part, And wing our words that they may reach The hid-den depths of man-y a heart.
4 Oh, fill us with your full-ness, Lord, Un-til our ver-y hearts o'er-flow In kin-dling thought and glow-ing word Your love to tell, your praise to show.

Text: Frances R. Havergal, 1836-79, abr., alt.
Tune: Robert A. Schumann, 1810-56, adapt.

CANONBURY
LM

EVANGELISM

562   **I Love to Tell the Story**

1. I love to tell the story Of unseen things above,
Of Jesus and his glory, Of Jesus and his love.
I love to tell the story Because I know it's true;
It satisfies my longings As nothing else can do.

2. I love to tell the story, For those who know it best
Seem hungering and thirsting To hear it like the rest.
And when in scenes of glory I sing the new, new song,
'Twill be the old, old story That I have loved so long.

EVANGELISM

Text: Arabella C. Hankey, 1834-1911, abr.
Tune: William G. Fischer, 1835-1912

HANKEY
76 76 D with Refrain

EVANGELISM

563 Go Labor On

1. Go labor on; spend and be spent— 'Tis joy to do the Father's will. It is the way the Master went; Should not the servant tread it still?

2. Go labor on; count not the cost— Your earthly loss is heav'nly gain. The world indeed will praise you not, But you will share in heaven's reign.

3. Go labor on while it is day; The world's dark night is hast'ning on. Speed, speed your work, do not delay, For it is thus that souls are won.

4. They die in darkness at your side Without a hope to cheer the tomb; Take up the torch and wave it wide, The torch that lights the thickest gloom.

5. Toil on, faint not, keep watch, and pray;
   Be wise the erring soul to win.
   Go forth into the world's wide way;
   Compel the wand'rer to come in.

6. Toil on and in your toil rejoice;
   For toil comes rest, for exile home.
   Soon shall you hear the Bridegroom's voice,
   The midnight cry, "Behold, I come!"

Text: Horatius Bonar, 1808-89, abr., alt.
Tune: *Antiphoner*, Grenoble, 1753
Setting published by permission of the executors of the late Dr. Basil Harwood

DEUS TUORUM MILITUM
LM
Alternate setting: 502

EVANGELISM

There Is a Balm in Gilead

564

There is a balm in Gil-e-ad to make the wound-ed whole;

There is a balm in Gil-e-ad to heal the sin-sick soul.

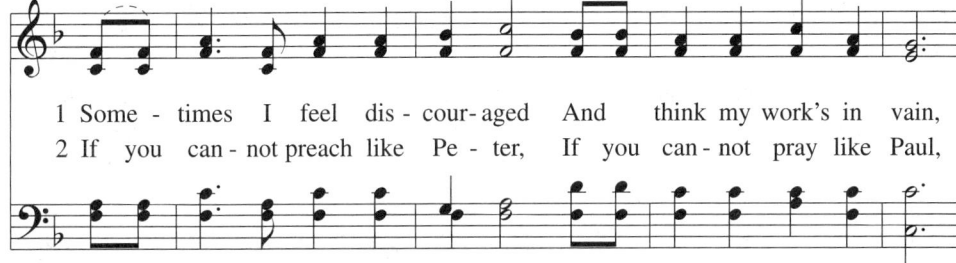

1 Some-times I feel dis-cour-aged And think my work's in vain,
2 If you can-not preach like Pe-ter, If you can-not pray like Paul,

Refrain

But then the Ho-ly Spir-it Re-vives my soul a-gain.
You can tell the love of Je-sus And say he died for all.

Text: African-American spiritual, abr.
Tune: African-American spiritual

BALM IN GILEAD
Irregular

Text: German hymn, 17th century; tr. William M. Czamanske, 1873-1964, alt.
Tune: Johann R. Ahle, 1625-73, alt.

ES IST GENUG
10 6 10 6 99 44

Text © 1941 Concordia Publishing House

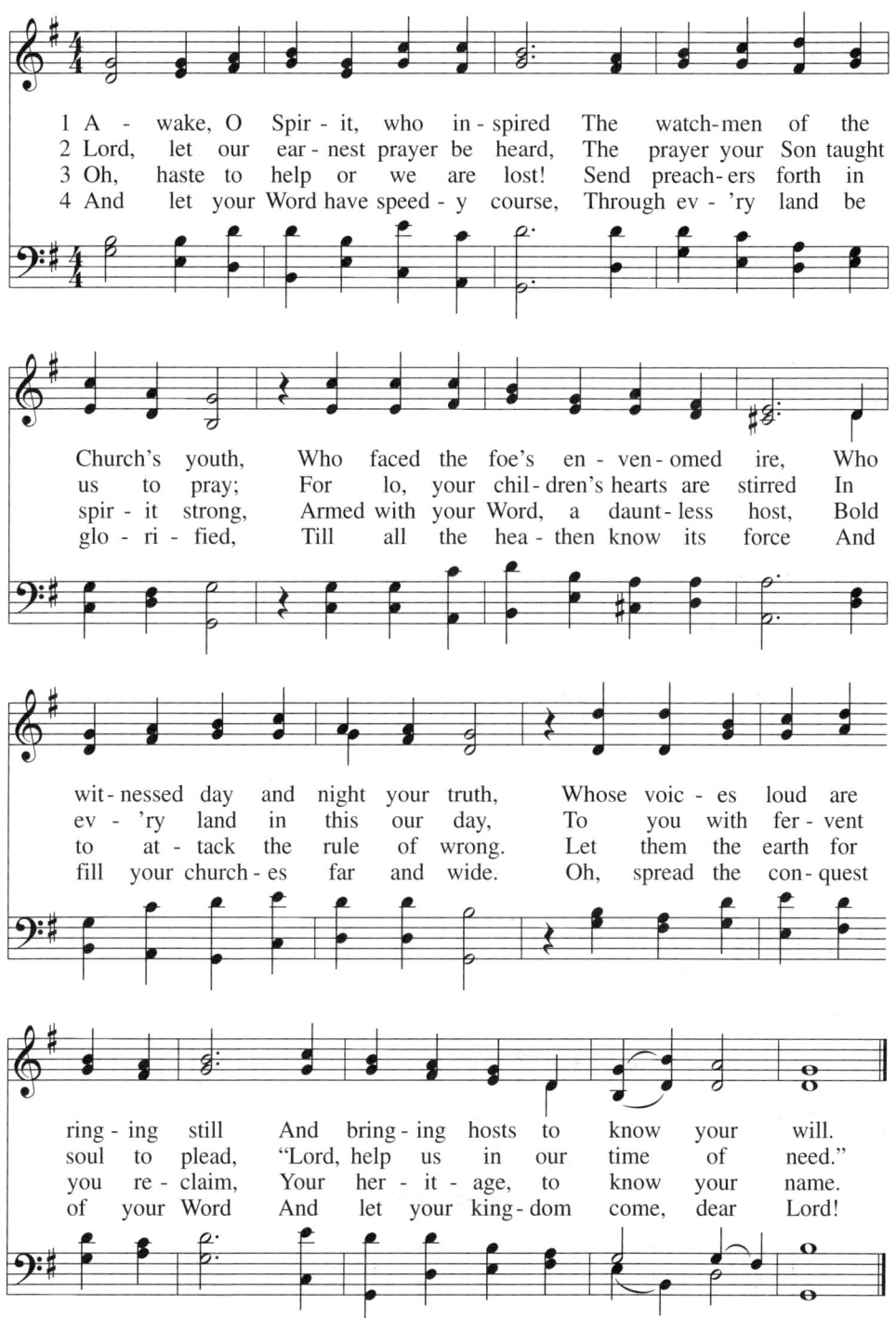

MISSIONS

O Christ, Our True and Only Light 569

1. O Christ, our true and only light, Enlighten those who sit in night; Let those afar now hear your voice And in your fold with us rejoice.

2. Fill with the radiance of your grace The souls now lost in error's maze And all whom in their secret minds Some dark delusion haunts and blinds.

3. Oh, gently call those gone astray That they may find the saving way! Let ev'ry conscience sore oppressed In you find peace and heav'nly rest.

4. Shine on the darkened and the cold; Recall the wand'rers to your fold. Unite all those who walk apart; Confirm the weak and doubting heart

5. That they with us may evermore
Such grace with wond'ring thanks adore
And endless praise to you be giv'n
By all your Church in earth and heav'n.

Text: Johann Heermann, 1585-1647, abr.; tr. Catherine Winkworth, 1827-78, alt.
Tune: *Andächtige Haus-Kirche*, Nürnberg, 1676, alt.

O JESU CHRISTE, WAHRES LICHT
LM

Alternate settings: 9, 383

MISSIONS

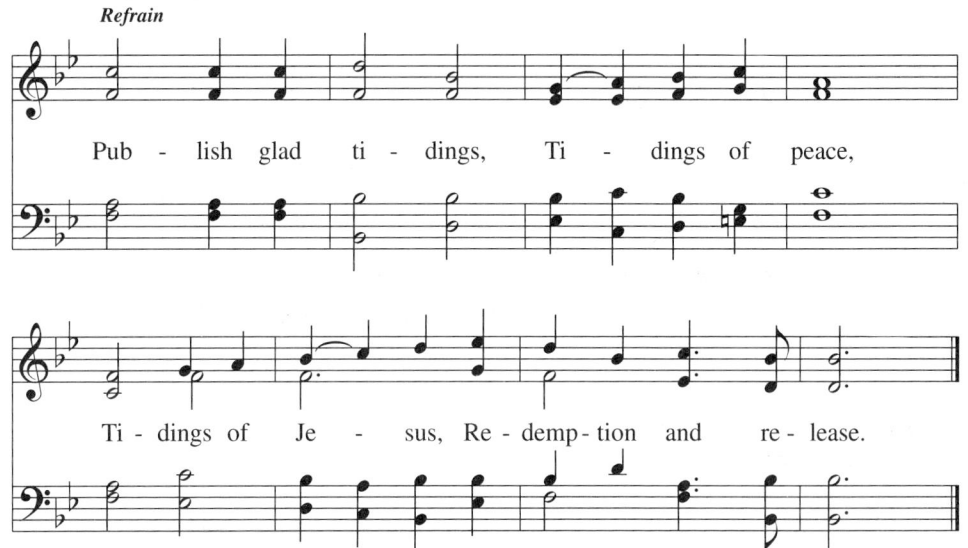

Text: Mary A. Thomson, 1834-1923, abr., alt.
Tune: Bruce R. Backer, b. 1929

REDEMPTION
11 10 11 10 with Refrain

Tune and Setting © 1993 Bruce R. Backer

MISSIONS

Send Forth, O Lord, to Every Place   572

1 Send forth, O Lord, to ev-'ry place Swift messen-gers before your face, The heralds of your wondrous grace, Where you yourself will come.
2 Send men whose eyes have seen the King, Men in whose ears his sweet words ring; Send them your lost ones home to bring; Send them where you will come—
3 To bring good news to souls in sin, The bruised and broken hearts to win, In ev-'ry place to bring them in Where you yourself will come.
4 Since you have died, your vic-t'ry claim; Assert, O Christ, your glory's name; And far to lands of pagan shame Send men where you will come.

5 Arm each one with the Spirit's sword,
The sword of your own deathless Word,
And make them conqu'rors, conqu'ring Lord,
Where you yourself will come.

Text: Mary C. Gates, 1842-1905, abr., alt.
Tune: Samuel Howard, 1710-82

ISLEWORTH
888 6
Alternate setting: 499

MISSIONS

573   Hark! The Voice of Jesus Crying

1 Hark! The voice of Jesus crying, "Who will go and work today? Fields are ripe and harvests waiting; Who will bear the sheaves away?" Loud and long the Master calleth; Rich reward he offers thee. Who will

2 If you cannot speak like angels, If you cannot preach like Paul, You can tell the love of Jesus; You can say he died for all. If you cannot rouse the wicked With the Judgment's dread alarms, You can

3 If you cannot be a watchman, Standing high on Zion's wall, Pointing out the path to heaven, Off'ring life and peace to all, With your prayers and with your off'rings You can do what God demands; You can

4 Let none hear you idly saying, "There is nothing I can do," While the multitudes are dying, And the Master calls for you. Take the task he gives you gladly; Let his work your pleasure be. Answer

MISSIONS

an - swer, glad - ly say - ing, "Here am I — send me, send me"?
lead the lit - tle chil - dren To the Sav - ior's wait - ing arms.
be like faith - ful Aar - on, Hold - ing up the proph - et's hands.
quick - ly when he call - eth, "Here am I — send me, send me!"

Text: Daniel March, 1816-1909, st. 1-2, 4, abr., alt.; unknown, st. 3, alt.
Tune: Joseph Barnby, 1838-96

GALILEAN
87 87 D

MISSIONS

Text: Martin Luther, 1483-1546; tr. Richard Massie, 1800-87, alt.
Tune: *Der Lxvj. Deus Misereatur*, Magdeburg, 1524, alt.

ES WOLLE GOTT UNS GNÄDIG SEIN
87 87 87 87 7

MISSIONS

575 How Shall They Hear the Word of God

1. How shall they hear the Word of God Unless the truth is told? How shall the sinful be set free, The sorrowful consoled? To all who speak the truth today Impart your Spirit, Lord, we pray.

2. How shall they call to God for help Unless they have believed? How shall the poor be given hope, The prisoner reprieved? To those who help the blind to see, Give light and love and charity.

3. How shall the gospel be proclaimed If heralds are not sent? How shall the world find peace at last If we are negligent? So send us, Lord, for we rejoice To speak of Christ with life and voice.

Text: Michael A. Perry, b. 1942, alt.
Tune: *Choralbuch für Volkschulen*, Magdeburg, 1816

AUCH JETZT MACHT GOTT
86 86 88

Text © 1982 Hope Publishing Co.

Spread, Oh, Spread the Mighty Word 576

1. Spread, oh, spread the mighty Word; Spread the kingdom of the Lord Ev'rywhere his breath has giv'n Life to beings meant for heav'n.

2. Tell them how the Father's will Made the world and keeps it still, How his only Son he gave All from sin and death to save.

3. Tell of our Redeemer's love, Who forever does remove By his holy sacrifice All the guilt that on us lies.

4. Tell them of the Spirit giv'n Now to guide us on to heav'n, Strong and holy, just and true, Working both to will and do.

5. Up! The rip'ning fields you see. Mighty shall the harvest be, But the reapers still are few; Great the work they have to do.

6. Lord of harvest, grant anew, Joy and strength to work for you, Till the gath'ring nations all See your light and heed your call.

Text: Jonathan F. Bahnmaier, 1774-1841, abr.; tr. Catherine Winkworth, 1827-78, alt.
Tune: *Erbaulicher Musicalisher Christen-Schatz*, Basel, 1745, alt.

HÖCHSTER PRIESTER
77 77

MISSIONS

577   Rise, O Light of Gentile Nations

1. Rise, O Light of Gentile nations, Jesus, bright and Morning Star; Let your Word, the gladsome tidings, Ring out loudly near and far, Bringing freedom to the captives, Peace and comfort to the slave, That the

2. Knowing you and your salvation, Grateful love dare never cease To proclaim your tender mercies, Gracious Lord, your heav'nly peace. Let us sound the gospel tidings To the earth's remotest bound That the

3. May our zeal to help the heathen Be increased from day to day, As we plead in true compassion And for their conversion pray. For the many faithful workers, For the gospel they proclaim, Let us

4. Savior, shine in all your glory On the nations near and far; From the highways and the byways Call them forth, O Morning Star. Guide them whom your grace has chosen Out of Satan's dreadful thrall To the

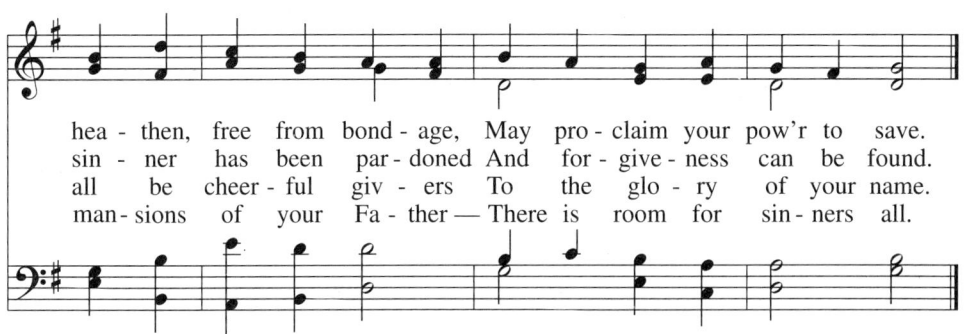

MORNING

Father, We Praise You 581

1 Father, we praise you, now the night is over. Active and watchful, standing now before you, Singing, we offer prayer and meditation; Thus we adore you.
2 Monarch of all things, fit us for your mansions; Banish our weakness, health and wholeness sending. Bring us to heaven, where your saints united Joy without ending.
3 All holy Father, Son, and equal Spirit, Trinity blessed, send us your salvation; Yours is the glory, gleaming and resounding Through all creation.

Text: attr. Gregory I, 540-604; tr. Percy Dearmer, 1867-1936, alt.
Tune: *Antiphoner*, Paris, 1681

CHRISTE SANCTORUM
11 11 11 5

Alternate setting: 343

582 Awake, My Soul, and with the Sun

1. Awake, my soul, and with the sun Your daily stage of duty run; Shake off your sleep and joyful rise To bring your morning sacrifice.
2. All praise to you, who safe have kept And have refreshed me while I slept. Grant, Lord, when I from death shall wake, I may of endless light partake.
3. Lord, all my prayers ascend to you: Disperse my sins as morning dew, Guard my first springs of thought and will, And with your light my spirit fill.
4. Direct, control, suggest this day All I design or do or say That all my pow'rs with all their might In your sole glory may unite.
5. Praise God, from whom all blessings flow;
Praise him, all creatures here below;
Praise him above, you heav'nly host —
Praise Father, Son, and Holy Ghost.

Text: Thomas Ken, 1637-1711, abr., alt.
Tune: François H. Barthelemon, 1741-1808

MORNING HYMN
LM

MORNING

Now that the Daylight Fills the Sky 583

1 Now that the daylight fills the sky, We lift our hearts to God on high That he, in all we do or say, Would keep us free from harm to-day,
2 Would guard our hearts and tongues from strife, From an-gry words would shield our life, From e-vil sights would turn our eyes, And close our ears to van-i-ties.
3 So we, when this new day is gone, And night in turn is draw-ing on, With con-science by the world un-stained, Shall praise his name for vic-t'ry gained.
4 "All praise to you, Cre-a-tor Lord! All praise to you, e-ter-nal Word! All praise to you, O Spir-it wise!" We sing as day-light fills the skies.

Text: Latin hymn, c. 8th century; tr. John M. Neale, 1818-66, alt.
Tune: Dale Wood, b. 1934

LAUREL
LM

Tune and Setting © Lutheran Church Press and Augsburg Publishing House

MORNING

584   O Blessed, Holy Trinity

1. O blessed, holy Trinity, Divine, eternal Unity—God Father, Son, and Holy Ghost— Be all this day my guide and host.
2. My soul and body keep from harm; O'er all I have extend your arm. Let Satan cause me no distress Nor bring me shame or wretchedness.
3. The Father's love shield me this day; The Son's pure wisdom cheer my way; The Holy Spirit's joy and light Drive from my heart the shades of night.
4. My Maker, hold me in your hand; Redeemer, be my dearest friend; Blest Comforter, stay at my side, That faith and love in me abide.
5. Lord, bless and keep me as your own;
   Lord, look in kindness from your throne;
   Lord, let your favor rest on me,
   And give me peace eternally.

Text: Martin Behm, 1557-1622, abr.; tr. Conrad H. L. Schuette, 1843-1926, alt.
Tune: Nikolaus Herman, c. 1480-1561, alt.

O HEILIGE DREIFALTIGKEIT
LM

Alternate settings: 480, 591

EVENING

Now Rest Beneath Night's Shadow   587

Text: Paul Gerhardt, 1607-76, abr.; tr. composite
Tune: Heinrich Isaac, c. 1450-1517, alt.

O WELT, ICH MUSS DICH LASSEN
776 778

Alternate setting: 113

EVENING

5 I need thy presence ev'ry passing hour.
  What but thy grace can foil the tempter's pow'r?
  Who like thyself my guide and stay can be?
  Through cloud and sunshine, oh, abide with me!

6 I fear no foe with thee at hand to bless;
  Ills have no weight and tears no bitterness.
  Where is death's sting? Where, grave, thy victory?
  I triumph still if thou abide with me.

7 Hold thou thy cross before my closing eyes;
  Shine through the gloom and point me to the skies.
  Heav'n's morning breaks, and earth's vain shadows flee;
  In life, in death, O Lord, abide with me!

Text: Henry F. Lyte, 1793-1847, abr., alt.
Tune: William H. Monk, 1823-89

EVENTIDE
10 10 10 10

Now the Day Is Over 589

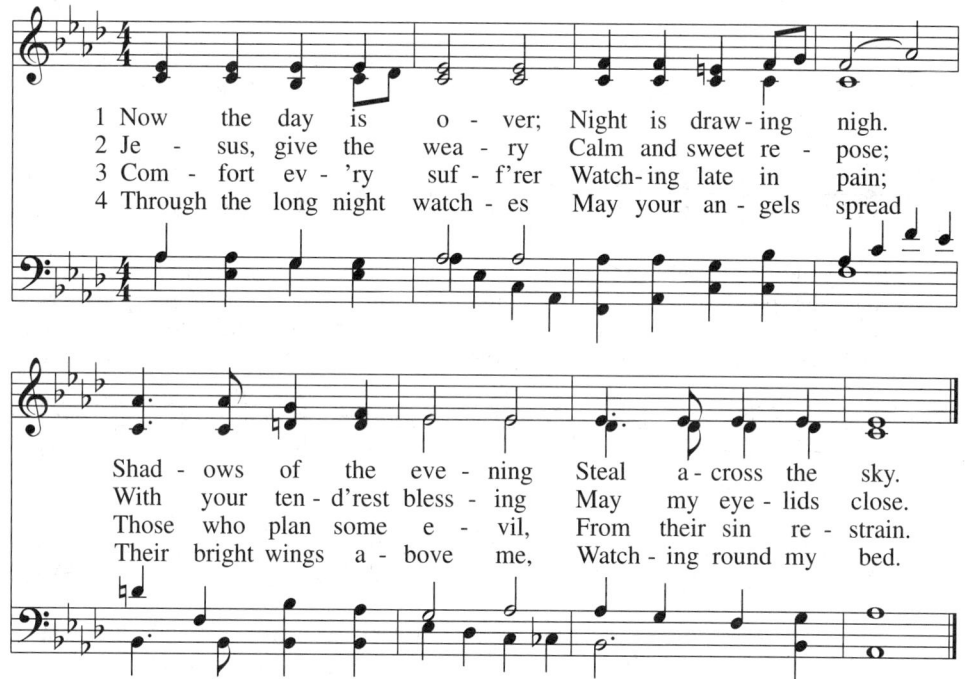

1 Now the day is over; Night is drawing nigh.
  Shadows of the evening Steal across the sky.
2 Jesus, give the weary Calm and sweet repose;
  With your ten-d'rest blessing May my eyelids close.
3 Comfort ev'ry suff'rer Watching late in pain;
  Those who plan some evil, From their sin restrain.
4 Through the long night watches May your angels spread
  Their bright wings above me, Watching round my bed.

5 When the morning wakens,
  Then may I arise
  Pure and fresh and sinless
  In your holy eyes.

Text: Sabine Baring-Gould, 1834-1924, abr., alt.
Tune: Joseph Barnby, 1838-96

MERRIAL
65 65

EVENING

O Trinity, Most Blessed Light
591

1. O Trinity, most blessed light, O Unity of sov-'reign might, As now the fiery sun departs, Oh, shine your light into our hearts.
2. To you our morning song of praise, To you our evening prayer we raise; May we your glory evermore In lowly reverence adore.
3. All praise to God the Father be And to the Son eternally, Whom with the Spirit we adore Forever and forevermore.

Text: attr. St. Ambrose, 340-97; tr. John M. Neale, 1818-66, alt.
Tune: Nikolaus Herman, c. 1480-1561, alt.

O HEILIGE DREIFALTIGKEIT
LM

Alternate settings: 480, 584

EVENING

self, and thee I, ere I sleep, at peace may be.
vig - 'rous make To serve my God when I a - wake.
heav'n - ly host; Praise Fa - ther, Son, and Ho - ly Ghost.

Text: Thomas Ken, 1637-1711, abr., alt.
Tune: Charles F. Gounod, 1818-93, adapt.

EVENING HYMN
LM D

Now the Light Has Gone Away 593

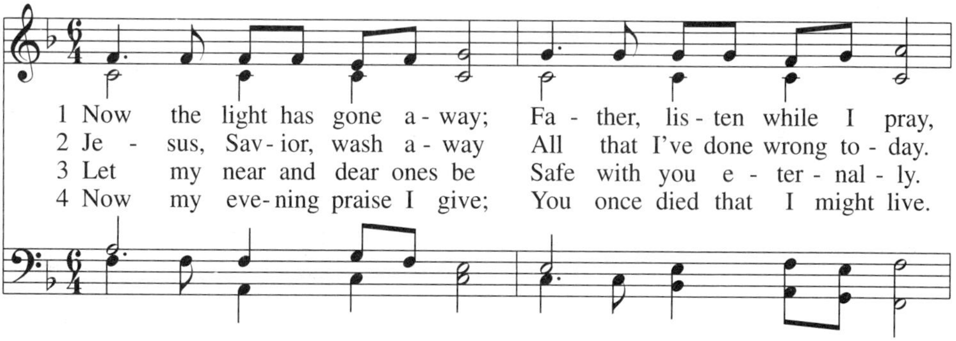

1 Now the light has gone a - way; Fa - ther, lis - ten while I pray,
2 Je - sus, Sav - ior, wash a - way All that I've done wrong to - day.
3 Let my near and dear ones be Safe with you e - ter - nal - ly.
4 Now my eve - ning praise I give; You once died that I might live.

Ask - ing you to watch and keep And to send me qui - et sleep.
Make me ev - er more like you, Good and gen - tle, kind and true.
Oh, bring me and all I love To your hap - py home a - bove.
All your pre - cious gifts are free — Oh, how good you are to me!

5 Ah, my best and kindest Friend,
You will love me to the end.
Let me love you more and more,
Always better than before.

Text: Frances R. Havergal, 1836-79, alt.
Tune: *Liederbuch für Kleinkinder-Schulen*, Kaiserwerth, 1842, alt.

MÜDE BIN ICH
77 77

EVENING

Before the Ending of the Day 595

1 Before the ending of the day, Creator of the world, we pray. Your grace and peace to us allow And guard and keep your people now.
2 From evil dreams defend our sight, From all the terrors of the night, From all deluding thoughts that creep On heedless minds disarmed by sleep.
3 O Father, this we ask be done Through Jesus Christ, your only Son, Whom with the Spirit we adore Forever and forevermore. A-men.

Text: Latin hymn, c. 6th century; tr. John M. Neale, 1818-66, alt.
Tune: Plainsong melody
Setting © 1969 Concordia Publishing House

JAM LUCIS
LM

CONFIRMATION

May God the Father of Our Lord 597

1 May God the Father of our Lord, Who called you by his holy Word, Perfect, establish, settle you, Keep you through faith forever true.
2 In Jesus Christ may you be blessed And brought to his eternal rest. The work he has in you begun, He will perform till all is done.
3 The Holy Spirit give you pow'r, The strength of prayer in ev'ry hour, The wisdom, knowledge, fear of God, That lifts above his chas't'ning rod.
4 May God the Father, God the Son, And God the Spirit, Three in One, Preserve you blameless till in grace You stand before his holy face.

Text: Dorothy I. Scharlemann, b. 1912
Tune: Thomas Tallis, c. 1505-85

TALLIS' CANON
LM

CONFIRMATION

Text: Johann J. Rambach, 1693-1735; tr. R. E. Taylor, d. 1938, alt.
Tune: Franz H. C. Meyer, 1705-67, alt.

MEIN SCHÖPFER, STEH MIR BEI
66 66 77 77 86

CONFIRMATION

599 Our Lord and God, Oh, Bless This Day

1 Our Lord and God, oh, bless this day And hear us, we implore you; None of your children turn away Who now appear before you. We come before your face And pray: let your rich grace Descend from heav'n above In all your love did them embrace.

2 Oh, bless your Word to all the young; Let them, your truth possessing, Bear witness true with heart and tongue, Their faith and ours confessing. From mother's arms your grace With love did Baptized into your name, As yours you them embrace.

3 And when they leave their childhood home, When Satan comes alluring, May their baptismal grace become A refuge reassuring. God's covenant is sure; His promises endure. They ne'er shall be undone Who trust in

CONFIRMATION

Text: Johan N. Brun, 1745-1816, abr.; tr. George A. T. Rygh, 1860-1942, st. 1, 3, alt.;
Carl Döving, 1867-1937, st. 2, alt.
Tune: Friedrich O. Reuter, 1863-1924

REUTER
87 87 66 66 7

Alternate setting: 536

MARRIAGE

Your Love, O God, Has Called Us Here   601

Text: Russell Schulz-Widmar, b. 1944
Tune: William Knapp, 1698-1768, alt.

Text © The Church Pension Fund

WAREHAM
LM

Alternate settings: 198, 466

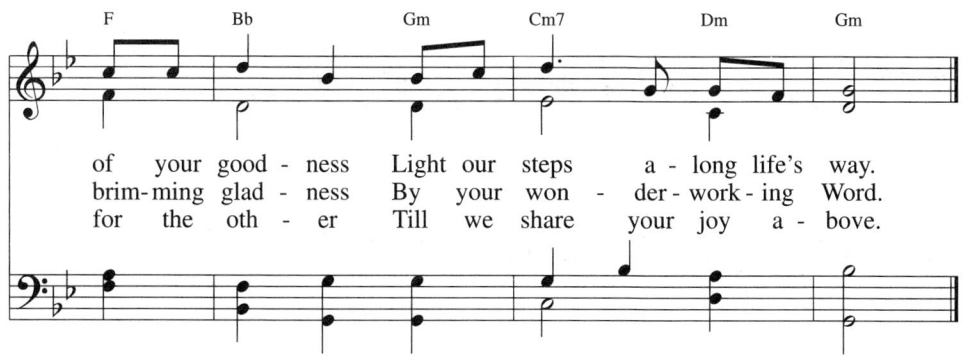

Text: Kurt J. Eggert, 1923-93
Tune: Kurt J. Eggert, 1923-93

GOD OF LOVE
87 87 89 87

Text and Tune © 1990 Kurt J. Eggert; Setting © 1993 Kermit G. Moldenhauer

MARRIAGE

603 Hear Us Now, Our God and Father

1 Hear us now, our God and Father; Send your
2 Give them joy to light-en sor-row; Give them

Spir - it from a - bove On this Chris - tian man and
hope to bright - en life. Go with them to face the

wom - an Who here make their vows of love.
mor - row; Stay with them in ev - 'ry strife.

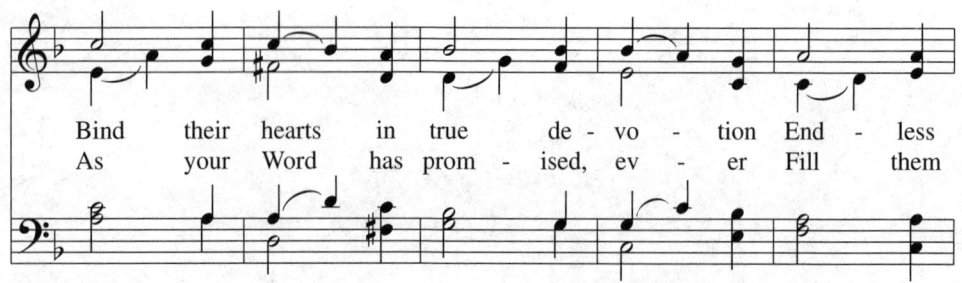

Bind their hearts in true de - vo - tion End - less
As your Word has prom - ised, ev - er Fill them

MARRIAGE

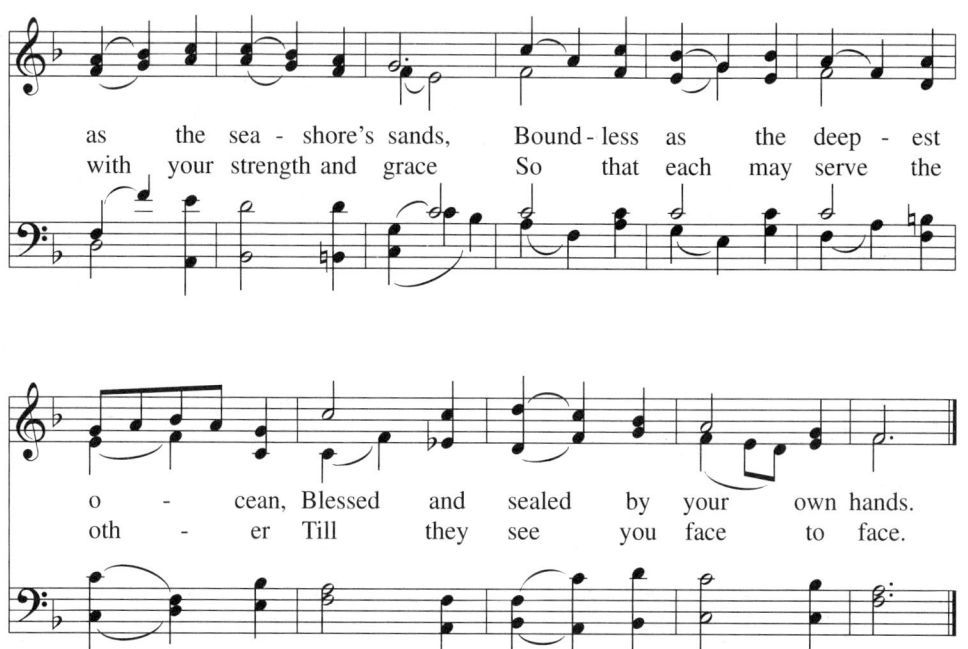

Text: Harry N. Huxhold, b. 1922
Tune: Rowland H. Prichard, 1811-87

Text st. 1,2 © 1978 *Lutheran Book of Worship*

HYFRYDOL
87 87 D

Alternate settings: 365, 486

MARRIAGE

604 O Love that Casts Out Fear

1. O love that casts out fear, O love that casts out sin,
Oh, stay no more with-out But come and dwell with-in.
True sun-light of the soul, Sur-round us as we go;
So shall our way be safe, Our feet no stray-ing know.

2. Great love of God, come in! O spring of last-ing peace,
O liv-ing wa-ter, come, Spring up and nev-er cease.
Love of the liv-ing God, Of Fa-ther and of Son,
Love of the Ho-ly Ghost, Make now our hearts as one.

Text: Horatius Bonar, 1808-89, alt.
Tune: *Musicalisches Gesangbuch,* Leipzig, 1736

ICH HALTE TREULICH STILL
66 66 D

DEATH AND BURIAL

Asleep in Jesus! Blessed Sleep 605

1 A-sleep in Je-sus! Bless-ed sleep, From which none ev-er wakes to weep, A calm and un-dis-turbed re-pose, Un-bro-ken by the last of foes.
2 A-sleep in Je-sus! Oh, how sweet To be for such a slum-ber meet, With ho-ly con-fi-dence to sing That death has lost his ven-omed sting!
3 A-sleep in Je-sus! Peace-ful rest, Whose wak-ing is su-preme-ly blest; No fear, no woe, shall dim that hour That man-i-fests the Sav-ior's pow'r.
4 A-sleep in Je-sus! Oh, for me May such a bliss-ful ref-uge be! Se-cure-ly shall my ash-es lie And wait the sum-mons from on high.

Text: Margaret Mackay, 1802-87, abr.
Tune: William B. Bradbury, 1816-68

REST
LM

DEATH AND BURIAL

606   For Me to Live Is Jesus

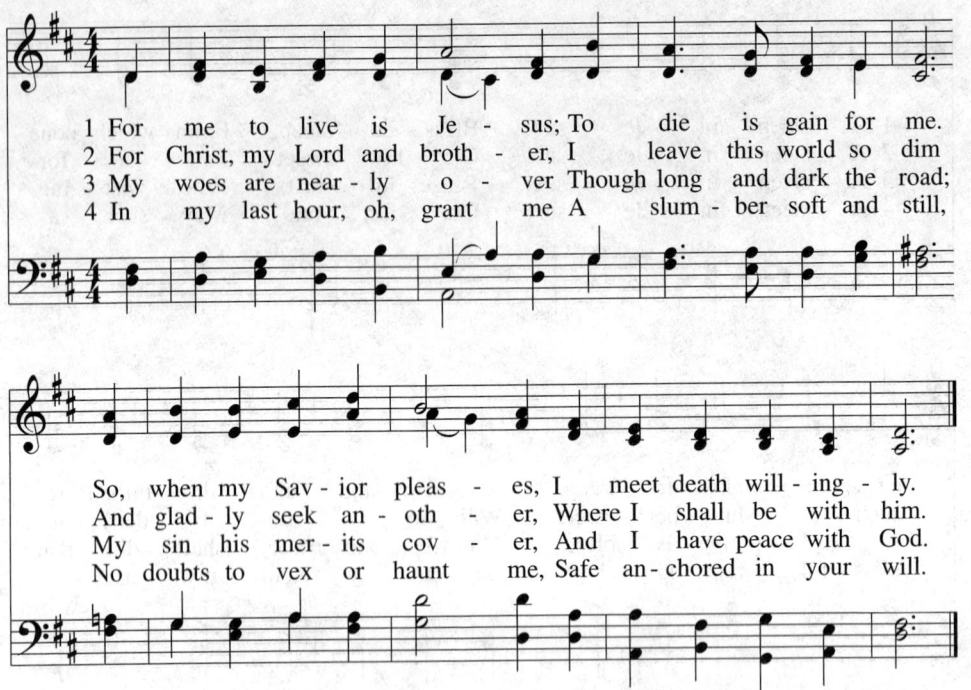

1. For me to live is Jesus; To die is gain for me.
So, when my Savior pleases, I meet death willingly.

2. For Christ, my Lord and brother, I leave this world so dim
And gladly seek another, Where I shall be with him.

3. My woes are nearly over Though long and dark the road;
My sin his merits cover, And I have peace with God.

4. In my last hour, oh, grant me A slumber soft and still,
No doubts to vex or haunt me, Safe anchored in your will.

5. Amen! For Christ my Savior
Will grant this unto me.
Your Spirit lead me ever
That I fare happily.

Text: *Ein schön geistlich Gesangbuch*, Jena, 1609, st. 1-4, abr.; unknown, st. 5;
     tr. Catherine Winkworth, 1827-78, st. 1-4, alt.; unknown, st. 5, alt.
Tune: Melchior Vulpius, c. 1570-1615, alt.
Setting © 1982 Concordia Publishing House

CHRISTUS, DER IST MEIN LEBEN
76 76

Alternate setting: 333

DEATH AND BURIAL

How Blest Are They

607

1. How blest are they who trust in Christ When we and those we love must part. We yield them up, for go we must, But do not lose them from our heart.
2. In ripened age, their harvest reaped, Or gone from us in youth or prime, In Christ they have eternal life, Released from all the bonds of time.
3. In Christ, who tasted death for us, We rise above our natural grief And witness to a stricken world The strength and splendor of belief.

Text: Fred Pratt Green, b. 1903, abr.
Tune: *Musicalisch Hand-Buch der Geistlichen Melodien,* Hamburg, 1690, alt.
Text © 1972 The Hymn Society

WINCHESTER NEW
LM

Alternate settings: 89, 133

DEATH AND BURIAL

608   I Fall Asleep in Jesus' Wounds

1 I fall asleep in Jesus' wounds; There pardon for my sin abounds. Yea, Jesus' blood and righteousness My beauty are, my glorious dress. In these before my God I'll stand When I shall reach the heav'nly land.

2 In peace and joy I now depart; God's child I am with all my heart. I thank you, death, for leading me To that true life, where I would be. So cleansed by Christ, I fear not death. Lord Jesus, strengthen now my faith.

Text: attr. Paul Eber, 1511-69; tr. Catherine Winkworth, 1827-78, alt.
Tune: attr. Martin Luther, 1483-1546

VATER UNSER IM HIMMELREICH, DER DU
88 88 88

Alternate settings: 306, 407, 479

THANKSGIVING

We Praise You, O God, Our Redeemer
609

1 We praise you, O God, our Redeemer, Creator!
In grateful devotion our tribute we bring:
We lay it before you; we kneel and adore you;
We bless your holy name; glad praises we sing.

2 We worship you, God of our fathers; we bless you.
Through trial and tempest our guide you have been;
When perils o'ertake us, you will not forsake us,
And with your help, O Lord, our battles we win.

3 With voices united our praises we offer;
To you, great Jehovah, glad anthems we raise.
Your strong arm will guide us; our God is beside us.
To you, our great Redeemer, for e'er be praise!

Text: Julia B. Cory, 1882-1963, alt.
Tune: *Nederlandtsch Gedenckclanck*, Haarlem, 1626

KREMSER
12 11 12 11

610 Now Thank We All Our God

THANKSGIVING

Text: Martin Rinkart, 1586-1649; tr. Catherine Winkworth, 1827-78, alt.
Tune: Johann Crüger, 1598-1662; Desc. Kermit G. Moldenhauer, b. 1949

NUN DANKET ALLE GOTT
67 67 66 66

Descant © 1993 Kermit G. Moldenhauer

THANKSGIVING

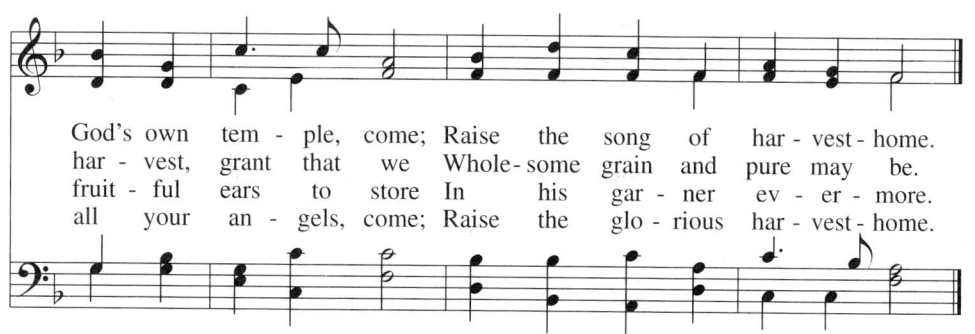

Text: Henry Alford, 1810-71, alt.
Tune: George J. Elvey, 1816-93

ST. GEORGE'S, WINDSOR
77 77 D

Alternate setting: 617

THANKSGIVING

616   *Feed Your Children, God Most Holy*

Feed your children, God most holy; Comfort sinners poor and lowly. Jesus, bread of life from heaven, Bless the food you here have given. As these gifts the body nourish, May our souls in graces flourish Till with saints in heav'nly splendor At your feast due thanks we render.

Text: Johann Heermann, 1585-1647; tr. *The Lutheran Hymnal,* St. Louis, 1941, alt.
Tune: Johann Crüger, 1598-1662, alt.

SCHMÜCKE DICH
LM D Trochaic

Setting © 1982 Concordia Publishing House

Alternate setting: 311

NATION

5 And when in pow'r he comes,
   Oh, may our native land
From all its rending tombs
   Send forth a glorious band,
A countless throng,
   And, joyful, sing
To heav'n's high King
   Salvation's song!

Text: Francis Scott Key, 1779-1843, alt.
Tune: John Darwall, 1731-89

DARWALL'S 148TH
66 66 4444

Alternate setting: 528

God Bless Our Native Land   619

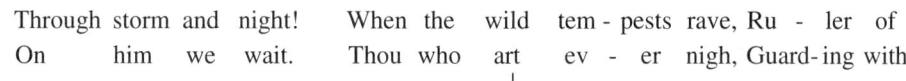

1 God bless our native land! Firm may she ev - er stand
2 For her our prayers shall rise To God a - bove the skies;

Through storm and night! When the wild tem - pests rave, Ru - ler of
On him we wait. Thou who art ev - er nigh, Guard-ing with

wind and wave, Do thou our coun - try save By thy great might.
watch - ful eye, To thee a - loud we cry, God save the state!

Text: Charles T. Brooks, 1813-83, st. 1, alt.; John S. Dwight, 1813-93, st. 2
Tune: *Thesaurus Musicus,* London, c. 1740

AMERICA
664 6664

NATION

620 — To You, Our God, We Fly

1. To you, our God, we fly For mercy and for grace.
2. The pow'rs that you ordained With heav'nly wisdom bless;
3. Give peace, Lord, in our time. Oh, let no foe draw nigh
4. Though vain and foolish, still We are your people, Lord.

Oh, hear our lowly cry And do not hide your face!
May evil be restrained, Replaced by righteousness.
Nor lawlessness and crime Insult your majesty!
Oh, bend us to your will; We'll serve no other God!

Refrain
O Lord, stretch forth your mighty hand
And guard and bless our native land.

Text: William W. How, 1823-97, abr., alt.
Tune: William Croft, 1678-1727

CROFT'S 136TH
66 66 88

CHURCH ANNIVERSARY

For Years on Years of Matchless Grace 621

1 For years on years of matchless grace We come, O
God, before your face; Your undeserved love and
care Rouse us to praise and stir to prayer.

2 For founding fathers filled with zeal To preach your
gospel and reveal Your love to sinners far and
wide, Let now your name be glorified.

3 For staunch confessors, praise, O Lord, For, bound and
governed by your Word, They led our church to firmer
ground, Though error flourished all around.

4 For growth in numbers, growth in grace, For missions
born in many a place, For gospel work in foreign
climes, We ring the glad thanksgiving chimes.

5 For many schools our thanks we pay,
The schools that teach the young your way,
The schools that train a ministry
Who want your will their will to be.

6 Oh, grant that we may never view
Your blessings as our right and due,
But see ourselves as beggars giv'n
To be your own and heirs of heav'n.

7 Lord, keep us steadfast, keep us true;
Give zeal your glorious work to do.
Until we join in heaven's song,
Your boundless grace to us prolong!

Text: Werner H. Franzmann, 1905-96, abr., alt.
Tune: James E. Engel, 1925-89

FOX VALLEY
LM

Text © 1993 Werner H. Franzmann; Tune and Setting © 1993 Mrs. James E. Engel.

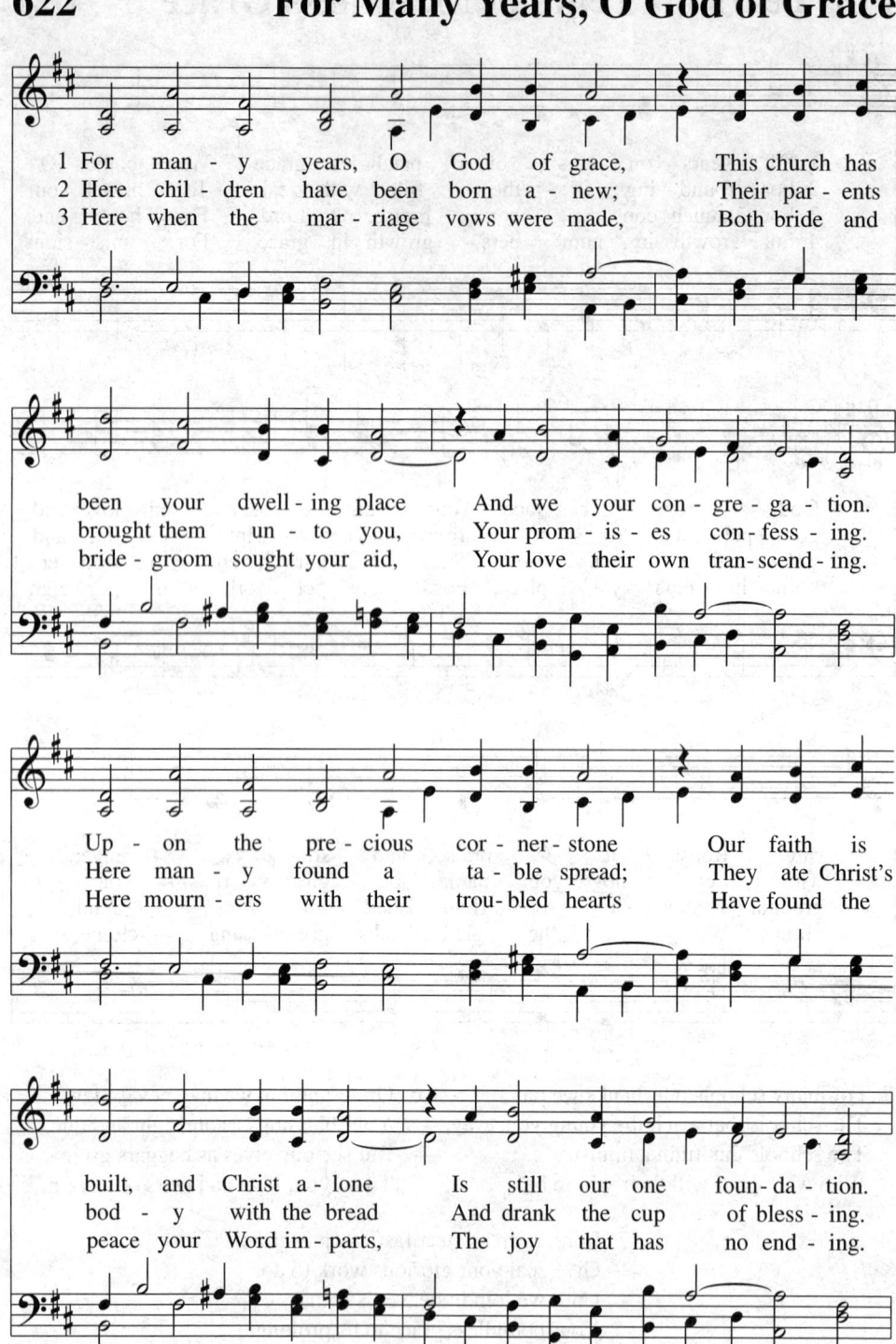

CHURCH ANNIVERSARY

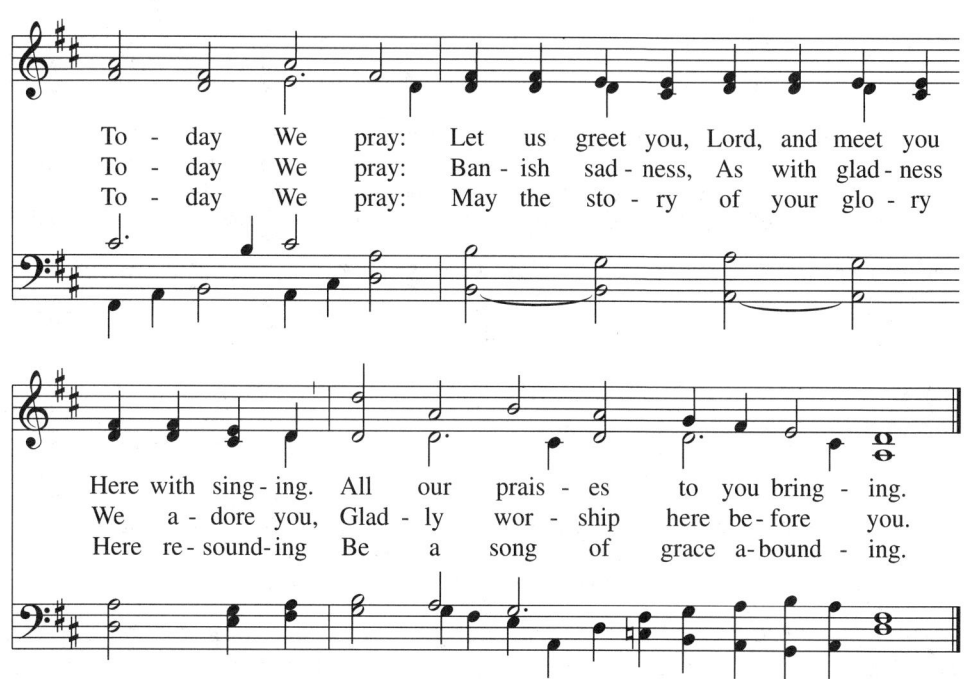

Text: William M. Czamanske, 1873-1964, alt.
Tune: Philipp Nicolai, 1556-1608, alt.
Text © 1941 Concordia Publishing House; Setting © 1981 Richard W. Gieseke

WIE SCHÖN LEUCHTET
887 887 22 44 48

Alternate setting: 79

CHURCH ANNIVERSARY

623 God the Father, Son, and Spirit

1 God the Father, Son, and Spirit, Ever-blessed Trinity, Humbly now our thanks we offer, All unworthy though we be. Freely you have showered blessings Countless as the ocean's sands, Blessings

2 Once you brought our fathers' footsteps To this land we hold so dear, Lengthening the cords and curtains Of their habitation here, Strengthening your temple's pillars As you have from age to age, Giving

3 Grant that we your Word may cherish And its purity retain. Lord, unless you are the builder, All our labor is in vain. Keep us from all pride and boasting, Vanity and foolish trust, Knowing

4 God of grace and love and blessing, Yours alone shall be the praise. Give us hearts to trust you truly, Hands to serve you all our days. Lord, bestow your future blessing Till we join the heav'nly host, There to

CHURCH ANNIVERSARY

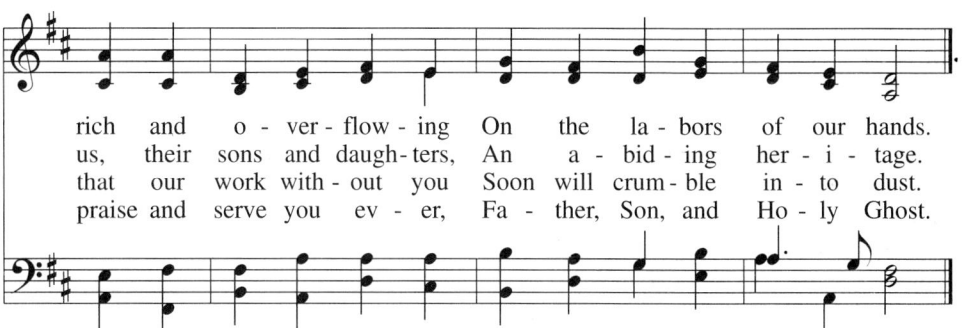

rich and o-ver-flow-ing On the la-bors of our hands.
us, their sons and daugh-ters, An a-bid-ing her-i-tage.
that our work with-out you Soon will crum-ble in-to dust.
praise and serve you ev-er, Fa-ther, Son, and Ho-ly Ghost.

Text: W. Gustave Polack, 1890-1950, alt.
Tune: Unknown

ST. HILARY
87 87 D

Text © 1941 Concordia Publishing House

INDEXES

Glossary	924
Personnel	925
Acknowledgments—Liturgical Materials	925
Acknowledgments—Hymns	927
Hymns with Descants	937
Hymns with Guitar Chords	937
Authors, Translators, and Sources of Hymns	937
Composers and Sources of Hymns	941
Tune Index	945
Metrical Index	948
First Line Index	955

GLOSSARY

abr.	abridged; one or more hymn stanzas have been deleted
adapt.	adapted; used for a text in which part of one stanza is combined with part of another or used when stanzas of one hymn are compiled from two or more earlier hymns; also applies to tunes that have been fashioned from a composer's earlier work
alt.	altered; indicates a text or tune where changes have been made to the original work
attr.	attributed to
b.	born
c.	circa; about
composite	a combined translation by various authors or a combined musical setting by various composers
d.	died
desc.	descant
ed.	edition
harm.	harmonization
ms.	manuscript
para.	paraphrased by
rev.	revised
st.	stanza
tr.	translator or translation

PERSONNEL

The Joint Hymnal Committee
C. T. Aufdemberge, Bruce Backer, Elfred Bloedel, Richard Buss,
Theodore Hartwig, Mark Jeske, Iver Johnson, Harlyn Kuschel, Arnold Lehmann,
Carl Nolte, Victor Prange, David Prillwitz, Loren Schaller, Wayne Schulz, James Tiefel

Hymnal Project Director
Kurt J. Eggert†

Hymnal Project Music Editor
Kermit G. Moldenhauer

Hymnal Project Secretary
Joanne Gruber

Cover Design and Interior Artwork
Zastrow Studios, Inc., Mequon, Wisconsin

Special Thanks
G. Jerome Albrecht†, Martin Albrecht†, Kurt Adams, David Bauer, Gary Baumler, Don Beutin, Mark Brunner, James Engel†, Marie Farley, James Fricke, Richard Hillert, Mentor Kujath, Laureen Reu Liu, Judith Lueck, Gordon Pape, Otto Schenk, Armin Schuetze, Mark Sikorski, Sharon Uekert, David Valleskey, Wayne and Esther Wiechmann

† *deceased*

ACKNOWLEDGMENTS

The publisher gratefully acknowledges the holders of copyright who have granted permission for material to be included in this book. Every effort has been made to determine the ownership of all tunes, texts, and settings used in this edition and to seek copyright permission for their use. The publisher regrets any error or oversight that may have occurred and will readily make proper acknowledgment in future editions. Acknowledgments are stated in accordance with the requirements of the individual copyright holder.

Copyrighted materials marked with an asterisk (*) may be reproduced in worship bulletins by congregations that have purchased multiple copies for regular worship services or Wisconsin Ev. Lutheran Synod organizations in meeting, without securing further permission from the publisher or individual copyright holders. Church schools may reproduce these materials for one-time use provided the copies are destroyed after use. Public domain materials have no copyright restrictions.

Liturgical Materials

All Scripture quotations, unless otherwise indicated, are taken from the HOLY BIBLE, NEW INTERNATIONAL VERSION®. NIV®. Copyright 1973, 1978, 1984 by International Bible Society. Used by permission of Zondervan Publishing House. All rights reserved.

The English translation of the Nicene Creed prepared by the English Language Liturgical Consultation (ELLC), 1988, altered.

The following authors, composers, and sources are acknowledged.

The Common Service
Texts revised from *The Lutheran Hymnal,* 1941.
Music from *The Lutheran Hymnal,* 1941, revised by James Engel.

ACKNOWLEDGMENTS

Service of Word and Sacrament
Kyrie, Song of Praise, Preface .... ***Tune:** © 1993 Kurt J. Eggert. Used by permission.
***Setting:**© 1993 Kermit G Moldenhauer. Used by permission.

Verse .... ***Tune and setting:** © 1993 Kermit G. Moldenhauer. Used by permission.
Sanctus, Agnus Dei .... ***Tune and setting:** © 1991 David Schack. Used by permission.
Thank the Lord .... **Tune and setting:** Richard Hillert. © 1978 *Lutheran Book of Worship*. Reprinted by permission of Augsburg Fortress.

Service of the Word
Oh, Taste and See, Verse .... ***Tune and setting:** © 1993 Kermit G. Moldenhauer. Used by permission.

Morning Praise
Texts revised from *The Lutheran Hymnal*, 1941.
Music from *The Lutheran Hymnal*, 1941, revised by Kermit G. Moldenhauer.

Evening Prayer
Texts revised from *The Lutheran Hymnal*, 1941.

Opening Versicles and Responses .... ***Tune:** © 1993 Kurt J. Eggert. Used by permission.
***Setting:** © 1993 Kermit G. Moldenhauer. Used by permission.
Song of Mary, Song of Simeon .... ***Tune:** © 1993 Kurt J. Eggert. Used by permission.
***Setting:** © 1993 Kermit G. Moldenhauer. Used by permission.
Service of Light .... © 1978 *Lutheran Book of Worship*. Reprinted by permission of Augsburg Fortress.
Let My Prayer Rise Before You .... **Tune and setting:** David Schack. © 1978 *Lutheran Book of Worship*. Reprinted by permission of Augsburg Fortress.

Psalms
Refrain, Psalm 1, 42/43, 71 .... **Tune and setting:** Robert J. Thompson. © 1986 GIA Publications, Inc., Chicago IL. All rights reserved. Used by permission.
Refrain, Psalm 2, 45, 51b, 96, 100, 139b .... ***Tune and setting:** © 1993 Kermit G. Moldenhauer. Used by permission.
Refrain, Psalm 8, 146 .... **Tune and setting:** Lynn Trapp. © 1989 MorningStar Music Publishers. All rights reserved. Used by permission.
Refrain, Psalm 6, 16, 19, 22, 23, 24, 116, 119b, 143, 145 .... **Tune and setting:** Richard Proulx. © 1986 GIA Publications, Inc., Chicago IL. All rights reserved. Used by permission.
Refrain, Psalm 18, 46, 47, 62, 67, 72 .... **Tune and setting:** Dale Wood. Reprinted from *Seasonal Psalms* © 1978 Augsburg Publishing House. Used by permission of Augsburg Fortress.
Refrain, Psalm 25, 33, 65, 118, 139a .... **Tune and setting:** Marty Haugen. © 1983 GIA Publications, Inc., Chicago IL. All rights reserved. Used by permission.
Refrain, Psalm 27 .... **Tune and setting:** David Haas. © 1983 GIA Publications, Inc., Chicago IL. All rights reserved. Used by permission.
Refrain, Psalm 30, 66, 89 .... **Tune and setting:** Steven Warner. © 1983 GIA Publications, Inc., Chicago IL. All rights reserved. Used by permission.
Refrain, Psalm 31, 73 .... **Tune and setting:** Jack Noble White. © 1976 Belwin-Mills Publishing Corp., c/o CPP/Belwin, Inc., Miami FL 33014. All rights reserved. Used by permission.
Refrain, Psalm 32, 130 .... **Tune and setting:** Michael Joncas. © 1986 GIA Publications, Inc., Chicago IL. All rights reserved. Used by permission.
Refrain, Psalm 34, 103, 133/34 .... **Tune and setting:** Columba Kelly. © 1986 GIA Publications, Inc., Chicago IL. All rights reserved. Used by permission.
Refrain, Psalm 38, 51a .... **Tune and setting:** Patricia Craig. © 1986 GIA Publications, Inc., Chicago IL. All rights reserved. Used by permission.
Refrain, Psalm 78, 119a, 119c .... ***Tune and setting:** © 1993 Joyce Schubkegel. Used by permission.
Refrain, Psalm 84 .... **Tune and setting:** David Clarke Isele. © 1979 GIA Publications, Inc., Chicago IL. All rights reserved. Used by permission.
Refrain, Psalm 85 .... **Tune and setting:** Reprinted from *The Psalmody For the Day, Series C*. © 1976 Fortress Press. Used by permission of Augsburg Fortress.
Refrain, Psalm 90 .... **Tune and setting:** Eugene Englert. © 1986 GIA Publications, Inc., Chicago IL. All rights reserved. Used by permission.
Refrain, Psalm 91, 121 .... **Tune and setting:** Reprinted from CGC-18 *Psalms Together* by Jane Marshall. © 1986 Choristers Guild. Used by permission.
Refrain, Psalm 92, 98, 111, 148 .... **Tune and setting:** J. Robert Carroll. © 1986 GIA Publications, Inc., Chicago IL. All rights reserved. Used by permission.
Refrain, Psalm 126, 150 .... **Tune and setting:** Walter Pelz. Reprinted from *Seasonal Psalms*. © 1978 Augsburg Publishing House. Used by permission of Augsburg Fortress.
Psalm Tone, Psalm 38, 51a .... ***Tune and setting:** Paul Bunjes. © 1982 Concordia Publishing House. Used by permission of CPH.
All other Psalm Tones .... ***Tune and setting:** © 1993 Kermit G. Moldenhauer. Used by permission.

Hymns

1 **Text and Tune:** public domain. *****Setting:** © 1993 Elfred Bloedel. Used by permission.
2 **Text and Tune:** public domain. *****Setting:** © 1993 Kermit G. Moldenhauer. Used by permission.
3 **Text, Tune, Setting:** public domain.
4 **Text, Tune, Setting:** public domain.
5 *****Text:** © 1993 Werner H. Franzmann. Used by permission. **Tune:** public domain. **Setting:** © A. R. Mowbray & Co., Ltd. Used by permission.
6 **Text, Tune, Setting:** public domain.
7 **Text and Tune:** public domain. **Setting:** © 1978 *Lutheran Book of Worship*. Reprinted by permission of Augsburg Fortress.
8 **Text, Tune, Setting:** public domain.
9 **Text and Tune:** public domain. *****Setting:** © 1993 Elfred Bloedel. Used by permission.
10 **Text, Tune, Setting:** public domain.
11 **Text, Tune, Setting:** public domain.
12 **Text, Tune, Setting:** public domain.
13 **Text and Tune:** public domain. **Setting:** From *The Hymnal 1982*, © The Church Pension Fund. Used by permission.
14 **Text and Tune:** public domain. *****Setting:** © 1993 Kermit G. Moldenhauer. Used by permission.
15 **Text, Tune, Setting, Descant:** public domain.
16 **Text and Tune:** public domain. **Setting:** © A. R. Mowbray & Co., Ltd. Used by permission.
17 **Text and Tune:** public domain. *****Setting:** © 1984 Jack Warren Burnam.
18 **Text, Tune, Setting:** public domain.
19 **Text and Tune:** public domain. *****Setting:** © 1970 by Bärenreiter-Verlag; reprinted by permission.
20 *****Text:** © 1941 Concordia Publishing House. Used by permission of CPH. **Tune and Setting:** public domain.
21 **Text, Tune, Setting:** public domain.
22 *****Text and Setting:** © 1969 Concordia Publishing House. Used by permission of CPH. **Tune:** public domain.
23 **Text, Tune, Setting:** public domain.
24 **Text and Tune:** public domain. **Setting:** © 1961 H. Freeman and Co., 95A St. George's Rd., Brighton Sussex UK.
25 **Text and Tune:** public domain. *****Setting:** © 1969 Concordia Publishing House. Used by permission of CPH.
26 **Text, Tune, Setting:** public domain.
27 **Text, Tune, Setting:** public domain.
28 **Text, Tune, Setting:** public domain.
29 **Text and Tune:** public domain. *****Setting:** © 1982 Concordia Publishing House. Used by permission of CPH.
30 **Text:** © 1928 Augustana Book Concern. Reprinted by permission of Augsburg Fortress. **Tune:** public domain. *****Setting:** © 1993 Kermit G. Moldenhauer. Used by permission.
31 **Text:** © 1993 World Library Publications, Inc. All rights reserved. Used with permission. **Tune:** public domain. *****Setting:** © 1993 Kermit G. Moldenhauer. Used by permission.
32 **Text and Tune:** public domain. *****Setting:** © 1993 Elfred Bloedel. Used by permission.
33 **Text, Tune, Setting:** public domain.
34 **Text and Tune:** public domain. *****Setting:** © 1993 Kermit G. Moldenhauer. Used by permission.
35 **Text and Tune:** public domain. *****Setting:** © 1982 Concordia Publishing House. Used by permission of CPH.
36 **Text, Tune, Setting:** public domain.
37 **Text, Tune, Setting:** public domain.
38 **Text, Tune, Setting:** public domain.
39 **Text, Tune, Setting:** public domain.
40 **Text and Tune:** public domain. *****Setting:** © 1993 Kermit G. Moldenhauer. Used by permission.
41 **Text, Tune, Setting:** public domain.
42 **Text and Tune:** public domain. *****Setting:** © 1993 Kermit G. Moldenhauer. Used by permission.
43 **Text and Tune:** public domain. *****Setting:** © 1993 Elfred Bloedel. Used by permission.
44 *****Text:** From *The Hymnal 1982*. © The Church Pension Fund. Used by permission. **Tune and Setting:** public domain.
45 **Text and Tune:** public domain. *****Setting:** © 1982 Concordia Publishing House. Used by permission of CPH.
46 **Text, Tune, Setting:** public domain.
47 **Text, Tune, Setting:** public domain.
48 **Text:** © 1978 *Lutheran Book of Worship*. Reprinted by permission of Augsburg Fortress. **Tune and Setting:** public domain.
49 **Text and Tune:** public domain. **Setting:** © 1981 Richard W. Gieseke, 835 Kentridge Ct., Manchester MO 63021-7568. Used by permission.
50 **Text and Tune:** public domain. **Setting:** © 1957 Novello & Company Ltd. Reprinted by permission of G. Schirmer, Inc.
51 *****Text st.1,4:** © 1982 Concordia Publishing House. Used by permission of CPH. **Text st.2,3,5:** © Augsburg Publishing House. Reprinted by permission of Augsburg Fortress. **Tune and Setting:** public domain.
52 **Text:** public domain. **Tune and Setting:** Collected and transcribed by Ralph Vaughan Williams. Reproduced by permission of Stainer & Bell Ltd., London England.
53 **Text, Tune, Setting:** public domain.
54 **Text:** © 1987 Jaroslav J. Vajda. Used by permission. **Tune and Setting:** Carl F. Schalk, b.1929 © 1987 by GIA Publications Inc., Chicago IL. All rights reserved. Used by permission.
55 **Text, Tune, Setting:** public domain. **Descant and harmony for st. 3,4** by David Willcocks. Reprinted by permission of Oxford University Press.
56 **Text and Tune:** public domain. *****Setting:** © 1993 Elfred Bloedel. Used by permission.
57 **Text:** From *American Negro Songs and Spirituals*. © 1940. Reprinted with permission of Mrs. Edith M. Work. **Tune and Setting:** public domain.
58 **Text, Tune, Setting:** public domain.
59 *****Text:** © 1941 Concordia Publishing House. Used by permission of CPH. **Tune and Setting:** public domain.
60 **Text, Tune, Setting:** public domain.
61 **Text, Tune, Setting:** public domain. **Descant and harmony for st.3** by David Willcocks. Reprinted by permission of Oxford University Press.
62 **Text, Tune, Setting:** public domain.

63 **Text, Tune, Setting:** public domain.
64 **Text, Tune, Setting:** public domain.
65 **Text, Tune, Setting:** public domain.
66 **Text and Tune:** public domain. **Setting:** Harmonized by Ralph Vaughan Williams. From the *English Hymnal* by permission of Oxford University Press.
67 **Text, Tune, Setting:** public domain.
68 **Text and Tune:** public domain. *****Setting:** © 1993 Mrs. James E. Engel. Used by permission.
69 **Text, Tune, Setting:** public domain.
70 **Text and Tune:** public domain. *****Setting:** © 1993 Kermit G. Moldenhauer. Used by permission.
71 **Text, Tune, Setting:** public domain.
72 **Text and Tune:** public domain. *****Setting:** © 1993 Kermit G. Moldenhauer. Used by permission.
73 **Text and Tune:** public domain. *****Setting:** © 1993 Kermit G. Moldenhauer. Used by permission.
74 **Text:** public domain. *****Tune and Setting:** © 1993 Kermit G. Moldenhauer. Used by permission.
75 **Text, Tune, Setting:** public domain.
76 **Text and Tune:** public domain. *****Setting:** © 1982 Concordia Publishing House. Used by permission of CPH.
77 **Text and Tune:** public domain. **Setting:** © 1981 Richard W. Gieseke, 835 Kentridge Ct., Manchester, MO 63021-7568. Used by permission.
78 **Text, Tune, Setting:** public domain.
79 **Text, Tune, Setting:** public domain. *****Descant:** © 1993 Kermit G. Moldenhauer.
80 **Text and Tune:** public domain. *****Setting:** © 1993 Kermit G. Moldenhauer. Used by permission.
81 *****Text:** © 1941 Concordia Publishing House. Used by permission of CPH. *****Tune and Setting:** © 1993 Bruce R. Backer. Used by permission.
82 **Text, Tune, Setting:** public domain.
83 **Text, Tune, Setting:** public domain.
84 **Text, Tune, Setting:** public domain.
85 **Text, Tune, Setting:** public domain.
86 **Text and Tune:** public domain. *****Setting:** © 1986 Bruce R. Backer. Used by permission.
87 **Text and Tune:** public domain. *****Setting:** © 1982 Concordia Publishing House. Used by permission of CPH.
88 **Text:** © 1976 Elizabeth Quitmeyer. **Tune:** public domain. **Setting:** © 1978 *Lutheran Book of Worship.* Reprinted by permission of Augsburg Fortress.
89 *****Text:** © 1993 James P. Tiefel. Used by permission. **Tune:** public domain. *****Setting:** © 1993 Elfred Bloedel. Used by permission.
90 **Text, Tune, Setting:** public domain.
91 **Text, Tune, Setting:** public domain.
92 **Text, Tune, Setting:** public domain.
93 **Text and Tune:** public domain. *****Setting:** © 1982 Concordia Publishing House. Used by permission of CPH.
94 **Text and Tune:** public domain. *****Setting:** © 1989 Ronald L. Shilling. Used by permission.
95 **Text, Tune, Setting:** public domain.
96 **Text and Tune:** public domain. *****Setting:** © 1969 Concordia Publishing House. Used by permission of CPH.
97 *****Text:** © 1968 Werner H. Franzmann. Used by permission. **Tune:** public domain. *****Setting:** © 1968 Richard Hillert. Used by permission.
98 **Text, Tune, Setting:** public domain.
99 *****Text, Tune, Setting:** © 1993 Kurt J. Eggert. Used by permission.
100 **Text, Tune, Setting:** public domain.
101 **Text, Tune, Setting:** public domain.
102 **Text and Tune:** public domain. *****Setting:** © 1982 Concordia Publishing House. Used by permission of CPH.
103 **Text, Tune, Setting:** public domain.
104 **Text, Tune, Setting:** public domain.
105 **Text, Tune, Setting:** public domain.
106 **Text, Tune, Setting:** public domain.
107 **Text and Tune:** © 1958 *Service Book and Hymnal.* Reprinted by permission of Augsburg Fortress. **Setting:** © 1978 *Lutheran Book of Worship.* Reprinted by permission of Augsburg Fortress.
108 **Text and Tune:** public domain. *****Setting:** © 1993 Kermit G. Moldenhauer. Used by permission.
109 **Text and Tune:** public domain. *****Setting:** © 1986 Bruce R. Backer. Used by permission.
110 **Text:** public domain. *****Tune and Setting:** © John Ireland Trust, c/o Mr. P.B.A. Taylor, 35 St. Mary's Mansions, St. Mary's Terrace, London W2 1SQ England.
111 **Text, Tune, Setting:** public domain.
112 **Text, Tune, Setting:** public domain.
113 **Text and Tune:** public domain. *****Setting:** © 1993 Kermit G. Moldenhauer. Used by permission.
114 **Text, Tune, Setting:** public domain.
115 **Text:** © 1982 by Hope Publishing Co., Carol Stream, IL 60188. All rights reserved. Used by permission. **Tune:** © 1958 *Service Book and Hymnal.* Reprinted by permission of Augsburg Fortress. **Setting:** © 1978 *Lutheran Book of Worship.* Reprinted by permission of Augsburg Fortress.
116 **Text, Tune, Setting:** public domain.
117 **Text and Tune:** public domain. *****Setting:** © 1993 Kermit G. Moldenhauer. Used by permission.
118 **Text:** From *The Book of Common Praise.* Reprinted by permission of A. R. Mowbray & Co. Ltd., London, England. **Tune:** public domain. *****Setting:** © 1993 Bruce R. Backer. Used by permission.
119 **Text, Tune, Setting:** public domain.
120 **Text and Tune:** public domain. *****Setting:** © 1993 Elfred Bloedel. Used by permission.
121 **Text and Tune:** public domain. **Setting:** © 1978 *Lutheran Book of Worship.* Reprinted by permission of Augsburg Fortress.
122 **Text:** public domain. *****Tune and Setting:** © 1967 Concordia Publishing House. Used by permission of CPH.
123 **Text, Tune, Setting:** public domain.
124 **Text, Tune, Setting:** public domain.
125 **Text, Tune, Setting:** public domain.
126 *****Text:** © 1941 Concordia Publishing House. Used by permission of CPH. **Tune and Setting:** public domain.
127 **Text and Tune:** public domain. *****Setting:** © 1982 Concordia Publishing House. Used by permission of CPH.
128 **Text, Tune, Setting:** public domain.
129 **Text, Tune, Setting:** public domain.
130 **Text, Tune, Setting:** public domain.
131 **Text and Tune:** public domain. *****Setting:** © Bärenreiter-Verlag; reprinted by permission. *****Descant:** © 1993 Kermit G. Moldenhauer. Used by permission.
132 **Text:** public domain. **Tune and Setting:** © 1941 renewed 1969 H. W. Gray Co., Inc., a Division of Belwin-Mills Publishing Corp., c/o CPP/Belwin, Inc., Miami FL 33014. All Rights Reserved. Used by permission.

ACKNOWLEDGMENTS

133 **Text, Tune, Setting:** public domain.
134 **Text, Tune, Setting:** public domain.
135 **Text, Tune, Setting:** public domain.
136 **Text, Tune, Setting:** public domain.
137 **Text and Tune:** public domain. ***Setting:** © 1982 Concordia Publishing House. Used by permission of CPH.
138 **Text, Tune, Setting:** public domain.
139 **Text, Tune, Setting:** public domain.
140 ***Text and Tune:** © 1993 Kurt J. Eggert. Used by permission. ***Setting:** © 1993 Kermit G. Moldenhauer. Used by permission.
141 **Text and Tune:** public domain. ***Setting:** © 1969 Concordia Publishing House. Used by permission of CPH.
142 **Text and Tune:** public domain. ***Setting:** © 1969 Concordia Publishing House. Used by permission of CPH.
143 ***Text:** © 1941 Concordia Publishing House. Used by permission of CPH. **Tune and Setting:** public domain.
144 ***Text:** © 1941 Concordia Publishing House. Used by permission of CPH. **Tune:** public domain. ***Setting:** © 1993 Kermit G. Moldenhauer. Used by permission.
145 **Text and Tune:** public domain. ***Setting:** © 1989 Ronald L. Shilling. Used by permission.
146 **Text:** © 1976 by Hope Publishing Co., Carol Stream IL 60188. All rights reserved. Used by permission. **Tune and Setting:** Traditional Angoni war song; adapt. Tom Colvin. © 1976 by Hope Publishing Co., Carol Stream IL 60188. All rights reserved. Used by permission.
147 **Text and Tune:** public domain. ***Setting:** © 1982 Concordia Publishing House. Used by permission of CPH.
148 **Text, Tune, Setting:** public domain.
149 **Text, Tune, Setting:** public domain.
150 **Text, Tune, Setting:** public domain.
151 ***Text, Tune, Setting:** © 1982 Concordia Publishing House. Used by permission of CPH.
152 **Text, Tune, Setting:** public domain. ***Descant:** ©1959 Concordia Publishing House. Used by permission of CPH.
153 **Text, Tune, Setting:** public domain.
154 **Text and Tune:** © 1973 The Word of God. Reprinted by permission of The Copyright Company. ***Setting:** ©1993 Bruce R. Backer. Used by permission.
155 **Text and Tune:** public domain. ***Setting:** From *The Hymnal 1982.* © The Church Pension Fund. Used by permission.
156 **Text, Tune, Setting:** public domain.
157 **Text, Tune, Setting:** public domain. **Descant:** From *Hymns Ancient and Modern* © 1955. Renewal 1983 by Hope Publishing Co., Carol Stream IL 60188. All rights reserved. Used by permission.
158 **Text, Tune, Setting:** public domain.
159 **Text, Tune, Setting:** public domain.
160 **Text:** From *Cowley Carol Book.* Reprinted by permission of A. R. Mowbray & Co., Ltd., London England. **Tune:** public domain. ***Setting:** © 1969 Concordia Publishing House. Used by permission of CPH.
161 **Text and Tune:** public domain. **Setting:** © 1981 Richard W. Gieseke, 835 Kentridge Ct., Manchester MO 63021-7568. Used by permission.
162 **Text and Tune:** public domain. **Setting:** © 1981 Richard W. Gieseke, 835 Kentridge Ct., Manchester MO 63021-7568. Used by permission.
163 **Text, Tune, Setting:** public domain.
164 ***Text:** © 1982 Concordia Publishing House. Used by permission of CPH. **Tune and Setting:** public domain.
165 **Text, Tune, Setting:** public domain.
166 **Text, Tune, Setting:** public domain.
167 **Text and Tune:** public domain. ***Setting:** © 1970 by Bärenreiter-Verlag; reprinted by permission.
168 ***Text and Setting:** © 1969 Concordia Publishing House. Used by permission of CPH. **Tune:** public domain.
169 **Text, Tune, Setting:** public domain.
170 **Text, Tune, Setting:** public domain.
171 **Text and Tune:** public domain. **Setting:** Reprinted from the *English Hymnal* by permission of Oxford University Press. **Descant:** public domain
172 **Text:** © Augsburg Publishing House. Reprinted by permission of Augsburg Fortress. **Tune and Setting:** © Henry V. Gerike. Used by permission.
173 ***Text:** © 1941 Concordia Publishing House. Used by permission of CPH. **Tune and Setting:** public domain.
174 **Text, Tune, Setting:** public domain.
175 **Text, Tune, Setting:** public domain.
176 **Text, Tune, Setting:** public domain.
177 **Text, Tune, Setting:** public domain.
178 **Text and Tune:** public domain. ***Setting:** © 1993 Kermit G. Moldenhauer. Used by permission.
179 **Text st.1,3:** From the *English Hymnal.* Reprinted by permission of Oxford University Press. ***Text st.2,4:** © 1993 Mark A. Jeske. Used by permission. **Tune and Setting:** From the *English Hymnal.* Reprinted by permission of Oxford University Press.
180 **Text, Tune, Setting:** public domain.
181 **Text and Tune:** public domain. ***Setting:** © 1993 Elfred Bloedel. Used by permission.
182 **Text:** Reprinted by permission of A. R. Mowbray & Co. Ltd., London England. **Tune:** public domain. ***Setting:** © 1969 Concordia Publishing House. Used by permission of CPH.
183 **Text, Tune, Setting:** public domain.
184 **Text, Tune, Setting:** public domain.
185 **Text, Tune, Setting:** public domain.
186 **Text and Tune:** public domain. ***Setting:** © 1993 Kermit G. Moldenhauer. Used by permission.
187 **Text:** © 1984 by Hope Publishing Co., Carol Stream IL 60188. All rights reserved. Used by permission. ***Tune and Setting:** © 1993 Bruce R. Backer. Used by permission.
188 **Text, Tune, Setting:** public domain.
189 **Text, Tune, Setting:** public domain.
190 **Text, Tune, Setting:** public domain.
191 **Text:** public domain. **Tune and Setting:** © 1987 MorningStar Music Publishers. All rights reserved. Used by permission.
192 **Text and Tune:** public domain. ***Setting:** © 1993 Kermit G. Moldenhauer. Used by permission.
193 **Text and Tune:** public domain. **Setting:** © 1972 by The Westminster Press; from *The Worshipbook.* Used by permission of Westminster/John Knox Press.
194 **Text, Tune, Setting:** public domain.
195 **Text, Tune, Setting:** public domain. ***Descant:** © 1993 Kermit G. Moldenhauer. Used by permission.
196 **Text and Tune:** public domain. ***Setting:** Published by permission of the executors of the late Dr. Basil Harwood.
197 **Text, Tune, Setting:** public domain.
198 **Text, Tune, Setting:** public domain.

ACKNOWLEDGMENTS

199 *Text: © 1993 Werner H. Franzmann. Used by permission. *Tune and Setting: © 1993 Martin Albrecht. Used by permission.
200 Text and Tune: public domain. *Setting: © 1970 by Bärenreiter-Verlag; reprinted by permission.
201 Text, Tune, Setting: public domain.
202 Text: public domain. Tune: From *Enlarged Songs of Praise* adapt. Ralph Vaughan Williams. Reprinted by permission of Oxford University Press. Setting: public domain.
203 Text, Tune, Setting: public domain.
204 *Text: © 1941 Concordia Publishing House. Used by permission of CPH. Tune and Setting: public domain.
205 Text and Tune: public domain. *Setting: © 1993 Bruce R. Backer. Used by permission.
206 Text and Tune: public domain. *Setting: © 1993 Kermit G. Moldenhauer. Used by permission.
207 Text, Tune, Setting: public domain.
208 Text and Tune: public domain. *Setting: © 1989 Ronald L. Shilling. Used by permission.
209 Text st.1-6: public domain. *Text st.7: © 1993 Mark A. Jeske. Used by permission. Tune and Setting: public domain.
210 Text, Tune, Setting: public domain.
211 Text, Tune, Setting: public domain.
212 Text, Tune, Setting: public domain.
213 Text, Tune, Setting: public domain.
214 Text, Tune, Setting: public domain.
215 Text: public domain. Tune and Setting: © 1938 J. Fischer & Bro. Renewed 1966 J. Fischer & Bro., A Division of Belwin-Mills Publishing Corp., c/o CPP/Belwin, Inc., Miami FL 33014. All Rights Reserved. Used by permission.
216 Text and Tune: public domain. *Setting: © 1993 Elfred Bloedel. Used by permission.
217 Text, Tune, Setting: public domain.
218 Text: © 1987 by Hope Publishing Co., Carol Stream IL 60188. All rights reserved. Used by permission. Tune and Setting: © 1969 by Hope Publishing Co., Carol Stream IL 60188. All rights reserved. Used by permission.
219 Text: public domain. *Tune and Setting: © 1993 Kurt J. Eggert. Used by permission.
220 Text, Tune, Setting: public domain.
221 Text, Tune, Setting: public domain.
222 Text, Tune, Setting: public domain.
223 *Text: © 1941 Concordia Publishing House. Used by permission of CPH. Tune and Setting: public domain.
224 Text, Tune, Setting: public domain.
225 Text, Tune, Setting: public domain.
226 Text, Tune, Setting: public domain.
227 Text, Tune, Setting: public domain.
228 Text and Tune: © 1973 by Hope Publishing Co., Carol Stream IL 60188. All rights reserved. Used by permission. Setting: © 1993 by Hope Publishing Co., Carol Stream IL 60188. All rights reserved. Used by permission.
229 Text and Tune: public domain. *Setting: © 1993 Elfred Bloedel. Used by permission.
230 Text, Tune, Setting: public domain.
231 Text, Tune, Setting: © 1969 by Hope Publishing Co., Carol Stream IL 60188. All rights reserved. Used by permission.
232 Text, Tune, Setting: public domain.
233 Text and Tune: public domain. *Setting: © 1982 Concordia Publishing House. Used by permission of CPH.
234 Text, Tune, Setting: public domain. Descant: © 1953 Novello & Company Ltd. Reprinted by permission of G. Schirmer, Inc.
235 *Text: © 1941 Concordia Publishing House. Used by permission of CPH. Tune and Setting: public domain.
236 Text, Tune, Setting: public domain.
237 *Text: © 1982 Margaret Stinton. Used by permission. Tune and Setting: public domain.
238 Text, Tune, Setting: public domain.
239 Text, Tune, Setting: public domain.
240 Text, Tune, Setting: public domain.
241 Text, Tune, Setting: public domain.
242 Text, Tune, Setting: public domain.
243 Text, Tune, Setting: public domain.
244 Text and Setting: © 1958 *Service Book and Hymnal*. Reprinted by permission of Augsburg Fortress. Tune: public domain.
245 Text and Tune: © 1973 by Hope Publishing Co., Carol Stream IL 60188. All rights reserved. Used by permission. Setting: © 1993 by Hope Publishing Co., Carol Stream IL 60188. All rights reserved. Used by permission.
246 Text: © 1981 by Hope Publishing Co., Carol Stream IL 60188. All rights reserved. Used by permission. Tune: © 1986 by GIA Publications, Inc., Chicago IL. All rights reserved. Used by permission. *Setting: © 1993 Elfred Bloedel. Used by permission.
247 Text, Tune, Setting: © 1968 Augsburg Publishing House. Reprinted by permission of Augsburg Fortress.
248 Text: © 1972 by Hope Publishing Co., Carol Stream IL 60188. All rights reserved. Used by permission. Tune and Setting: public domain.
249 Text, Tune, Setting: public domain.
250 Text and Tune: public domain. Setting: Ralph Vaughan Williams from the *English Hymnal*. Reprinted by permission of Oxford University Press.
251 Text, Tune, Setting: public domain.
252 Text, Tune, Setting: public domain.
253 Text and Tune: public domain. *Setting: © 1989 Ronald L. Shilling. Used by permission.
254 Text st.1,2,4 and Tune: public domain. *Text st.3: © 1993 Mark A. Jeske. Used by permission. *Setting: © 1993 Elfred Bloedel. Used by permission.
255 Text, Tune, Setting: public domain.
256 Text, Tune, Setting: © 1953. Renewed 1981 by Manna Music, Inc., 35255 Brooten Road, Pacific City, OR 97135. International copyright secured. All rights reserved. Used by permission.
257 Text, Tune, Setting: public domain.
258 Text, Tune, Setting: public domain.
259 Text, Tune, Setting: public domain.
260 Text: © 1939 renewed 1966 by E. C. Schirmer Music Company. Tune: public domain. Setting: © 1978 *Lutheran Book of Worship*. Reprinted by permission of Augsburg Fortress.
261 Text, Tune, Setting: public domain.
262 *Text: © 1941 Concordia Publishing House. Used by permission of CPH. Tune: public domain. *Setting: © 1990 Ronald L. Shilling. Used by permission.
263 Text st.1-3: public domain. *Text st.4: © 1993 Mark A. Jeske. Used by permission. Tune: public domain.

ACKNOWLEDGMENTS

Setting: © 1978 *Lutheran Book of Worship*. Reprinted by permission of Augsburg Fortress.
264 **Text:** © 1982 by Hope Publishing Co., Carol Stream IL 60188. All rights reserved. Used by permission. ***Tune:** © 1971 Walton Music Corporation. Used by permission. ***Setting:** © 1993 Elfred Bloedel. Used by permission.
265 **Text:** © 1978 *Lutheran Book of Worship*. Reprinted by permission of Augsburg Fortress. ***Tune and Setting:** © 1975, 1988 Richard Hillert. All rights reserved. Used by permission.
266 ***Text:** © 1941 Concordia Publishing House. Used by permission of CPH. **Tune:** public domain. ***Setting:** © 1993 Kermit G. Moldenauer. Used by permission.
267 **Text and Tune:** public domain. ***Setting:** © 1982 Concordia Publishing House. Used by permission of CPH.
268 **Text, Tune, Setting:** public domain.
269 **Text, Tune, Setting:** public domain.
270 **Text, Tune, Setting:** public domain.
271 **Text and Tune:** public domain. ***Setting:** © 1982 Concordia Publishing House. Used by permission of CPH.
272 ***Text, Tune, Setting:** Reprinted from *The Lutheran Hymnal* by permission of Concordia Publishing House.
273 ***Text, Tune, Setting:** Reprinted from *The Lutheran Hymnal* by permission of Concordia Publishing House.
274 ***Text:** © 1941 Concordia Publishing House. Used by permission of CPH. **Tune and Setting:** public domain.
275 **Text:** © 1973 by Hope Publishing Co., Carol Stream IL 60188. All rights reserved. Used by permission. **Tune:** public domain. ***Setting:** © 1993 Kermit G. Moldenauer. Used by permission.
276 **Text:** public domain. ***Tune and Setting:** © 1993 Kermit G. Moldenauer. Used by permission.
277 **Text:** ©1982 by Hope Publishing Co., Carol Stream IL 60188. All rights reserved. Used by permission. **Tune and Setting:** public domain.
278 **Text st.1,2,4:** public domain. ***Text st.3:** © 1993 Ruth Backer Glaeske. Used by permission. **Tune and Setting:** public domain.
279 **Text, Tune, Setting:** public domain.
280 ***Text:** © 1969 Concordia Publishing House. Used by permission of CPH. **Tune and Setting:** public domain.
281 **Text:** © 1953. Renewal 1981 by The Hymn Society, Texas Christian University, Fort Worth TX 76129. All rights reserved. Used by permission. **Tune and Setting:** public domain.
282 **Text st.1,3:** public domain. ***Text tr. st.2:** © 1993 Mark A. Jeske. Used by permission. **Tune:** public domain. ***Setting:** © 1993 Kermit G. Moldenauer. Used by permission.
283 **Text and Tune:** public domain. ***Setting:** © 1993 Elfred Bloedel. Used by permission.
284 **Text, Tune, Setting:** public domain.
285 **Text and Tune:** public domain. ***Setting:** © 1993 Kermit G. Moldenauer. Used by permission.
286 **Text, Tune, Setting:** public domain.
287 **Text, Tune, Setting:** public domain.
288 **Text and Tune:** public domain. ***Setting:** © 1993 Elfred Bloedel. Used by permission.
289 ***Text:** © 1941 Concordia Publishing House. Used by permission of CPH. **Tune and Setting:** public domain.
290 **Text, Tune, Setting:** public domain.
291 **Text, Tune, Setting:** public domain.

292 ***Text:** © 1980 Daniel Meeter, alt. Used by permission. ***Tune and Setting:** © 1987 CRC Publications, Grand Rapids MI 49560. All rights reserved. Used by permission.
293 **Text, Tune, Setting:** public domain.
294 **Text and Tune:** public domain. **Setting:** © 1981 Richard W. Gieseke, 835 Kentridge Ct., Manchester MO 63021-7568. Used by permission.
295 **Text, Tune, Setting:** public domain.
296 **Text, Tune, Setting:** public domain.
297 **Text:** © 1982 by Hope Publishing Co., Carol Stream IL 60188. All rights reserved. Used by permission. **Tune:** public domain. ***Setting:** © 1993 Kermit G. Moldenauer. Used by permission.
298 ***Text:** © 1941 Concordia Publishing House. Used by permission of CPH. **Tune and Setting:** public domain.
299 **Text, Tune, Setting:** public domain.
300 **Text:** © 1984 Jaroslav J. Vajda. Used by permission. **Tune and Setting:** public domain.
301 **Text:** © 1955 Judith O'Neill. Used by permission. **Tune and Setting:** public domain.
302 **Text, Tune, Setting:** public domain.
303 **Text, Tune, Setting:** public domain.
304 **Text, Tune, Setting:** public domain.
305 **Text st.1-3:** public domain. **Text st.4:** © 1978 *Lutheran Book of Worship*. Reprinted by permission of Augsburg Fortress. **Tune and Setting:** public domain.
306 **Text and Tune:** public domain. **Setting:** © 1981 Richard W. Gieseke, 835 Kentridge Ct., Manchester MO 63021-7568. Used by permission.
307 **Text: st.1** © 1978 *Lutheran Book of Worship*. **st.2** © Board of Publication, Lutheran Church in America. Reprinted by permission of Augsburg Fortress. **Tune and Setting:** public domain.
308 **Text, Tune, Setting:** public domain.
309 **Text, Tune, Setting:** public domain.
310 **Text, Tune, Setting:** public domain.
311 **Text, Tune, Setting:** public domain.
312 **Text, Tune, Setting:** public domain.
313 **Text, Tune, Setting:** public domain.
314 **Text and Tune:** public domain. ***Setting:** © 1982 Concordia Publishing House. Used by permission of CPH.
315 **Text and Tune:** public domain. ***Setting:** © 1969 Concordia Publishing House. Used by permission of CPH.
316 **Text and Tune:** public domain. ***Setting:** © 1982 Concordia Publishing House. Used by permission of CPH.
317 **Text and Tune:** public domain. ***Setting:** © 1993 Kermit G. Moldenauer. Used by permission.
318 **Text:** © 1964 World Library Publications, Inc. All rights reserved. Used With Permission. **Tune:** public domain. **Setting:** © 1978 *Lutheran Book of Worship*. Reprinted by permission of Augsburg Fortress.
319 **Text, Tune, Setting:** public domain.
320 **Text, Tune, Setting:** public domain.
321 **Text, Tune, Setting:** public domain.
322 **Text, Tune, Setting:** public domain.
323 **Text, Tune, Setting:** public domain.
324 **Text, Tune, Setting:** public domain.
325 **Text, Tune, Setting:** public domain.
326 **Text st.1,2:** public domain. **Text st.3:** © 1971 by GIA Publications, Inc., Chicago IL. All rights reserved. Used by permission. **Tune and Setting:** public domain.
327 **Text, Tune, Setting:** public domain.

ACKNOWLEDGMENTS

328 **Text:** public domain. **Tune and Setting:** Ralph Vaughan Williams from *Enlarged Songs of Praise*. Reprinted by permission of Oxford University Press.
329 **Text, Tune, Setting:** public domain.
330 **Text, Tune, Setting:** public domain.
331 **Text, Tune, Setting:** public domain.
332 **Text:** © 1983 Jaroslav J. Vajda. Used by permission. **Tune:** public domain. **Setting:** Harmonized by Ralph Vaughan Williams. From the *English Hymnal* by permission of Oxford University Press.
333 **Text, Tune, Setting:** public domain.
334 **Text, Tune, Setting:** public domain.
335 ***Text, Tune, Setting:** © 1969 Concordia Publishing House. Used by permission of CPH.
336 **Text and Tune:** public domain. ***Setting:** © 1982 Concordia Publishing House. Used by permission of CPH.
337 **Text, Tune, Setting:** public domain.
338 **Text, Tune, Setting:** public domain.
339 **Text, Tune, Setting:** public domain.
340 **Text, Tune, Setting:** public domain.
341 **Text, Tune, Setting:** public domain. **Descant:** Reprinted from *Crown Him with Many Crowns* by Walter Pelz, © 1963 Augsburg Publishing House. Used by permission of Augsburg Fortress.
342 **Text, Tune, Setting:** © 1978 *Lutheran Book of Worship*. Reprinted by permission of Augsburg Fortress.
343 **Text:** © 1969 by Hope Publishing Co., Carol Stream IL 60188. All rights reserved. Used by permission. **Tune:** public domain. ***Setting:** © 1969 Concordia Publishing House. Used by permission of CPH.
344 **Text:** public domain. **Tune and Setting:** Ralph Vaughan Williams from *Enlarged Songs of Praise*. Reprinted by permission of Oxford University Press.
345 **Text, Tune, Setting:** public domain.
346 **Text and Tune:** public domain. **Setting:** From *The Liturgical Year* © Oliver Ditson. Reprinted by permission of the publisher.
347 **Text, Tune, Setting:** public domain.
348 **Text, Tune, Setting:** public domain.
349 **Text and Tune:** public domain. ***Setting:** © 1982 Concordia Publishing House. Used by permission of CPH.
350 ***Text:** From *The Hymnal 1982* © The Church Pension Fund. Used by permission. **Tune and Setting:** © 1967 by The Bethany Press. Reprinted by permission of Chalice Press.
351 **Text, Tune, Setting:** public domain.
352 **Text and Tune:** public domain. ***Setting:** © 1969 Concordia Publishing House. Used by permission of CPH.
353 **Text:** © 1987 by Hope Publishing Co., Carol Stream IL 60188. All rights reserved. Used by permission. **Tune:** public domain. **Setting:** © 1978 *Lutheran Book of Worship*. Reprinted by permission of Augsburg Fortress.
354 **Text, Tune, Setting:** public domain.
355 **Text:** public domain. **Tune:** © 1980 by Hope Publishing Co., Carol Stream IL 60188. All rights reserved. Used by permission. **Setting:** © 1993 by Hope Publishing Co., Carol Stream IL 60188. All rights reserved. Used by permission.
356 **Text, Tune, Setting:** public domain.
357 **Text, Tune, Setting:** public domain.
358 **Text and Tune:** public domain. ***Setting:** © 1982 Concordia Publishing House. Used by permission of CPH.

359 **Text, Tune, Setting:** public domain.
360 **Text, Tune, Setting:** public domain.
361 **Text and Tune:** public domain. **Setting:** © 1978 *Lutheran Book of Worship*. Reprinted by permission of Augsburg Fortress.
362 **Text, Tune, Setting:** public domain.
363 ***Text:** © 1966, 1985 by Willard F. Jabusch, Calvert House, University of Chicago. Used by permission. **Tune:** public domain. ***Setting:** From *The Hymnal of the United Church of Christ*. Reprinted by permission of United Church Press.
364 **Text:** © Augsburg Publishing House. Reprinted by permission of Augsburg Fortress. **Tune and Setting:** public domain.
365 **Text, Tune, Setting:** public domain.
366 **Text, Tune, Setting:** public domain.
367 **Text:** © 1964 Renewal 1992 by Hope Publishing Co., Carol Stream, IL 60188. All rights reserved. Used by permission. **Tune:** public domain. ***Setting:** © 1982 Concordia Publishing House. Used by permission of CPH.
368 **Text, Tune, Setting:** public domain.
369 **Text, Tune, Setting:** public domain.
370 **Text, Tune, Setting:** public domain. **Descant:** © 1979 by GIA Publications, Inc., Chicago IL. All rights reserved. Used by permission.
371 **Text and Tune:** public domain. **Setting:** © 1985 by Hope Publishing Co., Carol Stream IL 60188. All rights reserved. Used by permission.
372 **Text, Tune, Setting:** public domain.
373 **Text, Tune, Setting:** public domain.
374 **Text and Tune:** public domain. ***Setting:** © 1993 Kermit G. Moldenhauer. Used by permission.
375 **Text, Tune, Setting:** public domain.
376 **Text, Tune, Setting:** public domain.
377 **Text, Tune, Setting:** public domain.
378 **Text, Tune, Setting:** public domain.
379 **Text and Tune:** public domain. **Setting:** © 1964 Abingdon Press. Reprinted from *The Book of Hymns* by permission.
380 **Text and Tune:** public domain. ***Setting:** © 1993 Elfred Bloedel. Used by permission.
381 **Text, Tune, Setting:** public domain.
382 **Text, Tune, Setting:** public domain.
383 **Text, Tune, Setting:** public domain.
384 **Text, Tune, Setting:** public domain.
385 **Text and Tune:** public domain. ***Setting:** © 1993 Kermit G. Moldenhauer. Used by permission.
386 **Text, Tune, Setting:** public domain.
387 **Text and Tune:** public domain. **Setting:** © 1978 *Lutheran Book of Worship*. Reprinted by permission of Augsburg Fortress.
388 **Text and Tune:** public domain. **Setting:** From the *Revised Church Hymnary 1927* by permission of Oxford University Press.
389 **Text, Tune, Setting:** public domain.
390 **Text, Tune, Setting:** public domain.
391 **Text, Tune, Setting:** public domain.
392 ***Text and Tune:** © 1975 Kurt J. Eggert. Used by permission. ***Setting:** © 1993 Mrs. James E. Engel. Used by permission.
393 **Text and Tune:** public domain. ***Setting:** © 1993 Kermit G. Moldenhauer. Used by permission.

ACKNOWLEDGMENTS

394 **Text, Tune, Setting:** public domain.
395 **Text, Tune, Setting:** public domain.
396 ***Text:** © 1969 Concordia Publishing House. Used by permission of CPH. ***Tune and Setting:** © 1993 Kurt J. Eggert. Used by permission.
397 **Text, Tune, Setting:** public domain.
398 **Text, Tune, Setting:** public domain.
399 **Text, Tune, Setting:** public domain.
400 **Text and Tune:** © 1978 *Lutheran Book of Worship.* Reprinted by permission of Augsburg Fortress. ***Setting:** © 1969 Concordia Publishing House. Used by permission of CPH.
401 **Text, Tune, Setting:** public domain.
402 **Text, Tune, Setting:** public domain.
403 **Text, Tune, Setting:** public domain.
404 **Text, Tune, Setting:** public domain.
405 **Text, Tune, Setting:** public domain.
406 **Text, Tune, Setting:** © 1980 by Hope Publishing Co., Carol Stream IL 60188. All rights reserved. Used by permission.
407 ***Text:** © 1969 Concordia Publishing House. Used by permission of CPH. **Tune and Setting:** public domain.
408 **Text, Tune, Setting:** public domain.
409 **Text, Tune, Setting:** public domain.
410 **Text, Tune, Setting:** public domain.
411 **Text, Tune, Setting:** public domain.
412 **Text and Tune:** public domain. ***Setting:** © 1993 Kermit G. Moldenhauer. Used by permission.
413 **Text and Tune:** public domain. ***Setting:** © 1982 Concordia Publishing House. Used by permission of CPH.
414 **Text, Tune, Setting:** public domain.
415 **Text:** public domain. **Tune:** © Breitkopf & Härtel, Wiesbaden. Used by permission. **Setting:** © 1933 Presbyterian Board of Christian Education. Renewed 1961; from *The Hymnbook.* Used by permission of Westminster/John Knox Press.
416 **Text, Tune, Setting:** public domain.
417 **Text, Tune, Setting:** public domain.
418 **Text, Tune, Setting:** public domain.
419 **Text and Tune:** public domain. ***Setting:** © 1993 Kermit G. Moldenhauer. Used by permission.
420 **Text and Tune:** public domain. ***Setting:** © 1993 Elfred Bloedel. Used by permission.
421 **Text, Tune, Setting:** public domain.
422 **Text, Tune, Setting:** public domain.
423 **Text, Tune, Setting:** public domain.
424 **Text, Tune, Setting:** public domain.
425 **Text:** By kind permission of The Lutheran World Federation. **Tune:** Melody adapt. Ralph Vaughan Williams from *Enlarged Songs of Praise* by permission of Oxford University Press. **Setting:** public domain.
426 **Text, Tune, Setting:** public domain.
427 **Text, Tune, Setting:** public domain.
428 **Text st.1-3:** public domain. ***Text st.4:** © 1993 Harlyn J. Kuschel. Used by permission. **Tune and Setting:** public domain.
429 **Text, Tune, Setting:** public domain.
430 **Text, Tune, Setting:** public domain.
431 **Text, Tune, Setting:** public domain.
432 **Text and Tune:** public domain. ***Setting:** © 1982 Concordia Publishing House. Used by permission of CPH.
433 **Text, Tune, Setting:** public domain.
434 **Text, Tune, Setting:** public domain.
435 **Text and Tune:** public domain. ***Setting:** © 1982 Concordia Publishing House. Used by permission of CPH.
436 **Text, Tune, Setting:** public domain.
437 **Text:** © 1967 Lutheran Council in the U.S.A. Reprinted by permission of Augsburg Fortress. **Tune and Setting:** public domain.
438 **Text and Tune:** public domain. ***Setting:** © 1993 Kermit G. Moldenhauer. Used by permission.
439 **Text:** © 1978 *Lutheran Book of Worship.* Reprinted by permission of Augsburg Fortress. **Tune and Setting:** public domain.
440 **Text and Tune:** © 1979, 1991, New Dawn Music, 5536 NE Hassalo, Portland, OR 97213. All rights reserved. Used with permission. ***Setting:** © 1993 Elfred Bloedel. Used by permission.
441 **Text, Tune, Setting:** public domain. **Descant:** From *55 Hymn Descants* © 1979 by GIA Publications, Inc., Chicago IL. All rights reserved. Used by permission.
442 ***Text and Tune:** From *Five Hymns* © 1973 Concordia Publishing House. Used by permission of CPH. **Setting:** public domain.
443 **Text and Tune:** public domain. **Setting:** © 1981 Richard W. Gieseke, 835 Kentridge Ct., Manchester, MO 63021-7568. Used by permission.
444 **Text, Tune, Setting:** public domain.
445 **Text and Tune:** public domain. ***Setting:** © 1993 Elfred Bloedel. Used by permission.
446 **Text, Tune, Setting:** public domain.
447 **Text, Tune, Setting:** public domain.
448 **Text and Tune:** public domain. ***Setting:** © 1993 Bruce R. Backer. Used by permission.
449 **Text:** © Board of Publication, Lutheran Church in America. Reprinted by permission of Augsburg Fortress. **Tune and Setting:** public domain.
450 ***Text:** © 1969 Concordia Publishing House. Used by permission of CPH. **Tune and Setting:** public domain.
451 **Text, Tune, Setting:** By Thomas A. Dorsey. © 1938 by Hill & Range Songs, Inc. © Renewed, assigned to Unichappell Music, Inc. (Rightsong Music, Publisher) International Copyright Secured. All rights reserved. Used by permission of Hal Leonard Publishing Corporation.
452 **Text, Tune, Setting:** public domain.
453 **Text, Tune, Setting:** public domain.
454 **Text, Tune, Setting:** public domain.
455 **Text and Tune:** public domain. ***Setting:** © 1970 by Bärenreiter-Verlag; reprinted by permission.
456 **Text:** public domain. ***Tune:** © 1981 Barry L. Bobb. Used by permission. ***Setting:** © 1982 Concordia Publishing House. Used by permission of CPH.
457 **Text, Tune, Setting:** public domain.
458 **Text, Tune, Setting:** public domain.
459 **Text, Tune, Setting:** public domain.
460 **Text and Tune:** public domain. ***Setting:** © 1993 Kermit G. Moldenhauer. Used by permission.
461 **Text and Tune:** public domain. ***Setting:** © 1982 Concordia Publishing House. Used by permission of CPH.
462 **Text, Tune, Setting:** public domain.
463 **Text, Tune, Setting:** public domain.
464 ***Text :** © 1941 Concordia Publishing House. Used by permission of CPH. **Tune:** public domain. ***Setting:** © 1993 Bruce R. Backer. Used by permission.

ACKNOWLEDGMENTS

465 **Text, Tune, Setting:** public domain.
466 **Text, Tune, Setting:** public domain.
467 **Text, Tune, Setting:** public domain.
468 *****Text:** © 1941 Concordia Publishing House. Used by permission of CPH. **Tune:** public domain. *****Setting:** © 1993 Elfred Bloedel. Used by permission.
469 **Text, Tune, Setting:** public domain.
470 **Text, Tune, Setting:** public domain.
471 **Text, Tune, Setting:** public domain.
472 **Text, Tune, Setting:** public domain.
473 **Text, Tune, Setting:** public domain.
474 **Text, Tune, Setting:** public domain.
475 **Text, Tune, Setting:** public domain.
476 **Text, Tune, Setting:** public domain.
477 **Text and Tune:** public domain. **Setting:** © 1981 Richard W. Gieseke, 835 Kentridge Ct., Manchester, MO 63021-7568. Used by permission.
478 *****Text:** © 1941 Concordia Publishing House. Used by permission of CPH. **Tune and Setting:** public domain.
479 **Text and Tune:** public domain. *****Setting:** © 1990 Ronald L. Shilling. Used by permission.
480 **Text and Tune:** public domain. *****Setting:** © 1982 Concordia Publishing House. Used by permission of CPH.
481 **Text:** © 1961 Renewal 1989 by The Hymn Society, Texas Christian University, Fort Worth TX 76129. All rights reserved. Used by permission. **Tune:** public domain. **Setting:** Reprinted by permission of Oxford University Press.
482 **Text:** © 1965. Renewal 1993 by The Hymn Society, Texas Christian University, Fort Worth TX 76129. All rights reserved. Used by permission. **Tune:** © Doris Wright Smith, 321 Sixth Ave S., Brigantine NJ 08303. *****Setting:** © 1969 Concordia Publishing House. Used by permission of CPH.
483 **Text:** © Albert F. Bayly. Used by permission of Oxford University Press. **Tune:** public domain. *****Setting:** © 1969 Concordia Publishing House. Used by permission of CPH.
484 **Text, Tune, Setting:** public domain.
485 **Text, Tune, Setting:** public domain.
486 **Text and Tune:** public domain. *****Setting:** © 1986 Bruce R. Backer. Used by permission.
487 **Text, Tune, Setting:** public domain.
488 **Text, Tune, Setting:** public domain.
489 **Text and Tune:** public domain. **Setting:** © 1986 by GIA Publications, Inc., Chicago IL. All rights reserved. Used by permission
490 *****Text and Tune:** © 1980 Concordia Publishing House; *****Setting:** © 1982 Concordia Publishing House. Used by permission of CPH.
491 *****Text and Tune:** public domain. *****Setting:** © 1993 Elfred Bloedel. Used by permission.
492 **Text and Tune:** public domain. *****Setting:** © 1986 James E. Engel. Used by permission of Mrs. James E. Engel.
493 **Text:** Used by permission of Oxford University Press. **Tune:** public domain. *****Setting:** © 1993 Bruce R. Backer. Used by permission.
494 **Text, Tune, Setting:** public domain.
495 **Text:** © 1985 by Hope Publishing Co., Carol Stream IL 60188; **Tune and Setting:** © 1969 by Hope Publishing Co., Carol Stream IL 60188. All rights reserved. Used by permission.

496 **Text and Setting:** © 1972 by GIA Publications, Inc., Chicago IL. All rights reserved. Used by permission. **Tune:** public domain.
497 **Text:** © 1969 James Quinn, SJ. Reproduced by permission of Geoffrey Chapman, a Division of Cassell. **Tune:** public domain. **Setting:** © Estate of T. H. Weaving.
498 **Text and Tune:** © 1972 by Hope Publishing Co., Carol Stream IL 60188. All rights reserved. Used by permission. **Setting:** © 1993 by Hope Publishing Co., Carol Stream IL 60188. All rights reserved. Used by permission.
499 **Text, Tune, Setting:** public domain.
500 **Text st. 1,3-5:** From *Book of Worship for U. S. Forces* published by U. S. Government Printing Office, Washington D.C. 20402 *****Text st. 2:** © 1993 Mark A. Jeske. **Tune:** public domain. *****Setting:** © 1982 Concordia Publishing House. Used by permission of CPH.
501 *****Text :** From *The Hymnal 1982* © The Church Pension Fund. Used by permission. **Tune and Setting:** public domain.
502 **Text:** © Albert F. Bayly. Used by permission of Oxford University Press. **Tune:** public domain. *****Setting:** © 1993 Kermit G. Moldenhauer. Used by permission.
503 **Text:** public domain. *****Tune and Setting:** © 1993 Kermit G. Moldenhauer. Used by permission.
504 **Text, Tune, Setting:** public domain.
505 *****Text:** © 1985 Donald E. Smith. Used by permission. **Tune:** public domain. *****Setting:** © 1993 Kermit G. Moldenhauer. Used by permission.
506 **Text, Tune, Setting:** public domain.
507 **Text:** © 1982 by Hope Publishing Co., Carol Stream IL 60188. All rights reserved. Used by permission. *****Tune and Setting:** © 1993 Kermit G. Moldenhauer. Used by permission.
508 **Text, Tune, Setting:** public domain.
509 **Text, Tune, Setting:** public domain.
510 **Text, Tune, Setting:** public domain.
511 *****Text:** © 1993 Dr. Oliver C. Rupprecht (b. 1903), Milwaukee WI. Used by permission. **Tune and Setting:** public domain.
512 *****Text:** © 1941 Concordia Publishing House. Used by permission of CPH. **Tune and Setting:** public domain.
513 *****Text and Setting:** © 1982 Concordia Publishing House. Used by permission of CPH. *****Tune:** © 1981 Barry L. Bobb. Used by permission.
514 **Text, Tune, Setting:** public domain.
515 **Text, Tune, Setting:** public domain.
516 *****Text:** © 1941 Concordia Publishing House. Used by permission of CPH. **Tune:** public domain. *****Setting:** © 1993 Elfred Bloedel. Used by permission.
517 *****Text:** From *The Hymnal 1982* © The Church Pension Fund. Used by permission. **Tune and Setting:** public domain.
518 **Text st.1,2,4,5:** © 1969 James Quinn, SJ. Reproduced by permission of Geoffrey Chapman, a Division of Cassell. *****Text st.3:** © 1993 Mark A. Jeske. Used by permission. **Tune and Setting:** public domain.
519 **Text, Tune, Setting:** public domain.
520 **Text and Tune:** public domain. **Setting:** Ralph Vaughan Williams by permission of Oxford University Press.
521 *****Text and Setting:** © 1969 Concordia Publishing House. Used by permission of CPH. **Tune:** public domain.
522 **Text:** By kind permission of The Lutheran World Federation. **Tune and Setting:** public domain.

934

ACKNOWLEDGMENTS

523 **Text and Tune:** public domain. ***Setting:*** © 1982 Concordia Publishing House. Used by permission of CPH.
524 **Text and Tune:** public domain. ***Setting:*** © 1993 Kermit G. Moldenhauer. Used by permission.
525 **Text:** © 1956 Renewal 1984 by The Hymn Society. Texas Christian University, Fort Worth TX 76129. All rights reserved. Used by permission. **Tune:** © Doris Wright Smith, 321 Sixth Ave. S., Brigantine NJ 08203. ***Setting:*** © 1993 Kermit G. Moldenhauer. Used by permission.
526 **Text:** © 1975 by Hope Publishing Co., Carol Stream IL 60188. **Tune and Setting:** © 1980 by Hope Publishing Co., Carol Stream IL 60188. All rights reserved. Used by permission.
527 **Text and Tune:** © 1949, 1977 by Chantry Music Press, Inc. Used by permission. **Setting:** Richard Proulx, © 1975 by GIA Publications, Inc., Chicago IL. All rights reserved. Used by permission.
528 **Text, Tune, Setting:** public domain.
529 **Text, Tune, Setting:** public domain.
530 **Text, Tune, Setting:** public domain.
531 **Text, Tune, Setting:** public domain.
532 **Text:** © 1979 by Hope Publishing Co., Carol Stream IL 60188. All rights reserved. Used by permission. **Tune:** public domain. **Setting:** © F. E. Röntgen c/o Johanna A. Rontgen, Mankestra 3, 2596 CJ Ben Haag, Holland.
533 **Text, Tune, Setting:** public domain
534 **Text, Tune, Setting:** public domain.
535 ***Text:*** © 1972 Concordia Publishing House. Used by permission of CPH. **Tune and Setting:** public domain.
536 **Text, Tune, Setting:** public domain.
537 **Text, Tune, Setting:** public domain.
538 **Text, Tune, Setting:** public domain. ***Descant:*** © 1993 Kermit G. Moldenhauer. Used by permission.
539 **Text st.1,4,5:** public domain***Text st.2:** © 1993 Mark A. Jeske. Used by permission. **Text st.3:** © 1982 by Hope Publishing Co., Carol Stream IL 60188. All rights reserved. Used by permission. **Tune and Setting:** © Harry T. Burleigh by permission of Harry T. Burleigh II.
540 **Text, Tune, Setting:** public domain.
541 **Text, Tune, Setting:** public domain.
542 ***Text:*** © 1941 Concordia Publishing House. Used by permission of CPH. **Tune and Setting:** public domain.
543 **Text, Tune, Setting:** public domain.
544 ***Text:*** © 1971 Mrs. Martin H. Franzmann. Used by permission. **Tune:** public domain. ***Setting:*** © 1969 Concordia Publishing House. Used by permission of CPH.
545 **Text and Tune:** public domain. ***Setting:*** © 1993 Elfred Bloedel. Used by permission.
546 **Text, Tune, Setting:** public domain.
547 **Text, Tune, Setting:** public domain.
548 ***Text:*** © 1993 Michael D. Schultz. Used by permission. **Tune and Setting:** public domain.
549 **Text, Tune, Setting:** public domain.
550 **Text st.1,2:** public domain. **Text st.3:** © 1978 *Lutheran Book of Worship*. Reprinted by permission of Augsburg Fortress. **Tune and Setting:** public domain.
551 **Text:** public domain. **Tune and Setting:** Ralph Vaughan Williams from the *English Hymnal* by permission of Oxford University Press.
552 ***Text st.1-4,6-27:*** From *The Hymnal 1982* © The Church Pension Fund. Used by permission. ***Text st.5:*** © 1993 Harlyn J. Kuschel. Used by permission. **Tune:** public domain. **Setting:** From the *Revised Church Hymnary 1927* by permission of Oxford University Press.
553 **Text:** © 1985 by Hope Publishing Co., Carol Stream IL 60188. All rights reserved. Used by permission. ***Tune and Setting:*** © 1993 Bruce R. Backer. Used by permission.
554 **Text, Tune, Setting:** public domain.
555 **Text and Tune:** public domain. ***Setting:*** © 1982 Concordia Publishing House. Used by permission of CPH.
556 **Text, Tune, Setting:** © Augsburg Publishing House. Reprinted by permission of Augsburg Fortress.
557 ***Text:*** © 1982 Concordia Publishing House. Used by permission of CPH. **Tune and Setting:** public domain.
558 **Text:** © 1984 by Hope Publishing Co., Carol Stream IL 60188. All rights reserved. Used by permission. **Tune and Setting:** public domain
559 **Text, Tune, Setting:** public domain.
560 ***Text:*** © 1993 John C. Lawrenz. Used by permission. **Tune and Setting:** public domain.
561 **Text, Tune, Setting:** public domain.
562 **Text, Tune, Setting:** public domain.
563 **Text and Tune:** public domain. ***Setting:*** Published by permission of the executors of the late Dr. Basil Harwood.
564 **Text, Tune, Setting:** public domain.
565 ***Text:*** © 1941 Concordia Publishing House. Used by permission of CPH. **Tune and Setting:** public domain.
566 **Text:** © 1986 by Hope Publishing Co., Carol Stream IL 60188. All rights reserved. Used by permission. **Tune and Setting:** public domain.
567 **Text, Tune, Setting:** public domain.
568 **Text:** © 1988 by Hope Publishing Co., Carol Stream IL 60188. All rights reserved. Used by permission. ***Tune and Setting:*** © 1993 Kermit G. Moldenhauer. Used by permission.
569 **Text, Tune, Setting:** public domain.
570 **Text:** public domain. ***Tune and Setting:*** © 1993 Bruce R. Backer. Used by permission.
571 **Text, Tune, Setting:** public domain.
572 **Text, Tune, Setting:** public domain.
573 **Text, Tune, Setting:** public domain.
574 **Text, Tune, Setting:** public domain.
575 **Text:** © 1982 by Hope Publishing Co., Carol Stream IL 60188. All rights reserved. Used by permission. **Tune and Setting:** public domain.
576 **Text, Tune, Setting:** public domain.
577 **Text and Tune:** public domain. ***Setting:*** © 1993 Kermit G. Moldenhauer. Used by permission.
578 **Text, Tune, Setting:** public domain.
579 **Text, Tune, Setting:** © 1974 by Hope Publishing Co., Carol Stream IL 60188. All rights reserved. Used by permission. **Descant:** © 1985 by GIA Publications, Inc., Chicago IL. All rights reserved. Used by permission.
580 **Text and Tune:** public domain. ***Setting:*** © 1993 Bruce R. Backer. Used by permission.
581 **Text, Tune, Setting:** public domain.
582 **Text, Tune, Setting:** public domain.
583 **Text:** public domain. **Tune and Setting:** © Lutheran Church Press and Augsburg Publishing House. Reprinted by permission of Augsburg Fortress.
584 **Text, Tune, Setting:** public domain.
585 **Text, Tune, Setting:** public domain.
586 **Text and Tune:** public domain. ***Setting:*** © 1982 Concordia Publishing House. Used by permission of CPH.

ACKNOWLEDGMENTS

587 **Text, Tune, Setting:** public domain.
588 **Text, Tune, Setting:** public domain.
589 **Text, Tune, Setting:** public domain.
590 **Text, Tune, Setting:** public domain.
591 **Text, Tune, Setting:** public domain.
592 **Text, Tune, Setting:** public domain.
593 **Text, Tune, Setting:** public domain.
594 **Text, Tune, Setting:** public domain.
595 **Text and Tune:** public domain. ***Setting:** © 1969 Concordia Publishing House. Used by permission of CPH.
596 **Text, Tune, Setting:** public domain.
597 **Text, Tune, Setting:** public domain.
598 **Text, Tune, Setting:** public domain.
599 **Text, Tune, Setting:** public domain.
600 **Text, Tune, Setting:** public domain.
601 *** Text:** From *The Hymnal 1982* © The Church Pension Fund. Used by permission. **Tune and Setting:** public domain.
602 *** Text and Tune:** © 1990 Kurt J. Eggert. Used by permission. *** Setting:** © 1993 Kermit G. Moldenhauer. Used by permission.
603 **Text st. 1,2:** © 1978 *Lutheran Book of Worship*. Reprinted by permission of Augsburg Fortress. **Tune and Setting:** public domain.
604 **Text, Tune, Setting:** public domain.
605 **Text, Tune, Setting:** public domain.
606 **Text and Tune:** public domain. *** Setting:** © 1982 Concordia Publishing House. Used by permission of CPH.
607 **Text:** © 1972 by the Hymn Society, Texas Christian University, Fort Worth TX 76129. All rights reserved. Used by permission. **Tune and Setting:** public domain.

608 **Text, Tune, Setting:** public domain.
609 **Text, Tune, Setting:** public domain.
610 **Text, Tune, Setting:** public domain. *** Descant:** © 1993 Kermit G. Moldenhauer. Used by permission.
611 **Text:** © 1970 by Hope Publishing Co., Carol Stream IL 60188. All rights reserved. Used by permission. **Tune:** public domain. **Setting:** Ralph Vaughan Williams from the *English Hymnal* by permission of Oxford University Press.
612 **Text, Tune, Setting:** public domain.
613 **Text, Tune, Setting:** public domain.
614 **Text and Tune:** public domain. *** Setting:** © 1969 Concordia Publishing House. Used by permission of CPH.
615 **Text, Tune, Setting:** public domain.
616 **Text and Tune:** public domain. *** Setting:** © 1982 Concordia Publishing House. Used by permission of CPH.
617 **Text and Tune:** public domain. **Setting:** © 1986 by GIA Publications, Inc., Chicago IL. All rights reserved. Used by permission.
618 **Text, Tune, Setting:** public domain.
619 **Text, Tune, Setting:** public domain.
620 **Text, Tune, Setting:** public domain.
621 *** Text:** © 1993 Werner H. Franzmann. Used by permission. *** Tune and Setting:** © 1993 Mrs. James E. Engel. Used by permission.
622 *** Text:** © 1941 Concordia Publishing House. Used by permission of CPH. **Tune:** public domain. **Setting:** © 1981 Richard W. Gieseke, 835 Kentridge Ct., Manchester, MO 63021-7568. Used by permission.
623 *** Text:** © 1941 Concordia Publishing House. Used by permission of CPH. **Tune and Setting:** public domain.

HYMNS WITH DESCANTS

A Hymn of Glory Let Us Sing	171
All Glory, Laud, and Honor	131
All Hail the Power of Jesus' Name	370
Crown Him with Many Crowns	341
Hark! A Thrilling Voice Is Sounding	15
Hark! The Herald Angels Sing	61
Holy, Holy, Holy, Lord God Almighty	195
How Lovely Shines the Morning Star	79
I Know that My Redeemer Lives	152
Jesus Christ Is Risen Today	157
Lift High the Cross	579
Now Thank We All Our God	610
O God, Our Help in Ages Past	441
Oh, Come, All Ye Faithful	55
Praise to the Lord, the Almighty	234
The Church's One Foundation	538

HYMNS WITH GUITAR CHORDS

Amazing Grace	379
Away in a Manger	68
Children of the Heavenly Father	449
Glorious in Majesty	496
Go, My Children, with My Blessing	332
God of Love and God of Marriage	602
Jerusalem, My Happy Home	215
Love Is the Gracious Gift	505
My Shepherd Will Supply My Need	374
O Dearest Lord, Thy Sacred Head	118
Sing a New Song to the Lord	245
What Child Is This	67

AUTHORS, TRANSLATORS, AND SOURCES OF HYMNS

Numbers in italics indicate translations.

A Collection of Hymns	351
A General Selection of . . . Spiritual Songs	120
A Selection of Hymns	370, 416
Addison, Joseph	259
African-American spiritual	57, 119, 564
Albinus, Johann G.	423
Albrecht von Preussen	435
Alderson, Eliza S.	486
Alexander, Cecil F.	50, 463
Alford, Henry	613
Allen, Oswald	339
Alte Catholische . . . Kirchengeseng	47
Ambrose	2, 586, 591
Andächtige Haus-Kirche	421
Ander Theil Des Dressdenischen GesangBuchs	64
Andrews, Carroll T.	326
Anna Sophia	283
Arends, Wilhelm E.	455
Armstrong, Richard S.	500
Arneson, Ole T.	*503*
Arthur, John W.	265
Astley, Charles T.	*427*
Ausserlesenes . . . GesangBuchlein	43
Bahnmaier, Jonathan F.	576
Baker, Henry W.	*35,* 138, 375, 388, 519
Barbauld, Anna L.	612
Baring-Gould, Sabine	24, 537, 589
Basque carol	24
Bateman, Henry	484
Bathurst, William H.	9, 405
Baughen, Michael A.	228
Bayly, Albert F.	483, 502
Bede, The Venerable	171
Behm, Martin	94, 584
Belsheim, Ole G.	*293*
Berg, Caroline V.	449
Bernard of Clairvaux	105, 373

AUTHORS, TRANSLATORS, SOURCES

Bernard of Cluny 214
Birken, Sigmund von 98, 452
Blumenfeld, Edward M. 525
Bogatzky, Karl H. von 567
Bohemian carol 59
Bonar, Horatius 239, 315, 338, 372, 401, 563, 604
Bonnus, Hermann 274
Borthwick, Jane L. *153, 415, 422*
Bourne, George H. 352
Bowring, John 345
Boye, Birgitte K. 49, 162, 180
Brauer, Alfred E. R. *235*
Bridges, Matthew 101, 341
Bridges, Robert S. *251*
Briggs, George W. 281
Brokering, Herbert F. 247
Brooks, Charles T. 619
Brooks, Phillips 65, 66
Brorson, Hans A. 46, 431, 550
Brownlie, John 25
Brun, Johan N. 325, 599
Burckhardt, Abel 48

Campbell, Robert *141*
Caswall, Edward *15*, 58, *103, 177, 178, 373*
Cawood, John 324
Celano, Thomas de 209
Chandler, John *1, 16, 528*
Church of England Magazine 232
Clausnitzer, Tobias 221, 270
Clement of Alexandria 515
Coffin, Charles 1, 16
Collyer, William B. 159, 208
Colvin, Tom 146
Composite 10, 18, 19, 47, 109, 121, 137, 171, 179, 190,
    194, 200, 201, 203, 234, 236, 241, 242, 253, 254, 268, 269,
    271, 283, 285, 304, 313, 330, 384, 386, 390, 393, 403, 410,
    428, 432, 435, 444, 445, 470, 539, 541, 546, 550, 585, 587, 590
Conder, Josiah 380
Cook, Henry 436
Cook, Joseph S. 56
Cory, Julia B. 609
Cothran, Jeff 496
Cowper, William 112, 420
Cox, Frances E. *145, 290*
Crasselius, Bartholomäus 189
Cronenwett, Emanuel *196*, 291, *312*
Crosby, Fanny J. 355, 399
Cross, Frank L. 481
Crossman, Samuel 110
Cruciger, Elizabeth 86
Crull, August *8, 27, 41, 72, 98, 123, 158, 170, 333,
    348, 391, 414, 424, 460, 461, 471, 477*
Czamanske, William M. *173, 298, 516, 565, 622*

D. M. Luthers . . . Geistliche Lieder und Psalmen 167
Dach, Simon 445, 554
Danish hymn 134
Davis, Katherine K. 260
Dayman, Edward A. 480
Dearmer, Percy *191, 581*
Decius, Nikolaus 263, 268
Denicke, David 460
Dexter, Henry M. *515*
Dix, William C. 67, 83, 169, 336
Doan, Gilbert E. *437*

Doane, George W. 356
Doddridge, Philip 12, 296, 381, 524
Dorsey, Thomas A. 451
Döving, Carl *49, 73, 306, 529, 599*
Dryden, John *188*
Dudley-Smith, Timothy 187, 245, 246, 367, 495,
    553, 558, 568
Duffield, George Jr. 474
Dwight, John S. 619
Dwight, Timothy 533

Eber, Paul 73, 413, 608
Edwards, Rusty 353, 566
Eggert, Kurt J. 99, 140, 392, 602
Ein schön geistlich Gesangbuch 606
Ellerton, John *163*, 321, 594
Elliott, Charlotte 397
Elven, Cornelius 303
Emilie Juliane 210
Enchiridion . . . zum Schwartzen Horn 204
English carol 52
Evangelical Lutheran Hymn-Book *114*
Evangelical Lutheran Hymnal *94, 506*

F. B. P. 215
Farrell, Melvin *31*
Fawcett, John 284, 329, 494
Fick, Herman 577
Findlater, Sarah B. *7*
Fischer, Christoph 123
Fischer, Eberhard L. 546
Fishel, Donald E. 154
Fortunatus, Venantius 122, 163, 179
Fosdick, Harry E. 523
Foster, Frederick W. *224*
Francis, Benjamin 347
Franck, Johann 78, 302, 311, 349
Franck, Salomo 414, 424
Franzmann, Martin H. 168, 280, 335, 396,
    400, 407, 527, 544
Franzmann, Werner H 5, 97, 151, 199, 621
Freystein, Johann B. 472
Funcke, Friedrich 170

Garve, Karl B. 153
Gates, Mary C. 572
Geisliche Lieder und Lobgesänge 453
Geistliche Psalmen 541
Geistreiches Gesangbuch 241
Geistreiches Gesang-Büchlein 221
Gellert, Christian F. 145
Gerhardt, Paul 18, 19, 37, 40, 42, 74, 100,
    105, 113, 156, 219, 253, 419,
    428, 430, 443, 479, 587
German folk hymn 317
German hymn 33, 144, 176, 190, 266, 545, 565
German litany 192
Germanus 36
Gesangbuch 596
Gesenius, Justus 109
Gieschen, Gerhard *81*
Glaeske, Ruth M. 278
Gramann, Johann 257
Grant, Robert 124, 243
Green, Fred Pratt 248, 343, 406, 532, 607, 611
Gregory I 581

Grigg, Joseph...347
Grindal, Gracia...*305*
Grundtvig, Nikolai F. S.............................293, 529
Gryphius, Andreas...289
Gurney, Dorothy F..600

Hamilton, James...69
Hankey, Arabella C..562
Harbaugh, Henry...617
Hardy, Henry E..118
Harjunpaa, Toivo K. I......................................*425*
Harmonia cantionum.....................................447
Hart, Joseph..354
Hastings, Thomas..337
Hausman, Julie K. von....................................439
Havergal, Frances R................368, 446, 454, 469, 561, 593
Hayn, Henrietta L. von....................................432
Heber, Reginald...21, 92, 195, 571
Heermann, Johann..............117, 121, 393, 459, 569, 616
Heiliges Lippen . . . Gesangbuch......................391
Held, Heinrich..28, 181
Helder, Bartholomäus..27
Helmbold, Ludwig............................418, 514, 516
Herbert, Petrus...404
Herklots, Rosamond E.....................................493
Herman, Nikolaus......................................41, 308
Herrnschmidt, Johann D.................................235
Herzberger, Frederick W.................................545
Heyder, Friedrich C...310
Hill, Rowland..549
Hine, Stuart W. K..256
Homburg, Ernst C...114
Hoppe, Anna B. D..30
Hopper, Edward..433
Hopson, Hal H...498
Horn, Johann..17
Hoskins, Joseph..466
How, William W........................76, 229, 279, 485, 551, 620
Hubert, Konrad...437
Humphreys, Joseph..394
Hus, John..313
Huxhold, Harry N..603
Hymnal and Order of Service...........................*408*
Hymns Ancient and Modern..............................*586*

Idle, Christopher M...................................115, 277
International Consultation on English Texts....276
Irons, Genevieve M...387
Irons, William J...*209*
Italian hymn...103

Jabusch, Willard F..363
Jeske, Mark A............179, 209, 254, 263, *282*, 500, 518, 539
Jillson, Marjorie A...442
John of Damascus...................................142, 166
Johnson, William..107
Joncas, Michael..440
Julian, John..85

Kahl, Johan..244
Kaiser, Oscar..*330*
Katholisches Gesangbuch.......................251, 278
Keimann, Christian..45
Kelly, John..74, 113, 156, 443
Kelly, Thomas...127, 216, 217
Ken, Thomas..334, 582, 592
Kennedy, Benjamin H.....................................*447*

Kethe, William..233
Key, Francis Scott...618
Kingo, Thomas H.............147, 299, 316, 319, 320, 470, 510
Kinner, Samuel...312
Kitchin, George W...579
Klug, Ronald A..556
Knapp, Albert...298
Koren, Ulrik V..252
Kretzmann, Paul E....................................*20, 464*
Krieger, W. Harry..535
Krohn, Julius L..425
Kuschel, Harlyn J.....................................428, 552

Landstad, Magnus B........................32, 211, 306, 503
Latin antiphon..522
Latin chant...273
Latin hymn................................15, 23, 31, 34, 96, 141,
                                  157, 191, 309, 528, 531, 583, 595
Latin sequence...150
Latin trope...266
Laudamus...*522*
Laufer, Calvin W...491
Laurenti, Laurentius...7
Lawrenz, John C...560
Leeson, Jane E...*150,* 508
Lettermann, Henry L................................513, 557
Lindemann, Johann..346
Little Children's Book......................................*68*
Liturgy of St. James..361
Longfellow, Henry Wadsworth........................*554*
Löwenstern, Matthäus Apelles von................258
Lowry, Somerset T. C......................................492
Loy, Matthias....................282, 287, 288, *308, 378, 514,* 596
Ludämilia Elisabeth..348
Lundeen, Joel W..*48,* 307
Luther, Martin...............2, 33, 38, 39, 53, 88, 161, 176, 190,
                                  200, 201, 202, 203, 205, 262,
                                  267, 269, 271, 285, 305, 313,
                                  317, 377, 410, 522, 534, 574
Lutheran Book of Worship..........................86, *439*
Lutherische Hand-Büchlein.............................230
Lyra Davidica..*157*
Lyte, Henry F...249, 465, 588

Mackay, Margaret...605
Madson, Norman A.................................*51, 510*
Magdeburg, Joachim......................................447
Mann, Frederick...468
Mant, Richard..555
March, Daniel...573
Mason, Arthur J..*316*
Massie, Richard.........39, 53, 161, 192, 377, 419, 430, 574
Mattes, John C...*186*
Maude, Mary F...426
Maurus, Rhabanus..................................177, 178, 188
Maxwell, Mary H...578
McComb, William...385
Medley, Samuel..152
Meeter, Daniel J...292
Melanchthon, Philipp.....................................196
Mentzer, Johann.............................194, 242, 536
Meyer, Anna M...*143*
Meyfart, Johann M..212
Miller, John...*224*
Milligan, James L..13
Milman, Henry H......................................132, 133

939

AUTHORS, TRANSLATORS, SOURCES

Mohr, Franz Joseph 60
Möller, Johann J. 158
Monsell, John S. B. 220, 457, 559, 614
Montgomery, James 80, 93, 104, 106, 116,
                               213, 222, 226, 412, 547
Morgen-und-Abend-segen 478
Morison, John 90
Mote, Edward 382
Moultrie, Gerard *361*
Mowbray, David 507
Mueller, John T. *274*
Mühlmann, Johannes 585
Münsterisch Gesangbuch 369
Murray, Robert 489

Nachtenhöfer, Kaspar F. 126
Neale, John M. *23, 35, 36, 91, 96, 122, 131*,
                         142, 165, 166, 197, 198, *214*,
                         309, 531, 583, 591, 595
Neander, Joachim 234
Nelson, Horatio B. 552
Neu-vermehrtes vollständiges Gesanbuch 393
Neumann, Caspar 461
Neumark, Georg C. 444
Neumeister, Erdmann 304, 403
Newbolt, Michael R. 579
Newton, John 322, 326, 358, 379, 409
Nicolai, Philipp 79, 206
Niedling, Johann 186
Noel, Caroline M. 344
Nouveau recueil de cantiques 63

O'Neill, Judith B. 301
Oakeley, Frederick *55*
Olearius, Johann G. 8, 20, 464
Olearius, Johannes 11, 282
Olson, Ernst W. *449*
Olsson, Olof *135*
Omeis, Magnus D. 126
Opitz, Martin 81
Osler, Edward 458, 524

Palmer, Ray 402
Perronet, Edward 370
Perry, Michael A. 264, 275, 575
Peter, Philip A. *207*
Petersen, Victor O. *134*
Pfefferkorn, Georg M. 477
Pfeil, Christoph C. L. von. 506
Phelps, Sylvanus D. 488
Phillimore, Greville 580
Pietsch, Frieda *366*
Pisek, Vincent *59*
Pisne duchovni . . . Cithara Sanctorum 450
Plumptre, Edward H. 520, 540
Polack, W. Gustave *126, 144, 204, 223, 262,
                                266, 478*, 542, 623
Pollock, Thomas B. 139
Pott, Francis *148*
Preiswerk, Samuel 530
Prudentius, Aurelius Clemens. 35
Psalm 51:10-12 272
Psalms and Hymns 208
Pye, Henry J. 77

Quinn, James 497, 518
Quitmeyer, Elizabeth *88*

Rambach, Johann J. 294, 598
Rankin, Jeremiah E. 327, 328
Reed, Andrew 183
Rees, John P. 379
Rees, Timothy 182
Reid, William W. Sr. 482
Reusner, Adam 448
Reynolds, William M *2*
Rimbach, J. Adam *452*
Ringwaldt, Bartholomäus 185, 207
Rinkart, Martin 610
Rist, Johann 44, 70, 137, 314
Ristad, Ditlef G. *431*
Robinson, Charles S. 473
Robinson, Joseph A. 95
Rodigast, Samuel 429
Rothe, Johann A. 386
Ruopp, Johann F. 471
Rupprecht, Oliver C. *164*, 511
Russell, Arthur T *14, 34, 86*
Ryden, Ernest E. *244, 425*
Rygh, George A. T. *147, 162, 180, 299, 599*

Savonarola, Girolamo 108
Saward, Michael 297
Scandinavian folk hymn 254
Scandinavian hymn 323
Schaefer, William J. *289, 536*
Schaeffer, Charles W. *181, 453*
Schalling, Martin M. 434
Scharlemann, Dorothy I. 597
Scheffler, Johann 453, 476
Scheidt, Christian L. 384
Schenck, Hartmann 330
Schirmer, Michael 184
Schlegel, Catharina A.von 415
Schmolck, Benjamin 255, 295
Schneegass, Cyriacus 72
Schröder, Johann H. 290
Schuette, Conrad H. L. *584*
Schultz, Dorothy R. 490
Schultz, Michael D 548
Schulz-Widmar, Russell 601
Schumacher, Bernhard 512
Schütz, Johann J. 236
Scriven, Joseph M. 411
Sedulius, Coelius 39, 91
Seiss, Joseph A. *369*
Selnecker, Nikolaus 541, 596
Seltz, Martin L. *22*
Shirley, Walter 111
Sloan, John M. *455*
Smeby, Oluf H. *32, 185, 325*
Smith, Donald E. 505
Smith, W. Chalmers 240
Spaeth, Harriet R. *46, 252, 362*
Spannaus, Olive Wise 521
Spee, Friedrich von 22, 137
Spegel, Haquin 135
Spencer, Robert N. 517
Spengler, Lazarus 378

Speratus, Paul 390
Spitta, Karl J. P. 427
Steele, Anne..102
Stegmann, Josua 333
Stephenson, Isabella S. 504
Steurlein, Johann 71
Sthen, Hans C. 362
Stinton, Margaret..237
Stolshagen, Kaspar 164
Stone, Samuel J. 538
Strömme, Peer O. *319, 320*
Svedberg, Jesper 408
Sveeggen, Peter A. *51, 364*
Swedish hymn 364
Symphonia Sirenum Selectarum 148

Taylor, R. E. *598*
Taylor, Thomas R. 417
Tersteegen, Gerhard 224
The Crown of Jesus, Part 2 63
The Lutheran Hymnal *14, 40, 42, 43, 79, 100, 105,*
117, 167, 176, 202, 205, 210,
219, 267, 310, 317, 349, 378,
418, 429, 448, 476, 534, 577, 616
The Lutheran Hymnary *211, 323*
The Psalms of David in Meeter 360
The Sabbath Hymn Book *33*
Theodulph of Orleans 131
Thilo, Valentin...14, 366
Thomas `a Kempis 371
Thomson, Mary A. 570
Threlfall, Jeannette 130
Thring, Godfrey...........................*26, 341, 499*
Tiefel, James P..89
Tisserand, Jean 165
Toplady, Augustus M. 381, 389
Troutbeck, John *44*
Tucker, F. Bland 350, 501
Tuttiett, Lawrence...75

Unknown 193, *221, 273, 419,* 573, *606,* 615

Vajda, Jaroslav J. 54, 172, 218, 231,
300, 332, 342, *450*
Vetter, Georg 168

Vineyard Songs..68
Voss, Arthur P. *395*

Wade, John F..55
Wallin, Johann O. 408
Walter, Johann 10
Walther, C. F. W..143
Walworth, Clarence A. *278*
Wandersleben, Martin 223
Watts, Isaac....................62, 84, 125, 128, 129, 136, 225,
227, 238, 250, 261, 286, 359, 374,
383, 398, 441, 462, 475, 509, 512
Webb, Benjamin *371*
Wegelin, Josua 173
Weingärtner, Sigismund 438
Weisse, Michael 155
Weissel, Georg 3, 4, *395*
Wendell, Claus A..307
Wesley, Charles 6, 29, 61, 149, 157, 175,
340, 357, 365, 456
Wesley, John B..*376, 479*
Westendorf, Omer E. 318
Wexelsen, Inger M. 51
Whiting, William 517
Wilde, Jane F. *108*
Wilkinson, Kate B. *467*
Williams, Peter *331*
Williams, William *331*
Winkworth, Catherine *3, 4, 11, 17, 28, 37, 38, 45, 64,*
70, 71, 78, 94, 114, 117, 137, 155,
167, 184, 189, 206, 212, 221, 230 , 255,
257, 258, 263, 270, 294, 295, 302, 305,
311, 314, 346, 349, 404, 413, 418, 421,
423, 434, 438, 448, 459, 472, 476, 506,
530, 567, 569, 576, 585, 606, 608, 610
Woodd, Basil 87
Woodward, George R. 160
Wordsworth, Christopher 82, 174, 487, 548
Work, John W. 57
Wortman, Denis..543
Wren, Brian A. 526

Young, John F. *60*

Zinzendorf, Nicolaus L. von...................*376, 422*

COMPOSERS AND SOURCES OF HYMNS

Numbers in italics indicate settings.

A Compilation of Genuine Church Music 374
A Supplement to the Kentucky Harmony 118, 493
African Angoni war song 146
African-American spiritual..................57, 119, 539, 564
Ahle, Johann R. 158, 221, 295, 330, 461, 565
Albrecht, Martin 199
Alte Catholische Geistliche Kirchengeseng 36, 47
American folk tune 215
Andächtige Haus-Kirche 9, 383, 569
Ander Theil Des Dressdenischen Gesangbuchs.................64
Ander Theil Des Erneuerten Gesang-Buchs................234
Anthes, Friedrich K. 336, 339, 560
Antiphoner (Grenoble).........................196, 502, 563
Antiphoner (Paris) 343, 558, 581
Arnatt, Ronald 264

As hymnodus sacer 170, 223, 404, 471, 514, 547
Ausserlesene. . .Geistliche Kirchengesäng..............171, 186,
250, 366
Ausserlesenes . . . GesangBuchlein 43

Bach, C. P. E..27
Bach, J. S. *44*, 95, *346, 424, 604*
Backer, Bruce R........................*81, 86, 109, 118,* 151, *154,*
187, 205, 228, 245, 448, 464,
486, 493, 553, 570, 580
Baker, Henry W. 446, 504
Bancroft, Henry H. 13
Barham-Gould, A. Cyril *467*
Barnby, Joseph *251, 387, 473, 488, 573, 589, 600*
Barthelemon, Francois H. *582*

941

COMPOSERS AND SOURCES

Basque carol 24
Beck, Theodore A. *25, 142, 352, 450*
Beethoven, Ludwig van 169
Bender, Jan O. *141*, 400, *614*
Bloedel, Elfred *1, 9, 32, 43, 56, 89, 120, 181, 216,*
229, 246, 254, 264, 283, 288, 380,
420, 440, 445, 468, 491, 498, 516, 545
Bobb, Barry L. 456, 513
Bohemian carol 59
Boltze, Georg G. 452
Bortniansky, Dimitri S. 548
Bourgeois, Louis 102, 378, 413
Bradbury, William B. 397, 605
Bunjes, Paul G. *22, 29, 35, 87, 93, 137, 147, 152,*
233, 247, 267, 271, 314, 316, 349, 358,
432, 435, 456, 500, 513, 523, 544, 547, 616
Burleigh, Harry T. *539*
Burnam, Jack W. 17

Cantica Laudis... 213
Cantionale Germanicum 71, 230, 288, 298, 516
Choral-Buch . . . Brüder-Gemeinen 432
Choralbuch für Volkschulen 575
Christlich Neu-vermehrt . . . Gesangbuch 212
Christliche Hauss und Tisch Musica 585
Cinquante Pseaumes 168
Clarke, Jeremiah 217, 301, 303, 308, 519
Columbian Harmony 379
Concentus novi 257, 403
Conkey, Ithamar 345
Converse, Charles C. 411
Corbeille, Pierre de 149, 175
Cothran, Jeff *496*
Croft, William 243, 441, 620
Crüger, Johann 18, 37, 40, 117, 145, 156, 167, 225,
227, 302, 311, 349, 512, 610, 616
Cummings, William H. *61*
Cutts, Peter W. 495

Dachstein, Wolfgang 100
Daman, William 128, 138
Darwall, John 322, 528, 618
Das grosse Cantional 114
Das . . . vollkommenes Musicalisch-Choral-Buch 348
Davids Himlische Harpffen 448
Davids Psalmen 160
Decius, Nikolaus 69, 263, 268
Den danske Psalmebog 325
Der Bussfertige Sünder 134
Der Lxvj. Deus Misereatur 574
Distler, Hugo 527
Doane, William H. 399
Dorsey, Thomas A. 451
Douglas, Charles W. 23, *119*
Drese, Adam 422
Dretzel, Cornelius H. 194, 384
Dykes, John B. 116, 136, 195, 338, 340, 373, 517, 542

Ebeling, Johann G. 394, 428, 430, 580
Edwards, John D. 501
Egenolff, Christian 202, 425
Eggert, Kurt J. 99, 140, 219, 392, 396, 602
Ein New Gesengbuchlen 180
Ein Schlesich singebüchlein 42
Elvey, George J. 82, 341, 376, 391, 613, 617
Emerson, Luther O. *590*

Emskirchner Choralbuch 70, 310
Enchiridion Geistlike Lede und Psalmen 163
Enchiridion...zum Schwartzen Horn 204, 511
Engel, James E. *48, 68, 151, 392, 492,* 621
English ballad 67
English carol 52
English folk tune 481, 520
English melody 66, 96, 371
Erbaulicher Musicalischer Christen-Schatz 108, 111, 354,
380, 576, 577
Etlich Christlich lider 72, 173, 299, 377, 390, 393
Evans, David *388, 552*
Ewing, Alexander C. 214
Eyn Enchiridion oder Handbüchlein 33, 39, 86,
109, 176, 205
Eyn schönn Lied 437

Ferguson, John *363*
Figulus, Wolfgang 73
Filitz, Friedrich 103, 436
Finnish folk tune 244, 388, 552
Fischer, William G. 562
Fishel, Donald E. 154
Frank, Peter 478
Fremder, Alfred *320*
French folk tune 29, 361
French melody 159, 222
Fritsch, Ahasverus 20, 477

Gaelic melody 297, 497, 505
Gardiner, William 360
Gastoldi, Giovanni G. 346
Gastorius, Severus 429
Gauntlett, Henry J. 50
Geistliche Deutsche Lieder 164
Geistliche lieder auffs new gebessert 21, 38, 177,
185, 207, 208,
291, 313, 506
Geistliche Lieder D. Martini Lutheri 541
Geistliche Lieder zu Wittemberg 203, 282, 287
Geistliche Volkslieder 127
Geistreiches Gesang-Buch (Darmstadt) 26, 126, 508
Geist-reiches Gesang-Buch (Halle) 3, 76, 87,
226, 351
Geist-reiches Gesang-Buch (Halle, 4th ed.) 431
George, Graham 132
Gerike, Henry V. 172
German folk tune 48, 197
German melody 34, 285
Gesang-Buch . . . der Herzogl . . . Hofkapelle ..130, 275, 615
Gesangbuch . . . Psalmen Geistliche Lieder ...188, 262, 567
Gesangbuch . . . Psalmen unnd KirchenLieder 101
Gesius, Bartholomäus 453
Geystliche gesangk Buchleyn 2, 28, 88, 190,
192, 269, 317
Giardini, Felice de 193
Gibbons, Orlando 183
Gieseke, Richard W. *49, 77, 161, 162, 294,*
306, 443, 477, 622
Gläser, Carl G. 491
Goss, John 58, 359
Gould, John E. 433
Gounod, Charles F. 592
Gradual (Prague) 450
Gray, Alan 15
Gruber, Franz X. 60

942

COMPOSERS AND SOURCES

Hammerschmidt, Andreas 45
Handel, George F. 62
Harding, James P. 92
Harmonischer Lieder-Schatz 261, 443, 476
Harwood, Basil *196, 563*
Hassler, Hans Leo *21,* 105
Hastings, Thomas 389
Hatton, John C. 152
Havergal, Frances R. 427
Havergal, William H. *249,* 462, *463,* 469
Haweis, Thomas 12
Haydn, Franz Joseph 277
Helder, Bartholomäus 97
Herman, Nikolaus 41, 90, 123, 480, 584, 586, 591
Hillert, Richard W. 88, 97, 265, 335, 342, *482, 521*
Himmlische Harmony 137
Hine, Stuart W. K. *256*
Hoff, Erik C. 252
Holden, Oliver 370
Hopkins, Edward J. 321
Hopp, Roy A. 292
Hopson, Hal H. 498
Horn, Johann 142
Howard, Samuel 499, 572
Hughes, John 237, 523
Hundert . . . geistlicher Arien 423, 472
Hymnal and Order of Service 7
Hymns Ancient and Modern 157

Ireland, John N. 110
Irish folk tune 367
Irish melody 375
Isaac, Heinrich 113, 587
Israeli melody 363

Jackisch, Frederick F. *121*
Jewish folk melody 496
Johann Störls . . . Noten-Buch 85, 535, 554
Johnson, David N. 247
Joncas, Michael 440
Joseph, Georg 274

Katholisches Gesangbuch 278
Kirbye, George 259
Kirchen gesenge 522
Kirchengeseng 141
Kirkpatrick, William J. 68
Knapp, William 198, 466, 601
Knecht, Justin H. 409, 426
Knudsen, Peder 51
Kocher, Conrad 83, 612
König, Johann B. 121, 242, 294, 296, 319, 386
Koral-Melodier 510
Kunwaldsky, Matthias 521
Kurtzweilige Teutsche Lieder 438

Lang, Craig Sellar 234
Latin credo melody 271
Latin melody 5, 16, 53, 144, 155, 161, 209, 534
Lawes, Henry 315, 483
Layriz, Friedrich L. C. 290
Lemke, August 4
Leonard, George *102, 127, 160, 336, 413, 606*
Leupold, Ulrich S. *244*
Lieder-Buch für Kleinkinder-Schulen 593

Lindeman, Ludvig M. 106, 153, 362, 529
Llyfr Tonau Cynulleidfaol 518
Löhner, Johann 421
Lovelace, Austin C. *379*
Löwenstern, Matthäus Apelles von 258
Luther, Martin 200, 201, 267, 305,
                                     306, 407, 410, 479, 608
Lyra Davidica 157

Mann, Arthur H. *50,* 368
Mason, Lowell 112, 125, 402, 458, 494, 515, 557, 571
Mayer, Johann D. 468, 487
Mendelssohn, Felix 61
Messiter, Arthur H. 540
Meyer, Franz H. C. 598
Möck, Christian 32, 210
Moldenhauer, Kermit G. *2, 14, 30, 31, 34, 40, 42, 70,*
                                     72, 73, 74, 79, 80, 108, 113,
                                     117, 131, 140, 144, 178, 186, 192,
                                     195, 206, 266, 275, 276, 282, 285,
                                     297, 317, 355, 374, 385, 393, 412,
                                     419, 438, 460, 502, 503, 505, 507,
                                     524, 525, 538, 568, 577, 602, 610
Monk, William H. 15, *133,* 216, 381,
                                            441, 485, 555, 588
Musae Sioniae, VII 10, 314
Musicalisch Hand-Buch 89, 133, 189, 229, 607
Musicalisches Gesangbuch 604
Musika Teutsch 445, 596

Neander, Joachim 224, 255
Nederlandtsch Gedenckclanck 609
Nelson, Ronald A. *7, 353, 361*
Neu-verfertigtes Darmstädtisches Gesang-Buch 8, 304
Neu-vermehrtes . . . Gesangbuch, 3rd ed. 78, 181, 270,
                                            279, 459, 460, 546
Neumark, Georg C. 414, 444
New Catechismus Gesangbüchlein 14
New Ordentlich Gesangbuch 424
New-vermehrte Christliche Seelenharpf 235
Nicholson, Sydney H. 579
Nicolai, Philipp 49, 79, 162, 184, 206, 241, 455, 622
Norwegian folk tune 364, 550
Nouveau recueil de cantiques 63

Oliver, Henry K. 347
Oude en Nieuwe Hollantse . . . Contradansen 182, 532
Owen, William 352

Palestrina, Giovanni P. da 148
Parry, Joseph 357
Pelz, Walter L. 341
Pettman, Charles E. 24
Pfälzische Kirchenordnung 273
Piae Cantiones Ecclesiasticae 56
Plainsong melody 23, 35, 266, 595
Porter, Hugh *57*
Praetorius, Michael *10, 36, 47*
Prichard, Rowland H. 365, 465, 486, 603
Proulx, Richard T. 246, 489, 527, 579, *617*
Psalmodia Evangelica, Part II 84
Purcell, Henry 77, 531

Quampen, Wilhelm *45, 76, 367, 461, 480, 555, 586*

943

COMPOSERS AND SOURCES

Recueil de plusieurs chansons 418
Redhead, Richard 104, 385
Redner, Lewis H. 65
Reimann, Johann B. 232
Reinagle, Alexander R. 358, 405, 509
Repository of Sacred Music, Part Second 25, 484
Reuter, Friedrich O. 293, 329, 536, 599
Reynolds, William J. *442*
Rheinfelssisch . . . Gesangbuch 22, 91, 544
Roberts, John *150*
Röntgen, Julius *532*

Sammlung alter und neuer . . . Melodien 135, 500
Sarum plainsong 31, 178
Sateren, Leland B. 107, 115, *318*
Schäffer-Belustigung . . . Hirthen-Lieder 464
Schalk, Carl F. 54, *96*, 122, *168, 182,* 218, 231,
                                263, *315, 343, 483, 522, 595*
Schmidt, Johann E. 30
Scholefield, Clement C. 594
Schop, Johann 44, 147, 253, 283, 408, 545
Schrader, Jack 406
Schreiber, Lawrence P. 350
Schröter, Leonhart 93, 289
Schultz, Ralph C. 490
Schulz, Johann A. P. 46
Schumacher, Bernhard 139, 416
Schumann, Robert A. 561
Scott, K. Lee 191
Second Supplement to Psalmody in Miniature 549
Sermisy, Claude de 435, 447
Shilling, Ronald L. 94, 145, 208, 253, *262, 479*
Sibelius, Jean J. C. 415
Silcher, P. Friedrich 439
Silesian folk tune 369
Smart, Henry T. 80, 166, 174, 281, 578
Smith, Alfred M. 482, 525
Smith, Kenneth D. *326, 530*
Sohren, Peter 312
Southern Harmony 120
Spanish melody 124
Stainer, John 382
Stanford, Charles V. 248
Steurlein, Johann 614
Stobäus, Johann 395
Störl, Johann G. C. 220
Sullivan, Arthur S. 417, 537
Swedish folk tune 256, 300, 449

Tallis, Thomas 597
Terry, R. Harold *260*
Teschner, Melchior 19, 94, 131, 419
The Christian Lyre 489
The CL Psalms of David 324, 356, 420
The Methodist Harmonist 457
The Parish Choir 401

The Revivalist 492
The Whole Booke of Psalmes 398, 412, 454, 524
Thesaurus Musicus 619
Tomer, William G. 327
Tredinnick, Noël H. 228
Trente quatre Pseaumes de David 11, 233, 286, 309, 316,
                                320, 323, 334, 470, 475, 543
Tscherlitzky, Johann H. 75

Unknown 6, 623

Vaughan Williams, Ralph 66, *171,* 179, 202, *250,*
                                328, *332,* 344, 425,
                                481, 520, 551, *611*
Vulpius, Melchior *28,* 98, 165, 236, 307, 333, 606

Wade, John F. 55
Walder, Johann J. 284
Walther, C. F. W. 143
Warren, George W. 331
Weaving, T. H. *497*
Webb, Charles H. *215*
Webb, George J. 474, 566
Weisse, Michael 17
Welsh folk tune 240, 260, 318
Welsh melody 332, 337, 590, 611
Werner, Johann G. 249
Wesley, Samuel S. 372, 538, 559
Weyse, Christoph E. F. 211, 254
Whinfield, Walter G. 239
White, Benjamin F. 353
Willcocks, David V. 55, 61
Williams, Aaron 1, 238, 533
Williams, Donna L. 355
Williams, J. Paul 355
Williams, Robert 150
Williams, Thomas J. 280
Wilson, David G. 245
Wilson, Hugh 129
Wilson, John W. 526
Winer, Johann G. 272
Witt, Christian F. 326, 463, 530
Wood, Dale 556, 583
Woodward, George R. 5, 16

Young, Michael E. 370, 441

Zimmermann, Heinz W. 442
Zwey Bücher . . . Tabulatur 434

TUNE INDEX

ABERYSTWYTH	357
ACCLAMATIONS	406
ACH BLEIB BEI UNS	541
ACH GOTT UND HERR	170
ACH GOTT VOM HIMMELREICHE	10, 314
ACH GOTT, VOM HIMMEL SIEH DAREIN	205
ACH, WAS SOLL ICH SÜNDER MACHEN	464
ADAM	396
ADESTE FIDELES	55
ALDINE	246
ALL EHR UND LOB	188, 262, 567
ALLEIN GOTT IN DER HÖH SEI EHR	69, 263
ALLEIN ZU DIR	437
ALLELUIA NO. 1	154
ALLES IST AN GOTTES SEGEN	421
AMERICA	619
AN WASSERFLÜSSEN BABYLON	100
ANGEL'S STORY	368
ANGELUS	274
ANTHES	336, 339, 560
ANTIOCH	62
AR HYD Y NOS	332, 590, 611
ASCENDED TRIUMPH	172
ASCENSION	13
AUCH JETZT MACHT GOTT	575
AUF, AUF, MEIN HERZ	156
AUF MEINEN LIEBEN GOTT	438
AURELIA	372, 538, 559
AUS MEINES HERZENS GRUNDE	14
AUS TIEFER NOT	305
AUSTRIA	277
AZMON	491
BALM IN GILEAD	564
BEACH SPRING	353
BEATITUDO	340
BEATUS VIR	521
BELMONT	360
BEVAN	359
BOYLSTON	494
BRIDEGROOM	495
BRYN CALFARIA	352
BUNESSAN	297, 505
CANONBURY	561
CANTATE DOMINO	245
CAPETOWN	436
CHESTERFIELD	12
CHRIST IST ERSTANDEN	144
CHRIST LAG IN TODESBANDEN	161
CHRIST UNSER HERR ZUM JORDAN KAM	88
CHRISTE SANCTORUM	343, 558, 581
CHRISTUM WIR SOLLEN LOBEN SCHON	39
CHRISTUS, DER IST MEIN LEBEN	333, 606
CHRISTUS IST ERSTANDEN	155
CONDITOR ALME SIDERUM	31
CONSOLATION	25
CONVERSE	411
CORDIS DONUM	43
CORONAE	216
CORONATION	370
COWPER	112
CRADLE SONG	68
CROFT'S 136TH	620
CRUCIFER	579
CWM RHONDDA	237, 523
DARWALL'S 148TH	322, 528, 618
DEN SIGNEDE DAG	211, 254
DENVER	292
DEO GRACIAS	96, 371
DER AM KREUZ	121, 319
DER LIEBEN SONNE LICHT UND PRACHT	431
DER TAG, DER IST SO FREUDENREICH	180
DETROIT	118, 493
DEUS TUORUM MILITUM	196, 502, 563
DIADEMATA	341
DIE GÜLDNE SONNE	430
DIES IRAE	209
DIR, DIR, JEHOVAH	189
DISTLER	527
DIVINUM MYSTERIUM	35
DIX	83, 612
DOROTHY	490
DOUSMAN	568
DU LEBENSBROT, HERR JESU CHRIST	312
DUKE STREET	152
DUNDEE	324, 356, 420
EARTH AND ALL STARS	247
EASTER HYMN	157
EBENEZER	280
ECCE AGNUS	101
EIN FESTE BURG	200, 201
EINS IST NOT	290
EIRENE	427
ELLACOMBE	130, 275, 615
ELLERS	321
ENERGY	381, 485, 555
ENGELBERG	248
EPIPHANY	81
ERHALT UNS, HERR	203, 282, 287
ERMUNTRE DICH	44
ES IST DAS HEIL	299, 390
ES IST EIN ROS	36, 47
ES IST GENUG	158, 565
ES IST GEWISSLICH	185, 207, 208
ES IST KEIN TAG	468, 487
ES WOLLE GOTT UNS GNÄDIG SEIN	574
EVAN	462
EVENING HYMN	592
EVENTIDE	588
EWING	214
FAHRE FORT	30
FANG DEIN WERK	478
FARLEY CASTLE	315, 483
FEDERAL STREET	347
FESTIVAL CANTICLE	265
FINLANDIA	415
FIRM FOUNDATION	416
FOREST GREEN	66
FORTUNATUS NEW	122
FOX VALLEY	621

TUNE INDEX

FRANCONIA	296
FRANKLIN	187, 553
FRED TIL BOD	153
FREDRICK PLACE	507
FREU DICH SEHR	11, 320, 470
FREUET EUCH, IHR CHRISTEN ALLE	45
FREUT EUCH, IHR LIEBEN CHRISTEN	93, 289
FRÖHLICH SOLL MEIN HERZE SPRINGEN	37
GABRIEL'S MESSAGE	24
GALILEAN	573
GAUDEAMUS PARITER	142
GEDULD, DIE SOLLN WIR HABEN	585
GELOBET SEIST DU, JESU CHRIST	33
GELOBT SEI GOTT	165
GETHSEMANE	104, 385
GIFT OF LOVE	498
GIVE ME JESUS	355
GLORIA	63
GLORIFICATION	75
GLORY BE TO THE FATHER	273
GO TELL IT	57
GOD BE WITH YOU	327
GOD OF LOVE	602
GOD WAS THERE ON CALVARY	140
GOTT DER VATER WOHN UNS BEI	192
GOTT SEI DANK DURCH ALLE WELT	76, 226
GOTT SEI GELOBET UND GEBENEDEIET	317
GOTTES SOHN IST KOMMEN	17
GOTTLOB, ES GEHT NUNMEHR ZU ENDE	135, 500
GRANTON	342
GREAT WHITE HOST	550
GREENSLEEVES	67
GROSSER GOTT, WIR LOBEN DICH	278
GUDS MENIGHED, SYNG	252
GUIDE ME	331
HAF TRONES LAMPA FÄRDIG	7
HAMBURG	125
HANKEY	562
HANOVER	243
HEAVEN IS MY HOME	417
HELFT MIR GOTT'S GÜTE PREISEN	73
HER KOMMER DINE ARME SMAA	46
HERR CHRIST, DER EINIG GOTTS SOHN	86, 109
HERR, ICH HABE MISSGEHANDELT	302
HERR JESU CHRIST, DICH ZU UNS WEND	71, 230, 288, 298, 516
HERR JESU CHRIST, MEINS	223, 404, 471, 514, 547
HERRE JESU KRIST	362
HERZLICH LIEB HAB ICH DICH, O HERR	434
HERZLICH TUT MICH VERLANGEN	105
HERZLIEBSTER JESU	117
HEUT TRIUMPHIERET GOTTES SOHN	164
HÖCHSTER PRIESTER	576
HOW GREAT THOU ART	256
HUMILITY	58
HYFRYDOL	365, 465, 486, 603
HYMN TO JOY	169
ICH DANK DIR, LIEBER HERRE	445, 596
ICH FREU MICH IN DEM HERREN	97
ICH HALTE TREULICH STILL	604
ICH SINGE DIR	261, 443
ICH STERBE TÄGLICH	70, 310
ICH WILL DICH LIEBEN	476
IN BABILONE	182, 532
IN DICH HAB ICH GEHOFFET	448
IN DIR IST FREUDE	346
IN DULCI JUBILO	34
IN GOTTES NAMEN FAHREN WIR	285
IN TREMBLING HANDS	199
INNOCENTS	159, 222
IRBY	50
ISLEWORTH	499, 572
ITALIAN HYMN	193
JAM LUCIS	595
JEG ER SAA GLAD	51
JEG VIL MIG HERREN LOVE	510
JERUSALEM, DU HOCHGEBAUTE STADT	212
JESAIA, DEM PROPHETEN	267
JESU KREUZ, LEIDEN UND PEIN	98, 307
JESU, MEINE FREUDE	349
JESU, MEINES LEBENS LEBEN	114
JESUS CHRISTUS, UNSER HEILAND, DER VON UNS	313
JESUS, JESUS, NICHTS ALS JESUS	348
JESUS, MEINE ZUVERSICHT	145, 167
JUBILATE DEO	228
JUST AS I AM	387
KING'S WESTON	344
KINGLY LOVE	335
KINGSFOLD	481, 520
KIRKEN DEN ER ET GAMMELT HUS	529
KOMM, GOTT SCHÖPFER	177
KOMM, HEILIGER GEIST, HERRE GOTT	176
KOMM, O KOMM, DU GEIST DES LEBENS	181
KREMSER	609
KUORTANE	388, 552
KYRIE, GOTT VATER	266
LADUE CHAPEL	264
LAKEWOOD	456, 513
LANCASHIRE	166
LAND OF REST	215
LASSET UNS MIT JESU ZIEHEN	452
LASST UNS ALLE	64
LASST UNS ERFREUEN	171, 250
LAUDES DOMINI	251
LAUREL	583
LIEBSTER JESU, WIR SIND HIER	221, 295, 330, 461
LITTLE FLOCK	442
LLANFAIR	150
LLEDROD	518
LOBE DEN HERREN	234
LOBE DEN HERREN, O MEINE SEELE	235
LOBT GOTT DEN HERREN, IHR HEIDEN ALL	236
LOBT GOTT, IHR CHRISTEN	41, 90
LORD, REVIVE US	492
LOVE UNKNOWN	110
MACHT HOCH DIE TÜR	3
MACHS MIT MIR, GOTT	453
MAGDALEN	382
MALDWYN	337
MANGER SONG	54
MARION	540
MARLEE	107, 115
MARTYRDOM	129
MCKEE	539

TUNE INDEX

MEIN SCHÖPFER, STEH MIR BEI 598
MEINEN JESUM LASS ICH NICHT 8, 304
MELITA 517, 542
MENDELSSOHN 61
MENDON 457
MERIBAH 458
MERRIAL 589
MERTON 15
MILWAUKEE 4
MISSIONARY HYMN 557, 571
MIT FREUDEN ZART 168
MIT FRIED UND FREUD 269
MITTEN WIR IM LEBEN SIND 534
MORNING HYMN 582
MORNING STAR 92
MÜDE BIN ICH 593
MUNICH 78, 279

NAAR MIT ÖIE 106
NARODIL SE KRISTUS PAN 59
NATIONAL CITY 350
NCHEU 146
NETTLETON 484
NEW BRITAIN 379
NEW ULM 329
NEW YEAR 74
NICAEA 195
NOT UNTO US 392
NOW 218, 231
NUN BITTEN WIR 190
NUN DANKET ALL 225, 227, 512
NUN DANKET ALLE GOTT 610
NUN FREUT EUCH,
  LIEBEN CHRISTEN 72, 173, 377, 393
NUN KOMM, DER HEIDEN HEILAND 2, 28
NUN LOB, MEIN SEEL 257, 403
NUN PREISET ALLE 258
NYT YLÖS, SIELUNI 244

O DASS ICH TAUSEND
  ZUNGEN HÄTTE (DRETZEL) 194, 384
O DASS ICH TAUSEND
  ZUNGEN HÄTTE (KÖNIG) 242, 294, 386
O DU LIEBE MEINER LIEBE 108, 380, 577
O DURCHBRECHER ALLER BANDE 87, 351
O GOTT, DU FROMMER GOTT (I) 424
O GOTT, DU FROMMER GOTT (II) 459, 460, 546
O GROSSER GOTT 85, 535
O HEILAND, REISS DIE HIMMEL AUF 22, 91, 544
O HEILIGE DREIFALTIGKEIT 480, 584, 586, 591
O HERRE GOTT, DEIN GÖTTLICH WORT 204, 511
O JERUSALEM, DU SCHÖNE 220
O JESU CHRIST, DEIN KRIPPLEIN IST 40
O JESU CHRISTE, WAHRES LICHT 9, 383, 569
O JESU, WARUM LEGST DU MIR 232
O JESULEIN SÜSS 186, 366
O LAMM GOTTES, UNSCHULDIG 268
O MEIN JESU, ICH MUSS STERBEN 127
O PERFECT LOVE 600
O TRAURIGKEIT, O HERZELEID 137
O WELT, ICH MUSS DICH LASSEN 113, 587
O WIE SELIG 554
OH, BLESSED HOME 503
OH, COME, MY SOUL 99
OLD 120TH 454
OLD 124TH 309, 543

OLD HUNDREDTH 233, 286, 316, 323, 334
OLIVET 402, 515
OM HIMMERIGES RIGE 325
ON EAGLES' WINGS 440
ORIENTIS PARTIBUS 149, 175

PÁN BŮH 450
PATMOS 469
PICARDY 29, 361
PILOT 433
PLEADING SAVIOR 489
POTSDAM 95
PRECIOUS LORD 451
PRINCESS EUGENIE 364
PROMISED ONE 363
PUER NOBIS NASCITUR 5, 16, 53

QUEM PASTORES 42

RANDOLPH 328
RATHBUN 345
RATISBON 249
REDEMPTION 570
REGENT SQUARE 80, 578
RESIGNATION 374
REST 605
REUTER 293, 536, 599
REX GLORIAE 174, 281
RHOSYMEDRE 501
RINGE RECHT 111, 354
ROCKINGHAM OLD 549

ST. AGNES 373
ST. ANNE 441
ST. CLEMENT 594
ST. COLUMBA 375
ST. CRISPIN 376, 391
ST. CROSS 136
ST. DENIO 240
ST. FLAVIAN 398, 412, 524
ST. GEORGE'S, WINDSOR 82, 613, 617
ST. GERTRUDE 537
ST. HILARY 6, 623
ST. JOHN 401
ST. LEONARD'S 467
ST. LOUIS 65
ST. LUKE 303, 308, 519
ST. MAGNUS 217, 301
ST. MARY MAGDALENE 116
ST. MICHAEL 475
ST. PETER 358, 405, 509
ST. PETERSBURG 548
ST. THOMAS 1, 238, 533
SALVE FESTA DIES 179
SCHAFFE IN MIR, GOTT 272
SCHMÜCKE DICH 311, 616
SCHÖNSTER HERR JESU 369
SCHUMANN 213
SEELENBRÄUTIGAM 422
SEI DU MIR GEGRÜSSET 163
SEPTEM VERBA 139
SHADES MOUNTAIN 191
SHIBBOLET BASADEH 496
SIEH, HIER BIN ICH, EHRENKÖNIG 26, 508
SINE NOMINE 551
SLANE 367

947

SO GEHST DU NUN 126
SO NIMM DENN MEINE HÄNDE 439
SOLLT ICH MEINEM GOTT NICHT SINGEN 253
SONG 13 183
SONNE DER GERECHTIGKEIT 141
SOUTHWELL 128, 138
SPANISH CHANT 124
STEPHANOS 446, 504
STILLE NACHT 60
STRAF MICH NICHT 423, 472
STUTTGART 326, 463, 530
SUANTRAI 497
SUCH, WER DA WILL 395
SURSUM CORDA 482, 525
SUSANNA 197
SUSSEX CAROL 52

TALLIS' CANON 597
TEMPUS ADEST FLORIDUM 56
THE ASH GROVE 260, 318
THE KING'S MAJESTY 132
TO GOD BE THE GLORY 399
TOPLADY 389
TRIUMPH 151
TRURO 84
TRYGGARE KAN INGEN VARA 300, 449

UNSER HERRSCHER 255

VALET WILL ICH DIR GEBEN 19, 94, 131, 419
VATER UNSER IM
    HIMMELREICH, DER DU 306, 407, 410, 479, 608
VENI CREATOR SPIRITUS 178
VENI, EMMANUEL 23
VERLEIH UNS FRIEDEN GNÄDIGLICH 522
VICTORY 148
VIENNA 409, 426
VOLLER WUNDER 394, 580
VOM HIMMEL HOCH 21, 38
VON GOTT WILL ICH NICHT LASSEN 418
VOX DILECTI 338
VRUECHTEN 160

WACHET AUF 206, 455
WÄCHTERLIED 202, 425
WALDER 284
WALTHER 143
WAREHAM 198, 466, 601
WARUM SOLLT ICH MICH DENN GRÄMEN 428
WAS FRAG ICH NACH DER WELT 20, 477
WAS GOTT TUT 429
WAS MEIN GOTT WILL 435, 447
WEBB 474, 566
WEDDING GLORY 219
WEIL ICH JESU SCHÄFLEIN BIN 432
WEIMAR 27
WEM IN LEIDENSTAGEN 103
WENN WIR IN
    HÖCHSTEN NÖTEN SEIN 102, 378, 413
WER NUR DEN LIEBEN GOTT 414, 444
WER WEISS, WIE NAHE 32, 210
WERDE MUNTER 147, 283, 408, 545
WERE YOU THERE 119
WESTMINSTER ABBEY 77, 531
WHITFIELD 526
WIE LIEBLICH IST DER MAIEN 614
WIE SCHÖN LEUCHTET 49, 79, 162, 184, 241, 622
WIE SOLL ICH DICH EMPFANGEN 18
WINCHESTER NEW 89, 133, 229, 607
WINCHESTER OLD 259
WINTERTON 473, 488
WIR DANKEN DIR, HERR JESU CHRIST 123
WIR GLAUBEN ALL AN EINEN GOTT 270
WIR GLAUBEN ALL AN EINEN GOTT 271
WIR HATTEN GEBAUET 48
WITTENBERG NEW 400
WO GOTT ZUM HAUS 291, 506
WO SOLL ICH FLIEHEN HIN 134
WOJTKIEWICZ 556
WONDROUS LOVE 120
WOODWORTH 397
WORCESTER 239
WUNDERBARER KÖNIG 224

METRICAL INDEX

44 11 D
O JESU CHRIST, DEIN KRIPPLEIN IST 40

44 776
O TRAURIGKEIT, O HERZELEID 137

447 444 7
HERRE JESU KRIST 362

447 447
ACH GOTT UND HERR 170

447 447 D Iambic (87 87 447 447 Iambic)
O HERRE GOTT, DEIN GÖTTLICH WORT 204
WAS MEIN GOTT WILL 447

447 447 44 447
SUCH, WER DA WILL 395

448 448 44 44 8
MIT FREUDEN ZART 168

448 88 (LM)
MENDON 457

457 457 with Refrain
EARTH AND ALL STARS 247

55 8 D
BUNESSAN 297

55 88 55
SEELENBRÄUTIGAM 422

557 558
SCHÖNSTER HERR JESU 369

METRICAL INDEX

56 56 9 10 10
NUN PREISET ALLE 258

64 64 6664
HEAVEN IS MY HOME 417
WINTERTON..473, 488

65 65
MERRIAL...589
WEM IN LEIDENSTAGEN 103

65 65 D
KING'S WESTON 344
ST. MARY MAGDALENE..116

65 65 D with Refrain
ST. GERTRUDE...537
SEI DU MIR GEGRÜSSET 163

65 65 55 88
NCHEU..146

66 11 66 11 D
THE ASH GROVE 260, 318

66 64 884
ECCE AGNUS..101

66 66 4444
DARWALL'S 148TH..528, 618
LOVE UNKNOWN...110

66 66 D
ICH HALTE TREULICH STILL..................................604

66 66 66
GOTTES SOHN IST KOMMEN 17
OLD 120TH..454

66 66 66 55
IN DULCI JUBILO 34

66 66 77 77 86
MEIN SCHÖPFER, STEH MIR BEI 598

66 66 88
BEVAN...359
CROFT'S 136TH..620
DARWALL'S 148TH...322
FREDRICK PLACE...507
MARLEE..107, 115
ST. JOHN...401

66 66 888
RHOSYMEDRE...501

66 76 6
LITTLE FLOCK 442

66 77 77
AUF MEINEN LIEBEN GOTT 438
WO SOLL ICH FLIEHEN HIN 134

66 86 66
FRANKLIN 187, 553

66 86 66 44 6
DOUSMAN 568

66 88 66
SUSANNA..197

664 6664
AMERICA 619
ITALIAN HYMN 193
OLIVET..402, 515

665 665 34 86
JESU, MEINE FREUDE 349

666 666
LAUDES DOMINI...251

668 668 33 66
WUNDERBARER KÖNIG..224

67 67 with Refrain
VRUECHTEN 160

67 67 66 66
NUN DANKET ALLE GOTT......................................610
O GOTT, DU FROMMER GOTT (I)...........................424
O GOTT, DU FROMMER GOTT (II) 459, 460, 546
WAS FRAG ICH NACH DER WELT...............20, 477

67 87 89 6
FAHRE FORT 30

74 74 D
SO NIMM DENN MEINE HÄNDE 439

74 74 with Refrain
NARODIL SE KRISTUS PAN 59

75 75 D
GLORIFICATION..75

76 76
CHRISTUS, DER IST MEIN LEBEN 333, 606

76 76 Trochaic
LASST UNS ALLE 64

76 76 D
ACH GOTT VOM HIMMELREICHE 10, 314
ANGEL'S STORY 368
ANTHES...336, 339, 560
AURELIA..372, 538, 559
DISTLER..527
ELLACOMBE 130, 275, 615
EWING...214
FREUT EUCH, IHR LIEBEN CHRISTEN 93, 289
GEDULD, DIE SOLLN WIR HABEN 585
HAF TRONES LAMPA FÄRDIG 7
HERZLICH TUT MICH VERLANGEN 105
ICH DANK DIR, LIEBER HERRE 445, 596
ICH FREU MICH IN DEM HERREN 97
JEG VIL MIG HERREN LOVE...................................510
KUORTANE..388, 552
LANCASHIRE 166
MISSIONARY HYMN 557, 571

949

METRICAL INDEX

MUNICH 78, 279
TEMPUS ADEST FLORIDUM 56
VALET WILL ICH DIR GEBEN 19, 94, 131, 419
WEBB 474, 566
WIE LIEBLICH IST DER MAIEN 614
WIE SOLL ICH DICH EMPFANGEN 18

76 76 D Trochaic
FANG DEIN WERK 478
GAUDEAMUS PARITER 142
JESU KREUZ, LEIDEN UND PEIN 98, 307

76 76 D with Refrain
HANKEY 562

76 76 33 66
STRAF MICH NICHT 423, 472

76 76 66 66
AUF, AUF, MEIN HERZ 156

76 76 67 76
AUS MEINES HERZENS GRUNDE 14
HELFT MIR GOTT'S GÜTE PREISEN 73
VON GOTT WILL ICH NICHT LASSEN 418

76 76 676
ES IST EIN ROS 36, 47

76 76 76
WIR HATTEN GEBAUET 48

76 76 776
HERR CHRIST, DER EINIG GOTTS SOHN 86, 109

76 76 776 776
DER TAG, DER IST SO FREUDEN REICH 180

76 76 88 86
CORDIS DONUM 43

768 D with Refrain
SHIBBOLET BASADEH 496

77 11 8
CANTATE DOMINO 245

77 75
GOD WAS THERE ON CALVARY 140

77 77
GOTT SEI DANK DURCH ALLE WELT 76, 226
HÖCHSTER PRIESTER 576
INNOCENTS 159, 222
MÜDE BIN ICH 593
NUN KOMM, DER HEIDEN HEILAND 2, 28
ORIENTIS PARTIBUS 149, 175
PATMOS 469
SONG 13 183
VIENNA 409, 426

77 77 Iambic
NEW YEAR 74

77 77 with Refrain
GLORIA 63
HUMILITY 58

77 77 with Alleluias
EASTER HYMN 157
LLANFAIR 150

77 77 D
ABERYSTWYTH 357
SPANISH CHANT 124
ST. GEORGE'S, WINDSOR 82, 613, 617

77 77 D with Refrain
MENDELSSOHN 61

77 77 4
CHRISTUS IST ERSTANDEN 155
SONNE DER GERECHTIGKEIT 141

77 77 77
DIX 83, 612
FRED TIL BOD 153
GETHSEMANE 104, 385
PILOT 433
RATISBON 249
TOPLADY 389
VOLLER WUNDER 394, 580

77 77 77 7 D
GOTT DER VATER WOHN UNS BEI 192

77 77 778
O LAMM GOTTES, UNSCHULDIG 268

77 88 77
WEIL ICH JESU SCHÄFLEIN BIN 432

776 778
EPIPHANY 81
O WELT, ICH MUSS DICH LASSEN 113, 587

777 5
CAPETOWN 436

777 6
SEPTEM VERBA 139

78 76 76 76
GO, TELL IT 57

78 78 76 76 76 76
NUN LOB, MEIN SEEL 257, 403

78 78 77
GROSSER GOTT, WIR LOBEN DICH 278
JESUS, MEINE ZUVERSICHT 145, 167
MEINEN JESUM LASS ICH NICHT 8, 304

78 78 78 78 78 78 87 63
NOW 218, 231

78 78 88
LIEBSTER JESU, WIR SIND HIER 221, 295, 330, 461

78 88 88 8 10 8
KOMM, HEILIGER GEIST, HERRE GOTT 176

METRICAL INDEX

8 33 6 D
FRÖHLICH SOLL MEIN HERZE SPRINGEN 37
WARUM SOLLT ICH MICH DENN GRÄMEN 428

84 84 88 84
AR HYD Y NOS 332

84 84 888 4
AR HYD Y NOS 590, 611

85 83
STEPHANOS 446, 504

85 84 77
MIT FRIED UND FREUD 269

86 446 76 446
FOREST GREEN 66
ST. LOUIS 65

86 86 86
CORONATION 370

86 86 88
AUCH JETZT MACHT GOTT 575
O JESU, WARUM LEGST DU MIR 232

86 866
LOBT GOTT, IHR CHRISTEN 41, 90

87 77 77
WIR GLAUBEN ALL AN EINEN GOTT 270

87 85
ST. LEONARD'S 467

87 87
DOROTHY 490
JUBILATE DEO 228
MERTON 15
RATHBUN 345
RINGE RECHT 111, 354
STUTTGART 326, 463, 530

87 87 Iambic
ST. COLUMBA 375

87 87 with Refrain
GIVE ME JESUS 355

87 87 D
AUSTRIA 277
BEACH SPRING 353
CONVERSE 411
EBENEZER 280
GALILEAN 573
HYFRYDOL 365, 465, 486, 603
HYMN TO JOY 169
IN BABILONE 182, 532
LADUE CHAPEL 264
LORD, REVIVE US 492
NETTLETON 484
O DU LIEBE MEINER LIEBE 108, 380, 577
O DURCHBRECHER ALLER BANDE 87, 351

O MEIN JESU, ICH MUSS STERBEN 127
PLEADING SAVIOR 489
REX GLORIAE 174, 281
ST. HILARY 6, 623

87 87 6
BRIDEGROOM 495

87 87 8
VERLEIH UNS FRIEDEN GNÄDIGLICH 522

87 87 12 12 11 11
EINS IST NOT 290

87 87 44 77
WAS GOTT TUT 429

87 87 47
CORONAE 216
GUIDE ME 331
WORCESTER 239

87 87 444 77
BRYN CALFARIA 352

87 87 447
O JERUSALEM, DU SCHÖNE 220

87 87 447 447 Iambic (447 447 D Iambic)
O HERRE GOTT, DEIN GÖTTLICH WORT 511
SO GEHST DU NUN 126
WAS MEIN GOTT WILL 435

87 87 55 56 7
EIN FESTE BURG 200, 201

87 87 65 66 7
REUTER 536

87 87 66 66 7
REUTER 293, 599

87 87 66 88
DER LIEBEN SONNE LICHT UND PRACHT 431

87 87 68 67
GREENSLEEVES 67

87 87 77
IRBY 50
JESUS, JESUS, NICHTS ALS JESUS 348
KOMM, O KOMM, DU GEIST DES LEBENS 181
NAAR MIT ÖIE 106
UNSER HERRSCHER 255

87 87 77 88
DER AM KREUZ 121, 319
FREU DICH SEHR 11, 320, 470
WERDE MUNTER 147, 283, 408, 545

87 87 78 74
CHRIST LAG IN TODESBANDEN 161

951

87 87 87
ASCENDED TRIUMPH 172
FORTUNATUS NEW 122
NEW ULM 329
PICARDY 29, 361
REGENT SQUARE 80, 578
SIEH, HIER BIN ICH, EHRENKÖNIG 26, 508
WESTMINSTER ABBEY 77, 531

87 87 87 78 77
SOLLT ICH MEINEM GOTT NICHT SINGEN 253

87 87 87 87 7
CHRIST UNSER HERR ZUM JORDAN KAM..............88
ES WOLLE GOTT UNS GNÄDIG SEIN....................574

87 87 877
CWM RHONDDA 237, 523
DIVINUM MYSTERIUM 35

87 87 877 877
LASSET UNS MIT JESU ZIEHEN 452

87 87 88
HERR, ICH HABE MISSGEHANDELT.......................302
MACHS MIT MIR, GOTT 453

87 87 88 77
ERMUNTRE DICH 44
JESU, MEINES LEBENS LEBEN 114

87 87 88 848
ALLEIN ZU DIR 437

87 87 887
ACH GOTT, VOM HIMMEL SIEH DAREIN 205
ALLEIN GOTT IN DER HÖH SEI EHR................69, 263
AUS TIEFER NOT 305
DU LEBENSBROT, HERR JESU CHRIST 312
ES IST DAS HEIL 299, 390
ES IST GEWISSLICH...........................185, 207, 208
LOBT GOTT DEN HERREN, IHR HEIDEN ALL 236
NUN FREUT EUCH,
    LIEBEN CHRISTEN 72, 173, 377, 393
WÄCHTERLIED 202, 425

87 87 887 887
AN WASSERFLÜSSEN BABYLON 100
WEDDING GLORY 219

87 87 89 87
GOD OF LOVE 602

877 877
ACH, WAS SOLL ICH SÜNDER MACHEN 464

877 877 with Refrain
FREUET EUCH, IHR CHRISTEN ALLE.......................45

88 44 8
OH, COME, MY SOUL 99

88 78
JESUS CHRISTUS, UNSER HEILAND,
    DER VON UNS 313

88 87
QUEM PASTORES 42

88 87 4
IN GOTTES NAMEN FAHREN WIR 285

88 88 88
ALL EHR UND LOB 188, 262, 567
MAGDALEN 382
MELITA 517, 542
ST. PETERSBURG 548
SUSSEX CAROL 52
VATER UNSER IM
    HIMMELREICH, DER ZU 306, 407, 410, 479, 608

88 88 88 8
KIRKEN DEN ER ET GAMMELT HUS 529

88 88 88 66
MACHT HOCH DIE TÜR 3
MILWAUKEE 4

88 88 88 88 88
WIR GLAUBEN ALL AN EINEN GOTT 271

886 886
MERIBAH 458

887 88 77
OM HIMMERIGES RIGE 325

887 447
IN DICH HAB ICH GEHOFFET 448

887 887
ALLES IST AN GOTTES SEGEN 421

887 887 22 44 48
WIE SCHÖN LEUCHTET 49, 79, 162, 184, 241, 622

887 887 7
OH, BLESSED HOME 503

887 887 88 88 488
HERZLICH LIEB HAB ICH DICH, O HERR 434

888
DIES IRAE 209

888 with Alleluias
GELOBT SEI GOTT 165

888 4
ES IST KEIN TAG 468, 487

888 4 with Alleluias
VICTORY 148

888 6
ISLEWORTH 499, 572
JUST AS I AM 387

888 888
HEUT TRIUMPHIERET GOTTES SOHN 164

METRICAL INDEX

888 888 with Alleluias
LASST UNS ERFREUEN 171, 250

898 898 664 448
WACHET AUF 206, 455

9 10 9 10 10 10
DIR, DIR, JEHOVAH 189

98 89
RANDOLPH 328

98 89 with Refrain
GOD BE WITH YOU 327

98 98
DENVER 292
ST. CLEMENT 594

98 98 86
ICH WILL DICH LIEBEN 476

98 98 98
DEN SIGNEDE DAG 211, 254

98 98 88
ICH STERBE TÄGLICH 70, 310
O DASS ICH TAUSEND
    ZUNGEN HÄTTE (DRETZEL) 194, 384
O DASS ICH TAUSEND
    ZUNGEN HÄTTE (KÖNIG) 242, 294, 386
WER NUR DEN LIEBEN GOTT 414, 444
WER WEISS, WIE NAHE 32, 210

99 11 10 4
NUN BITTEN WIR 190

10 6 10 6 76 76
JERUSALEM, DU HOCHGEBAUTE STADT 212

10 6 10 6 99 44
ES IST GENUG 158, 565

10 8 10 8 88 8
LOBE DEN HERREN, O MEINE SEELE 235

10 8 88 10
O JESULEIN SÜSS 186, 366

10 10 5 10
O WIE SELIG 554

10 10 10 with Alleluia
ENGELBERG 248
NATIONAL CITY 350

10 10 10 with Alleluias
SINE NOMINE 551

10 10 10 10
CRUCIFER 579
ELLERS 321
EVENTIDE 588
FARLEY CASTLE 315, 483

OLD 124TH 309, 543
PRINCESS EUGENIE 364
SURSUM CORDA 482, 525

10 10 10 10 10 10
FINLANDIA 415

10 10 11 11
HANOVER 243

10 10 12 10
GABRIEL'S MESSAGE 24

10 10 14 10
WERE YOU THERE 119

10 11 11 6
CHRISTE SANCTORUM 343

10 47 56 5
PÁN BŮH 450

11 5 12 9
GUDS MENIGHED, SYNG 252

11 10 11 10
EIRENE 427
MORNING STAR 92
O PERFECT LOVE 600

11 10 11 10 with Refrain
HOW GREAT THOU ART 256
REDEMPTION 570

11 11 11 5
CHRISTE SANCTORUM 581
HERZLIEBSTER JESU 117
SHADES MOUNTAIN 191
WOJTKIEWIECZ 556

11 11 11 6
CHRISTE SANCTORUM 558

11 11 11 11
CRADLE SONG 68
FIRM FOUNDATION 416
MALDWYN 337
ST. DENIO 240
WALTHER 143

11 11 11 11 with Refrain
TO GOD BE THE GLORY 399

11 12 12 10
NICAEA 195

12 9 66 12 9
WONDROUS LOVE 120

12 10 13 10
NOT UNTO US 392

12 11 12 11
KREMSER 609

953

METRICAL INDEX

12 12 with Refrain
PROMISED ONE 363

12 12 10 10
MANGER SONG 54

12 12 12
ACCLAMATIONS 406

14 14 478
LOBE DEN HERREN 234

SM (Short Meter — 66 86)
BOYLSTON 494
ENERGY 381, 485, 555
FRANCONIA 296
POTSDAM 95
ST. MICHAEL 475
ST. THOMAS 1, 238, 533
SCHUMANN 213
SOUTHWELL 128, 138

SM with Refrain
MARION 540
TRIUMPH 151

SM D (Short Meter Double — 66 86 66 86)
DIADEMATA 341

CM (Common Meter — 86 86)
ADAM 396
AZMON 491
BEATITUDO 340
BELMONT 360
CHESTERFIELD 12
CONSOLATION 25
COWPER 112
DETROIT 118, 493
DUNDEE 324, 356, 420
EVAN 462
ICH SINGE DIR 261, 443
JEG ER SAA GLAD 51
LAND OF REST 215
MARTYRDOM 129
MCKEE 539
NEW BRITAIN 379
NUN DANKET ALL 225, 227, 512
ST. AGNES 373
ST. ANNE 441
ST. FLAVIAN 398, 412, 524
ST. MAGNUS 217, 301
ST. PETER 358, 405, 509
WALDER 284
WINCHESTER OLD 259

CM with Repeat
ANTIOCH 62

CM D (Common Meter Double — 86 86 86 86)
KINGSFOLD 481, 520
RESIGNATION 374
VOX DILECTI 338

LM (Long Meter — 88 88)
ACH BLEIB BEI UNS 541
ANGELUS 274
BEATUS VIR 521
CANONBURY 561
CHRISTUM WIR SOLLEN LOBEN SCHON 39
CONDITOR ALME SIDERUM 31
DEO GRACIAS 96, 371
DEUS TUORUM MILITUM 196, 502, 563
DUKE STREET 152
ERHALT UNS, HERR 203, 282, 287
FEDERAL STREET 347
FOX VALLEY 621
GIFT OF LOVE 498
GOTTLOB, ES GEHT NUNMEHR ZU ENDE 135, 500
HAMBURG 125
HER KOMMER DINE ARME SMAA 46
HERR JESU CHRIST,
 DICH ZU UNS WEND 71, 230, 288, 298, 516
HERR JESU CHRIST, MEINS 223, 404, 471, 514, 547
IN TREMBLING HANDS 199
JAM LUCIS 595
KOMM, GOTT SCHÖPFER 177
LAKEWOOD 456, 513
LAUREL 583
LLEDROD 518
MORNING HYMN 582
O HEILAND, REISS DIE HIMMEL AUF 22, 91, 544
O HEILIGE DREIFALTIGKEIT 480, 584, 586, 591
O JESU CHRISTE, WAHRES LICHT 9, 383, 569
OLD HUNDREDTH 233, 286, 316, 323, 334
PUER NOBIS NASCITUR 5, 16, 53
REST 605
ROCKINGHAM OLD 549
ST. CRISPIN 376, 391
ST. CROSS 136
ST. LUKE 303, 308, 519
SUANTRAI 497
TALLIS' CANON 597
THE KING'S MAJESTY 132
TRURO 84
VENI CREATOR SPIRITUS 178
VOM HIMMEL HOCH 21, 38
WAREHAM 198, 466, 601
WEIMAR 27
WENN WIR IN HÖCHSTEN
 NÖTEN SEIN 102, 378, 413
WINCHESTER NEW 89, 133, 229, 607
WIR DANKEN DIR, HERR JESU CHRIST 123
WO GOTT ZUM HAUS 291, 506
WOODWORTH 397

LM Trochaic
TRYGGARE KAN INGEN VARA 300, 449

LM with Alleluia
GELOBET SEIST DU, JESU CHRIST 33

LM with Refrain
VENI, EMMANUEL 23

LM D (Long Meter Double — 88 88 88 88)
EVENING HYMN 592
O GROSSER GOTT 85, 535
WITTENBERG NEW 400

LM D Trochaic
SCHMÜCKE DICH...311, 616

PM (Peculiar Meter)
CHRIST IST ERSTANDEN..144
DIE GÜLDNE SONNE 430
GLORY BE TO THE FATHER 273
GOTT SEI GELOBET UND GEBENEDEIET.....................317
GREAT WHITE HOST 550
IN DIR IST FREUDE 346
JESAIA, DEM PROPHETEN 267
KINGLY LOVE..335
KYRIE, GOTT VATER 266
MITTEN WIR IM LEBEN SIND..534
NYT YLÖS, SIELUNI 244
SCHAFFE IN MIR, GOTT..272

Irregular
ADESTE FIDELES 55
ALDINE...246
ASCENSION 13
BALM IN GILEAD 564
BUNESSAN 505
GRANTON 342
ON EAGLES' WINGS 440
PRECIOUS LORD 451
SALVE FESTA DIES..179
SLANE...367
STILLE NACHT..60
WHITFIELD..526

Irregular with Refrain
ALLELUIA NO. 1 154
FESTIVAL CANTICLE..265

FIRST LINE INDEX

Indented lines indicate first lines by which some hymns are known.

A Great and Mighty Wonder 36
A Hymn of Glory Let Us Sing 171
A Lamb Goes Uncomplaining Forth......................................100
A Mighty Fortress Is Our God 200, 201
Abide, O Dearest Jesus 333
Abide with Me 588
Across the Sky the Shades of Night...69
Alas! and Did My Savior Bleed 129
All Depends on Our Possessing 421
All Glory Be to God Alone 262
All Glory Be to God on High...263
All Glory, Laud, and Honor 131
All Hail the Power of Jesus' Name 370
All Mankind Fell in Adam's Fall 378
    All My Heart This Night Rejoices 37
All People that on Earth Do Dwell 233
All Praise Be Yours..350
All Praise to God Who Reigns Above 236
All Praise to Thee, My God, This Night 592
All Praise to You, Eternal God 33
All Who Believe and Are Baptized..299
Alleluia, Alleluia, Give Thanks 154
Alleluia! Jesus Lives 153
Alleluia! Let Praises Ring..241
Alleluia! Sing to Jesus..169
Almighty Father, Bless the Word 323
Almighty Father, Heaven and Earth 480

Almighty Father, Strong to Save..517
Almighty God, Your Word Is Cast 324
Amazing Grace—How Sweet the Sound..............................379
Amid the World's Bleak Wilderness 342
Angels from the Realms of Glory 80
Angels We Have Heard on High..63
Arise and Shine in Splendor...81
Arise, My Soul, Arise 244
Arise, O Christian People...14
Around the Throne, A Glorious Band....................................549
Around the Throne of God a Band...198
As Angels Joyed with One Accord 5
As Surely as I Live, God Said..308
As We Begin Another Week..223
As with Gladness Men of Old..83
Asleep in Jesus! Blessed Sleep 605
At the Lamb's High Feast We Sing 141
At the Name of Jesus 344
Awake, My Heart, with Gladness 156
Awake, My Soul, and with the Sun 582
Awake, O Spirit, Who Inspired..567
    Awake, Thou Spirit, Who Didst Fire 567
Away in a Manger..68

Baptized in Water 297
Baptized into Your Name Most Holy 294
Be Still, My Soul..415

955

FIRST LINE INDEX

Beautiful Savior 369
Before the Ending of the Day 595
Before the Lord We Bow 618
 Before Thee, God, Who Knowest All 306
Before You, God, the Judge of All 306
Behold, a Branch Is Growing 47
Behold a Host, Arrayed in White 550
Behold the Lamb of God 101
Bless Our Loved Ones, Holy Father 504
Blessed Are the Saints of God 394
Blessed Are They, Forever Blest 383
Blessed Jesus, at Your Word 221
Blest Be the God of Israel 275
Blest Be the Tie that Binds 494
 Blest Is the Man, Forever Blest 383
Break Forth, O Beauteous Heavenly Light 44
Brightest and Best 92
Brothers, Sisters, Let Us Gladly 484
Built on the Rock 529
By All Your Saints Still Striving 552
By Grace I'm Saved 384

Chief of Sinners Though I Be 385
Children of the Heavenly Father 449
Christ Be My Leader 367
Christ, by Heavenly Hosts Adored 617
Christ High-Ascended 558
Christ Is Arisen 144
Christ Is Made the Sure Foundation 531
Christ Is Our Cornerstone 528
Christ Is the World's Light 343
Christ Jesus Lay in Death's Strong Bands 161
Christ, the Life of All the Living 114
Christ the Lord Is Risen Again 155
Christ the Lord Is Risen Today 149
Christ the Lord Is Risen Today; Alleluia 150
Christ the Lord to Us Is Born 59
Christians, While on Earth Abiding 408
Come, Follow Me, the Savior Spoke 453
Come, Holy Ghost, Creator Blest 177, 178
Come, Holy Ghost, God and Lord 176
Come, Let Us Join Our Cheerful Songs 227
 Come, My Soul, Thy Suit Prepare 409
Come, My Soul, with Every Care 409
Come, Now, Almighty King 193
Come, O Long-Expected Jesus 6
Come, O Precious Ransom, Come 8
Come, Oh, Come, Life-Giving Spirit 181
Come, Rejoice before Your Maker 228
Come to Calvary's Holy Mountain 106
Come unto Me, Ye Weary 336
Come, You Faithful, Raise the Strain 142
Come, You Thankful People, Come 613
Come, Your Hearts and Voices Raising 42
Comfort, Comfort All My People 11
Create in Me a Clean Heart, O God 272
Creator Spirit, by Whose Aid 188
Crown Him with Many Crowns 341

Day of Wrath, Oh, Day of Mourning 209
Dear Christians, One and All, Rejoice 377
Dear Father, You Have Made Us All 298
Dear Lord, to Your True Servants Give 542
Dearest Jesus, We Are Here 295
Deep Were His Wounds 107
Delay Not! Delay Not 337
Down from the Mount of Glory 97

Draw Near and Take the Body of the Lord 309
Draw Us to Thee 170
Drawn to the Cross 387

Earth and All Stars 247
Enslaved by Sin and Bound in Chains 102
Evening and Morning 430
Every Morning Mercies New 580

Faith Is a Living Power from Heaven 404
Father, Let Me Dedicate 75
Father Most Holy, Merciful, and Tender 191
Father, We Praise You 581
Feed Your Children, God Most Holy 616
Fight the Good Fight 457
For All the Saints 551
For All Your Saints, O Lord 555
For Christian Homes, O Lord, We Pray 500
For Many Years, O God of Grace 622
For Me to Live Is Jesus 606
For the Fruit of His Creation 611
For Years on Years of Matchless Grace 621
Forever with the Lord 213
Forgive Our Sins as We Forgive 493
Forgive Us, Lord 482
Forth in the Peace of Christ We Go 518
Forth in Your Name, O Lord , I Go 456
From All that Dwell below the Skies 250
From Depths of Woe I Cry to You 305
From Eternity, O God 461
 From God Shall Naught Divide Me 418
From Greenland's Icy Mountains 571
From Heaven Above to Earth I Come 38

Gentle Mary Laid Her Child 56
Give Thanks to God on High 553
Glorious in Majesty 496
Glory Be to God in Heaven 264
Glory Be to God the Father 239
Glory Be to Jesus 103
Glory Be to the Father 273
Go Labor On 563
Go, My Children, with My Blessing 332
Go, Tell It on the Mountain 57
Go to Dark Gethsemane 104
God Be with You till We Meet Again 327, 328
God Bless Our Native Land 619
God Has Spoken by His Prophets 281
God Himself Is Present 224
God Is Here! As We His People 532
God Loved the World So that He Gave 391
God Moves in a Mysterious Way 420
God, My Lord, My Strength 450
God of Grace and God of Glory 523
God of Love and God of Marriage 602
God of Mercy, God of Grace 249
God of the Prophets 543
 God the Father, Be Our Stay 192
God the Father, Son, and Spirit 623
God Was There on Calvary 140
God, We Praise You 277
God, Who Made the Earth and Heaven 590
God's Own Son Most Holy 17
God's Word Is Our Great Heritage 293
Good News of God Above 568
Grace Has a Thrilling Sound 381
 Grace, 'Tis a Charming Sound 381

FIRST LINE INDEX

Gracious Savior, Gentle Shepherd 508
Grant Peace, We Pray, in Mercy, Lord 522
Great God, What Do I See and Hear 208
Guide Me, O Thou Great Jehovah 331

Hail, O Once-Despised Jesus 351
Hail, O Source of Every Blessing 87
Hail the Day that Sees Him Rise 175
Hail Thee, Festival Day 179
Hail to the Lord's Anointed 93
Hark! A Thrilling Voice Is Sounding 15
Hark! The Church Proclaims Her Honor 530
Hark the Glad Sound! The Savior Comes 12
Hark! The Herald Angels Sing 61
Hark! The Voice of Jesus Crying 573
Have No Fear, Little Flock 442
He Is Arisen! Glorious Word 162
He Stood before the Court 115
      He that Believes and Is Baptized 299
He's Risen, He's Risen 143
Hear Us Now, Our God and Father 603
Help Us, O Lord, for Now We Enter 70
Here, O My Lord, I See You Face to Face 315
His Battle Ended There 146
      Holy Father, in Thy Mercy 504
Holy God, We Praise Your Name 278
Holy, Holy, Holy! Lord God Almighty 195
Holy Spirit, Ever Dwelling 182
Holy Spirit, God of Love 180
Holy Spirit, Light Divine 183
Hosanna, Loud Hosanna 130
Hosanna to the Coming Lord 21
How Blest Are They 607
How Blest Are They Who Hear 325
How Can I Thank You, Lord 460
How Firm a Foundation 416
How Good, Lord, to Be Here 95
How Great Thou Art 256
How Lovely Shines the Morning Star 79
How Precious Is the Book Divine 284
How Shall the Young Secure Their Hearts 509
How Shall They Hear the Word of God 575
How Sweet the Name of Jesus Sounds 358

I Am Content! My Jesus Lives Again 158
I Am Jesus' Little Lamb 432
I Am So Glad When Christmas Comes 51
I Am Trusting You, Lord Jesus 446
I Come, O Savior, to Your Table 310
I Fall Asleep in Jesus' Wounds 608
I Gave My Life for Thee 454
I Hear the Savior Calling 560
I Heard the Voice of Jesus Say 338
I Know My Faith Is Founded 403
I Know of a Sleep in Jesus' Name 211
I Know that My Redeemer Lives 152
I Lay My Sins on Jesus 372
I Leave All Things to God's Direction 414
I Love to Tell the Story 562
I Love Your Kingdom, Lord 533
I Pray You, Dear Lord Jesus 510
I Trust, O Christ, in You Alone 437
I Walk in Danger All the Way 431
I Will Sing My Maker's Praises 253
If God Had Not Been on Our Side 202
If God Himself Be for Me 419

If Thou but Suffer God to Guide Thee 444
If You But Trust in God to Guide You 444
If Your Beloved Son, O God 393
I'm But a Stranger Here 417
Immortal, Invisible, God Only Wise 240
In Adam We Have All Been One 396
In Christ There Is No East or West 539
In God, My Faithful God 438
In His Temple Now Behold Him 77
In Peace and Joy I Now Depart 269
In the Cross of Christ I Glory 345
In the Hour of Trial 116
In the Midst of Earthly Life 534
      In Thee Alone, O Christ, My Lord 437
      In Thee, Lord, Have I Put My Trust 448
In Trembling Hands, Lord God, We Hold 199
In You Is Gladness 346
In You, O Lord, I Put My Trust 448
Isaiah, Mighty Seer in Days of Old 267

Jehovah, Let Me Now Adore You 189
Jerusalem, My Happy Home 215
Jerusalem the Golden 214
Jerusalem, Thou City Fair and High 212
Jesus! and Shall It Ever Be 347
Jesus Calls Us O'er the Tumult 463
Jesus Came, the Heavens Adoring 26
Jesus Christ Is Risen Today 157
Jesus Christ, My Pride and Glory 464
Jesus Christ, My Sure Defense 167
Jesus Christ, Our Blessed Savior 313
Jesus, Grant that Balm and Healing 121
Jesus, I My Cross Have Taken 465
Jesus, I Will Ponder Now 98
Jesus, in Your Dying Woes 139
Jesus, Jesus, Only Jesus 348
Jesus, Lead Us On 422
Jesus Lives! The Victory's Won 145
Jesus, Lover of My Soul 357
Jesus, My Great High Priest 359
Jesus! Name of Wondrous Love 76
Jesus, Priceless Treasure 349
Jesus, Refuge of the Weary 108
Jesus, Savior, Pilot Me 433
Jesus Shall Reign Where'er the Sun 84
Jesus, Shepherd of the Sheep 436
Jesus Sinners Does Receive 304
Jesus, Your Blood and Righteousness 376
Jesus, Your Boundless Love to Me 479
Jesus, Your Church with Longing Eyes 9
Joy to the World 62
Just As I Am, without One Plea 397

Kyrie, God Father in Heaven Above 266

Lamb of God, Pure and Holy 268
Lamb of God, We Fall before You 354
Let All Mortal Flesh Keep Silence 361
Let All Things Now Living 260
Let All Together Praise Our God 41
Let Children Hear the Mighty Deeds 512
Let Me Be Yours Forever 596
Let the Earth Now Praise the Lord 28
      Let Thoughtless Thousands Choose 466
Let Us All with Gladsome Voice 64
Let Us Ever Walk with Jesus 452

957

Lift High the Cross	579
Lift Up Your Heads, You Mighty Gates	3, 4
Like the Golden Sun Ascending	147
Lo, He Comes with Clouds Descending	29
Lord, Dismiss Us with Your Blessing	329
Lord, Enthroned in Heavenly Splendor	352
Lord God, to You We All Give Praise	196
Lord, Help Us Ever to Retain	514
Lord Jesus Christ, Be Present Now	230
Lord Jesus Christ, My Savior Blest	362
Lord Jesus Christ, the Children's Friend	513
Lord Jesus Christ, the Church's Head	536
Lord Jesus Christ, with Us Abide	541
Lord Jesus Christ, You Have Prepared	312
Lord Jesus Christ, You Set Us Free	123
Lord Jesus, We Give Thanks to Thee	123
Lord Jesus, You Are Going Forth	126
Lord Jesus, You Have Come	546
Lord, Keep Us Steadfast in Your Word	203
Lord of All Good	483
Lord of All Nations, Grant Me Grace	521
Lord of Glory, You Have Bought Us	486
Lord of Lords, the Sparkling Heavens	237
Lord of My Life, Whose Tender Care	232
Lord of Our Growing Years	507
Lord of the Home	502
Lord of the Living Harvest	559
Lord, Open Now My Heart to Hear	282
Lord, Speak to Us that We May Speak	561
Lord, Take My Hand and Lead Me	439
Lord, Teach Us How to Pray Aright	412
Lord, 'Tis Not that I Did Choose You	380
Lord, to You I Make Confession	302
Lord, We Confess Our Numerous Faults	398
Lord, When Your Glory I Shall See	219
Lord, You I Love with All My Heart	434
Lord, You Love the Cheerful Giver	489
Love Divine, All Love Excelling	365
Love in Christ Is Strong and Living	490
Love Is the Gracious Gift	505
May God Bestow on Us His Grace	574
May God the Father of Our Lord	597
May the Grace of Christ Our Savior	326
May the Mind of Christ My Savior	467
May We Your Precepts, Lord, Fulfill	458
Morning Breaks upon the Tomb	159
My Faith Looks Up to Thee	402
My God, My Father, Make Me Strong	468
My God Will Never Leave Me	418
My Heart Is Longing	364
My Hope Is Built on Nothing Less	382
My Maker Be Thou Nigh	598
My Maker, Be with Me	598
My Shepherd Will Supply My Need	374
My Song Is Love Unknown	110
My Soul Now Magnifies the Lord	274
My Soul, Now Bless Your Maker	257
Not All the Blood of Beasts	128
Not for Tongues of Heaven's Angels	495
Not in Anger, Mighty God	423
Not unto Us	392
Now I Have Found the Firm Foundation	386
Now Let All Loudly	258
Now Let Us Come before Him	74
Now Praise We Christ, the Holy One	39
Now Rest Beneath Night's Shadow	587
Now Sing We, Now Rejoice	34
Now Thank We All Our God	610
Now that the Daylight Fills the Sky	583
Now the Day Is Over	589
Now, the Hour of Worship O'er	330
Now the Light Has Gone Away	593
Now the Silence	231
O Blessed, Holy Trinity	584
O Bride of Christ, Rejoice	134
O Christ, Our True and Only Light	569
O Christians, Haste	570
O Dearest Jesus	117
O Dearest Lord, Thy Sacred Head	118
O Fount of Good, for All Your Love	524
O God, Forsake Me Not	424
O God from God, O Light from Light	85
O God, My Faithful God	459
O God, O Lord of Heaven and Earth	400
O God of Love, O King of Peace	519
O God of Mercy, God of Might	499
O God, Our Help in Ages Past	441
O God, Our Lord, Your Holy Word	204
O God, Your Hand the Heavens Made	481
O Holy Spirit, Enter In	184
O Holy Spirit, Grant Us Grace	185
O Jesus, Blessed Lord, to Thee	316
O Jesus Christ, Your Manger Is	40
O Jesus, King Most Wonderful	373
O Jesus, King of Glory	94
O Jesus, Lamb of God, You Are	27
O Jesus So Sweet, O Jesus So Mild	366
O Kingly Love, that Faithfully	335
O Light of Gentile Nations	78
O Little Town of Bethlehem	65, 66
O Living Bread from Heaven	314
O Lord, How Shall I Meet You	18, 19
O Lord, in Prayer You Spent the Night	548
O Lord, Look Down from Heaven	205
O Lord of Heaven and Earth and Sea	487
O Lord of Light, Who Made the Stars	31
O Lord, Our Father, Thanks and Praise	72
O Lord, Our God, Your Gracious Hand	511
O Lord, We Praise You	317
O Lord, You Have in Your Pure Grace	407
O Love that Casts Out Fear	604
O Master of the Loving Heart	491
O Perfect Love	600
O Sacred Head, Now Wounded	105
O Savior, Precious Savior	368
O Savior, Rend the Heavens Wide	22
O Sons and Daughters of the King	165
O Spirit of Life, O Spirit of God	186
O Splendor of God's Glory Bright	586
O Trinity, Most Blessed Light	591
O Word of God Incarnate	279
O'er the Distant Mountains Breaking	220
Of the Father's Love Begotten	35
Oh, Bless the Lord, My Soul	238
Oh, Blessed Home, Where Man and Wife	503
Oh, Blest the House, Whate'er Befall	506
Oh, Come, All Ye Faithful	55
Oh, Come, My Soul	99
Oh, Come, Oh, Come, Emmanuel	23

Oh, Darkest Woe	137
Oh, for a Faith that Will Not Shrink	405
Oh, for a Thousand Tongues to Sing	340
Oh, How Blest Are They	554
Oh, Love, How Deep	371
Oh, Perfect Life of Love	138
Oh, Rejoice, All Christians, Loudly	45
Oh, Sing, My Soul, Your Maker's Praise	425
Oh, Sing to the Lord	252
Oh, that I Had a Thousand Voices	194
Oh, that I Had a Thousand Voices	242
Oh, that the Lord Would Guide My Ways	462
Oh, Wondrous Type! Oh, Vision Fair	96
Oh, Worship the King	243
On Christ's Ascension I Now Build	173
On Christmas Night All Christians Sing	52
On Eagles' Wings	440
On Galilee's High Mountain	557
On Jordan's Bank the Baptist's Cry	16
On My Heart Imprint Your Image	319, 320
On What Has Now Been Sown	322
Once Again My Heart Rejoices	37
Once He Came in Blessing	17
Once in Royal David's City	50
One Thing's Needful	290
Onward, Christian Soldiers	537
Open Now Thy Gates of Beauty	255
Our Children Jesus Calls	296
Our Father, by Whose Name	501
Our Father, Who from Heaven Above	410
Our Father's God in Years Long Gone	535
Our God, Our Help in Ages Past	441
Our Lord and God, Oh, Bless This Day	599

Praise Be to the Lord	276
Praise God, from Whom All Blessings Flow	334
Praise God, the Lord, Ye Sons of Men	41
Praise the Almighty; My Soul, Adore Him	235
Praise the One Who Breaks the Darkness	353
Praise to God, Immortal Praise	612
Praise to the Lord, the Almighty	234
Praise to You and Adoration	470
Preach You the Word	544
Precious Lord, Take My Hand	451
Preserve Your Word, O Savior	289

Redeemed, Restored, Forgiven	388
Rejoice, My Heart, Be Glad and Sing	443
Rejoice, O Pilgrim Throng	540
Rejoice, Rejoice, Believers	7
Rejoice, Rejoice, This Happy Morn	49
Renew Me, O Eternal Light	471
Ride On, Ride On in Majesty	132, 133
Rise, Arise	30
Rise, My Soul, to Watch and Pray	472
Rise, O Light of Gentile Nations	577
Rise, Shine, You People	556
Rise! to Arms! With Prayer Employ You	455
Rock of Ages, Cleft for Me	389

Saints, Behold! The Sight Is Glorious	216
Saints of God, the Dawn Is Brightening	578
Salvation unto Us Has Come	390
Savior, Again to Thy Dear Name	321
Savior, I Follow On	473
Savior of the Nations, Come	2

Savior, Thy Dying Love	488
Savior, When in Dust to You	124
See in Yonder Manger Low	58
See, the Conqueror Mounts in Triumph	174
See This Wonder in the Making	300
Seek Where You May to Find a Way	395
Send Forth, O Lord, to Every Place	572
Send, O Lord, Your Holy Spirit	545
Sent Forth by God's Blessing	318
Shepherd of Tender Youth	515
Silent Night! Holy Night	60
Sing a New Song to the Lord	245
Sing, My Tongue, the Glorious Battle	122
Sing to the Lord of Harvest	614
Son of God, Eternal Savior	492
Songs of Praise the Angels Sang	222
Songs of Thankfulness and Praise	82
Soul, Adorn Yourself with Gladness	311
Speak, O Lord, Thy Servant Heareth	283
Speak, O Savior; I Am Listening	283
Spread, Oh, Spread the Mighty Word	576
Stand Up, Stand Up for Jesus	474
Stricken, Smitten, and Afflicted	127
Sweet the Moments, Rich in Blessing	111

Take My Life and Let It Be	469
Take the World, but Give Me Jesus	355
That Man a Godly Life Might Live	285
The Advent of Our King	1
The Angel Gabriel from Heaven Came	24
The Bridegroom Soon Will Call Us	10
The Church's One Foundation	538
The Day Full of Grace	254
The Day Is Surely Drawing Near	207
The Day of Resurrection	166
The Day You Gave Us, Lord, Is Ended	594
The Death of Jesus Christ, Our Lord	135
The Gospel Shows the Father's Grace	288
The Head that Once Was Crowned	217
The King of Glory Comes	363
The King of Love My Shepherd Is	375
The King Shall Come	25
The Law Commands and Makes Us Know	286
The Law of God Is Good and Wise	287
The Lord Is God; There Is No Other	292
The Lord's My Shepherd; I'll Not Want	360
The Man Is Ever Blest	475
The Old Year Now Has Passed Away	71
The Only Son from Heaven	86
The People that in Darkness Sat	90
The Savior Kindly Calls	296
The Son of God, Our Christ	525
The Star Proclaims the King Is Here	91
The Stars Declare His Glory	246
The Strife Is O'er, the Battle Done	148
The Ten Commandments Are the Law	285
The Will of God Is Always Best	435
Thee Will I Love, My Strength, My Tower	476
Then the Glory	218
There Is a Balm in Gilead	564
There Is a Fountain Filled with Blood	112
There Still Is Room	565
There's a Voice in the Wilderness Crying	13
They Leave Their Place on High	197
Thine Forever, God of Love	426
This Day at Your Creating Word	229

FIRST LINE INDEX

This Is My Will 497
This Is the Day the Lord Has Made 225
This Is the Feast of Victory 265
This Is the Threefold Truth 406
This Joyful Eastertide 160
    Thou Art the Way; to Thee Alone 356
    Thou Light of Gentile Nations 78
    Thou Who the Night in Prayer Didst Spend 548
Though I May Speak with Bravest Fire 498
Though Thoughtless Thousands Choose 466
Through Jesus' Blood and Merit 445
Thy Strong Word 280
    Thy Works, Not Mine, O Christ 401
    'Tis Good, Lord, to Be Here 95
To God Be the Glory 399
To God the Anthem Raising 73
To Jordan Came the Christ, Our Lord 88
To Jordan's River Came Our Lord 89
To Shepherds as They Watched by Night 53
To Thee My Heart I Offer 43
    To Thy Temple I Repair 226
To You, Our God, We Fly 620
To Your Temple I Draw Near 226
Today in Triumph Christ Arose 164
Today Your Mercy Calls Us 339
Triumphant from the Grave 151
Triune God, Oh, Be Our Stay 192
'Twas on that Dark, that Doleful Night 136

Up Through Endless Ranks of Angels 172
Upon the Cross Extended 113

Wake, Awake, for Night Is Flying 206
We All Are One in Mission 566
We All Believe in One True God 270
We All Believe in One True God 271
We Are the Lord's 427
We Are Your People 526
We Bid You Welcome in the Name 547
We Give Thee but Thine Own 485
We Have a Sure Prophetic Word 291
We Now Implore God the Holy Ghost 190
We Praise You, Lord 301

We Praise You, O God, Our Redeemer 609
We Sing the Almighty Power of God 261
We Thank You for Your Blessings 615
Weary of All Trumpeting 527
Welcome, Happy Morning 163
Were You There 119
What a Friend We Have in Jesus 411
What Child Is This 67
What God Ordains Is Always Good 429
What Is the World to Me 477
What Wondrous Love Is This 120
When All the World Was Cursed 20
When All Your Mercies, O My God 259
When Christmas Morn Is Dawning 48
When God the Spirit Came 187
When I Survey the Wondrous Cross 125
When in Our Music God Is Glorified 248
When in the Hour of Utmost Need 413
When Morning Gilds the Skies 251
When O'er My Sins I Sorrow 109
When Sinners See Their Lost Condition 32
Where Shepherds Lately Knelt 54
While Yet the Morn Is Breaking 585
Who Knows When Death 210
Who Trusts in God, a Strong Abode 447
Why Should Cross and Trial Grieve Me 428
With Broken Heart and Contrite Sigh 303
With High Delight Let Us Unite 168
With the Lord Begin Your Task 478
Wondrous Are Your Ways, O God 307

Ye Lands, to the Lord Make a Jubilant Noise ... 252
    Ye Parents, Hear What Jesus Taught 516
    Ye Sons and Daughters of the King 165
    Ye Sons of Men, O Hearken 14
    Yea, As I Live, Jehovah Saith 308
You Are the Way; through You Alone 356
You Parents, Hear What Jesus Taught 516
Your Hand, O Lord, in Days of Old 520
Your Little Ones, Dear Lord, Are We 46
Your Love, O God, Has Called Us Here 601
Your Works, Not Mine, O Christ 401
Yours Forever, God of Love 426